הטה אזנך לרנתי

FROM YOUR LIPS TO GOD'S EARS

THE BOOK OF PSALMS

Reuben Ebrahimoff

This work pays tribute to the memory of

Mr. Sami Rohr ז"ל

ר' שמואל ב"ר יהושע אליהו ז"ל

who served his Maker with joy
and whose far-reaching vision, warm open hand, love of Torah,
and love for every Jew were catalysts for the revival and growth of
vibrant Jewish life in the former Soviet Union
and in countless communities the world over,

and to the memory of his beloved wife

Mrs. Charlotte Rohr (née Kastner) ע"ה

שרה בת ר' יקותיאל יהודה ע"ה

who survived the fires of the Shoah to become
the elegant and gracious matriarch,
first in Colombia and later in the United States,
of three generations of a family
nurtured by her love and unstinting devotion.
She found grace in the eyes of all those whose lives she touched

Together they merited to see all their children
build lives enriched by faithful commitment
to the spreading of Torah and *Ahavat Yisrael*

Dedicated with love by

The Rohr Family

New York, USA

RABBINICAL COURT
NEW YORK

בית דין צדק
בניו יורק

160 01 Union Turnpike Hilcrest 11865 phone number 718-249-5903

****

Rabbi Eliyahu Ben-Chaim
Chairman

Brought before me was an explanation and interpretation on the Book of Tehillim containing great insights authored by my dear friend and colleague Reb Reuven Gavriel ben Nissim Ebrahimoff. I found its contents to be entirely lovely as golden apples and decorated with silver. The Book of Tehillim is always used by the Jewish people in times of trouble and moments of joy. Therefore a majority of our prayers in daily life are comprised of this Holy book.

My dear friend Reuven researched tirelessly to explain each and every sentence, to bring to light the design of the ancient instruments that accompanied the writing of this Holy text.

There is no doubt that all that engage in this book will enjoy it and gain deeper understanding with the explanations of the verses of Tehillim. He made accessible this Holy book to every person that wants and desires to understand the words that we say in this Holy book.

May your strength endure.

I bless Rav Reuven, that is mentioned above, may it be God's will that wisdom spreads out from your eyes outwardly and let the Torah grow and be great.

Be strong and have courage.

3 Menachem Av 5776

Signed: Rabbi Eliyahu Ben-Chaim

RABBINICAL COURT
NEW YORK

בית דין צדק
ניו יורק

180 01 Union Turnpike Hilcrest 11365 phone number 718-249-5903

****

Rabbi Eliyahu Ben-Chaim
Chairman

בס"ד

הובאו לפני פירוש וביאור על ספר תהילים וחידושים
נפלאים שכתב ידידי ורעי הר' ראובן גבריאל בן נסים
אברמוב וראיתי שאת הכל עשה יפה בעתו דבר דבור
על אופניו תפוחי זהב במשכיות כסף, ספר תהילים
תמיד כל יהודי קורא בו גם בעת צרה וגם בעת שמחה
וכן רוב התפילה בכל יום אנו מתפללים הוא מספר קדוש זה
ידידי הנ"ל איזה טרח ועמל להסביר כל פסוק ופסוק וכן להביא
ביורים עתיקים לפי הנגינה הכתובים בספר הקדוש הזה
אין ספק שכולנו נהנה מעבודתו זו שאסף וקיבץ מתוך
דברי רבותינו הקדושים את הביאורים לפסוקים של תהילים
והפק את הספר הקדוש לכל אדם הרוצה והחפץ להבין
את הדברים שאנו אומרים בספר הקדוש הזה.
ישר כח
ואני מברך את הרב הנ"ל יהי רצון שיפוצו מעינותיך
חוצה ויגדיל תורה ויאדיר חזק ואמץ

ז' מנחם אב תשע"ו
נאום אליהו בן חיים

ACKNOWLEDGEMENTS

I would like to thank the following people, who each in their own ways has inspired and molded me:

Thank you, Sylvia Kelaty Ebrahimoff a"h, my mother, and Nissim Ebrahimoff z"l, my father, for enrolling me into Yeshiva Dov Revel of Forest Hills in 1966, making me one of the first Persian Jews from Mashad to be enrolled in a Jewish day school in the United States.

Thank you, George Rohr, for your generous support of the Tehillim Book.

Thank you, Rabbi Shimon Kessin, for challenging me to find a mitzvah to revive. I chose to speak about the Haftorahs which led me to become known as The Haftorahman.

Thank you, Roberta Lebowitz, without whom this book would not have been completed. Thank you for giving of your time and spending countless hours over the past four years on this book, improving on the text and scrupulously looking at each word to ensure perfection. I'm extraordinarily grateful for all of your contributions to this project.

Thank you, Avram Herzog, who edited and proofread this book. His efforts went far beyond my expectations, and after seeing the improvements he had brought to the text, the book took on much deeper meaning and clarity, and made the information within it easily accessible to anybody.

Thank you, Rabbi Marc Schneier, who for more than a decade permitted me to speak from his pulpit at the Hampton Synagogue. It is there that some of the happiest moments of my life have taken place. The weekly teaching of his congregants is one of my greatest joys.

Thank you, Rabbi Adam Mintz, for permitting me to speak at Kehilat Rayim Ahuvim. He made available the pulpit for me to speak at, and because of him, I was able to hone my craft and develop a mastery of public speaking.

Thank you, Michael Schwerd, for being my best friend since first grade. Since then, many of our discussions have formed me into who I am today.

Thank you, Rabbi Shaul Shimon Deutsch, for putting in the time to review my book, and for providing the Talmud on the Tehillim and their introductions.

Thank you, Rabbi Kornfeld and Avraham Davis, of the Metsudah Company, who provided the

English translation of Tehillim.

Thank you, **Ariel Mintz**, for providing the content for what became the biblical personalities, biblical locations, and biblical peoples referenced to in the book.

Thank you, **Moshe Frumin**, for providing the images of his handmade ancient musical instruments.

Thank you, **Dennis McCorkle**, author of *The Davidic Cipher*, which greatly enhanced my understanding of the music of the Psalms. He shared with me his understanding of how the Levitical orchestra might have sounded.

Thank you, **Chazzan Netanel Hershtik**, who provided me with a greater understanding of the music in the times of the Temple.

Thank you, **Dr. Edward de Bono**, who is recognized as the world's leading expert on creativity, for mentoring me to use my imagination.

Thank you, **Shlomo Moussaieff z"l**, who considered me his spiritual son. He made his collection of biblical antiquities accessible to me, allowing me to learn the deep connection between antiquities and biblical text.

Thank you, **Donnie Berman**, who is like a big brother to me. He has taught me so much and opened so many doors for me.

Thank you, **Yair Medina** of Jerusalem Fine Art Prints, for taking my manuscript and transforming it into a visual masterpiece. You bring great beauty to the Jewish world and beyond.

Thank you, **Irit Harel**, for providing your extraordinary talents and skills to the design of this book. You brilliantly molded this book into a piece of artwork.

Thank you, **Malky Weinstock**, who early on was able to take my words and put them into writing.

Thank you, **Amanda Weiss**, of the Bible Lands Museum in Jerusalem, for making it possible for me to understand the history of the Jewish people in antiquity.

Table of Contents

INTRODUCTION TO SEFER TEHILLIM - THE BOOK OF PSALMS

FOR MILLENNIA, SEFER TEHILLIM, THE BOOK OF PSALMS, HAS BEEN A JEW'S FAITHFUL COMPANION, EXPRESSING THE FULL RANGE OF OUR FAITH, BOTH IN TIMES OF SORROW AND TIMES OF JOY. BUT WHAT HAS PERHAPS GOTTEN LOST THROUGH THE GENERATIONS IS THE "SOUL" OF THE BOOK. FOR THAT, A LITTLE HISTORY IS IN ORDER.

Since the first moment of man's creation, the soul within seeks to connect with its Divine Source, Hashem (God). A true connection with Hashem requires both action and speech, physical activity and verbal affirmation/communication—Mitzvot (deeds) and Tefillah (prayer).

The Temple service epitomized this synthesis: The Kohanim (Priests in the Temple) brought Korbanot (sacrifices) while the Levites sang praises to Hashem. Their music was the ultimate sound system, vibrant and transformative, evoking the soul's yearning to bond with God. These praises, Psalms—The Greek word for "Songs"—were composed primarily by the beloved King David (see "Tehillim Composers" for further explanation). Composed throughout his life, commemorating good times and bad, David's Tehillim dealt with the full gamut of emotions linked not only to personal experiences and occasions of his generation, but to all future generations. Each sentence holds an eternal message, perfectly phrased to facilitate a dynamic and passionate conversation with God. Thus, they were perfectly suited to complement the Korbanot; together, they served as the combination of the precise actions and words to channel Divine influence, thereby

fulfilling the needs of His beloved children, the Jewish People.

With the Temple's destruction, the Psalms of David took on a new form. No longer a counterpart to the sacrifices, they became the framework for its replacement. With this new need to compensate for the physical services of the Temple which fostered closeness to God, Tehillim was the clear, perfect prototype from which to compile a structured prayer. For this reason, Jewish liturgy is replete with King David's artfully worded prose.

The mission of this book is to bring Tehillim back to life; to revive the orchestra, the Levite Symphony that was the Tehillim, which uplifted, transformed and connected the Jewish people to Their Beloved and Awesome Father in Heaven. It is a user's guide for evoking the spiritual craving within each of us, to bond with God today in the here and now; for every moment, God is the source of life and all blessings. And Tehillim is a blueprint for spiritual growth, to prepare us for the imminent Redemption when the sound of the Levites Symphony will once again fill our ears, our hearts, and indeed, our souls.

PRAYING WITH TEHILLIM

AS MENTIONED, NUMEROUS PORTIONS OF SEFER TEHILLIM WERE INTEGRATED INTO MANY OF OUR DAILY PRAYERS. HOWEVER, THERE ARE DIFFERENT TIMES AND OCCASIONS TO RECITE TEHILLIM AS A WAY TO COMMUNICATE AND FORM A BOND WITH THE CREATOR.

CYCLES

Many have a custom to recite all of Tehillim over a consecutive period of days. One of the reasons for this, is referenced in the prayer said immediately before Tehillim. There, we ask God that He should consider our recitation of the Psalms as if the Psalmist had said them himself. Because it is impossible for us to know every little nuance and connotation that the author had in mind, those who complete Sefer Tehillim on a consistent basis are sure to have prayed for all of their needs, even those of which they were unaware.

There are two universally used recitation programs, which complete Sefer Tehillim every 7 or 30 days, respectively:

The Monthly Cycle

This method divides Sefer Tehillim's 150 chapters into thirty sections, corresponding to the thirty days in the Jewish month.

Note: Jewish months consist of twenty nine or thirty days. In the shorter months, Tehillim for day 30 are combined with those of day 29.

Day of the Month	Chapter	Day of the Month	Chapter
1st	1-9	16th	79-82
2nd	10-17	17th	83-87
3rd	18-22	18th	88-89
4th	23-28	19th	90-96
5th	29-34	20th	97-103
6th	35-38	21st	104-105
7th	39-43	22nd	106-107
8th	44-48	23rd	108-112
9th	49-54	24th	113-118
10th	55-59	25th	119 א-ל
11th	60-65	26th	119 מ-ת
12th	66-68	27th	120-134
13th	69-71	28th	135-139
14th	72-76	29th	140-144
15th	77-78	30th	145-150

The Weekly Cycle

This method divides Sefer Tehillim's 150 chapters into seven sections, corresponding to the seven days of the week.

Day of the Week	Chapter
Sunday	1-29
Monday	30-50
Tuesday	51-72
Wednesday	73-89
Thursday	90-106
Friday	107-119
Saturday	120-150

OCCASIONS

Isaiah 55:6 states: "Seek God while He can be found." We learn from this that our ability and the methods we use to connect to God are different depending on the time and day. This is evidenced throughout structured prayer, where what one says in the morning is different from what is said at night, weekday from Shabbat, a holiday from a fast. So it is for Tehillim: different psalms are more apt to channel God's influence at different times. Thus, many have the custom of saying particular chapters of Tehillim on certain days and for certain occasions.

Shir Shel Yom (Song of the Day)

The Levites would sing these psalms in the Temple, praising God differently each day of the week. It has become the universal custom to say the appropriate chapter at the end of Morning Services.

Day of the Week	Chapter
Sunday	24
Monday	48
Tuesday	82
Wednesday	94; 95:1-3
Thursday	81
Friday	93
Saturday	92

One's Birthday

Some have the custom to recite the daily psalm that corresponds to the years of one's life. For example, a 20-year-old recites Chapter 21 (since on one's 20th birthday, one begins the 21st year of their life).

Breslov Chassidim

The Breslov Chassidim have the custom to recite daily a compilation of 10 chapters of Tehillim called Tikkun Klali (General Remedy), for spiritual correction. The following psalms are recited: 16, 32, 41, 42, 59, 77, 90, 105, 137, 150.

In Times of Need

Originally, man prayed on a reactionary basis, asking when in need, thanking upon receipt. While structured prayers were instituted by the Men of the Great Assembly during the Second Temple period, this form of prayer is still used throughout Judaism. Choosing a psalm that relates to the person's request, one asks Hashem that his request should be answered as was the psalmist's.

In addition to the above, we have included in this book the Shimush Tehillim, Usages of Psalms, listing each particular psalm and an explanation of the connection to the occasion. This has been both integrated into each chapter and in its own section listed alphabetically.

Group Prayer

Group prayer has more influence than an individual's. As such, there are five main ways in which a congregation recites Tehillim:

- The congregation repeats each verse after the chazzan (cantor).
- The congregation repeats a standard refrain after every verse recited by the chazzan.
- The chazzan begins a verse, and the congregation completes it.
- The chazzan sings the incipit of the unit, and the congregation repeats the incipit and completes the unit.
- The chazzan sings the whole psalm, and the congregation repeats it.

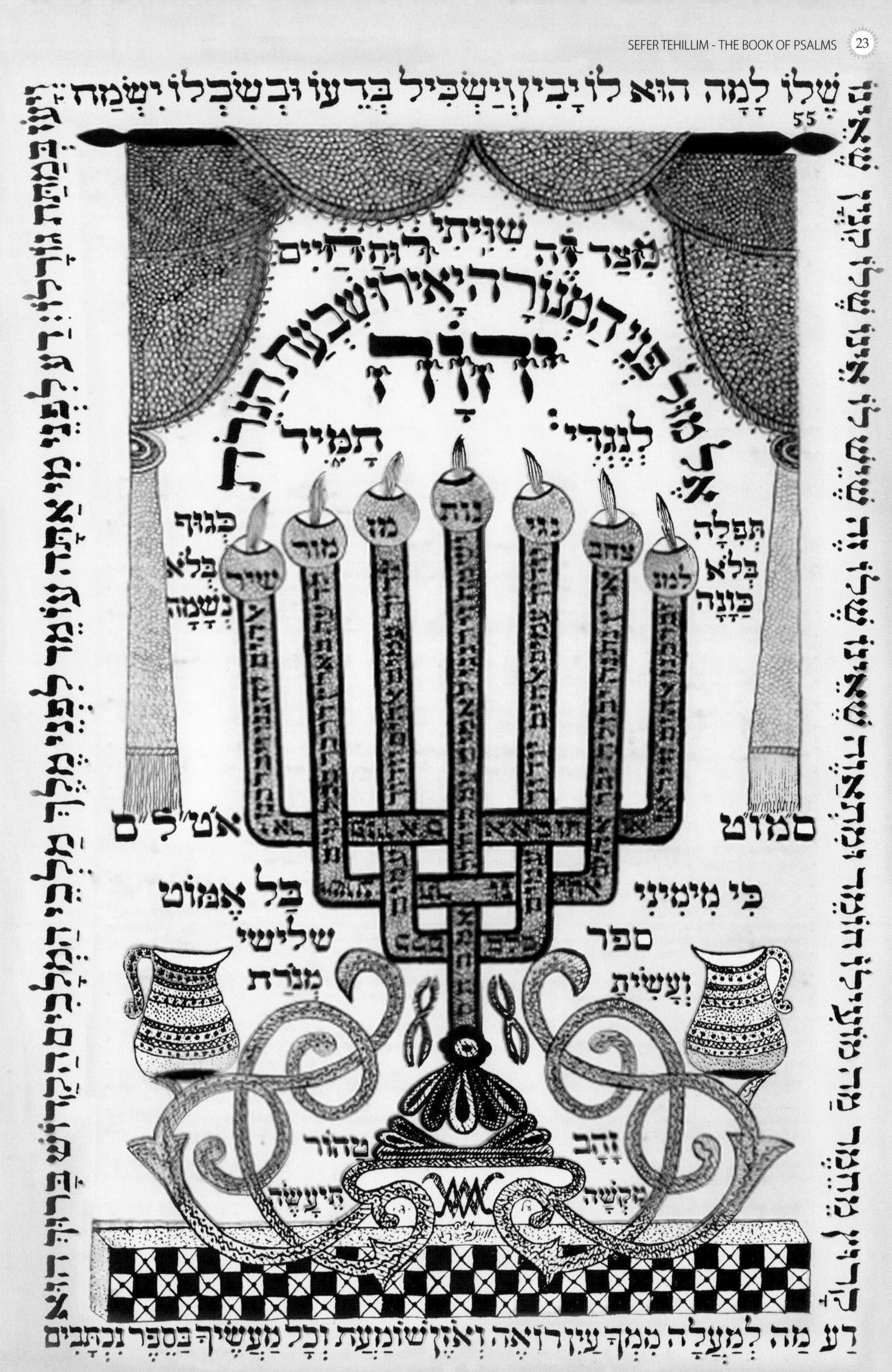

Cover of Handwritten Tehillim by Moshe Weinberg

THE 7 MAIN SELECTIONS OF SEFER TEHILLIM IN THE SIDDUR - PRAYER BOOK

SEFER TEHILLIM -THE BOOK OF PSALMS IS 150 CHAPTERS LONG.
IT IS THE LONGEST BOOK IN THE BIBLE.
MORE THAN 1,000 VERSES AND ALMOST 50 FULL CHAPTERS FROM SEFER TEHILLIM HAVE MADE ITS WAY INTO THE SIDDUR.

1. שיר של יום - Shir Shel Yom (The Song of The Day)

The legendary Beit HaMikdash, King Solomon's Temple, stood in Jerusalem from 995 BCE - 586 BCE. In its courtyards, the Kohanim (Priests) performed the various sacrifices while the Levi'im (Levites) sang in a choir accompanied by their brethren who played in the Levitical orchestra.

Every day, from Sunday through Shabbat, the Levites would sing the Shir Shel Yom, the designated Psalm of The Day.

The Psalm of the Day was chanted by the Levites daily, during the Temple service (Mishnah Tamid 7:4). The seven daily psalms allude to the 7 days of creation (Talmud Rosh Hashanah 31a). Each day, before reciting the selected Psalm of the Day, the Levites would proclaim an introductory statement declaring what day it was in relation to Shabbat. For instance, on Sunday they declared "Hayom Yom Rishon B'Shabbat", "This is the First Day of the Week towards Shabbat"; on Monday they declared "Hayom Yom Sheini B'Shabbat", "This is the Second Day of the Week towards Shabbat"; culminating on Shabbat itself, on which they declared "Hayom Yom Shabbat Kodesh", "Today is the Day of the Holy Shabbat."

2. פסוקי דזימרא - Pesukei Dezimra (Verses of Song)

Psalms 145-150

In Keeping with the Talmudic dictum that a person should always formulate praise of God before prayer (Talmud Berachot 32a), these psalms were adapted into the Siddur largely constituting Pesukei Dezimra, the introductory section of praise for Tefillat Shacharit, the daily Morning Service. Pesukei Dezimra culminates with "Az Yashir", "The Song of Moses" (Exodus 14:30-15:18), sung by the Jewish People after they experienced the miraculous salvation from the advancing Egyptian army with Keriat Yam Suf, the Splitting of the Sea.

3. פסוקי דזימרא של שבת ויום טוב – Pesukei Dezimra for Shabbat and Yom Tov (Festivals)

On Shabbat and Yom Tov, these additional psalms are inserted into the Pesukei Dezimra: 19, 34, 90, 91, 135, 136, 33, 93.

4. קבלת שבת - Kabbalat Shabbat (Welcoming the Shabbat Prayer)

Psalms 95, 96, 97, 98, 99, 29, 92, 93.

These psalms are recited to welcome the Shabbat on Friday night. Together with Lechah Dodi, written by Shlomo HaLevi Alkabetz (1500-1580), a rabbi, kabbalist and poet, these psalms constitute the main body of Kabbalat Shabbat.

The Kabalat Shabbat Prayer contains six psalms prior to Lechah Dodi, representing the 6 work days of the week. The initial letters of the six selected psalms have the numerical value of 430, equal to that of the word nefesh, soul.

5. הלל - Hallel (Psalms of Praise)

Psalms 113-118

These psalms constitute the Hallel Prayer which is recited on Rosh Chodesh, Chanukah, and the Festivals. Some also recite Hallel on Yom Ha'Atzma'ut (Israel's Independence Day), and Yom Yerushalayim (the Day of the Reunification of Jerusalem).

6. שיר המעלות - Shir HaMa'alot (The Songs of Ascent)

Psalms 120-134

These are a group of fifteen psalms which were sung as a Pilgrimage Song, as Jews made their way up to the Beit HaMikdash, a journey of more than two weeks for many, to celebrate the Shalosh Regalim, the Three Pilgrimage Festivals, which can be viewed as the core of national and religious life.

Beginning with the first Shabbat after Sukkot until Shabbat HaGadol (the Shabbat preceding Passover), some have a custom to read one Shir HaMa'alot per week following the Shabbat Minchah service.

Psalm 126, Shir HaMa'alot Beshuv Hashem, is sung on Shabbat and Festivals before Birkat HaMazon, The Grace after Meals.

There are fifteen chapters of Tehillim – Psalms 120-134 – that begin with the words "Shir HaMa'alot – Song of Ascent." There are three widely accepted interpretations as to what the ambiguous term "ascent" refers:

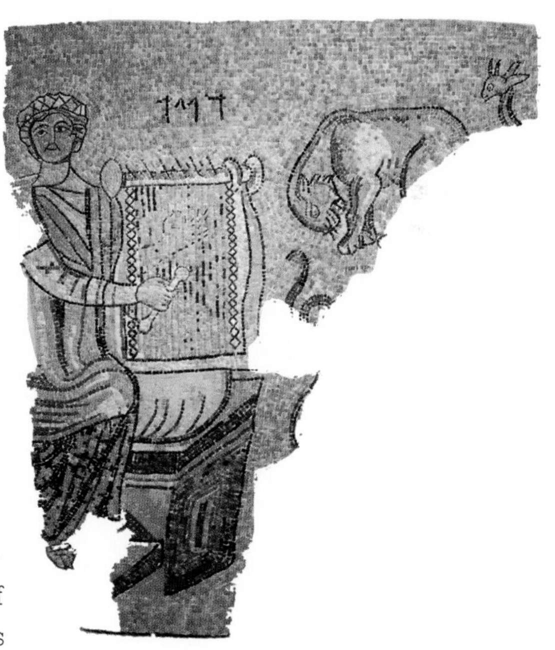

Mosaic of King David Playing the Harp

a. These fifteen psalms correspond to the fifteen steps which led to the inner courtyard of the Beit HaMikdash. The Levites would play instruments and recite these psalms as they ascended these steps.

b. These chapters of Tehillim were recited by the Jewish people as they made their three annual trips to the Beit HaMikdash for the Shalosh Regalim (Pilgrimage Festivals), Pesach, Sukkot, and Shavu'ot. First, they would ritually immerse themselves in the waters of the Siloam Pool in Jerusalem. They would then recite the Songs of Ascent as they ascended from there to the Temple Mount.

c. It was the voices of the singers in the Levitical choir that ascended louder and louder as they sang Shir HaMa'alot.

7. Contemporary Songs

Many lyrics of the most popular Jewish Hebrew Songs are indeed verses of the Tehillim.

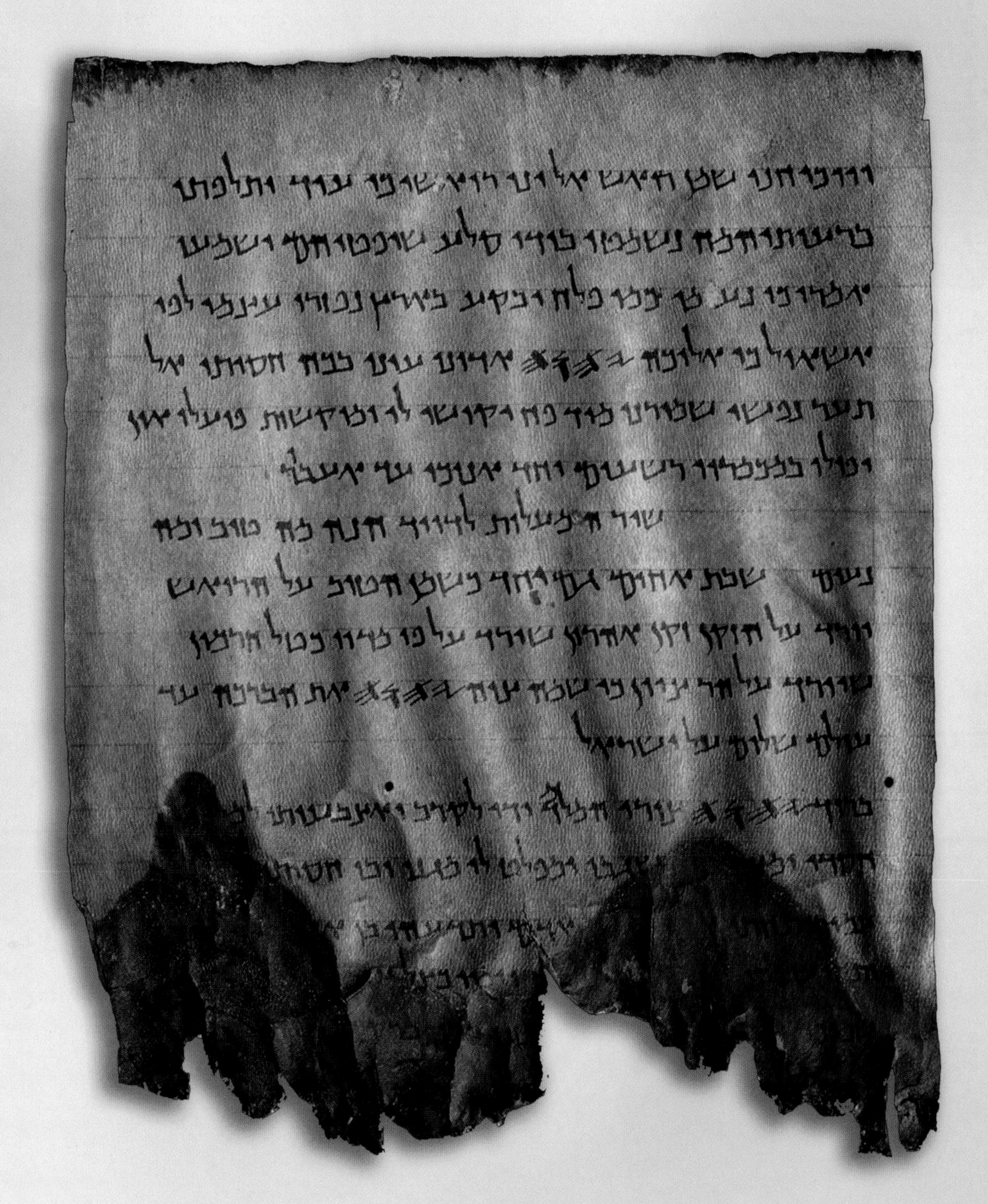

Tehillim Scroll

TEHILLIM COMPOSERS

ALTHOUGH AS A WHOLE, SEFER TEHILLIM IS ATTRIBUTED TO KING DAVID, RASHI — THE MOST HIGHLY ACCLAIMED BIBLICAL AND TALMUDIC COMMENTATOR (ELEVENTH CENTURY) —NOTES THAT THERE WERE ACTUALLY TEN AUTHORS (SEE TALMUD BAVA BATRA 14B) OF THE VARIOUS PSALMS INCLUDED IN SEFER TEHILLIM. THE TALMUD (PESACHIM 117A) MAINTAINS THAT EVERY CHAPTER OF "SHIROT VETISHBACHOT" ("SONGS AND PRAISES") WAS AUTHORED BY KING DAVID HIMSELF. GIVEN THE ABOVE, IT WOULD BE MOST ACCURATE TO ASSERT THAT KING DAVID REDACTED, RATHER THAN ACTUALLY PENNED, THE ENTIRETY OF SEFER TEHILLIM, WHILE AT THE SAME TIME AUTHORED MANY CHAPTERS HIMSELF.

Below is a list and short biographies of the most widely accepted view as to the many authors of Tehillim:

דָּוִד הַמֶּלֶךְ - King David

Second king of Israel, composer of the majority of the psalms which comprise Sefer Tehillim. The meaning of the name David is "beloved." He was a descendent of Ruth the Moabite, and the son of Yishai (Jesse) and Nitzevet Bat Adael. David had a ruddy complexion. As a youth, he was a shepherd, tending to flocks of sheep. He was a noted and gifted warrior; despite his young age he killed the mighty giant Goliath with a single slingshot. David was a musician who played music to calm Shaul (Saul), his father-in-law and former king of Israel. He was a faithful friend of Shaul's son, Yonatan (Jonathan). David prepared the initial blueprint for the Beit HaMikdash (Holy Temple). His son, Shlomo (Solomon) succeeded him as King of Israel. David is the ancestor of the foretold Mashiach (Messiah). He was born in Beit Lechem (Bethlehem) and passed away in Jerusalem, at the age of 70. The Talmud (Pesachim 117a) discusses whether in his Tehillim King David was referring to himself or the nation as a whole, or, alternatively, referring to himself in some chapters and to the Jewish people in others.

The following chapters are attributed to King David:
3-9, 11-32, 34-41, 51-61, 62*, 63-65, 68-70, 72**, 86, 101, 103, 108-110, 122, 124, 127**, 131-133, 138-145.

* Perhaps co-authored with Yedutun.

** Perhaps written and dedicated by King David to his son Shlomo (Solomon), his successor to the throne.

אָסָף - Asaf

Ancestor of one of the principal Levite families of singers in the Beit HaMikdash (Holy Temple). His father was Berachyah, the appointed guardian of the Aron HaKodesh (Ark of the Covenant). So talented was Asaf, that King David appointed him in charge of the music that heralded the arrival of the Aron HaKodesh. Asaf set to music many of the chapters of Tehillim authored by King David and inspired by God. Asaf and his fourteen sons were instrumental in the Levitical choir. According to the midrash, they infused such an awesome degree of spiritual power into their music and song that it indeed induced prophecy in those prepared for it. Asaf enjoyed a long and prosperous life. According to one view, he lived through the reigns of David, Shlomo and Shlomo's son, Rechavam. According to another opinion, he was a son of Korach, and thereby lived considerably earlier, during the time of Moses and Aaron. The midrash (Tana Devei Eliyahu Rabbah 30) states that he was a Navi (prophet). (See also Midrash Rabbah, Vayikra 10, 17).

The following chapters are attributed to Asaf:
50, 73-76, 77*, 78-83.

*Perhaps co-authored with Yedutun.

מֹשֶׁה - Moses

The Jewish leader chosen by God to lead the Jewish nation out of Egypt and to receive the Torah at Mount Sinai. Moses is considered Israel's greatest prophet and the most humble man of all time, both descriptions being spelled out in the Torah text itself! Moses was the leader and advocate of the Jewish people when they were established as a nation, leading them through the forty years in the Sinai Desert.

The following chapters are attributed to Moses : possibly 90-100

בְּנֵי-קֹרַח - The Sons of Korach

Korach, Moses 's first cousin and a Levite, he infamously attempted to usurp Moses 's leadership. The three sons of Korach, Assir, Elkanah and Aviasaf, repented and therefore did not perish along with him and his followers. The term "Sons of Korach" refers to the clan of Korach's descendants who sang in the Beit HaMikdash. Their psalms were not composed by any one individual, but rather were passed down from generation to generation.

The following chapters are attributed to B'nei Korach: 42, 44-49, 84-85, 87-88*

*According to tradition, co-authored with Heiman HaEzrachi.

שְׁלֹמֹה הַמֶּלֶךְ - King Solomon

The son of King David. The name Shlomo derives from the word meaning "peace" or "prosperity." He was crowned as king of Israel at the age of 12. He began building the Beit HaMikdash when he was sixteen, a process which took 7 years. He was also extremely wealthy. He is referred to as the smartest man who ever lived; the Midrash explains that he was able to give 3,000 explanations of every pasuk (verse) in the Torah. The Midrash adds that he was fluent in all 70 languages spoken in the world during his time, as well as being able to communicate with all the living creatures in the animal kingdom. He authored three books: Kohelet (Ecclesiastes), Mishlei (Proverbs), and Shir Hashirim (Song of Songs). Shlomo ruled for forty years; he passed away at the age of 52.

The following chapters are attributed to Shlomo: 72*, 127**

* Possibly begun by King David and finished by King Shlomo, or, according to another tradition, written completely by King David and dedicated to his son Shlomo, the future king of Israel.

** Possibly written by King David and dedicated to his son King Shlomo.

הֵימָן - Heiman

As there are several individuals known by the name Heiman, it is not clear which Heiman is considered a contributor to Tehillim. According to one account, the Heiman in question is a son of Yehudah, considered a great, wise man exceeded in wisdom only by King Solomon himself. According to another, this is none other than Heiman HaEzrachi—the son of Zerach and grandson of Judah. Heiman HaEzrachi was one of five sons, trained by their father to sing and play instruments in the Levitical choir. He was the brother of Zimri, Eitan, Kalchol, and Darda. He was one of three chief Levi'im appointed by King David to direct the musical service, together with the aforementioned Asaf and Yedutun. Heiman is also referred to as Chozeh HaMelech, Seer of the King. Heiman co-authored Psalm 88 with Korach's sons. (See Sanhedrin 44b).

The following chapter is attributed to Heiman: *88

*Perhaps co-authored with the sons of Korach.

אֵיתָן - Eitan

Also known as Eitan HaEzrachi, the son of Zerach and brother of Heiman HaEzrachi. He was a singer in the Levitical choir. The Talmud (Sanhedrin 44b) identifies Eitan HaEzrachi with Avraham Avinu (Abraham, the first of our patriarchs).

The following chapter is attributed to Eitan: possibly 89

יְדוּתוּן - Yedutun

From the family of Merari the son of Levi, he was a director, along with Hemian, of the Levitical orchestra and choir. He stood to the left of Heiman at the helm and opposite the singers. (See the Talmud, Bava Batra 14b).

The following chapters are attributed to Yedutun: 39, 62

Unknown or Debated Authorship

The following chapters are of unknown or debated authorship: 1, 2, 10, 33, 43, 66, 67, 71, 102, 104-107, 111-121, 123, 125, 126, 128-130, 134-137, 146-150.

According to Rashi, The Book of Tehillim is recorded with ten expressions of song, corresponding to the ten individuals who originally recited Tehillim: Adam, Malki Tzedek, Abraham, Moses, David, Solomon, Asaf and the three sons of Korach. Additionally, the Talmud (Berachot 10a) states that any psalm that begins or ends with the word "Ashrei—Praiseworthy" was composed by King David, and was considered particularly dear to him. The Tosafists (a group of Talmudic scholars comprised primarily of Rashi's grandchildren) extend this to all psalms that begin and/or end with the word "Haleluyah—Praise God", as they share a similar formula.

THE 10 INTRODUCTORY WORDS TO THE BOOK OF TEHILLIM

THERE ARE 10 INTRODUCTORY WORDS WHICH BEGIN MANY OF THE CHAPTERS OF TEHILLIM. FOLLOWING IS A CHART FURTHER EXPLAINING THESE WORDS, IDENTIFIED HERE AS "EXPRESSIONS OF SONG".

THE 10 EXPRESSIONS OF SONG

#	Hebrew	English	Example	Text
1	בניצוח	Conducting	4:1	לַמְנַצֵּחַ בִּנְגִינוֹת מִזְמוֹר לְדָוִד׃
2	בניגון	Melody	4:1	לַמְנַצֵּחַ בִּנְגִינוֹת מִזְמוֹר לְדָוִד׃
3	במזמור	Musical Accompaniment	92:1	מִזְמוֹר שִׁיר לְיוֹם הַשַּׁבָּת׃
4	בשיר	Song	92:1	מִזְמוֹר שִׁיר לְיוֹם הַשַּׁבָּת׃
5	בהלל	Praise	117:1	הַלְלוּ אֶת־יְהוָה כָּל־גּוֹיִם שַׁבְּחוּהוּ כָּל־הָאֻמִּים׃

#	Hebrew	English	Example	Text
6	בתפילה	Prayer	90:1	תְּפִלָּה לְמֹשֶׁה אִישׁ־הָאֱלֹהִים אֲדֹנָי מָעוֹן אַתָּה הָיִיתָ לָּנוּ בְּדֹר וָדֹר׃
7	בברכה	Blessing	144:1	לְדָוִד ׀ בָּרוּךְ יְהוָה ׀ צוּרִי הַמְלַמֵּד יָדַי לַקְרָב אֶצְבְּעוֹתַי לַמִּלְחָמָה׃
8	בהודאה	Thanksgiving	136:1	הוֹדוּ לַיהוָה כִּי־טוֹב כִּי לְעוֹלָם חַסְדּוֹ׃
9	באשרי	Praiseworthy	145:1	אַשְׁרֵי יוֹשְׁבֵי בֵיתֶךָ עוֹד יְהַלְלוּךָ סֶּלָה׃
10	בהללויה	Praise of Hashem	150:1	הַלְלוּ יָהּ ׀ הַלְלוּ־אֵל בְּקָדְשׁוֹ הַלְלוּהוּ בִּרְקִיעַ עֻזּוֹ׃

The above list follows the opinion of Rashi. An alternative list (Talmud, Pesachim 117a) adds "Maskil" ("A Discerning Individual") and deletes "Berachah" ("Blessing").

THE MUSİCAL İNSTRUMENTS FOUND İN THE BOOK OF TEHİLLİM

ALL THE MUSİCAL İNSTRUMENTS İN THE LEVİTİCAL ORCHESTRA CAN BE CATEGORİZED İNTO FOUR MAİN SECTİONS:

1. STRİNG İNSTRUMENTS
2. DRUMS
3. HORNS
4. CYMBALS

A KINOR - HARP

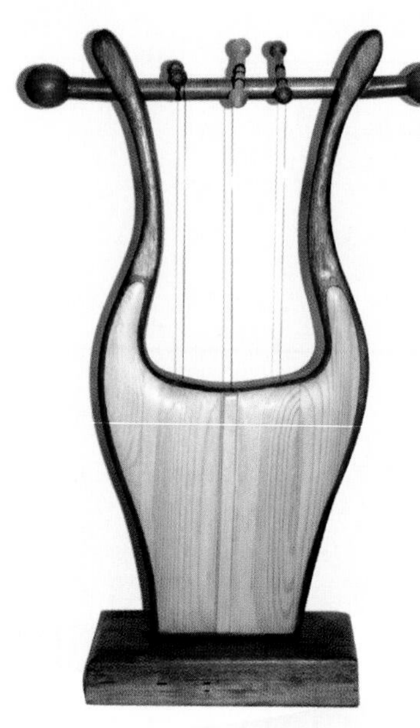

Bar Kochba Coin

Wooden Harp

B TOF - FRAMED DRUM

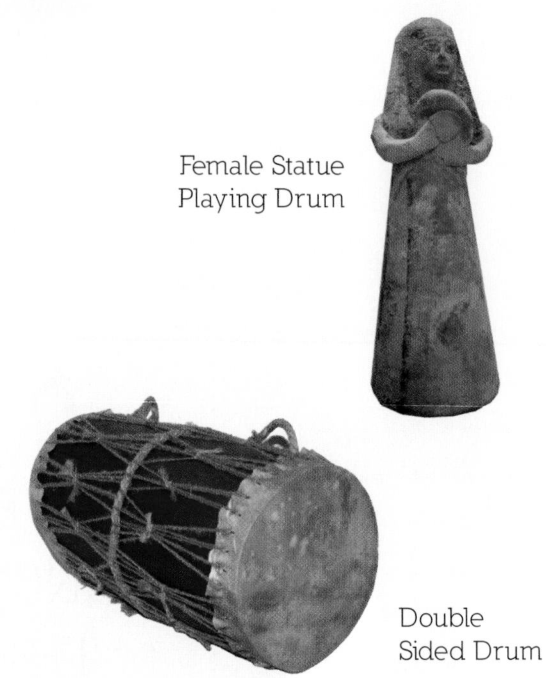

Female Statue Playing Drum

Double Sided Drum

C NEVEL - LYRE

Bar Kochba Coin

Wooden Lyre

D TOF - DRUM

Female Statue Playing Drum

Hand Drum

E SHOFAR - RAM'S HORN

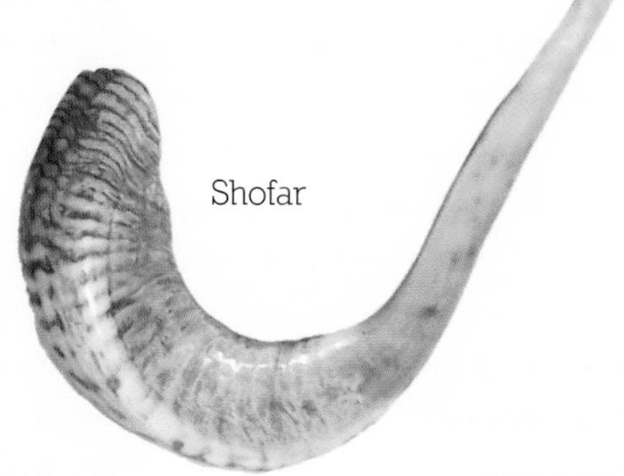

Shofar

Mosaic with Shofar

F TZİLZELİM - CYMBALS

Finger Cymbals

Oil Lamp

G CHATZOTZROT - SİLVER TRUMPETS

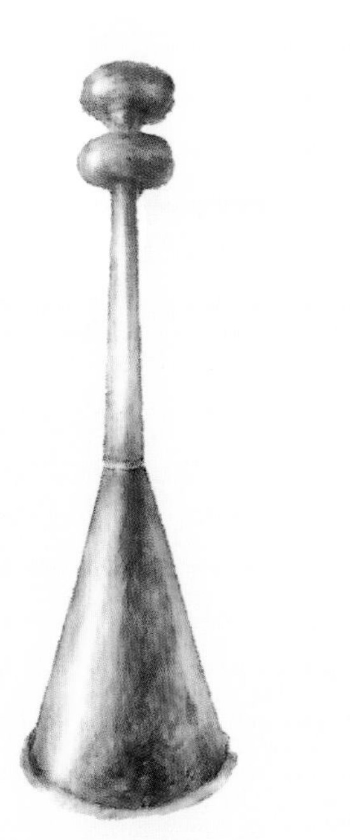

Chatzotrot

Bar Kochba Coin

H TZİLZELEİ TERUAH - CYMBAL CLAPPERS

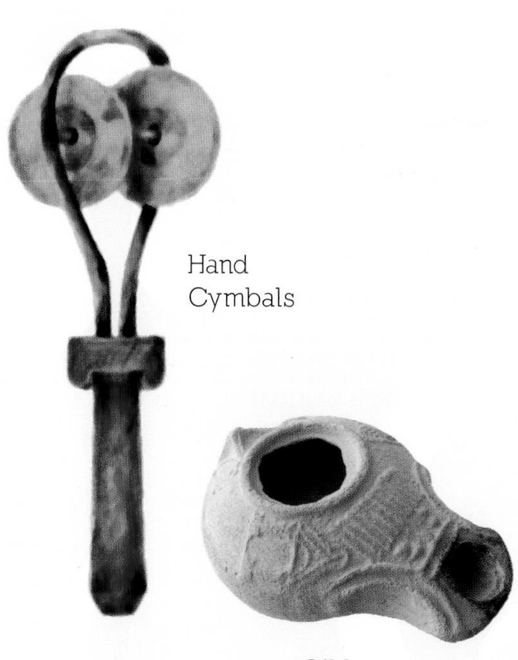

Hand Cymbals

Oil Lamp

MUSİCAL İNSTRUMENTS MENTİONED İN THE BOOK OF TEHİLLİM

שׁוֹפָר

Signaling instrument

Blown Instrument

Hebrew: עָלָה אֱלֹהִים, בִּתְרוּעָה; יְהוָה, בְּקוֹל שׁוֹפָר

Transliteration: Shofar

Description:

A non-musical signaling device made from the hollow horn of a kosher animal, traditionally a ram. It was light portable, easy to make, and was readily available to the common people. It's distinctive and piercing sound, varying sequences of long and short tone, could be heard over long distances.

1st Appearance in Tehillim: 47:6

Occurrences in Tehillim: 4

חֲצֹצְרוֹת

Signaling instruments

Blown Instrument

Hebrew: בַּחֲצֹצְרוֹת, וְקוֹל שׁוֹפָר-הָרִיעוּ, לִפְנֵי הַמֶּלֶךְ יְהוָה

Transliteration: Chatzotzrot

English: Two silver trumpets

Description:

A pair of non-musical, metal signaling devices used by the Kohanim to signal the assembly of the nation, the breaking of camp and in conjunction with various ritual functions. Originally crafted as a pair out of a solid piece of beaten silver, the instruments consisted of a mouthpiece and a straight bore body which terminated in a flared bell.

1st Appearance in Tehillim: 98:6

Occurrences in Tehillim: 1

כִּנּוֹר

Musical Instruments

String Instruments

Hebrew: הוֹדוּ לַיהוָה בְּכִנּוֹר; בְּנֵבֶל עָשׂוֹר, זַמְּרוּ-לוֹ

Transliteration: Kinor

English: Harp

Description:

A generic term for an ancient class of 'gut' string instruments used to accompany the voice or another instrument. Along with the lyre and melodic cymbals, the harp was one of the three primary instruments of song used by the Levites in their musical ensembles.

1st Appearance in Tehillim: 33:2

Occurrences in Tehillim: 13

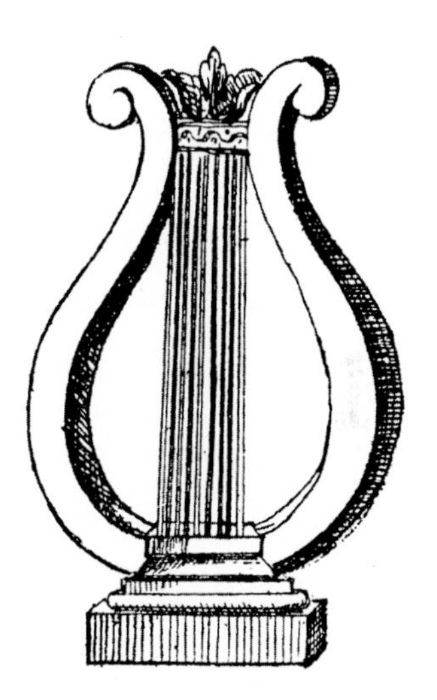

עֲלָמוֹת

Musical instruments

String Instrument

Hebrew: לַמְנַצֵּחַ לִבְנֵי-קֹרַח - עַל-עֲלָמוֹת שִׁיר

Transliteration: Alamos

Description:

An unidentified instrument - probably a harp.

1st Appearance in Tehillim: 46:1

Occurrences in Tehillim: 1

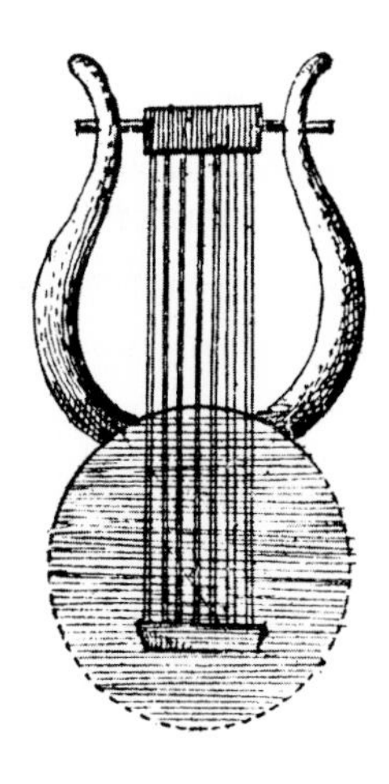

נֵבֶל

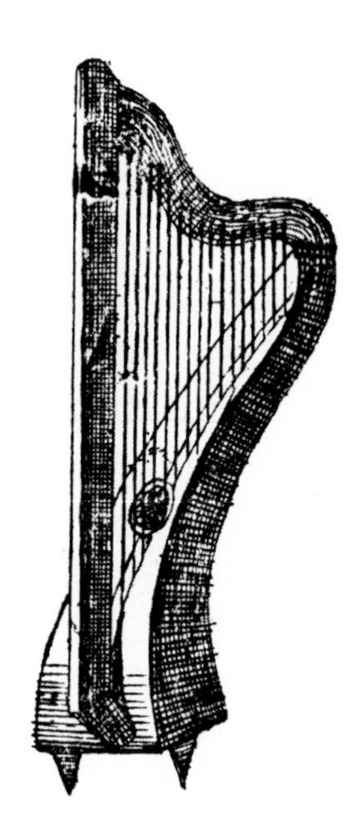

Musical Instruments

String Instrument

Hebrew: הודוּ לַיהוָה בְּכִנּוֹר; בְּנֵבֶל עָשׂוֹר, זַמְּרוּ-לוֹ

Transliteration: Nevel

Description:

An ancient string instrument of ten or more strings used to accompany the vocal presentations of the Levites. Standing almost three feet tall, the nevel had strings that were played in much the same manner as a modern harp—by plucking with the fingers.

1st Appearance in Tehillim: 71:22

Occurrences in Tehillim: 5

נֵבֶל עָשׂוֹר

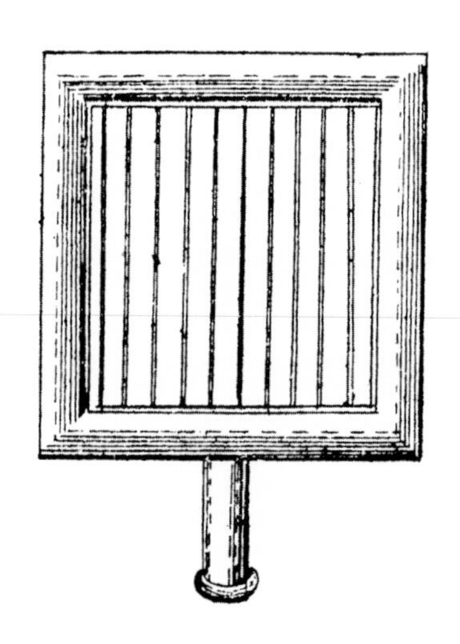

Musical Instruments

String Instrument

Hebrew: הודוּ לַיהוָה בְּכִנּוֹר; בְּנֵבֶל עָשׂוֹר, זַמְּרוּ-לוֹ

Transliteration: Nevel Asor

Description:

A Ten-Stringed Handheld Lyre

1st Appearance in Tehillim: 33:2

Occurrences in Tehillim: 3

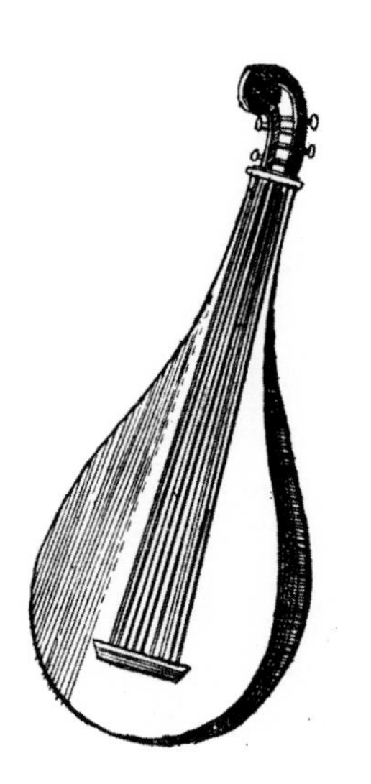

שְׁמִינִית

Musical Instruments

String Instrument

Hebrew: לַמְנַצֵּחַ בִּנְגִינוֹת, עַל-הַשְּׁמִינִית; מִזְמוֹר לְדָוִד

Transliteration: Sheminit

Description:

An eight-stringed harp

1st Appearance in Tehillim: 6:1

Occurrences in Tehillim: 2

גִּתִּית

Musical instruments

String Instrument

Hebrew: לַמְנַצֵּחַ עַל-הַגִּתִּית, מִזְמוֹר לְדָוִד

Transliteration: Gittis

Description:

Probably an instrument from the city of Gath. These psalms may have been sung at the Tabernacle as a musical accompaniment during the procedure of treading the new wine.

1st Appearance in Tehillim: 8:1

Occurrences in Tehillim: 3

עֻגָב

Musical instruments

Wind instruments

Hebrew: הַלְלוּהוּ, בְתֹף וּמָחוֹל; הַלְלוּהוּ, בְּמִנִּים וְעֻגָב

Transliteration: Ugav

English: Flute or multiple pipe flute

Description:

A generic name for a family of hollow, tubular musical wind instruments. Closed on one end and made of bone, bamboo, wood, or metal its sound is created by gently blowing across the tube. Mentioned only five times within the Bible in limited contexts, the ugav is one of the instruments of the scriptures we know very little about. Due to the inconsistent renderings as a string instrument, harp, pipe, organ, and even a song in various translations, an exact description and classification of this instrument is problematic.

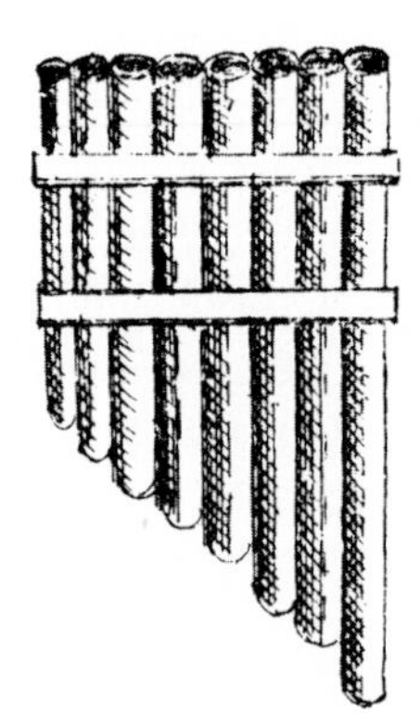

1st Appearance in Tehillim: 150:4

Occurrences in Tehillim: 1

שֹׁשַׁנִּים

Concussion Instruments

Hebrew: לַמְנַצֵּחַ עַל-שֹׁשַׁנִּים, לִבְנֵי-קֹרַח; מַשְׂכִּיל, שִׁיר יְדִידֹת

Transliteration: Shoshanim

English: On the roses or lilies

Description:

According to Rashi it is either a six-stringed instrument whose name comes from the root shesh or six. Another explanation is that shoshan is a musical instrument in the shape of a lily or rose.

1st Appearance in Tehillim: 45:1

Occurrences in Tehillim: 3

נְגִינוֹת

Musical instruments

String Instrument

Hebrew: לַמְנַצֵּחַ בִּנְגִינוֹת, מִזְמוֹר לְדָוִד

Transliteration: Neginos

English: A psalm accompanied by stringed instruments

Description:

Either a stringed instrument, or music with the accompaniment of strings.

1st Appearance in Tehillim: 4:1

Occurrences in Tehillim: 7

נְּחִילוֹת

Musical Instruments

Wind Instruments

Hebrew: לַמְנַצֵּחַ אֶל-הַנְּחִילוֹת, מִזְמוֹר לְדָוִד

Transliteration: Nechilot

English: Wind instrument

Description:

Instruments such as the pipes or flutes that accompanied the psalms.

1st Appearance in Tehillim: 5:1

Occurrences in Tehillim: 1

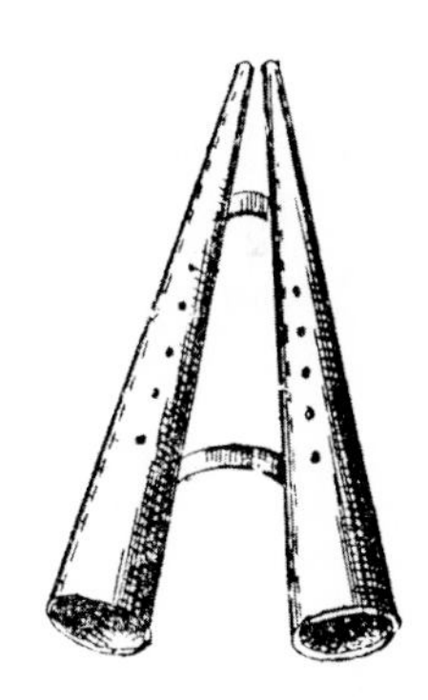

מָחוֹל

Musical Instruments

Wind Instruments

Hebrew: הַלְלוּהוּ, בְתֹף וּמָחוֹל; הַלְלוּהוּ, בְּמִנִּים וְעֻגָב

Transliteration: Machol

English: Flutes

Description:

A reedless wind instrument or possibly a dance.

1st Appearance in Tehillim: 150:1

Occurrences in Tehillim: 1

צִלְצְלֵיים / מְצִלְתַּיִם

Musical Instruments

Concussion Instruments

Hebrew: הַלְלוּהוּ בְצִלְצְלֵי-שָׁמַע; הַלְלוּהוּ, בְּצִלְצְלֵי תְרוּעָה

Transliteration: Mitzaltayim, Zelzelim

English: Melodic cymbals

Description:

The larger variety of the ancient cymbals (3½" to 4¾") , today referred to as crotales—pitched or tuned cymbals, which produce specific, refined musical tone. Always referenced as a set, the melodic cymbals were used by the Levite singers, as part of the Levite musical production. They consisted of two individual cymbal plates (one held by the right hand and one by the left) that were concussively struck together, serving three primary functions: providing a tuning reference for the lyres and harps; starting pitches for singers; and praising the name of God.

1st Appearance in Tehillim: 150:5

Occurrences in Tehillim: 1

צִלְצְלֵי-שָׁמַע

Musical Instruments

Percussion Instruments

Hebrew: הַלְלוּהוּ בְצִלְצְלֵי-שָׁמַע; הַלְלוּהוּ, בְּצִלְצְלֵי תְרוּעָה

Transliteration: TselTselai Shama

English: Pitched cymbals

Description:

Cymbals of melodious sounds .

1st Appearance in Tehillim: 150:5

Occurrences in Tehillim: 1

תּוֹף

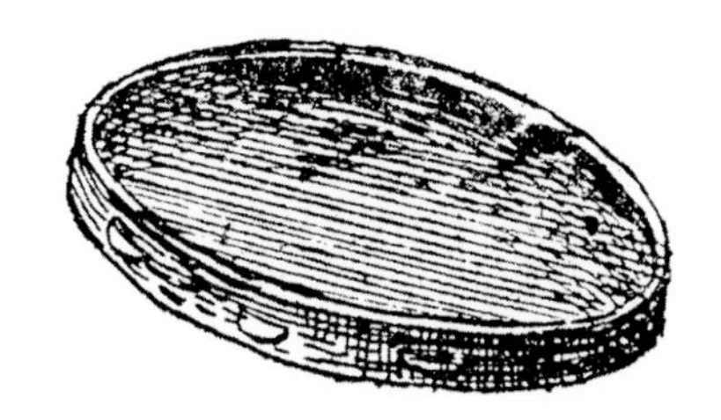

Rhythm Instruments
Percussion Instruments
Hebrew: קִדְּמוּ שָׁרִים, אַחַר נֹגְנִים; בְּתוֹךְ עֲלָמוֹת, תּוֹפֵפוֹת
Transliteration: Tof
English: Framed hand drum
Description:
A large, thin drum, made with wood and animal hide, in conjunction with dance, and often played by women. The frame-drum was held with the left hand and played by striking the head of the drum with the alternating thumb and forefingers of the right hand in various rhythmic patterns.
1st Appearance in Tehillim: 68:26
Occurrences in Tehillim: 4

צִלְצְלֵי תְרוּעָה

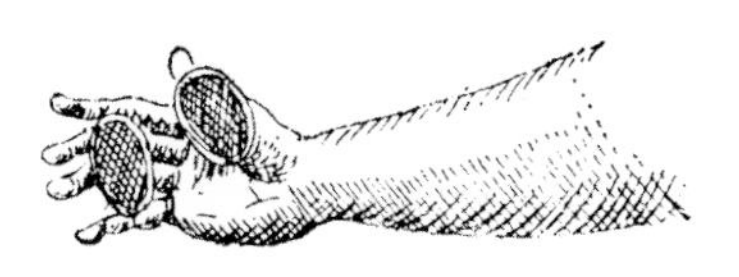

Rhythm Instruments
Concussion Instruments
Hebrew: הַלְלוּהוּ בְצִלְצְלֵי-שָׁמַע; הַלְלוּהוּ, בְּצִלְצְלֵי תְרוּעָה
Transliteration: TselTselai Teruah
English: Cymbal clappers
Description:
A pair of small cymbals (1½" to 2½"), individually mounted on flexible prongs that would be shaken rapidly (the teruah) causing the cymbal plates to concussively strike each other. Unlike finger cymbals, this cymbal clapper requires very little skill to execute.
1st Appearance in Tehillim: 150:5
Occurrences in Tehillim: 1

SHIMUSH TEHILLIM INDEX - WHEN TO SAY - THE USAGES OF TEHILLIM

SHIMUSH TEHILLIM IS A USEFUL GUIDE TO UNDERSTANDING WHY WE SAY A PARTICULAR CHAPTER OF TEHILLIM WHEN PRAYING FOR SPECIAL REQUESTS AND OUTCOMES.

SHIMUSH TEHILLIM

Shimush Tehillim, The Usages of Psalms, was written by Rav Hai Gaon (939-1038), the head of the Talmudic Academy of Pumbedita (today the location of the modern city Fallujah, Iraq), during the era of the Abbasid Caliphate. His work is an exhaustive index, listing when it is appropriate to recite each particular psalm, accompanied by his reasoning of the connection. We have integrated Shimush Tehillim into the introduction of each chapter. (See the section titled "How to Use This Book" for further explanation).

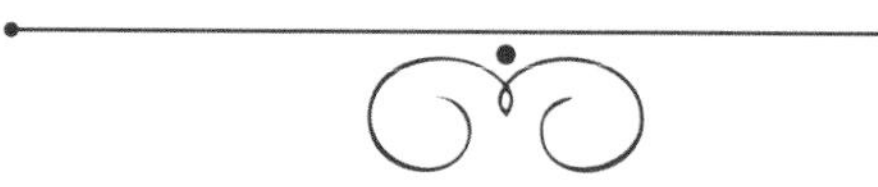

INDEX - Shimush Tehillim

The list below, following the guidelines of Shimush Tehillim, is organized alphabetically along with the chapter(s) to be recited. In the case of chapter 119, comprised of eight verses for each letter of the Hebrew Alphabet, a Hebrew letter following the chapter number indicates that one should recite the eight verses beginning with that Hebrew letter.

HOW TO USE THIS BOOK

HOW TO USE THIS BOOK

The following information accompanies each chapter of this book, where applicable.

1. Chapter: A listing of the chapter number in Hebrew and English.
Example: Psalms Chapter 1 | **תהלים פרק א**

2. Cycle Chart: A chart corresponding to the recitation of the psalms according to the weekly cycle, the monthly cycle or by the five book division.

Example:

Weekly Cycle	Monthly Cycle	Book Number
Sunday	1st day of the month	Book 1

3. Edge Index: Positioned on the right side of each of the 150 chapters of psalms is an index to be used to locate a specific chapter or the different cycles of its recitation.

Book 1 - The 150 chapters are grouped into five books, so that the recitation of the entire Book of Psalms can be completed every five days. The books are marked in the index as Book 1 through Book 5.

Day of the Week - The 150 chapters are grouped into seven portions, so that the recitation of the entire Book of Psalms can be completed every week. The days are marked in the index from Sunday through Saturday.

Day of the Month - The 150 chapters are grouped into thirty portions, so that the entire Book of Psalms can be completed every Jewish month. The days of the month are marked in the index from 1-30.

Chapter Number - For easy access to finding any given chapter, the chapter numbers (1-150) are placed horizontally in the edge index.

4. Author: A listing of the individual(s) who authored the chapter. For a biography of all of the authors, see the section titled "Tehillim Composers".

5. Genre: A listing of the genre of that particular chapter. There are many types of psalms, the major groupings of which are: Songs of Praise, Songs of Thanksgiving, and Prayers of Lament.

6. Chapter Summary: A brief overview of each chapter.

7. Introductory Word: A listing of introductory words and phrases pertaining to the particular chapter, based on the commentary of Rashi. On the 1st verse of the Book of Tehillim, Rashi lists ten expressions of song with which many of the chapters begin. (See; Chart of 10 Expressions of Song).

8. Musical Instruments: A listing of instrument(s) which accompanied the recitation of the chapter by the Levitical orchestra. Where a specific instrument is mentioned in the text of the psalm, it is noted.

9. Technical Terminology: A listing of obscure words and/or phrases appearing in the particular chapter. Each entry is translated and transliterated as well.

10. Shimush Tehillim: A list of occasions upon which to recite the particular psalm, based on the work Shimush Tehillim (the Usages of Tehillim). Where applicable, the reasoning behind the specific occasion has been integrated as well. (See Shimush Tehillim Index - When to Say).

11. Interesting Facts: Assorted interesting facts and figures regarding aspects of the particular chapter.

12. Where in the Siddur (Prayer Book): A cross referencing of the particular chapter of the Book of Tehillim to the arrangement of the Siddur. Here the reader will find where many of the verses and chapters appear in Jewish liturgy.

13. Biblical Peoples: A brief description of the nations mentioned in the chapter. All such nations were geographically Israel's neighbors. In some instances they were also Israel's enemies.

14. Biblical Personalities: A list of each individual mentioned in the particular chapter, accompanied by a brief biography.

15. Biblical Places: A list of many otherwise unfamiliar locations in and around the land of Israel as referenced in the particular chapter.

16. Contemporary Song: A list of contemporary, popular songs composed with lyrics from verses of that particular chapter.

17. Talmud on Tehilim: Talmudic explanations and insights of various passages of the particular chapter.

PRAYERS TO BE RECİTED BEFORE SAYİNG TEHİLLİM - PSALMS

תפילה קודם אמירת תהלים - Prayer Before Reciting Tehillim

יְהִי רָצוֹן מִלְּפָנֶיךָ,	May it be the will before You,
יהוה אֱלֹהֵינוּ וֵאלֹהֵי אֲבוֹתֵינוּ-	Hashem, our God, and the God of our forefathers -
הַבּוֹחֵר בְּדָוִד עַבְדּוֹ	Who chose David His servant
וּבְזַרְעוֹ אַחֲרָיו,	and his offspring after him,
וְהַבּוֹחֵר בְּשִׁירוֹת וְתִשְׁבָּחוֹת-	and Who chose songs and praises -
שֶׁתֵּפֶן בְּרַחֲמִים אֶל קְרִיאַת מִזְמוֹרֵי תְהִלִּים	that you attend with mercy to the recitation of psalms
שֶׁאֶקְרָא כְּאִלּוּ אֲמָרָם	that I shall merit. and consider it as if they were recited
דָּוִד הַמֶּלֶךְ	by King David,
עָלָיו הַשָּׁלוֹם בְּעַצְמוֹ,	of blessed memory himself,
זְכוּתוֹ יָגֵן עָלֵינוּ.	may his merit be a shield over us.
וְיַעֲמָד לָנוּ זְכוּת	And stand in our favor may the merit
פְּסוּקֵי תְהִלִּים -	of the verses of the psalms -
וּזְכוּת תֵּבוֹתֵיהֶם,	together with the merit of their words
וְאוֹתִיּוֹתֵיהֶם,	and their letters
וּנְקוּדּוֹתֵיהֶם,	and their vowels
וְטַעֲמֵיהֶם,	and their cantillations,
וְהַשֵּׁמוֹת	and together with the Holy Names
הַיּוֹצְאִים מֵהֶם,	that are formed from them,
מֵרָאשֵׁי תֵבוֹת	from the initial (letters) of the words
וּמִסּוֹפֵי תֵבוֹת-	and from the final (letters) of the words -
לְכַפֵּר	may their merit serve to bring atonement
פְּשָׁעֵינוּ	for our transgressions,
וַעֲוֹנוֹתֵינוּ וְחַטֹּאתֵינוּ,	iniquities, and sins,
וּלְזַמֵּר עָרִיצִים,	and to cut down ruthless men,
וּלְהַכְרִית כָּל הַחוֹחִים וְהַקּוֹצִים	and slash away all the thorns and briars
הַסּוֹבְבִים אֶת הַשּׁוֹשַׁנָּה הָעֶלְיוֹנָה	which surround the Celestial Rose;
וּלְחַבֵּר אֵשֶׁת נְעוּרִים עִם דּוֹדָהּ,	and to unite the Bride of Youth with her Beloved
בְּאַהֲבָה וְאַחֲוָה וְרֵיעוּת.	in love, brotherhood, and companionship.
וּמִשָּׁם יִמָּשֵׁךְ לָנוּ	And from that may be drawn to us
שֶׁפַע לְנֶפֶשׁ רוּחַ וּנְשָׁמָה	an abundant blessing to our spirit, breath and soul,
לְטַהֲרֵנוּ מֵעֲוֹנוֹתֵינוּ	to purify us of our iniquities,
וְלִסְלוֹחַ חַטֹּאתֵינוּ וּלְכַפֵּר פְּשָׁעֵינוּ,	to forgive our sins and to atone for our transgressions,
כְּמוֹ שֶׁסָּלַחְתָּ לְדָוִד	just as You forgave David
שֶׁאָמַר מִזְמוֹרִים אֵלּוּ לְפָנֶיךָ	who recited these very same psalms before You -
כְּמוֹ שֶׁנֶּאֱמַר:	as it is said:
גַּם יהוה הֶעֱבִיר חַטָּאתְךָ לֹא תָמוּת.	Hashem also has forgiven your sin, you shall not die.

וְאַל תִּקָּחֵנוּ מֵהָעוֹלָם הַזֶּה	May you not take us from This World
קוֹדֶם זְמַנֵּנוּ	before our time,
עַד מְלֹאת שְׁנוֹתֵינוּ	until the completion of our years,
(בָּהֶם שִׁבְעִים שָׁנָה)	(among them are seventy years),
בְּאוֹפֶן שֶׁנּוּכַל	in a manner that we be able
לְתַקֵּן אֶת אֲשֶׁר שִׁחַתְנוּ.	to rectify anything that we have ruined.
וּזְכוּת דָּוִד הַמֶּלֶךְ עָלָיו הַשָּׁלוֹם	May the merit of King David, of blessed memory,
יָגֵן עָלֵינוּ וּבַעֲדֵנוּ	shield over us and for us;
שֶׁתַּאֲרִיךְ אַפְּךָ	that You may be patient (with us),
עַד שׁוּבֵנוּ אֵלֶיךָ	until we return to You
בִּתְשׁוּבָה שְׁלֵמָה לְפָנֶיךָ.	in repentance that is complete before You.
וּמֵאוֹצַר מַתְּנַת	From your treasury of grace that is undeserved,
חִנָּם חָנֵּנוּ	be gracious to us -
כְּדִכְתִיב:	as it is written:
וְחַנֹּתִי אֶת אֲשֶׁר אָחֹן	I am Compassionate to those whom I favor,
וְרִחַמְתִּי אֶת אֲשֶׁר אֲרַחֵם.	and I am Merciful to those upon whom I have mercy.
וּכְשֵׁם שֶׁאָנוּ אוֹמְרִים לְפָנֶיךָ	And just as we recite before You
שִׁירָה בְּעוֹלָם הַזֶּה	a song in This World,
כַּךְ נִזְכֶּה לוֹמַר לְפָנֶיךָ	so let us merit to recite before You -
יהוה אֱלֹהֵינוּ	O Hashem, our God -
שִׁיר וּשְׁבָחָה לָעוֹלָם הַבָּא.	songs and praises in the World to Come.
וְעַל יְדֵי אֲמִירַת תְּהִלִּים	And through the recitation of the psalms
תִּתְעוֹרֵר חֲבַצֶּלֶת הַשָּׁרוֹן	arouse the Rose of Sharon
וְלָשִׁיר בְּקוֹל נָעִים בְּגִילַת וְרַנֵּן,	to sing with a voice that is pleasant, with ecstasy and joy.
כְּבוֹד הַלְּבָנוֹן נִתַּן לָהּ,	May the glory of the Lebanon be given to her,
הוֹד וְהָדָר בְּבֵית אֱלֹהֵינוּ	majesty and splendor in the House of our God,
בִּמְהֵרָה בְיָמֵינוּ אָמֵן סֶלָה.	speedily in our days. Amen. Selah!

On the Sabbath and Festivals, begin here (Psalms 95:1-3):

לְכוּ, נְרַנְּנָה לַיהוָה;	Come, let us sing praises to the Lord;
נָרִיעָה,	let us shout
לְצוּר יִשְׁעֵנוּ.	to the rock of our salvation.
נְקַדְּמָה פָנָיו בְּתוֹדָה;	Let us greet His presence with thanksgiving;
בִּזְמִרוֹת, נָרִיעַ לוֹ.	let us shout to Him with songs.
כִּי אֵל גָּדוֹל יְהוָה;	For the Lord is a great God
וּמֶלֶךְ גָּדוֹל, עַל כָּל אֱלֹהִים.	and a great King over all divine powers.

SEFER TEHİLLİM - THE BOOK OF PSALMS - İNTRODUCTİON, TEXT AND TRANSLATİON

BOOK 1

פרק א Chapter 1

Weekly Cycle	Monthly Cycle	Book Number
Sunday	1st day of the month	Book 1

Author

Unknown, perhaps דָּוִד הַמֶּלֶךְ—King David—the second king of Israel and father of the Davidic royal and messianic dynasty. David composed over seventy of the 150 psalms of Sefer Tehillim.

Genre

Psalm of Wisdom – This psalm contains teachings and wise advice and is meant to instruct people on how to live a Godly life.

Chapter Summary

This psalm, along with the following one, serves as an introduction to the entire Sefer Tehillim (Book of Psalms). Together they are described in the Talmud (Berachot 9b) as one unit, and in fact, only at a later date were subdivided into two separate chapters.

The psalmist, in this introduction, reveals to us the golden rule for spiritual success: only one who departs from evil and does good is truly happy and firmly rooted. The first verse explains it all: "Fortunate is the man who has not walked in the counsel of the wicked, and in the way of the sinful he has not stood, and in the seat of the scornful he has not sat."

This psalm consists of six verses, subdivided into three parts.
In verses 1 & 2, the psalmist speaks of the difference between the deeds of the righteous and those of the wicked.
In verses 3 & 4, he contrasts the righteous and the wicked by way of a simile. The righteous and their deeds are compared to a fruit-bearing tree while the wicked and their deeds are compared to valueless chaff blown away by the wind
In verses 5 & 6, he describes the rewards to be reaped by the righteous and the punishment to be exacted upon the wicked.

Introductory Word

אַשְׁרֵי—Ashrei—Fortunate—Praiseworthy—Happy

Shimush Tehillim - When to Say

To prevent miscarriage—Verse 3 refers to a tree which produces fruit in its natural time. Similarly, a person who is dedicated to righteousness will see the fruits of his/her labor in a timely fashion.

Contemporary Song

Verses 1 & 2

Talmud on Tehillim

Verse 1: "אַשְׁרֵי"—"Ashrei"—"Fortunate; Praiseworthy; Happy"
The Talmud, Berachot 10a, states: "Any chapter [of Psalms] that was especially dear to King David,

he opened with a verse containing the word אַשְׁרֵי (Fortunate), and/or concluded with a verse containing the word אַשְׁרֵי (Fortunate)".

Amulet Plaque with Menorah and Birds

פֶּרֶק א

א אַשְׁרֵי־הָאִישׁ אֲשֶׁר ׀ לֹא הָלַךְ
בַּעֲצַת רְשָׁעִים
וּבְדֶרֶךְ חַטָּאִים
לֹא עָמָד
וּבְמוֹשַׁב לֵצִים לֹא יָשָׁב׃
ב כִּי אִם בְּתוֹרַת יְהוָה
חֶפְצוֹ
וּבְתוֹרָתוֹ יֶהְגֶּה יוֹמָם וָלָיְלָה׃
ג וְהָיָה כְּעֵץ
שָׁתוּל עַל־פַּלְגֵי מָיִם
אֲשֶׁר פִּרְיוֹ ׀ יִתֵּן בְּעִתּוֹ
וְעָלֵהוּ לֹא־יִבּוֹל
וְכֹל אֲשֶׁר־יַעֲשֶׂה יַצְלִיחַ׃
ד לֹא־כֵן הָרְשָׁעִים
כִּי אִם־כַּמֹּץ
אֲשֶׁר־תִּדְּפֶנּוּ רוּחַ׃
ה עַל־כֵּן ׀
לֹא־יָקֻמוּ רְשָׁעִים בַּמִּשְׁפָּט
וְחַטָּאִים
בַּעֲדַת צַדִּיקִים׃
ו כִּי־יוֹדֵעַ יְהוָה
דֶּרֶךְ צַדִּיקִים
וְדֶרֶךְ רְשָׁעִים תֹּאבֵד׃

Chapter 1

1 Fortunate is the man who has not walked
in the counsel of the wicked,
and in the way of the sinful
he has not stood,
and in the seat of the scornful he has not sat.
2 But only in the Torah of Adonoy
is his desire,
and in his Torah he meditates day and night.
3 He will be like a tree
set into the ground near streams of water,
which yields its fruit in its season,
and whose leaf does not wither;
and in whatever he does he will succeed.
4 Not so the wicked
who are like the chaff
which the wind drives away.
5 Therefore,
the wicked will not stand up in judgment,
nor the sinful
in the assembly of the righteous.
6 For Adonoy regards
the way of the righteous,
and the way of the wicked will be lost.

פרק ב Chapter 2

Weekly Cycle	Monthly Cycle	Book Number
Sunday	1st day of the month	Book 1

Author

Unknown; perhaps דָּוִד הַמֶּלֶךְ—King David—the second king of Israel and father of the Davidic royal and messianic dynasty. David composed over seventy of the 150 psalms of Sefer Tehillim.

When & Why

David might have written this psalm at the time of his inaugruation, encouraging the Israelites to respect the new king, who is God's annointed one.

Genre

Psalm of Royalty - This psalm describes how God reigns supreme. It focuses on the human king of Israel, or upon God as King of Israel.

Chapter Summary

This psalm speaks of the suffering that befell the author, symbolizing and anticipating the sufferings of both the individual Jew and the Jewish People throughout the generations. It seeks to inspire the Jew with hope and strength during the long exile, until the arrival of the Mashiach (Messiah).

This psalm consists of twelve verses, subdivided into four parts.
In verses 1-3, the nations of the world shout out against God and His anointed.
In verses 4-6, God speaks to the nations.
In verses 7-9, the psalmist speaks of and relates God's words to him.
In verses 10-12, the psalmist himself addresses the nations.

Shimush Tehillim - When to Say

For a Headache —Verse 9 refers to "Break them with a rod of iron, as a potter's vessel, shatter them."

For a Stormy Sea—Verse 12 exhorts the reader to " Do homage in purity [of heart], lest He be angry and you will be lost on your way, for His wrath is kindled suddenly; fortunate are all who take refuge in Him."

Biblical Places

צִיּוֹן—Zion—often used as a synonym for Jerusalem. The term Zion originally referred only to the area where a Jebbusite fortress once stood, also the location of the City of David. Zion was later used by prophets and psalmists as another name for the expanded Jerusalem.

Talmud on Tehillim

Verse 7: "אֲסַפְּרָה אֶל-חֹק" —"I will tell of the decree."
The Talmud, Sukkah 52a, relates this verse to the Mashiach (Messiah), the descendant of David.

פֶּרֶק ב

א לָמָּה רָגְשׁוּ גוֹיִם
וּלְאֻמִּים יֶהְגּוּ־רִיק׃
ב יִתְיַצְּבוּ ׀ מַלְכֵי־אֶרֶץ
וְרוֹזְנִים נוֹסְדוּ־יָחַד
עַל־יְהוָה
וְעַל־מְשִׁיחוֹ׃
ג נְנַתְּקָה אֶת־מוֹסְרוֹתֵימוֹ
וְנַשְׁלִיכָה מִמֶּנּוּ עֲבֹתֵימוֹ׃
ד יוֹשֵׁב בַּשָּׁמַיִם יִשְׂחָק
אֲדֹנָי יִלְעַג־לָמוֹ׃
ה אָז יְדַבֵּר אֵלֵימוֹ בְאַפּוֹ
וּבַחֲרוֹנוֹ יְבַהֲלֵמוֹ׃
ו וַאֲנִי נָסַכְתִּי מַלְכִּי
עַל־צִיּוֹן הַר־קָדְשִׁי׃
ז אֲסַפְּרָה אֶל חֹק
יְהוָה אָמַר אֵלַי בְּנִי אַתָּה
אֲנִי הַיּוֹם יְלִדְתִּיךָ׃
ח שְׁאַל מִמֶּנִּי
וְאֶתְּנָה גוֹיִם נַחֲלָתֶךָ
וַאֲחֻזָּתְךָ
אַפְסֵי־אָרֶץ׃
ט תְּרֹעֵם בְּשֵׁבֶט בַּרְזֶל
כִּכְלִי יוֹצֵר תְּנַפְּצֵם׃
י וְעַתָּה מְלָכִים הַשְׂכִּילוּ
הִוָּסְרוּ שֹׁפְטֵי אָרֶץ׃
יא עִבְדוּ אֶת־יְהוָה בְּיִרְאָה
וְגִילוּ בִּרְעָדָה׃
יב נַשְּׁקוּ־בַר
פֶּן־יֶאֱנַף ׀
וְתֹאבְדוּ דֶרֶךְ
כִּי־יִבְעַר כִּמְעַט אַפּוֹ
אַשְׁרֵי כָּל־חוֹסֵי בוֹ׃

Chapter 2

1 Why do the nations congregate
and [why do] peoples think of worthless plans?
2 [Why do] the earth's kings set themselves,
and the rulers take counsel together,
against Adonoy
and against His annointed [saying],
3 "Let us remove their bands
and cast away from us their cords."
4 He Who sits in heaven will laugh,
my Master will mock them.
5 Then He will speak to them in His anger,
and in His rage He will terrify them.
6 "But it is I Who have annointed My king,
upon Zion, My holy mountain."
7 I will tell of the decree:
Adonoy said to me, "You are My son,
I have this day begotten you.
8 Ask of Me
and I will give you nations as your inheritance,
and your possessions
will extend to the ends of the earth.
9 Break them with a rod of iron,
as a potter's vessel, shatter them."
10 Now, therefore, kings be wise,
be admonished judges of the earth.
11 Serve Adonoy with fear
and rejoice with trembling.
12 Do homage in purity [of heart],
lest He be angry
and you will be lost on your way,
for His wrath is kindled suddenly;
fortunate are all who take refuge in Him.

Royal Capital

פרק ג׳ Chapter 3

Weekly Cycle	Monthly Cycle	Book Number
Sunday	1st day of the month	Book 1

Author

דָּוִד הַמֶּלֶךְ—King David—the second king of Israel and father of the Davidic royal and messianic dynasty. David composed over seventy of the 150 psalms of Sefer Tehillim.

When & Why

David wrote this psalm after he escaped from his son Absalom, who was attempting to usurp David's throne. David stresses his belief that God will save him from Absalom.

Genre

Psalm of Individual Lament - This psalm was written from the perspective of the individual worshipper, who cries out to God in his time of need. It is characterized as an address to God involving a complaint, followed by a request and ending with an expression of trust.

Chapter Summary

This psalm relates David's unwavering trust in God even when his son Absalom drove him from his throne and pursued him. It is intended to instill hope in one's heart in the face of tragedy, for it is God's decision to free us, and not ours.

This psalm consists of nine verses, subdivided into three parts.
Verse 1 serves as an introduction, and refers to King David's fleeing from his son Absalom.
In verses 2 & 3, the Psalmist expands upon his trouble and personal struggle.
In verses 4-7, he describes his trust in God to deliver him.
In verses 8 & 9, he further beseeches the Almighty to save him.

Introductory Word

מִזְמוֹר—Mizmor—Musical Accompaniment

Technical Terminology

סֶלָה—Selah—Verse 3 contains the first appearance of the word "selah" in the Book of Tehillim. It occurs 71 times, most often as the last word of a psalm. While its meaning is unclear, the most familiar opinion is that it is a musical notation, instructing the Levitical orchestra to pause its singing and playing of instruments. Alternatively, "selah" may mean "everlasting".

Shimush Tehillim - When to Say

For a Headache—Verse 4 asks God to protect one's honor and lift up his head.
For a Shoulderache—Verse 6 expresses one's ability to wake up from sleep, as it is God who sustains him.

Where in the Siddur

Verses 2-9 are part of the prayers of the bedtime Shema.
Verse 9 comprises the eighth verse of V'hu Rachum of Pesukei Dezimra (introductory Verses of

Praise to the Shacharit morning service).

Verse 9 is also found in the Motza'ei Shabbat (Saturday night) Havdalah service.

Biblical Personalities

אַבְשָׁלוֹם—Absalom—King David's son, who attempted to seize the throne from his father and was killed in battle fighting against his father's army.

Talmud on Tehillim

Verse 8: "שִׁנֵּי רְשָׁעִים שִׁבַּרְתָּ"—"the teeth of the wicked, You have broken."

The Talmud, Berachot 54b, reinterprets this to be read not only as "shibarta"—"you have broken", but also as "shirbavta"—"you have extended". The implication, by way of allegory, is that Moses was ten amot (cubits) tall. He then took an axe that was ten amot long, jumped ten amot upwards, and smote Og, King of Bashan, at the ankles of his feet and killed him.

פרק ג

א מִזְמוֹר לְדָוִד
בְּבָרְחוֹ מִפְּנֵי | אַבְשָׁלוֹם בְּנוֹ:
ב יְהוָה מָה־רַבּוּ צָרָי
רַבִּים קָמִים עָלָי:
ג רַבִּים אֹמְרִים לְנַפְשִׁי
אֵין יְשׁוּעָתָה לּוֹ
בֵאלֹהִים סֶלָה:
ד וְאַתָּה יְהוָה מָגֵן בַּעֲדִי
כְּבוֹדִי וּמֵרִים רֹאשִׁי:
ה קוֹלִי אֶל־יְהוָה אֶקְרָא
וַיַּעֲנֵנִי
מֵהַר קָדְשׁוֹ סֶלָה:
ו אֲנִי שָׁכַבְתִּי וָאִישָׁנָה
הֱקִיצוֹתִי כִּי יְהוָה יִסְמְכֵנִי:
ז לֹא־אִירָא מֵרִבְבוֹת עָם
אֲשֶׁר סָבִיב שָׁתוּ עָלָי:
ח קוּמָה יְהוָה | הוֹשִׁיעֵנִי אֱלֹהַי
כִּי־הִכִּיתָ אֶת־כָּל־אֹיְבַי
לֶחִי
שִׁנֵּי רְשָׁעִים שִׁבַּרְתָּ:
ט לַיהוָה הַיְשׁוּעָה
עַל־עַמְּךָ בִרְכָתֶךָ סֶּלָה:

Chapter 3

1 A Psalm of David,
when he fled from Absalom his son.
2 Adonoy, how many are my tormentors!
The great rise up against me.
3 The great say of my soul,
There is no deliverance for him
from God, Selah."
4 But You Adonoy are as a shield about me;
my glory and lifter of my head.
5 With my voice I call out to Adonoy,
and He answered me
from out of His holy mountain, Selah.
6 I lay down and I slept;
I awoke, for Adonoy sustains me.
7 I will not fear the myriads of people
that have set themselves around me.
8 Arise Adonoy, deliver me My God;
for You have smitten all of my enemies
upon the jawbone,
the teeth of the wicked, You have broken.
9 To Adonoy belongs deliverance,
upon Your people is Your blessing. Selah.

פרק ד Chapter 4

Weekly Cycle	Monthly Cycle	Book Number
Sunday	1st day of the month	Book 1

Author

דָּוִד הַמֶּלֶךְ—King David—the second king of Israel and father of the Davidic royal and messianic dynasty. David composed over seventy of the 150 psalms of Sefer Tehillim.

When & Why

David wrote this psalm after he was betrayed and his location was revealed to Saul.

Genre

Psalm of Individual Lament - This psalm was written from the perspective of the individual worshipper, who cries out to God in his time of need. It is characterized as an address to God involving a complaint, followed by a request and ending with an expression of trust.

Psalm of Individual Confidence - In this psalm, the worshipper expresses absolute certainty that his prayers will be heard.

Chapter Summary

King David joyously thanks God for his kindness. Although engulfed in troubles and surrounded by the vindictiveness of his enemies, he strives to rise above despair and rejoice in the Divine Presence. He admonishes his enemies and advises them to repent.

This psalm consists of nine verses, subdivided into three parts.
Verse 1 serves as a heading.
In verse 2, King David addresses God.
In Verses 3–6, he addresses "the children of great men".
In verses 7-9, he turns once again to God, addressing Him in the more intimate second person.

Introductory Words

לַמְנַצֵּחַ—Lamnatsei'ach—To the Conductor
מִזְמוֹר—Mizmor—Musical Accompaniment

Technical Terminology

נְגִינוֹת—Neginos—Tunes
סֶלָה—Selah—While its meaning is unclear, the most familiar opinion is that it is a musical notation, instructing the Levitical orchestra to pause its singing and playing of instruments. Alternatively, "Selah" may mean "everlasting".

Shimush Tehillim - When to Say

For success against other people (recite every morning)—
For a request to be granted from others (recite seven times)—
Verse 2 requests of God to accept one's general petitions. Verse 5 asks that one's opponents should

realize that he is correct. Finally, verse 9 asks for one to be able to be rest assured.

Where in the Siddur

Verse 5 is part of the prayers of the bedtime Shema.

Verse 7 is part of the "Prayer for Sustenance" recited by some on the High Holidays.

Talmud on Tehillim

Verse 5: "רִגְזוּ, וְאַל תֶּחֱטָאוּ: אִמְרוּ בִלְבַבְכֶם, עַל מִשְׁכַּבְכֶם; וְדֹמּוּ סֶלָה" —"Tremble and do not sin, reflect in your hearts upon your bed, and be still Selah."

The Talmud, Berachot 5a, teaches us that a person should constantly agitate his good inclination to fight against his evil inclination. The root of the word "rigzu"—"tremble" also connotes anger. While anger is usually a bad trait, it does have its proper place too; one should vent his anger against the evil inclination, because anger can prevent sin.

The Talmud, Pesachim 119a, interprets the verse to mean: "Recite it "bilvavchem"—"in your heart", "al mishkavchem"—"on your beds", and then "v'domu"—"be utterly silent" and (immediately) fall asleep after reciting these words. One should therefore recite the Shema immediately before going to sleep, even if one had already recited it earlier in the evening.

פרק ד

א לַמְנַצֵּחַ בִּנְגִינוֹת
מִזְמוֹר לְדָוִד:
ב בְּקָרְאִי עֲנֵנִי |
אֱלֹהֵי צִדְקִי
בַּצָּר הִרְחַבְתָּ לִּי
חָנֵּנִי וּשְׁמַע תְּפִלָּתִי:
ג בְּנֵי אִישׁ
עַד־מֶה כְבוֹדִי לִכְלִמָּה
תֶּאֱהָבוּן רִיק
תְּבַקְשׁוּ כָזָב סֶלָה:
ד וּדְעוּ כִּי־הִפְלָה יְהוָה
חָסִיד לוֹ
יְהוָה יִשְׁמַע בְּקָרְאִי אֵלָיו:
ה רִגְזוּ וְאַל־תֶּחֱטָאוּ
אִמְרוּ בִלְבַבְכֶם עַל־מִשְׁכַּבְכֶם
וְדֹמּוּ סֶלָה:
ו זִבְחוּ זִבְחֵי־צֶדֶק
וּבִטְחוּ אֶל־יְהוָה:
ז רַבִּים אֹמְרִים
מִי־יַרְאֵנוּ טוֹב
נְסָה־עָלֵינוּ אוֹר פָּנֶיךָ יְהוָה:

Chapter 4

1 To the Chief Musician, on Neginos,
a Psalm of David.
2 When I call, answer me,
God of my righteousness;
when I was in distress You set me free;
be gracious to me and hear my prayer.
3 Children of great men,
how long will you put my honor to shame,
you who love vanity,
and seek deception Selah?
4 Know that Adonoy has set apart
the devoted one to Himself;
Adonoy will hear when I call to Him.
5 Tremble and do not sin,
reflect in your hearts upon your bed,
and be still Selah.
6 Offer the sacrifices of righteousness
and trust in Adonoy.
7 Many say,
"Who will show us good?"
Lift up unto us a sign—the light of Your face, Adonoy.

נָתַתָּה שִׂמְחָה בְלִבִּי מֵעֵת דְּגָנָם וְתִירוֹשָׁם רָבּוּ׃	ח	8	You have put joy in my heart, more than when their grain and their wine increase.
בְּשָׁלוֹם יַחְדָּו אֶשְׁכְּבָה וְאִישָׁן כִּי־אַתָּה יְהוָה לְבָדָד לָבֶטַח תּוֹשִׁיבֵנִי׃	ט	9	In peaceful unity I lay down and sleep; for You, Adonoy, will let me dwell alone [and] in security.

פרק ה Chapter 5

Weekly Cycle	Monthly Cycle	Book Number
Sunday	1st day of the month	Book 1

Author

דָּוִד הַמֶּלֶךְ—King David—the second king of Israel and father of the Davidic royal and messianic dynasty. David composed over seventy of the 150 psalms of Sefer Tehillim.

When & Why

This psalm was written to be read aloud immediately before a battle.

Genre

Psalm of Individual Lament - This psalm was written from the perspective of the individual worshipper, who cries out to God in his time of need. It is characterized as an address to God involving a complaint, followed by a request and ending with an expression of trust.

Summary

King David declares his trust in God who watches over the righteous and admonishes the wicked. He asks for Divine guidance to smooth the way before him, and calls for retribution of the wicked.

This psalm consists of thirteen verses, subdivided into three parts.
Verse 1 serves as an introduction.
In verses 2-4, the Psalmist accepts God as King and Lord, and asks that his prayer be accepted.
In verses 5-8, he further praises God for hiding his face from the wicked and drawing close those who fear Him.
In verses 9-13, King David requests that God lead him in the path of righteousness.

Introductory Words

לַמְנַצֵּחַ—Lamnatsei'ach—To the Conductor
מִזְמוֹר—Mizmor—Musical Accompaniment

Musical Instrument

נְחִילוֹת—Nechilot—A Type of Flute

Shimush Tehillim - When to Say

For being pursued by an evil spirit—Verse 5 states that God does not desire any evil, nor does he want it to dwell in man's midst. In verse 12, the Psalmist writes: "And they will rejoice, all who take refuge in You."

For being liked by an authority or boss—Verse 12 adds: "and they will exult in You, who love your Name."

Where in the Siddur

Verses 2 & 3 are a part of the Selichot (Penitential Service) recited in the evenings leading up to Rosh HaShanah and Yom Kippur.

Verse 8 comprises the second verse of Ma Tovu, recited during the Birchot HaShachar (Morning Blessings).

Biblical Places

הֵיכַל—Heichal—Holy Temple—a term used to refer to the inner sanctuary of the Temple in Jerusalem. The Heichal contained the Holy of Holies, the resting place of the Aron HaKodesh (Holy Ark)*.

It also housed the Menorah, Altar of Incense, and Table of the Showbread.

*The Aron HaKodesh, while present in the first Beit HaMikdash (Temple), was buried, and hence its location was not known, during the period of the second Beit HaMikdash.

Contemporary Song

Verse 8

Talmud on Tehillim

Verse 8: "וַאֲנִי בְּרֹב חַסְדְּךָ, אָבוֹא בֵיתֶךָ; אֶשְׁתַּחֲוֶה אֶל הֵיכַל קָדְשְׁךָ, בְּיִרְאָתֶךָ"—"As for me, through Your abundant kindness I will enter Your house; I will prostrate myself toward Your Holy Sanctuary in awe of You."

The Talmud, Berachot 30b, teaches that one should not rise to pray the Shemoneh Esrei (Silent Meditation) except out of an attitude of reverence. We learn from here that prayer must be approached with awe and an understanding of the seriousness of standing before God, and not something done just by force of habit.

פֶּרֶק ה			**Chapter 5**
לַמְנַצֵּחַ אֶל־הַנְּחִילוֹת מִזְמוֹר לְדָוִד׃	א	1	To the Chief Musician, with wind instruments, a Psalm of David.
אֲמָרַי הַאֲזִינָה ׀ יְהוָה בִּינָה הֲגִיגִי׃	ב	2	To my words, give ear, Adonoy, consider my meditation.
הַקְשִׁיבָה ׀ לְקוֹל שַׁוְעִי מַלְכִּי וֵאלֹהָי כִּי־אֵלֶיךָ אֶתְפַּלָּל׃	ג	3	Listen to the voice of my cry, my King and my God, for to You I pray.

ד	יְהוָה בֹּקֶר תִּשְׁמַע קוֹלִי	4	Adonoy, in the morning You hear my voice,
	בֹּקֶר אֶעֱרָךְ־לְךָ		in the morning I arrange [my prayer] to You,
	וַאֲצַפֶּה׃		and I wait expectantly.
ה	כִּי ׀ לֹא אֵל־	5	For You are not an Almighty
	חָפֵץ רֶשַׁע ׀ אָתָּה		Who desires wickedness;
	לֹא יְגֻרְךָ רָע׃		evil does not sojourn with You.
ו	לֹא־יִתְיַצְּבוּ הוֹלְלִים	6	The boasters will not stand
	לְנֶגֶד עֵינֶיךָ		before Your eyes;
	שָׂנֵאתָ כָּל־פֹּעֲלֵי אָוֶן׃		You hate all evil doers.
ז	תְּאַבֵּד דֹּבְרֵי כָזָב	7	You will destroy speakers of deception;
	אִישׁ־דָּמִים וּמִרְמָה		a man of murder and deceit,
	יְתָעֵב ׀ יְהוָה׃		Adonoy detests.
ח	וַאֲנִי	8	As for me,
	בְּרֹב חַסְדְּךָ		through Your abundant kindness
	אָבוֹא בֵיתֶךָ		I will enter Your house;
	אֶשְׁתַּחֲוֶה		I will prostrate myself
	אֶל־הֵיכַל־קָדְשְׁךָ		toward Your Holy Sanctuary
	בְּיִרְאָתֶךָ׃		in awe of You.
ט	יְהוָה ׀ נְחֵנִי בְצִדְקָתֶךָ	9	Adonoy, lead me in Your righteousness,
	לְמַעַן שׁוֹרְרָי		because of those who lie in wait for me,
	הַיְשַׁר לְפָנַי דַּרְכֶּךָ׃		straighten before me Your way.
י	כִּי אֵין בְּפִיהוּ נְכוֹנָה	10	For in their mouth there is no sincerity,
	קִרְבָּם הַוּוֹת		their inner thought is deceit;
	קֶבֶר־פָּתוּחַ גְּרוֹנָם		an open grave is their throat,
	לְשׁוֹנָם יַחֲלִיקוּן׃		[with] their tongue they make smooth [talk].
יא	הַאֲשִׁימֵם ׀ אֱלֹהִים	11	Condemn them God,
	יִפְּלוּ מִמֹּעֲצוֹתֵיהֶם		let them fall by their own counsels;
	בְּרֹב פִּשְׁעֵיהֶם הַדִּיחֵמוֹ		for their many sins cast them aside
	כִּי־מָרוּ בָךְ׃		for they have rebelled against You.
יב	וְיִשְׂמְחוּ	12	And they will rejoice,
	כָל־חוֹסֵי בָךְ		all who take refuge in You
	לְעוֹלָם יְרַנֵּנוּ		forever they will sing joyously,
	וְתָסֵךְ עָלֵימוֹ		and You will shelter them;
	וְיַעְלְצוּ בְךָ		and they will exult in You,
	אֹהֲבֵי שְׁמֶךָ׃		who love Your Name.
יג	כִּי־אַתָּה תְּבָרֵךְ צַדִּיק	13	For You will bless the righteous,
	יְהוָה כַּצִּנָּה רָצוֹן תַּעְטְרֶנּוּ׃		Adonoy, as a shield You encompass him with favor.

פרק ו Chapter 6

Weekly Cycle	Monthly Cycle	Book Number
Sunday	1st day of the month	Book 1

Author

דָוִד הַמֶּלֶךְ—King David—the second king of Israel and father of the Davidic royal and messianic dynasty. David composed over seventy of the 150 psalms of Sefer Tehillim.

When & Why

David wrote this psalm after recovering from a serious sickness.

Genre

Psalm of Individual Lament - This psalm was written from the perspective of the individual worshipper, who cries out to God in his time of need. It is characterized as an address to God involving a complaint, followed by a request and ending with an expression of trust.

Chapter Summary

David composed this psalm in the midst of his illness and pain, and thus prays for deliverance and life. He also addresses his enemies: "Ashamed and utterly terrified will all my foes be, they will return and be instantaneously ashamed." Likewise, he hints at the suffering and martyrdom of the Jewish people throughout the ages.

This psalm consists of eleven verses, subdivided into three parts.
Verse 1 serves as a heading.
In verses 2-6, King David addresses his supplications directly to God.
In verses 7-8, he describes his grief as if talking to himself.
In verses 9-11, he speaks out against his enemies and commands them to depart from his midst.

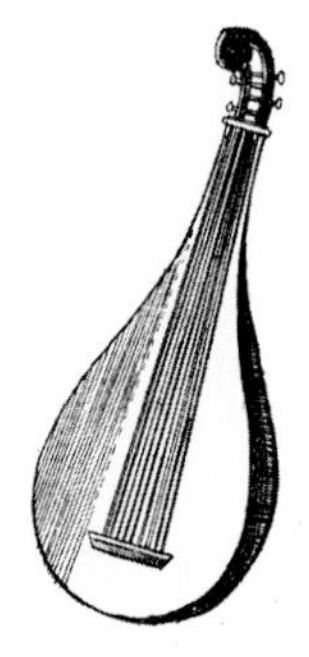

Introductory Words

לַמְנַצֵּחַ—Lamnatsei'ach—To the Conductor
מִזְמוֹר—Mizmor—Musical Accompaniment

Musical Instrument

שְׁמִינִית—Sheminit—An Eight-Stringed Harp

Technical Terminology

נְגִינוֹת—Neginos—Tunes

Shimush Tehillim - When to Say

For troubles at sea or on land—The letters yud-shin-ayin-yud—constituting the word "yishi"—"my savior"—are alluded to in the following verses: yud from the name of God in verse 2—"Do not rebuke me with Your anger, nor chastise me with Your rage."; shin from "shuva" in verse 5—"free my soul, deliver me for the sake of Your lovingkidness"; ayin from "asheshah" in verse 8—"My eye is dimmed from anger, it has aged because of my tormentors."; yud from "yeivoshu" in verse 11—"Ashamed and utterly terrified will all my foes be."

Where in the Siddur

Verses 2-11 constitute the Tachanun (Supplication Prayer), recited after Shemoneh Esrei (Silent Meditation).

Verse 5 is found in the Vidui (Confession Prayer), recited on various occasions throughout the year.

Biblical Places

שְׁאוֹל—Sheol—Lower or Underworld; the abode of the dead.

פרק ו			**Chapter 6**
לַמְנַצֵּחַ בִּנְגִינוֹת	א	1	To the Chief Musician, on Neginos,
עַל־הַשְּׁמִינִית מִזְמוֹר לְדָוִד׃			on the eight stringed harp, a Psalm of David.
יְהוָה אַל־בְּאַפְּךָ תוֹכִיחֵנִי	ב	2	Adonoy, do not rebuke me with Your anger,
וְאַל־בַּחֲמָתְךָ תְיַסְּרֵנִי׃			nor chastise me with Your rage.
חָנֵּנִי יְהוָה	ג	3	Be gracious unto me, Adonoy,
כִּי אֻמְלַל אָנִי			for I am desolate,
רְפָאֵנִי יְהוָה כִּי נִבְהֲלוּ עֲצָמָי׃			heal me Adonoy, for my bones are terrified.
וְנַפְשִׁי נִבְהֲלָה מְאֹד	ד	4	My soul, [too,] is utterly terrified,
וְאַתָּה יְהוָה עַד־מָתָי׃			and You Adonoy, how long?
שׁוּבָה יְהוָה חַלְּצָה נַפְשִׁי	ה	5	Return Adonoy, free my soul,
הוֹשִׁיעֵנִי לְמַעַן חַסְדֶּךָ׃			deliver me for the sake of Your lovingkindness.
כִּי אֵין בַּמָּוֶת זִכְרֶךָ	ו	6	For in death there is no mention of You;
בִּשְׁאוֹל מִי יוֹדֶה־לָּךְ׃			in the lower world who will thank You?
יָגַעְתִּי ׀ בְּאַנְחָתִי	ז	7	I am worn out with my sighing,
אַשְׂחֶה בְכָל־לַיְלָה מִטָּתִי			every night I cause my bed to float;
בְּדִמְעָתִי עַרְשִׂי אַמְסֶה׃			with my tears, I melt my couch.
עָשְׁשָׁה מִכַּעַס עֵינִי	ח	8	My eye is dimmed from anger,
עָתְקָה בְּכָל־צוֹרְרָי׃			it has aged because of my tormentors.
סוּרוּ מִמֶּנִּי כָּל־פֹּעֲלֵי אָוֶן	ט	9	Depart from me, all you evildoers,
כִּי־שָׁמַע יְהוָה קוֹל בִּכְיִי׃			for Adonoy has heard the voice of my weeping.
שָׁמַע יְהוָה תְּחִנָּתִי	י	10	Adonoy has heard my supplication,
יְהוָה תְּפִלָּתִי יִקָּח׃			Adonoy will (also) accept my prayer.
יֵבֹשׁוּ ׀ וְיִבָּהֲלוּ מְאֹד	יא	11	Ashamed and utterly terrified
כָּל־אֹיְבָי			will all my foes be,
יָשֻׁבוּ			they will return
יֵבֹשׁוּ רָגַע׃			and be instantaneously ashamed.

פרק ז Chapter 7

Weekly Cycle	Monthly Cycle	Book Number
Sunday	1st day of the month	Book 1

Author

דָּוִד הַמֶּלֶךְ—King David—the second king of Israel and father of the Davidic royal and messianic dynasty. David composed over seventy of the 150 psalms of Sefer Tehillim.

When & Why

David sings to God concerning Cush, a Benjaminite. Cush was likely another partisan of Saul against David. David wrote this psalm to thank God for saving him from Saul.

Genre

Psalm of Individual Lament - This psalm was written from the perspective of the individual worshipper, who cries out to God in his time of need. It is characterized as an address to God involving a complaint, followed by a request and ending with an expression of trust.

Chapter Summary

King David gives thanks for having been saved from his enemies who lurk to destroy him. It may seem that this righteous man is helpless against those who rise up against him, but he dare not despair. With God's mercy, the wicked will ultimately fall victim to their own schemes.

This psalm consists of eighteen verses, subdivided into seven parts.
Verse 1 serves as a heading.
In verses 2 & 3, King David turns to God and pleads for deliverance.
In verses 4-6, he takes an oath condemning himself if he has indeed done wrong.
In verses 7 & 8, he calls out to God to rise up against his enemies.
In verses 9 & 10, the Psalmist publicly calls on God to reveal His righteousness.
In verses 11-14, he expresses his confidence in God's justice.
In verses 15-17, he expresses his faith that the wicked will be destroyed by their own mischief.
In verse 18, he concludes by taking upon himself to thank God for His deliverance.

Technical Terminology

שִׁגָּיוֹן—Shiggayon—Song of Lament
סֶלָה—Selah—While its meaning is unclear, the most familiar opinion is that it is a musical notation, instructing the Levitical orchestra to pause its singing and playing of instruments. Alternatively, "Selah" may mean "everlasting".

Shimush Tehillim - When to Say

For protection against enemies—Verse 1 refers to the lament David expressed after Saul's death.
For a successful judgment—Verse 2 states: "deliver me from all my pursuers and rescue me." Further, in verse 18, David thanks God for a good outcome.

Biblical Personalities

כּוּשׁ בֶּן-יְמִינִי—Cush the Benjaminite—a follower of King Saul and an enemy of King David.

פרק ז

א שִׁגָּיוֹן לְדָוִד
אֲשֶׁר־שָׁר לַיהוָה
עַל־דִּבְרֵי־כוּשׁ בֶּן־יְמִינִי:
ב יְהוָה אֱלֹהַי בְּךָ חָסִיתִי
הוֹשִׁיעֵנִי מִכָּל־רֹדְפַי
וְהַצִּילֵנִי:
ג פֶּן־יִטְרֹף כְּאַרְיֵה נַפְשִׁי
פֹּרֵק
וְאֵין מַצִּיל:
ד יְהוָה אֱלֹהַי אִם־עָשִׂיתִי זֹאת
אִם־יֶשׁ־עָוֶל בְּכַפָּי:
ה אִם־גָּמַלְתִּי שׁוֹלְמִי רָע
וָאֲחַלְּצָה צוֹרְרִי רֵיקָם:
ו יִרַדֹּף אוֹיֵב | נַפְשִׁי
וְיַשֵּׂג
וְיִרְמֹס לָאָרֶץ חַיָּי
וּכְבוֹדִי | לֶעָפָר יַשְׁכֵּן סֶלָה:
ז קוּמָה יְהוָה | בְּאַפֶּךָ
הִנָּשֵׂא
בְּעַבְרוֹת צוֹרְרָי
וְעוּרָה אֵלַי
מִשְׁפָּט צִוִּיתָ:
ח וַעֲדַת לְאֻמִּים
תְּסוֹבְבֶךָּ
וְעָלֶיהָ לַמָּרוֹם שׁוּבָה:
ט יְהוָה יָדִין עַמִּים
שָׁפְטֵנִי יְהוָה
כְּצִדְקִי
וּכְתֻמִּי עָלָי:
י יִגְמָר־נָא רַע | רְשָׁעִים
וּתְכוֹנֵן צַדִּיק
וּבֹחֵן לִבּוֹת וּכְלָיוֹת
אֱלֹהִים צַדִּיק:
יא מָגִנִּי עַל־אֱלֹהִים
מוֹשִׁיעַ יִשְׁרֵי־לֵב:

Chapter 7

1 A shiggayon of David,
which he sang to Adonoy,
concerning Cush, a Benjamite.
2 Adonoy, my God, in You I have taken refuge,
deliver me from all my pursuers
and rescue me.
3 Lest he tear my soul like a lion,
rending it in pieces,
while there is no rescuer.
4 Adonoy, my God, if I have done this;
if there is iniquity in my hands.
5 If I have repaid my friends with evil,
I who released my unprovoked adversary.
6 Then let the enemy pursue my soul
and overtake it,
and trample my life to the earth,
and lay my glory in the dust selah.
7 Rise up Adonoy in Your anger,
lift Yourself up
in indignation against my tormentors;
awaken for me
the judgment which You commanded.
8 And a gathering of nations
will then surround You,
and above it return on high.
9 Adonoy will punish the nations;
judge me, Adonoy,
according to my righteousness
and my integrity.
10 Let an end come to the evil of the wicked,
and establish the righteous;
You Who tests hearts and minds,
God is righteous.
11 My shield rests with God;
He delivers the upright in heart.

יב אֱלֹהִים שׁוֹפֵט צַדִּיק וְאֵל זֹעֵם בְּכָל־יוֹם׃	12 God is a righteous Judge, and the Almighty is angered every day.
יג אִם־לֹא יָשׁוּב חַרְבּוֹ יִלְטוֹשׁ קַשְׁתּוֹ דָרַךְ וַיְכוֹנְנֶהָ׃	13 If he does not repent; He will sharpen his sword, He has bent His bow and made it ready.
יד וְלוֹ הֵכִין כְּלֵי־מָוֶת חִצָּיו לְדֹלְקִים יִפְעָל׃	14 And for him He has prepared deadly weapons; He has made His arrows for swift pursuers.
טו הִנֵּה יְחַבֶּל־אָוֶן וְהָרָה עָמָל וְיָלַד שָׁקֶר׃	15 Behold, he labors with iniquity, conceives mischief, and brings forth falsehood.
טז בּוֹר כָּרָה וַיַּחְפְּרֵהוּ וַיִּפֹּל בְּשַׁחַת יִפְעָל׃	16 He has dug a pit and hollowed it, and then fell into the ditch which he made.
יז יָשׁוּב עֲמָלוֹ בְרֹאשׁוֹ וְעַל קָדְקֳדוֹ חֲמָסוֹ יֵרֵד׃	17 His mischief will return upon his own head, and on his own skull his violence will come down.
יח אוֹדֶה יְהוָה כְּצִדְקוֹ וַאֲזַמְּרָה שֵׁם־יְהוָה עֶלְיוֹן׃	18 I will thank Adonoy according to His righteousness, and I will sing praise to the Name of Adonoy, Most High.

פרק ח Chapter 8

Weekly Cycle	Monthly Cycle	Book Number
Sunday	1st day of the month	Book 1

Author

דָּוִד הַמֶּלֶךְ—King David—the second king of Israel and father of the Davidic royal and messianic dynasty. David composed over seventy of the 150 psalms of Sefer Tehillim.

Genre

Psalm of Praise – This is a psalm of celebration, often the result of a victory. It declares God's goodness and urges all of creation to worship.

Chapter Summary

The Singer boasts of the Almighty's supervision over His creatures and acclaims the excellence of the man who lives in accordance with his Maker's will. He acknowledges: "How mighty is Your Name over all the earth."

This psalm consists of ten verses, subdivided into four sections.
Verse 1 serves as a heading.
In verses 2 & 3, King David proudly proclaims that God's greatness is manifest everywhere, and that the wicked are destined for destruction.
In verses 4 & 5, he tells of man's insignificance in relation to the heavens and the stars.
In verses 6-9, he speaks of man's greatness and dominion over the world and all living things.
In verse 10, he concludes in the same way he begins, with words of praise to God.

Introductory Words

לַמְנַצֵּחַ—Lamnatsei'ach—To the Conductor
מִזְמוֹר—Mizmor—Musical Accompaniment

Musical Instrument

גִּתִּית—Gittis—A Stringed Instrument; perhaps from the city of Gath.

Shimush Tehillim - When to Say

To find favor amongst others—Verse 6 refers to man's greatness being only slightly less than that of the angels, crowned with honor and glory.
For a crying child—Verse 3 refers to the mouth of a nursing child, bringing him strength.

Where in the Siddur

Recited during the week of Parashat Bereishit in some traditions.
Recited on Simchat Torah in some traditions.
Verse 2 (and repeated in Verse 10) are recited by the Kohanim during the Birkat Kohanim (Priestly Blessing), and in Hoshanot (Sukkot Salvation Service) in some traditions.

פֶּרֶק ח

א לַמְנַצֵּחַ
עַל־הַגִּתִּית
מִזְמוֹר לְדָוִד׃
ב יְהוָה אֲדֹנֵינוּ
מָה־אַדִּיר שִׁמְךָ בְּכָל־הָאָרֶץ
אֲשֶׁר תְּנָה הוֹדְךָ עַל־הַשָּׁמָיִם׃
ג מִפִּי עוֹלְלִים ׀ וְיֹנְקִים
יִסַּדְתָּ עֹז
לְמַעַן צוֹרְרֶיךָ
לְהַשְׁבִּית אוֹיֵב וּמִתְנַקֵּם׃
ד כִּי־אֶרְאֶה שָׁמֶיךָ
מַעֲשֵׂי אֶצְבְּעֹתֶיךָ
יָרֵחַ וְכוֹכָבִים
אֲשֶׁר כּוֹנָנְתָּה׃

Chapter 8

1 1. To the Chief Musician,
on the Gitis—
a Psalm of David.
2 Adonoy, our Master,
how mighty is Your Name over all the earth;
Who has set Your glory above the heavens.
3 Out of the mouths of babes and sucklings
You have founded strength,
because of Your tormentors;
to still foe and avenger.
4 When I look at Your heavens,
the work of Your fingers;
the moon and the stars
which You have established.

מָה־אֱנוֹשׁ כִּי־תִזְכְּרֶנּוּ וּבֶן־אָדָם כִּי תִפְקְדֶנּוּ׃	ה	5	What then is man that You remember him? and the son of man that You are mindful of him?
וַתְּחַסְּרֵהוּ מְּעַט מֵאֱלֹהִים וְכָבוֹד וְהָדָר תְּעַטְּרֵהוּ׃	ו	6	Yet You have made him slightly less than the angels; and with honor and dignity You have crowned him.
תַּמְשִׁילֵהוּ בְּמַעֲשֵׂי יָדֶיךָ כֹּל שַׁתָּה תַחַת־רַגְלָיו׃	ז	7	You gave him dominion over the works of Your hands; You put everything at his feet.
צֹנֶה וַאֲלָפִים כֻּלָּם וְגַם בַּהֲמוֹת שָׂדָי׃	ח	8	Sheep and cattle, all of them; also, the beasts of the field.
צִפּוֹר שָׁמַיִם וּדְגֵי הַיָּם עֹבֵר אָרְחוֹת יַמִּים׃	ט	9	The fowl of the sky and the fish of the sea; whatever passes through the seas.
יְהוָה אֲדֹנֵינוּ מָה־אַדִּיר שִׁמְךָ בְּכָל־הָאָרֶץ׃	י	10	Adonoy, our Master, how mighty is Your Name over all the earth.

פרק ט Chapter 9

Weekly Cycle	Monthly Cycle	Book Number
Sunday	1st day of the month	Book 1

Author

דָּוִד הַמֶּלֶךְ—King David—the second king of Israel and father of the Davidic royal and messianic dynasty. David composed over seventy of the 150 psalms of Sefer Tehillim.

When & Why

David wrote this psalm to thank God for saving him from a military enemy.

Genre

Psalm of Individual Lament - This psalm was written from the perspective of the individual worshipper, who cries out to God in his time of need. It is characterized as an address to God involving a complaint, followed by a request and ending with an expression of trust.

Psalm of Individual Thanksgiving - This psalm emphasizes gratitude for what God has done for the individual.

Acrostic

A literary composition in which the writer has used the letters of the Hebrew alphabet in their order as the initial letters for a sequence of verses. i.e. **א.ב.ג.ד**

Chapter Summary

King David composed this psalm after having defeated his enemies who harassed the Israelites. He expresses his joy at the manifestation of God's presence in the affairs of this world, and in particular, in His judgment.

This psalm consists of twenty-one verses. As mentioned above, it is one of the psalms arranged in alphabetical order.

Introductory Words

לַמְנַצֵּחַ—Lamnatsei'ach—To the Conductor
מִזְמוֹר—Mizmor—Musical Accompaniment

Technical Terminology

עַל מוּת לַבֵּן—Al-mut Labain—Upon the death of Labain—There are two major opinions as to what Al-mut Labain means. The first is that it was a musical instruction to sing in a high pitched falsetto voice or Labain was a biblical personality. See explanation below.
הִגָּיוֹן סֶלָה—Higgayon Selah—Reflective Interlude

Shimush Tehillim - When to Say

For an ill child—Verse 1 refers to "mut laben", which, as mentioned above, indicates a falsetto, yet alternatively may refer to a child on his deathbed.
To be saved from enemies—Verse 4 states: "When my enemies are turned back, they will stumble and perish."

Where in the Siddur

Verse 4 is found in the repetition of the Shmoneh Esrei (Silent Meditation) of Rosh HaShanah.
Verse 9 is found in Kabbalat Shabbat (Friday night service), with a slight textual variation.
Verse 11 is found in Pesukei Dezimra (Introductory Verses of Praise to the Shacharit morning service).
Verse 13 is a part of Av HaRachamim, a memorial prayer recited just prior to Musaf on Shabbat.

Biblical Personalities

לַבֵּן—Labain, a King who threatened Israel in the time of King David. David defeated him and offered this psalm of thanks to God.

Biblical Places

שְׁאוֹל—Sheol—Lower or Underworld; abode of the dead.
צִיּוֹן—Zion—often used as a synonym for Jerusalem. The term Zion originally referred only to the area where a Jebbusite fortress once stood, also the location of the City of David. It was later used by prophets and psalmists as another name for Jerusalem.

פֶּרֶק ט׳

א לַמְנַצֵּחַ
עַלְמוּת לַבֵּן
מִזְמוֹר לְדָוִד׃
ב אוֹדֶה יְהוָה בְּכָל־לִבִּי
אֲסַפְּרָה כָּל־נִפְלְאוֹתֶיךָ׃
ג אֶשְׂמְחָה וְאֶעֶלְצָה בָךְ
אֲזַמְּרָה שִׁמְךָ עֶלְיוֹן׃
ד בְּשׁוּב־אוֹיְבַי אָחוֹר
יִכָּשְׁלוּ וְיֹאבְדוּ מִפָּנֶיךָ׃
ה כִּי־עָשִׂיתָ מִשְׁפָּטִי
וְדִינִי
יָשַׁבְתָּ לְכִסֵּא שׁוֹפֵט צֶדֶק׃
ו גָּעַרְתָּ גוֹיִם
אִבַּדְתָּ רָשָׁע
שְׁמָם מָחִיתָ
לְעוֹלָם וָעֶד׃
ז הָאוֹיֵב | תַּמּוּ
חֳרָבוֹת לָנֶצַח
וְעָרִים נָתַשְׁתָּ
אָבַד זִכְרָם הֵמָּה׃
ח וַיהוָה לְעוֹלָם יֵשֵׁב
כּוֹנֵן לַמִּשְׁפָּט כִּסְאוֹ׃
ט וְהוּא יִשְׁפֹּט־תֵּבֵל
בְּצֶדֶק
יָדִין לְאֻמִּים
בְּמֵישָׁרִים׃
י וִיהִי יְהוָה מִשְׂגָּב לַדָּךְ
מִשְׂגָּב לְעִתּוֹת בַּצָּרָה׃
יא וְיִבְטְחוּ בְךָ
יוֹדְעֵי שְׁמֶךָ
כִּי לֹא־עָזַבְתָּ
דֹרְשֶׁיךָ יְהוָה׃
יב זַמְּרוּ לַיהוָה יֹשֵׁב צִיּוֹן
הַגִּידוּ בָעַמִּים עֲלִילוֹתָיו׃
יג כִּי־דֹרֵשׁ דָּמִים
אוֹתָם זָכָר
לֹא־שָׁכַח צַעֲקַת עֲנָוִים׃
יד חָנְנֵנִי יְהוָה

Chapter 9

1 To the Chief Musician,
upon the death of Labain,
a Psalm of David.
2 I will thank Adonoy with all my heart;
I will tell of all Your wonders.
3 I will rejoice and exult in You;
I will sing praise to Your Name, Most High.
4 When my enemies are turned back,
they will stumble and perish at Your presence.
5 For You have rendered my judgment
and [maintained] my cause;
You sat upon the throne as the righteous Judge.
6 You have rebuked nations,
You have destroyed the wicked;
their name You have blotted out
forever and ever.
7 The enemy is finished—
[those whose] daggers [of hatred] were eternal;
and the cities which You uprooted,
their remembrance has perished.
8 But Adonoy is forever enthroned;
He has established His throne for judgment.
9 And He will judge the inhabited world
with righteousness.
He will minister judgment to the people
with equity.
10 Adonoy will be a fortress for the oppressed,
a fortress in times of trouble.
11 And they will trust in You,
those who know Your Name
for You have never forsaken
those who seek You, Adonoy.
12 Sing praises to Adonoy Who dwells in Zion;
declare among the nations His deeds.
13 For He Who avenges blood
has remembered them;
He has not forgotten the cry of the humble.
14 Be gracious to me, Adonoy,

רְאֵה עָנְיִי, מִשֹּׂנְאָי;	see my affliction [caused] by my enemies;
מְרוֹמְמִי,	You Who has raised me up
מִשַּׁעֲרֵי מָוֶת.	from the gates of death.
טו לְמַעַן אֲסַפְּרָה כָּל־תְּהִלָּתֶיךָ	15 That I may tell of all Your praises
בְּשַׁעֲרֵי בַת־צִיּוֹן	in the gates of the daughter of Zion;
אָגִילָה בִּישׁוּעָתֶךָ:	that I may rejoice in Your deliverance.
טז טָבְעוּ גוֹיִם	16 The nations have sunk down
בְּשַׁחַת עָשׂוּ	in the pit which they made;
בְּרֶשֶׁת־זוּ טָמָנוּ	in the same net which they hid
נִלְכְּדָה רַגְלָם:	their own foot was caught.
יז נוֹדַע ׀ יְהוָה	17 Adonoy has made Himself known,
מִשְׁפָּט עָשָׂה	He has executed judgment;
בְּפֹעַל כַּפָּיו	in the work of his own hands,
נוֹקֵשׁ רָשָׁע	the wicked is snared;
הִגָּיוֹן סֶלָה:	reflect upon this. Selah.
יח יָשׁוּבוּ רְשָׁעִים לִשְׁאוֹלָה	18 The wicked will return to the grave,
כָּל־גּוֹיִם שְׁכֵחֵי אֱלֹהִים:	[as will] all nations that forget God.
יט כִּי לֹא לָנֶצַח יִשָּׁכַח אֶבְיוֹן	19 For not forever will the needy be forgotten,
תִּקְוַת עֲנִיִּים תֹּאבַד לָעַד:	nor will the hope of the poor perish forever.
כ קוּמָה יְהוָה	20 Rise up, Adonoy,
אַל־יָעֹז אֱנוֹשׁ	let not man [evil] prevail;
יִשָּׁפְטוּ גוֹיִם	let the nations be judged
עַל־פָּנֶיךָ:	because of Your anger.
כא שִׁיתָה יְהוָה ׀ מוֹרָה לָהֶם	21 Adonoy, set [Your] mastery over them;
יֵדְעוּ גוֹיִם	let the nations know
אֱנוֹשׁ הֵמָּה סֶּלָה:	they are but men. Selah.

According to some opinions this chapter is a continuation of the previous chapter which is attributed to King David

Hexagonal Glass Jar with Menorah (Courtesy of Shlomo Moussaieff Collection)

פרק י Chapter 10

Weekly Cycle	Monthly Cycle	Book Number
Sunday	2nd day of the month	Book 1

Author
Unknown

Genre
Psalm of Individual Lament - This psalm was written from the perspective of the individual worshipper, who cries out to God in his/her time of need. It is characterized as an address to God involving a complaint, followed by a request and ending with an expression of trust.
Psalm of Individual Thanksgiving - This psalm emphasizes gratitude for what God has done for the individual.
Acrostic - A literary composition in which the writer has used the letters of the Hebrew alphabet in their order as the initial letters for a sequence of verses. i.e. **א.ב.ג.ד**

Chapter Summary
The wicked man oppresses the poor and helpless with impunity, symbolic of the Jewish people's suffering under foreign rule. The psalmist thus pleads for Heaven's intervention:"Why, Adonoy, do You stand far off, hiding [Yourself] in times of trouble?", he asks.

This psalm consists of eighteen verses, subdivided into three parts.
In verse 1, the psalmist laments God's seeming distance from him. He expresses his longing for closeness.
In verses 2-11, he describes the thoughts and actions of the wicked.
In verses 12-18, he prays that the wicked will be destroyed and that God will reveal His sovereignty and judge the world in righteousness.

Shimush Tehillim - When to Say
For protection from a demon—Verse 2 states: "Through the haughtiness of the wicked the poor is hotly pursued, and is caught in the devices which they have conceived."

Where in the Siddur
Recited during the Ten Days of Repentance in some traditions.
Verse 16 is part of both the eighth and ninth verses of Yehi Chevod, the introductory paragraph to Ashrei of Pesukei Dezimra (Introductory Verses of Praise to the Shacharit morning service). It is also found in Baruch Hashem Le'olam of Ma'ariv (evening service), as well as in the bedtime Shema.
Verse 17 is found in the repetition of the Shmoneh Esrei (Silent Meditation) of Rosh HaShanah.

Talmud on Tehillim
Verse 5: "יָחִילוּ דְרָכָו בְּכָל-עֵת-מָרוֹם מִשְׁפָּטֶיךָ מִנֶּגְדּוֹ"—"His ways prosper at all times; Your judgments are far beyond him."

The Talmud, Berachot 7b, teaches us not to contend with a wicked person who appears to be successful. During the period of success granted him, heavenly judgments will not befall him, but in the end, he will be judged and punished for his sins.
Verse 17: "תָּכִין לִבָּם, תַּקְשִׁיב אָזְנֶךָ"—"guide their heart, let Your ear be attentive." The Talmud, Berachot 31a, instructs that one who prays must direct his heart toward heaven. In so doing, his prayer is more acceptable.

Lion

פרק י	Chapter 10
א לָמָה יְהוָה תַּעֲמֹד בְּרָחוֹק	1 Why, Adonoy, do You stand far off,
תַּעְלִים לְעִתּוֹת בַּצָּרָה׃	hiding [Yourself] in times of trouble?
ב בְּגַאֲוַת רָשָׁע	2 Through the haughtiness of the wicked
יִדְלַק עָנִי	the poor is hotly pursued,
יִתָּפְשׂוּ ׀ בִּמְזִמּוֹת	and is caught in the devices
זוּ חָשָׁבוּ׃	which they have conceived.
ג כִּי־הִלֵּל רָשָׁע	3 When the wicked boasts
עַל־תַּאֲוַת נַפְשׁוֹ	of [achieving] his heart's desire
וּבֹצֵעַ בֵּרֵךְ	and the brazen robber utters a blessing;
נִאֵץ ׀ יְהוָה׃	he has mocked Adonoy.
ד רָשָׁע כְּגֹבַהּ	4 The wicked in the pride
אַפּוֹ	of his countenance [says,]
בַּל־יִדְרֹשׁ	"He will not avenge."
אֵין אֱלֹהִים כָּל־מְזִמּוֹתָיו׃	"There is no God" are all his thoughts.
ה יָחִילוּ דְרָכָיו ׀ בְּכָל־עֵת	5 His ways prosper at all times,
מָרוֹם מִשְׁפָּטֶיךָ מִנֶּגְדּוֹ	Your judgments are far above and beyond him;
כָּל־צוֹרְרָיו	[as for] all his tormentors
יָפִיחַ בָּהֶם׃	he puffs at them.
ו אָמַר בְּלִבּוֹ	6 He said in his heart,
בַּל־אֶמּוֹט	"I will not be moved;
לְדֹר וָדֹר אֲשֶׁר לֹא־בְרָע׃	for all generations I will not be in adversity."
ז אָלָה פִּיהוּ מָלֵא	7 His mouth is full of curses

וּמִרְמוֹת וָתֹךְ	with deceit and evil thoughts;
תַּחַת לְשׁוֹנוֹ עָמָל וָאָוֶן׃	under his tongue is mischief and falsehood.
ח יֵשֵׁב ׀	8 He sits [lurking]
בְּמַאְרַב חֲצֵרִים	in the secret places of open villages,
בַּמִּסְתָּרִים יַהֲרֹג נָקִי	in hidden places he murders the innocent;
עֵינָיו לְחֵלְכָה יִצְפֹּנוּ׃	his eyes are on the lookout for the helpless.
ט יֶאֱרֹב בַּמִּסְתָּר ׀	9 He lies in wait in a hidden place,
כְּאַרְיֵה בְסֻכֹּה	as a lion in his lair;
יֶאֱרֹב לַחֲטוֹף עָנִי	he lies in wait to snatch the poor;
יַחְטֹף עָנִי	he snatches the poor
בְּמָשְׁכוֹ בְרִשְׁתּוֹ׃	when he draws him into his net.
י יִדְכֶּה יָשֹׁחַ	10 He crouches, he bows down;
וְנָפַל בַּעֲצוּמָיו חֵיל כָּאִים׃	and into his might falls the helpless.
יא אָמַר בְּלִבּוֹ	11 He said in his heart,
שָׁכַח אֵל	"the Almighty has forgotten;
הִסְתִּיר פָּנָיו בַּל־רָאָה לָנֶצַח׃	He has hidden His face, He will never see."
יב קוּמָה יְהוָה	12 Rise up, Adonoy,
אֵל נְשָׂא יָדֶךָ	Almighty, lift up Your hand;
אַל־תִּשְׁכַּח עֲנָוִים׃	do not forget the humble.
יג עַל־מֶה ׀ נִאֵץ רָשָׁע ׀ אֱלֹהִים	13 Why does the wicked mock God
אָמַר בְּלִבּוֹ	by saying in his heart,
לֹא תִדְרֹשׁ׃	"You will not seek [revenge]"?
יד רָאִתָה	14 You indeed have seen it,
כִּי־אַתָּה ׀ עָמָל וָכַעַס ׀ תַּבִּיט	for You observe mischief and anger,
לָתֵת בְּיָדֶךָ	and it is in Your power to allow it;
עָלֶיךָ יַעֲזֹב חֵלֶכָה	[Nevertheless] upon You the helpless relies,
יָתוֹם אַתָּה ׀ הָיִיתָ עוֹזֵר׃	for the orphan You have been the Helper.
טו שְׁבֹר זְרוֹעַ רָשָׁע	15 Break the arm of the wicked [nations];
וָרָע	and as for the evil man;
תִּדְרוֹשׁ־רִשְׁעוֹ בַל־תִּמְצָא׃	search for his wickedness till none be found.
טז יְהוָה מֶלֶךְ עוֹלָם וָעֶד	16 Adonoy will reign for all eternity,
אָבְדוּ גוֹיִם מֵאַרְצוֹ׃	when the nations have perished from His earth.
יז תַּאֲוַת עֲנָוִים שָׁמַעְתָּ	17 The desire of the humble You have heard,
יְהוָה	Adonoy;
תָּכִין לִבָּם תַּקְשִׁיב אָזְנֶךָ׃	guide their heart, let Your ear be attentive.
יח לִשְׁפֹּט יָתוֹם	18 To do justice for the orphan
וָדָךְ	and the oppressed
בַּל־יוֹסִיף עוֹד לַעֲרֹץ	so that no longer will the wicked ones terrify
אֱנוֹשׁ מִן־הָאָרֶץ׃	the weak from the earth.

פרק יא Chapter 11

Weekly Cycle	Monthly Cycle	Book Number
Sunday	2nd day of the month	Book 1

Author

דָּוִד הַמֶּלֶךְ—King David—the second king of Israel and father of the Davidic royal and messianic dynasty. David composed over seventy of the 150 psalms of Sefer Tehillim.

When & Why

David wrote this psalm after saving the people of the city of Ke'ilah from an army of Phillistines. Ke'ilah was located within the tribal territory of Judeah, which obligated King David to save them from their enemies, the Philistines. (Samuel I Ch. 23, v. 1-13)

Genre

Psalm of Individual Confidence - In this psalm, the worshipper expresses absolute certainty that his prayers will be heard.

Chapter Summary

King David speaks against those who pursue and humiliate him, entreating God to sanctify His name by paying them back in accordance with their deeds. He also addresses the issue of why it is that the righteous suffer, while the wicked prosper.

This psalm consists of seven verses, subdivided into two parts.
In verse 1-3, King David declares his trust in the Almighty.
Men advise the Psalmist to flee his home from the threat posed by the wicked. He does not heed their advice, as only God is his refuge.
In verses 4-7, he explains the principles of Divine Providence by which God examines and investigates man's deeds, and judges him accordingly.

Introductory Word

לַמְנַצֵּחַ—Lamnatsei'ach—To the Conductor

Shimush Tehillim - When to Say

For protection against evil spirits, wicked individuals, and danger—Verse 2 states: "For behold, the wicked bend the bow, they have made ready their arrow upon the bowstring; that they may shoot in darkness, at the upright in heart."
Verse 7 states: "For Adonoy is righteous, He loves righteousness the upright will behold His face."

Biblical Places

הֵיכָל—Heichal—Holy Temple—a term used to refer to the inner sanctuary of the Temple in Jerusalem. The Heichal contained the Holy of Holies, the resting place of the Aron HaKodesh (Holy Ark)*.
It also housed the Menorah, Altar of Incense, and Table of the Showbread.

*The Aron HaKodesh, while present in the first Beit HaMikdash (Temple), was buried, and hence its location was not known, during the period of the second Beit HaMikdash.

Tiberius Synagogue Menorahs and Ark

פֶּרֶק יא

Chapter 11

א לַמְנַצֵּחַ
לְדָוִד
בַּיהוָה | חָסִיתִי
אֵיךְ תֹּאמְרוּ לְנַפְשִׁי
נוּדִי הַרְכֶם צִפּוֹר׃

1 To the Chief Musician,
[a Psalm] of David.
In Adonoy I have taken refuge;
how do you say to my soul,
"Flee to your mountain [as a] bird."

ב כִּי הִנֵּה הָרְשָׁעִים
יִדְרְכוּן קֶשֶׁת
כּוֹנְנוּ חִצָּם
עַל־יֶתֶר
לִירוֹת בְּמוֹ־אֹפֶל
לְיִשְׁרֵי־לֵב׃

2 For behold, the wicked
bend the bow,
they have made ready their arrow
upon the bowstring;
that they may shoot in darkness,
at the upright in heart.

ג כִּי הַשָּׁתוֹת יֵהָרֵסוּן
צַדִּיק מַה־פָּעָל׃

3 When the foundations are destroyed,
what has the righteous done?

ד יְהוָה | בְּהֵיכַל קָדְשׁוֹ
יְהוָה בַּשָּׁמַיִם כִּסְאוֹ
עֵינָיו יֶחֱזוּ
עַפְעַפָּיו יִבְחֲנוּ בְּנֵי אָדָם׃

4 Adonoy is in His Holy Temple,
Adonoy, in the heaven is His throne;
His eyes behold,
His eyelids examine the children of man.

ה יְהוָה צַדִּיק יִבְחָן
וְרָשָׁע
וְאֹהֵב חָמָס
שָׂנְאָה נַפְשׁוֹ׃

5 Adonoy examines the righteous,
but the wicked
and the lover of violence,
His soul hates.

ו יַמְטֵר עַל־רְשָׁעִים פַּחִים
אֵשׁ וְגָפְרִית וְרוּחַ זִלְעָפוֹת
מְנָת כּוֹסָם׃

6 He will rain coal upon the wicked;
fire and brimstone and burning wind
is the portion of their cup.

ז כִּי־צַדִּיק יְהוָה
צְדָקוֹת אָהֵב
יָשָׁר יֶחֱזוּ פָנֵימוֹ׃

7 For Adonoy is righteous,
He loves righteousness;
the upright will behold His face.

פרק יב Chapter 12

Weekly Cycle	Monthly Cycle	Book Number
Sunday	2nd day of the month	Book 1

Author
דָּוִד הַמֶּלֶךְ—King David—the second king of Israel and father of the Davidic royal and messianic dynasty. David composed over seventy of the 150 psalms of Sefer Tehillim.

When & Why
David wrote this psalm concerning the Israelites who betrayed him and revealed his location to Saul.

Genre
Psalm of Individual Lament - This psalm was written from the perspective of the individual worshipper, who cries out to God in his time of need. It is characterized as an address to God involving a complaint, followed by a request and ending with an expression of trust.

Chapter Summary
King David protests the early death of the righteous, contrasting it with the longevity of those who speak with false and flattering lips. "Deliver [us], Adonoy", he pleads on behalf of the downtrodden, "for the devoted man has ceased, for the faithful have disappeared from among the sons of man."

This psalm consists of nine verses, subdivided into two equal parts of four verses each.
Verse 1 serves as a heading.
In verses 2-5, King David describes the evil deeds of the wicked.
In verses 6-9, he describes the deeds of God. He beseeches that God should hear the sighs of the needy and bring them redemption, and wage war against such a vile generation.

Introductory Word
לַמְנַצֵּחַ—Lamnatsei'ach—To the Conductor
מִזְמוֹר—Mizmor—Musical Accompaniment

Musical Instrument
שְׁמִינִית—Sheminit—An Eight-Stringed Harp

Shimush Tehillim - When to Say
To be saved from bad advice—Verse 2 states: "for the devoted man has ceased."
Verse 3 adds: "Falsehood they speak one man with his neighbor." Verses 4 and 5 proclaim further: "May Adonoy cut off all smooth lips, the tongue which speaks of great [haughty] things. Who have said, with our tongue we will prevail."
To avoid sin—Verse 9 refers to the defeat of the wicked who surround the righteous.

Talmud on Tehillim

Verse 7: "אִמְרוֹת יְהוָה, אֲמָרוֹת טְהֹרוֹת: כֶּסֶף צָרוּף, בַּעֲלִיל לָאָרֶץ; מְזֻקָּק, שִׁבְעָתָיִם"—"The words of Adonoy are pure words, as purified silver, clearly visible [to all] on earth refined seven times."

The Talmud, Rosh HaShanah 21b, teaches that the word "alil"—"crucible" connotes both purity and clarity. It also deduces that forty-nine ("sevenfold" - seven times seven) of the fifty "gates of understanding" were revealed to Moses exclusively. The final gate was revealed to all of Israel at Mount Sinai.

פֶּרֶק יב			**Chapter 12**
לַמְנַצֵּחַ	א	1	To the Chief Musician,
עַל־הַשְּׁמִינִית			on the eight stringed harp,
מִזְמוֹר לְדָוִד:			a Psalm of David.
הוֹשִׁיעָה יְהוָה	ב	2	Deliver [us], Adonoy;
כִּי־גָמַר חָסִיד			for the devoted man has ceased,
כִּי־פַסּוּ אֱמוּנִים			for the faithful have disappeared
מִבְּנֵי אָדָם:			from among the sons of man.
שָׁוְא ׀ יְדַבְּרוּ	ג	3	Falsehood they speak
אִישׁ אֶת־רֵעֵהוּ			one man with his neighbor;
שְׂפַת חֲלָקוֹת בְּלֵב			with a smooth lip and with a double heart
וָלֵב יְדַבֵּרוּ:			do they speak.
יַכְרֵת יְהוָה	ד	4	May Adonoy cut off
כָּל־שִׂפְתֵי חֲלָקוֹת			all smooth lips,
לָשׁוֹן מְדַבֶּרֶת			the tongue which speaks
גְּדֹלוֹת:			of great [haughty] things.
אֲשֶׁר אָמְרוּ ׀	ה	5	Who have said,
לִלְשֹׁנֵנוּ נַגְבִּיר			With our tongue we will prevail;
שְׂפָתֵינוּ אִתָּנוּ			our lips are with us,
מִי אָדוֹן לָנוּ:			who is master over us?"
מִשֹּׁד עֲנִיִּים	ו	6	"On account of the oppression of the poor,
מֵאַנְקַת אֶבְיוֹנִים			on account of the sighing of the needy,
עַתָּה אָקוּם יֹאמַר יְהוָה			now I will arise" says Adonoy;
אָשִׁית בְּיֵשַׁע			I will grant him deliverance"
יָפִיחַ לוֹ:			He says to him.
אִמֲרוֹת יְהוָה אֲמָרוֹת טְהֹרוֹת	ז	7	The words of Adonoy are pure words,
כֶּסֶף צָרוּף			as purified silver,
בַּעֲלִיל לָאָרֶץ			clearly visible [to all] on earth
מְזֻקָּק שִׁבְעָתָיִם:			refined seven times.

ח	אַתָּה־יְהוָה תִּשְׁמְרֵם תִּצְּרֶנּוּ | מִן־הַדּוֹר זוּ לְעוֹלָם׃	8 You, Adonoy, will preserve them; You will keep them secure from such a [vile] generation forever.
ט	סָבִיב רְשָׁעִים יִתְהַלָּכוּן כְּרֻם זֻלּוּת	9 The wicked walk on every side when the scorned are exalted
י	לִבְנֵי אָדָם׃	among the sons of man.

Mosaic with the Ark, Menorahs and Lions

פרק י״ג Chapter 13

Weekly Cycle	Monthly Cycle	Book Number
Sunday	2nd day of the month	Book 1

Author

דָּוִד הַמֶּלֶךְ—King David—the second king of Israel and father of the Davidic royal and messianic dynasty. David composed over seventy of the 150 psalms of Sefer Tehillim.

Genre

Psalm of Individual Lament - This psalm was written from the perspective of the individual worshipper, who cries out to God in his time of need. It is characterized as an address to God involving a complaint, followed by a request and ending with an expression of trust.

Chapter Summary

King David teaches us to ask God not to forget us, and not to hide His face from us. "Until when", he asks. How long must each Jew suffer unrelenting persecutions at the hands of his enemies? Yet, he answers, trusting in God's kindness will see us through.

This psalm consists of six verses, subdivided into three parts.

Verse 1 is an introduction.

In verses 2 & 3, King David laments: "Until when, Adonoy, will You forget me, forever? Until when will You hide Your face from me?"
In verses 4 & 5, he further beseeches God to hear his prayer.
In verse 6, he concludes by expressing his hope and trust in Gods' deliverance.

Introductory Words

לַמְנַצֵּחַ—Lamnatsei'ach—To the Conductor
מִזְמוֹר— Mizmor—Musical Accompaniment

Shimush Tehillim - When to Say

To avoid unnatural death and for illness of the eyes—Verse 4 states: "brighten my eyes lest I slumber into death."

Where in the Siddur

Verse 4 is recited as part of the bedtime Shema.
Verse 6 is the ninth verse of Hoshi'a Et Amecha of Pesukei Dezimra (Introductory Verses of Praise to the Shacharit morning service).

פֶּרֶק יג			**Chapter 13**
לַמְנַצֵּחַ	א	1	To the Chief Musician,
מִזְמוֹר לְדָוִד׃			a Psalm of David.
עַד־אָנָה יְהוָה	ב	2	Until when, Adonoy,
תִּשְׁכָּחֵנִי נֶצַח			will You forget me, forever?
עַד־אָנָה ׀			Until when
תַּסְתִּיר אֶת־פָּנֶיךָ מִמֶּנִּי׃			will You hide Your face from me?
עַד־אָנָה	ג	3	Until when
אָשִׁית עֵצוֹת בְּנַפְשִׁי			must I devise plans within my soul
יָגוֹן בִּלְבָבִי יוֹמָם			[to be free of] sorrow in my heart by day?
עַד־אָנָה ׀			Until when
יָרוּם אֹיְבִי עָלָי׃			will my enemy rise high above me?
הַבִּיטָה	ד	4	Look [at my troubled life and]
עֲנֵנִי יְהוָה אֱלֹהָי			answer me, Adonoy, my God;
הָאִירָה עֵינַי			brighten my eyes
פֶּן־אִישַׁן הַמָּוֶת׃			lest I slumber into death.
פֶּן־יֹאמַר אֹיְבִי	ה	5	Lest my enemy say,
יְכָלְתִּיו			I have prevailed against him;"
צָרַי יָגִילוּ כִּי אֶמּוֹט׃			my tormentors rejoice when I waver.
וַאֲנִי ׀ בְּחַסְדְּךָ בָטַחְתִּי	ו	6	I trust in Your loving kindness,
יָגֵל לִבִּי בִּישׁוּעָתֶךָ			my heart will exult in Your deliverance.
אָשִׁירָה לַיהוָה			I will sing to Adonoy,
כִּי גָמַל עָלָי׃			for He has dealt kindly with me.

פרק יד Chapter 14

Weekly Cycle	Monthly Cycle	Book Number
Sunday	2nd day of the month	Book 1

Author
דָּוִד הַמֶּלֶךְ—King David—the second king of Israel and father of the Davidic royal and messianic dynasty. David composed over seventy of the 150 psalms of Sefer Tehillim.

When & Why
David wrote this psalm concerning the Israelites who betrayed him and revealed his location to Saul.

Genre
Psalm of Individual Lament - This psalm was written from the perspective of the individual worshipper, who cries out to God in his time of need. It is characterized as an address to God involving a complaint, followed by a request and ending with an expression of trust.

Chapter Summary
King David speaks against those who deny Divine Providence. He rejects the wicked man's belief that one can act with impunity. "Oh that out of Zion would come Israel's deliverance!", he cries.

This psalm consists of seven verses, subdivided into three parts.
In verses 1-3, King David laments how his people have deviated from the path of righteousness and gone astray.
In verses 4-6, he rebukes the wicked and tells of the punishment to come.
In verse 7, he expresses his hope for salvation.

Introductory Word
לַמְנַצֵּחַ—Lamnatsei'ach—To the Conductor

Shimush Tehillim - When to Say
For salvation from harmful words of others—Verse 7 states: "Oh that out of Zion would come Israel's deliverance! When Adonoy returns the captivity of His people, Jacob will exult, Israel will rejoice."

Biblical People
יַעֲקֹב—Ya'akov— Jacob, also called Israel, son of Isaac and Rebekah and grandson of Abraham, was the third Hebrew patriarch and the traditional ancestor of the people of Israel.
יִשְׂרָאֵל—Yisrael—The Nation of Israel.

Biblical Places
צִיּוֹן—Zion—often used as a synonym for Jerusalem. The term Zion originally referred only to the area where a Jebbusite fortress once stood, also the location of the City of David. Zion was later used by prophets and psalmists as another name for Jerusalem.

פרק יד

א לַמְנַצֵּחַ
לְדָוִד
אָמַר נָבָל בְּלִבּוֹ
אֵין אֱלֹהִים
הִשְׁחִיתוּ הִתְעִיבוּ עֲלִילָה
אֵין עֹשֵׂה־טוֹב׃
ב יְהוָה מִשָּׁמַיִם
הִשְׁקִיף עַל־בְּנֵי־אָדָם
לִרְאוֹת הֲיֵשׁ מַשְׂכִּיל
דֹּרֵשׁ אֶת־אֱלֹהִים׃
ג הַכֹּל סָר
יַחְדָּו נֶאֱלָחוּ
אֵין עֹשֵׂה־טוֹב
אֵין גַּם־אֶחָד׃
ד הֲלֹא יָדְעוּ
כָּל־פֹּעֲלֵי אָוֶן
אֹכְלֵי עַמִּי
אָכְלוּ לֶחֶם
יְהוָה לֹא קָרָאוּ׃
ה שָׁם ׀ פָּחֲדוּ פָחַד
כִּי־אֱלֹהִים בְּדוֹר צַדִּיק׃
ו עֲצַת־עָנִי
תָבִישׁוּ
כִּי יְהוָה מַחְסֵהוּ׃
ז מִי יִתֵּן מִצִּיּוֹן
יְשׁוּעַת יִשְׂרָאֵל
בְּשׁוּב יְהוָה
שְׁבוּת עַמּוֹ
יָגֵל יַעֲקֹב
יִשְׂמַח יִשְׂרָאֵל׃

Chapter 14

1 1. To the Chief Musician,
[a Psalm] of David.
The degenerate said in his heart,
"There is no God."
They have acted corruptly and abominably,
there is no doer of good.
2 Adonoy, from heaven,
looked down upon [these] sons of man,
to see if there were any man of understanding
searching for God.
3 They were all gone astray
together they became corrupt,
there was no doer of good,
none, not even one.
4 Do they not know,
all the workers of iniquity,
who would devour My people
as they devour bread,
[and] unto Adonoy they call not?
5 There they were in great fear,
for God is with the righteous generation.
6 The counsel of the poor
you would put to shame,
that Adonoy is his refuge.
7 Oh that out of Zion
would come Israel's deliverance!
When Adonoy returns
the captivity of His people,
Jacob will exult,
Israel will rejoice.

פרק טו Chapter 15

Weekly Cycle	Monthly Cycle	Book Number
Sunday	2nd day of the month	Book 1

Author
דָּוִד הַמֶּלֶךְ—King David—the second king of Israel and father of the Davidic royal and messianic dynasty. David composed over seventy of the 150 psalms of Sefer Tehillim.

Genre
Psalm of Wisdom - This psalm contains teachings and wise advice and is meant to instruct people on how to live a Godly life.

Chapter Summary
In contrast to the wicked man, the Tzaddik (righteous man) has many virtues. Because of his perfections of character, good works, and faith in God, he merits to dwell with the Almighty and behold His pleasure.

This psalm consists of a mere five verses.
In verse 1, the Psalmist poses the question of who is fit to sit in God's sanctuary.
In veres 2-5, he attempts to answer that very question.
In total, King David lists eleven virtuous qualities in this psalm. In verse 5, he adds his assurance that one who succeeds in obtaining these qualities will not falter.

Introductory Word
מִזְמוֹר—Mizmor—Musical Accompaniment

Shimush Tehillim - When to Say
To find favor in people's eyes
To banish a demon

Where in the Siddur
Recited as part of the traditional burial service.
Verse 4 is found in the repetition of the Musaf Amidah (Silent Meditation) of Rosh HaShanah.

Biblical Places
אָהֳלֶךָ—God's tent; הַר קָדְשֶׁךָ—God's Holy Mount—both are references to the Temple in Jerusalem.

Talmud on Tehillim
Verse 5: "כַּסְפּוֹ לֹא נָתַן בְּנֶשֶׁךְ, וְשֹׁחַד עַל נָקִי לֹא לָקָח. עֹשֵׂה אֵלֶּה לֹא יִמּוֹט לְעוֹלָם"—"His money he has not lent out as usury and a bribe against the innocent he has not taken."
The Talmud, Baba Metzia 71a, applies this verse to one who has the means and yet lends without taking interest, and reinforces the notion that he will not falter.
The converse is implied: If one does not conform to the above and lends with interest, then he indeed will eventually falter, and his possessions will in turn diminish.

פֶּרֶק טו			Chapter 15
מִזְמוֹר לְדָוִד	א	1	A Psalm of David.
יְהוָה מִי־יָגוּר בְּאָהֳלֶךָ			Adonoy, who will sojourn in Your Tabernacle?
מִי־יִשְׁכֹּן בְּהַר קָדְשֶׁךָ׃			Who will dwell upon Your holy mountain?
הוֹלֵךְ תָּמִים	ב	2	He who walks in wholehearted integrity
וּפֹעֵל צֶדֶק			and deals righteously
וְדֹבֵר אֱמֶת בִּלְבָבוֹ׃			and speaks truth in his heart.
לֹא־רָגַל | עַל־לְשֹׁנוֹ	ג	3	He who has no slander on his tongue,
לֹא־עָשָׂה לְרֵעֵהוּ רָעָה			who has done his friend no evil,
וְחֶרְפָּה לֹא־נָשָׂא עַל־קְרֹבוֹ׃			nor cast disgrace upon his fellow man.
נִבְזֶה | בְּעֵינָיו נִמְאָס	ד	4	In whose eyes a vile person is despised,
וְאֶת־יִרְאֵי יְהוָה יְכַבֵּד			and those who fear Adonoy he honors;
נִשְׁבַּע לְהָרַע			though he swears to his own hurt,
וְלֹא יָמִר׃			he does not change [his oath].
כַּסְפּוֹ | לֹא־נָתַן בְּנֶשֶׁךְ	ה	5	His money he has not lent out at usury
וְשֹׁחַד עַל־נָקִי			and a bribe against the innocent
לֹא לָקָח			he has not taken;
עֹשֵׂה־אֵלֶּה			whoever does these things
לֹא יִמּוֹט לְעוֹלָם׃			will not be moved forever.

פרק טז — Chapter 16

Weekly Cycle	Monthly Cycle	Book Number
Sunday	2nd day of the month	Book 1

Author

דָּוִד הַמֶּלֶךְ—King David—the second king of Israel and father of the Davidic royal and messianic dynasty. David composed over seventy of the 150 psalms of Sefer Tehillim.

Genre

Psalm of Individual Confidence - In this psalm, the worshipper expresses absolute certainty that his prayers will be heard.

Chapter Summary

This psalm rebukes idol worshippers and those drawn after foolishness, contrasting them with the humble and sincere servant of God. "You are my Master, I have no well being without You." This provides the Tzaddik (righteous man) with security so that he may rejoice and anticipate the World To Come.

This psalm consists of eleven verses, subdivided into three parts.
Verse 1 serves as a heading, with the request that God preserve those who put their trust in Him.
In verses 2-4, King David affirms his distancing himself from idol worship.
In verses 5-8, he thanks God for bestowing upon him a goodly portion.
In verses 9-11, he expresses the gladness in his heart and gives the reason for his joy, proclaiming that God protects the lives of His faithful.

Technical Terminology

מִכְתָּם—Michtam—an engraving, perhaps of simple fashion (Targum Yonatan); alternatively, made of fine gold (Ibn Ezra).

Shimush Tehillim - When to Say

To catch a thief
To inspire one's heart towards God
To make peace with an enemy
To alleviate distress—Verse 6 states: "The portions that have fallen to me are in pleasant places; a beautiful inheritance is mine." The letters chet and yud, comprising the word חי—chai—life, are alluded to in the first letter of the word "chavalim"—"portions", and the last letter of the word "alai—"to me."

Where in the Siddur

Recited as part of the cemetery service.
Verse 3 is found in Pirkei Avot (Ethics of the Fathers), 6:10.
Verse 8 is often inscribed on or above the Aron Kodesh (Holy Ark).

Biblical Places

שְׁאוֹל—Sheol—Lower or Underworld; abode of the dead.

Talmud on Tehillim

Verse 10: "כִּי לֹא-תַעֲזֹב נַפְשִׁי לִשְׁאוֹל לֹא-תִתֵּן חֲסִידְךָ לִרְאוֹת שָׁחַת"— "For You will not abandon my soul to the grave, nor will You allow Your devoted one to see the pit."
The Talmud, Yoma 87a, states: "כָּל הַמְזַכֶּה אֶת הָרַבִּים, אֵין חֵטְא בָּא עַל יָדוֹ"—"Whoever causes the community to do good will not be given the opportunity to sin". God prevents the righteous from falling into Geihinom while his disciples have found their resting place in Gan Eden—the Garden of Eden. And while God does not interfere with one's free will, the goal is achieved through God's assuring that the opportunity to sin does not come their way.

פרק טז

א מִכְתָּם לְדָוִד
שָׁמְרֵנִי אֵל
כִּי־חָסִיתִי בָךְ׃
ב אָמַרְתְּ לַיהוָה
אֲדֹנָי אָתָּה
טוֹבָתִי בַּל־עָלֶיךָ׃
ג לִקְדוֹשִׁים אֲשֶׁר־בָּאָרֶץ הֵמָּה
וְאַדִּירֵי
כָּל־חֶפְצִי־בָם׃
ד יִרְבּוּ עַצְּבוֹתָם
אַחֵר מָהָרוּ
בַּל־אַסִּיךְ נִסְכֵּיהֶם מִדָּם
וּבַל־אֶשָּׂא אֶת־שְׁמוֹתָם
עַל־שְׂפָתָי׃
ה יְהוָה מְנָת־חֶלְקִי
וְכוֹסִי
אַתָּה תּוֹמִיךְ גּוֹרָלִי׃
ו חֲבָלִים נָפְלוּ־לִי
בַּנְּעִמִים
אַף־נַחֲלָת שָׁפְרָה עָלָי׃
ז אֲבָרֵךְ אֶת־יְהוָה
אֲשֶׁר יְעָצָנִי
אַף־לֵילוֹת
יִסְּרוּנִי כִלְיוֹתָי׃
ח שִׁוִּיתִי יְהוָה לְנֶגְדִּי תָמִיד
כִּי מִימִינִי
בַּל־אֶמּוֹט׃
ט לָכֵן ׀ שָׂמַח לִבִּי
וַיָּגֶל כְּבוֹדִי
אַף־בְּשָׂרִי יִשְׁכֹּן לָבֶטַח׃
י כִּי ׀ לֹא־תַעֲזֹב נַפְשִׁי
לִשְׁאוֹל
לֹא־תִתֵּן חֲסִידְךָ
לִרְאוֹת שָׁחַת׃
יא תּוֹדִיעֵנִי
אֹרַח חַיִּים
שֹׂבַע שְׂמָחוֹת אֶת־פָּנֶיךָ
נְעִמוֹת בִּימִינְךָ נֶצַח׃

Chapter 16

1 A Michtam of David.
Preserve me, Almighty,
for I have taken refuge in You.
2 You said to Adonoy,
"You are my Master,
I have no well being without You."
3 Due to the holy that are in the earth,
and the mighty,
are all my desires [fulfilled].
4 Let their sufferings multiply,
those who follow another [sovereignty];
I will not pour their libations of blood
nor carry their names
upon my lips.
5 Adonoy is the portion of my inheritance
and of my cup;
You guide my fate.
6 The portions that have fallen to me
are in pleasant places;
a beautiful inheritance is mine.
7 I will bless Adonoy
Who has given me counsel;
even for the nights
in which my mind admonished me.
8 I have set Adonoy before me always;
for surely He is at my right hand,
I will not be moved.
9 Therefore my heart rejoiced
and my soul exulted;
also my flesh will dwell in safety.
10 For You will not abandon my soul
to the grave,
nor will You allow Your devoted one
to see the pit.
11 You will make known to me
the path of life;
fullness of joy is in Your presence;
pleasantness is at Your right hand, evermore.

פרק יז Chapter 17

Weekly Cycle	Monthly Cycle	Book Number
Sunday	2nd day of the month	Book 1

Author

דָּוִד הַמֶּלֶךְ—King David—the second king of Israel and father of the Davidic royal and messianic dynasty. David composed over seventy of the 150 psalms of Sefer Tehillim.

When & Why

David wrote this psalm as a prayer to God to save him from his enemies.

Genre

Psalm of Individual Lament - This psalm was written from the perspective of the individual worshipper, who cries out to God in his time of need. It is characterized as an address to God involving a complaint, followed by a request and ending with an expression of trust.

Chapter Summary

David offers a plea to God, appealing for deliverance, as his heart is pure. "Rise up, Adonoy, confront him, bring him to his knees", he declares of his enemy. These words are also understood as referring to man's evil inclination and the angel of death.

This psalm contains fifteen verses, subdivided into three parts.
In verses 1-5, King David asks that his prayers be accepted, as God has already purified him with suffering which cleanses a person of sin.
In verses 6-12, he once again requests that his prayers be accepted, and describes the wickedness of his enemies, thereby elucidating the suffering referenced above.
In verses 13-15, he asks that God rescue him from his enemies and that he receive his fair share in this world as well as in the world to come.

Introductory Word

תְּפִלָּה—Tefilah—Prayer

Shimush Tehillim - When to Say

For traveling on a journey—Verse 4 states: "I have preserved [my soul] by avoiding the way of the lawbreakers."

Where in the Siddur

Verse 2 is found in the repetition of the Amidah of Rosh HaShanah.
Verse 8 is part of the prayers of the bedtime Shema. It is also paraphrased as part of the blessings following the Shema of Ma'ariv.

Talmud on Tehillim

Verse 15: "אֲנִי בְּצֶדֶק, אֶחֱזֶה פָנֶיךָ; אֶשְׂבְּעָה בְהָקִיץ, תְּמוּנָתֶךָ"—"As for me, in righteousness I will behold Your presence; I will be satisfied when I awake, with Your likeness."

The Talmud, Bava Batra 10a, explains: When one brings a large gift to a king, it is questionable whether or not the king's palace servants will accept the gift on the king's behalf. And, if it is accepted, it is still questionable whether the visitor will be granted a personal audience with the king. However, when one gives a perutah, a small coin, to a pauper, he is immediately deserving and receives the Divine Presence.

The Talmud further infers that this verse refers to Talmidei Chachamim (Torah scholars), who remain awake late at night studying Torah, thereby lacking sleep. God therefore satisfies them in the world to come with the Divine Presence.

Seal of Shema

פרק יז	**Chapter 17**
א תְּפִלָּה לְדָוִד	1 A prayer of David.
שִׁמְעָה יְהוָֹה | צֶדֶק	Hear, Adonoy, that which is right,
הַקְשִׁיבָה רִנָּתִי	be attentive to my cry;
הַאֲזִינָה תְפִלָּתִי	give ear to my prayer
בְּלֹא שִׂפְתֵי מִרְמָה:	which is not from lips of deceit.
ב מִלְּפָנֶיךָ	2 From before You
מִשְׁפָּטִי יֵצֵא	let my judgment come forth;
עֵינֶיךָ תֶּחֱזֶינָה מֵישָׁרִים:	let Your eyes behold [my] uprightness.
ג בָּחַנְתָּ לִבִּי |	3 You have examined my heart,
פָּקַדְתָּ לַּיְלָה	You have inspected it in the night,
צְרַפְתַּנִי	You have tested me
בַל־תִּמְצָא	and You did not find [what You sought];
זַמֹּתִי	my presumptuous thoughts
בַּל־יַעֲבָר־פִּי:	will no longer pass my mouth.
ד לִפְעֻלּוֹת אָדָם	4 That the deeds of man
בִּדְבַר שְׂפָתֶיךָ	[may follow] the word of Your lips,
אֲנִי שָׁמַרְתִּי	I have preserved [my soul]
אָרְחוֹת פָּרִיץ:	by avoiding the way of the lawbreakers.

ה תָּמֹךְ אֲשֻׁרַי בְּמַעְגְּלוֹתֶיךָ
בַּל־נָמוֹטּוּ פְעָמָי׃

5 Let my steps hold fast to Your paths
so that my feet do not slip.

ו אֲנִי־קְרָאתִיךָ
כִי־תַעֲנֵנִי אֵל
הַט־אָזְנְךָ לִי
שְׁמַע אִמְרָתִי׃

6 I called out to You,
for You will answer me, Almighty;
incline Your ear to me,
hear my speech.

ז הַפְלֵה חֲסָדֶיךָ
מוֹשִׁיעַ חוֹסִים
מִמִּתְקוֹמְמִים
בִּימִינֶךָ׃

7 Set aside Your kindliness,
to deliver those who take refuge [in You],
from those who revolt against You,
with Your right hand.

ח שָׁמְרֵנִי כְּאִישׁוֹן בַּת־עָיִן
בְּצֵל כְּנָפֶיךָ תַּסְתִּירֵנִי׃

8 Preserve me as the apple of the eye,
in the shadow of Your wings hide me.

ט מִפְּנֵי רְשָׁעִים זוּ שַׁדּוּנִי
אֹיְבַי בְּנֶפֶשׁ יַקִּיפוּ עָלָי׃

9 From the wicked who have devastated me;
my soul's enemies surround me.

י חֶלְבָּמוֹ סָּגְרוּ
פִּימוֹ דִּבְּרוּ בְגֵאוּת׃

10 In their gross fat they are shut,
with their mouth they spoke proudly.

יא אַשֻּׁרֵינוּ עַתָּה סְבָבוּנוּ
עֵינֵיהֶם יָשִׁיתוּ
לִנְטוֹת בָּאָרֶץ׃

11 At our [every] step they now surround us,
they set their eyes
to extend [their power] over the earth.

יב דִּמְיֹנוֹ כְּאַרְיֵה
יִכְסוֹף לִטְרוֹף
וְכִכְפִיר
יֹשֵׁב בְּמִסְתָּרִים׃

12 He is like a lion
eager to tear [his prey] into pieces
and like a young lion
who lurks in hiding.

יג קוּמָה יְהוָֹה קַדְּמָה פָנָיו
הַכְרִיעֵהוּ
פַּלְּטָה נַפְשִׁי מֵרָשָׁע
חַרְבֶּךָ׃

13 Rise up, Adonoy, confront him,
bring him to his knees;
rescue my soul from the wicked
[who act as] Your sword.

יד מִמְתִים
יָדְךָ ׀ יְהוָֹה
מִמְתִים מֵחֶלֶד
חֶלְקָם בַּחַיִּים
וּצְפוּנְךָ
תְּמַלֵּא בִטְנָם
יִשְׂבְּעוּ בָנִים
וְהִנִּיחוּ יִתְרָם לְעוֹלְלֵיהֶם׃

14 [Rather, I prefer being] from [among] those whose death
is by Your hand, Adonoy,
from men who die of old age,
whose portion is eternal life,
and with Your hidden treasure
You fill their stomach,
who are satisfied with children,
and leave their abundance to their offspring.

טו אֲנִי
בְּצֶדֶק אֶחֱזֶה פָנֶיךָ
אֶשְׂבְּעָה בְהָקִיץ
תְּמוּנָתֶךָ׃

15 As for me,
in righteousness I will behold Your presence;
I will be satisfied when I awake,
with Your likeness.

As for me, in righteousness
I will behold Your presence;
I will be satisfied when I awake,
with Your likeness.

פרק יח Chapter 18

Weekly Cycle	Monthly Cycle	Book Number
Sunday	3rd day of the month	Book 1

Author

דָּוִד הַמֶּלֶךְ—King David—the second king of Israel and father of the Davidic royal and messianic dynasty. David composed over seventy of the 150 psalms of Sefer Tehillim.

When & Why

David wrote this psalm at a later stage in his life, and in it, he reflects on how God delivered him from his enemies and established his kingdom.

Genre

Psalm of Individual Thanksgiving - This psalm emphasizes gratitude for what God has done for the individual.

Psalm of Royalty - This psalm describes how God reigns supreme. It focuses on the human king of Israel, or upon God as King of Israel.

Chapter Summary

With all his battles completed, King David sings praises of thanksgiving to God in whom he has taken refuge. God alone has shielded him and straightened his path, in the process giving him strength and teaching him how to battle. Unlike Saul, whose kingdom was short lived, "He increases the deliverance of His king, and does kindness with His annointed, to David and his seed, for evermore."

This psalm contains fifty-one verses, subdivided into two parts.
Verse 1 serves as an introduction.
In verses 2-32, King David describes his prayer in time of trouble, and illustrates how God's strength saved him from his enemies. He further explains how God has rewarded him according to his merits.
In verses 33-51, King David describes the battle and victory, and, paralleling the verses above, illustrates how God allowed him to go out, pursue and overtake his enemies. He ends the psalm with praise and gratitude to God.

Introductory Words

לַמְנַצֵּח—Lamnatsei'ach—To the Conductor
שִׁירָה—Shirah—Song

Shimush Tehillim - When to Say

To ward off bandits—Verse 1 demonstrates how God delivered the Psalmist from the hand of his enemies. In verse 18 he states: "He rescued me from my mighty enemy", and in verse 49 he declares: "You rescue me from my enemies."

Where in the Siddur

This psalm is a mirror reflection of Shmu'el Bet (Samuel II), chapter 22, recited as the Haftarah of the seventh day of Passover.

Verse 32 is recited before Ein K'Eilokeinu (one of the concluding prayers of Shacharit).

Verse 51 is part of the weekday version of Birkat HaMazon—Grace after Meals.

Biblical Personalities

שָׁאוּל—Shaul—Saul—the first King of Israel. After Saul disobeyed God's command to destroy all of Amalek, the prophet Samuel dethroned Saul and annointed David to start a new monarchic line.

Biblical Places

הֵיכָל—Heichal—Holy Temple—a term used to refer to the inner sanctuary of the Temple in Jerusalem. The Heichal contained the Holy of Holies, the resting place of the Aron HaKodesh (Holy Ark)*. It also housed the Menorah, Altar of Incense, and Table of the Showbread.

*The Aron HaKodesh, while present in the first Beit HaMikdash (Temple), was buried, and hence its location was not known, during the period of the second Beit HaMikdash.

שְׁאוֹל—Sheol—Lower or Underworld; abode of the dead

Contemporary Song

Verse 3

פֶּרֶק יח

א לַמְנַצֵּחַ ׀
לְעֶבֶד יְהֹוָה לְדָוִד
אֲשֶׁר דִּבֶּר ׀ לַיהֹוָה
אֶת־דִּבְרֵי הַשִּׁירָה הַזֹּאת
בְּיוֹם הִצִּיל־יְהֹוָה אוֹתוֹ
מִכַּף כָּל־אֹיְבָיו
וּמִיַּד שָׁאוּל:

ב וַיֹּאמַר
אֶרְחָמְךָ יְהֹוָה חִזְקִי:

ג יְהֹוָה ׀ סַלְעִי וּמְצוּדָתִי
וּמְפַלְטִי
אֵלִי צוּרִי אֶחֱסֶה־בּוֹ
מָגִנִּי וְקֶרֶן־יִשְׁעִי
מִשְׂגַּבִּי:

ד מְהֻלָּל אֶקְרָא יְהֹוָה
וּמִן־אֹיְבַי אִוָּשֵׁעַ:

ה אֲפָפוּנִי חֶבְלֵי־מָוֶת
וְנַחֲלֵי בְלִיַּעַל יְבַעֲתוּנִי:

Chapter 18

1 To the Chief Musician,
[a Psalm] of the servant of Adonoy, of David,
who spoke to Adonoy
the words of this song,
on the day Adonoy rescued him
from the palm of all his enemies,
and from the hand of Saul.

2 And he said:
I love You, Adonoy, my strength.

3 Adonoy is my rock, and my fortress,
and my rescuer;
my Almighty, my Rock, I take refuge in Him;
my shield, and the horn of my salvation,
my stronghold.

4 With praises I call out to Adonoy,
and from my enemies I am delivered.

5 I was often surrounded by bands of death,
and floods of despicable people alarmed me.

ו חֶבְלֵי שְׁאוֹל סְבָבוּנִי
קִדְּמוּנִי מוֹקְשֵׁי מָוֶת׃

6 Bands of the wicked surrounded me,
I was confronted by the snares of death.

ז בַּצַּר־לִי | אֶקְרָא יְהוָה
וְאֶל־אֱלֹהַי אֲשַׁוֵּעַ
יִשְׁמַע מֵהֵיכָלוֹ קוֹלִי
וְשַׁוְעָתִי לְפָנָיו | תָּבוֹא בְאָזְנָיו׃

7 In my distress I called out to Adonoy
and to my God I cried;
out of His Sanctuary He heard my voice,
and my cry before Him reached His ears.

ח וַתִּגְעַשׁ וַתִּרְעַשׁ | הָאָרֶץ
וּמוֹסְדֵי
הָרִים יִרְגָּזוּ
וַיִּתְגָּעֲשׁוּ כִּי־חָרָה לוֹ׃

8 The earth shook and quaked,
and the foundations
of the mountains trembled;
they were shaken because He was wroth.

ט עָלָה עָשָׁן | בְּאַפּוֹ
וְאֵשׁ־מִפִּיו תֹּאכֵל
גֶּחָלִים בָּעֲרוּ מִמֶּנּוּ׃

9 Smoke arose from His nostrils,
devouring fire from His mouth;
coals flamed forth from Him.

י וַיֵּט שָׁמַיִם וַיֵּרַד
וַעֲרָפֶל תַּחַת רַגְלָיו׃

10 He bent the heavens and came down;
and clouds of darkness were under His feet.

יא וַיִּרְכַּב עַל־כְּרוּב וַיָּעֹף
וַיֵּדֶא עַל־כַּנְפֵי־רוּחַ׃

11 And He rode upon a cherub and flew;
He swooped down upon the wings of the wind.

יב יָשֶׁת חֹשֶׁךְ | סִתְרוֹ
סְבִיבוֹתָיו סֻכָּתוֹ
חֶשְׁכַת־מַיִם עָבֵי שְׁחָקִים׃

12 He made darkness His hiding place,
His immediate surroundings His shelter;
darkness of waters, thick clouds of the skies.

יג מִנֹּגַהּ נֶגְדּוֹ
עָבָיו עָבְרוּ
בָּרָד וְגַחֲלֵי־אֵשׁ׃

13 At the brightness that is before Him
His thick clouds [that] passed through
brought hailstones and coals of fire.

יד וַיַּרְעֵם בַּשָּׁמַיִם | יְהוָה
וְעֶלְיוֹן יִתֵּן קֹלוֹ
בָּרָד וְגַחֲלֵי־אֵשׁ׃

14 And Adonoy thundered in the heavens,
and the Most High gave forth His voice;
[in the form of] hailstones and coals of fire.

טו וַיִּשְׁלַח חִצָּיו
וַיְפִיצֵם
וּבְרָקִים רָב
וַיְהֻמֵּם׃

15 And He sent out His arrows
and scattered them;
and He shot forth lightning
and confounded them.

טז וַיֵּרָאוּ | אֲפִיקֵי מַיִם
וַיִּגָּלוּ מוֹסְדוֹת תֵּבֵל
מִגַּעֲרָתְךָ יְהוָה
מִנִּשְׁמַת רוּחַ אַפֶּךָ׃

16 And [original] streams of water appeared,
and the foundations of the earth were revealed
at Your rebuke, Adonoy,
at the blast of the breath of Your nostrils.

יז יִשְׁלַח מִמָּרוֹם יִקָּחֵנִי
יַמְשֵׁנִי מִמַּיִם רַבִּים׃

17 He sent forth on high, He took me,
He drew me out of mighty waters.

יח יַצִּילֵנִי מֵאֹיְבִי עָז
וּמִשֹּׂנְאַי
כִּי־אָמְצוּ מִמֶּנִּי׃

18 He rescued me from my mighty enemy
and from those who hate me,
for they were too powerful for me.

יט יְקַדְּמוּנִי
בְיוֹם־אֵידִי
וַיְהִי־יְהוָה לְמִשְׁעָן לִי׃

19 When they confronted me
on the day of my calamity,
Adonoy was a support to me.

כ וַיּוֹצִיאֵנִי לַמֶּרְחָב
יְחַלְּצֵנִי כִּי חָפֵץ בִּי׃

20 He brought me into spaciousness
He released me because he desired me.

כא יִגְמְלֵנִי יְהוָה
כְּצִדְקִי
כְּבֹר יָדַי
יָשִׁיב לִי׃

21 Adonoy rewarded me
according to my righteousness,
according to the purity of my hands
He recompensed me.

כב כִּי־שָׁמַרְתִּי דַּרְכֵי יְהוָה
וְלֹא־רָשַׁעְתִּי מֵאֱלֹהָי׃

22 For I have kept the ways of Adonoy,
and I have not wickedly forsaken my God.

כג כִּי כָל־מִשְׁפָּטָיו לְנֶגְדִּי
וְחֻקֹּתָיו לֹא־אָסִיר מֶנִּי׃

23 For all His ordinances were before me,
and His statutes I did not dismiss from me.

כד וָאֱהִי תָמִים עִמּוֹ
וָאֶשְׁתַּמֵּר מֵעֲוֺנִי׃

24 And I was wholehearted with Him,
and I guarded myself from iniquity.

כה וַיָּשֶׁב־יְהוָה לִי
כְצִדְקִי
כְּבֹר יָדַי
לְנֶגֶד עֵינָיו׃

25 And Adonoy recompensed me
according to my righteousness
according to the purity of my hands
before His eyes.

כו עִם־חָסִיד תִּתְחַסָּד
עִם־גְּבַר תָּמִים
תִּתַּמָּם׃.

26 With the devout You act devoutly,
with the wholehearted man,
You act wholeheartedly.

כז עִם־נָבָר תִּתְבָּרָר
וְעִם־עִקֵּשׁ תִּתְפַּתָּל׃

27 With the pure You act purely,
and with the pervert You act perversely.

כח כִּי־אַתָּה עַם־עָנִי תוֹשִׁיעַ
וְעֵינַיִם רָמוֹת תַּשְׁפִּיל׃

28 For You deliver an afflicted people
and haughty eyes You humble.

כט כִּי־אַתָּה תָּאִיר נֵרִי
יְהוָה אֱלֹהַי יַגִּיהַּ חָשְׁכִּי׃

29 For You give light to my lamp;
Adonoy, my God, brighten my darkness.

ל כִּי־בְךָ
אָרֻץ גְּדוּד
וּבֵאלֹהַי אֲדַלֶּג־שׁוּר׃

30 Because of You
I [am able to] run through a troop;
and [with the help of] my God, I scale a wall.

לא הָאֵל תָּמִים דַּרְכּוֹ
אִמְרַת־יְהוָה צְרוּפָה
מָגֵן הוּא
לְכֹל ׀ הַחֹסִים בּוֹ׃

31 As for the Almighty, His way is perfect,
the word of Adonoy is refined;
He is a shield
to all who take refuge in Him.

לב כִּי מִי אֱלוֹהַּ מִבַּלְעֲדֵי יְהוָה
וּמִי צוּר זוּלָתִי אֱלֹהֵינוּ׃

32 For who is God, save Adonoy,
and who is a rock, besides our God?

לג הָאֵל הַמְאַזְּרֵנִי חָיִל
וַיִּתֵּן תָּמִים דַּרְכִּי׃

33 The Almighty that girded me with strength,
and made my way faultless.

לד מְשַׁוֶּה רַגְלַי כָּאַיָּלוֹת	34 He made my feet [swift] like the hinds;
וְעַל בָּמוֹתַי יַעֲמִידֵנִי׃	and upon my high places He stood me.
לה מְלַמֵּד יָדַי לַמִּלְחָמָה	35 He trained my hands for war,
וְנִחֲתָה קֶשֶׁת־נְחוּשָׁה זְרוֹעֹתָי׃	and my arms to bend a bow of bronze.
לו וַתִּתֶּן־לִי	36 And You have given me
מָגֵן יִשְׁעֶךָ	the shield of Your salvation,
וִימִינְךָ תִסְעָדֵנִי	and Your right hand has upheld me;
וְעַנְוַתְךָ	and Your humility
תַרְבֵּנִי׃	was most generous toward me.
לז תַּרְחִיב צַעֲדִי תַחְתָּי	37 You have expanded my stride beneath me,
וְלֹא מָעֲדוּ קַרְסֻלָּי׃	and my ankles have not slipped.
לח אֶרְדּוֹף אוֹיְבַי	38 I have pursued my enemies
וְאַשִּׂיגֵם	and overtaken them,
וְלֹא־אָשׁוּב	and I did not turn back
עַד־כַּלּוֹתָם׃	until they were consumed.
לט אֶמְחָצֵם	39 I have smitten them
וְלֹא־יֻכְלוּ קוּם	so that they were unable to rise;
יִפְּלוּ תַּחַת רַגְלָי׃	they fell under my feet.
מ וַתְּאַזְּרֵנִי חַיִל	40 You have girded me with strength
לַמִּלְחָמָה	for the battle,
תַּכְרִיעַ קָמַי	You have made my adversaries kneel
תַּחְתָּי׃	beneath me.
מא וְאֹיְבַי	41 And [regarding] my enemies
נָתַתָּה לִּי עֹרֶף	You have given me [the back of] their necks;
וּמְשַׂנְאַי אַצְמִיתֵם׃	and my adversaries I cut off.
מב יְשַׁוְּעוּ	42 They cried out,
וְאֵין־מוֹשִׁיעַ	but there was no one to deliver them
עַל־יְהוָה	even unto Adonoy,
וְלֹא עָנָם׃	but He did not answer them.
מג וְאֶשְׁחָקֵם כְּעָפָר	43 I ground them as the dust
עַל־פְּנֵי־רוּחַ	before the wind,
כְּטִיט חוּצוֹת אֲרִיקֵם׃	as the mire of the streets, I poured them out.
מד תְּפַלְּטֵנִי	44 You have rescued me
מֵרִיבֵי עָם	from the contentions of the people,
תְּשִׂימֵנִי לְרֹאשׁ גּוֹיִם	You placed me at the head of nations;
עַם לֹא־יָדַעְתִּי יַעַבְדוּנִי׃	a people whom I have not known serves me.
מה לְשֵׁמַע אֹזֶן יִשָּׁמְעוּ לִי	45 As soon as they hear me, they obey me;
בְּנֵי־נֵכָר	the sons of the stranger
יְכַחֲשׁוּ־לִי׃	pretend loyalty to me.

מו בְּנֵי־נֵכָר יִבֹּלוּ וְיַחְרְגוּ מִמִּסְגְּרוֹתֵיהֶם׃	46 The sons of the stranger wither away, and are terrified by their confinement.
מז חַי־יְהוָה וּבָרוּךְ צוּרִי וְיָרוּם אֱלוֹהֵי יִשְׁעִי׃	47 Adonoy lives, and blessed is my Rock; and may exalted be the God of my deliverance.
מח הָאֵל הַנּוֹתֵן נְקָמוֹת לִי וַיַּדְבֵּר עַמִּים תַּחְתָּי׃	48 The Almighty that gives me revenge to me, and subdues people under me.
מט מְפַלְּטִי מֵאֹיְבָי אַף מִן־קָמַי תְּרוֹמְמֵנִי מֵאִישׁ חָמָס תַּצִּילֵנִי׃	49 You rescue me from my enemies, and above my adversaries You raise me; from the violent man You save me.
נ עַל־כֵּן ׀ אוֹדְךָ בַגּוֹיִם ׀ יְהוָה וּלְשִׁמְךָ אֲזַמֵּרָה׃	50 Therefore I thank You among the nations, Adonoy; and to Your Name I will sing praises.
נא מַגְדִּיל יְשׁוּעוֹת מַלְכּוֹ וְעֹשֶׂה חֶסֶד ׀ לִמְשִׁיחוֹ לְדָוִד וּלְזַרְעוֹ עַד־עוֹלָם׃	51 He increases the deliverance of His king, and does kindness with His annointed, to David and his seed, for evermore.

Synagogue Screen Fragments, Ashkelon

פרק יט Chapter 19

Weekly Cycle	Monthly Cycle	Book Number
Sunday	3rd day of the month	Book 1

Author

דָּוִד הַמֶּלֶךְ—King David—the second king of Israel and father of the Davidic royal and messianic dynasty. David composed over seventy of the 150 psalms of Sefer Tehillim.

Genre

Psalm of Praise – This is a psalm of celebration, often the result of a victory. It declares God's goodness and urges all of creation to worship.

Psalm of Wisdom - This psalm contains teachings and wise advice and is meant to instruct people on how to live a Godly life.

Chapter Summary

The Singer declares that God's glory is revealed in this world in two ways: through creation and through Torah. However, as he points out, the Torah's excellence exceeds that of creation in its ability to bring man to perfection and fulfillment in life.

This psalm contains fifteen verses, subdivided into two parts.
Verse 1 serves as a heading.
In verses 2-7, King David praises God for the wonder of the heavens, calling them a testimony to God's greatness.
In verses 8-15, he praises the Torah and expresses his yearning to fulfill its commandments.

Introductory Words

לַמְנַצֵּחַ—Lamnatsei'ach—To the Conductor
מִזְמוֹר—Mizmor—Musical Accompaniment

Shimush Tehillim - When to Say

To ward off an evil spirit (say this 7 times)
For an overdue childbirth (say this 7 times)—Verse 6 states: "And it [the sun] is like a groom departing his bridal chamber, happy as a warrior to run on course."
To inspire one's heart towards Torah—Verse 9 states: "The precepts of Adonoy, are upright, rejoicing the heart."

Where in the Siddur

Recited in its entirety as part of Pesukei Dezimra (Introductory Verses of Praise to the Shacharit morning service) of Shabbat and Yom Tov (Festivals).
Recited at weddings in some traditions.
Recited on the first day of Shavu'ot in some traditions.
Verses 8 & 9 are recited upon the removal of the Torah from the Aron Kodesh (Holy Ark).
Verse 14 is found in the repetition of the Musaf Amidah of Rosh HaShanah.
Verse 15 is found at the conclusion of Shemoneh Esrei (Silent Meditation), the bedtime Shema, as well as upon the removal of the Torah from the Ark. (See Talmud Berachot, 4b, for further explanation).

Contemporary Song

Verses 8

Talmud on Tehillim

Verse 15: "יִהְיוּ לְרָצוֹן אִמְרֵי פִי, וְהֶגְיוֹן לִבִּי לְפָנֶיךָ: יְהוָה, צוּרִי וְגֹאֲלִי"— "May they be acceptable— the words of my mouth and the thoughts of my heart before You, Adonoy, my Rock and my Redeemer."

The Talmud, Berachot 9b, states that just as King David said these words after the composition of eighteen psalms, so too we say this verse after the eighteen blessings of the daily Amidah (Silent Meditation). While the observant reader will notice that this verse concludes chapter 19, and not chapter 18, it has been noted in the opening remarks to chapter 1 that chapters 1 and 2 were originally one chapter and later subdivided into two; the original chapter 18 then became chapter 19 as we find it today.

פֶּרֶק יט

Chapter 19

א לַמְנַצֵּחַ
מִזְמוֹר לְדָוִד:

1 To the Chief Musician,
a Psalm of David.

ב הַשָּׁמַיִם מְסַפְּרִים כְּבוֹד־אֵל
וּמַעֲשֵׂה יָדָיו מַגִּיד הָרָקִיעַ

2 The skies recount the glory of the Almighty,
and His handiwork is related by the firmament.

ג יוֹם לְיוֹם יַבִּיעַ אֹמֶר
וְלַיְלָה לְּלַיְלָה יְחַוֶּה־דָּעַת:

3 Day to day makes speech flow,
and night to night expresses wisdom.

ד אֵין־אֹמֶר וְאֵין דְּבָרִים
בְּלִי נִשְׁמָע קוֹלָם:

4 There is no speech, and there are no words;
their voice is never heard.

ה בְּכָל־הָאָרֶץ | יָצָא קַוָּם
וּבִקְצֵה תֵבֵל
מִלֵּיהֶם
לַשֶּׁמֶשׁ
שָׂם־אֹהֶל בָּהֶם:

5 Throughout the earth, their line extends,
and to the edge of the inhabited world
their words,
for the sun
He has set a tent in their midst.

ו וְהוּא כְּחָתָן
יֹצֵא מֵחֻפָּתוֹ
יָשִׂישׂ כְּגִבּוֹר לָרוּץ אֹרַח:

6 And it [the sun] is like a groom
departing his bridal chamber,
happy as a warrior to run on course.

ז מִקְצֵה הַשָּׁמַיִם | מוֹצָאוֹ
וּתְקוּפָתוֹ עַל־קְצוֹתָם
וְאֵין נִסְתָּר מֵחַמָּתוֹ:

7 From one end of the skies is its rising
and its circuit is to their [other] end;
there is no escaping its heat.

ח תּוֹרַת יְהוָה תְּמִימָה
מְשִׁיבַת נָפֶשׁ
עֵדוּת יְהוָה נֶאֱמָנָה
מַחְכִּימַת פֶּתִי:

8 The Torah of Adonoy, is perfect,
restoring the soul;
the testimony of Adonoy, is trustworthy,
making wise the simple [man].

ט פִּקּוּדֵי יְהוָה יְשָׁרִים
מְשַׂמְּחֵי־לֵב
מִצְוַת יְהוָה בָּרָה
מְאִירַת עֵינָיִם:

9 The precepts of Adonoy, are upright,
rejoicing the heart;
the commandment of Adonoy, is lucid,
enlightening the eyes.

י יִרְאַת יְהוָה | טְהוֹרָה
עוֹמֶדֶת לָעַד
מִשְׁפְּטֵי־יְהוָה אֱמֶת
צָדְקוּ יַחְדָּו:

10 The fear of Adonoy, is pure,
it endures forever;
the judgments of Adonoy, are true,
they are righteous in unison.

יא הַנֶּחֱמָדִים מִזָּהָב
וּמִפַּז רָב
וּמְתוּקִים מִדְּבַשׁ
וְנֹפֶת צוּפִים:

11 More desirable than gold,
even more than quantities of fine gold;
and sweeter than honey,
or the drippings of honeycombs.

יב גַּם־עַבְדְּךָ נִזְהָר בָּהֶם
בְּשָׁמְרָם עֵקֶב רָב:

12 Even Your servant is careful of them,
since they guard great reward.

יג שְׁגִיאוֹת מִֽי־יָבִ֑ין	13 Errors—who can comprehend?
מִנִּסְתָּר֥וֹת נַקֵּֽנִי׃	From hidden [faults], cleanse me.
יד גַּ֤ם מִזֵּדִ֨ים ׀	14 Also from willful [sins]
חֲשֹׂ֬ךְ עַבְדֶּ֗ךָ	spare Your servant,
אַֽל־יִמְשְׁלוּ־בִ֣י	let them not rule me,
אָ֣ז אֵיתָ֑ם	then I will be strong
וְ֝נִקֵּ֗יתִי מִפֶּ֥שַׁע רָֽב׃	and will be cleansed of gross transgression.
טו יִהְי֤וּ לְרָצ֨וֹן ׀	15 May they be acceptable—
אִמְרֵי־פִ֡י	the words of my mouth
וְהֶגְי֣וֹן לִבִּ֣י לְפָנֶ֑יךָ	and the thoughts of my heart before You,
יְ֝הוָ֗ה צוּרִ֥י וְגֹאֲלִֽי׃	Adonoy, my Rock and my Redeemer.

Bread Stamp with Menorah

פֶּרֶק כ — Chapter 20

Weekly Cycle	Monthly Cycle	Book Number
Sunday	3rd day of the month	Book 1

Author

דָּוִד הַמֶּלֶךְ—King David—the second king of Israel and father of the Davidic royal and messianic dynasty. David composed over seventy of the 150 psalms of Sefer Tehillim.

When & Why

David wrote this psalm during wartime and he read it when his armies went out to battle.

Genre

Psalm of Royalty - This psalm describes how God reigns supreme. It focuses on the human king of Israel, or upon God as King of Israel.

Chapter Summary

This psalm was intended to be recited as a blessing offered by the nation of Israel to its king. It was also chanted by King David every time he dispatched his troops into battle.

This psalm consists of ten verses, subdivided into two parts.
Verse 1 serves as a heading.
In verses 2-6, the people speak to the king and bless him. While this psalm is a prayer recited on behalf of a mortal king, God, the ultimate King, is alluded to here as well. "May Adonoy answer you on the day of distress", beseeches the Psalmist. "May He grant you what your heart desires, and fulfill all your plans."
In verses 7-9, King David offers an expression of confidence in God's salvation.
In verse 10, King David concludes by calling upon God to send deliverance.

Introductory Words

לַמְנַצֵּחַ—Lamnatsei'ach—To the Conductor

Shimush Tehillim - When to Say

For success in a court case
In times of distress, particularly by women suffering the pangs of childbirth

Technical Terminology

סֶלָה—Selah—While its meaning is unclear, the most familiar opinion is that it is a musical notation, instructing the Levitical orchestra to pause its singing and playing of instruments. Alternatively, "Selah" may mean "everlasting".

Where in the Siddur

Recited in its entirety towards the end of the daily Shacharit (morning service)—except on Shabbat, Yom Tov (Festivals), Rosh Chodesh (New Moon), Chol HaMo'eid (Intermediate Days of Sukkot and Passover), Tishah BeAv (Fast of the Ninth of Av), Hanukkah, Purim, Shushan Purim, the 14th and 15th of Adar 1 in a leap year, and the day before Yom Kippur and Passover—between the second Ashrei and Uva Letzion. In this context it is referred to simply as "Lamnatsei'ach" (the first word of the psalm).
Verses 2 and 10 are part of the opening paragraph of the long Tachanun (Supplication Prayer) recited on Mondays and Thursdays.
Verse 10 is also the 11th verse of V'hu Rachum in Pesukei Dezimra (Introductory Verses of Praise to the Shacharit morning service), the final verse of Yehi Kivod in Pesukei Dezimra, one of the verses of Uva Letzion, the second of two verses recited as an introduction to Ma'ariv (evening service), as well as part of the Motza'ei Shabbat Havdalah service.

Biblical Places

צִיּוֹן—Zion—a place name often used as a synonym for Jerusalem. The term Zion originally referred only to the area where a Jebbusite fortress once stood, which was also the location of the City of David. Zion was later used by prophets and psalmists as another name for Jerusalem.

Contemporary Song

Verses 8-10

Talmud on Tehillim

Verse 2: "יַעַנְךָ יְהוָה, בְּיוֹם צָרָה; יְשַׂגֶּבְךָ, שֵׁם אֱלֹהֵי יַעֲקֹב"—"May Adonoy answer you on the day of distress; May the Name of Jacob's God fortify you."

Rashi, commenting on the Talmud, Berachot 64a, explains that David would recite this psalm on behalf of the Jews when they would go out to do battle. Why was it, he asks, that when King David would beseech God on behalf of the Jews he would do so specifically in the merit of Jacob and not in the merit of Abraham and Isaac as well? He answers that as Jacob was the patriarch of all the twelve tribes of Israel, it was therefore his unique privilege and responsibility to pray for their mercy.

פרק כ			**Chapter 20**
לַמְנַצֵּחַ	א	1	To the Chief Musician,
מִזְמוֹר לְדָוִד׃			a Psalm of David
יַעַנְךָ יְהוָה	ב	2	May Adonoy answer you
בְּיוֹם צָרָה			on the day of distress;
יְשַׂגֶּבְךָ שֵׁם | אֱלֹהֵי יַעֲקֹב׃			May the Name of Jacob's God fortify you.
יִשְׁלַח־עֶזְרְךָ מִקֹּדֶשׁ	ג	3	May He send your help from the Sanctuary,
וּמִצִּיּוֹן יִסְעָדֶךָּ׃			and support you from Zion.
יִזְכֹּר כָּל־מִנְחֹתֶךָ	ד	4	May He remember all your meal offerings
וְעוֹלָתְךָ יְדַשְּׁנֶה סֶלָה׃			and accept your burnt sacrifices, Selah.
יִתֶּן־לְךָ כִלְבָבֶךָ	ה	5	May He grant you what your heart desires,
וְכָל־עֲצָתְךָ יְמַלֵּא׃			and fulfill all your plans.
נְרַנְּנָה | בִּישׁוּעָתֶךָ	ו	6	We will sing at Your deliverance,
וּבְשֵׁם־אֱלֹהֵינוּ נִדְגֹּל			and in the Name of our God, raise our banners;
יְמַלֵּא יְהוָה כָּל־מִשְׁאֲלוֹתֶיךָ׃			May Adonoy fulfill all your wishes.
עַתָּה יָדַעְתִּי	ז	7	Now I know
כִּי הוֹשִׁיעַ | יְהוָה מְשִׁיחוֹ			that Adonoy has delivered His anointed one,
יַעֲנֵהוּ מִשְּׁמֵי קָדְשׁוֹ			He will answer him from His holy heavens
בִּגְבֻרוֹת יֵשַׁע יְמִינוֹ׃			with the mighty deliverance of His right hand.
אֵלֶּה בָרֶכֶב	ח	8	Some [rely] upon chariots
וְאֵלֶּה בַסּוּסִים			and some upon horses, but as for us,
וַאֲנַחְנוּ |			but as for us,
בְּשֵׁם־יְהוָה אֱלֹהֵינוּ נַזְכִּיר׃			upon the Name of Adonoy, our God, we call.
הֵמָּה כָּרְעוּ וְנָפָלוּ	ט	9	They have bowed down and fallen,
וַאֲנַחְנוּ קַּמְנוּ וַנִּתְעוֹדָד׃			but we have risen and stand firm.
יְהוָה הוֹשִׁיעָה הַמֶּלֶךְ	י	10	Adonoy, deliver [us],
יַעֲנֵנוּ בְיוֹם־קָרְאֵנוּ׃			the King will answer us on the day we call.

Mosaic of King David Playing the Harp

פרק כא Chapter 21

Weekly Cycle	Monthly Cycle	Book Number
Sunday	3rd day of the month	Book 1

Author

דָּוִד הַמֶּלֶךְ—King David—the second king of Israel and father of the Davidic royal and messianic dynasty. David composed over seventy of the 150 psalms of Sefer Tehillim.

When & Why

David wrote this psalm during wartime and he read it when his armies went out to battle.

Genre

Psalm of Royalty - This psalm describes how God reigns supreme. It focuses on the human king of Israel, or upon God as King of Israel.

Chapter Summary

King David composed this psalm for the Jewish people to recite after every victorious battle. It is an expression of thanksgiving to God for all the ways that He had favored him personally and all of Israel as a whole.

This psalm consists of fourteen verses, subdivided into three parts.
Verse 1 serves as a heading.
In verses 2-7, King David describes the joy of the king who is blessed by God.
In verses 8-13, he blesses the king and prays that he will be victorious over his enemies.
In verse 14, the people ask to see God's strength and proceed to praise him for his power.

Introductory Words

לַמְנַצֵּח—Lamnatsei'ach—To the Conductor
מִזְמוֹר—Mizmor—Musical Accompaniment

Technical Terminology

סֶלָה—Selah—While its meaning is unclear, the most familiar opinion is that it is a musical notation, instructing the Levitical orchestra to pause its singing and playing of instruments. Alternatively, "Selah" may mean "everlasting".

Shimush Tehillim - When to Say

When facing an important authority or rabbi—Verse 3 states: "His heart's desire You have given him, and the utterance of his lips You have not withheld."
For a storm at sea—Verse 5 proclaims: "Life he asked of You, You gave it to him."

פרק כא

א לַמְנַצֵּחַ
מִזְמוֹר לְדָוִד׃
ב יְהוָה בְּעָזְּךָ יִשְׂמַח־מֶלֶךְ
וּבִישׁוּעָתְךָ מַה־יָּגֶל מְאֹד׃
ג תַּאֲוַת לִבּוֹ נָתַתָּה לּוֹ
וַאֲרֶשֶׁת שְׂפָתָיו
בַּל־מָנַעְתָּ סֶּלָה׃
ד כִּי־תְקַדְּמֶנּוּ
בִּרְכוֹת טוֹב
תָּשִׁית לְרֹאשׁוֹ עֲטֶרֶת פָּז׃
ה חַיִּים ׀ שָׁאַל מִמְּךָ
נָתַתָּה לּוֹ
אֹרֶךְ יָמִים עוֹלָם וָעֶד׃
ו גָּדוֹל כְּבוֹדוֹ בִּישׁוּעָתֶךָ
הוֹד וְהָדָר תְּשַׁוֶּה עָלָיו׃
ז כִּי־תְשִׁיתֵהוּ בְרָכוֹת לָעַד
תְּחַדֵּהוּ בְשִׂמְחָה אֶת־פָּנֶיךָ׃
ח כִּי־הַמֶּלֶךְ בֹּטֵחַ בַּיהוָה
וּבְחֶסֶד עֶלְיוֹן
בַּל־יִמּוֹט׃
ט תִּמְצָא יָדְךָ לְכָל־אֹיְבֶיךָ
יְמִינְךָ תִּמְצָא שֹׂנְאֶיךָ׃
י תְּשִׁיתֵמוֹ ׀ כְּתַנּוּר אֵשׁ
לְעֵת פָּנֶיךָ
יְהוָה בְּאַפּוֹ יְבַלְּעֵם
וְתֹאכְלֵם אֵשׁ׃
יא פִּרְיָמוֹ מֵאֶרֶץ תְּאַבֵּד
וְזַרְעָם
מִבְּנֵי אָדָם׃
יב כִּי־נָטוּ עָלֶיךָ רָעָה
חָשְׁבוּ מְזִמָּה
בַּל־יוּכָלוּ׃
יג כִּי תְּשִׁיתֵמוֹ שֶׁכֶם
בְּמֵיתָרֶיךָ
תְּכוֹנֵן עַל־פְּנֵיהֶם׃
יד רוּמָה יְהוָה בְעֻזֶּךָ
נָשִׁירָה וּנְזַמְּרָה גְּבוּרָתֶךָ׃

Chapter 21

1 To the Chief Musician,
a Psalm of David.
2 Adonoy, in Your strength the king rejoices,
and in Your deliverance how greatly he exults.
3 His heart's desire You have given him,
and the utterance of his lips
You have not withheld, Selah.
4 For You have preceded him
with blessings of the good;
You set on his head a crown of pure gold.
5 Life he asked of You,
You gave it to him;
length of days forever and ever.
6 Great is his glory in Your deliverance;
beauty and splendor You placed upon him.
7 For You appoint him for blessings forever;
You make him glad with joy in Your presence.
8 For the king trusts in Adonoy,
and in the loving kindness of the Most High;
he will not be moved.
9 Your hand will find all Your enemies,
Your right hand will find Your adversaries.
10 You will make them as a fiery oven
in the time of Your anger;
may Adonoy, in His wrath, consume them,
and let a fire devour them.
11 Destroy their offspring from the earth,
and their children
from among the children of man.
12 For they intended evil against You,
they devised a plan
[with which] they will not prevail.
13 For You will make them as [Israel]'s portion,
with Your bowstring
which You aim at their faces.
14 Be exalted, Adonoy, in Your strength;
we will sing and chant of Your power.

פרק כב Chapter 22

Weekly Cycle	Monthly Cycle	Book Number
Sunday	3rd day of the month	Book 1

Author
דָוִד הַמֶּלֶךְ—King David—the second king of Israel and father of the Davidic royal and messianic dynasty. David composed over seventy of the 150 psalms of Sefer Tehillim.

Genre
Psalm of Individual Lament - This psalm was written from the perspective of the individual worshipper, who cries out to God in his time of need. It is characterized as an address to God involving a complaint, followed by a request and ending with an expression of trust.

Chapter Summary
With the Holy Spirit upon him, King David authored this psalm as a prayer for deliverance from one's enemies, and for the nation's deliverance from future exiles. He expresses confidence that in the end, God's humble servants will be redeemed.

This psalm consists of thirty-two verses, subdivided into two parts.
Verse 1 serves as a heading.
In verses 2-22, feeling abandoned by God, King David cries out in distress.
In verses 23-32, he vows to offer gratitude for his salvation.

Introductory Words
לַמְנַצֵּחַ—Lamnatsei'ach—To the Conductor
מִזְמוֹר—Mizmor—Musical Accompaniment

Technical Terminology
עַל-אַיֶּלֶת הַשַּׁחַר—Al Ayelet HaShachar—On the Doe of the Dawn.

Shimush Tehillim - When to Say
When preparing to face an enemy—Verse 6 states: "To You they cried out and were delivered."
To purify oneself (recite seven times)—Verse 10 states: "For you took me out of the womb." This verse is compared to the emerging from a Mikveh.
To cross over a river—Verse 15 states: "Like waters I am poured out." The Talmud compares this to a person in fear, as their stomach "melts like water."
To be saved from wild animals—Verse 22 states: " Deliver me from the lion's mouth; for from the horns of Re'emim You have answered me."
To inspire one's heart in Torah and closeness to God—Verse 27 states: "Let the humble eat and be satisfied, let them praise Adonoy, those who seek Him; may your hearts be alive forever."

Where in the Siddur
Verse 4 is one of the opening verses of Uva Letzion, a concluding prayer of the weekday Shacharit

morning service, as well as after the Amidah (Silent Meditation) of Motza'ei Shabbat.
Verse 29 is appended to Az Yashir—the Song of Moses (Exodus), recited in Shacharit (morning service).
Verse 29 is also found in the Malchuyot (Kingship) section of Musaf of Rosh HaShanah.

Biblical Personalities

יַעֲקֹב—Yaakov—Jacob, also referred to as Yisrael—Israel—the third patriarch, the father of the twelve tribes of Israel. He was a twin of Esau, and was married to Leah and Rachel.
יִשְׂרָאֵל—Yisrael—The Nation of Israel

Biblical Places

בָּשָׁן—Bashan—a country located in modern day Syria, not to be confused with Mount Bashan also referenced in this chapter.

פֶּרֶק כב		**Chapter 22**
א לַמְנַצֵּחַ	1	To the Chief Musician,
עַל־אַיֶּלֶת הַשַּׁחַר		upon Aiyelet haShachar,
מִזְמוֹר לְדָוִד׃		a Psalm of David.
ב אֵלִי אֵלִי	2	My God my God,
לָמָה עֲזַבְתָּנִי		why have You forsaken me—
רָחוֹק מִישׁוּעָתִי		so far from my deliverance,
דִּבְרֵי שַׁאֲגָתִי׃		from the words of my cry?
ג אֱלֹהַי אֶקְרָא יוֹמָם	3	My God, I call out by day
וְלֹא תַעֲנֶה		but You do not answer;
וְלַיְלָה		and at night
וְלֹא־דוּמִיָּה לִי׃		and there is no relief for me.
ד וְאַתָּה קָדוֹשׁ	4	And You, Holy One,
יוֹשֵׁב תְּהִלּוֹת יִשְׂרָאֵל׃		are enthroned upon the praises of Israel.
ה בְּךָ בָּטְחוּ אֲבֹתֵינוּ	5	In You our fathers trusted;
בָּטְחוּ וַתְּפַלְּטֵמוֹ׃		they trusted, and You saved them.
ו אֵלֶיךָ זָעֲקוּ וְנִמְלָטוּ	6	To You they cried out and were delivered;
בְּךָ בָטְחוּ וְלֹא־בוֹשׁוּ׃		in You they trusted and were not ashamed.
ז וְאָנֹכִי תוֹלַעַת וְלֹא־אִישׁ	7	But I am a worm, and not a man;
חֶרְפַּת אָדָם וּבְזוּי עָם׃		scorn of man and despised by people.
ח כָּל־רֹאַי יַלְעִגוּ לִי	8	All who see me taunt me;
יַפְטִירוּ בְשָׂפָה		they reject me with a curled lip
יָנִיעוּ רֹאשׁ׃		[and with] a shake of the head.
ט גֹּל אֶל־יְהוָה	9	Let him commit himself to Adonoy,
יְפַלְּטֵהוּ		let Him save him,
יַצִּילֵהוּ כִּי חָפֵץ בּוֹ׃		let Him rescue him, for He desires him.

כִּי־אַתָּה גֹחִי מִבָּטֶן	י	10	For You took me out of the womb;
מַבְטִיחִי			You made me secure
עַל־שְׁדֵי אִמִּי׃			[when I was] upon my mother's breast.
עָלֶיךָ הָשְׁלַכְתִּי מֵרָחֶם	יא	11	Upon You I have been cast from birth;
מִבֶּטֶן אִמִּי אֵלִי אָתָּה׃			from my mother's womb You are my God.
אַל־תִּרְחַק מִמֶּנִּי	יב	12	Be not far from me;
כִּי־צָרָה קְרוֹבָה			for trouble is near;
כִּי־אֵין עוֹזֵר׃			for there is no help.
סְבָבוּנִי פָּרִים רַבִּים	יג	13	Many bulls have surrounded me;
אַבִּירֵי בָשָׁן כִּתְּרוּנִי׃			strong bulls of Bashan have encircled me.
פָּצוּ עָלַי פִּיהֶם	יד	14	They gaped their mouth upon me,
אַרְיֵה טֹרֵף וְשֹׁאֵג׃			[as] a slashing, roaring lion.
כַּמַּיִם נִשְׁפַּכְתִּי	טו	15	Like waters I am poured out,
וְהִתְפָּרְדוּ כָּל־עַצְמוֹתָי			and all my bones became disjointed;
הָיָה לִבִּי כַּדּוֹנָג			my heart has become like wax,
נָמֵס בְּתוֹךְ מֵעָי׃			it melts in my innermost parts.
יָבֵשׁ כַּחֶרֶשׂ | כֹּחִי	טז	16	My strength is dried up like a potsherd,
וּלְשׁוֹנִי מֻדְבָּק מַלְקוֹחָי			and my tongue cleaves to my palate;
וְלַעֲפַר־מָוֶת תִּשְׁפְּתֵנִי׃			and in the dust of death You set me.
כִּי סְבָבוּנִי כְּלָבִים	יז	17	For dogs have surrounded me
עֲדַת מְרֵעִים הִקִּיפוּנִי			a company of evil doers have enclosed me;
כָּאֲרִי יָדַי וְרַגְלָי׃			as a lion at my hands and feet.
אֲסַפֵּר כָּל־עַצְמוֹתָי	יח	18	I count all my bones;
הֵמָּה יַבִּיטוּ יִרְאוּ־בִי׃			they look and stare at me.
יְחַלְּקוּ בְגָדַי לָהֶם	יט	19	They divide my garments among them,
וְעַל־לְבוּשִׁי יַפִּילוּ גוֹרָל׃			and for my clothing they cast lots.
וְאַתָּה יְהוָה אַל־תִּרְחָק	כ	20	But You, Adonoy, be not far off;
אֱיָלוּתִי לְעֶזְרָתִי חוּשָׁה׃			my strength, hasten to help me.
הַצִּילָה מֵחֶרֶב נַפְשִׁי	כא	21	Rescue my soul from the sword,
מִיַּד־כֶּלֶב יְחִידָתִי׃			from the grip of the dog, my very soul.
הוֹשִׁיעֵנִי מִפִּי אַרְיֵה	כב	22	Deliver me from the lion's mouth;
וּמִקַּרְנֵי רֵמִים			for from the horns of Re'emim
עֲנִיתָנִי׃			You have answered me.
אֲסַפְּרָה שִׁמְךָ לְאֶחָי	כג	23	I will declare Your Name to my brethren;
בְּתוֹךְ קָהָל			in the midst of the congregation
אֲהַלְלֶךָּ׃			I will praise You.
יִרְאֵי יְהוָה | הַלְלוּהוּ	כד	24	You who fear Adonoy, praise Him,
כָּל־זֶרַע יַעֲקֹב			all of you, the seed of Jacob,
כַּבְּדוּהוּ			glorify Him;

וְגוּרוּ מִמֶּנּוּ	and be in fear of Him,
כׇּל־זֶרַע יִשְׂרָאֵל׃	all of you, seed of Israel.
כה כִּי לֹא־בָזָה	25 For He has neither despised
וְלֹא שִׁקַּץ עֱנוּת עָנִי	nor abhorred the lowliness of the poor,
וְלֹא־הִסְתִּיר פָּנָיו מִמֶּנּוּ	nor has He hid His face from him,
וּבְשַׁוְּעוֹ אֵלָיו שָׁמֵעַ׃	and when he cried to Him, He heard.
כו מֵאִתְּךָ תְּהִלָּתִי	26 From You comes my praise,
בְּקָהָל רָב	in the great congregation;
נְדָרַי אֲשַׁלֵּם	I will pay my vows
נֶגֶד יְרֵאָיו׃	in the presence of those who fear Him.
כז יֹאכְלוּ עֲנָוִים | וְיִשְׂבָּעוּ	27 Let the humble eat and be satisfied,
יְהַלְלוּ יְהוָה דֹּרְשָׁיו	let them praise Adonoy, those who seek Him;
יְחִי לְבַבְכֶם לָעַד׃	may your hearts be alive forever.
כח יִזְכְּרוּ | וְיָשֻׁבוּ אֶל־יְהוָה	28 They will remember and return to Adonoy,
כׇּל־אַפְסֵי־אָרֶץ	all the ends of the earth;
וְיִשְׁתַּחֲווּ לְפָנֶיךָ	and they will bow down before You
כׇּל־מִשְׁפְּחוֹת גּוֹיִם׃	all the families of nations.
כט כִּי לַיהוָה הַמְּלוּכָה	29 For the kingship is Adonoy's
וּמֹשֵׁל בַּגּוֹיִם׃	and He rules over nations.
ל אָכְלוּ וַיִּשְׁתַּחֲווּ |	30 They have eaten and bowed down;
כׇּל־דִּשְׁנֵי־אֶרֶץ	all the fat of the earth
לְפָנָיו יִכְרְעוּ	before Him will kneel
כׇּל־יוֹרְדֵי עָפָר	all who go down to the dust,
וְנַפְשׁוֹ לֹא חִיָּה׃	but He will not revive their soul.
לא זֶרַע יַעַבְדֶנּוּ	31 [Through] the seed [who] will serve Him,
יְסֻפַּר	it will be told
לַאדֹנָי לַדּוֹר׃	to the [next] generation; of the Lord.
לב יָבֹאוּ	32 They will come
וְיַגִּידוּ צִדְקָתוֹ	and declare His righteousness
לְעַם נוֹלָד	to a newborn people,
כִּי עָשָׂה׃	that which He has done.

Guardian Lions (Courtesy of the Shlomo Moussaieff Collection)

פרק כג Chapter 23

Weekly Cycle	Monthly Cycle	Book Number
Sunday	4th day of the month	Book 1

Author

דָוִד הַמֶּלֶךְ—King David—the second king of Israel and father of the Davidic royal and messianic dynasty. David composed over seventy of the 150 psalms of Sefer Tehillim.

When & Why

David wrote this psalm when he was fleeing from Saul.

Genre

Psalm of Individual Confidence - In this psalm, the worshipper expresses absolute certainty that his prayers will be heard.

Chapter Summary

King David composed this psalm to praise God for His supervision and guidance, and to beseech him for the future. He asks that he always be joyous, content with his portion, and lack nothing in the World to Come.

This psalm consists of a mere six verses.
Verse 1 opens with a dedication, afterwhich the chapter is subdivided into two parts.
In verses 1-4, King David compares himself to a lamb and likens God to a shepherd.
In verses 5 & 6, he compares himself to a guest in the house of God.

Introductory Words

מִזְמוֹר—Mizmor—Musical Accompaniment

Shimush Tehillim - When to Say

To request positive and pleasant dreams: Verse 4 states: "Though I walk in the valley of the shadow of death, I will fear no evil, for You are with me." The Talmud informs us that sleep is equal to 1/60th of death.
To rise to greatness: Verse 5 states: "You anointed my head with oil."

Interesting Facts

The most popular and well known psalm.

Where in the Siddur

Recited as part of the funeral service. It has become particularly associated with funeral liturgy in the English-speaking world, and films with funeral scenes often depict a graveside recitation of the psalm.
Recited in some congregations after the Amidah of Kabbalat Shabbat (Friday night service).
Often sung at Se'udah Sh'lishit—the Third Meal of Shabbat, usually eaten towards the end of the day.

פרק כג			Chapter 23
מִזְמוֹר לְדָוִד יְהוָה רֹעִי לֹא אֶחְסָר:	א	1	A Psalm of David, Adonoy is my shepherd, I shall lack nothing.
בִּנְאוֹת דֶּשֶׁא יַרְבִּיצֵנִי עַל־מֵי מְנֻחוֹת יְנַהֲלֵנִי:	ב	2	In lush pastures He makes me lie, besides tranquil waters, He leads me.
נַפְשִׁי יְשׁוֹבֵב יַנְחֵנִי בְמַעְגְּלֵי־צֶדֶק לְמַעַן שְׁמוֹ:	ג	3	My soul, He restores, He directs me in paths of righteousness for the sake of His Name.
גַּם כִּי־אֵלֵךְ בְּגֵיא צַלְמָוֶת לֹא־אִירָא רָע כִּי־אַתָּה עִמָּדִי שִׁבְטְךָ וּמִשְׁעַנְתֶּךָ הֵמָּה יְנַחֲמֻנִי:	ד	4	Though I walk in the valley of the shadow of death, I will fear no evil for You are with me, Your rod and Your staff, they comfort me.
תַּעֲרֹךְ לְפָנַי	שֻׁלְחָן נֶגֶד צֹרְרָי דִּשַּׁנְתָּ בַשֶּׁמֶן רֹאשִׁי כּוֹסִי רְוָיָה:	ה	5	You prepare a table for me in the full presence of my enemies, You annointed my head with oil; my cup overflows.
אַךְ	טוֹב וָחֶסֶד יִרְדְּפוּנִי כָּל־יְמֵי חַיָּי וְשַׁבְתִּי בְּבֵית־יְהוָה לְאֹרֶךְ יָמִים:	ו	6	[May] only good and kindness pursue me all the days of my life, and I shall dwell in the House of Adonoy for long days.

פרק כד Chapter 24

Weekly Cycle	Monthly Cycle	Book Number
Sunday	4th day of the month	Book 1

Author

דָּוִד הַמֶּלֶךְ—King David—the second king of Israel and father of the Davidic royal and messianic dynasty. David composed over seventy of the 150 psalms of Sefer Tehillim.

When & Why

David wrote this psalm to be read at the time when the Ark was being brought into the Temple.

Genre

Psalm of Wisdom - This psalm contains teachings and wise advice and is meant to instruct people on how to live a Godly life.

Chapter Summary

This psalm clarifies that the purpose of creation is to establish the kingship of God in this world. This goal, the Singer tells us, is accomplished when men purify their souls, thereby becoming worthy of ascending Har Hashem—God's mountain, the site of the Beit HaMikdash (Holy Temple).

This psalm consists of ten verses, subdivided into three parts. It is worth noting that this chapter opens with the words "L'David Mizmor— "Of David, [a Psalm]". This and all such introductions may have been written by David himself, or may simply be an introduction to his words.

In verses 1 and 2, King David offers praise to God, Creator of the universe.

In verses 3 and 4, King David asks and answers the question: "Who may ascend the mountain of Adonoy."

In verses 7-10, the Psalmist calls out to the gates that they should open to allow the "King of Glory" to enter.

Introductory Words

מִזְמוֹר—Mizmor—Musical Accompaniment

Technical Terminology

סֶלָה—Selah—While its meaning is unclear, the most familiar opinion is that it is a musical notation, instructing the Levitical orchestra to pause its singing and playing of instruments. Alternatively, "Selah" may mean "everlasting".

Shimush Tehillim - When to Say

For protection against floods—Verse 2 states: "For He founded it (the earth) upon the seas."

For achieving spiritual greatness—Verse 3 asks: "Who may ascend the mountain of Adonoy." (A similar thought is expressed in chapter 92).

Where in the Siddur

Recited as the Shir Shel Yom—the Psalm of the Day, of Sunday Recited upon returning the Torah scroll to the Aron Kodesh (Holy Ark), except on Shabbat.

Verse 1 is included in the Mishnah (Tamid 7:4).

Verses 7-10 are found in the Amidah (Silent Meditation) of Musaf of Rosh HaShanah.

Recited responsively upon the conclusion of the Amidah of Ma'ariv (evening service) of Rosh HaShanah.

Contemporary Song

Verses 7 and 8

Talmud on Tehillim

Verse 1: "לַיהוָה הָאָרֶץ וּמְלוֹאָהּ"—"The earth is Adonoy's and the fullness thereof." The Talmud, Rosh HaShanah 31a, states, as mentioned above, that the Levi'im sang this chapter in the Beit HaMikdash on the first day of the week.

The Talmud, Berachot 35a, teaches: "Whoever derives benefit from this world without first reciting a blessing, is regarded as if he has derived benefit from the consecrated property of [God in] heaven."

Verses 7- 10: The Talmud, Shabbat 30a, relates that when King Solomon built the Beit HaMikdash, he sought to bring the Ark into the Holy of Holies. The gates, however, could not be opened.

Solomon therefore recited 24 songs of prayer, yet still the gates remained closed. He then recited Psalm 24, verses 7-10, and the gates ran after him, attempting to swallow him. They said to him: "Who is the King of Glory" to whom you refer?" Solomon replied that he was not referring to himself, but rather to God, the mighty and strong. The gates however still remained closed until he asked God to remember the pieties of his father David. Thereupon the gates finally opened. At that moment, the faces of David's enemies turned dark with humiliation, for they saw that God had forgiven David for his sin with Bath Sheba .

פֶּרֶק כד

א לְדָוִד מִזְמוֹר
לַיהוָה הָאָרֶץ וּמְלוֹאָהּ
תֵּבֵל וְיֹשְׁבֵי בָהּ׃
ב כִּי־הוּא עַל־יַמִּים יְסָדָהּ
וְעַל־נְהָרוֹת יְכוֹנְנֶהָ׃
ג מִי־יַעֲלֶה בְהַר־יְהוָה
וּמִי־יָקוּם
בִּמְקוֹם קָדְשׁוֹ׃
ד נְקִי כַפַּיִם וּבַר־לֵבָב
אֲשֶׁר | לֹא־נָשָׂא לַשָּׁוְא נַפְשִׁי
וְלֹא נִשְׁבַּע לְמִרְמָה׃
ה יִשָּׂא בְרָכָה מֵאֵת יְהוָה
וּצְדָקָה
מֵאֱלֹהֵי יִשְׁעוֹ׃
ו זֶה דּוֹר
דֹּרְשָׁיו
מְבַקְשֵׁי פָנֶיךָ
יַעֲקֹב סֶלָה׃
ז שְׂאוּ שְׁעָרִים | רָאשֵׁיכֶם
וְהִנָּשְׂאוּ
פִּתְחֵי עוֹלָם
וְיָבוֹא מֶלֶךְ הַכָּבוֹד׃
ח מִי זֶה מֶלֶךְ הַכָּבוֹד
יְהוָה עִזּוּז וְגִבּוֹר
יְהוָה גִּבּוֹר מִלְחָמָה׃
ט שְׂאוּ שְׁעָרִים | רָאשֵׁיכֶם

Chapter 24

1 Of David, [a Psalm]:
the earth is Adonoy's and the fullness thereof,
the inhabited world and those who dwell in it.
2 For He founded it upon the seas,
and established it upon rivers.
3 Who may ascend the mountain of Adonoy,
and who may stand
in the place of His holiness?
4 The clean of hands and the pure of heart,
who has not borne my soul in vain,
and has not sworn deceitfully.
5 He will bear Adonoy's blessing
and righteousness
from the God of his deliverance.
6 This is the generation
of those who seek Him,
the seekers of Your Presence,
[God of] Jacob, selah.
7 Lift up your heads, gates,
and be uplifted
[you] entranceways to eternity,
so that the King of Glory may enter.
8 Who is this King of Glory?
Adonoy, strong and mighty;
Adonoy, the Mighty One in battle.
9 Lift up your heads, gates,

וּשְׂאוּ פִּתְחֵי עוֹלָם	and lift, entranceways to eternity,
וְיָבֹא מֶלֶךְ הַכָּבוֹד:	so that the King of Glory may enter.
י מִי הוּא זֶה מֶלֶךְ הַכָּבוֹד	10 Who is He, this King of Glory?
יְהוָה צְבָאוֹת	Adonoy of Hosts,
הוּא מֶלֶךְ הַכָּבוֹד סֶלָה:	He is the King of Glory. Selah.

פרק כה Chapter 25

Weekly Cycle	Monthly Cycle	Book Number
Sunday	4th day of the month	Book 1

Author

דָּוִד הַמֶּלֶךְ—King David—the second king of Israel and father of the Davidic royal and messianic dynasty. David composed over seventy of the 150 psalms of Sefer Tehillim.

When & Why

David wrote this psalm as an entreaty to God to save him from his enemies

Genre

Psalm of Individual Lament - This psalm was written from the perspective of the individual worshipper, who cries out to God in his time of need. It is characterized as an address to God involving a complaint, followed by a request and ending with an expression of trust.
Acrostic: A literary composition in which the writer has used the letters of the Hebrew alphabet in their order as the initial letters for a sequence of verses. i.e. א.ב.ג.ד

Chapter Summary

King David composed this psalm as a sincere plea for atonement for both his sins and those of the entire community of Israel. He acclaims God's kindnesses towards those who observe His covenant, and asks that all those who seek refuge in Him, be redeemed. He profers four specific requests: salvation from his enemies, pardon for his sins, knowledge of God's ways, and God's help in walking in the path of justice and integrity.

This psalm consists of twenty-two verses, subdivided into ten parts. It is arranged in order of the Hebrew alphabet (excluding the letters ב, ו, and ק (bet, vav and koof).
Verse 1 is an introduction, in which King David expresses a yearning for God.
In verses 2 and 3, he declares complete trust in God.
In verses 4 and 5, he requests to know the ways of God.
In verses 6 and 7, he similarly pleads for mercy.
In verses 8-10, God's attributes of goodness and lovingkindness are extolled.
In verse 11, he asks God for forgiveness.
In verses 12-14, he rejoices in the happiness of the man who fears God.

In verse 15, he expresses his constant hope in God's salvation.
In verses 16-20, he petitions God for deliverance from troubles and enemies.
In verse 21, he beseeches God to help in following the path of integrity and uprightness.
In verse 22, he extends his request for deliverance and redemption to all of Israel.

Shimush Tehillim - When to Say

To rise to spiritual greatness—Verse 20 states: "Preserve my soul and rescue me, let me not be ashamed for I have taken refuge in You."
For distress (say every morning)—Verse 22 states: "God, Redeem Israel from all its troubles."

Where in the Siddur

Verse 4 is recited responsively during the repetition of the Amidah (Silent Meditation) of Rosh HaShanah.
Verse 6 is the third verse of V'hu Rachum of Pesukei Dezimra (Introductory Verses of praise to the Shacharit morning service), one of the opening verses of the long Tachanun (Supplication prayer) recited on Mondays and Thursdays, as well as part of the final paragraph of the regular daily Tachanun.

פֶּרֶק כה

א לְדָוִד
אֵלֶיךָ יְהוָה נַפְשִׁי אֶשָּׂא׃
ב אֱלֹהַי בְּךָ בָטַחְתִּי
אַל־אֵבוֹשָׁה
אַל־יַעַלְצוּ אֹיְבַי לִי׃
ג גַּם כָּל־קֹוֶיךָ
לֹא יֵבֹשׁוּ
יֵבֹשׁוּ
הַבּוֹגְדִים רֵיקָם׃
ד דְּרָכֶיךָ יְהוָה הוֹדִיעֵנִי
אֹרְחוֹתֶיךָ לַמְּדֵנִי׃
ה הַדְרִיכֵנִי בַאֲמִתֶּךָ | וְלַמְּדֵנִי
כִּי־אַתָּה אֱלֹהֵי יִשְׁעִי
אוֹתְךָ קִוִּיתִי כָּל־הַיּוֹם׃
ו זְכֹר־רַחֲמֶיךָ יְהוָה
וַחֲסָדֶיךָ
כִּי מֵעוֹלָם הֵמָּה׃
ז חַטֹּאות נְעוּרַי |
וּפְשָׁעַי אַל־תִּזְכֹּר
כְּחַסְדְּךָ

Chapter 25

1 Of David [a Psalm].
To You, Adonoy, I lift up my soul.
2 My God, in You I have put my trust,
let me not be ashamed;
let not my enemies gloat over me.
3 Also, all those who hope for You
will not be ashamed;
let them be ashamed—
the treacherous who impoverish [the poor].
4 Your ways, Adonoy, make known to me;
Your paths, teach [them to] me.
5 Guide me in Your truth and teach me,
for You are the God of my salvation;
for You I have hoped all day.
6 Remember Your mercies, Adonoy,
and Your kindness,
for they are from the beginning of the world.
7 The sins of my youth
and my transgressions remember not;
according to Your kindness

זְכׇר־לִי־אַתָּה		may You remember me,
לְמַעַן טוּבְךָ יְהוָה׃		for the sake of Your goodness, Adonoy.
ח טוֹב־וְיָשָׁר יְהוָה	8	Good and upright is Adonoy;
עַל־כֵּן יוֹרֶה חַטָּאִים בַּדָּרֶךְ׃		therefore, He instructs sinners in the way.
ט יַדְרֵךְ עֲנָוִים בַּמִּשְׁפָּט	9	He guides the humble with justice,
וִילַמֵּד עֲנָוִים דַּרְכּוֹ׃		and He teaches the humble His way.
י כׇּל־אׇרְחוֹת יְהוָה	10	All the paths of Adonoy
חֶסֶד וֶאֱמֶת		are kindness and truth,
לְנֹצְרֵי בְרִיתוֹ		to those who keep his covenant
וְעֵדֹתָיו׃		and His testimonies.
יא לְמַעַן־שִׁמְךָ יְהוָה	11	For Your name's sake, Adonoy;
וְסָלַחְתָּ לַעֲוֺנִי כִּי רַב־הוּא׃		pardon my iniquity, for it is great.
יב מִי־זֶה הָאִישׁ יְרֵא יְהוָה	12	Who is the man that fears Adonoy;
יוֹרֶנּוּ		He will instruct him how to walk
בְּדֶרֶךְ יִבְחָר׃		in the way that he chose.
יג נַפְשׁוֹ בְּטוֹב תָּלִין	13	His soul will abide in goodness,
וְזַרְעוֹ יִירַשׁ אָרֶץ׃		and his seed will inherit the earth.
יד סוֹד יְהוָה	14	The secret counsel of Adonoy
לִירֵאָיו		is with those who fear Him,
וּבְרִיתוֹ לְהוֹדִיעָם׃		and His covenant He makes known to them.
טו עֵינַי תָּמִיד אֶל־יְהוָה	15	My eyes are ever directed toward Adonoy,
כִּי הוּא־יוֹצִיא מֵרֶשֶׁת רַגְלָי׃		for He will free my feet from the net.
טז פְּנֵה־אֵלַי וְחׇנֵּנִי	16	Turn to me and favor me,
כִּי־יָחִיד וְעָנִי אָנִי׃		for I am alone and poor.
יז צָרוֹת לְבָבִי הִרְחִיבוּ	17	The troubles of my heart have spread,
מִמְּצוּקוֹתַי הוֹצִיאֵנִי׃		bring me out from my distress.
יח רְאֵה עׇנְיִי וַעֲמָלִי	18	Behold my affliction and my travail,
וְשָׂא לְכׇל־חַטֹּאותָי׃		and bear all my sins.
יט רְאֵה־אוֹיְבַי	19	Behold my enemies
כִּי־רָבּוּ		for they have multiplied,
וְשִׂנְאַת חָמָס		and with unjustified hatred
שְׂנֵאוּנִי׃		they hate me.
כ שׇׁמְרָה נַפְשִׁי וְהַצִּילֵנִי	20	Preserve my soul and rescue me,
אַל־אֵבוֹשׁ		let me not be ashamed
כִּי־חָסִיתִי בָךְ׃		for I have taken refuge in You.
כא תֹּם־וָיֹשֶׁר יִצְּרוּנִי	21	Integrity and uprightness will protect me,
כִּי קִוִּיתִיךָ׃		for I have hoped for You.
כב פְּדֵה אֱלֹהִים אֶת־יִשְׂרָאֵל	22	God, Redeem Israel
מִכֹּל צָרוֹתָיו׃		from all its troubles.

פרק כו Chapter 26

Weekly Cycle	Monthly Cycle	Book Number
Sunday	4th day of the month	Book 1

Author

דָּוִד הַמֶּלֶךְ—King David—the second king of Israel and father of the Davidic royal and messianic dynasty. David composed over seventy of the 150 psalms of Sefer Tehillim.

When & Why

David wrote this psalm as a way of reaffirming that his sin with Bath Sheba was an exception to the rule and that he is truly a faithful servant of God, even though he sinned.

Genre

Psalm of Individual Lament - This psalm was written from the perspective of the individual worshipper, who cries out to God in his time of need. It is characterized as an address to God involving a complaint, followed by a request and ending with an expression of trust.

Chapter Summary

The righteous man trusts in the Lord and appeals to Him to avenge his enemies. He asks that God alone judge him, for he is certain that the Holy One will not forsake him.

This psalm consists of twelve verses, subdivided into three sections.
Verse 1 is an introduction, and is comprised of King David's request of God to judge him favorably.
In verses 2-10, King David justifies his request, pointing to his own righteousness.
In verses 11 & 12, King David comes full circle, once again beseeching God and affirming the righteous path he has taken.

Shimush Tehillim - When to Say

For one who is in distress, whether at sea or on land, or for one who is in captivity, to be saved from his distress.

Where in the Siddur

Verse 8 is the third verse of Ma Tovu, recited by some upon entry into the synagogue in the morning. Originally coined by Bilam, the seer hired by Balak, king of Moav, to curse Israel, who in turn blessed Israel instead, the verse Ma Tovu extolls the beauty of the "tents of Jacob, the dwelling places of Israel", a reference to the synagogue.

Talmud on Tehillim

Verse 6: "אֶרְחַץ בְּנִקָּיוֹן כַּפָּי; וַאֲסֹבְבָה אֶת מִזְבַּחֲךָ יְהוָה."—"I will wash my hands in purity, and I will encircle Your altar, Adonoy."
The Talmud, Berachot 15a, deduces that the performing of the morning rituals of washing ones hands, laying Tefillin (phylacteries) and reciting the Shema is comparable to building an altar and sacrificing upon it to God.

פֶּרֶק כו

א לְדָוִ֨ד ׀
שָׁפְטֵ֤נִי יְהוָ֗ה
כִּֽי־אֲ֭נִי בְּתֻמִּ֣י הָלַ֑כְתִּי
וּבַיהוָ֥ה בָּ֝טַ֗חְתִּי
לֹ֣א אֶמְעָֽד׃
ב בְּחָנֵ֣נִי יְהוָ֣ה וְנַסֵּ֑נִי
צָרְפָ֖ה כִלְיוֹתַ֣י וְלִבִּֽי׃
ג כִּֽי־חַ֭סְדְּךָ לְנֶ֣גֶד עֵינָ֑י
וְ֝הִתְהַלַּ֗כְתִּי בַּאֲמִתֶּֽךָ׃
ד לֹא־יָ֭שַׁבְתִּי
עִם־מְתֵי־שָׁ֑וְא
וְעִ֥ם נַ֝עֲלָמִ֗ים
לֹ֣א אָבֽוֹא׃
ה שָׂ֭נֵאתִי קְהַ֣ל מְרֵעִ֑ים
וְעִם־רְ֝שָׁעִ֗ים לֹ֣א אֵשֵֽׁב׃
ו אֶרְחַ֣ץ בְּנִקָּי֣וֹן כַּפָּ֑י
וַאֲסֹבְבָ֖ה אֶת־מִזְבַּחֲךָ֣ יְהוָֽה׃
ז לַ֭שְׁמִעַ
בְּק֣וֹל תּוֹדָ֑ה
וּ֝לְסַפֵּ֗ר כָּל־נִפְלְאוֹתֶֽיךָ׃
ח יְֽהוָ֗ה אָ֭הַבְתִּי מְע֣וֹן בֵּיתֶ֑ךָ
וּ֝מְק֗וֹם מִשְׁכַּ֥ן כְּבוֹדֶֽךָ׃
ט אַל־תֶּאֱסֹ֣ף
עִם־חַטָּאִ֣ים נַפְשִׁ֑י
וְעִם־אַנְשֵׁ֖י דָמִ֣ים חַיָּֽי׃
י אֲשֶׁר־בִּידֵיהֶ֥ם זִמָּ֑ה
וִֽ֝ימִינָ֗ם מָ֣לְאָה שֹּֽׁחַד׃
יא וַ֭אֲנִי
בְּתֻמִּ֥י אֵלֵ֗ךְ
פְּדֵ֣נִי וְחָנֵּֽנִי׃
יב רַ֭גְלִי עָמְדָ֣ה בְמִישׁ֑וֹר
בְּ֝מַקְהֵלִ֗ים אֲבָרֵ֥ךְ יְהוָֽה׃

Chapter 26

1 Of David, [a Psalm].
Judge me, Adonoy,
for in my wholeheartedness I have walked,
and in Adonoy I have trusted,
I will not waver.
2 Examine me, Adonoy, and test me,
refine [purify] my mind and my heart.
3 For Your kindness is before my eyes,
and I have walked in Your truth.
4 I have not sat down
with men of falsehood,
and with those who sin in secret
I do not associate.
5 I have hated the gathering of evildoers,
and with the wicked I will not sit.
6 I will wash my hands in purity,
and I will encircle Your altar, Adonoy.
7 To make [myself] heard
in a voice of thanksgiving,
and tell of all Your wonders.
8 Adonoy, I love the Dwelling, Your House,
and the place where Your glory resides.
9 Gather not
my soul with sinners,
nor my life with men of blood.
10 For in their hands is mischief,
and their right hand is full of bribes.
11 As for me,
I will walk in my wholeheartedness;
redeem me and favor me.
12 My foot stands on a straight path,
in the congregations will I bless Adonoy.

פרק כז Chapter 27

Weekly Cycle	Monthly Cycle	Book Number
Sunday	4th day of the month	Book 1

Author

דָּוִד הַמֶּלֶךְ—King David—the second king of Israel and father of the Davidic royal and messianic dynasty. David composed over seventy of the 150 psalms of Sefer Tehillim.

When & Why

David wrote this psalm as a prayer to God that he be saved from his enemies and that he have the strength to serve God in the best way.

Genre

Psalm of Individual Confidence - In this psalm, the worshipper expresses absolute certainty that his prayers will be heard.

Psalm of Individual Lament - This psalm was written from the perspective of the individual worshipper, who cries out to God in his time of need. It is characterized as an address to God involving a complaint, followed by a request and ending with an expression of trust.

Chapter Summary

With this psalm, King David seeks to strengthen his own resolve, and that of his warriors, to fight and pray for victory. He intends to teach us that Divine Providence and guidance are directly related to the degree of one's cleaving to God.

This psalm consists of fourteen verses, subdivided into three parts.
In verses 1-3, King David describes his complete trust in God.
In verses 4-6, he puts forth his request of God.
In verses 7-14, he further elaborates on his request, beseeching the reader to "Adonoy, hear my voice, when I call; be gracious to me and answer me."

Shimush Tehillim - When to Say

To calm an animal (say this in the animal's ear)—Verse 1 acknowledges God as one's light and salvation, and as the source of all animal life. Why, then, should one fear?

Where in the Siddur

Recited twice daily during the entire month of Elul through Shemini Atzeret, days considered by the Midrash to be an auspicious time period for repentance.
Verse 14 is found in some siddurim as the introductory verse to Ein Keloheinu, recited towards the end of Shacharit, in some communities daily, and in others only on Shabbat.

Contemporary Song

Verse 4

Talmud on Tehillim

Verse 13: "לוּלֵא הֶאֱמַנְתִּי, לִרְאוֹת בְּטוּב יְהוָה בְּאֶרֶץ חַיִּים"—"Had I not believed that I would see the goodness of Adonoy in the land of living."

The Talmud, Berachot 4a, explains that King David trusted that God gives just rewards to the righteous in the World to Come. He did not know, however, whether he himself had a portion among them. While sure of his devoutness, he wasn't certain that he merited to be rewarded, and was further afraid that any sins on his part may cause him to lose any reward he had indeed earned.

Verse 14:" קַוֵּה אֶל יְהוָה: חֲזַק, וְיַאֲמֵץ לִבֶּךָ, וְקַוֵּה אֶל יְהוָה"—"Hope to Adonoy, be strong and He will give you courage; and hope to Adonoy."

The Talmud, Berachot 32b, deduces that the repetitive phrase "chazak veya'ameitz"—"be strong and brave", indicates the need for extra effort in this endeavor. The Talmud advises further: "If a person sees that his prayers have not been answered, he should pray again." One must constantly strengthen himself during prayer to ensure proper concentration.

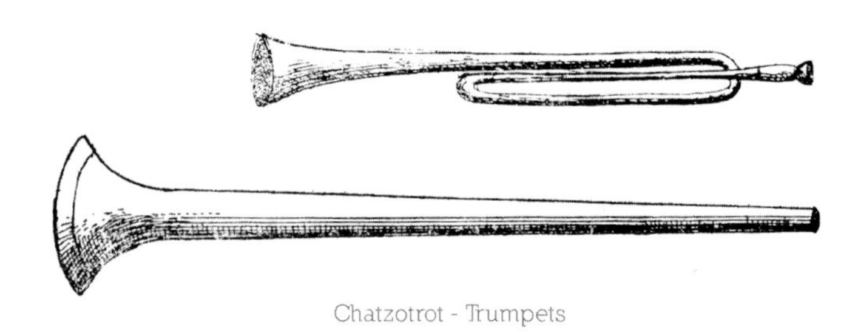

Chatzotrot - Trumpets

פֶּרֶק כז			**Chapter 27**
לְדָוִד |	א	1	Of David, [a Psalm]:
יְהוָה | אוֹרִי וְיִשְׁעִי			Adonoy is my light and my salvation,
מִמִּי אִירָא			whom shall I fear?
יְהוָה מָעוֹז־חַיַּי			Adonoy is the strength of my life,
מִמִּי אֶפְחָד:			of whom shall I be afraid?
בִּקְרֹב עָלַי | מְרֵעִים	ב	2	When evildoers approach me
לֶאֱכֹל אֶת־בְּשָׂרִי			to devour my flesh—
צָרַי וְאֹיְבַי לִי			my tormentors and my foes,
הֵמָּה כָשְׁלוּ וְנָפָלוּ:			they stumble and fall.
אִם־תַּחֲנֶה עָלַי | מַחֲנֶה	ג	3	If an army should encamp against me,
לֹא־יִירָא לִבִּי			my heart would not fear;
אִם־תָּקוּם עָלַי מִלְחָמָה			if war were to rise against me
בְּזֹאת אֲנִי בוֹטֵחַ:			in this I trust.

ד אַחַת | שָׁאַלְתִּי מֵאֵת־יְהוָה	4 One thing I request of Adonoy,
אוֹתָהּ אֲבַקֵּשׁ	[only] that shall I seek:
שִׁבְתִּי בְּבֵית־יְהוָה	that I may dwell in the House of Adonoy
כָּל־יְמֵי חַיַּי	all the days of my life,
לַחֲזוֹת בְּנֹעַם־יְהוָה	to behold the pleasantness of Adonoy,
וּלְבַקֵּר בְּהֵיכָלוֹ׃	and to meditate in His Sanctuary.
ה כִּי יִצְפְּנֵנִי | בְּסֻכֹּה	5 For He will hide me in His Tabernacle
בְּיוֹם רָעָה	on the day of distress,
יַסְתִּרֵנִי בְּסֵתֶר אָהֳלוֹ	He will conceal me in the shelter of His Tent,
בְּצוּר יְרוֹמְמֵנִי׃	upon a rock He will lift me.
ו וְעַתָּה יָרוּם רֹאשִׁי	6 And now my head is raised high
עַל אֹיְבַי סְבִיבוֹתַי	above my enemies around me;
וְאֶזְבְּחָה בְאָהֳלוֹ	and I will offer in His Tent,
זִבְחֵי תְרוּעָה	sacrifices [accompanied] with trumpets of joy;
אָשִׁירָה וַאֲזַמְּרָה לַיהוָה׃	I will sing and chant to Adonoy.
ז שְׁמַע־יְהוָה קוֹלִי אֶקְרָא	7 Adonoy, hear my voice when I call;
וְחָנֵּנִי וַעֲנֵנִי׃	be gracious to me and answer me.
ח לְךָ | אָמַר לִבִּי	8 Of You, my heart has said,
בַּקְּשׁוּ פָנָי	"seek My Presence";
אֶת־פָּנֶיךָ יְהוָה אֲבַקֵּשׁ׃	Your Presence, Adonoy I will seek.
ט אַל־תַּסְתֵּר פָּנֶיךָ | מִמֶּנִּי	9 Conceal not Your Presence from me,
אַל־תַּט־בְּאַף עַבְדֶּךָ	do not turn Your servant away in anger.
עֶזְרָתִי הָיִיתָ	You have been my help;
אַל־תִּטְּשֵׁנִי וְאַל־תַּעַזְבֵנִי	neither cast me off nor abandon me,
אֱלֹהֵי יִשְׁעִי׃	God of my deliverance.
י כִּי־אָבִי וְאִמִּי עֲזָבוּנִי	10 When my father and mother abandon me,
וַיהוָה יַאַסְפֵנִי׃	Adonoy will gather me up.
יא הוֹרֵנִי יְהוָה דַּרְכֶּךָ	11 Adonoy, teach me Your way,
וּנְחֵנִי בְּאֹרַח מִישׁוֹר	and lead me in the path of uprightness,
לְמַעַן שׁוֹרְרָי׃	because of my watchers.
יב אַל־תִּתְּנֵנִי	12 Do not deliver me
בְּנֶפֶשׁ צָרָי	to the will of my tormentors,
כִּי קָמוּ־בִי עֵדֵי־שֶׁקֶר	for false witnesses have risen against me,
וִיפֵחַ חָמָס׃	who breathe violence.
יג לוּלֵא הֶאֱמַנְתִּי לִרְאוֹת	13 Had I not believed that I would see
בְּטוּב־יְהוָה בְּאֶרֶץ חַיִּים׃	the goodness of Adonoy in the land of living.
יד קַוֵּה אֶל־יְהוָה	14 Hope to Adonoy,
חֲזַק וְיַאֲמֵץ לִבֶּךָ	be strong and He will give you courage;
וְקַוֵּה אֶל־יְהוָה׃	and hope to Adonoy.

פרק כח Chapter 28

Weekly Cycle	Monthly Cycle	Book Number
Sunday	4th day of the month	Book 1

Author
דָּוִד הַמֶּלֶךְ—King David—the second king of Israel and father of the Davidic royal and messianic dynasty. David composed over seventy of the 150 psalms of Sefer Tehillim.

When & Why
David wrote this psalm as a lament of his enemies, who praised him outwardly, but hated him inwardly and plotted against him.

Genre
Psalm of Individual Lament - This psalm was written from the perspective of the individual worshipper, who cries out to God in his time of need. It is characterized as an address to God involving a complaint, followed by a request and ending with an expression of trust.

Chapter Summary
David calls upon God to hear his supplications and grant his request. He asks to be free to devote himself to the needs of the soul and to serving God, spared from those who pay no heed to the Lord.

This psalm consists of nine verses, subdivided into three parts.
In verses 1 & 2, King David requests that his prayer be accepted.
In verses 3-5, he delineates his request, praying to not be drawn to the behavior of the wicked, and to be protected against his enemies.
In verses 6-9, he expresses his gratitude for having his prayers answered by God.

Shimush Tehillim - When to Say
For peace with an enemy —The concluding verse states: "Deliver Your people and bless Your inheritance; tend them and uplift them forever."

Where in the Siddur
Verse 9 is the first verse of the paragraph Hoshi'a et Amecha of Pesukei Dezimra (introductory Verses of Praise to the Shacharit morning service). This verse, because of its ten words, is often used for counting the ten men needed for a minyan, as Jewish law forbids direct, numerical counting of individuals.

Contemporary Song
Verse 9

פֶּרֶק כח

א לְדָוִד
אֵלֶיךָ יְהוָה | אֶקְרָא
צוּרִי אַל־תֶּחֱרַשׁ מִמֶּנִּי
פֶּן־תֶּחֱשֶׁה מִמֶּנִּי
וְנִמְשַׁלְתִּי
עִם־יוֹרְדֵי בוֹר:
ב שְׁמַע קוֹל תַּחֲנוּנַי
בְּשַׁוְּעִי אֵלֶיךָ
בְּנָשְׂאִי יָדַי
אֶל־דְּבִיר קָדְשֶׁךָ:
ג אַל־תִּמְשְׁכֵנִי עִם־רְשָׁעִים
וְעִם־פֹּעֲלֵי אָוֶן
דֹּבְרֵי שָׁלוֹם עִם־רֵעֵיהֶם
וְרָעָה בִּלְבָבָם:
ד תֶּן־לָהֶם כְּפָעֳלָם
וּכְרֹעַ מַעַלְלֵיהֶם
כְּמַעֲשֵׂה יְדֵיהֶם תֵּן לָהֶם
הָשֵׁב גְּמוּלָם לָהֶם:
ה כִּי לֹא יָבִינוּ אֶל־פְּעֻלֹּת יְהוָה
וְאֶל־מַעֲשֵׂה יָדָיו
יֶהֶרְסֵם
וְלֹא יִבְנֵם:
ו בָּרוּךְ יְהוָה
כִּי־שָׁמַע קוֹל תַּחֲנוּנָי:
ז יְהוָה | עֻזִּי וּמָגִנִּי
בּוֹ בָטַח לִבִּי
וְנֶעֱזָרְתִּי
וַיַּעֲלֹז לִבִּי
וּמִשִּׁירִי אֲהוֹדֶנּוּ:
ח יְהוָה עֹז־לָמוֹ
וּמָעוֹז יְשׁוּעוֹת
מְשִׁיחוֹ הוּא:
ט הוֹשִׁיעָה | אֶת־עַמֶּךָ
וּבָרֵךְ אֶת־נַחֲלָתֶךָ
וּרְעֵם וְנַשְּׂאֵם עַד־הָעוֹלָם:

Chapter 28

1 Of David, [a Psalm].
To You, Adonoy, I call;
my Rock, be not deaf unto me,
for if You will be silent to me
I shall be likened
to them that go down to the grave.
2 Hear the voice of my supplications
when I cry out to You,
when I lift my hands
toward the Holy of Holies of Your Sanctuary.
3 Draw me not away with the wicked
and with the workers of iniquity;
who speak peace with their neighbors
though evil is in their hearts.
4 Give them according to their deeds
and according to the evil of their endeavors;
according to the work of their hands give them,
render to them their due.
5 For they regard not the deeds of Adonoy
nor the work of His hands;
[therefore] He will destroy them
and not rebuild them.
6 Blessed is Adonoy,
for He has heard the voice of my supplications.
7 Adonoy is my strength and my shield,
in Him my heart trusts;
in Him my heart trusts;
and my heart was overjoyed,
and with my song I will praise Him.
8 Adonoy is a strength to them,
and He is a stronghold of deliverance
to His annointed.
9 Deliver Your people
and bless Your inheritance;
tend them and uplift them forever.

פרק כט Chapter 29

Weekly Cycle	Monthly Cycle	Book Number
Sunday	5th day of the month	Book 1

Author

דָּוִד הַמֶּלֶךְ—King David—the second king of Israel and father of the Davidic royal and messianic dynasty. David composed over seventy of the 150 psalms of Sefer Tehillim.

When & Why

David wrote this psalm to praise God on the creation of the world, the Exodus from Egypt, and the giving of the Torah at Sinai.

Genre

Psalm of Praise – This is a psalm of celebration, often the result of a victory. It declares God's goodness and urges all of creation to worship.

Chapter Summary

The Psalmist proudly proclaims the awesome wonders of the Creator on earth, and the manifestations of His power in nature. He concludes with a blessing of strength and peace for the Jewish people.

This psalm consists of eleven verses, subdivided into three parts.
Verses 1 & 2 serve as an introduction, in which King David turns to the angels and asks them to praise God.
In verses 3-9, he describes the voice of the Lord.
In verses 10 & 11, he further describes God's reign and His blessing of strength and peace to His people.

Introductory Word

מִזְמוֹר—Mizmor—Musical Accompaniment

Shimush Tehillim - When to Say

For an evil spirit——The concluding verse states: "Adonoy will give strength to His people; Adonoy will bless His people with peace."

Where in the Siddur

Recited on Friday night as the sixth paragraph of Kabbalat Shabbat (Friday night service).
Recited on Shabbat morning upon returning the Torah Scroll to the Aron Kodesh (Holy Ark).
Recited before Ma'ariv (evening service) of Motza'ei Shabbat in some congregations.
Verse 9 is recited as the final verse of Birkat HaMazon (Grace after Meals).
Verse 9 is recited as part of the prayers following Ma'ariv of Motza'ei Shabbat Maariv in some congregations.
Verse 9 is also recited as one of the verses of Atah Horeita, a responsive reading introducing the

Hakafot dancing ceremony on Simchat Torah.

Interesting Fact

This psalm provides the framework for the blessings of praise that begin every Amidah (Silent Meditation). It is also the source for the inclusion of eighteen original blessings in the weekday Amidah, also known as Shmoneh Esrei, as this psalm mentions the name of God eighteen times. While Shmoneh Esrei, which translated means "eighteen", actually contains nineteen berachot, the twelfth, "V'lamalshinim", is a later addition.

Biblical Places

הֵיכָל—Heichal—Holy Temple—a term used to refer to the inner sanctuary of the Temple in Jerusalem. The Heichal contained the Holy of Holies, the resting place of the Aron HaKodesh (Holy Ark)*. It also housed the Menorah, Altar of Incense, and Table of the Showbread.

*The Aron HaKodesh, while present in the first Beit HaMikdash (Temple), was buried, and hence its location was not known, during the period of the second Beit HaMikdash.

לְבָנוֹן וְשִׂרְיֹן—Lebanon and Siryon—mountains located in the north of Israel.

מִדְבַּר קָדֵשׁ—Wilderness of Kadesh—a desert located east of the Jordan River. Thirty-eight of the Israelites forty year sojourn in the wilderness were spent in Kadesh.

Talmud on Tehillim

Verse 1: "הָבוּ לַיהוָה, בְּנֵי אֵלִים :"— "Ascribe to Adonoy—you sons of the mighty."

According to the Talmud, Sukkah 55a, this verse was sung on the first day of Chol HaMo'eid Sukkot (Intermediate Days of Sukkot) in the Beit HaMikdash (Temple).

Verse 3: "קוֹל יְהוָה עַל-הַמָּיִם... יְהוָה, עַל-מַיִם רַבִּים"—"Adonoy's voice is upon the water... Adonoy is upon [the] many waters."

The Talmud, Pesachim 112a, states that one who drinks water on Tuesday and Friday nights is in danger of being harmed by the evil spirit. Accordingly, one should remedy this danger by reciting these verses.

פרק כט			Chapter 29
מִזְמוֹר לְדָוִד הָבוּ לַיהוָה בְּנֵי אֵלִים הָבוּ לַיהוָה כָּבוֹד וָעֹז:	א	1	A Psalm of David. Ascribe to Adonoy—you sons of the mighty— ascribe to Adonoy glory and might.
הָבוּ לַיהוָה כְּבוֹד שְׁמוֹ הִשְׁתַּחֲווּ לַיהוָה בְּהַדְרַת-קֹדֶשׁ:	ב	2	Ascribe to Adonoy the glory due His Name, prostrate yourselves before Adonoy in the splendor of holiness.
קוֹל יְהוָה עַל-הַמָּיִם אֵל-הַכָּבוֹד הִרְעִים יְהוָה עַל-מַיִם רַבִּים:	ג	3	Adonoy's voice is upon the waters. Almighty of glory thunders, Adonoy is upon [the] many waters.

קוֹל־יְהוָה בַּכֹּחַ	ד	4	The voice of Adonoy is in power,
קוֹל יְהוָה בֶּהָדָר׃			the voice of Adonoy is in beauty.
קוֹל יְהוָה שֹׁבֵר אֲרָזִים	ה	5	The voice of Adonoy breaks cedars,
וַיְשַׁבֵּר יְהוָה			Adonoy shatters
אֶת־אַרְזֵי הַלְּבָנוֹן׃			the cedars of Lebanon.
וַיַּרְקִידֵם כְּמוֹ־עֵגֶל	ו	6	He makes them leap like a calf,
לְבָנוֹן וְשִׂרְיֹן כְּמוֹ בֶן־רְאֵמִים׃			Lebanon and Sirion like unicorns.
קוֹל־יְהוָה	ז	7	The voice of Adonoy
חֹצֵב לַהֲבוֹת אֵשׁ׃			hews out flames of fire.
קוֹל יְהוָה יָחִיל מִדְבָּר	ח	8	The voice of Adonoy makes the desert tremble,
יָחִיל יְהוָה מִדְבַּר קָדֵשׁ׃			Adonoy makes tremble the desert of Kadesh.
קוֹל יְהוָה ׀ יְחוֹלֵל אַיָּלוֹת	ט	9	The voice of Adonoy causes hinds to calve,
וַיֶּחֱשֹׂף יְעָרוֹת			and strips the forests bare;
וּבְהֵיכָלוֹ			and in His Sanctuary
כֻּלּוֹ אֹמֵר כָּבוֹד׃			all proclaim [His] glory.
יְהוָה לַמַּבּוּל יָשָׁב	י	10	Adonoy sat enthroned (even) at the flood
וַיֵּשֶׁב יְהוָה מֶלֶךְ לְעוֹלָם׃			Adonoy is enthroned as King forever.
יְהוָה עֹז לְעַמּוֹ יִתֵּן	יא	11	11. Adonoy will give strength to His people;
יְהוָה ׀ יְבָרֵךְ אֶת־עַמּוֹ בַשָּׁלוֹם׃			Adonoy will bless His people with peace.

Mosaic of Unicorn

פרק ל Chapter 30

Weekly Cycle	Monthly Cycle	Book Number
Monday	5th day of the month	Book 1

Author

דָּוִד הַמֶּלֶךְ—King David—the second king of Israel and father of the Davidic royal and messianic dynasty. David composed over seventy of the 150 psalms of Sefer Tehillim.

When & Why

David wrote this psalm to be sung during the consecration of the Temple in the times of Solomon.

Genre

Psalm of Individual Thanksgiving – This psalm emphasizes gratitude for what God has done for the individual.

Chapter Summary

This psalm was composed by King David in honor of the dedication of the Beit HaMikdash, the Holy Temple. Though he himself would not be worthy of building God's house, the promise that the Temple would be built by his son, Solomon, was sufficient vindication against the taunts and derision of his enemies.

This psalm consists of thirteen verses, subdivided into four parts.
Verse 1 serves as an introduction.
In verses 2-4, King David expresses his thanks to God.
In verses 5 & 6, he calls upon the pious to give thanks to God as well, for God's anger passes quickly.
In verses 7-10, the Psalmist describes his struggles.
In verses 11-13, he offers his thanksgiving for deliverance from his hardship.

Introductory Word

מִזְמוֹר—Mizmor—Musical Accompaniment
שִׁיר—Shir—Song

Interesting Facts

This psalm is commonly referred to by its first two words, "Mizmor shir".
While originally recited as part of the dedication ceremony of the Beit HaMikdash (Temple), it was reintroduced as part of the daily prayer during the 17th century.

Shimush Tehillim - When to Say

For deliverance from a bad occurrence—Verse 11 states: "Hear [me] Adonoy, and be gracious to me. Adonoy, be a help to me."

Where in the Siddur

Recited as the opening prayer to Pesukei Dezimra (introductory Verses of Praise to the Shacharit morning service). In some congregations, it is incorporated into the body of Pesukei Dezimra itself.

Recited as the Shir Shel Yom (Psalm for the Day) of Hanukkah. In some congregations, it is recited in addition to the regular daily psalm. In others, it replaces the daily psalm.

Verse 13 is part of Uva Letzion, one of the closing prayers of the weekday Shacharit and Ma'ariv of Motza'ei Shabbat.

Biblical Places

שְׁאוֹל—Sheol—Lower or Underworld; abode of the dead.

Talmud on Tehillim

Verse 6:"כִּי רֶגַע בְּאַפּוֹ, חַיִּים בִּרְצוֹנוֹ"— "For His anger lasts only a moment."

The Talmud, Berachot 7a, deduces from this verse that God's anger at Israel lasts for only a fleeting moment. When Bilam, a diviner, tried to curse Israel, he timed his curse to coincide precisely with this moment of anger.

	פרק ל		**Chapter 30**
א	מִזְמוֹר	1	A Psalm,
	שִׁיר־חֲנֻכַּת הַבַּיִת		a song for the inauguration of the Temple,
	לְדָוִד׃		by David.
ב	אֲרוֹמִמְךָ יְהוָה	2	I will exalt You, Adonoy,
	כִּי דִלִּיתָנִי		for You have upheld me,
	וְלֹא־שִׂמַּחְתָּ אֹיְבַי לִי׃		and not let my foes rejoice over me.
ג	יְהוָה אֱלֹהָי	3	Adonoy, my God,
	שִׁוַּעְתִּי אֵלֶיךָ וַתִּרְפָּאֵנִי׃		I cried out to You, and You healed me.
ד	יְהוָה	4	Adonoy,
	הֶעֱלִיתָ מִן־שְׁאוֹל נַפְשִׁי		You have raised my soul from the Lower World.
	חִיִּיתַנִי מִיָּרְדִי־בוֹר׃		You have kept me alive, lest I descend to the Pit.
ה	זַמְּרוּ לַיהוָה חֲסִידָיו	5	Sing to Adonoy, [you,] His pious ones,
	וְהוֹדוּ לְזֵכֶר קָדְשׁוֹ׃		and give thanks to His holy Name.
ו	כִּי רֶגַע	בְּאַפּוֹ	6	For His anger lasts only a moment,
	חַיִּים בִּרְצוֹנוֹ		but there is [long] life, in His conciliation.
	בָּעֶרֶב יָלִין בֶּכִי		In the evening, one retires weeping,
	וְלַבֹּקֶר רִנָּה׃		but in the morning there is [a cry of] joy!
ז	וַאֲנִי אָמַרְתִּי בְשַׁלְוִי	7	I said, in my serenity,
	בַּל־אֶמּוֹט לְעוֹלָם׃		I would never be moved.

Scale Model of the Beit HaMikdash (Second Temple), located in Israel Museum

ח יְהוָה בִּרְצוֹנְךָ הֶעֱמַדְתָּה לְהַרְרִי עֹז הִסְתַּרְתָּ פָנֶיךָ הָיִיתִי נִבְהָל׃	8 [But,] Adonoy, it was Your will [alone] that established my mountain as a stronghold. When You concealed Your Presence, I was terrified.
ט אֵלֶיךָ יְהוָה אֶקְרָא וְאֶל־אֲדֹנָי אֶתְחַנָּן׃	9 To You, Adonoy, I called, and my Master I beseeched.
י מַה־בֶּצַע בְּדָמִי בְּרִדְתִּי אֶל־שָׁחַת הֲיוֹדְךָ עָפָר הֲיַגִּיד אֲמִתֶּךָ׃	10 What gain is there in [the shedding of] my blood? In my going down to destruction? Will the dust acknowledge You? Will it proclaim Your truth?
יא שְׁמַע־יְהוָה וְחָנֵּנִי יְהוָה הֱיֵה־עֹזֵר לִי׃	11 Hear [me] Adonoy, and be gracious to me. Adonoy, be a help to me.
יב הָפַכְתָּ מִסְפְּדִי לְמָחוֹל לִי פִּתַּחְתָּ שַׂקִּי וַתְּאַזְּרֵנִי שִׂמְחָה׃	12 You have turned my mourning into dancing. You have loosened my sackcloth and supported me with joy.
יג לְמַעַן | יְזַמֶּרְךָ כָבוֹד וְלֹא יִדֹּם יְהוָה אֱלֹהַי לְעוֹלָם אוֹדֶךָּ׃	13 In order that my soul might sing to You and not be stilled, Adonoy, my God, forever will I thank You.

פרק לא Chapter 31

Weekly Cycle	Monthly Cycle	Book Number
Monday	5th day of the month	Book 1

Author

דָּוִד הַמֶּלֶךְ—King David—the second king of Israel and father of the Davidic royal and messianic dynasty. David composed over seventy of the 150 psalms of Sefer Tehillim.

When & Why

David wrote this psalm when he was escaping from Saul. In it, he prays that God should save him from his enemies and pursuants.

Genre

Psalm of Individual Lament - This psalm was written from the perspective of the individual worshipper, who cries out to God in his time of need. It is characterized as an address to God involving a complaint, followed by a request and ending with an expression of trust.

Chapter Summary

To merit Divine Protection, even through supernatural means, one must completely trust in God. Here, David thanks the Almighty for having miraculously saved him from Saul, and further prays for God's deliverance from all other adversaries as well.

This psalm consists of twenty-five verses, subdivided into two parts.
Verse 1 serves as a heading.
In verses 2-9, King David pleads for salvation and expresses gratitude for his rescue.
In verses 10-25, he beseeches God to be gracious to him in his distress, and again pleads for salvation and for the downfall of the wicked. He then once again expresses thanks for his deliverance, and calls to those who fear God to love Him and put their trust in Him.

Introductory Word

לַמְנַצֵּחַ—Lamnatsei'ach—To the Conductor
מִזְמוֹר—Mizmor—Musical Accompaniment

Shimush Tehillim - When to Say

For protection against the evil eye—Verses 14 & 15 state: "For I have heard the whispering of many, terror all around; when they took counsel together against me, they planned to take my soul [life]. But, as for me, in You I have trusted, Adonoy, I said, "You are my God."

Where in the Siddur

Verse 6 is one of the verses comprising Baruch Hashem Le'olam, one of the blessings surrounding Shema of Ma'ariv (evening service).
Verse 6 is also recited as one of the verses of the longer version of the bedtime Shema (Talmud, Berachot, 5a).

Biblical Places

שְׁאוֹל—Sheol—Lower or Underworld; abode of the dead.

Talmud on Tehillim

Verse 13: "נִשְׁכַּחְתִּי כְּמֵת מִלֵּב; הָיִיתִי כִּכְלִי אֹבֵד"—"I am forgotten like a dead man from the heart, I have become like a lost vessel."

The Talmud, Berachot 58b, states: "The dead is not forgotten from the heart until after twelve months." The verse draws an analogy between forgetting a dead person and abandoning a lost object. From here the Talmud deduces that just as a lost object is abandoned by its owner only after twelve months, so too, the loss of a loved one only leaves one's heart after twelve months. This verse serves as a prooftext for the twelve month mourning period for one's parents.

	פֶּרֶק לא		Chapter 31
א	לַמְנַצֵּחַ	1	To the Chief Musician,
	מִזְמוֹר לְדָוִד׃		a Psalm of David.
ב	בְּךָ יְהוָה חָסִיתִי	2	In You, Adonoy, I have taken refuge,
	אַל־אֵבוֹשָׁה לְעוֹלָם		let me not be ashamed, ever;
	בְּצִדְקָתְךָ פַלְּטֵנִי׃		in Your righteousness, let me escape.
ג	ה הַטֵּה אֵלַי | אָזְנְךָ	3	Incline to me Your ear,
	מְהֵרָה הַצִּילֵנִי		speedily rescue me,
	הֱיֵה לִי | לְצוּר־מָעוֹז		be to me a rock of strength,
	לְבֵית מְצוּדוֹת לְהוֹשִׁיעֵנִי׃		a fortress of defense, to deliver me.
ד	כִּי־סַלְעִי וּמְצוּדָתִי אָתָּה	4	For my rock and my fortress are You,
	וּלְמַעַן שִׁמְךָ		and for the sake of Your Name,
	תַּנְחֵנִי וּתְנַהֲלֵנִי׃		lead me and guide me.
ה	תּוֹצִיאֵנִי מֵרֶשֶׁת זוּ	5	Bring me out from this net
	טָמְנוּ לִי		which they have hidden for me,
	כִּי־אַתָּה מָעוּזִּי׃		for You are my stronghold.
ו	בְּיָדְךָ אַפְקִיד רוּחִי	6	Into Your hand, I commit my spirit;
	פָּדִיתָה אוֹתִי		You have liberated me,
	יְהוָה אֵל אֱמֶת׃		Adonoy, Almighty of truth.
ז	שָׂנֵאתִי הַשֹּׁמְרִים	7	I hate those who anticipate [salvation from]
	הַבְלֵי־שָׁוְא		useless vanities;
	וַאֲנִי אֶל־יְהוָה בָּטָחְתִּי׃		as for me, in Adonoy do I trust.
ח	אָגִילָה וְאֶשְׂמְחָה בְּחַסְדֶּךָ	8	I will exult and rejoice in Your kindness,
	אֲשֶׁר רָאִיתָ אֶת־עָנְיִי		for You have seen my affliction.
	יָדַעְתָּ בְּצָרוֹת נַפְשִׁי׃		You know the troubles of my soul.
ט	וְלֹא הִסְגַּרְתַּנִי	9	And You have not imprisoned me

בְּיַד־אוֹיֵב	in the hand of the enemy;
הֶעֱמַדְתָּ בַמֶּרְחָב רַגְלָי׃	[but] stood my feet in a wide [open] place.
י חָנֵּנִי יְהוָה	10 Favor me, Adonoy,
כִּי צַר־לִי	for I am in distress;
עָשְׁשָׁה בְכַעַס עֵינִי	dimmed by anger is my eye,
נַפְשִׁי וּבִטְנִי׃	my soul and my stomach [are wasted away].
יא כִּי כָלוּ בְיָגוֹן חַיַּי	11 For my life is spent in sorrow,
וּשְׁנוֹתַי בַּאֲנָחָה	and my years in sighing;
כָּשַׁל בַּעֲוֹנִי כֹחִי	because of my iniquity my strength failed,
וַעֲצָמַי עָשֵׁשׁוּ׃	and my bones are wasted away.
יב מִכָּל־צֹרְרַי	12 Because of all my adversaries
הָיִיתִי חֶרְפָּה	I became disgraced,
וְלִשְׁכֵנַי ׀ מְאֹד	and to my neighbors exceedingly;
וּפַחַד לִמְיֻדָּעָי	and a dread to my acquaintances,
רֹאַי בַּחוּץ נָדְדוּ מִמֶּנִּי׃	those who see me outside flee from me.
יג נִשְׁכַּחְתִּי כְּמֵת	13 I am forgotten like a dead man
מִלֵּב	from the heart,
הָיִיתִי כִּכְלִי אֹבֵד׃	I have become like a lost vessel.
יד כִּי שָׁמַעְתִּי ׀ דִּבַּת רַבִּים	14 For I have heard the whispering of many,
מָגוֹר מִסָּבִיב	terror all around;
בְּהִוָּסְדָם יַחַד עָלַי	when they took counsel together against me,
לָקַחַת נַפְשִׁי זָמָמוּ׃	they planned to take my soul [life].
טו וַאֲנִי ׀	15 But, as for me,
עָלֶיךָ בָטַחְתִּי יְהוָה	in You I have trusted, Adonoy,
אָמַרְתִּי אֱלֹהַי אָתָּה׃	I said, ``You are my God."
טז בְּיָדְךָ עִתֹּתָי	16 In Your hand are my times;
הַצִּילֵנִי מִיַּד־אוֹיְבַי	rescue me from the hand of my enemies
וּמֵרֹדְפָי׃	and from my pursuers.
יז הָאִירָה פָנֶיךָ עַל־עַבְדֶּךָ	17 Shine Your face upon Your servant,
הוֹשִׁיעֵנִי בְחַסְדֶּךָ׃	deliver me in Your kindness.
יח יְהוָה אַל־אֵבוֹשָׁה	18 Adonoy, let me not be ashamed
כִּי קְרָאתִיךָ	for having called out to You;
יֵבֹשׁוּ רְשָׁעִים	let the wicked be ashamed,
יִדְּמוּ לִשְׁאוֹל׃	let them be silenced in the grave.
יט תֵּאָלַמְנָה שִׂפְתֵי שָׁקֶר	19 Let them be muted, the lying lips,
הַדֹּבְרוֹת	[lips] which speak
עַל־צַדִּיק עָתָק	arrogantly against the righteous,
בְּגַאֲוָה וָבוּז׃	with pride and contempt.
כ מָה רַב־טוּבְךָ	20 . How abundant is Your goodness

Saul Attacking David

אֲשֶׁר־צָפַנְתָּ			which You have hidden as a treasure
לִּירֵאֶיךָ			for those who fear You;
פָּעַלְתָּ			which You have made
לַחֹסִים בָּךְ			for those who take refuge in You
נֶגֶד בְּנֵי אָדָם׃			in the presence of the sons of man.
תַּסְתִּירֵם |	כא	21	Conceal them
בְּסֵתֶר פָּנֶיךָ			in the covert of Your presence,
מֵרֻכְסֵי אִישׁ			from bands of the wicked;
תִּצְפְּנֵם בְּסֻכָּה			hide them as a treasure in a shelter
מֵרִיב לְשֹׁנוֹת׃			from the strife of tongues.
בָּרוּךְ יְהוָה	כב	22	Blessed is Adonoy
כִּי הִפְלִיא חַסְדּוֹ לִי			for His wondrous kindness He has shown me
בְּעִיר מָצוֹר׃			in a city besieged.
וַאֲנִי | אָמַרְתִּי בְחָפְזִי	כג	23	And I said in my haste,
נִגְרַזְתִּי מִנֶּגֶד עֵינֶיךָ			``I am cut off from before Your eyes,"
אָכֵן שָׁמַעְתָּ קוֹל תַּחֲנוּנַי			but You heard the voice of my supplications
בְּשַׁוְּעִי אֵלֶיךָ׃			when I cried out to You.
אֶהֱבוּ אֶת־יְהוָה כָּל־חֲסִידָיו	כד	24	Love Adonoy, all His devoted ones;
אֱמוּנִים נֹצֵר יְהוָה			the faithful, Adonoy preserves.
וּמְשַׁלֵּם עַל־יֶתֶר			And He repays with exactness
עֹשֵׂה גַאֲוָה׃			those who act haughtily.
חִזְקוּ וְיַאֲמֵץ לְבַבְכֶם	כה	25	Be strong and take courage in your hearts,
כָּל־הַמְיַחֲלִים לַיהוָה׃			all who wait for Adonoy.

פרק לב Chapter 32

Weekly Cycle	Monthly Cycle	Book Number
Monday	5th day of the month	Book 1

Author

דָּוִד הַמֶּלֶךְ—King David—the second king of Israel and father of the Davidic royal and messianic dynasty. David composed over seventy of the 150 psalms of Sefer Tehillim.

When & Why

David wrote this psalm after his sin with Bath Sheba as a way to bolster his faith in the power of penance and in God's readiness to forgive sinners who repent.

Genre

Psalm of Wisdom - This psalm contains teachings and wise advice and is meant to instruct people on how to live a Godly life.

Chapter Summary

King David addresses those whose sins have caused them to despair of personal salvation. Nothing can stand in the way of repentance, he tells them. If one admits his sins, expresses regret, and bridles his passions, there indeed is hope!

This psalm consists of eleven verses, subdivided into two parts.
Verses 1 & 2 serve as an introduction, with declarations of "Fortunate is he." "Fortunate is the man."
In verses 3-7, King David describes his suffering, confession and ensuing salvation.
In verses 8-11, he humbly acknowledges lessons learned, with a call to rejoice in God.

Technical Terminology

מַשְׂכִּיל—Maskil—a discerning person; alternatively, a giver of instruction, perhaps denoting a translator of the chapter (Rashi).
סֶלָה—Selah—While its meaning is unclear, the most familiar opinion is that it is a musical notation, instructing the Levitical orchestra to pause its singing and playing of instruments. Alternatively, "Selah" may mean "everlasting".

Shimush Tehillim - When to Say

For mercy (say daily)—Verse 10 states: "But he who trusts in Adonoy kindness surrounds him."

Where in the Siddur

Verse 8 is found in Yesod HaTeshuvah (Foundation of Repentance) recited in some congregations on the eve of Rosh Hashanah. Some recite Yesod HaTeshuvah immediately following Hatarat Nedarim (Annulment of Vows).

Talmud on Tehillim

Verse 6: "עַל זֹאת, יִתְפַּלֵּל כָּל חָסִיד אֵלֶיךָ לְעֵת מְצֹא"—"For this, let every man of devotion pray to You, in a time when You may be found."

The Midrash Tanchuma, Bereishit 43:9, deduces from this verse that one should pray to find a suitable spouse.

Menorah Glass Pendant (Courtesy of the Shlomo Moussaieff Collection)

פֶּרֶק לב

א לְדָוִד מַשְׂכִּיל
אַשְׁרֵי נְשׂוּי־פֶּשַׁע
כְּסוּי חֲטָאָה׃
ב אַשְׁרֵי אָדָם
לֹא יַחְשֹׁב יְהוָה לוֹ עָוֺן
וְאֵין בְּרוּחוֹ רְמִיָּה׃
ג כִּי־הֶחֱרַשְׁתִּי
בָּלוּ עֲצָמָי
בְּשַׁאֲגָתִי כָּל־הַיּוֹם׃

Chapter 32

1 [A Psalm] of David, an instruction.
Fortunate is he whose transgression is borne,
whose sin is covered.
2 Fortunate is the man
to whom Adonoy does not count iniquity,
and in whose spirit there is no deceit.
3 When I kept silent,
my bones wasted away
through my groaning all day long.

ד כִּי ׀ יוֹמָם וָלַיְלָה	4 For day and night
תִּכְבַּד עָלַי יָדֶךָ	Your hand was heavy upon me;
נֶהְפַּךְ לְשַׁדִּי	my marrow turned dry
בְּחַרְבֹנֵי קַיִץ סֶלָה׃	as by the droughts of summer, Selah.
ה חַטָּאתִי אוֹדִיעֲךָ	5 [Therefore] my sin I acknowledge to You,
וַעֲוֺנִי לֹא־כִסִּיתִי	and my iniquity I do not hide;
אָמַרְתִּי	[when] I said,
אוֹדֶה עֲלֵי פְשָׁעַי לַיהוָה	``I will confess my transgressions to Adonoy,"
וְאַתָּה נָשָׂאתָ	You had [already] forgiven
עֲוֺן חַטָּאתִי סֶלָה׃	the iniquity of my sin, Selah.
ו עַל־זֹאת	6 For this,
יִתְפַּלֵּל כָּל־חָסִיד ׀ אֵלֶיךָ	let every man of devotion pray to You,
לְעֵת מְצֹא	in a time when You may be found;
רַק לְשֵׁטֶף מַיִם רַבִּים	indeed when mighty waters threaten
אֵלָיו לֹא יַגִּיעוּ׃	they will not reach him.
ז אַתָּה ׀ סֵתֶר לִי	7 You are my shelter,
מִצַּר תִּצְּרֵנִי	from distress You preserve me;
רָנֵּי פַלֵּט	with glad song of rescue,
תְּסוֹבְבֵנִי סֶלָה׃	You envelop me, Selah.
ח אַשְׂכִּילְךָ ׀ וְאוֹרְךָ	8 I will instruct you and teach you
בְּדֶרֶךְ־זוּ תֵלֵךְ	in the way in which you should go;
אִיעֲצָה עָלֶיךָ עֵינִי׃	I will signal you with [the winking of] my eye.
ט אַל־תִּהְיוּ ׀ כְּסוּס כְּפֶרֶד	9 Be not as the horse or as the mule,
אֵין הָבִין	devoid of understanding;
בְּמֶתֶג־וָרֶסֶן	who with a bit and bridle
עֶדְיוֹ לִבְלוֹם	must be restrained when being groomed,
בַּל קְרֹב אֵלֶיךָ׃	so that they do not come near you.
י רַבִּים מַכְאוֹבִים לָרָשָׁע	10 Many are the sorrows of the wicked
וְהַבּוֹטֵחַ בַּיהוָה	But he who trusts in Adonoy
חֶסֶד יְסוֹבְבֶנּוּ׃	kindness surrounds him.
יא שִׂמְחוּ בַיהוָה	11 Rejoice in Adonoy,
וְגִילוּ צַדִּיקִים	and exult, righteous ones,
וְהַרְנִינוּ	and sing for joy
כָּל־יִשְׁרֵי־לֵב׃	all who are upright in heart.

פרק לג Chapter 33

Weekly Cycle	Monthly Cycle	Book Number
Monday	5th day of the month	Book 1

Author

Unknown

When & Why

David might have written this psalm as a prayer of thanks to God for delivering him from his opponents in battle.

Genre

Psalm of Praise – This is a psalm of celebration, often the result of a victory. It declares God's goodness and urges all of creation to worship.

Chapter Summary

The singer composed this psalm on the occasion of a great victory achieved by him and his people. He proclaims that deliverance is not due to the might of the victors, but rather comes by the will of God. Some suggest that the author is allegorically referring to man's ongoing, inner struggle.

This psalm consists of twenty-two verses, subdivided into three parts.
Verses 1-3 serve as an introduction, in which the psalmist calls for praise of God.
In verses 4-19, he describes and expands upon God's praises.
In verses 20-22, he concludes with his expressions of trust in God, as well as prays for His lovingkindness.

Musical Instruments

כִּנּוֹר—Kinor—A Small Handheld Harp - played with a plecturm (pick).
נֶבֶל עָשׂוֹר—Nevel Asor—A Ten-Stringed Lyre

Shimush Tehillim - When to Say

For a place that suffers from distress—Verse 14 states: "From His dwelling place, He watches intently all inhabitants of the earth."
For a woman whose children pass away—Verse 19 proclaims: "To rescue their soul from death."

Where in the Siddur

Recited as part of Pesukei Dezimra (introductory Verses of Praise to the the Shacharit morning service) of Yom Tov (Festivals), and Hoshana Rabbah (seventh day of Sukkot).
Verse 1 is included in Shochein Ad, an addition to Pesukei Dezimra of Shabbat and Yom Tov.
Verses 9-11, rearranged, comprise part of Yehi Chevod, the paragraph preceding Ashrei of Pesukei Dezimra.
Verses 20-22 comprise a part of Pesukei Dezimra.

Verse 22 is included in Tachanun (Penitential Prayer) following the Amidah Of Shacharit, as well as in Baruch Hashem Le'olam, one of the blessings of Shema of Ma'ariv.

Recited by some as part of Tashlich—a prayer recited on Rosh HaShanah afternoon, usually by a body of water, in which we beseech God to "cast away" our sins into the depths of the sea.

Verse 15 serves as the basis for the tenth of Maimonides' thirteen Principles of Faith.

Talmud on Tehillim

Verse 5: "אֹהֵב צְדָקָה וּמִשְׁפָּט"—"He loves righteousness and justice."

The Talmud, Sukkah 49b, teaches: "One who does what is just and right is considered to have filled the world with kindness."

Verse 6: "בִּדְבַר יְהוָה, שָׁמַיִם נַעֲשׂוּ; וּבְרוּחַ פִּיו, כָּל צְבָאָם"—"By the word of God, the heavens were made, and by the breath of His mouth, all their hosts."

The Talmud, Shabbat 119b, deduces from this verse that speech is considered equivalent to action, for the heavens were made simply by God's spoken word.

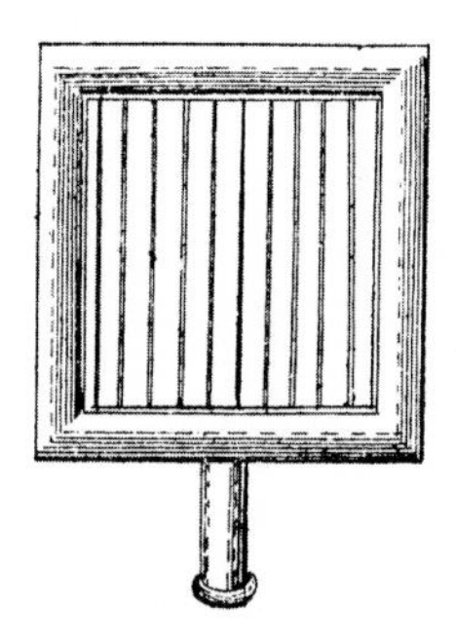

Nevel Asor - A Ten-Stringed Handheld Lyre

פֶּרֶק לג	Chapter 33
א רַנְּנוּ צַדִּיקִים בַּיהוָה לַיְשָׁרִים נָאוָה תְהִלָּה:	1 Joyfully exult in Adonoy, [you] righteous ones, for the upright, praise is fitting.
ב הוֹדוּ לַיהוָה בְּכִנּוֹר בְּנֵבֶל עָשׂוֹר זַמְּרוּ־לוֹ:	2 Thank Adonoy with the harp, with the ten-stringed lyre sing to Him.
ג שִׁירוּ־לוֹ שִׁיר חָדָשׁ הֵיטִיבוּ נַגֵּן בִּתְרוּעָה:	3 Sing Him a new song, play skillfully with jubilation.
ד כִּי־יָשָׁר דְּבַר־יְהוָה וְכָל־מַעֲשֵׂהוּ בֶּאֱמוּנָה:	4 For upright is the word of Adonoy and all His deeds [are done] with faithfulness.
ה אֹהֵב צְדָקָה וּמִשְׁפָּט חֶסֶד יְהוָה מָלְאָה הָאָרֶץ:	5 He loves righteousness and justice the kindliness of Adonoy fills the earth.
ו בִּדְבַר יְהוָה שָׁמַיִם נַעֲשׂוּ וּבְרוּחַ פִּיו כָּל־צְבָאָם:	6 By the word of God, the heavens were made, and by the breath of His mouth, all their hosts.
ז כֹּנֵס כַּנֵּד מֵי הַיָּם	7 He gathers like a mound the waters of the sea,

נֹתֵן בְּאֹצָרוֹת תְּהוֹמוֹת׃

He places in vaults the deep waters.

ח יִירְאוּ מֵיְהוָה כָּל־הָאָרֶץ
מִמֶּנּוּ יָגוּרוּ
כָּל־יֹשְׁבֵי תֵבֵל׃

8 Fear Adonoy, all the earth,
of Him, be in dread
all dwellers of the inhabited world.

ט כִּי הוּא אָמַר וַיֶּהִי
הוּא־צִוָּה וַיַּעֲמֹד׃

9 For He spoke and it became;
He commanded and it stood.

י יְהוָה הֵפִיר עֲצַת־גּוֹיִם
הֵנִיא מַחְשְׁבוֹת עַמִּים׃

10 Adonoy annuls the counsel of nations,
He disrupts the intention of peoples.

יא עֲצַת יְהוָה לְעוֹלָם תַּעֲמֹד
מַחְשְׁבוֹת לִבּוֹ
לְדֹר וָדֹר׃

11 The counsel of Adonoy will stand forever,
the thoughts of His heart
throughout all generations.

יב אַשְׁרֵי הַגּוֹי
אֲשֶׁר־יְהוָה אֱלֹהָיו
הָעָם | בָּחַר לְנַחֲלָה לוֹ׃

12 Fortunate is the nation
for whom Adonoy is their God,
the people He chose as His heritage.

יג מִשָּׁמַיִם הִבִּיט יְהוָה
רָאָה אֶת־כָּל־בְּנֵי הָאָדָם׃

13 From the heavens, Adonoy looks [down],
He sees all mankind.

יד מִמְּכוֹן־שִׁבְתּוֹ
הִשְׁגִּיחַ
אֶל כָּל־יֹשְׁבֵי הָאָרֶץ׃

14 From His dwelling place,
He watches intently
all the inhabitants of the earth.

טו הַיֹּצֵר יַחַד לִבָּם
הַמֵּבִין אֶל־כָּל־מַעֲשֵׂיהֶם׃

15 He forms their hearts all together;
He perceives all their doings.

טז אֵין־הַמֶּלֶךְ נוֹשָׁע בְּרָב־חָיִל
גִּבּוֹר לֹא־יִנָּצֵל
בְּרָב־כֹּחַ׃

16 A king is not saved by a great army;
a mighty man is not rescued
with [his] great strength.

יז שֶׁקֶר הַסּוּס
לִתְשׁוּעָה
וּבְרֹב חֵילוֹ
לֹא יְמַלֵּט׃

17 A horse is deceptive [assurance]
for deliverance,
and with its great strength
it provides no escape.

יח הִנֵּה עֵין יְהוָה
אֶל־יְרֵאָיו
לַמְיַחֲלִים לְחַסְדּוֹ׃

18 Behold, the eye of Adonoy
is on those who fear Him,
on those who wait for His kindliness.

יט לְהַצִּיל מִמָּוֶת נַפְשָׁם
וּלְחַיּוֹתָם בָּרָעָב׃

19 To rescue their soul from death,
and to keep them alive during famine.

כ נַפְשֵׁנוּ חִכְּתָה לַיהוָה
עֶזְרֵנוּ וּמָגִנֵּנוּ הוּא׃

20 Our soul yearned for Adonoy,
our help and our shield is He.

כא כִּי־בוֹ יִשְׂמַח לִבֵּנוּ
כִּי בְשֵׁם קָדְשׁוֹ בָטָחְנוּ׃

21 For in Him our heart will rejoice,
for in His holy Name we trust,

כב יְהִי־חַסְדְּךָ יְהוָה עָלֵינוּ
כַּאֲשֶׁר יִחַלְנוּ לָךְ׃

22 May Your kindliness, Adonoy, be upon us,
as we have waited for You.

פרק לד Chapter 34

Weekly Cycle	Monthly Cycle	Book Number
Monday	5th day of the month	Book 1

Author

דָוִד הַמֶּלֶךְ—King David—the second king of Israel and father of the Davidic royal and messianic dynasty. David composed over seventy of the 150 psalms of Sefer Tehillim.

When & Why

David wrote this psalm as a prayer of thanks to God, after escaping from Saul and arriving safely in the Philistine city of Gat.

Genre

Psalm of Individual Thanksgiving - This psalm emphasizes gratitude for what God has done for the individual.

Psalm of Wisdom - This psalm contains teachings and wise advice and is meant to instruct people on how to live a Godly life.

Acrostic - A literary composition in which the writer has used the letters of the Hebrew alphabet in their order as the initial letters for a sequence of verses. i.e. א.ב.ג.ד

Chapter Summary

This psalm relates David's miraculous salvation from the hands of Achish, king of Gath.

The verses are arranged alphabetically (excluding the letter vav), indicating the need for every man to praise God.

This psalm consists of twenty-three verses, subdivided into five parts. Verse 1 serves as a heading.

Verse 1 serves as a heading.

In verses 2-4, King David praises God.

In verses 5-8, he speaks of his deliverance from all the calamities of which he was fearful.

In verses 9-11, he calls upon the congregation of Israel to fear God and seek His refuge.

In verses 12-15, he outlines the principles of conduct that a God-fearing person should follow.

In verses 16-23, the Psalmist praises God who destroys the wicked and saves the righteous.

Shimush Tehillim - When to Say

For traveling on a journey—The opening verse describes the sudden, successful exit of King David from Avimelech, the Philistine king.

Before delivering a speech—Verse 5 states: "from all my fears He saved me", a reference to David's fear of speaking up before Avimelech.

Before facing an important authority—Verse 18 states: "They cry out and Adonoy hears and from all their troubles, He saves them."

Where in the Siddur

Recited in its entirety as part of Pesukei Dezimra (introductory Verses of Praise to the Shacharit morning service) of Shabbat, Yom Tov (Festivals), and Hoshana Rabbah.
Verse 4 is recited upon removing the Torah scroll from the Aron Kodesh (Holy Ark).
Verses 10 & 11 are part of the final paragraph of Birkat HaMazon (Grace after Meals).
Verse 14 forms the basis of the closing paragraph of the Amidah (Silent Meditation).

Biblical Personalities

אֲבִימֶלֶךְ—Avimelech—a Philistine king who freed King David when David disguised himself by pretending to be insane. Avimelech is technically a title of all Philistine kings, much as Pharoh is a title of all Egyptian kings.

Contemporary Song

Verses 13-15

Talmud on Tehillim

Verse 4: "גַּדְּלוּ לַיהוָה אִתִּי; וּנְרוֹמְמָה שְׁמוֹ יַחְדָּו"— "Declare the greatness of Adonoy with me, and let us exalt His Name together."
The Talmud, Berachot 45a, instructs that three who eat bread together are required to join in zimun—an invitation to bless God as a community. The Talmud further deduces that it is preferable to recite Birkat HaMazon (Grace after Meals) in a group of three or more. Furthermore, three who eat together are not permitted to break up the group and recite Birkat Hamazon individually.

פרק לד

א לְדָוִד
בְּשַׁנּוֹתוֹ אֶת־טַעְמוֹ
לִפְנֵי אֲבִימֶלֶךְ
וַיְגָרְשֵׁהוּ
וַיֵּלַךְ׃
ב אֲבָרְכָה אֶת־יְהוָה בְּכָל־עֵת
תָּמִיד תְּהִלָּתוֹ בְּפִי׃
ג בַּיהוָה תִּתְהַלֵּל נַפְשִׁי
יִשְׁמְעוּ עֲנָוִים וְיִשְׂמָחוּ׃
ד גַּדְּלוּ לַיהוָה אִתִּי
וּנְרוֹמְמָה שְׁמוֹ יַחְדָּו׃
ה דָּרַשְׁתִּי אֶת־יְהוָה וְעָנָנִי
וּמִכָּל־מְגוּרוֹתַי הִצִּילָנִי׃
ו הִבִּיטוּ אֵלָיו וְנָהָרוּ
וּפְנֵיהֶם אַל־יֶחְפָּרוּ׃
ז זֶה עָנִי קָרָא וַיהוָה שָׁמֵעַ
וּמִכָּל־צָרוֹתָיו הוֹשִׁיעוֹ׃

Chapter 34

1 Of David,
When he acted insane
in the presence of Avimelech
and he [Avimelech] drove him away,
and he [David] left.
2 I will bless Adonoy at all times
constantly is His praise in my mouth.
3 In Adonoy does my soul take pride,
the humble will hear [this] and rejoice.
4 Declare the greatness of Adonoy with me,
and let us exalt His Name together.
5 I sought Adonoy and He responded to me;
and from all my fears He saved me.
6 [Those who] look to Him are enlightened
and their faces are never darkened [humiliated].
7 This poor man called and Adonoy heard;
and from all his troubles, He delivered him.

ח	חֹנֶה מַלְאַךְ־יְהוָה סָבִיב לִירֵאָיו וַיְחַלְּצֵם׃	8	The angel of Adonoy encamps around those who fear Him and sets them free.
ט	טַעֲמוּ וּרְאוּ כִּי־טוֹב יְהוָה אַשְׁרֵי הַגֶּבֶר יֶחֱסֶה־בּוֹ׃	9	Taste and see that Adonoy is good; fortunate is the man who takes refuge in Him.
י	יְראוּ אֶת־יְהוָה קְדֹשָׁיו כִּי־אֵין מַחְסוֹר לִירֵאָיו׃	10	Fear Adonoy, [you] His holy ones, for there is no deprivation for those who fear Him.
יא	כְּפִירִים רָשׁוּ וְרָעֵבוּ וְדֹרְשֵׁי יְהוָה לֹא־יַחְסְרוּ כָל־טוֹב׃	11	Young lions feel want and hunger, but those who seek Adonoy will not lack any good thing.
יב	לְכוּ־בָנִים שִׁמְעוּ־לִי יִרְאַת יְהוָה אֲלַמֶּדְכֶם׃	12	Come children, listen to me, fear of Adonoy will I teach you.
יג	מִי־הָאִישׁ הֶחָפֵץ חַיִּים אֹהֵב יָמִים לִרְאוֹת טוֹב׃	13	Who is the man who desires life, and loves days that he may see good?
יד	נְצֹר לְשׁוֹנְךָ מֵרָע וּשְׂפָתֶיךָ מִדַּבֵּר מִרְמָה׃	14	Guard your tongue from evil, and your lips from speaking deceitfully.
טו	סוּר מֵרָע וַעֲשֵׂה־טוֹב בַּקֵּשׁ שָׁלוֹם וְרָדְפֵהוּ׃	15	Turn from evil and do good, seek peace and pursue it.
טז	עֵינֵי יְהוָה אֶל־צַדִּיקִים וְאָזְנָיו אֶל־שַׁוְעָתָם׃	16	The eyes of Adonoy are toward the righteous, and His ears [are open] to their cry.
יז	פְּנֵי יְהוָה בְּעֹשֵׂי רָע לְהַכְרִית מֵאֶרֶץ זִכְרָם׃	17	The face of Adonoy is set against evildoers to excise from earth, their memory.
יח	צָעֲקוּ וַיהוָה שָׁמֵעַ וּמִכָּל־צָרוֹתָם הִצִּילָם׃	18	They cry out and Adonoy hears and from all their troubles, He saves them.
יט	קָרוֹב יְהוָה לְנִשְׁבְּרֵי־לֵב וְאֶת־דַּכְּאֵי־רוּחַ יוֹשִׁיעַ׃	19	Adonoy is close to the broken-hearted and those crushed in spirit, He delivers.
כ	רַבּוֹת רָעוֹת צַדִּיק וּמִכֻּלָּם יַצִּילֶנּוּ יְהוָה׃	20	Many evils befall a righteous man, and from all of them, Adonoy saves him.
כא	שֹׁמֵר כָּל־עַצְמוֹתָיו אַחַת מֵהֵנָּה לֹא נִשְׁבָּרָה׃	21	He preserves all his bones, not one of them is broken.
כב	תְּמוֹתֵת רָשָׁע רָעָה וְשֹׂנְאֵי צַדִּיק יֶאְשָׁמוּ׃	22	The cause of death of the wicked is evil; and the haters of the righteous are doomed.
כג	פּוֹדֶה יְהוָה נֶפֶשׁ עֲבָדָיו וְלֹא יֶאְשְׁמוּ כָּל־הַחֹסִים בּוֹ׃	23	Adonoy liberates the soul of His servants, and none are doomed who take refuge in Him.

סור מרע
ועשה טוב
בקש שלום
ורדפהו

Turn from evil and do good, seek peace and pursue it.

פרק לה Chapter 35

Weekly Cycle	Monthly Cycle	Book Number
Monday	6th day of the month	Book 1

Author

דָּוִד הַמֶּלֶךְ—King David—the second king of Israel and father of the Davidic royal and messianic dynasty. David composed over seventy of the 150 psalms of Sefer Tehillim.

When & Why

David wrote this psalm as a prayer to God that He should fight Saul on David's behalf and rescue David without David needing to kill Saul.

Genre

Psalm of Individual Lament - This psalm was written from the perspective of the individual worshipper, who cries out to God in his time of need. It is characterized as an address to God involving a complaint, followed by a request and ending with an expression of trust.

Chapter Summary

King David pleads for Divine assistance in the wars against his enemies, both those who openly oppose him and those who repay his friendship with hostility.

This psalm consists of twenty-eight verses, subdivided into three parts.
In verses 1-10, King David prays for the defeat of his enemies.
In verses 11-18, he further complains of the treachery of his enemies.
In verses 19-28, he prays for the day that God will only be recognized and praised for His salvation.

Shimush Tehillim - When to Say

To overcome people who verbally attack—The opening verse states: "Strive, Adonoy, against those who strive against me; battle against those who battle against me."

Where in the Siddur

Verse 10 is part of Nishmat Kol Chai, the closing paragraph of Pesukei DeZimra (introductory Verses of Praise to the Shacharit morning service) of Shabbat and Yom Tov (Festivals).

Talmud on Tehillim

Verse 13: "וַאֲנִי, בַּחֲלוֹתָם לְבוּשִׁי שָׂק"—"But as for me, when they were sick, my clothing was sackcloth." The Talmud, Berachot 12b, deduces from here that a Torah scholar who does not pray for a sick person will in turn be afflicted by sickness himself.

פֶּרֶק לה

א לְדָוִד ׀
רִיבָה יְהוָה
אֶת־יְרִיבַי
לְחַם אֶת־לֹחֲמָי׃
ב הַחֲזֵק מָגֵן וְצִנָּה
וְקוּמָה בְּעֶזְרָתִי׃
ג וְהָרֵק חֲנִית
וּסְגֹר לִקְרַאת רֹדְפָי
אֱמֹר לְנַפְשִׁי
יְשֻׁעָתֵךְ אָנִי׃
ד יֵבֹשׁוּ וְיִכָּלְמוּ
מְבַקְשֵׁי נַפְשִׁי
יִסֹּגוּ אָחוֹר וְיַחְפְּרוּ
חֹשְׁבֵי רָעָתִי׃
ה יִהְיוּ כְּמֹץ לִפְנֵי־רוּחַ
וּמַלְאַךְ יְהוָה דּוֹחֶה׃
ו יְהִי־דַרְכָּם חֹשֶׁךְ וַחֲלַקְלַקּוֹת
וּמַלְאַךְ יְהוָה רֹדְפָם׃
ז כִּי־חִנָּם
טָמְנוּ־לִי שַׁחַת רִשְׁתָּם
חִנָּם חָפְרוּ לְנַפְשִׁי׃
ח תְּבוֹאֵהוּ שׁוֹאָה לֹא־יֵדָע
וְרִשְׁתּוֹ אֲשֶׁר־טָמַן
תִּלְכְּדוֹ
בְּשׁוֹאָה יִפָּל־בָּהּ׃
ט וְנַפְשִׁי תָּגִיל בַּיהוָה
תָּשִׂישׂ בִּישׁוּעָתוֹ׃
י כָּל עַצְמוֹתַי ׀ תֹּאמַרְנָה
יְהוָה מִי כָמוֹךָ
מַצִּיל עָנִי
מֵחָזָק מִמֶּנּוּ
וְעָנִי וְאֶבְיוֹן
מִגֹּזְלוֹ׃
יא יְקוּמוּן עֵדֵי חָמָס
אֲשֶׁר לֹא־יָדַעְתִּי
יִשְׁאָלוּנִי׃
יב יְשַׁלְּמוּנִי רָעָה תַּחַת טוֹבָה

Chapter 35

1 Of David, [a Psalm].
Strive, Adonoy,
against those who strive against me;
battle against those who battle against me.
2 Take hold of shield and armour,
and rise up in my help.
3 And draw out the spear
and bar the way against my pursuers;
say to my soul,
``Your deliverance am I."
4 Let them be ashamed and disgraced,
those who seek my soul;
let them be turned back and humiliated,
those who devise my hurt.
5 Let them be as chaff before the wind,
with the angel of Adonoy thrusting them away.
6 Let their way be dark and slippery,
with the angel of Adonoy pursuing them.
7 For without cause
they camouflaged a pit for me with their net;
without cause have they dug [pits] for my soul.
8 Let desolation come upon him, unawares,
and as for his own net that he hid,
let it trap him,
in desolation let him fall.
9 And my soul will exult in Adonoy,
it will rejoice in His deliverance.
10 All my bones will say:
Adonoy! who is like You?"
You save the poor man
from one stronger than he,
and the poor and needy
from one who would rob him.
11 Malicious witnesses rise [against me]
things of which I know nothing
they demand of me.
12 They repay me evil for good;

שְׁכ֣וֹל לְנַפְשִׁי׃			bereavement for my soul.
וַאֲנִ֤י ׀ בַּחֲלוֹתָ֡ם	יג	13	But as for me, when they were sick,
לְב֬וּשִׁי שָׂ֗ק			my clothing was sackcloth,
עִנֵּ֣יתִי בַצּ֣וֹם נַפְשִׁ֑י			I afflicted my soul with fasting,
וּ֝תְפִלָּתִ֗י			and my prayer,
עַל־חֵיקִ֥י תָשֽׁוּב׃			upon my own bosom let it return.
כְּרֵֽעַ־כְּאָ֣ח לִ֭י	יד	14	As if it had been my friend or my brother
הִתְהַלָּ֑כְתִּי			I went about;
כַּאֲבֶל־אֵ֝֗ם			as one mourns for his mother,
קֹדֵ֥ר שַׁחֽוֹתִי׃			I mournfully bowed down.
וּבְצַלְעִ֣י שָׂמְח֣וּ	טו	15	But when I limped, they rejoiced
וְ֭נֶאֱסָפוּ			and gathered together—
נֶאֶסְפ֬וּ עָלַ֣י נֵ֭כִים			against me gathered the lame,
וְלֹ֣א יָדַ֑עְתִּי			and [even] those whom I do not know;
קָֽרְע֥וּ וְלֹא־דָֽמּוּ׃			they tore at me and did not cease.
בְּ֭חַנְפֵי לַעֲגֵ֣י	טז	16	For their flattery and mockery
מָע֑וֹג			[for which] they received [free] meals
חָרֹ֖ק עָלַ֣י שִׁנֵּֽימוֹ׃			they gnash at me with their teeth.
אֲדֹנָי֮ כַּמָּ֪ה תִּ֫רְאֶ֥ה	יז	17	My Master, how long will You look on?
הָשִׁ֣יבָה֮ נַ֭פְשִׁי מִשֹּׁאֵיהֶ֑ם			Return my soul from their desolation,
מִ֝כְּפִירִ֗ים יְחִידָתִֽי׃			from the lions my one and only soul.
א֭וֹדְךָ בְּקָהָ֣ל רָ֑ב	יח	18	I will thank You in a great congregation,
בְּעַ֖ם עָצ֣וּם אֲהַלְלֶֽךָּ׃			among a mighty gathering I will praise You.
אַֽל־יִשְׂמְחוּ־לִ֣י	יט	19	Let them not rejoice over me,
אֹיְבַ֣י שֶׁ֑קֶר			these, my enemies, who bear false witness;
שֹׂנְאַ֥י חִ֝נָּ֗ם			nor let those who hate me without cause
יִקְרְצוּ־עָֽיִן׃			wink their eye.
כִּ֤י לֹ֥א שָׁל֗וֹם יְדַ֫בֵּ֥רוּ	כ	20	For it is not of peace that they speak;
וְעַ֥ל רִגְעֵי־אֶ֑רֶץ			but against the oppressed in the land,
דִּבְרֵ֥י מִ֝רְמ֗וֹת יַחֲשֹׁבֽוּן׃			deceitful matters they scheme.
וַיַּרְחִ֥יבוּ עָלַ֗י פִּ֫יהֶ֥ם	כא	21	And they opened their mouths against me,
אָ֭מְרוּ הֶאָ֥ח ׀ הֶאָ֗ח			they said, "O joy, O joy,
רָאֲתָ֥ה עֵינֵֽינוּ׃			our eye has seen it."
רָאִ֣יתָה יְ֭הוָה	כב	22	You have seen, Adonoy,
אַֽל־תֶּחֱרַ֑שׁ			keep not silent,
אֲ֝דֹנָ֗י אַל־תִּרְחַ֥ק מִמֶּֽנִּי׃			my Master be not far from me.
הָעִ֣ירָה וְ֭הָקִיצָה	כג	23	Rouse and awake [the Heavenly Tribunal]
לְמִשְׁפָּטִ֑י			for my judgment,
אֱלֹהַ֖י וַאדֹנָ֣י לְרִיבִֽי׃			my God and my Master for my cause.

Pergamon Lion

כד שְׁפָטֵנִי כְצִדְקְךָ
יְהוָה אֱלֹהָי
וְאַל־יִשְׂמְחוּ־לִי׃

24 Judge me according to Your righteousness,
Adonoy, my God;
and let them not rejoice over me.

כה אַל־יֹאמְרוּ בְלִבָּם
הֶאָח נַפְשֵׁנוּ
אַל־יֹאמְרוּ
בִּלַּעֲנוּהוּ׃

25 Let them not say in their heart
O joy, we have our desire";
let them not say,
"We have swallowed him up."

כו יֵבֹשׁוּ
וְיַחְפְּרוּ | יַחְדָּו
שְׂמֵחֵי רָעָתִי
יִלְבְּשׁוּ־בֹשֶׁת וּכְלִמָּה
הַמַּגְדִּילִים עָלָי׃

26 Let them be ashamed
and humiliated together,
those who rejoice at my hurt;
let them be clothed in shame and disgrace,
those who magnify themselves against me.

כז יָרֹנּוּ וְיִשְׂמְחוּ
חֲפֵצֵי צִדְקִי
וְיֹאמְרוּ תָמִיד
יִגְדַּל יְהוָה
הֶחָפֵץ שְׁלוֹם עַבְדּוֹ׃

27 Let those shout for joy and rejoice
who desire my righteousness;
let them say always,
"Magnified be Adonoy,"
He Who desires the peace of His servant.

כח וּלְשׁוֹנִי
תֶּהְגֶּה צִדְקֶךָ
כָּל־הַיּוֹם תְּהִלָּתֶךָ׃

28 And my tongue
will speak of Your righteousness,
all day long, of Your praise.

פרק לו Chapter 36

Weekly Cycle	Monthly Cycle	Book Number
Monday	6th day of the month	Book 1

Author

דָּוִד הַמֶּלֶךְ—King David—the second king of Israel and father of the Davidic royal and messianic dynasty. David composed over seventy of the 150 psalms of Sefer Tehillim.

When & Why

David wrote this psalm about the heretics who pretend they are righteous and lie about their true beliefs.

Genre

Psalm of Individual Lament - This psalm was written from the perspective of the individual worshipper, who cries out to God in his time of need. It is characterized as an address to God involving a complaint, followed by a request and ending with an expression of trust.

Psalm of Wisdom - This psalm contains teachings and wise advice and is meant to instruct people on how to live a Godly life.

Chapter Summary

King David warns man against being led astray by the false arguments of the wicked. Man must know and acknowledge his Master, David implores, and realize that it is He who dispenses reward for good and retribution for evil.

This psalm consists of thirteen verses, subdivided into three parts. The first verse serves as a heading.

In verses 2-5, King David describes the thoughts and actions of the wicked.

In verses 6-10, he expresses his trust that God's lovingkindness is so great that " in the heavens is Your kindness, Your faithfulness is as far as the skies." He also speaks of God's faithfulness to those who keep His covenant.

In verses 11-13, the Psalmist offers a prayer for protection against the wicked.

Introductory Word

לַמְנַצֵּחַ—Lamnatsei'ach—To the Conductor

Shimush Tehillim - When to Say

For protection against evil tidings—Verse 12 states: "and let not the hand of the wicked move me away."

Where in the Siddur

Verse 7 is one of the verses of Tzidkatcha, a short prayer following the Amidah of Minchah (afternoon service) of Shabbat. It is interesting to note that all three verses of this prayer begin with the word "tzidkatcha", literally meaning "Your righteousness".

Verses 8-11 are recited following the wrapping of the Tallit prior to Shacharit (morning service).

פֶּרֶק לו

Chapter 36

א לַמְנַצֵּחַ ׀
לְעֶבֶד־יְהֹוָה לְדָוִד׃

1 To the Chief Musician,
[a Psalm] of the servant of Adonoy, of David.

ב נְאֻם־פֶּשַׁע לָרָשָׁע
בְּקֶרֶב לִבִּי
אֵין־פַּחַד אֱלֹהִים לְנֶגֶד עֵינָיו׃

2 A discourse of transgression to the wicked
is in the midst of my heart;
there is no fear of God before his eyes.

ג כִּי־הֶחֱלִיק אֵלָיו בְּעֵינָיו
לִמְצֹא עֲוֺנוֹ
לִשְׂנֹא׃

3 For it smoothes [the way] before his eyes,
causing Him [God] to discover his iniquity
for which He will hate him.

ד דִּבְרֵי־פִיו
אָוֶן וּמִרְמָה
חָדַל לְהַשְׂכִּיל לְהֵיטִיב׃

4 The words of his mouth
[are] iniquity and deceit,
he has ceased to apply his mind to do good.

ה אָוֶן ׀ יַחְשֹׁב עַל־מִשְׁכָּבוֹ
יִתְיַצֵּב עַל־דֶּרֶךְ לֹא־טוֹב
רָע לֹא יִמְאָס׃

5 Iniquity he devises on his bed,
he sets himself on a path of no good;
evil he does not abhor.

ו יְהֹוָה בְּהַשָּׁמַיִם חַסְדֶּךָ
אֱמוּנָתְךָ עַד־שְׁחָקִים׃

6 Adonoy, in the heavens is Your kindness,
Your faithfulness is as far as the skies.

ז צִדְקָתְךָ ׀
כְּהַרְרֵי־אֵל
מִשְׁפָּטֶךָ תְּהוֹם רַבָּה
אָדָם־וּבְהֵמָה תוֹשִׁיעַ יְהֹוָה׃

7 Your righteousness
is like the mighty mountains,
Your judgements like the great deep;
man and beast, You deliver, Adonoy.

ח מַה־יָּקָר חַסְדְּךָ אֱלֹהִים
וּבְנֵי אָדָם
בְּצֵל כְּנָפֶיךָ יֶחֱסָיוּן׃

8 How precious is Your kindness, O God;
the children of man
take refuge in the shadow of Your wings.

ט יִרְוְיֻן
מִדֶּשֶׁן בֵּיתֶךָ
וְנַחַל עֲדָנֶיךָ
תַשְׁקֵם׃

9 They will be filled
from the abundance of Your House,
and from the stream of Your delights
You will give them to drink.

י כִּי־עִמְּךָ מְקוֹר חַיִּים
בְּאוֹרְךָ נִרְאֶה־אוֹר׃

10 For with You is the source of life,
in Your light shall we see light.

יא מְשֹׁךְ חַסְדְּךָ
לְיֹדְעֶיךָ
וְצִדְקָתְךָ לְיִשְׁרֵי־לֵב׃

11 Extend Your kindness
to those who know You,
and Your righteousness to the upright in heart.

יב אַל־תְּבוֹאֵנִי רֶגֶל גַּאֲוָה
וְיַד־רְשָׁעִים
אַל־תְּנִדֵנִי׃

12 Let not the foot of egoism, overtake me
and let not the hand of the wicked
move me away.

יג שָׁם נָפְלוּ פֹּעֲלֵי אָוֶן
דֹּחוּ
וְלֹא־יָכְלוּ קוּם׃

13 There have the workers of iniquity fallen,
they were thrust down
and were not able to rise.

פרק לז Chapter 37

Weekly Cycle	Monthly Cycle	Book Number
Monday	6th day of the month	Book 1

Author

דָּוִד הַמֶּלֶךְ—King David—the second king of Israel and father of the Davidic royal and messianic dynasty. David composed over seventy of the 150 psalms of Sefer Tehillim.

Genre

Psalm of Wisdom - This psalm contains teachings and wise advice and is meant to instruct people on how to live a Godly life.
Acrostic - A literary composition in which the writer has used the letters of the Hebrew alphabet in their order as the initial letters for a sequence of verses. i.e. א.ב.ג.ד

Chapter Summary

In this psalm, King David admonishes the Jewish People not to be impressed and discouraged by the capacity and success of evildoers. Their very success, he espouses, is, in the end, to their detriment.

This psalm consists of forty verses, subdivided into five sections. The verses are arranged, for the most part, in the order of the Hebrew alphabet.
In verses 1-11, The Psalmist teaches us that we should trust in God, for He will destroy the wicked, while the righteous will be rewarded with blessings and peace.
In verses 12-17, he expands upon this idea and declares that the righteous are saved from the sword of the wicked.
In verses 18-29, he speaks of the righteous man, who is saved from famine.
In verses 30-33, he further describes how the righteous man is saved from false charges.
Verses 34-40 serve as a conclusion, whereupon King David admonishes his people to put their trust in God and to take refuge in Him.

Shimush Tehillim - When to Say

For one who is drunk—Verse 33 states: "Adonoy will not leave him in his hand, nor will He condemn him when he is judged."

Where in the Siddur

Verse 21 is found in Pirkei Avot—Ethics of the Fathers, 2:14.
Verse 25 is included in the final paragraph of Birkat HaMazon (Grace After Meals).

Contemporary Song

Verse 25

Talmud on Tehillim

Verse 4: "וְהִתְעַנַּג עַל יְהוָה"—"Trust in Adonoy."

The Talmud, Shabbat 118b, learns from this verse that "all who express their true joy in Shabbat are granted their hearts' desires."

Verse 11: "וַעֲנָוִים יִירְשׁוּ אָרֶץ; וְהִתְעַנְּגוּ עַל רֹב שָׁלוֹם"—"And the humble will inherit the land, and they will delight themselves in the abundance of peace."

The Talmud, Sukkah 29b, deduces from this verse that those who publicly display their wealth, thereby arousing jealousy and anger in others, will in turn lose their riches.

Verse 32: "צוֹפֶה רָשָׁע לַצַּדִּיק, וּמְבַקֵּשׁ לַהֲמִיתוֹ"—"The wicked watches for the righteous and seeks to slay him."

The Talmud, Sukkah 52b, teaches that the evil inclination attempts daily to convince people to sin; without God's assistance, one would not be able to withstand its pressure. (See the Talmud, Kiddushin 30b, for further elaboration on this concept).

פֶּרֶק לז

א לְדָוִד ׀
אַל־תִּתְחַר בַּמְּרֵעִים
אַל־תְּקַנֵּא בְּעֹשֵׂי עַוְלָה׃

ב כִּי כֶחָצִיר מְהֵרָה יִמָּלוּ
וּכְיֶרֶק דֶּשֶׁא יִבּוֹלוּן׃

ג בְּטַח בַּיהוָה וַעֲשֵׂה־טוֹב
שְׁכָן־אֶרֶץ
וּרְעֵה אֱמוּנָה׃

ד וְהִתְעַנַּג עַל־יְהוָה
וְיִתֶּן־לְךָ מִשְׁאֲלֹת לִבֶּךָ׃

ה גּוֹל עַל־יְהוָה דַּרְכֶּךָ
וּבְטַח עָלָיו וְהוּא יַעֲשֶׂה׃

ו וְהוֹצִיא כָאוֹר
צִדְקֶךָ
וּמִשְׁפָּטֶךָ כַּצָּהֳרָיִם׃

ז דּוֹם ׀ לַיהוָה וְהִתְחוֹלֵל לוֹ
אַל־תִּתְחַר בְּמַצְלִיחַ דַּרְכּוֹ
בְּאִישׁ עֹשֶׂה מְזִמּוֹת׃

ח הֶרֶף מֵאַף וַעֲזֹב חֵמָה
אַל־תִּתְחַר
אַךְ־לְהָרֵעַ׃

ט כִּי־מְרֵעִים יִכָּרֵתוּן
וְקֹוֵי יְהוָה
הֵמָּה יִירְשׁוּ־אָרֶץ׃

Chapter 37

1 [A Psalm] of David.
Grieve not over [the success of] evildoers,
nor envy wrongdoers.

2 For like grass they will soon be cut,
and as the green herb, they will fade.

3 Trust in Adonoy and do good;
[that you may] dwell in the land
and be nourished by [your] faith.

4 And take delight in Adonoy,
and He will give you the desires of your heart.

5 Commit to Adonoy your path;
and trust in Him and He will do [for you].

6 And He will bring forth as the light,
your righteousness,
and your judgment as the noonday.

7 Be silent before Adonoy and hope unto Him;
grieve not over him who prospers in his way,
of the man who devises evil plans.

8 Cease from anger and forsake wrath,
do not grieve,
for it brings only harm.

9 For evildoers will be cut off;
but those who hope to Adonoy,
they will inherit the land.

י וְעוֹד מְעַט
וְאֵין רָשָׁע
וְהִתְבּוֹנַנְתָּ עַל־מְקוֹמוֹ
וְאֵינֶנּוּ׃

10 [Wait] only a little while,
and the wicked will be no more;
and you will look closely at his place
and he will be gone.

יא וַעֲנָוִים יִירְשׁוּ־אָרֶץ
וְהִתְעַנְּגוּ
עַל־רֹב שָׁלוֹם׃

11 And the humble will inherit the land,
and they will delight themselves
in the abundance of peace.

יב זֹמֵם רָשָׁע לַצַּדִּיק
וְחֹרֵק עָלָיו שִׁנָּיו׃

12 The wicked plots against the righteous
and gnashes at him [with] his teeth.

יג אֲדֹנָי יִשְׂחַק־לוֹ
כִּי־רָאָה כִּי־יָבֹא יוֹמוֹ׃

13 My Master laughs at him
for He sees that his day is coming.

יד חֶרֶב | פָּתְחוּ רְשָׁעִים
וְדָרְכוּ קַשְׁתָּם
לְהַפִּיל עָנִי וְאֶבְיוֹן
לִטְבוֹחַ יִשְׁרֵי־דָרֶךְ׃

14 The wicked have drawn out the sword
and bent their bow,
to cast down the poor and the needy,
to slaughter those who walk upright in the path.

טו חַרְבָּם תָּבוֹא בְלִבָּם
וְקַשְּׁתוֹתָם תִּשָּׁבַרְנָה׃

15 Their sword will enter into their own heart,
and their bows will be broken.

טז טוֹב מְעַט לַצַּדִּיק
מֵהֲמוֹן רְשָׁעִים רַבִּים׃

16 Better the few with [who help] the righteous,
than the multitude of many wicked.

יז כִּי זְרוֹעוֹת רְשָׁעִים
תִּשָּׁבַרְנָה
וְסוֹמֵךְ צַדִּיקִים יְהוָה׃

17 For the arms of the wicked
will be broken,
but the support of the righteous is Adonoy.

יח יוֹדֵעַ יְהוָה
יְמֵי תְמִימִם
וְנַחֲלָתָם לְעוֹלָם תִּהְיֶה׃

18 Adonoy knows
the days of the wholehearted
and their inheritance will be forever.

יט לֹא־יֵבֹשׁוּ בְּעֵת רָעָה
וּבִימֵי רְעָבוֹן יִשְׂבָּעוּ׃

19 They will not be ashamed in the time of evil,
and in the days of famine they will be satisfied.

כ כִּי רְשָׁעִים | יֹאבֵדוּ
וְאֹיְבֵי יְהוָה
כִּיקַר כָּרִים
כָּלוּ בֶעָשָׁן כָּלוּ׃

20 For the wicked will perish,
and the enemies of Adonoy
will be like the fat of rams,
consumed, in smoke they are consumed.

כא לֹוֶה רָשָׁע וְלֹא יְשַׁלֵּם
וְצַדִּיק חוֹנֵן וְנוֹתֵן׃

21 The wicked borrows and does not repay,
but the righteous person is gracious and gives.

כב כִּי מְבֹרָכָיו
יִירְשׁוּ אָרֶץ
וּמְקֻלָּלָיו יִכָּרֵתוּ׃

22 For those blessed by Him
will inherit the land,
and those cursed by Him will be cut off.

כג מֵיְהוָה
מִצְעֲדֵי־גֶבֶר כּוֹנָנוּ
וְדַרְכּוֹ יֶחְפָּץ׃

23 It is from Adonoy
that a man's footsteps are established,
and it is his path that He desires.

כד כִּֽי־יִפֹּל
לֹא־יוּטָל
כִּֽי־יְהֹוָה סוֹמֵךְ יָדוֹ׃

24 Though he falls
he will not remain cast down,
for Adonoy supports his hand.

כה נַעַר | הָיִיתִי גַּם־זָקַנְתִּי
וְלֹא־רָאִיתִי צַדִּיק נֶעֱזָב
וְזַרְעוֹ מְבַקֶּשׁ־לָחֶם׃

25 I was young and I have grown old,
yet I have never seen a righteous man forsaken,
nor his children begging for bread.

כו כָּל־הַיּוֹם חוֹנֵן וּמַלְוֶה
וְזַרְעוֹ לִבְרָכָה׃

26 All day long he is gracious and lends,
and his seed is blessed.

כז סוּר מֵרָע וַעֲשֵׂה־טוֹב
וּשְׁכֹן לְעוֹלָם׃

27 Turn away from evil and do good;
and dwell [in security] forever.

כח כִּי יְהֹוָה | אֹהֵב מִשְׁפָּט
וְלֹא־יַעֲזֹב אֶת־חֲסִידָיו
לְעוֹלָם נִשְׁמָרוּ
וְזֶרַע רְשָׁעִים נִכְרָת׃

28 For Adonoy loves justice
and will not forsake His devoted ones;
they will forever be preserved,
but the seed of the wicked will be cut off.

כט צַדִּיקִים יִירְשׁוּ־אָרֶץ
וְיִשְׁכְּנוּ לָעַד עָלֶיהָ׃

29 The righteous will inherit the land
and dwell forever upon it.

ל פִּי־צַדִּיק יֶהְגֶּה חָכְמָה
וּלְשׁוֹנוֹ תְּדַבֵּר מִשְׁפָּט׃

30 The mouth of the righteous utters wisdom,
and his tongue speaks justice.

לא תּוֹרַת אֱלֹהָיו בְּלִבּוֹ
לֹא תִמְעַד אֲשֻׁרָיו׃

31 The Torah of his God is in his heart,
his footsteps will not stumble.

לב צוֹפֶה רָשָׁע לַצַּדִּיק
וּמְבַקֵּשׁ לַהֲמִיתוֹ׃

32 The wicked watches for the righteous
and seeks to slay him.

לג יְהֹוָה לֹא־יַעַזְבֶנּוּ בְיָדוֹ
וְלֹא יַרְשִׁיעֶנּוּ בְּהִשָּׁפְטוֹ׃

33 Adonoy will not leave him in his hand,
nor will He condemn him when he is judged.

לד קַוֵּה אֶל־יְהֹוָה |
וּשְׁמֹר דַּרְכּוֹ
וִירוֹמִמְךָ לָרֶשֶׁת אָרֶץ
בְּהִכָּרֵת רְשָׁעִים תִּרְאֶה׃

34 Hope to Adonoy
and preserve His way,
and He will exalt you to inherit the land;
when the wicked are cut off, you will see.

לה רָאִיתִי רָשָׁע
עָרִיץ
וּמִתְעָרֶה כְּאֶזְרָח רַעֲנָן׃

35 I have seen the wicked tyrant,
strong, well_rooted
like an evergreen tree in its native soil.

לו וַיַּעֲבֹר
וְהִנֵּה אֵינֶנּוּ
וָאֲבַקְשֵׁהוּ וְלֹא נִמְצָא׃

36 And he passed by
and behold, he was no more;
and I sought him, but he could not be found.

לז שְׁמָר־תָּם
וּרְאֵה יָשָׁר
כִּי־אַחֲרִית לְאִישׁ שָׁלוֹם׃

37 Observe the wholehearted
and look upon the upright,
for there is a future for the man of peace.

לח וּפֹשְׁעִים
נִשְׁמְדוּ יַחְדָּו

38 But transgressors
will be destroyed together,

אַחֲרִית רְשָׁעִים נִכְרָתָה׃	the future of the wicked will be cut off.
לט וּתְשׁוּעַת צַדִּיקִים	39 But the deliverance of the righteous
מֵיְהֹוָה	is from Adonoy,
מָעוּזָּם בְּעֵת צָרָה׃	their strength in time of trouble.
מ וַיַּעְזְרֵם יְהֹוָה	40 And Adonoy helped them
וַיְפַלְּטֵם	and rescued them;
יְפַלְּטֵם מֵרְשָׁעִים	He will rescue them from the wicked
וְיוֹשִׁיעֵם	and deliver them,
כִּי־חָסוּ בוֹ׃	because they have taken refuge in Him.

פרק לח Chapter 38

Weekly Cycle	Monthly Cycle	Book Number
Monday	6th day of the month	Book 1

Author

דָּוִד הַמֶּלֶךְ—King David—the second king of Israel and father of the Davidic royal and messianic dynasty. David composed over seventy of the 150 psalms of Sefer Tehillim.

Genre

Psalm of Individual Lament - This psalm was written from the perspective of the individual worshipper, who cries out to God in his time of need. It is characterized as an address to God involving a complaint, followed by a request and ending with an expression of trust.

Chapter Summary

In this psalm, King David reminds us that God afflicts man because of his transgressions, and further prays to God for salvation from his afflictions. David's additional intention here is to instill in man the responsibility to bless God for the bad just as one blesses Him for the good.

This psalm consists of twenty-three verses, subdivided into five parts. The first verse serves as a heading.

In verses 2-8, King David describes his various illnesses and ailments, attributing them to God.
In verses 9-13, he expresses his loneliness.
In verses 14-16, he gives voice to the tension between his silence and his hope.
In verses 17-21, he elaborates upon his fear of his enemies due to his sins.
In verses 22 and 23, he concludes by pleading for salvation.

Introductory Word

מִזְמוֹר—Mizmor—Musical Accompaniment

Technical Terminology

לְהַזְכִּיר—Lehazkir—For rememberance

Shimush Tehillim - When to Say

Against people who speak evil gossip—Verse 13 states: "and those who seek my hurt speak of destruction, and upon deceits, all day do they meditate."

Where in the Siddur

Verse 22 is included in the long version of the Tachanun (Penitential Prayer), recited on Mondays and Thursdays upon the conclusion of the Amidah (Silent Meditation) of Shacharit (morning service).

Talmud on Tehillim

Verse 11: "לִבִּי סְחַרְחַר, עֲזָבַנִי כֹחִי"—"My heart is engulfed in grief, my strength has forsaken me." The Talmud, Gittin 70a, deduces from here that three things weaken the body of a person: fear, travel and sin.

פרק לח

א מִזְמוֹר לְדָוִד לְהַזְכִּיר׃
ב יְהֹוָה אַל־בְּקֶצְפְּךָ תוֹכִיחֵנִי
וּבַחֲמָתְךָ תְיַסְּרֵנִי׃
ג כִּי־חִצֶּיךָ נִחֲתוּ בִי
וַתִּנְחַת עָלַי יָדֶךָ׃
ד אֵין־מְתֹם בִּבְשָׂרִי
מִפְּנֵי זַעְמֶךָ
אֵין־שָׁלוֹם בַּעֲצָמַי
מִפְּנֵי חַטָּאתִי׃
ה כִּי עֲוֺנֹתַי עָבְרוּ רֹאשִׁי
כְּמַשָּׂא כָבֵד
יִכְבְּדוּ מִמֶּנִּי׃
ו הִבְאִישׁוּ נָמַקּוּ חַבּוּרֹתָי
מִפְּנֵי אִוַּלְתִּי׃
ז נַעֲוֵיתִי שַׁחֹתִי עַד־מְאֹד
כָּל־הַיּוֹם קֹדֵר הִלָּכְתִּי׃
ח כִּי־כְסָלַי מָלְאוּ נִקְלֶה
וְאֵין מְתֹם בִּבְשָׂרִי׃
ט נְפוּגוֹתִי וְנִדְכֵּיתִי עַד־מְאֹד
שָׁאַגְתִּי מִנַּהֲמַת לִבִּי׃

Chapter 38

1 A Psalm of David, to serve as a memorial.
2 Adonoy, with Your anger, rebuke me not
nor with Your wrath, chasten me.
3 For Your arrows were fired [deep] into me,
and down upon me has Your hand come.
4 There is no unmarred spot in my flesh
because of Your rage;
there is no peace in my bones
because of my sin.
5 For my iniquities have gone over my head,
as an onerous burden,
they are too heavy for me.
6 Festered and rotted are my wounds,
because of my foolishness.
7 I am bent and bowed down greatly,
all day in dark melancholy, I go.
8 For my inner thoughts were filled with futility
and there is no unmarred spot in my flesh.
9 I was faint and crushed exceedingly;
I roared from the moaning of my heart.

י אֲדֹנָי	10 My Master,
נֶגְדְּךָ כָל־תַּאֲוָתִי	before You are all my desires [needs],
וְאַנְחָתִי מִמְּךָ לֹא־נִסְתָּרָה׃	and my sighing is not hidden from You.
יא לִבִּי סְחַרְחַר	11 My heart is engulfed in grief,
עֲזָבַנִי כֹחִי	my strength has forsaken me,
וְאוֹר־עֵינַי	and the light of my eyes,
גַּם־הֵם אֵין אִתִּי׃	it, too, is gone from me.
יב אֹהֲבַי ׀ וְרֵעַי	12 My friends and my companions
מִנֶּגֶד נִגְעִי יַעֲמֹדוּ	stand aloof from my affliction,
וּקְרוֹבַי מֵרָחֹק עָמָדוּ׃	and my kinsmen stand at a distance.
יג וַיְנַקְשׁוּ ׀	13 They laid snares for me,
מְבַקְשֵׁי נַפְשִׁי	those who seek my soul
וְדֹרְשֵׁי רָעָתִי	and those who seek my hurt
דִּבְּרוּ הַוּוֹת	speak of destruction,
וּמִרְמוֹת כָּל־הַיּוֹם יֶהְגּוּ׃	and upon deceits, all day do they meditate.
יד וַאֲנִי כְחֵרֵשׁ לֹא אֶשְׁמָע	14 But I am as a deaf man, I do not hear,
וּכְאִלֵּם לֹא יִפְתַּח־פִּיו׃	and as a mute who does not open his mouth.
טו וָאֱהִי כְּאִישׁ אֲשֶׁר לֹא־שֹׁמֵעַ	15 I became as a man that does not hear,
וְאֵין בְּפִיו תּוֹכָחוֹת׃	and in whose mouth there are no rebuttals.
טז כִּי־לְךָ יְהוָה הוֹחָלְתִּי	16 For You, Adonoy, did I wait,
אַתָּה תַעֲנֶה אֲדֹנָי אֱלֹהָי׃	You will answer, my Master, my God.
יז כִּי־אָמַרְתִּי פֶּן־יִשְׂמְחוּ־לִי	17 For I said lest they rejoice over me;
בְּמוֹט רַגְלִי	when my foot slips,
עָלַי הִגְדִּילוּ׃	they exalt themselves over me.
יח כִּי־אֲנִי לְצֶלַע נָכוֹן	18 For I am prone to limp [suffer]
וּמַכְאוֹבִי נֶגְדִּי תָמִיד׃	and my pain is continually before me.
יט כִּי־עֲוֺנִי אַגִּיד	19 For my iniquity I declare [in my heart],
אֶדְאַג מֵחַטָּאתִי׃	I am anxious because of my sin.
כ וְאֹיְבַי חַיִּים עָצֵמוּ	20 But my foes abound with life
וְרַבּוּ	and multiplied
שֹׂנְאַי שָׁקֶר׃	are those who hate me without cause.
כא וּמְשַׁלְּמֵי רָעָה תַּחַת טוֹבָה	21 And those who repay evil for good
יִשְׂטְנוּנִי תַּחַת רָדְפִי־טוֹב׃	denounce me because of my pursuit of good.
כב אַל־תַּעַזְבֵנִי יְהוָה אֱלֹהַי	22 Forsake me not, Adonoy, my God,
אַל־תִּרְחַק מִמֶּנִּי׃	be not far from me.
כג חוּשָׁה לְעֶזְרָתִי	23 Hasten to help me,
אֲדֹנָי תְּשׁוּעָתִי׃	my Master, my deliverance.

פרק לט Chapter 39

Weekly Cycle	Monthly Cycle	Book Number
Monday	7th day of the month	Book 1

Author

דָוִד הַמֶּלֶךְ—King David—the second king of Israel and father of the Davidic royal and messianic dynasty. David composed over seventy of the 150 psalms of Sefer Tehillim.

Possibly composed for Yedutun - a noted singer and composer of several psalms.

When & Why

David wrote this psalm when he was sick and he needed God's help to recover from his illness.

Genre

Psalm of Individual Lament - This psalm was written from the perspective of the individual worshipper, who cries out to God in his time of need. It is characterized as an address to God involving a complaint, followed by a request and ending with an expression of trust.

Chapter Summary

King David's suffering prompts him to realize how fleeting man's time is on this earth. He pleads to God to allow him to recover from his suffering, so that he may return to fulfilling His will.

This psalm contains fourteen verses, subdivided into three parts. The first verse serves as a heading.

In verses 2-4, King David apologizes for the harsh words he is about to speak to God.

In verses 5-7, he laments that man is driven by vanity.

In verses 8-14, he expresses his hope for God and offers a prayer to Him.

Introductory Words

לַמְנַצֵּחַ—Lamnatsei'ach—To the Conductor

מִזְמוֹר—Mizmor—Musical Accompaniment

Technical Terminology

סֶלָה—Selah—While its meaning is unclear, the most familiar opinion is that it is a musical notation, instructing the Levitical orchestra to pause its singing and playing of instruments. Alternatively, "Selah" may mean "everlasting".

Shimush Tehillim - When to Say

For spiritual growth—Verse 14 states: " Let me alone so that I may become strong, before I go away and cease to be."

Where in the Siddur

Verse 8 is found in the repetition of the Amidah (Silent Meditation) of Musaf of Rosh HaShanah.

Talmud on Tehillim

Verse 3: "נֶאֱלַמְתִּי דוּמִיָּה, הֶחֱשֵׁיתִי מִטּוֹב"—"I became mute with silence, I was silent from the [hope of] good things."

The Talmud, Berachot 5a, deduces from here that one who has the opportunity to study Torah, but does not do so, brings suffering upon himself. The word "tov"—"good" here is interpreted as referring to Torah study.

Verse 7: "אַךְ בְּצֶלֶם יִתְהַלֶּךְ אִישׁ, אַךְ הֶבֶל יֶהֱמָיוּן; יִצְבֹּר, וְלֹא יֵדַע מִי אֹסְפָם"—"Surely in darkness does man make his way, surely for vanity they are in turmoil; he heaps up riches and does not know who will gather them."

The Talmud Yerushalmi—Jerusalem Talmud, Shekalim 2:5, deduces that when repeating something one heard in learning, he should imagine that the one who originally shared these words is standing before him.

Verse 13: "שִׁמְעָה תְפִלָּתִי יְהוָה, וְשַׁוְעָתִי הַאֲזִינָה אֶל דִּמְעָתִי, אַל תֶּחֱרַשׁ"—"Hear my prayer, Adonoy, and give ear to my cry; to my tears be not silent."

The Talmud, Berachot 32b, teaches: "The gates of prayer were closed since the destruction of the Beit HaMikdash (Holy Temple); even so, the gates of tears were not." The Talmud is instructing us that if one cries out to Hashem his prayers will indeed be heard. (See the Talmud Bava Metzia, 49a for more on this idea).

פֶּרֶק לט	**Chapter 39**
א לַמְנַצֵּחַ לִידוּתוּן	1 To the Chief Musician; for Yedusun,
מִזְמוֹר לְדָוִד:	a Psalm of David.
ב אָמַרְתִּי אֶשְׁמְרָה דְרָכַי	2 I said, "I will guard my ways
מֵחֲטוֹא בִלְשׁוֹנִי	from sinning with my tongue;
אֶשְׁמְרָה לְפִי מַחְסוֹם	I will guard my mouth as with a muzzle,
בְּעֹד רָשָׁע לְנֶגְדִּי:	while the wicked one is before me."
ג נֶאֱלַמְתִּי דוּמִיָּה	3 I became mute with silence,
הֶחֱשֵׁיתִי מִטּוֹב	I was silent from the [hope of] good things
וּכְאֵבִי נֶעְכָּר:	and my pain was stirred.
ד חַם־לִבִּי ׀ בְּקִרְבִּי	4 My heart grew hot within me,
בַּהֲגִיגִי תִבְעַר־אֵשׁ	while I was musing the fever increased,
דִּבַּרְתִּי בִּלְשׁוֹנִי:	finally I spoke out with my tongue.
ה הוֹדִיעֵנִי יְהוָה ׀ קִצִּי	5 "Make known to me, Adonoy, my end
וּמִדַּת יָמַי מַה־הִיא	and the measure of my days what is it;
אֵדְעָה מֶה־חָדֵל אָנִי:	let me know how short lived I am.
ו הִנֵּה	6 Behold,
טְפָחוֹת ׀ נָתַתָּה יָמַי	as handbreadths have You made my days,
וְחֶלְדִּי כְאַיִן נֶגְדֶּךָ	and my life span is as nothing before You;

אַךְ כָּל־הֶבֶל כָּל־אָדָם נִצָּב סֶלָה׃	but all is vanity, all mankind's existence, forever."
ז אַךְ־בְּצֶלֶם | יִתְהַלֶּךְ־אִישׁ	7 Surely in darkness does man make his way,
אַךְ־הֶבֶל יֶהֱמָיוּן	surely for vanity they are in turmoil;
יִצְבֹּר	he heaps up riches
וְלֹא־יֵדַע מִי־אֹסְפָם׃	and does not know who will gather them.
ח וְעַתָּה מַה־קִּוִּיתִי אֲדֹנָי	8 And now, for what do I hope, my Master,
תּוֹחַלְתִּי לְךָ הִיא׃	for what do I yearn from You?
ט מִכָּל־פְּשָׁעַי הַצִּילֵנִי	9 From all my transgressions rescue me;
חֶרְפַּת נָבָל	a disgrace among the degenerate
אַל־תְּשִׂימֵנִי׃	do not make me.
י נֶאֱלַמְתִּי לֹא אֶפְתַּח־פִּי	10 I became mute, I will not open my mouth,
כִּי אַתָּה עָשִׂיתָ׃	because You have done it.
יא הָסֵר מֵעָלַי נִגְעֶךָ	11 Remove from me Your affliction,
מִתִּגְרַת יָדְךָ	from the harassment of Your hand
אֲנִי כָלִיתִי׃	I am consumed.
יב בְּתוֹכָחוֹת עַל־עָוֺן |	12 With rebukes for iniquity
יִסַּרְתָּ אִישׁ	You chasten man,
וַתֶּמֶס כָּעָשׁ חֲמוּדוֹ	and You make his charm rot like a moth,
אַךְ הֶבֶל כָּל־אָדָם סֶלָה׃	surely vanity is all mankind, forever.
יג שִׁמְעָה־תְפִלָּתִי | יְהוָה	13 Hear my prayer, Adonoy,
וְשַׁוְעָתִי | הַאֲזִינָה	and give ear to my cry;
אֶל־דִּמְעָתִי אַל־תֶּחֱרַשׁ	to my tears be not silent,
כִּי גֵר אָנֹכִי עִמָּךְ	for a stranger am I with You,
תּוֹשָׁב כְּכָל־אֲבוֹתָי׃	a sojourner as all my fathers were.
יד הָשַׁע מִמֶּנִּי וְאַבְלִיגָה	14 Let me alone so that I may become strong,
בְּטֶרֶם אֵלֵךְ וְאֵינֶנִּי׃	before I go away and cease to be.

Oil Lamp with Harp (Courtesy of the Shlomo Moussaieff Collection)

פרק מ Chapter 40

Weekly Cycle	Monthly Cycle	Book Number
Monday	7th day of the month	Book 1

Author
דָּוִד הַמֶּלֶךְ—King David—the second king of Israel and father of the Davidic royal and messianic dynasty. David composed over seventy of the 150 psalms of Sefer Tehillim.

When & Why
David wrote this psalm when he recovered from his sickness and brought thanksgiving offerings to God.

Genre
Psalm of Individual Thanksgiving - This psalm emphasizes gratitude for what God has done for the individual.
Psalm of Wisdom - This psalm contains teachings and wise advice and is meant to instruct people on how to live a Godly life.

Chapter Summary
David gives thanks to God for healing him from his maladies. His goal in proclaiming a new song (see verse 4) is to teach man that in times of deep affliction he should put his trust in God alone.

This psalm consists of eighteen verses, subdivided into two parts. The first verse serves as a heading.
In verses 2-11, King David thanks God for having delivered him in the past, and prays that God will save him from his current distress. He describes his previous deliverance and expresses his gratitude by observing God's law.
In verses 12-18, the Psalmist expands upon his prayer for deliverance, and asks God to reveal His mercy.

Introductory Words
לַמְנַצֵּחַ—Lamnatsei'ach—To the Conductor
מִזְמוֹר—Mizmor—Musical Accompaniment

Shimush Tehillim - When to Say
For protection against evil spirits—Verse 18 states: "my Master, be aware of me; my help and my rescuer are You, my God, tarry not."

Where in the Siddur
Verse 2 is found in the repetition of the Amidah (Silent Meditation) of Musaf of Rosh HaShanah.
Verse 12 comprises the second verse of V'hu Rachum, one of the passages of Pesukei Dezimra (introductory Verses of Praise to the Shacharit morning service), as well as the long Tachanun (Penitential Prayer) following the Amidah of Shacharit, recited on Mondays and Thursdays.

פֶּרֶק מ

א לַמְנַצֵּחַ
לְדָוִד מִזְמוֹר׃
ב קַוֹּה קִוִּיתִי יְהוָה
וַיֵּט אֵלַי וַיִּשְׁמַע שַׁוְעָתִי׃
ג וַיַּעֲלֵנִי | מִבּוֹר שָׁאוֹן
מִטִּיט הַיָּוֵן
וַיָּקֶם עַל־סֶלַע רַגְלַי
כּוֹנֵן אֲשֻׁרָי׃
ד וַיִּתֵּן בְּפִי | שִׁיר חָדָשׁ
תְּהִלָּה לֵאלֹהֵינוּ
יִרְאוּ רַבִּים וְיִירָאוּ
וְיִבְטְחוּ בַּיהוָה׃
ה אַשְׁרֵי הַגֶּבֶר
אֲשֶׁר־שָׂם יְהוָה מִבְטַחוֹ
וְלֹא־פָנָה אֶל־רְהָבִים
וְשָׂטֵי כָזָב׃
ו רַבּוֹת עָשִׂיתָ |
אַתָּה | יְהוָה אֱלֹהַי
נִפְלְאֹתֶיךָ וּמַחְשְׁבֹתֶיךָ
אֵלֵינוּ
אֵין | עֲרֹךְ אֵלֶיךָ
אַגִּידָה וַאֲדַבֵּרָה
עָצְמוּ מִסַּפֵּר׃
ז זֶבַח וּמִנְחָה |
לֹא־חָפַצְתָּ
אָזְנַיִם כָּרִיתָ לִּי
עוֹלָה וַחֲטָאָה
לֹא שָׁאָלְתָּ׃
ח אָז אָמַרְתִּי הִנֵּה־בָאתִי
בִּמְגִלַּת־סֵפֶר כָּתוּב עָלָי׃
ט לַעֲשׂוֹת־רְצוֹנְךָ אֱלֹהַי
חָפָצְתִּי
וְתוֹרָתְךָ בְּתוֹךְ מֵעָי׃
י בִּשַּׂרְתִּי צֶדֶק |
בְּקָהָל רָב
הִנֵּה שְׂפָתַי לֹא אֶכְלָא
יְהוָה אַתָּה יָדָעְתָּ׃
יא צִדְקָתְךָ

Chapter 40

1 To the Chief Musician,
a Psalm of David.
2 I have hoped continually for Adonoy,
and He inclined [His ear] to me and heard my cry.
3 And He raised me from the turbulent pit,
out of the miry mud;
and He set my feet upon a rock,
He firmly established my steps.
4 And He put in my mouth a new song,
praise to our God;
many will see and fear
and will trust in Adonoy.
5 Fortunate is the man
who has made Adonoy his trust,
and has not turned to the arrogant
and to those who stray after falsehood.
6 Many things have You done,
You Adonoy, my God,
Your wondrous works and Your thoughts
are for us,
there is none that can compare to You;
to declare and speak of them [is impossible]
[for] they are too numerous to be told.
7 Sacrifice and meal offering
You did not desire,
my ears You have opened;
[for] burnt offering and sin offering
You have not asked.
8 Then I said, ``Here I have come;
in the Scroll of a Book is written of me.
9 To fulfill Your will, my God,
I desired,
and Your Torah is in my innermost parts."
10 I have proclaimed [Your] righteousness
in the great congregation,
behold, my lips I will not refrain;
Adonoy, You know.
11 Your righteousness

Hebrew	English
לֹא־כִסִּיתִי ׀ בְּתוֹךְ לִבִּי	I have not concealed within my heart;
אֱמוּנָתְךָ וּתְשׁוּעָתְךָ	Your faithfulness and Your deliverance
אָמָרְתִּי	I have declared;
לֹא־כִחַדְתִּי חַסְדְּךָ וַאֲמִתְּךָ	I have not hidden Your kindness and Your truth
לְקָהָל רָב׃	from the great congregation.
יב אַתָּה יְהֹוָה	12 You, Adonoy,
לֹא־תִכְלָא רַחֲמֶיךָ מִמֶּנִּי	withhold not Your mercy from me;
חַסְדְּךָ וַאֲמִתְּךָ	may Your kindness and Your truth
תָּמִיד יִצְּרוּנִי׃	always protect me.
יג כִּי אָפְפוּ־עָלַי ׀ רָעוֹת	13 For encompassed about me are evils
עַד־אֵין מִסְפָּר	too many to enumerate,
הִשִּׂיגוּנִי עֲוֹנֹתַי	my iniquities have overtaken me
וְלֹא־יָכֹלְתִּי לִרְאוֹת	and I was unable to see;
עָצְמוּ	they were more numerous
מִשַּׂעֲרוֹת רֹאשִׁי	than the hairs of my head,
וְלִבִּי עֲזָבָנִי׃	and my heart has failed me.
יד רְצֵה יְהֹוָה לְהַצִּילֵנִי	14 May it please You, Adonoy, to rescue me;
יְהֹוָה לְעֶזְרָתִי חוּשָׁה׃	Adonoy, to my help, hasten.
טו יֵבֹשׁוּ וְיַחְפְּרוּ ׀	15 Let them be ashamed and humiliated
יַחַד	together,
מְבַקְשֵׁי נַפְשִׁי לִסְפּוֹתָהּ	those who seek my soul to remove it;
יִסֹּגוּ אָחוֹר וְיִכָּלְמוּ	let them fall back and be disgraced
חֲפֵצֵי רָעָתִי׃	those who desire my hurt.
טז יָשֹׁמּוּ	16 Let them be appalled
עַל־עֵקֶב בָּשְׁתָּם	at the extent of their shame,
הָאֹמְרִים לִי הֶאָח ׀ הֶאָח׃	those who say to me, "Aha, aha."
יז יָשִׂישׂוּ וְיִשְׂמְחוּ ׀ בְּךָ	17 Let them exult and rejoice in You,
כָּל־מְבַקְשֶׁיךָ	all those who seek You;
יֹאמְרוּ תָמִיד	let them say continually,
יִגְדַּל יְהֹוָה	"Be magnified, Adonoy,"
אֹהֲבֵי תְּשׁוּעָתֶךָ׃	those who love Your deliverance.
יח וַאֲנִי ׀ עָנִי וְאֶבְיוֹן	18 As for me, being poor and needy,
אֲדֹנָי יַחֲשָׁב לִי	my Master, be aware of me;
עֶזְרָתִי וּמְפַלְטִי אַתָּה	my help and my rescuer are You,
אֱלֹהַי אַל־תְּאַחַר׃	my God, tarry not.

פרק מא Chapter 41

Weekly Cycle	Monthly Cycle	Book Number
Monday	7th day of the month	Book 1

Author

דָוִד הַמֶּלֶךְ—King David—the second king of Israel and father of the Davidic royal and messianic dynasty. David composed over seventy of the 150 psalms of Sefer Tehillim.

When & Why

David wrote this when he was struggling with a serious illness.

Genre

Psalm of Individual Lament - This psalm was written from the perspective of the individual worshipper, who cries out to God in his time of need. It is characterized as an address to God involving a complaint, followed by a request and ending with an expression of trust.

Chapter Summary

In this chapter, King David describes the happiness of the man who, in his afflictions, turns to God for help. The Psalmist concludes with thanksgiving to the Almighty for enabling him to complete the "first book" of Psalms.

This psalm consists of fourteen verses, subdivided into four parts. The first verse serves as an introduction.

In verses 2-4, King David describes how God attends to the sick and heals them.

In verses 5-11, he complains about those who speak evil of him.

In verses 12-13, he expresses his confidence that God is pleased with him and that his prayer has been accepted.

In verse 14, he concludes by declaring "Baruch Hashem meiha'olam v'ad ha'olam"—"Blessed is Adonoy, the God of Israel, from all times past throughout all times to come."

Introductory Words

לַמְנַצֵּחַ—Lamnatsei'ach—To the Conductor

מִזְמוֹר—Mizmor—Musical Accompaniment

Technical Terminology

מַשְׂכִּיל—Maskil—a discerning person; alternatively, a giver of instruction, perhaps denoting a translator of the chapter (Rashi).

Shimush Tehillim - When to Say

To request Heavenly advice for a bad dream (fast and recite this chapter 7 times)—Verse 4 states: "Adonoy will support him on the bed of illness."

One whose job was replaced by another (recite this and the next two chapters)—Verse 12 states: "By this I will know that You are delighted in me, that my enemy does not shout triumphantly over me."

Where in the Siddur

Verse 4 is found in the repetition of the Amidah (Silent Meditation) of Musaf of Rosh HaShanah, as well as in Tashlich (a prayer recited on Rosh HaShanah afternoon, usually by a body of water, in which we beseech God to "cast away" our sins into the depths of the sea).

Talmud on Tehillim

Verse 2: "אַשְׁרֵי מַשְׂכִּיל אֶל דָּל"—"Fortunate is he who understands the [needs of the] lowly."
The Talmud Yerushalmi—Jerusalem Talmud, Shekalim 5:4, infers that this verse refers to one who contemplates how to perform the mitzvot (commandments) in the best possible manner.
Verse 4: "יְהוָה יִסְעָדֶנּוּ, עַל עֶרֶשׂ דְּוָי"—"Adonoy will support him on the bed of illness."
The Talmud, Shabbat 12b, states that from this we learn that the Shechinah (Divine Presence) visits and rejuvenates the choleh (the sick).

Hebrew			English
פרק מא			**Chapter 41**
לַמְנַצֵּחַ	א	1	To the Chief Musician,
מִזְמוֹר לְדָוִד׃			A Psalm of David.
אַשְׁרֵי מַשְׂכִּיל	ב	2	Fortunate is he who understands
אֶל־דָּל			the [needs of the] lowly.
בְּיוֹם רָעָה יְמַלְּטֵהוּ יְהוָה׃			On the day of evil, Adonoy will save him.
יְהוָה | יִשְׁמְרֵהוּ	ג	3	Adonoy will preserve him
וִיחַיֵּהוּ			and keep him alive,
וְאֻשַּׁר בָּאָרֶץ			he will be fortunate on earth,
וְאַל־תִּתְּנֵהוּ			and You will not give him [up]
בְּנֶפֶשׁ אֹיְבָיו׃			to the will of his enemies.
יְהוָה יִסְעָדֶנּוּ	ד	4	Adonoy will support him
עַל־עֶרֶשׂ דְּוָי			on the bed of illness,
כָּל־מִשְׁכָּבוֹ הָפַכְתָּ			all his restfulness You overturned
בְחָלְיוֹ׃			during his sickness.
אֲנִי־אָמַרְתִּי	ה	5	As for me, I said,
יְהוָה חָנֵּנִי			"Adonoy, be gracious to me,
רְפָאָה נַפְשִׁי כִּי־חָטָאתִי לָךְ׃			heal my soul for I have sinned against You."
אוֹיְבַי יֹאמְרוּ רַע לִי	ו	6	My enemies speak evil of me;
מָתַי יָמוּת וְאָבַד שְׁמוֹ׃			"When will he die and his name perish?"
וְאִם־בָּא לִרְאוֹת |	ז	7	And if one [does] come to see [visit me],
שָׁוְא יְדַבֵּר			he speaks falsehood [in my presence]
לִבּוֹ			but in his heart
יִקְבָּץ־אָוֶן לוֹ			he gathers thoughts of iniquity
יֵצֵא לַחוּץ יְדַבֵּר׃			[and] when he goes outside he speaks of it.
יַחַד עָלַי יִתְלַחֲשׁוּ	ח	8	Together they whisper against me,

כָּל־שֹׂנְאָ֑י
עָלַ֓י ׀ יַחְשְׁב֖וּ
רָעָ֣ה לִֽי׃
ט דְּֽבַר־בְּ֭לִיַּעַל יָצ֣וּק בּ֑וֹ
וַאֲשֶׁ֥ר שָׁ֝כַ֗ב לֹא־יוֹסִ֥יף לָקֽוּם׃
י גַּם־אִ֤ישׁ שְׁלוֹמִ֨י ׀
אֲשֶׁר־בָּטַ֣חְתִּי ב֭וֹ אוֹכֵ֣ל לַחְמִ֑י
הִגְדִּ֖יל עָלַ֣י עָקֵֽב׃
יא וְאַתָּ֤ה יְהֹוָ֗ה חָנֵּ֥נִי
וַהֲקִימֵ֑נִי
וַאֲשַׁלְּמָ֥ה לָהֶֽם׃
יב בְּזֹ֣את יָ֭דַעְתִּי
כִּֽי־חָפַ֣צְתָּ בִּ֑י
כִּ֤י לֹֽא־יָרִ֖יעַ אֹיְבִ֣י
עָלָֽי׃
יג וַאֲנִ֗י
בְּ֭תֻמִּי
תָּמַ֣כְתָּ בִּ֑י
וַתַּצִּיבֵ֖נִי לְפָנֶ֣יךָ לְעוֹלָֽם׃
יד בָּ֘ר֤וּךְ יְהֹוָ֨ה ׀ אֱלֹהֵ֬י יִשְׂרָאֵ֗ל
מֵֽהָעוֹלָם֮
וְעַ֤ד הָעוֹלָ֗ם
אָ֘מֵ֥ן ׀ וְאָמֵֽן׃

all my enemies;
about me, they imagine,
why evil has befallen me.
9 "[His] wicked actions are cast upon him
and now that he lays may he rise no more."
10 Also, my own intimate friend,
in whom I trusted, who ate my bread,
has lifted his heel against me [in contempt.]
11 But You, Adonoy, be gracious to me
and raise me up
and then I will repay them.
12 By this I will know
that You are delighted in me,
that my enemy does not shout triumphantly
over me.
13 And as for me,
because of my integrity
You have supported me,
and You set me before You forever.
14 Blessed is Adonoy, the God of Israel,
from all times past
throughout all times to come,
Amen and Amen.

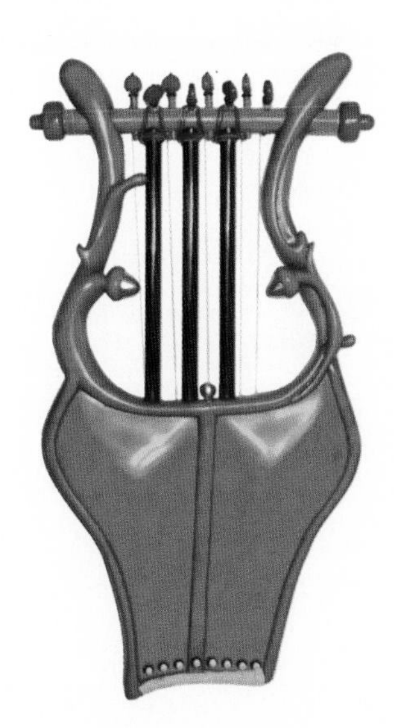

Kinor - Harp

BOOK 2

פרק מב Chapter 42

Weekly Cycle	Monthly Cycle	Book Number
Monday	7th day of the month	Book 2

Author
בְּנֵי-קֹרַח—Sons of Korach—Korach rebelled against his cousins Moshe and Aharon (Moses and Aaron) and challenged their authority. Korach and his cohorts perished in the aftermath of the rebellion, yet his sons, who repented, survived.

When & Why
The sons of Korach wrote this psalm after they repented and were saved from the deadly punishment that their father received.

Genre
Psalm of Individual Lament - This psalm was written from the perspective of the individual worshipper, who cries out to God in his time of need. It is characterized as an address to God involving a complaint, followed by a request and ending with an expression of trust.

Chapter Summary
This psalm begins the "second book", and foretells and speaks of the exiles to be suffered by the Jewish People. It was spoken by means of Ruach HaKodesh (Divine Inspiration), and expresses the depth of Israel's longing for deliverance.

This psalm, consisting of twelve verses, is directly connected to the following psalm, chapter 43, consisting of five verses; they are therefore considered as one unit. Together they are subdivided into three parts. The first verse of Psalm 42 serves as an introduction. Each of the three main sections ends with a refrain.
In Psalm 42, verses 2-5, the psalmists describe their thirst for the living God, and then continues with a refrain, consisting of words of comfort, found in verse 6.
In Psalm 42, verses 7-11, the psalmists complain about their distress and repeat the refrain: "Why are you cast down, my soul? and why do you yearn for me?", found in verse 12.
In Psalm 43, verses 1-4, the psalmists pray for deliverance and salvation, and conclude with the previous refrain, found in verse 5.

Introductory Word
לַמְנַצֵּחַ—Lamnatsei'ach—To the Conductor

Technical Terminology
מַשְׂכִּיל—Maskil—a discerning person; alternatively, a giver of instruction, perhaps denoting a translator of the chapter (Rashi).

Shimush Tehillim - When to Say
One whose job was replaced by another (recite this, the previous, and the following chapter)—

Verse 12 states: "Why are you cast down, my soul? and why do you yearn for me? Hope in God, for I will yet thank Him, for He is my deliverance, the light of my countenance, and my God."

Where in the Siddur

Parts of verses 6 & 12 are paraphrased in Lechah Dodi (one of the prayers of Kabbalat Shabbat (Friday night service).

Biblical Places

חֶרְמוֹן—Hermon—a tall mountain in the most northern part of Israel.

יַרְדֵּן—Yardein—Jordan—located to the east of Israel. God stopped the flow of the Jordan River in order to enable Yehoshua (Joshua) and the Israelites to cross into Israel.

פֶּרֶק מב			**Chapter 42**
לַמְנַצֵּחַ	א	1	To the Chief Musician,
מַשְׂכִּיל לִבְנֵי־קֹרַח:			an instruction of the sons of Korach.
כְּאַיָּל תַּעֲרֹג	ב	2	As the hart cries out in thirst
עַל־אֲפִיקֵי־מָיִם			for the springs of water,
כֵּן נַפְשִׁי תַעֲרֹג			so does my soul cry out in thirst
אֵלֶיךָ אֱלֹהִים:			for You, O God.
צָמְאָה נַפְשִׁי | לֵאלֹהִים	ג	3	My soul thirsts for God,
לְאֵל חָי			for the living Almighty,
מָתַי אָבוֹא וְאֵרָאֶה פְּנֵי אֱלֹהִים:			when will I come and appear before God?
הָיְתָה־לִּי דִמְעָתִי	ד	4	My tear has been
לֶחֶם יוֹמָם וָלָיְלָה			my bread day and night,
בֶּאֱמֹר אֵלַי כָּל־הַיּוֹם			while they say to me all the day,
אַיֵּה אֱלֹהֶיךָ:			"Where is your God?"
אֵלֶּה אֶזְכְּרָה |	ה	5	These do I remember
וְאֶשְׁפְּכָה עָלַי | נַפְשִׁי			and pour out my soul within me
כִּי אֶעֱבֹר | בַּסָּךְ			how I passed on with the throng
אֶדַּדֵּם עַד־בֵּית אֱלֹהִים			and led them slowly up to the House of God,
בְּקוֹל־רִנָּה וְתוֹדָה			with loud rejoicing and thanksgiving,
הָמוֹן חוֹגֵג:			a multitude gathering for a holiday.
מַה־תִּשְׁתּוֹחֲחִי | נַפְשִׁי	ו	6	Why are you cast down, my soul?
וַתֶּהֱמִי עָלָי			and why do you yearn for me?
הוֹחִילִי לֵאלֹהִים כִּי־עוֹד אוֹדֶנּוּ			Hope in God for I will yet thank Him
יְשׁוּעוֹת			for deliverance
פָּנָיו:			[that will come from] His countenance.

ז אֱלֹהַי עָלַי נַפְשִׁי תִשְׁתּוֹחָח
עַל־כֵּן אֶזְכָּרְךָ
מֵאֶרֶץ יַרְדֵּן
וְחֶרְמוֹנִים
מֵהַר מִצְעָר׃

7 My God, my soul is cast down within me;
therefore do I remember You
from the land of the Jordan,
and Hermon's peaks,
from the young mountain [Sinai].

ח תְּהוֹם־אֶל־תְּהוֹם קוֹרֵא
לְקוֹל צִנּוֹרֶיךָ
כָּל־מִשְׁבָּרֶיךָ וְגַלֶּיךָ
עָלַי עָבָרוּ׃

8 Deep calls to deep
to the commotion of Your canals;
all Your billows and Your waves
have gone over me.

ט יוֹמָם | יְצַוֶּה יְהוָה | חַסְדּוֹ
וּבַלַּיְלָה
שִׁירוֹ עִמִּי
תְּפִלָּה לְאֵל חַיָּי׃

9 By day, Adonoy will command His kindness,
and in the night
His resting place will be with me;
[my] prayer to the Almighty of my life.

י אוֹמְרָה | לְאֵל סַלְעִי
לָמָה שְׁכַחְתָּנִי
לָמָּה־קֹדֵר אֵלֵךְ
בְּלַחַץ אוֹיֵב׃

10 I will say to the Almighty, my Rock,
"Why have You forgotten me?
Why do I go about mourning
under the oppression of my enemy?"

יא בְּרֶצַח | בְּעַצְמוֹתַי
חֵרְפוּנִי צוֹרְרָי
בְּאָמְרָם אֵלַי כָּל־הַיּוֹם
אַיֵּה אֱלֹהֶיךָ׃

11 Like a sword in my bones
are the taunts of my adversaries,
by saying to me all the day
"Where is your God?"

יב מַה־תִּשְׁתּוֹחֲחִי | נַפְשִׁי
וּמַה־תֶּהֱמִי עָלָי
הוֹחִילִי לֵאלֹהִים כִּי־עוֹד אוֹדֶנּוּ
יְשׁוּעֹת
פָּנַי וֵאלֹהָי׃

12 Why are you cast down, my soul?
and why do you yearn for me?
Hope in God, for I will yet thank Him,
for He is my deliverance,
the light of my countenance, and my God.

Bar Kochba Coin with a Depiction of a Kinor - Harp

פרק מג Chapter 43

Weekly Cycle	Monthly Cycle	Book Number
Monday	7th day of the month	Book 2

Author

Probably authored by בְּנֵי-קֹרַח—Sons of Korach - Korach rebelled against his cousins Moshe and Aharon (Moses and Aaron) and challenged their authority. Korach and his cohorts perished in the aftermath of the rebellion, yet his sons, who repented, survived.

When & Why

This is a continuation of the previous psalm, which was written by the sons of Korach after they were saved from the punishment that was visited upon their father.

Genre

Psalm of Individual Lament - This psalm was written from the perspective of the individual worshipper, who cries out to God in his time of need. It is characterized as an address to God involving a complaint, followed by a request and ending with an expression of trust.

Chapter Summary

The singer prays for deliverance from the many who taunt and vilify him. Some also see in this psalm a cry against exile by the Congregation of Israel, as well as a request that God exact vengeance from, and meet judgment upon, her enemies.

This psalm consists of five verses. This and the previous psalm comprise one unit. (See the notes to chapter 42 for further elaboration).

In verses 1-4, the psalmist prays for deliverance and salvation.

In verse 5, he concludes with the same lamenting refrain found in chapter 42.

Musical Instrument

כִּנּוֹר—Kinor—A Small Handheld Harp - played with a plecturm (pick).

Shimush Tehillim - When to Say

One whose job was replaced by another (recite the previous 2 chapters and this one)—Verse 5 states: "Why are you cast down, my soul? and why do you yearn for me? Hope in God for I will yet thank Him, for He is my deliverance, the light of my countenance and my God."

פרק מג	Chapter 43
א שָׁפְטֵנִי אֱלֹהִים ׀ וְרִיבָה רִיבִי מִגּוֹי לֹא־חָסִיד מֵאִישׁ־מִרְמָה וְעַוְלָה תְפַלְּטֵנִי׃	1 Judge [avenge] me, O God, and plead my cause against a nation without kindness; from a deceitful and unjust man, rescue me.

ב כִּי־אַתָּה ׀ אֱלֹהֵי מָעוּזִּי לָמָה זְנַחְתָּנִי לָמָּה־קֹדֵר אֶתְהַלֵּךְ בְּלַחַץ אוֹיֵב׃	2	For You are the God of my strength, why have You forsaken me? Why do I go about mourning under the oppression of the enemy?
ג שְׁלַח־אוֹרְךָ וַאֲמִתְּךָ הֵמָּה יַנְחוּנִי יְבִיאוּנִי אֶל־הַר־קָדְשְׁךָ וְאֶל־מִשְׁכְּנוֹתֶיךָ׃	3	Send Your light and Your truth, let them lead me; let them bring me to the mountain of Your Holy Sanctuary and to Your dwelling places.
ד וְאָבוֹאָה ׀ אֶל־מִזְבַּח אֱלֹהִים אֶל־אֵל שִׂמְחַת גִּילִי וְאוֹדְךָ בְכִנּוֹר אֱלֹהִים אֱלֹהָי׃	4	Then I will come to the altar of God, to the Almighty, the [source of] joy of my exultation; and I will praise You upon the harp, God, my God.
ה מַה־תִּשְׁתּוֹחֲחִי ׀ נַפְשִׁי וּמַה־תֶּהֱמִי עָלָי הוֹחִילִי לֵאלֹהִים כִּי־עוֹד אוֹדֶנּוּ יְשׁוּעֹת פָּנַי וֵאלֹהָי׃	5	Why are you cast down, my soul? and why do you yearn for me? Hope in God for I will yet thank Him, for He is my deliverance, the light of my countenance and my God.

פרק מד — Chapter 44

Weekly Cycle	Monthly Cycle	Book Number
Monday	8th day of the month	Book 2

Author

בְּנֵי-קֹרַח—Sons of Korach—Korach rebelled against his cousins Moshe and Aharon (Moses and Aaron) and challenged their authority. Korach and his cohorts perished in the aftermath of the rebellion, yet his sons, who repented, survived.

Genre

Psalm of Communal Lament - This psalm focuses on expressing deep sorrow for the travails of a nation and as a group asking for God's blessing or intervention.

Chapter Summary

As in the previous psalm, this one, too, foretells and describes the future exile. The singers depict the hardships that will ensue, appealing to the soul not to lose hope.

This psalm consists of twenty-seven verses, subdivided into two parts. The first verse serves as a heading.

In verses 2-9, the psalmists tell of God's wondrous deeds performed on behalf of those who conquered the Land of Israel in days of old, and speak of the salvation that God has brought in his generation as well.

In verses 10-27, they speak of the people's defeat and shame, and talk of their loyalty to God's covenant. Even after their enemies mock and slaughter them, they pray to God for salvation.

Introductory Word

לַמְנַצֵּחַ—Lamnatsei'ach—To the Conductor

Technical Terminology

מַשְׂכִּיל—Maskil—a discerning person; alternatively, a giver of instruction, perhaps denoting a translator of the chapter (Rashi).

סֶלָה—Selah—While its meaning is unclear, the most familiar opinion is that it is a musical notation, instructing the Levitical orchestra to pause its singing and playing of instruments. Alternatively, "Selah" may mean "everlasting".

Shimush Tehillim - When to Say

For salvation from enemies—Verse 8 states: "But You have delivered us from our adversaries, and those who cause hatred against us have You shamed."

Where in the Siddur

Verse 9 is found in the repetition of the Amidah (Silent Meditation) of Musaf of Rosh HaShanah.

Segments of verses 14 and 23 form one of the verses of the long Tachanun (Penitential Prayer), recited on Mondays and Thursdays.

Verse 27 comprises one of the verses of Hoshi'a et Amecha, one of the paragraphs of Pesukei Dezimra (introductory Verses of Praise to the Shacharit morning service).

Contemporary Song

Verse 5

Talmud on Tehillim

Verse 7: "כִּי לֹא בְקַשְׁתִּי אֶבְטָח; וְחַרְבִּי לֹא תוֹשִׁיעֵנִי"—"For not in my bow do I trust nor does my sword deliver me."

The Talmud, Bava Batra 123a, explains that Ya'akov (Jacob) acquired the land not by mighty swords or bows and arrows, but rather through his prayers and supplications. By equating the words "charbi"—"my sword", and "kashti"—"my bow" of this verse with the same terms used by Ya'akov in blessing his sons prior to his death, the Talmud deduces that "charbi" refers to prayer, and "kashti" refers to a bakashah—request. The Talmud is further employing a play on words here, as the word "kashti" is written in the above verses with the prefix "ב"—"b"—"in", and thus is read and pronounced similarly to the word "בקשה"—"bakashah"—request.

פֶּרֶק מד

Chapter 44

א לַמְנַצֵּחַ
לִבְנֵי־קֹרַח מַשְׂכִּיל׃

1 To the Chief Musician,
a Psalm of the sons of Korach, an instruction.

ב אֱלֹהִים ׀ בְּאָזְנֵינוּ שָׁמַעְנוּ
אֲבוֹתֵינוּ סִפְּרוּ־לָנוּ
פֹּעַל פָּעַלְתָּ בִימֵיהֶם
בִּימֵי קֶדֶם׃

2 God, with our ears we have heard,
our fathers have told us;
of the work You did in their days,
in the days of old.

ג אַתָּה ׀ יָדְךָ גּוֹיִם הוֹרַשְׁתָּ
וַתִּטָּעֵם
תָּרַע לְאֻמִּים וַתְּשַׁלְּחֵם׃

3 You, [with] Your hand,drove out the nations
and You planted them [our fathers] therein;
You afflicted peoples and drove them away.

ד כִּי לֹא בְחַרְבָּם
יָרְשׁוּ אָרֶץ
וּזְרוֹעָם לֹא־הוֹשִׁיעָה לָּמוֹ
כִּי־יְמִינְךָ וּזְרוֹעֲךָ
וְאוֹר פָּנֶיךָ
כִּי רְצִיתָם׃

4 For not by their own sword
did they inherit the land,
nor did their own arm deliver them,
but Your right hand and Your arm,
and the light of Your countenance;
because You favored them.

ה אַתָּה־הוּא מַלְכִּי אֱלֹהִים
צַוֵּה יְשׁוּעוֹת יַעֲקֹב׃

5 You are my King, God;
command the deliverance of Jacob.

ו בְּךָ צָרֵינוּ נְנַגֵּחַ
בְּשִׁמְךָ נָבוּס
קָמֵינוּ׃

6 Through You will we gore our adversaries;
with Your Name will we trample
those who rise up against us.

ז כִּי לֹא בְקַשְׁתִּי אֶבְטָח
וְחַרְבִּי לֹא תוֹשִׁיעֵנִי׃

7 For not in my bow do I trust
nor does my sword deliver me.

ח כִּי הוֹשַׁעְתָּנוּ
מִצָּרֵינוּ
וּמְשַׂנְאֵינוּ
הֱבִישׁוֹתָ׃

8 But You have delivered us
from our adversaries,
and those who cause hatred against us
have You shamed.

ט בֵּאלֹהִים הִלַּלְנוּ כָל־הַיּוֹם
וְשִׁמְךָ ׀ לְעוֹלָם נוֹדֶה סֶלָה׃

9 In God we gloried all the day,
and Your Name we will thank forever, Selah.

י אַף־זָנַחְתָּ
וַתַּכְלִימֵנוּ
וְלֹא־תֵצֵא בְּצִבְאוֹתֵינוּ׃

10 Even though You have cast off
and disgraced us,
and You do not go forth with our hosts.

יא וּתְשִׁיבֵנוּ אָחוֹר מִנִּי־צָר
וּמְשַׂנְאֵינוּ
שָׁסוּ לָמוֹ׃

11 You made us retreat from the adversary
and those who cause hatred against us
plunder for themselves.

יב תִּתְּנֵנוּ כְּצֹאן מַאֲכָל
וּבַגּוֹיִם זֵרִיתָנוּ׃

12 You gave us up like sheep to be eaten,
and among the nations You have scattered us.

יג תִּמְכֹּר־עַמְּךָ בְלֹא־הוֹן
וְלֹא־רִבִּיתָ בִּמְחִירֵיהֶם׃

13 You sold Your people without gain,
and have not set their value high.

יד תְּשִׂימֵנוּ חֶרְפָּה לִשְׁכֵנֵינוּ לַעַג וָקֶלֶס לִסְבִיבוֹתֵינוּ׃	14 You humililated us to our neighbors, a scorn and a mockery to those who surround us.
טו תְּשִׂימֵנוּ מָשָׁל בַּגּוֹיִם מְנוֹד־רֹאשׁ בַּל־אֻמִּים׃	15 You made us a byword among the nations, a [cause for] shaking of the head among the peoples.
טז כָּל־הַיּוֹם כְּלִמָּתִי נֶגְדִּי וּבֹשֶׁת פָּנַי כִּסָּתְנִי׃	16 All the day my disgrace is before me, and the shame of my face has covered me.
יז מִקּוֹל מְחָרֵף וּמְגַדֵּף מִפְּנֵי אוֹיֵב וּמִתְנַקֵּם׃	17 Before the voice of the taunter and the blasphemer, before the enemy and the avenger.
יח כָּל־זֹאת בָּאַתְנוּ וְלֹא שְׁכַחֲנוּךָ וְלֹא־שִׁקַּרְנוּ בִּבְרִיתֶךָ׃	18 All this has come upon us and yet we have not forgotten You, nor have we been false to Your covenant.
יט לֹא־נָסוֹג אָחוֹר לִבֵּנוּ וַתֵּט אֲשֻׁרֵינוּ מִנִּי אָרְחֶךָ׃	19 Our heart has not turned back, nor have our steps turned away from Your path.
כ כִּי דִכִּיתָנוּ בִּמְקוֹם תַּנִּים וַתְּכַס עָלֵינוּ בְצַלְמָוֶת׃	20 [Even] though You crushed us in a place of reptiles, and covered us in the shadow of death.
כא אִם־שָׁכַחְנוּ שֵׁם אֱלֹהֵינוּ וַנִּפְרֹשׂ כַּפֵּינוּ לְאֵל זָר׃	21 Have we forgotten the Name of our God, and stretched out our hands to a strange god?
כב הֲלֹא אֱלֹהִים יַחֲקָר־זֹאת כִּי־הוּא יֹדֵעַ תַּעֲלֻמוֹת לֵב׃	22 Would God not have searched this out, for He knows the secrets of the heart.
כג כִּי־עָלֶיךָ הֹרַגְנוּ כָל־הַיּוֹם נֶחְשַׁבְנוּ כְּצֹאן טִבְחָה׃	23 For it is for Your sake that we are killed all the day; we are considered as sheep for the slaughter.
כד עוּרָה | לָמָּה תִישַׁן | אֲדֹנָי הָקִיצָה אַל־תִּזְנַח לָנֶצַח׃	24 Awake, why do You [appear to] sleep, my Master? Arouse Yourself, cast [us] not off forever.
כה לָמָּה־פָנֶיךָ תַסְתִּיר תִּשְׁכַּח עָנְיֵנוּ וְלַחֲצֵנוּ׃	25 Why do You conceal Your face and forget our affliction and our oppression?
כו כִּי שָׁחָה לֶעָפָר נַפְשֵׁנוּ דָּבְקָה לָאָרֶץ בִּטְנֵנוּ׃	26 For bowed down to the dust is our soul, clinging to the earth is our belly.
כז קוּמָה עֶזְרָתָה לָּנוּ וּפְדֵנוּ לְמַעַן חַסְדֶּךָ׃	27 Arise, come to our aid and redeem us for the sake of Your kindness.

פרק מה Chapter 45

Weekly Cycle	Monthly Cycle	Book Number
Monday	8th day of the month	Book 2

Author
בְּנֵי-קֹרַח—Sons of Korach—Korach rebelled against his cousins Moshe and Aharon (Moses and Aaron) and challenged their authority. Korach and his cohorts perished in the aftermath of the rebellion, yet his sons, who repented, survived.

Genre
Psalm of Royalty - This psalm describes how God reigns supreme. It focuses on the human king of Israel, or upon God as King of Israel.

Chapter Summary
This psalm describes the virtues of the ideal monarch of the Jewish people, perhaps an allusion to the high stature of Torah scholars. Alternatively, it is perhaps a reference to the righteousness of the messianic king and the redemption he will usher in.

This psalm consists of eighteen verses, subdivided into three parts. The first verse serves as a heading; the final verse serves as a conclusion.
In verse 2, the psalmists praise their composition and present their song to "the king" (see Chapter Summary above).
In verses 3-8, they praise the king and his virtues.
In verses 9-17, they describe a royal wedding and praise the bride, perhaps alluding to the messianic era.

Introductory Words
לַמְנַצֵּחַ—Lamnatsei'ach—To the Conductor
שִׁיר—Shir—Song

Musical Instrument
מַשְׂכִּיל—Maskil—a discerning person; alternatively, a giver of instruction, perhaps denoting a translator of the chapter (Rashi).

Techinical Terminology
שֹׁשַׁנִּים—Shoshanim—a musical instrument which resembled a bell with petals attached, likening it to a lily or rose.

Shimush Tehillim - When to Say
For one who has an evil spouse —Verse 14 states: "All honor [awaits] the princess within [the palace], greater than golden settings is her raiment."

Biblical Places
אוֹפִיר—Ophir—a country that exported gold to Israel and other countries in the Middle East and

North Africa. The exact location of Ophir is unknown.
צֹר—Tzor—Tyre—a city located on the southwest coast of Lebanon, just to the north of Israel. It was particularly known for the production of a rare and extraordinarily expensive purple dye, known as Tyrian purple, perhaps produced from the murex shellfish. This color was, in many cultures of ancient times, reserved for the use of nobility. A variant form of this dye was techeilet, of sky blue color, used to color the tzitzit fringes of the four cornered garment.

Talmud on Tehillim

Verse 4: "חֲגוֹר חַרְבְּךָ עַל יָרֵךְ"—"Gird your sword on the thigh."
The Talmud, Shabbat 63a, deduces from this verse that a weapon may be carried in the public domain on Shabbat, if being worn as a ceremonial object or jewelry. The Talmudic sages are perhaps also teaching, by way of allegory, that one should be careful to review his/her learning. Just as a sword stands ready upon the thigh of a mighty warrior, enabling him to triumph in battle, so too having one's Torah study "upon the thigh", at the ready to recall and engage in debate, will enable him to succeed in the application of his learning, and is thus ultimately his "jewelry"—his glory and spendor.
Verse 5: "וַהֲדָרְךָ, צְלַח"— "In your glory, be successful."
The Talmud, Shabbat 63a, teaches: "Two scholars who sharpen each other in halachah (Jewish law), God grants them success."

פֶּרֶק מה

Chapter 45

א לַמְנַצֵּחַ עַל־שֹׁשַׁנִּים
לִבְנֵי־קֹרַח מַשְׂכִּיל
שִׁיר יְדִידֹת׃

1 To the Chief Musician, upon shoshanim,
[a Psalm] of the sons of Korach, an instruction,
a song of endearment.

ב רָחַשׁ לִבִּי ׀ דָּבָר טוֹב
אֹמֵר אָנִי מַעֲשַׂי לְמֶלֶךְ
לְשׁוֹנִי עֵט ׀ סוֹפֵר מָהִיר׃

2 My heart is moved with a noble theme:
I say, ``My works are in honor of a king,
my tongue is like the pen of an expert writer."

ג יָפְיָפִיתָ מִבְּנֵי אָדָם
הוּצַק חֵן בְּשִׂפְתוֹתֶיךָ
עַל־כֵּן בֵּרַכְךָ אֱלֹהִים לְעוֹלָם׃

3 You are fairer than [other] sons of man,
grace is poured upon your lips;
therefore God has blessed you forever.

ד חֲגוֹר־חַרְבְּךָ עַל־יָרֵךְ גִּבּוֹר
הוֹדְךָ וַהֲדָרֶךָ׃

4 Gird your sword on the thigh, mighty one,
[it is] your beauty and your splendor.

ה וַהֲדָרְךָ ׀ צְלַח
רְכַב עַל־דְּבַר־אֱמֶת
וְעַנְוָה־צֶדֶק
וְתוֹרְךָ נוֹרָאוֹת יְמִינֶךָ׃

5 And with your splendor be successful,
mount and ride on behalf of truth
and righteous humility,
let your right hand teach you awesome things.

ו חִצֶּיךָ שְׁנוּנִים
עַמִּים תַּחְתֶּיךָ יִפְּלוּ
בְּלֵב
אוֹיְבֵי הַמֶּלֶךְ׃

6 Your arrows are sharpened,
peoples will fall under you,
[the arrows sink] into the heart
of the enemies of the king.

ז כִּסְאֲךָ אֱלֹהִים עוֹלָם וָעֶד

7 Your throne, O judge, is forever and ever;

שֵׁבֶט מִישֹׁר			the scepter of equity
שֵׁבֶט מַלְכוּתֶךָ׃			is the scepter of your kingdom.
אָהַבְתָּ צֶּדֶק וַתִּשְׂנָא רֶשַׁע	ח	8	You love righteousness and hate wickedness,
עַל־כֵּן ׀ מְשָׁחֲךָ אֱלֹהִים אֱלֹהֶיךָ			therefore God, your God, has annointed you
שֶׁמֶן שָׂשׂוֹן מֵחֲבֵרֶיךָ׃			with the oil of rejoicing, above your fellows.
מֹר־וַאֲהָלוֹת קְצִיעוֹת	ט	9	Myrrh and aloes, and cassia,
כָּל־בִּגְדֹתֶיךָ			are all your garments,
מִן־הֵיכְלֵי שֵׁן			[more splendid] than ivory palaces
מִנִּי שִׂמְּחוּךָ׃			are Mine that will make you rejoice.
בְּנוֹת מְלָכִים בְּיִקְּרוֹתֶיךָ	י	10	Daughters of kings visit you,
נִצְּבָה שֵׁגַל לִימִינְךָ			the queen stands at your right hand
בְּכֶתֶם אוֹפִיר׃			in the golden jewelry of Ophir.
שִׁמְעִי־בַת וּרְאִי	יא	11	``Listen, daughter, and observe
וְהַטִּי אָזְנֵךְ			and incline your ear;
וְשִׁכְחִי עַמֵּךְ			and forget your people
וּבֵית אָבִיךְ׃			and your father's house.
וְיִתְאָו הַמֶּלֶךְ יָפְיֵךְ	יב	12	So that the King will desire your beauty,
כִּי־הוּא אֲדֹנַיִךְ			for He is your Master,
וְהִשְׁתַּחֲוִי־לוֹ׃			and prostrate yourself before Him.
וּבַת־צֹר ׀	יג	13	And the daughter of Tyre,
בְּמִנְחָה פָּנַיִךְ יְחַלּוּ			with a gift will seek your presence—
עֲשִׁירֵי עָם׃			[those who are] the richest of the people.
כָּל־כְּבוּדָּה בַת־מֶלֶךְ	יד	14	All honor [awaits] the princess
פְּנִימָה			within [the palace],
מִמִּשְׁבְּצוֹת זָהָב לְבוּשָׁהּ׃			greater than golden settings is her raiment.
לִרְקָמוֹת	טו	15	In embroidered clothing
תּוּבַל לַמֶּלֶךְ			will she be brought to the King,
בְּתוּלוֹת אַחֲרֶיהָ רֵעוֹתֶיהָ			the virgins in her train are her companions,
מוּבָאוֹת לָךְ׃			being brought to you.
תּוּבַלְנָה	טז	16	They are brought
בִּשְׂמָחֹת וָגִיל			with rejoicing and gladness,
תְּבֹאֶינָה בְּהֵיכַל מֶלֶךְ׃			they enter into the palace of the King.
תַּחַת אֲבֹתֶיךָ יִהְיוּ בָנֶיךָ	יז	17	In place of your fathers will be your sons;
תְּשִׁיתֵמוֹ לְשָׂרִים			You will appoint them as princes
בְּכָל־הָאָרֶץ׃			in all the land.
אַזְכִּירָה שִׁמְךָ	יח	18	I will cause Your Name to be remembered
בְּכָל־דֹּר וָדֹר			in all generations;
עַל־כֵּן עַמִּים יְהוֹדֻךָ			therefore the peoples will praise You
לְעֹלָם וָעֶד׃			forever and ever.

פרק מו Chapter 46

Weekly Cycle	Monthly Cycle	Book Number
Monday	8th day of the month	Book 2

Author

בְּנֵי-קֹרַח—Sons of Korach—Korach rebelled against his cousins Moshe and Aharon (Moses and Aaron) and challenged their authority. Korach and his cohorts perished in the aftermath of the rebellion, yet his sons, who repented, survived.

When & Why

The sons of Korach wrote this psalm about the coming of the Messiah and salvation of Israel in the end of days.

Genre

Psalm of Communal Confidence - In this psalm, the community expresses absolute certainty that their prayers will be heard.

Psalm of Praise – This is a psalm of celebration, often the result of a victory. It declares God's goodness and urges all of creation to worship.

Psalm of Zion - This psalm glorifies God's city and His holy mount in which He has placed His abode.

Chapter Summary

While some of the psalms composed by the sons of the Korach spoke prophetically of exile and redemption, this psalm speaks of redemption and the pangs of the messianic age and the war launched by Gog and Magog—a precursor to the messianic era.

This psalm consists of twelve verses, subdivided into two parts. The first verse serves as a heading. Each of the two parts is followed by the refrain, "Adonoy of Hosts is with us, a stronghold for us is the God of Jacob, The Lord of hosts is with us. The God of Jacob, Selah." (verses 8 and 12).
In verses 2-7, the psalmists describe the effects of, and God's involvement in, an earthquake.
In verses 9-11, they describe how God ceases wars.

Introductory Words

לַמְנַצֵּחַ—Lamnatsei'ach—To the Conductor
שִׁיר—Shir—Song

Musical Instrument

עֲלָמוֹת—Alamos—An Unidentified Instrument - probably a Harp.

Techinical Terminology

סֶלָה—Selah—While its meaning is unclear, the most familiar opinion is that it is a musical notation, instructing the Levitical orchestra to pause its singing and playing of instruments. Alternatively, "Selah" may mean "everlasting".

Shimush Tehillim - When to Say

For a man who hates his wife—Verse 10 states: "He causes wars to cease to the end of the earth," an allusion to personal wars.

Where in the Siddur

Verse 8 (repeated as verse 12) is one of the verses of V'hu Rachum, one of the paragraphs comprising Pesukei Dezimra (introductory Verses of Praise to the Shacharit morning service). Verse 8 is also found in Uva Letzion—one of the closing prayers of Shacharit.

פֶּרֶק מו			**Chapter 46**
לַמְנַצֵּחַ	א	1	To the Chief Musician,
לִבְנֵי־קֹרַח			[a Psalm] of the sons of Korach,
עַל־עֲלָמוֹת שִׁיר׃			upon Alamos, a song.
אֱלֹהִים לָנוּ מַחֲסֶה וָעֹז	ב	2	God is our refuge and strength,
עֶזְרָה בְצָרוֹת			a help in times of trouble,
נִמְצָא מְאֹד׃			He is most accessible.
עַל־כֵּן לֹא־נִירָא	ג	3	Therefore we will not fear
בְּהָמִיר אָרֶץ			when He transforms the earth,
וּבְמוֹט הָרִים			when mountains are hurled
בְּלֵב יַמִּים׃			into the midst of the sea.
יֶהֱמוּ יֶחְמְרוּ מֵימָיו	ד	4	Though its waters roar and foam,
יִרְעֲשׁוּ־הָרִים בְּגַאֲוָתוֹ			and though mountains shake before His glory,
סֶלָה׃			Selah.
נָהָר	ה	5	There is a river—
פְּלָגָיו			its streams
יְשַׂמְּחוּ עִיר־אֱלֹהִים			will make the City of God rejoice,
קְדֹשׁ מִשְׁכְּנֵי עֶלְיוֹן׃			the holiest of dwelling places of the Most High.
אֱלֹהִים בְּקִרְבָּהּ בַּל־תִּמּוֹט	ו	6	God is in its midst, it will not be moved,
יַעְזְרֶהָ אֱלֹהִים לִפְנוֹת בֹּקֶר׃			God will help it at the approach of morning.
הָמוּ גוֹיִם מָטוּ מַמְלָכוֹת	ז	7	Nations roared, kingdoms were moved,
נָתַן בְּקוֹלוֹ תָּמוּג אָרֶץ׃			He uttered His voice, the earth melted.
יְהוָה צְבָאוֹת עִמָּנוּ	ח	8	Adonoy of Hosts is with us,
מִשְׂגָּב־לָנוּ אֱלֹהֵי יַעֲקֹב			a stronghold for us is the God of Jacob,
סֶלָה׃			Selah.
לְכוּ־חֲזוּ מִפְעֲלוֹת יְהוָה	ט	9	Go, behold the works of Adonoy,
אֲשֶׁר־שָׂם שַׁמּוֹת בָּאָרֶץ׃			Who has made desolations in the land.

מַשְׁבִּית מִלְחָמוֹת	י	10	He causes wars to cease
עַד־קְצֵה הָאָרֶץ			to the end of the earth,
קֶשֶׁת יְשַׁבֵּר			the bow He will break
וְקִצֵּץ חֲנִית			and He will cut the spear [to pieces]
עֲגָלוֹת יִשְׂרֹף בָּאֵשׁ:			chariots He will burn in the fire.
הַרְפּוּ וּדְעוּ	יא	11	"Desist, and know
כִּי אָנֹכִי אֱלֹהִים			that I am God,
אָרוּם בַּגּוֹיִם			I will be exalted among the nations,
אָרוּם בָּאָרֶץ:			I will be exalted upon the earth."
יהוה צְבָאוֹת עִמָּנוּ	יב	12	Adonoy of Hosts is with us,
מִשְׂגָּב לָנוּ אֱלֹהֵי יַעֲקֹב			a stronghold for us is the God of Jacob,
סֶלָה:			Selah.

פרק מז Chapter 47

Weekly Cycle	Monthly Cycle	Book Number
Monday	8th day of the month	Book 2

Author

בְּנֵי-קֹרַח—Sons of Korach—Korach rebelled against his cousins Moshe and Aharon (Moses and Aaron) and challenged their authority. Korach and his cohorts perished in the aftermath of the rebellion, yet his sons, who repented, survived.

Genre

Psalm of Enthronement - This psalm extols God's royal role in the universe.
Psalm of Praise – This is a psalm of celebration, often the result of a victory. It declares God's goodness and urges all of creation to worship.

Chapter Summary

This psalm describes the great rejoicing of the Jewish people following their deliverance, and speaks of the establishment of the Kingdom of God that will ensue.

This psalm consists of ten verses, subdivided into three parts. The first verse serves as a heading.
In verses 2-5, the psalmists turn to all the nations of the world, and invite them to come and raise their voices in praise to God.
In verses 6-8, they describe the moment that God ascends His throne, accompanied by Shofar blasts and songs of praise.

In verses 9 & 10, they proudly proclaim God's kingship and declare that all the nations have gathered together to accept His sovereignty.

Introductory Words

לַמְנַצֵּחַ—Lamnatsei'ach—To the Conductor
מִזְמוֹר—Mizmor—Musical Accompaniment

Techinical Terminology

סֶלָה—Selah—While its meaning is unclear, the most familiar opinion is that it is a musical notation, instructing the Levitical orchestra to pause its singing and playing of instruments. Alternatively, "Selah" may mean "everlasting".

Shimush Tehillim - When to Say

To be accepted by others and find favor in their eyes (say 7 times)—Verse 5 states: "He chose for us our inheritance, the pride of Jacob whom He loves."

Interesting Fact

Verse 2 is written proof that people would originally clap their hands when singing Psalms.

Where in the Siddur

Recited on Rosh HaShanah as part of the introduction to the blowing of the Shofar.

Biblical Personalities

אַבְרָהָם—Avraham—together with his wife Sarah—the first person to proactively spread the idea of monotheism throughout the world, as well as the first to enter into a covenant with God.
It is for this reason that he was chosen as the first of our forefathers, and Sarah as the first of our foremothers. Today, Avraham is considered to be the founder of the world's three monotheistic religions: Judaism, Christianity and Islam. In fact, this is alluded to in the name Avraham. When God changes his name from Avram to Avraham, by the addition of the letter "hei", God tells him that he has now made him an "אַב הֲמוֹן גּוֹיִם"—"Av hamon goyim"—"father of many nations".
יַעֲקֹב—Yaakov—Jacob, also called Yisrael—Israel—the third patriarch, known as the father of the twelve tribes of Israel. He was married to Rachel and Leah, and was the twin brother of Eisav.

פרק מז	Chapter 47
א לַמְנַצֵּחַ ׀ לִבְנֵי־קֹרַח מִזְמוֹר׃	1 To the Chief Musician, a Psalm of the sons of Korach.
ב כָּל־הָעַמִּים תִּקְעוּ־כָף הָרִיעוּ לֵאלֹהִים בְּקוֹל רִנָּה׃	2 All peoples clap hands, shout to God with the voice of joyous song.
ג כִּי־יְהוָה עֶלְיוֹן נוֹרָא מֶלֶךְ גָּדוֹל עַל־כָּל־הָאָרֶץ׃	3 For Adonoy is Most High, awesome; a great King over all the earth.
ד יַדְבֵּר עַמִּים תַּחְתֵּינוּ וּלְאֻמִּים תַּחַת רַגְלֵינוּ׃	4 He subdues peoples under us, and nations under our feet.

יִבְחַר־לָנוּ אֶת־נַחֲלָתֵנוּ	ה	5	He chose for us our inheritance,
אֶת גְּאוֹן יַעֲקֹב אֲשֶׁר־אָהֵב			the pride of Jacob whom He loves,
סֶלָה׃			Selah.
עָלָה אֱלֹהִים בִּתְרוּעָה	ו	6	God has ascended with a blast,
יְהוָֹה בְּקוֹל שׁוֹפָר׃			Adonoy, with the sound of the shofar.
זַמְּרוּ אֱלֹהִים זַמֵּרוּ	ז	7	Sing praises to God, sing praises;
זַמְּרוּ לְמַלְכֵּנוּ זַמֵּרוּ׃			sing praises to our King, sing praises.
כִּי מֶלֶךְ כָּל־הָאָרֶץ אֱלֹהִים	ח	8	For King of all the earth is God;
זַמְּרוּ מַשְׂכִּיל׃			sing praises with skillful art.
מָלַךְ אֱלֹהִים עַל־גּוֹיִם	ט	9	God has reigned over nations,
אֱלֹהִים יָשַׁב ׀ עַל־כִּסֵּא קָדְשׁוֹ׃			God is seated upon His holy throne.
נְדִיבֵי	י	10	The nobles [converts]
עַמִּים ׀ נֶאֱסָפוּ			among the peoples gathered,
עַם אֱלֹהֵי אַבְרָהָם			[joining] the people of the God of Abraham;
כִּי לֵאלֹהִים מָגִנֵּי־אֶרֶץ			for God has the power to shield the earth,
מְאֹד נַעֲלָה׃			He is greatly exalted.

King David Playing the Harp

פֶּרֶק מוז Chapter 48

Weekly Cycle	Monthly Cycle	Book Number
Monday	8th day of the month	Book 2

Author

בְּנֵי-קֹרַח—Sons of Korach—Korach rebelled against his cousins Moshe and Aharon (Moses and Aaron) and challenged their authority. Korach and his cohorts perished in the aftermath of the rebellion, yet his sons, who repented, survived.

Genre

Psalm of of Praise - This is a psalm of celebration, often the result of a victory. It declares God's goodness and urges all of creation to worship.

Psalm of Zion – This psalm glorifies God's city and His holy mount in which He has placed His abode.

Chapter Summary

The sons of Korach composed this psalm to express the many excellent qualities of the holy city of Jerusalem. Its superiority stems mainly from its being the site of the Beit HaMikdash (Holy Temple).

This psalm consists of fifteen verses, subdivided into five parts. The first verse serves as a heading.

In verses 2-4, the psalmists praise Zion for its beauty and strength, which in turn is a testimony to God's greatness.

In verses 5-8, they describe how even the kings were afraid and trembled at what they saw.

In verses 9-11, they praise the Almighty as the one who dwells in His city.

In verses 12-14, the authors call upon the daughters of Yehudah (Judah) to rejoice and to walk around Zion and encircle her.

In verse 15, they close by declaring that "this is God, our God forever and ever, He will lead us like children."

Introductory Words

מִזְמוֹר—Mizmor—Musical Accompaniment

שִׁיר—Shir—Song

Shimush Tehillim - When to Say

To scare away one's enemy (say 7 times)—Verse 7 states: "Trembling siezed them there, like the pangs of a woman in labor."

Where in the Siddur

Recited as the Shir Shel Yom (Psalm of the Day) for Monday.

Verse 2 comprises one of the verses found in the Mishnah (Tamid 7:4), recited after Ein K'Eilokeinu upon the conclusion of Musaf of Shabbat.

Biblical Places

תַּרְשִׁישׁ—Tarshish—a seaport, which had a fleet at sea along with the fleet of Hiram. Once in three years the fleet of Tarshish would arrive at the Port of Yafo (Jaffa) bearing gold, silver, ivory, monkeys and parrots.

צִיּוֹן—Zion—often used as a synonym for Jerusalem. The term Zion originally referred only to the area where a Jebbusite fortress once stood, also the location of the City of David. Zion was later used by prophets and psalmists to refer to all of Jerusalem.

Talmud on Tehillim

Verse 2: "גָּדוֹל יְהוָה וּמְהֻלָּל מְאֹד"—"Adonoy is great and highly extolled."

The Talmud, Rosh Hashanah 31a, states that this chapter was sung by the Levites every Monday in the Beit HaMikdash (Temple). Indeed, the introductory phrase to the Shir Shel Yom (Psalm of the Day), states: "The Levites would recite [the following] in the Beit HaMikdash."

פֶּרֶק מ״ח	Chapter 48
א שִׁיר מִזְמוֹר לִבְנֵי־קֹרַח׃	1 A song, a Psalm by the sons of Korach.
ב גָּדוֹל יְהוָה וּמְהֻלָּל מְאֹד בְּעִיר אֱלֹהֵינוּ הַר־קָדְשׁוֹ׃	2 Adonoy is great and highly extolled in the city of our God, the mountain of His Sanctuary.
ג יְפֵה נוֹף מְשׂוֹשׂ כָּל־הָאָרֶץ הַר־צִיּוֹן יַרְכְּתֵי צָפוֹן קִרְיַת מֶלֶךְ רָב׃	3 Beautiful in its panoramic vista, the joy of all the earth is Mount Zion, on the northern extremities (of Jerusalem); the city of the great King.
ד אֱלֹהִים בְּאַרְמְנוֹתֶיהָ נוֹדַע לְמִשְׂגָּב׃	4 God, in its palaces, has become known as a Stronghold.
ה כִּי־הִנֵּה הַמְּלָכִים נוֹעֲדוּ עָבְרוּ יַחְדָּו׃	5 For behold, the kings assembled, they passed by together.
ו הֵמָּה רָאוּ כֵּן תָּמָהוּ נִבְהֲלוּ נֶחְפָּזוּ׃	6 They saw and were astounded, they panicked and fled in haste.
ז רְעָדָה אֲחָזָתַם שָׁם חִיל כַּיּוֹלֵדָה׃	7 Trembling seized them there, like the pangs of a woman in labor.
ח בְּרוּחַ קָדִים תְּשַׁבֵּר אֳנִיּוֹת תַּרְשִׁישׁ׃	8 With an east wind You smashed the ships of Tarshish.
ט כַּאֲשֶׁר שָׁמַעְנוּ | כֵּן רָאִינוּ בְּעִיר־יְהוָה צְבָאוֹת בְּעִיר אֱלֹהֵינוּ אֱלֹהִים יְכוֹנְנֶהָ עַד־עוֹלָם סֶלָה׃	9 As we heard, so we saw, in the city of Adonoy of Hosts, in the city of our God; may God establish it for eternity, Selah.
י דִּמִּינוּ אֱלֹהִים חַסְדֶּךָ בְּקֶרֶב הֵיכָלֶךָ׃	10 We hoped, God, for Your lovingkindness in the midst of Your Sanctuary.
יא כְּשִׁמְךָ אֱלֹהִים כֵּן תְּהִלָּתְךָ עַל־קַצְוֵי־אֶרֶץ צֶדֶק מָלְאָה יְמִינֶךָ׃	11 As Your Name, God, so is Your praise— to the ends of the earth; Your right hand is full of righteousness.
יב יִשְׂמַח | הַר־צִיּוֹן תָּגֵלְנָה בְּנוֹת יְהוּדָה לְמַעַן מִשְׁפָּטֶיךָ׃	12 Let Mount Zion rejoice, let the daughters of Judah exult, because of Your judgments.
יג סֹבּוּ צִיּוֹן וְהַקִּיפוּהָ סִפְרוּ מִגְדָּלֶיהָ׃	13 Rally around Zion and encircle her, count her towers.
יד שִׁיתוּ לִבְּכֶם | לְחֵילָה פַּסְּגוּ אַרְמְנוֹתֶיהָ לְמַעַן תְּסַפְּרוּ לְדוֹר אַחֲרוֹן׃	14 Consider well her ramparts, raise high her citadels, that you may recount it to future generations.
טו כִּי זֶה | אֱלֹהִים אֱלֹהֵינוּ עוֹלָם וָעֶד הוּא יְנַהֲגֵנוּ עַל־מוּת׃	15 That this is God, our God forever and ever, He will lead us like children.

פרק מט Chapter 49

Weekly Cycle	Monthly Cycle	Book Number
Monday	9th day of the month	Book 2

Author

בְּנֵי-קֹרַח—Sons of Korach—Korach rebelled against his cousins Moshe and Aharon (Moses and Aaron) and challenged their authority. Korach and his cohorts perished in the aftermath of the rebellion, yet his sons, who repented, survived.

Genre

Psalm of of Wisdom - This psalm contains teachings and wise advice and are meant to instruct people on how to live a Godly life.

Chapter Summary

This psalm serves as a reminder that there is so much more to life than physical pleasures. Happiness is not measured solely by material wealth, and misery not by a lack thereof. Rather, it is the pursuit of spiritual wealth through which one attains true happiness.

This psalm consists of twenty-one verses, subdivided into five parts. The first verse serves as a heading.
In verses 2-5, the psalmists inform the reader that the following words of wisdom, understanding and riddles, to be accompaniedby the music of the harp, are directed at all of mankind.
In verses 6-11, they proclaim their trust in God, and remind us that death is the end of all men, from which one cannot be freed with material wealth.
In verses 12-15, they direct their attention to the wealthy who fool themselves into thinking that through their wealth they can achieve eternal life.
In verses 16-21, they again proclaim their trust in God, and repeat the refrain that a man's wealth is of no help to him once he is dead.

Introductory Words

לַמְנַצֵּחַ—Lamnatsei'ach—To the Conductor
מִזְמוֹר—Mizmor—Musical Accompaniment

Musical Instrument

כִּנּוֹר—Kinor—A Small Handheld Harp - played with a plecturm (pick).

Techinical Terminology

סֶלָה—Selah—While its meaning is unclear, the most familiar opinion is that it is a musical notation, instructing the Levitical orchestra to pause its singing and playing of instruments. Alternatively, "Selah" may mean "everlasting".

Shimush Tehillim - When to Say

For a fever—Verse 16 states: "But God will redeem my soul from the [grasp of] the grave, for He will take me [to Himself]."

Where in the Siddur

Recited on the Shabbat of Parashat Shekalim (one of the four special readings during the months of Adar and Nisan).

Recited following the Shacharit (morning service) and Ma'ariv (evening service) in a house of mourning.

Recited at the graveside burial service.

Verse 16 is found in the Yizkor memorial service recited on Yom Kippur and the Shalosh Regalim—the Festivals of Shemini Atzeret (eighth day of Sukkot), Pesach and Shavu'ot.

Verse 6 is found in Yesod HaTeshuvah (Foundation of Repentance) recited in some congregations on the eve of Rosh Hashanah. Some recite Yesod HaTeshuvah immediately following Hatarat Nedarim (Annulment of Vows).

Biblical Places

שְׁאוֹל—Sheol—Lower or Underworld; abode of the dead.

פֶּרֶק מט

א לַמְנַצֵּחַ |
לִבְנֵי־קֹרַח מִזְמוֹר׃
ב שִׁמְעוּ־זֹאת כָּל־הָעַמִּים
הַאֲזִינוּ כָּל־יֹשְׁבֵי חָלֶד׃
ג גַּם־בְּנֵי אָדָם גַּם־בְּנֵי־אִישׁ
יַחַד עָשִׁיר וְאֶבְיוֹן׃
ד פִּי יְדַבֵּר חָכְמוֹת
וְהָגוּת לִבִּי תְבוּנוֹת׃
ה אַטֶּה לְמָשָׁל אָזְנִי
אֶפְתַּח
בְּכִנּוֹר
חִידָתִי׃
ו לָמָּה אִירָא בִּימֵי רָע
עֲוֺן עֲקֵבַי יְסוּבֵּנִי׃
ז הַבֹּטְחִים עַל־חֵילָם
וּבְרֹב עָשְׁרָם יִתְהַלָּלוּ׃
ח אָח לֹא־פָדֹה יִפְדֶּה אִישׁ
לֹא־יִתֵּן לֵאלֹהִים כָּפְרוֹ׃
ט וְיֵקַר פִּדְיוֹן נַפְשָׁם
וְחָדַל לְעוֹלָם׃

Chapter 49

1 To the Chief Musician,
a Psalm by the sons of Korach.
2 Hear this all peoples,
listen all inhabitants of the decaying world!
3 Sons of Adam and sons of men,
rich and poor together.
4 My mouth shall speak wisdom
and the meditation of my heart shall be of understanding.
5 I will incline my ear to a parable,
I will begin to solve,
to the accompaniment of a harp,
my riddle.
6 Why should I fear in the days of evil?
The iniquity I trod upon surrounds me.
7 Those who trust in their wealth
and take pride in their great riches.
8 A man will not redeem his brother
neither can he give to God his ransom.
9 The redemption of their soul is too costly
and it shall cease to be forever.

י וִֽיחִי־ע֥וֹד לָנֶ֑צַח
לֹ֖א יִרְאֶ֣ה הַשָּֽׁחַת׃

10 Shall he then live forever,
shall he never see the grave?

יא כִּ֤י יִרְאֶ֨ה ׀ חֲכָמִ֤ים יָמ֗וּתוּ
יַ֤חַד כְּסִ֣יל וָבַ֣עַר יֹאבֵ֑דוּ
וְעָזְב֖וּ לַאֲחֵרִ֣ים חֵילָֽם׃

11 For he sees that wise men die,
the fools and senseless perish equally
and leave their wealth to others.

יב קִרְבָּ֤ם
בָּתֵּ֨ימוֹ ׀ לְֽעוֹלָ֗ם
מִ֭שְׁכְּנֹתָם לְדֹ֣ר וָדֹ֑ר
קָֽרְא֥וּ בִ֝שְׁמוֹתָ֗ם
עֲלֵ֣י אֲדָמֽוֹת׃

12 Their inner thoughts are
that their houses [will last] forever,
their homes for generation after generation;
(for) they have proclaimed their names
throughout the lands.

יג וְאָדָ֣ם בִּ֭יקָר בַּל־יָלִ֑ין
נִמְשַׁ֖ל כַּבְּהֵמ֣וֹת נִדְמֽוּ׃

13 But man does not endure in his splendor,
he is likened to the silenced animals.

יד זֶ֣ה דַ֭רְכָּם
כֵּ֣סֶל לָ֑מוֹ
וְאַחֲרֵיהֶ֓ם ׀
בְּפִיהֶ֖ם יִרְצ֣וּ סֶֽלָה׃

14 This is their way—
their folly remains with them,
and [yet] their descendants
take pleasure in their speech, Selah.

טו כַּצֹּ֤אן ׀ לִשְׁא֥וֹל שַׁ֗תּוּ
מָ֤וֶת יִרְעֵ֗ם
וַיִּרְדּ֤וּ בָ֨ם יְשָׁרִ֨ים ׀
לַבֹּ֗קֶר
וְצוּרָם֮ לְבַלּ֥וֹת שְׁאוֹל
מִזְּבֻ֥ל לֽוֹ׃

15 Like sheep—they are destined for the grave;
death shall be their shepherd,
and the upright shall dominate them
at morning,
and their form will be consumed in the grave;
[it will not remain] their dwelling-place.

טז אַךְ־אֱלֹהִ֗ים יִפְדֶּ֣ה נַ֭פְשִׁי
מִֽיַּד־שְׁא֑וֹל
כִּ֖י יִקָּחֵ֣נִי סֶֽלָה׃

16 But God will redeem my soul
from the [grasp of] the grave,
for He will take me [to Himself] Selah.

יז אַל־תִּ֭ירָא כִּֽי־יַעֲשִׁ֣ר אִ֑ישׁ
כִּֽי־יִ֝רְבֶּה כְּב֣וֹד בֵּיתֽוֹ׃

17 Fear not when a man grows rich,
when the glory of his house is increased.

יח כִּ֤י לֹ֣א בְ֭מוֹתוֹ
יִקַּ֣ח הַכֹּ֑ל
לֹא־יֵרֵ֖ד אַחֲרָ֣יו כְּבוֹדֽוֹ׃

18 For when he dies,
he shall carry nothing away,
his glory will not descend after him.

יט כִּֽי־נַ֭פְשׁוֹ בְּחַיָּ֣יו יְבָרֵ֑ךְ
וְ֝יוֹדֻ֗ךָ
כִּֽי־תֵיטִ֥יב לָֽךְ׃

19 Because while he lived, he blessed his soul,
(saying): they will praise you
because you have done well for yourself.

כ תָּ֭בוֹא עַד־דּ֣וֹר אֲבוֹתָ֑יו
עַד־נֵ֝֗צַח לֹ֣א יִרְאוּ־אֽוֹר׃

20 He will join the generation of his fathers,
they shall not see light, for all eternity.

כא אָדָ֣ם בִּ֭יקָר
וְלֹ֣א יָבִ֑ין
נִמְשַׁ֖ל כַּבְּהֵמ֣וֹת נִדְמֽוּ׃

21 Man with [all] his splendor,
[but] without understanding
is likened to the silenced animals.

King David Playing the Harp

פרק נ Chapter 50

Weekly Cycle	Monthly Cycle	Book Number
Monday	9th day of the month	Book 2

Author
אָסָף—Asaf—a composer of several psalms and patriarch of a family of singers in the Beit HaMikdash (Temple).

Genre
Psalm of of Wisdom - This psalm contains teachings and wise advice and is meant to instruct people on how to live a Godly life.

Chapter Summary
Asaf praises God as Creator of the world. As such, He has no need for sacrificial offerings. While a sacrifice indeed brings honor to God, if the proper attitude of remorse and repentance are lacking, the offering becomes meaningless. The author concludes by declaring that God will show His salvation to the person who improves his ways.

This psalm consists of twenty-three verses, subdivided into four parts.
The first verse serves as a heading.
In verses 2-7, the psalmist describes, with beautiful imagery, the revelation of the Divine Presence.
In verses 8-15, God Himself offers words of rebuke relating to the sincerity of sacrifices.
In verses 16-21, God directs his rebuke toward the wicked who associate with robbers and adulterers.
In verses 22 &23, Asaf concludes by declaring that God desires the sacrifices offered with a pure heart and with the proper intentions.

Introductory Words
מִזְמוֹר—Mizmor—Musical Accompaniment

Techinical Terminology
סֶלָה—Selah—While its meaning is unclear, the most familiar opinion is that it is a musical notation, instructing the Levitical orchestra to pause its singing and playing of instruments. Alternatively, "Selah" may mean "everlasting".

Shimush Tehillim - When to Say
To be saved from enemies and bandits—Verses 15 & 16 state: "And call upon Me in the day of trouble; I will free you, and you will honor Me. But to the wicked, God said, "What does it avail you to recount my statutes, while you bear My covenant [only] upon your mouth?"

Biblical Places
צִיּוֹן—Zion—a place name often used as a synonym for Jerusalem. The term Zion originally referred only to the area where a Jebbusite fortress once stood, also the location of the City of David. Zion

was later used by prophets and psalmists as another name for Jerusalem.

Talmud on Tehillim

Verse 16: "וְלָרָשָׁע, אָמַר אֱלֹהִים"—"But to the wicked, God said."

The Talmud, Sukkah 55a, teaches that this verse was sung in the Beit HaMikdash (Holy Temple) on the second day of Chol HaMo'eid Sukkot (Intermediate Days of Sukkot), just prior to the opening of the Simchat Beit HaSho'eivah, a celebration of the drawing in of water to Jerusalem. As Jerusalem is located in a mountainous area, water was drawn in annually on the Festival of Sukkot. This verse admonished all present to rid themselves of any ill feelings, and to be happy and thankful to God on this joyous occasion.

פֶּרֶק נ

א מִזְמוֹר לְאָסָף
אֵל | אֱלֹהִים יְהוָֹה דִּבֶּר
וַיִּקְרָא־
אָרֶץ
מִמִּזְרַח־שֶׁמֶשׁ עַד־מְבֹאוֹ:
ב מִצִּיּוֹן מִכְלַל־יֹפִי
אֱלֹהִים הוֹפִיעַ:
ג יָבֹא אֱלֹהֵינוּ
וְאַל־יֶחֱרַשׁ
אֵשׁ־לְפָנָיו תֹּאכֵל
וּסְבִיבָיו נִשְׂעֲרָה מְאֹד:
ד יִקְרָא אֶל־הַשָּׁמַיִם מֵעָל
וְאֶל־הָאָרֶץ לָדִין עַמּוֹ:
ה אִסְפוּ־לִי חֲסִידָי
כֹּרְתֵי בְרִיתִי
עֲלֵי־זָבַח:
ו וַיַּגִּידוּ שָׁמַיִם צִדְקוֹ
כִּי־אֱלֹהִים | שֹׁפֵט הוּא סֶלָה:
ז שִׁמְעָה עַמִּי | וַאֲדַבֵּרָה
יִשְׂרָאֵל וְאָעִידָה בָּךְ
אֱלֹהִים אֱלֹהֶיךָ אָנֹכִי:
ח לֹא עַל־זְבָחֶיךָ
אוֹכִיחֶךָ
וְעוֹלֹתֶיךָ
לְנֶגְדִּי תָמִיד:

Chapter 50

1 A Psalm of Asaph.
Almighty God, Adonoy, has spoken,
and He called
[all] the [inhabitants of the] earth,
from the rising of the sun to its setting.
2 Out of Zion, perfect beauty,
God shines forth.
3 Our God will come
and He will not keep silent,
a fire before Him, devours [His enemies]
and round about Him it storms furiously.
4 He calls upon the heavens from above
and to the earth, to judge His people.
5 "Gather My devoted ones to Me,
those who made a covenant with Me
by sacrifice."
6 And the heavens declared His righteousness,
that God is the Judge, Selah.
7 "Hear My people and I will speak;
Israel, and I will testify against you;
God, your God, am I.
8 Not for [the lack of] your sacrifices
will I reprove you,
nor for your burnt offerings
that are [not] before Me continually.

ט	לֹא־אֶקַּח מִבֵּיתְךָ פָר	9	I will not take from your house a bullock,
	מִמִּכְלְאֹתֶיךָ עַתּוּדִים׃		nor from your corral any he-goats.
י	כִּי־לִי כָל־חַיְתוֹ־יָעַר	10	For Mine is every beast of the forest;
	בְּהֵמוֹת בְּהַרְרֵי־אָלֶף׃		the Behemoth upon a thousand hills.
יא	יָדַעְתִּי כָּל־עוֹף הָרִים	11	I know every bird of the mountains;
	וְזִיז שָׂדַי עִמָּדִי׃		the teeming life of fields is Mine.
יב	אִם־אֶרְעַב לֹא־אֹמַר לָךְ	12	Were I hungry I would not tell you,
	כִּי־לִי תֵבֵל		for Mine is the inhabitated world
	וּמְלֹאָהּ׃		and its fullness.
יג	הַאוֹכַל בְּשַׂר אַבִּירִים	13	Do I eat the flesh of bulls;
	וְדַם עַתּוּדִים אֶשְׁתֶּה׃		the blood of he-goats, do I drink?"
יד	זְבַח לֵאלֹהִים תּוֹדָה	14	[First] offer to God confession,
	וְשַׁלֵּם לְעֶלְיוֹן נְדָרֶיךָ׃		and then pay to the Most High your vows.
טו	וּקְרָאֵנִי בְּיוֹם צָרָה	15	"And call upon Me in the day of trouble;
	אֲחַלֶּצְךָ וּתְכַבְּדֵנִי׃		I will free you, and you will honor Me."
טז	וְלָרָשָׁע ׀ אָמַר אֱלֹהִים	16	But to the wicked, God said,
	מַה־לְּךָ		"What does it avail you
	לְסַפֵּר חֻקָּי		to recount my statutes,
	וַתִּשָּׂא בְרִיתִי		while you bear My covenant
	עֲלֵי־פִיךָ׃		[only] upon your mouth?
יז	וְאַתָּה שָׂנֵאתָ מוּסָר	17	For you hated discipline,
	וַתַּשְׁלֵךְ דְּבָרַי אַחֲרֶיךָ׃		and you cast My words behind you.
יח	אִם־רָאִיתָ גַנָּב וַתִּרֶץ עִמּוֹ	18	When you saw a thief, you sanctioned him,
	וְעִם מְנָאֲפִים חֶלְקֶךָ׃		and with adulterers was your portion.
יט	פִּיךָ שָׁלַחְתָּ בְרָעָה	19	Your mouth you let loose for evil,
	וּלְשׁוֹנְךָ תַּצְמִיד מִרְמָה׃		and harness your tongue to deceit.
כ	תֵּשֵׁב בְּאָחִיךָ תְדַבֵּר	20	You sit, against your brother you speak;
	בְּבֶן־אִמְּךָ תִּתֶּן־דֹּפִי׃		to your mother's son you bring contempt.
כא	אֵלֶּה עָשִׂיתָ ׀ וְהֶחֱרַשְׁתִּי	21	These have you done and I kept silent,
	דִּמִּיתָ הֱיוֹת־אֶהְיֶה כָמוֹךָ		Did you think I was like yourself;
	אוֹכִיחֲךָ		[but] I will reprove you
	וְאֶעֶרְכָה לְעֵינֶיךָ׃		and set it before your eyes.
כב	בִּינוּ־נָא זֹאת	22	Understand this, please I ask
	שֹׁכְחֵי אֱלוֹהַּ		you who have forgotten God,
	פֶּן־אֶטְרֹף		lest I tear [you] into pieces
	וְאֵין מַצִּיל׃		and there be no one to rescue [you].
כג	זֹבֵחַ תּוֹדָה יְכַבְּדָנְנִי	23	He who offers confession honors Me,
	וְשָׂם דֶּרֶךְ		and [I will] prepare the way;
	אַרְאֶנּוּ בְּיֵשַׁע אֱלֹהִים׃		I will show him the deliverance of God."

פרק נא Chapter 51

Weekly Cycle
Tuesday

Monthly Cycle
9th day of the month

Book Number
Book 2

Author

דָּוִד הַמֶּלֶךְ—King David—the second king of Israel and father of the Davidic royal and messianic dynasty. David composed over seventy of the 150 psalms of Sefer Tehillim.

When & Why

David wrote this psalm after he was rebuked by Nathan for sinning with Bath Sheba. In it, he prays to God to forgive him.

Genre

Psalm of Individual Lament - This psalm was written from the perspective of the individual worshipper, who cries out to God in his time of need. It is characterized as an address to God involving a complaint, followed by a request and ending with an expression of trust.

Chapter Summary

King David composed this psalm, known as "The Psalm of Repentance", as a prayer for forgiveness. It is considered suitable for one who wants to repent for his sins.

This psalm consists of twenty-one verses, subdivided into four parts. The first verse serves as a heading.

In verses 2-7, King David confesses his sin with Bath Sheba , and requests for mercy.

In verses 8-14, he further requests forgiveness.

In verses 15-19, he vows to teach the ways of God.

In verses 20-21, he concludes with a request to build the city of Jerusalem, where God will accept the sacrifices of the righteous.

Introductory Words

לַמְנַצֵּחַ—Lamnatsei'ach—To the Conductor

מִזְמוֹר—Mizmor—Musical Accompaniment

Shimush Tehillim - When to Say

For someone who has sinned (say in the evening, morning, and afternoon)— Verse 4 states: "Wash me thoroughly from my iniquity, and from my sin cleanse me."

Where in the Siddur

Recited as one of the passages of Arizal's (Rabbi Isaac Luria's) weekday bedtime Shema.

Recited as part of Tikkun Chatzot—a prayer recited by some at midnight, in which the author laments the destruction of the Beit HaMikdash (Temple).

Recited by some along with Parashat Parah, the Torah portion describing the ritual of the "red heifer", read in preparation for Passover.

Verse 13 is found in the Selichot (Penitential Service) recited in the evenings leading up to Rosh HaShanah and Yom Kippur.

Verse 17 comprises the introductory verse to the Amidah (Silent Meditation), as it is the central prayer of the three daily services (see Talmud, Berachot 4b).

Verse 20 is recited (in Ashkenazic liturgy) as the Torah scroll is removed from the Ark on Shabbat and Yom Tov (Festivals).

Biblical Personalities

בַּת-שָׁבַע—Bath Sheba —the wife of Uriah the Hittite, later taken in marriage by King David.

נָתָן הַנָּבִיא—Natan HaNavi—Nathan the Prophet—King David's personal prophet. He came to David to reprimand him over his committing adultery with Bathsheva while she was still the wife of Uriah the Hittite.

Biblical Places

יְרוּשָׁלַםִ—Yerushalayim—Jerusalem—the capital city of the kingdom of Israel, conquered by King David 3,000 years ago. David established Jerusalem as both the religious and political center of Israel.

צִיּוֹן—Zion—a place name often used as a synonym for Jerusalem. The term Zion originally referred only to the area where a Jebbusite fortress once stood, also the location of the City of David. Zion was later used by prophets and psalmists as another name for Jerusalem.

Contemporary Song

Verses 12 & 13

פֶּרֶק נא	Chapter 51
א לַמְנַצֵּחַ	1 To the Chief Musician,
מִזְמוֹר לְדָוִד׃	a Psalm of David.
ב בְּבוֹא־אֵלָיו נָתָן הַנָּבִיא	2 When Nathan the prophet came to him,
כַּאֲשֶׁר־בָּא אֶל־בַּת־שָׁבַע׃	after he had come to Bath Sheba.
ג חָנֵּנִי אֱלֹהִים	3 Be gracious to me, God,
כְּחַסְדֶּךָ	according to Your kindness;
כְּרֹב רַחֲמֶיךָ	according to the abundance of Your mercies
מְחֵה פְשָׁעָי׃	blot out my transgressions.
ד הֶרֶב כַּבְּסֵנִי מֵעֲוֹנִי	4 Wash me thoroughly from my iniquity,
וּמֵחַטָּאתִי טַהֲרֵנִי׃	and from my sin cleanse me.
ה כִּי־פְשָׁעַי אֲנִי אֵדָע	5 For of my transgressions I am cognizant
וְחַטָּאתִי נֶגְדִּי תָמִיד׃	and my sin is before me always.
ו לְךָ לְבַדְּךָ ׀ חָטָאתִי	6 Against You alone, have I sinned,
וְהָרַע בְּעֵינֶיךָ	and [only] that which is evil in Your eyes
עָשִׂיתִי	have I done,
לְמַעַן תִּצְדַּק בְּדָבְרֶךָ	that You may be justified when You speak,
תִּזְכֶּה בְשָׁפְטֶךָ׃	and just in Your verdict.

ז הֵן־בְּעָווֹן חוֹלָלְתִּי
וּבְחֵטְא יֶחֱמַתְנִי אִמִּי׃

7 Behold, in iniquity I was formed,
and in sin did my mother conceive me.

ח הֵן־
אֱמֶת חָפַצְתָּ בַטֻּחוֹת
וּבְסָתֻם
חָכְמָה תוֹדִיעֵנִי׃

8 Behold,
You desire truth with inner conviction;
and in my innermost heart,
have You shown me wisdom.

ט תְּחַטְּאֵנִי בְאֵזוֹב וְאֶטְהָר
תְּכַבְּסֵנִי וּמִשֶּׁלֶג אַלְבִּין׃

9 Purge me with hyssops, and I will be pure;
wash me, and I will be whiter than snow.

י תַּשְׁמִיעֵנִי שָׂשׂוֹן וְשִׂמְחָה
תָּגֵלְנָה עֲצָמוֹת דִּכִּיתָ׃

10 Make me hear gladness and rejoicing,
so that they will rejoice—the bones You have crushed.

יא הַסְתֵּר פָּנֶיךָ מֵחֲטָאָי
וְכָל־עֲוֺנֹתַי מְחֵה׃

11 Hide Your face from my sins,
and all my iniquities blot out.

יב לֵב טָהוֹר בְּרָא־לִי אֱלֹהִים
וְרוּחַ נָכוֹן חַדֵּשׁ בְּקִרְבִּי׃

12 A pure heart create for me, God;
and a spirit of correctness renew within me.

יג אַל־תַּשְׁלִיכֵנִי מִלְּפָנֶיךָ
וְרוּחַ קָדְשְׁךָ אַל־תִּקַּח מִמֶּנִּי׃

13 Cast me not away from Your Presence,
and Your Holy Spirit take not from me.

יד הָשִׁיבָה לִּי שְׂשׂוֹן יִשְׁעֶךָ
וְרוּחַ נְדִיבָה תִסְמְכֵנִי׃

14 Restore to me the joy of Your deliverance,
and with a generous spirit, support me.

טו אֲלַמְּדָה פֹשְׁעִים דְּרָכֶיךָ
וְחַטָּאִים אֵלֶיךָ יָשׁוּבוּ׃

15 [Then] I will teach transgressors Your ways,
and [how] sinners [may] return to You.

טז הַצִּילֵנִי מִדָּמִים ׀
אֱלֹהִים אֱלֹהֵי תְּשׁוּעָתִי
תְּרַנֵּן לְשׁוֹנִי
צִדְקָתֶךָ׃

16 Rescue me from the guilt of blood,
God, God of my deliverance;
let my tongue sing joyously
of Your righteousness.

יז אֲדֹנָי שְׂפָתַי תִּפְתָּח
וּפִי יַגִּיד תְּהִלָּתֶךָ׃

17 My Master, open my lips,
and my mouth will declare Your praise.

יח כִּי ׀ לֹא־תַחְפֹּץ זֶבַח
וְאֶתֵּנָה
עוֹלָה לֹא תִרְצֶה׃

18 For You do not want sacrifice,
otherwise I would give it;
a burnt offering You do not desire.

יט זִבְחֵי אֱלֹהִים
רוּחַ נִשְׁבָּרָה
לֵב־נִשְׁבָּר וְנִדְכֶּה
אֱלֹהִים לֹא תִבְזֶה׃

19 The [correct] offerings to God
is a broken spirit,
a broken and humbled heart;
God, You will not despise.

כ הֵיטִיבָה בִרְצוֹנְךָ אֶת־צִיּוֹן
תִּבְנֶה חוֹמוֹת יְרוּשָׁלָםִ׃

20 Do good, as You see fit, to Zion.
May You rebuild the walls of Jerusalem.

כא אָז תַּחְפֹּץ
זִבְחֵי־צֶדֶק
עוֹלָה וְכָלִיל
אָז יַעֲלוּ עַל־מִזְבַּחֲךָ פָרִים׃

21 Then will You desire
the sacrifices of righteousness,
burnt offering and whole offering;
bullocks will then be offered upon Your altar.

פרק נב Chapter 52

Weekly Cycle	Monthly Cycle	Book Number
Tuesday	9th day of the month	Book 2

Author

דָּוִד הַמֶּלֶךְ—King David—the second king of Israel and father of the Davidic royal and messianic dynasty. David composed over seventy of the 150 psalms of Sefer Tehillim.

Genre

Psalm of Individual Lament - This psalm was written from the perspective of the individual worshipper, who cries out to God in his time of need. It is characterized as an address to God involving a complaint, followed by a request and ending with an expression of trust.

Chapter Summary

King David speaks against Doeg the Edomite, and in so doing laments all who allow themselves to be misled by their evil inclinations.

This psalm consists of eleven verses, subdivided into two sections.
Verses 1 & 2 serve as a heading.
In verses 3-7, King David rebukes the wicked, evil man for his moral corruption, and further describes his punishment.
In verses 8-11, he records what the righteous will say in their rejoicing in the downfall of the wicked.

Introductory Words

לַמְנַצֵּחַ—Lamnatsei'ach—To the Conductor

Technical Terminology

מַשְׂכִּיל—Maskil—a discerning person; alternatively, a giver of instruction, perhaps denoting a translator of the chapter (Rashi).
סֶלָה—Selah—While its meaning is unclear, the most familiar opinion is that it is a musical notation, instructing the Levitical orchestra to pause its singing and playing of instruments. Alternatively, "Selah" may mean "everlasting".

Shimush Tehillim - When to Say

To stop speaking evil gossip—Verse 4 states: "Wickedness does your tongue devise, like a sharpened razor, working deceitfully." Verse 10 adds: "But I am like an evergreen olive tree in the House of God; I put my trust in the kindness of God, forever and ever."

Biblical Personalities

אֲחִימֶלֶךְ—Achimelech—the Kohen (Priest).
שָׁאוּל—Shaul—Saul—the first King of Israel. After Saul disobeyed God's command to destroy all of Amalek, the prophet Shmuel (Samuel) dethroned Saul and annointed David.
דוֹאֵג הָאֲדֹמִי—Doeg the Edomite—King Saul's chief herdsman. Saul was jealous of David and was

looking to murder him. When David fled to the priestly city of Nov, near Jerusalem, where the Tabernacle was placed, Achimelech gave him bread and a sword. Doeg reported it to Saul, intimating that Achimelech desired to pronounce David the King over Israel. This aroused Saul's anger causing him to condemn the entire city of Nov to death.

פרק נב

א לַמְנַצֵּחַ
מַשְׂכִּיל לְדָוִד׃
ב בְּבוֹא | דּוֹאֵג הָאֲדֹמִי
וַיַּגֵּד לְשָׁאוּל וַיֹּאמֶר לוֹ
בָּא דָוִד אֶל־בֵּית אֲחִימֶלֶךְ׃
ג מַה־תִּתְהַלֵּל בְּרָעָה
הַגִּבּוֹר
חֶסֶד אֵל כָּל־הַיּוֹם׃
ד הַוּוֹת תַּחְשֹׁב לְשׁוֹנֶךָ
כְּתַעַר מְלֻטָּשׁ עֹשֵׂה רְמִיָּה׃
ה אָהַבְתָּ רָּע מִטּוֹב
שֶׁקֶר | מִדַּבֵּר צֶדֶק
סֶלָה׃
ו אָהַבְתָּ כָל־דִּבְרֵי־בָלַע
לְשׁוֹן מִרְמָה׃
ז גַּם־
אֵל יִתָּצְךָ לָנֶצַח
יַחְתְּךָ וְיִסָּחֲךָ מֵאֹהֶל
וְשֵׁרֶשְׁךָ מֵאֶרֶץ חַיִּים סֶלָה׃
ח וְיִרְאוּ צַדִּיקִים וְיִירָאוּ
וְעָלָיו יִשְׂחָקוּ׃
ט הִנֵּה הַגֶּבֶר
לֹא יָשִׂים אֱלֹהִים מָעוּזּוֹ
וַיִּבְטַח בְּרֹב עָשְׁרוֹ
יָעֹז בְּהַוָּתוֹ׃
י וַאֲנִי | כְּזַיִת רַעֲנָן
בְּבֵית אֱלֹהִים
בָּטַחְתִּי בְחֶסֶד־אֱלֹהִים
עוֹלָם וָעֶד׃
יא אוֹדְךָ לְעוֹלָם
כִּי עָשִׂיתָ
וַאֲקַוֶּה שִׁמְךָ כִי־טוֹב
נֶגֶד חֲסִידֶיךָ׃

Chapter 52

1 To the Chief Musician,
an instruction of David.
2 When Doeg the Edomite came
and told Saul, and said to him,
David has come to the house of Achimelech."
3 Why do you pride yourself with evil
mighty man?
The kindness of Almighty is all the day.
4 Wickedness does your tongue devise,
like a sharpened razor, working deceitfully.
5 You love evil more than good,
falsehood more than speaking righteousness,
Selah.
6 You love all devouring words,
[and] the deceitful tongue.
7 Likewise,
the Almighty will shatter you forever,
He will break you and pluck you from the tent;
and uproot you from the land of the living, Selah.
8 And the righteous will see and be in fear,
and at him they will laugh.
9 "Behold, this is the man
who did not make God his stronghold,
but he trusted in the abundance of his wealth,
and strengthened himself in his wickedness."
10 But I am like an ever-green olive tree
in the House of God;
I put my trust in the kindness of God,
forever and ever.
11 I will thank You forever
for what You have done
and I will put hope in Your Name,
for [You are] good to Your devoted ones.

פרק נג ∽ Chapter 53

Weekly Cycle	Monthly Cycle	Book Number
Tuesday	9th day of the month	Book 2

Author

דָּוִד הַמֶּלֶךְ—King David—the second king of Israel and father of the Davidic royal and messianic dynasty. David composed over seventy of the 150 psalms of Sefer Tehillim.

When & Why

David wrote this psalm prophetically about the destruction of the second Temple.

Genre

Psalm of Individual Lament - This psalm was written from the perspective of the individual worshipper, who cries out to God in his time of need. It is characterized as an address to God involving a complaint, followed by a request and ending with an expression of trust.

Chapter Summary

In this psalm, David speaks against those who destroyed the second Temple as well as those who deny Divine Providence.

This psalm consists of seven verses, subdivided into three parts. The first verse serves as a heading.
In verses 2-4, the Psalmist speaks of the wicked, corrupt fools, who think that man's actions are not subject to reward and punishment.
In verses 5 & 6, he rebukes those who engage in iniquity.
In verse 7, the concluding verse, King David offers a prayer for salvation.

Introductory Words

לַמְנַצֵּחַ—Lamnatsei'ach—To the Conductor

Technical Terminology

מָחֲלַת—Machalat—a musical instrument; alternatively, a prayer for forgiveness.
מַשְׂכִּיל—Maskil—Maskil—a discerning person; alternatively, a giver of instruction, perhaps denoting a translator of the chapter (Rashi).

Shimush Tehillim - When to Say

To scare an enemy (say every day)—Verses 5 & 6 state: "Do they not know, workers of iniquity, who devour My people as they eat bread, and unto Adonoy they had not called? There they were in great fear, a fear such as never was, for God has scattered the bones of those who encamped against you; you have put them to shame because God has rejected them."

Biblical Personalities

יַעֲקֹב—Yaakov—Jacob—also called Israel, the third patriarch is considered the father of the twelve tribes of Israel. He was the brother of Esau, and was married to Leah and Rachel.

Biblical People

יִשְׂרָאֵל—Yisrael—The Nation of Israel

Biblical Places

צִיּוֹן—Zion—a place name often used as a synonym for Jerusalem. The term Zion originally referred only to the area where a Jebbusite fortress once stood, also the location of the City of David. Zion was later used by prophets and psalmists as another name for Jerusalem.

פֶּרֶק נג

א לַמְנַצֵּחַ
עַל־מָחֲלַת
מַשְׂכִּיל לְדָוִד׃
ב אָמַר נָבָל בְּלִבּוֹ
אֵין אֱלֹהִים
הִשְׁחִיתוּ וְהִתְעִיבוּ עָוֶל
אֵין עֹשֵׂה־טוֹב׃
ג אֱלֹהִים מִשָּׁמַיִם
הִשְׁקִיף עַל־בְּנֵי אָדָם
לִרְאוֹת הֲיֵשׁ מַשְׂכִּיל
דֹּרֵשׁ אֶת־אֱלֹהִים׃
ד כֻּלּוֹ סָג
יַחְדָּו נֶאֱלָחוּ
אֵין עֹשֵׂה־טוֹב
אֵין גַּם־אֶחָד׃
ה הֲלֹא יָדְעוּ פֹּעֲלֵי אָוֶן
אֹכְלֵי עַמִּי אָכְלוּ לֶחֶם
אֱלֹהִים לֹא קָרָאוּ׃
ו שָׁם | פָּחֲדוּ־פַחַד
לֹא־הָיָה פָחַד
כִּי־אֱלֹהִים פִּזַּר
עַצְמוֹת חֹנָךְ
הֱבִשֹׁתָה
כִּי־אֱלֹהִים מְאָסָם׃
ז מִי יִתֵּן מִצִּיּוֹן
יְשֻׁעוֹת יִשְׂרָאֵל
בְּשׁוּב אֱלֹהִים שְׁבוּת עַמּוֹ
יָגֵל יַעֲקֹב יִשְׂמַח יִשְׂרָאֵל׃

Chapter 53

1 To the Chief Musician,
upon the Machalas,
an instruction of David.
2 The degenerate says in his heart,
"There is no God."
They have acted corruptly and abominably,
there is no doer of good.
3 God, from heaven,
looked down upon these sons of man,
to see if there was any man of understanding
searching for God.
4 They all were depraved
together they became corrupt,
there was no doer of good,
none, not even one.
5 Do they not know, workers of iniquity,
who devour My people as they eat bread,
and unto Adonoy they had not called?
6 There they were in great fear,
a fear such as never was,
for God has scattered
the bones of those who encamped against you;
you have put them to shame
because God has rejected them.
7 May it be that out of Zion
[would come] Israel's deliverances!
When God returns the captivity of His people,
Jacob will exult, Israel will rejoice.

פרק נד Chapter 54

Weekly Cycle	Monthly Cycle	Book Number
Tuesday	9th day of the month	Book 2

Author

דָּוִד הַמֶּלֶךְ—King David—the second king of Israel and father of the Davidic royal and messianic dynasty. David composed over seventy of the 150 psalms of Sefer Tehillim.

When & Why

David wrote this psalm after he was saved from the inhabitants of the city of Zif, who tried to hand him over to Saul.

Genre

Psalm of Individual Lament - This psalm was written from the perspective of the individual worshipper, who cries out to God in his time of need. It is characterized as an address to God involving a complaint, followed by a request and ending with an expression of trust.

Chapter Summary

As explained earlier, King David views his personal woes as a parallel to the troubles of the Jewish people. Just as he trusted in God when imperiled by Saul and his men, similarly Israel must trust in God in her times of trouble. Only then will she merit to be saved.

This psalm consists of nine verses, subdivided into two parts.
Verses 1 & 2 serve as a heading.
In verses 3-5, King David prays for God's salvation, and further asks that his prayer be heard.
In verses 6-9, he expresses his trust that salvation will indeed come.

Introductory Words

לַמְנַצֵּחַ—Lamnatsei'ach—To the Conductor

Technical Terminology

נְגִינֹת—Neginos—Tunes
מַשְׂכִּיל—Maskil—Maskil—a discerning person; alternatively, a giver of instruction, perhaps denoting a translator of the chapter (Rashi).
סֶלָה—Selah—While its meaning is unclear, the most familiar opinion is that it is a musical notation, instructing the Levitical orchestra to pause its singing and playing of instruments. Alternatively, "Selah" may mean "everlasting".

Shimush Tehillim - When to Say

For protection from an enemy—Verse 7 states: " He will repay the evil to those who watch for my downfall with Your truth destroy them."

Biblical Personalities

שָׁאוּל—Shaul—Saul—the first King of Israel. After Saul disobeyed God's command to destroy all of Amalek, the prophet Shmuel (Samuel) dethroned Saul and annointed David to start a new monarchic line.

זִיפִים—Ziphites—men from an area called Ziph. They were from the tribe of Judah, as was David, but they didn't hesitate to betray him. David and his men had taken refuge in the wilderness of Ziph after their escape from Saul. When the Ziphites discovered them, they immediately reported their hideout to Saul. Their trechery was considered even greater than that of Doeg, who was not related to David as were the Zifim. (See Psalm 52).

פרק נד

א לַמְנַצֵּחַ
בִּנְגִינֹת
מַשְׂכִּיל לְדָוִד׃
ב בְּבוֹא הַזִּיפִים וַיֹּאמְרוּ לְשָׁאוּל
הֲלֹא דָוִד מִסְתַּתֵּר עִמָּנוּ׃
ג אֱלֹהִים בְּשִׁמְךָ הוֹשִׁיעֵנִי
וּבִגְבוּרָתְךָ תְדִינֵנִי׃
ד אֱלֹהִים שְׁמַע תְּפִלָּתִי
הַאֲזִינָה לְאִמְרֵי־פִי׃
ה כִּי זָרִים | קָמוּ עָלַי
וְעָרִיצִים בִּקְשׁוּ נַפְשִׁי
לֹא שָׂמוּ אֱלֹהִים לְנֶגְדָּם סֶלָה׃
ו הִנֵּה אֱלֹהִים עֹזֵר לִי
אֲדֹנָי בְּסֹמְכֵי נַפְשִׁי׃
ז יָשִׁיב הָרַע
לְשֹׁרְרָי
בַּאֲמִתְּךָ הַצְמִיתֵם׃
ח בִּנְדָבָה
אֶזְבְּחָה־לָּךְ
אוֹדֶה שִּׁמְךָ יְהוָה
כִּי־טוֹב׃
ט כִּי מִכָּל־צָרָה הִצִּילָנִי
וּבְאֹיְבַי
רָאֲתָה עֵינִי׃

Chapter 54

1 To the Chief Musician,
with string music,
an instruction of David.
2 When the Ziphites came and said to Saul,
"Does not David hide himself with us?"
3 God, by Your Name deliver me,
and judge [vindicate] me by Your might.
4 God, hear my prayer;
listen to the words of my mouth.
5 For strangers have risen up against me,
and violent men have sought my soul;
they have not set God before them, Selah.
6 Behold, God is my helper;
my Master is with those who support my soul.
7 He will repay the evil
to those who watch for my downfall
with Your truth destroy them.
8 With a free will offering
will I sacrifice to You;
I will thank Your Name, Adonoy,
for it is good.
9 For from all trouble He has rescued me,
and upon my enemies [downfall]
has my eye gazed.

פרק נה Chapter 55

Weekly Cycle	Monthly Cycle	Book Number
Tuesday	10th day of the month	Book 2

Author

דָּוִד הַמֶּלֶךְ—King David—the second king of Israel and father of the Davidic royal and messianic dynasty. David composed over seventy of the 150 psalms of Sefer Tehillim.

When & Why

David wrote this psalm after he was forced to escape Jerusalem because he was being chased by Absalom, and after he was informed that one of his top advisors had betrayed him.

Genre

Psalm of Individual Lament - This psalm was written from the perspective of the individual worshipper, who cries out to God in his time of need. It is characterized as an address to God involving a complaint, followed by a request and ending with an expression of trust.

Chapter Summary

In this psalm, King David is perhaps alluding to the servants of Saul who pretended to love him, yet, in the end, betrayed him. Alternatively, he may have composed it when fleeing from his son Absalom, who sought to murder him.

This psalm consists of twenty-four verses, subdivided into two parts. The first verse serves as a heading.

In verses 2-16, King David requests that his prayers be heard. He expresses fear of his enemies and requests that they be punished. He further laments a betrayal by a trusted friend.

In verses 17-24, he now expresses trust that his prayer will indeed be heard and that salvation will come.

Introductory Words

לַמְנַצֵּחַ—Lamnatsei'ach—To the Conductor

Technical Terminology

נְגִינֹת—Neginos—Tunes

מַשְׂכִּיל—Maskil—Maskil—a discerning person; alternatively, a giver of instruction, perhaps denoting a translator of the chapter (Rashi).

סֶלָה—Selah—While its meaning is unclear, the most familiar opinion is that it is a musical notation, instructing the Levitical orchestra to pause its singing and playing of instruments. Alternatively, "Selah" may mean "everlasting".

Shimush Tehillim - When to Say

To bring retribution against an enemy—Verse 16 states: "May He incite death against them let them go down into the grave, alive, for evil is in their dwelling and within them."

Where in the Siddur

Verse 2 is found in the Vidui (Confession Service), recited on the days leading up to, and including, Yom Kippur. Interestingly, the Vidui service is not recited on Rosh HaShanah itself.

Verse 3 is found in the Musaf service of Rosh HaShanah and Yom Kippur.

Verse 3 is also found in the Kinot (Lamentations) of Tishah Be'Av (Fast of the Ninth of Av) in a kinah which speaks of the Crusades.

Verse 14 is found in Pirkei Avot (Ethics of the Fathers), 6:3.

Verse 19 is found in the prayers recited by some following Ma'ariv (evening service) of Motza'ei Shabbat.

Verse 24 is found in Pirkei Avot (Ethics of the Fathers), 5:22.

Verse 24 also comprises one of the verses recited at a siyum—the completion of a masechet (tractate) of Talmud.

Biblical Places

שְׁאוֹל—Sheol—Lower or Underworld; abode of the dead.

Talmud on Tehillim

Verse 19: "פָּדָה בְשָׁלוֹם נַפְשִׁי, מִקְּרָב לִי, כִּי בְרַבִּים הָיוּ עִמָּדִי"— "He has redeemed my soul in peace, from impending battle, for the sake of the many that were with me."

The Talmud, Berachot 8a, deduces from this verse that when a congregation prays together, it is an eit ratzon, a time of favor before God.

פרק נה

א לַמְנַצֵּחַ
בִּנְגִינֹת
מַשְׂכִּיל לְדָוִד׃
ב הַאֲזִינָה אֱלֹהִים תְּפִלָּתִי
וְאַל־תִּתְעַלַּם מִתְּחִנָּתִי׃
ג הַקְשִׁיבָה לִּי וַעֲנֵנִי
אָרִיד בְּשִׂיחִי וְאָהִימָה׃
ד מִקּוֹל אוֹיֵב
מִפְּנֵי עָקַת רָשָׁע
כִּי־יָמִיטוּ עָלַי אָוֶן
וּבְאַף יִשְׂטְמוּנִי׃
ה לִבִּי יָחִיל בְּקִרְבִּי
וְאֵימוֹת מָוֶת נָפְלוּ עָלָי׃
ו יִרְאָה וָרַעַד יָבֹא בִי
וַתְּכַסֵּנִי פַּלָּצוּת׃

Chapter 55

1 To the Chief Musician,
with string music,
an instruction of David.
2 Listen God, to my prayer,
and hide not from my supplication.
3 Hearken to me and answer me;
I lament in my prayer and I moan.
4 Because of the [raging] voice of the enemy,
because of the oppression of the wicked;
for they accuse me of iniquity
and in anger they hate me bitterly.
5 My heart shudders within me,
and the terrors of death have fallen upon me.
6 Fear and trembling come upon me,
and I am overwhelmed with horrors.

ז וָאֹמַר	7 And I said,
מִי־יִתֶּן־לִּי אֵבֶר כַּיּוֹנָה	"Oh that I had wings like a dove,
אָעוּפָה וְאֶשְׁכֹּנָה׃	I would fly away and be at rest.
ח הִנֵּה אַרְחִיק נְדֹד	8 Behold, then I will wander far off,
אָלִין בַּמִּדְבָּר סֶלָה׃	I would lodge in the wilderness, Selah.
ט אָחִישָׁה מִפְלָט לִי	9 I would hurry to a shelter
מֵרוּחַ סֹעָה מִסָּעַר׃	from the stormy wind, from the tempest."
י בַּלַּע אֲדֹנָי	10 Consume them, my Master,
פַּלַּג לְשׁוֹנָם	and confuse their tongue;
כִּי־רָאִיתִי חָמָס	for I have seen violence
וְרִיב בָּעִיר׃	and strife in the city.
יא יוֹמָם וָלַיְלָה	11 Day and night
יְסוֹבְבֻהָ עַל־חוֹמֹתֶיהָ	[they] encircle it upon its walls,
וְאָוֶן וְעָמָל בְּקִרְבָּהּ׃	and iniquity and mischief are within it.
יב הַוּוֹת בְּקִרְבָּהּ	12 Wickedness is within it,
וְלֹא־יָמִישׁ מֵרְחֹבָהּ	never leaving its broad place
תֹּךְ וּמִרְמָה׃	are guile and deceit.
יג כִּי לֹא־אוֹיֵב יְחָרְפֵנִי	13 For no enemy ever taunted me
וְאֶשָּׂא	that I would endure it;
לֹא־מְשַׂנְאִי עָלַי הִגְדִּיל	nor does my foe enlarge himself against me,
וְאֶסָּתֵר מִמֶּנּוּ׃	that I would have hidden myself from him.
יד וְאַתָּה אֱנוֹשׁ כְּעֶרְכִּי	14 But you are a man of my equal,
אַלּוּפִי וּמְיֻדָּעִי׃	my guide and my close confidante.
טו אֲשֶׁר יַחְדָּו נַמְתִּיק סוֹד	15 Together we held sweet counsel,
בְּבֵית אֱלֹהִים	into the House of God
נְהַלֵּךְ בְּרָגֶשׁ׃	we walked with the throng.
טז יַשִּׁי מָוֶת ׀ עָלֵימוֹ	16 May He incite death against them
יֵרְדוּ שְׁאוֹל חַיִּים	let them go down into the grave, alive,
כִּי־רָעוֹת בִּמְגוּרָם בְּקִרְבָּם׃	for evil is in their dwelling and within them.
יז אֲנִי אֶל־אֱלֹהִים אֶקְרָא	17 As for me, upon God will I call,
וַיהוָה יוֹשִׁיעֵנִי׃	and Adonoy will deliver me.
יח עֶרֶב וָבֹקֶר וְצָהֳרַיִם	18 Evening, and morning, and noontime,
אָשִׂיחָה וְאֶהֱמֶה	I pray and moan;
וַיִּשְׁמַע קוֹלִי׃	and He heard my voice.
יט פָּדָה בְשָׁלוֹם נַפְשִׁי	19 He has redeemed my soul in peace,
מִקְּרָב־לִי	from impending battle,
כִּי־בְרַבִּים הָיוּ עִמָּדִי׃	for the sake of the many that were with me.
כ יִשְׁמַע ׀ אֵל ׀ וְיַעֲנֵם	20 Almighty will hear them and answer them,
וְיֹשֵׁב קֶדֶם	He Who is enthroned from days of old,

David and Absalom

סֶלָה	Selah.
אֲשֶׁר	against those
אֵין חֲלִיפוֹת לָמוֹ	who are not concerned of change,
וְלֹא יָרְאוּ אֱלֹהִים׃	and have no fear of God.
כא שָׁלַח יָדָיו	21 He extended his hands
בִּשְׁלֹמָיו	against those who were at peace with him,
חִלֵּל בְּרִיתוֹ׃	he has profaned his own covenant.
כב חָלְקוּ	מַחְמָאֹת	22 Smoother than butter
פִּיו	were the words of his mouth,
וּקְרָב־לִבּוֹ	but in his heart was war;
רַכּוּ דְבָרָיו מִשֶּׁמֶן	his words were softer than oil,
וְהֵמָּה פְתִחוֹת׃	yet they were curses.
כג הַשְׁלֵךְ עַל־יְהֹוָה	יְהָבְךָ	23 Cast upon Adonoy your burden
וְהוּא יְכַלְכְּלֶךָ	and He will sustain you;
לֹא־יִתֵּן לְעוֹלָם	He will never allow
מוֹט לַצַּדִּיק׃	the faltering of the righteous.
כד וְאַתָּה אֱלֹהִים	תּוֹרִדֵם		24 But You, God, will lower them
לִבְאֵר שַׁחַת	into the pit of destruction,
אַנְשֵׁי דָמִים וּמִרְמָה	men of blood and deceit
לֹא־יֶחֱצוּ יְמֵיהֶם	will not live out half their days;
וַאֲנִי אֶבְטַח־בָּךְ׃	but as for me, I will trust in You.

פרק נו Chapter 56

Weekly Cycle	Monthly Cycle	Book Number
Tuesday	10th day of the month	Book 2

Author

דָּוִד הַמֶּלֶךְ—King David—the second king of Israel and father of the Davidic royal and messianic dynasty. David composed over seventy of the 150 psalms of Sefer Tehillim.

When & Why

David wrote this psalm after he fled to Philistia to escape Saul. In Philistia he pretended to be demented so that Goliath would not murder him.

Genre

Psalm of Individual Lament - This psalm was written from the perspective of the individual worshipper, who cries out to God in his time of need. It is characterized as an address to God involving a complaint, followed by a request and ending with an expression of trust.

Chapter Summary

King David calls out to God for assistance upon being captured by the Pelishtim (Philistines). He concludes with a request that his prayer be accepted by the Almighty, and a vow in which he thanks God for salvation.

This psalm consists of fourteen verses, subdivided into three parts. The first verse serves as a heading.

In verses 2-9, the Psalmist prays to God for salvation from his captors.
In verses 10-12, he expresses his trust that the day will come when his enemies will retreat.
In verses 13 & 14, King David affirms that, on that day, he will fulfill his vows of thanksgiving to the Almighty.

Introductory Words

לַמְנַצֵּחַ—Lamnatsei'ach—To the Conductor

Technical Terminology

עַל יוֹנַת אֵלֶם רְחֹקִים—Al yonat eilem rechokim—Over a silent dove in the distance (perhaps a reference to King David himself).
מִכְתָּם—Michtam—an engraving, perhaps of simple fashion (Targum Yonatan); alternatively, made of fine gold (Ibn Ezra).

Shimush Tehillim - When to Say

For someone bound in chains—Verse 1 states: "When the Philistines seized him in Gath."
To fight the evil inclination—Verse 10 states: "Then will my enemies turn back on the day that I call out; for this I know, that God is for me."

Biblical Personalities

פְּלִשְׁתִּים—Pelishtim—Philistines—an enemy nation that dwelled on the southwestern coast of Israel.

Biblical Places

גַּת—Gath—one of five Philistine city-states. The other four were Gaza, Ashkelon, Ashdod and Ekron.

פֶּרֶק נו

א לַמְנַצֵּחַ ׀
עַל־יוֹנַת אֵלֶם רְחֹקִים
לְדָוִד מִכְתָּם
בֶּאֱחֹז אֹתוֹ פְלִשְׁתִּים בְּגַת:
ב חָנֵּנִי אֱלֹהִים
כִּי־שְׁאָפַנִי אֱנוֹשׁ
כָּל־הַיּוֹם לֹחֵם יִלְחָצֵנִי:
ג שָׁאֲפוּ שׁוֹרְרַי כָּל־הַיּוֹם
כִּי־רַבִּים לֹחֲמִים לִי מָרוֹם:
ד יוֹם אִירָא
אֲנִי אֵלֶיךָ אֶבְטָח:
ה בֵּאלֹהִים
אֲהַלֵּל דְּבָרוֹ
בֵּאלֹהִים בָּטַחְתִּי
לֹא אִירָא
מַה־יַּעֲשֶׂה בָשָׂר לִי:
ו כָּל־הַיּוֹם דְּבָרַי יְעַצֵּבוּ
עָלַי כָּל־מַחְשְׁבֹתָם לָרָע:
ז יָגוּרוּ ׀
יִצְפּוֹנוּ
הֵמָּה עֲקֵבַי יִשְׁמֹרוּ
כַּאֲשֶׁר קִוּוּ נַפְשִׁי:
ח עַל אָוֶן
פַּלֶּט לָמוֹ
בְּאַף עַמִּים ׀ הוֹרֵד אֱלֹהִים:
ט נֹדִי סָפַרְתָּה אָתָּה
שִׂימָה דִמְעָתִי בְנֹאדֶךָ
הֲלֹא בְּסִפְרָתֶךָ:

Chapter 56

1 To the Chief Musician,
upon yonas ailem rechokim,
[a Psalm] of David, a Miktam,
when the Philistines seized him in Gath.
2 Be gracious to me, God,
for man yearns to swallow me;
each day the fighter oppresses me.
3 My watchers yearn to swallow me each day,
for many battle against me, Most High.
4 In the day when I am afraid,
I will put my trust in You.
5 Through God's judgment
I will praise His word,
in God I have put my trust;
I will not fear,
for what can [mortal] flesh do to me?
6 Each day they cause my words to be sad;
about me all their thoughts are for evil.
7 They gather together,
they lie in ambush,
they watch my footsteps
as they wait for my soul.
8 For [their] iniquity
should they anticipate rescue?
In anger cast down the nations, God.
9 My wanderings You have counted,
place my tear into Your flask;
Are they not in Your account?

י אָז יָשׁוּבוּ אוֹיְבַי אָחוֹר בְּיוֹם אֶקְרָא זֶה־יָדַעְתִּי כִּי־אֱלֹהִים לִי׃	10 Then will my enemies turn back on the day that I call out; for this I know, that God is for me.
יא בֵּאלֹהִים אֲהַלֵּל דָּבָר בַּיהוָה אֲהַלֵּל דָּבָר׃	11 Through God's judgment I will praise [His] word; through Adonoy's kindness I will praise [His] word.
יב בֵּאלֹהִים בָּטַחְתִּי לֹא אִירָא מַה־יַּעֲשֶׂה אָדָם לִי׃	12 In God I have put my trust; I will not fear, for what can man do to me?
יג עָלַי אֱלֹהִים נְדָרֶיךָ אֲשַׁלֵּם תּוֹדֹת לָךְ׃	13 Upon me, God, are Your vows I will bring thanksgiving offerings to You.
יד כִּי הִצַּלְתָּ נַפְשִׁי מִמָּוֶת הֲלֹא רַגְלַי מִדֶּחִי לְהִתְהַלֵּךְ לִפְנֵי אֱלֹהִים בְּאוֹר הַחַיִּים׃	14 For You have rescued my soul from death, even my feet from stumbling, so that I may walk before God in the light of life.

פרק נז Chapter 57

Weekly Cycle	Monthly Cycle	Book Number
Tuesday	10th day of the month	Book 2

Author

דָּוִד הַמֶּלֶךְ—King David—the second king of Israel and father of the Davidic royal and messianic dynasty. David composed over seventy of the 150 psalms of Sefer Tehillim.

When & Why

David wrote this psalm after he escaped a near encounter with Saul, who had unknowingly entered the cave in which David was hiding.

Genre

Psalm of Individual Lament - This psalm was written from the perspective of the individual worshipper, who cries out to God in his time of need. It is characterized as an address to God involving a complaint, followed by a request and ending with an expression of trust.

Chapter Summary

Hiding in the depths of the cave where an unsuspecting Saul had come to relieve himself, David prays that he not be destroyed.

This psalm consists of twelve verses, subdivided into two parts. The first verse serves as a heading.
In verses 2-5, King David calls out to God to save him from his enemies.
In verses 6-12, he expresses thanks for his salvation.

Introductory Words

לַמְנַצֵּחַ—Lamnatsei'ach—To the Conductor

Technical Terminology

אַל-תַּשְׁחֵת—Al Tashcheit—Do not destroy. This phrase is perhaps the author's, or printer's, notation indicating that the associated manuscript was from another source, and should not be thrown away or destroyed.

מִכְתָּם—Michtam—an engraving, perhaps of simple fashion (Targum Yonatan); alternatively, made of fine gold (Ibn Ezra).

סֶלָה—Selah—While its meaning is unclear, the most familiar opinion is that it is a musical notation, instructing the Levitical orchestra to pause its singing and playing of instruments. Alternatively, "Selah" may mean "everlasting".

Musical Instruments

כִּנּוֹר—Kinor—A Small Handheld Harp - played with a plecturm (pick).

נֵבֶל—Nevel—A Large Handheld Lyre - played by plucking with fingers.

Shimush Tehillim - When to Say

For success and good fortune—Verse 4 states: "He will send from heaven and deliver me."

Where in the Siddur

Verse 3 is found in the repetition of the Amidah (Silent Meditation) of Musaf of Rosh HaShanah.

Biblical Personalities

שָׁאוּל—Shaul—Saul—the first King of Israel. After Saul disobeyed God's command to destroy all of Amalek, the prophet Samuel dethroned Saul and annointed David to start a new monarchic line.

Contemporary Song

Verse 9

Talmud on Tehillim

Verse 9: "עוּרָה כְבוֹדִי עוּרָה, הַנֵּבֶל וְכִנּוֹר; אָעִירָה שָּׁחַר"—"Awake my soul, awake lyre and harp, I will awaken the dawn."

The Talmud, Berachot 4a, deduces from here that King David had servants play a lyre and a harp in order to awaken him at midnight from his sleep. In contrast to other kings who were awakened by the dawn, David would personally "awaken the dawn" himself.

Verse 11: "כִּי גָדֹל עַד שָׁמַיִם חַסְדֶּךָ"—"For great until the heavens is Your kindness."

The Talmud, Pesachim 50b, delineates two levels of mitzvah performance. This verse refers to those who have ulterior motives in their worship of God, and worship "until the heavens". In contrast, psalm 108 speaks of those who perform a mitzvah for its own sake, for no purpose other than to fulfill the will of God, and who recognize that "your faithfulness is higher than the heavens."

פרק נז

א לַמְנַצֵּחַ
אַל־תַּשְׁחֵת לְדָוִד מִכְתָּם
בְּבָרְחוֹ מִפְּנֵי־שָׁאוּל בַּמְּעָרָה׃
ב חָנֵּנִי אֱלֹהִים | חָנֵּנִי
כִּי בְךָ חָסָיָה נַפְשִׁי
וּבְצֵל־כְּנָפֶיךָ אֶחְסֶה
עַד יַעֲבֹר הַוּוֹת׃
ג אֶקְרָא לֵאלֹהִים עֶלְיוֹן
לָאֵל גֹּמֵר עָלָי׃
ד יִשְׁלַח מִשָּׁמַיִם | וְיוֹשִׁיעֵנִי
חֵרֵף
שֹׁאֲפִי
סֶלָה
יִשְׁלַח אֱלֹהִים חַסְדּוֹ וַאֲמִתּוֹ׃
ה נַפְשִׁי | בְּתוֹךְ לְבָאִם
אֶשְׁכְּבָה לֹהֲטִים
בְּנֵי־אָדָם שִׁנֵּיהֶם חֲנִית וְחִצִּים
וּלְשׁוֹנָם חֶרֶב חַדָּה׃
ו רוּמָה עַל־הַשָּׁמַיִם אֱלֹהִים
עַל כָּל־הָאָרֶץ כְּבוֹדֶךָ׃
ז רֶשֶׁת | הֵכִינוּ לִפְעָמַי
כָּפַף נַפְשִׁי
כָּרוּ לְפָנַי שִׁיחָה
נָפְלוּ בְתוֹכָהּ סֶלָה׃
ח נָכוֹן לִבִּי אֱלֹהִים
נָכוֹן לִבִּי
אָשִׁירָה וַאֲזַמֵּרָה׃
ט עוּרָה כְבוֹדִי
עוּרָה הַנֵּבֶל וְכִנּוֹר
אָעִירָה שָּׁחַר׃
י אוֹדְךָ בָעַמִּים | אֲדֹנָי
אֲזַמֶּרְךָ בַּל־אֻמִּים׃
יא כִּי־גָדֹל עַד־שָׁמַיִם חַסְדֶּךָ
וְעַד־שְׁחָקִים אֲמִתֶּךָ׃
יב רוּמָה עַל־שָׁמַיִם אֱלֹהִים
עַל כָּל־הָאָרֶץ כְּבוֹדֶךָ׃

Chapter 57

1 To the Chief Musician,
al tashchais, [a Psalm] of David, a Miktam,
when he fled from Saul, in the cave.
2 Be gracious to me, God, be gracious to me,
for in You my soul has taken refuge;
and in the shadow of Your wings will I take refuge
until the wickedness passes by.
3 I will call to God, Most High;
to the Almighty Who fulfills my purpose.
4 He will send from heaven and deliver me
from the humiliation
of those who yearn to swallow me,
Selah;
God will send His kindness and His truth.
5 My soul is among lions,
I lie beside those who are aflame;
sons of man whose teeth are spears and arrows,
and their tongue is a sharp sword.
6 Be exalted above the heavens, God,
above all the earth be Your glory.
7 A net they have prepared for my feet,
my soul they bent down,
they have dug a pit before me,
they have fallen into it, Selah.
8 My heart is steadfast, God,
my heart is steadfast;
I will sing and chant praises.
9 Awake my soul,
awake lyre and harp,
I will awaken the dawn.
10 I will thank You among peoples, my Master,
I will sing praises to You among nations.
11 For great until the heavens is Your kindness,
and until the clouds is Your truth.
12 Be exalted above the heavens, God,
above all the earth be Your glory.

פרק נח Chapter 58

Weekly Cycle	Monthly Cycle	Book Number
Tuesday	10th day of the month	Book 2

Author

דָוִד הַמֶּלֶךְ—King David—the second king of Israel and father of the Davidic royal and messianic dynasty. David composed over seventy of the 150 psalms of Sefer Tehillim.

When & Why

David wrote this psalm after Saul's judges fabricated charges against him and unjustly sentenced him to death for rebelling against the king.

Genre

Psalm of Individual Lament - This psalm was written from the perspective of the individual worshipper, who cries out to God in his time of need. It is characterized as an address to God involving a complaint, followed by a request and ending with an expression of trust.

Chapter Summary

In this psalm, King David warns against judges who pervert justice. The Psalmist is perhaps alluding to Saul's ministers who falsely accused David of rebelling against the throne.

This psalm consists of twelve verses, subdivided into two parts. The first verse serves as a heading.
In verses 2-6, King David harshly laments the deeds of the wicked.
In verses 7-12, he offers a prayer to God that a great revenge should befall the wicked, enabling the righteous to then rejoice.

Introductory Words

לַמְנַצֵּחַ—Lamnatsei'ach—To the Conductor

Technical Terminology

אַל-תַּשְׁחֵת—Al Tashcheit—Do not destroy. This phrase is perhaps the author's, or printer's, notation indicating that the associated manuscript was from another source, and should not be thrown away or destroyed.
מִכְתָּם—Michtam—an engraving, perhaps of simple fashion (Targum Yonatan); alternatively, made of fine gold (Ibn Ezra).

Shimush Tehillim - When to Say

For protection from a vicious dog—Verse 7 states: "God, break their teeth in their mouth, the incisors of young lions smash, Adonoy."

פֶּרֶק נ״ח			**Chapter 58**
לַמְנַצֵּחַ אַל־תַּשְׁחֵת	א	1	To the Chief Musician, al tashchais,
לְדָוִד מִכְתָּם׃			[a Psalm] of David, a Miktam.
הַאֻמְנָם אֵלֶם	ב	2	Can Your silence be justified
צֶדֶק			[at a time] when righteousness
תְּדַבֵּרוּן			you should speak,
מֵישָׁרִים			[when] with equity
תִּשְׁפְּטוּ בְּנֵי אָדָם׃			you should judge the sons of man?
אַף־בְּלֵב	ג	3	Indeed, in [your] heart
עוֹלֹת תִּפְעָלוּן בָּאָרֶץ			you commit wrongs in the land,
חֲמַס יְדֵיכֶם			the violence of your hands,
תְּפַלֵּסוּן׃			outweighs [the good].
זֹרוּ רְשָׁעִים מֵרָחֶם	ד	4	Estranged are the wicked from the womb;
תָּעוּ מִבֶּטֶן דֹּבְרֵי כָזָב׃			astray from birth go the speakers of lies.
חֲמַת־לָמוֹ כִּדְמוּת חֲמַת־נָחָשׁ	ה	5	Their venom is like the venom of a serpent,
כְּמוֹ־פֶתֶן חֵרֵשׁ יַאְטֵם אָזְנוֹ׃			like a deaf viper which closes its ear.
אֲשֶׁר לֹא־יִשְׁמַע	ו	6	So as not to hearken
לְקוֹל מְלַחֲשִׁים			to the voice of charmers
חוֹבֵר חֲבָרִים מְחֻכָּם׃			of the most cunning spellbinder.
אֱלֹהִים הֲרׇס־שִׁנֵּימוֹ בְּפִימוֹ	ז	7	God, break their teeth in their mouth,
מַלְתְּעוֹת כְּפִירִים נְתֹץ ׀ יְהוָה׃			the incisors of young lions smash, Adonoy.
יִמָּאֲסוּ כְמוֹ־מַיִם	ח	8	Let them melt away as water
יִתְהַלְּכוּ־לָמוֹ			that is always running
יִדְרֹךְ חִצָּיו			when He aims his arrows
כְּמוֹ יִתְמֹלָלוּ׃			let it be as though they are cut down.
כְּמוֹ שַׁבְּלוּל	ט	9	[Let them be] as the snail which
תֶּמֶס יַהֲלֹךְ			melts and slithers away,
נֵפֶל אֵשֶׁת			like the stillbirth of a mole
בַּל־חָזוּ שָׁמֶשׁ׃			that has not seen the sun.
בְּטֶרֶם יָבִינוּ	י	10	Before the development
סִּירֹתֵיכֶם אָטָד			of your tender shoots into hardened thorns,
כְּמוֹ־חַי כְּמוֹ־חָרוֹן			with His might, with His wrath,
יִשְׂעָרֶנּוּ׃			He will sweep them away as with a whirlwind.
יִשְׂמַח צַדִּיק	יא	11	The righteous will rejoice
כִּי־חָזָה נָקָם			when he sees the vengeance,
פְּעָמָיו יִרְחַץ			his feet he will wash
בְּדַם הָרָשָׁע׃			in the blood of the wicked.
וְיֹאמַר אָדָם	יב	12	And man will say,

אַךְ־פְּרִי לַצַּדִּיק אַךְ יֵשׁ־אֱלֹהִים שֹׁפְטִים בָּאָרֶץ׃	"Indeed there is reward for the righteous, indeed there is a Judge [God] administering justice in the land."

פרק נט Chapter 59

Weekly Cycle	Monthly Cycle	Book Number
Tuesday	10th day of the month	Book 2

Author

דָּוִד הַמֶּלֶךְ—King David—the second king of Israel and father of the Davidic royal and messianic dynasty. David composed over seventy of the 150 psalms of Sefer Tehillim.

When & Why

David wrote this psalm after he escaped from the guards who Saul sent to break into his house at night and murder him.

Genre

Psalm of Individual Lament - This psalm was written from the perspective of the individual worshipper, who cries out to God in his time of need. It is characterized as an address to God involving a complaint, followed by a request and ending with an expression of trust.

Chapter Summary

King David composed this psalm after Saul had dispatched agents to watch his house all night and kill him in the morning. He offers thanks to God for the miracle of being given enough time to escape his pursuers.

This psalm consists of eighteen verses, subdivided into two parts. The first verse serves as a heading.

In verses 2-10, King David requests of God to be delivered from evildoers, and then prays for the downfall of wicked traitors.

In verses 11-18, King David expresses his trust that God will indeed bring about the downfall of his enemies, and further declares that their punishment should be exile and death. He concludes this section with a song of victory and thanksgiving.

Introductory Words

לַמְנַצֵּחַ—Lamnatsei'ach—To the Conductor

Technical Terminology

אַל-תַּשְׁחֵת—Al Tashcheit—Do not destroy. This phrase is perhaps the author's, or printer's, notation indicating that the associated manuscript was from another source, and should not be thrown away or destroyed.

מִכְתָּם—Michtam—an engraving, perhaps of simple fashion (Targum Yonatan); alternatively, made of fine gold (Ibn Ezra).

סֶלָה—Selah—While its meaning is unclear, the most familiar opinion is that it is a musical notation, instructing the Levitical orchestra to pause its singing and playing of instruments. Alternatively, "Selah" may mean "everlasting".

Shimush Tehillim - When to Say

Against the evil inclination (say 3 times daily)—Verse 2 states: "Rescue me from my enemies, my God; from those who rise up against me, strengthen me."

Biblical Personalities

שָׁאוּל—Shaul—Saul—the first King of Israel. After Saul disobeyed God's command to destroy all of Amalek, the prophet Samuel dethroned Saul and annointed David to start a new monarchic line.

יַעֲקֹב—Yaakov—Jacob, also called Yisrael—Israel, the third patriarch, and known as the father of the twelve tribes of Israel. He was married to Rachel and Leah, and was the brother of Eisav.

פֶּרֶק נט			**Chapter 59**
לַמְנַצֵּחַ אַל־תַּשְׁחֵת לְדָוִד מִכְתָּם בִּשְׁלֹחַ שָׁאוּל וַיִּשְׁמְרוּ אֶת־הַבַּיִת לַהֲמִיתוֹ:	א	1	To the Chief Musician, al tashchais, [a Psalm] of David, a Miktam, when Saul sent and they watched the house to kill him.
הַצִּילֵנִי מֵאֹיְבַי ׀ אֱלֹהָי מִמִּתְקוֹמְמַי תְּשַׂגְּבֵנִי:	ב	2	Rescue me from my enemies, my God; from those who rise up against me, strengthen me.
הַצִּילֵנִי מִפֹּעֲלֵי אָוֶן וּמֵאַנְשֵׁי דָמִים הוֹשִׁיעֵנִי:	ג	3	Rescue me from the workers of iniquity, and from the bloodthirsty men deliver me.
כִּי הִנֵּה אָרְבוּ לְנַפְשִׁי יָגוּרוּ עָלַי עַזִּים לֹא־פִשְׁעִי וְלֹא־חַטָּאתִי יְהוָה:	ד	4	For behold, they lie in ambush for my soul against me gather the impudent; I have not transgressed [against them] nor have I sinned [against them], Adonoy.
בְּלִי־עָוֺן יְרוּצוּן וְיִכּוֹנָנוּ עוּרָה לִקְרָאתִי וּרְאֵה:	ה	5	Without iniquity [on my part] they run and prepare themselves, awake towards me and behold.
וְאַתָּה יְהוָה־אֱלֹהִים ׀ צְבָאוֹת אֱלֹהֵי יִשְׂרָאֵל הָקִיצָה לִפְקֹד כָּל־הַגּוֹיִם אַל־תָּחֹן כָּל־בֹּגְדֵי אָוֶן סֶלָה:	ו	6	And You, Adonoy, God of Hosts, God of Israel, arouse Yourself to remember all the nations; do not favor any iniquitous traitors, Selah.
יָשׁוּבוּ לָעֶרֶב יֶהֱמוּ כַכָּלֶב וִיסוֹבְבוּ עִיר:	ז	7	They return toward evening, they howl like the dog, and go round about the city.

ח הִנֵּה ׀ יַבִּיעוּן
בְּפִיהֶם
חֲרָבוֹת בְּשִׂפְתוֹתֵיהֶם
כִּי־מִי שֹׁמֵעַ׃

8 Behold, they bark
with their mouth,
swords are in their lips,
for [they say in their hearts] ``Who hears it?"

ט וְאַתָּה יְהוָה תִּשְׂחַק־לָמוֹ
תִּלְעַג לְכָל־גּוֹיִם׃

9 But You, Adonoy, You laugh at them,
You mock all nations.

י עֻזּוֹ
אֵלֶיךָ אֶשְׁמֹרָה
כִּי־אֱלֹהִים מִשְׂגַּבִּי׃

10 [Because of] his strength,
for You [Your help] I will wait,
for God is my stronghold.

יא אֱלֹהֵי חַסְדִּי יְקַדְּמֵנִי
אֱלֹהִים יַרְאֵנִי בְשֹׁרְרָי׃

11 The God of my kindness will precede me;
God will let me gaze upon my watchful foes.

יב אַל־תַּהַרְגֵם ׀ פֶּן־יִשְׁכְּחוּ עַמִּי
הֲנִיעֵמוֹ
בְחֵילְךָ
וְהוֹרִידֵמוֹ
מָגִנֵּנוּ אֲדֹנָי׃

12 Slay them not, lest my people would forget;
remove them from prosperity,
with Your power,
and bring them down,
our shield, my Master.

יג חַטַּאת־פִּימוֹ
דְּבַר־שְׂפָתֵימוֹ
וְיִלָּכְדוּ בִגְאוֹנָם
וּמֵאָלָה וּמִכַּחַשׁ יְסַפֵּרוּ׃

13 For the sin of their mouth
is the word of their lips,
and they will be caught in their pride,
because of curses and lies that they tell.

יד כַּלֵּה בְחֵמָה
כַּלֵּה וְאֵינֵמוֹ
וְיֵדְעוּ
כִּי־אֱלֹהִים מֹשֵׁל בְּיַעֲקֹב
לְאַפְסֵי הָאָרֶץ סֶלָה׃

14 Consume them in wrath,
consume them that they be no more;
and then will they know
that God rules in Jacob,
unto the ends of the earth, Selah.

טו וְיָשֻׁבוּ לָעֶרֶב
יֶהֱמוּ כַכָּלֶב
וִיסוֹבְבוּ עִיר׃

15 And they return toward evening,
they howl like the dog,
and go round about the city.

טז הֵמָּה יְנִיעוּן לֶאֱכֹל
אִם־לֹא יִשְׂבְּעוּ וַיָּלִינוּ׃

16 They wander about [seeking food] to eat
and tarry all night until they are satiated.

יז וַאֲנִי ׀
אָשִׁיר עֻזֶּךָ
וַאֲרַנֵּן לַבֹּקֶר
חַסְדֶּךָ
כִּי־הָיִיתָ מִשְׂגָּב לִי
וּמָנוֹס בְּיוֹם צַר־לִי׃

17 But as for me,
I will sing of Your strength,
and I will sing aloud in the morning
of Your kindness;
for You have been my stronghold
and a refugein the day of my distress.

יח עֻזִּי אֵלֶיךָ אֲזַמֵּרָה
כִּי־אֱלֹהִים מִשְׂגַּבִּי
אֱלֹהֵי חַסְדִּי׃

18 My strength, to You I will sing praises,
for God is my stronghold,
the God of my kindness.

באלהים
נעשה
חיל
והוא יבוס
צרינו

Through God we will emerge with might
and He will trample our adversaries.

פרק ס Chapter 60

Weekly Cycle	Monthly Cycle	Book Number
Tuesday	11th day of the month	Book 2

Author
דָוִד הַמֶּלֶךְ—King David—the second king of Israel and father of the Davidic royal and messianic dynasty. David composed over seventy of the 150 psalms of Sefer Tehillim.

When & Why
David wrote this psalm when his armies were being defeated by the armies of Aram and Edom. In it, he prays to God to make his soldiers victorious in battle.

Genre
Psalm of Communal Lament - This psalm focuses on expressing deep sorrow for the travails of a nation and as a group asking for God's blessing or intervention.

Chapter Summary
Here, David speaks of the wars he waged against Israel's belligerent neighbors. He also addresses his deliverance from these enemies, acknowledging that his successes come from the hand of the Almighty.

This psalm consists of fourteen verses, subdivided into three parts.
1 & 2 serve as a heading.
In verses 3-6, King David bemoans his defeat in a difficult war.
In verses 7-10, he prays for the fulfillment of a prophetic promise of salvation and endurance in the Holy Land, and further petitions God on behalf of the people of Israel.
In verses 11-14, he expresses his trust that God will indeed bring defeat upon Israel's enemies.

Introductory Words
לַמְנַצֵּחַ—Lamnatsei'ach—To the Conductor

Technical Terminology
עַל שׁוּשַׁן עֵדוּת—Al Shushan Eidut—a musical instrument shaped like a rose; alternatively, a reference to the tune or melody in which this chapter was sung.
מִכְתָּם—Michtam—an engraving, perhaps of simple fashion (Targum Yonatan); alternatively, made of fine gold (Ibn Ezra).
לְלַמֵּד—Lelameid—To instruct
סֶלָה—Selah—While its meaning is unclear, the most familiar opinion is that it is a musical notation, instructing the Levitical orchestra to pause its singing and playing of instruments. Alternatively, "Selah" may mean "everlasting".

Shimush Tehillim - When to Say
When going to war (say 7 times)—Verses 13 and 14 state: "Give us help against the adversary; futile is the help of man. Through God we will emerge with might and He will trample our

adversaries."

Where in the Siddur

Verse 7 comprises one of the verses of the closing paragraph of the Amidah (Silent Meditation).

Biblical Personalities

אֱדוֹם—Edom—descendants of Eisav (Esau), the brother of Yaakov (Jacob). The sibling rivalry between them persisted for centuries, most strongly expressed when the Edomites looted Jerusalem as it was being overrun by the Babylonians.

מְנַשֶּׁה, אֶפְרַיִם, וִיהוּדָה—Menasheh, Ephraim and Judah—three of the twelve tribes of Israel. Menasheh and Ephraim were the sons of Yosef (Joseph), and King David himself was a descendant of Yehudah (Judah).

מוֹאָב—Moab—biblical enemies of the Israelites, located on the eastern shore of the Dead Sea.

פְּלֶשֶׁת—Pelishtim—Philistines—an enemy nation that dwelled on the southwestern coast of Israel.

יוֹאָב—Yoav—Joab—King David's chief general.

Biblical Places

אֲרַם נַהֲרַיִם—Aram Naharayim—a city-state bordering on two rivers, one of which was the Euphrates. It is identified with Mesopotamia, north of Damascus.

אֲרַם צוֹבָה—Aram Zobah—a city-state northwest of Damascus, identified with Aleppo of today, located in Southern Syria. Its king, Hadadezer bar Rehob, allied with Ammon against David, and Arameans from across the Euphrates came to Hadadezer's aid. Still, David defeated Zobah and made the kingdom a tributary to Israel.

עֵמֶק סֻכּוֹת—Eimek Sukkot—Valley of Sukkot— a valley to the east of the Jordan river, located near Shechem.

גֵיא-מֶלַח—Gei Melach—a valley located to the south of the Dead Sea.

גִלְעָד—Gilead—an area located just east of the Jordan River, divided among the tribes of Gad and Menasheh.

שְׁכֶם—Shechem—an Israelite city of the tribe of Manasseh and the first capital of the Kingdom of Israel.

פרק ס	**Chapter 60**
א לַמְנַצֵּחַ עַל־שׁוּשַׁן עֵדוּת מִכְתָּם לְדָוִד לְלַמֵּד:	1 To the Chief Musician, upon Shushan Aidus, a Miktam of David to teach.
ב הַצּוֹתוֹ | אֶת אֲרַם נַהֲרַיִם וְאֶת־אֲרַם צוֹבָה וַיָּשָׁב יוֹאָב וַיַּךְ אֶת־אֱדוֹם בְּגֵיא־מֶלַח שְׁנֵים עָשָׂר אָלֶף:	2 When he battled with Aram Naharayim and with Aram Tsovah, and Joab returned and smote Edom in Gei Melach, twelve thousand men.

ג אֱלֹהִים זְנַחְתָּנוּ
פְרַצְתָּנוּ
אָנַפְתָּ
תְּשׁוֹבֵב לָנוּ׃

3 God, You have forsaken us,
You have breached us,
You have been angry with us;
[please] grant us respite.

ד הִרְעַשְׁתָּה אֶרֶץ
פְּצַמְתָּהּ
רְפָה שְׁבָרֶיהָ כִי־מָטָה׃

4 You have made the land shake,
You have torn it open;
heal its fragments for it totters.

ה הִרְאִיתָה עַמְּךָ קָשָׁה
הִשְׁקִיתָנוּ יַיִן תַּרְעֵלָה׃

5 You have shown Your people hardship,
You made us drink the wine of bewilderment.

ו נָתַתָּה לִּירֵאֶיךָ
נֵּס לְהִתְנוֹסֵס
מִפְּנֵי קֹשֶׁט סֶלָה׃

6 You have given to those who fear You
a test by which to be proven,
for the sake of [Your] truth, Selah.

ז לְמַעַן יֵחָלְצוּן יְדִידֶיךָ
הוֹשִׁיעָה יְמִינְךָ וַעֲנֵנִי׃

7 In order that Your loved ones be released,
deliver [with] Your right hand and answer me.

ח אֱלֹהִים | דִּבֶּר בְּקָדְשׁוֹ
אֶעְלֹזָה
אֲחַלְּקָה שְׁכֶם
וְעֵמֶק סֻכּוֹת אֲמַדֵּד׃

8 God spoke in His [spirit of] holiness—
that I would exult [in His deliverance]that I would divide Shechem,
and the valley of Succos I would apportion.

ט לִי גִלְעָד | וְלִי מְנַשֶּׁה
וְאֶפְרַיִם מָעוֹז רֹאשִׁי
יְהוּדָה מְחֹקְקִי׃

9 Mine is Gilad and mine is Menasheh,
and Ephraim is the stronghold of my head;
Judah is my lawgiver.

י מוֹאָב | סִיר רַחְצִי
עַל־אֱדוֹם אַשְׁלִיךְ נַעֲלִי
עָלַי פְּלֶשֶׁת הִתְרֹעָעִי׃

10 Moav is my wash basin,
upon Edom will I cast my lock,
Philistia, join yourself with me.

יא מִי יֹבִלֵנִי עִיר מָצוֹר
מִי נָחַנִי עַד־אֱדוֹם׃

11 Who will bring me into the fortified city,
who will lead me unto Edom?

יב הֲלֹא־אַתָּה אֱלֹהִים זְנַחְתָּנוּ
וְלֹא־תֵצֵא אֱלֹהִים
בְּצִבְאוֹתֵינוּ׃

12 Have not You, God, forsaken us
and You do not go forth, God,
with our hosts?

יג הָבָה־לָּנוּ עֶזְרָת מִצָּר
וְשָׁוְא תְּשׁוּעַת אָדָם׃

13 Give us help against the adversary;
futile is the help of man.

יד בֵּאלֹהִים נַעֲשֶׂה־חָיִל
וְהוּא יָבוּס צָרֵינוּ׃

14 Through God we will emerge with might
and He will trample our adversaries.

פרק סא Chapter 61

Weekly Cycle	Monthly Cycle	Book Number
Tuesday	11th day of the month	Book 2

Author

דָּוִד הַמֶּלֶךְ—King David—the second king of Israel and father of the Davidic royal and messianic dynasty. David composed over seventy of the 150 psalms of Sefer Tehillim.

When & Why

David wrote this psalm when he was in exile hiding from Saul. In it, he prays to God to help him return to Jerusalem so that he can continue building the foundation of the Temple.

Genre

Psalm of Individual Lament - This psalm was written from the perspective of the individual worshipper, who cries out to God in his time of need. It is characterized as an address to God involving a complaint, followed by a request and ending with an expression of trust.

Chapter Summary

King David composed this psalm when he was being pursued by those who sought to take his life. He prays for tranquility in his personal life and in his kingdom. Looking forward, he also adds a prayer concerning the future exile of the Jewish people.

This psalm consists of nine verses, subdivided into two parts. The first verse serves as a heading.
In verses 2-5, King David begs God for protection from his enemies.
In verses 6-9, he asks to be allowed to conquer the land granted as an inheritance to the Children of Israel, and further prays for his welfare as king.

Introductory Words

לַמְנַצֵּחַ—Lamnatsei'ach—To the Conductor

Technical Terminology

נְגִינוֹת—Neginos—Tunes
סֶלָה—Selah—While its meaning is unclear, the most familiar opinion is that it is a musical notation, instructing the Levitical orchestra to pause its singing and playing of instruments. Alternatively, "Selah" may mean "everlasting".

Shimush Tehillim - When to Say

For one who is apprehensive about going home —Verse 5 states: "I will dwell in Your Tent forever, I will take refuge in the shelter of Your wings."

Talmud on Tehillim

Verse 8: "יֵשֵׁב עוֹלָם, לִפְנֵי אֱלֹהִים; חֶסֶד וֶאֱמֶת, מַן יִנְצְרֻהוּ"—"May he be enthroned forever before God, kindness and truth appoint that they may preserve him."
The Talmud, Eiruvin 86a, states: "Rabbi Akiva and Rebbe (Rabbi Yehudah HaNasi) honored the

wealthy who assisted the poor, per the inference of Rava bar Mari [from this verse]." Those who help the poor are compared to those who dwell in God's presence, as they are indeed truly spiritually wealthy.

פרק סא

א לַמְנַצֵּחַ ׀
עַל־נְגִינַת לְדָוִד׃
ב שִׁמְעָה אֱלֹהִים רִנָּתִי
הַקְשִׁיבָה תְּפִלָּתִי׃
ג מִקְצֵה הָאָרֶץ ׀
אֵלֶיךָ אֶקְרָא
בַּעֲטֹף לִבִּי
בְּצוּר־יָרוּם מִמֶּנִּי תַנְחֵנִי׃
ד כִּי־הָיִיתָ מַחְסֶה לִי
מִגְדַּל־עֹז
מִפְּנֵי אוֹיֵב׃
ה אָגוּרָה בְאָהָלְךָ עוֹלָמִים
אֶחֱסֶה
בְסֵתֶר כְּנָפֶיךָ סֶּלָה׃
ו כִּי־אַתָּה אֱלֹהִים
שָׁמַעְתָּ לִנְדָרָי
נָתַתָּ יְרֻשַּׁת
יִרְאֵי שְׁמֶךָ׃
ז יָמִים עַל־יְמֵי־מֶלֶךְ תּוֹסִיף
שְׁנוֹתָיו
כְּמוֹ־דֹר וָדֹר׃
ח יֵשֵׁב עוֹלָם לִפְנֵי אֱלֹהִים
חֶסֶד וֶאֱמֶת מַן
יִנְצְרֻהוּ׃
ט כֵּן אֲזַמְּרָה שִׁמְךָ לָעַד
לְשַׁלְּמִי נְדָרַי יוֹם ׀ יוֹם׃

Chapter 61

1 To the Chief Musician,
on neginas [a Psalm] of David.
2 Hear, God, my singing,
hearken to my prayer.
3 From the end of the earth
to You I will call out,
when my heart is exhausted;
to a rock that is higher than I, lead me.
4 For You have been a refuge for me,
a tower of strength
in the face of the enemy.
5 I will dwell in Your Tent forever,
I will take refuge
in the shelter of Your wings, Selah.
6 For You, God,
have heard my vows,
You have granted the heritage
of those who fear Your Name.
7 May You add days to the days of the king,
[may the length of] his years
be as generation after generation.
8 May he be enthroned forever before God,
kindness and truth appoint
that they may preserve him.
9 Likewise will I praise Your Name forever,
that I may pay my vows daily.

פרק סב Chapter 62

Weekly Cycle	Monthly Cycle	Book Number
Tuesday	11th day of the month	Book 2

Author
דָּוִד הַמֶּלֶךְ—King David—the second king of Israel and father of the Davidic royal and messianic dynasty. David composed over seventy of the 150 psalms of Sefer Tehillim; possibly composed for יְדוּתוּן—Yedutun—a noted singer and composer of several psalms.

When & Why
David wrote this psalm when he was in the desolate Judean desert hiding from Saul. In it, he prays to God to allow him to return to God's city, Jerusalem.

Genre
Psalm of Individual Confidence - In this psalm, the worshipper expresses absolute certainty that his prayers will be heard.

Chapter Summary
King David addresses his soul, encouraging it to trust in God in times of trouble. He also directly speaks to his enemies who conspire to do evil against him. Finally, he concludes with an admonition and a reminder that God judges the earth.

This psalm consists of thirteen verses, subdivided into two parts, each of which opens with a refrain (verses 2-3 and 6-7 respectively) conveying the idea that the Psalmist trusts only in God. The first verse serves as a heading.
In verses 4 and 5, King David describes the treacherous deeds of the wicked and addresses his enemies directly.
In verses 8-13, he addresses all God-fearing individuals, urging them to have faith that God will protect them and punish their enemies. Like vapor, asserts the Psalmist, one's enemies, too, are but temporary.

Introductory Words
לַמְנַצֵּחַ—Lamnatsei'ach—To the Conductor
מִזְמוֹר—Mizmor—Musical Accompaniment

Musical Instrument
יְדוּתוּן—Yedutun—perhaps a musical instrument; alternatively, the name of a singer and/or composer.

Technical Terminology
סֶלָה—Selah—While its meaning is unclear, the most familiar opinion is that it is a musical notation, instructing the Levitical orchestra to pause its singing and playing of instruments. Alternatively, "Selah" may mean "everlasting".

Shimush Tehillim

To build trust in God—Verse 9 states: "Trust in Him at all times, people; pour out your hearts before Him, God is a refuge for us."

Where in the Siddur

Verse 9 is recited by some following Ma'ariv (evening service) of Sunday night and the Minchah (afternoon service) of Monday afternoon.

פֶּרֶק סב

א לַמְנַצֵּחַ עַל־יְדוּתוּן
מִזְמוֹר לְדָוִד׃
ב אַךְ אֶל־אֱלֹהִים דּוּמִיָּה נַפְשִׁי
מִמֶּנּוּ יְשׁוּעָתִי׃
ג אַךְ־הוּא צוּרִי וִישׁוּעָתִי
מִשְׂגַּבִּי לֹא־אֶמּוֹט רַבָּה׃
ד עַד־אָנָה | תְּהוֹתְתוּ
עַל אִישׁ
תְּרָצְּחוּ כֻלְּכֶם
כְּקִיר נָטוּי גָּדֵר הַדְּחוּיָה׃
ה אַךְ מִשְּׂאֵתוֹ |
יָעֲצוּ לְהַדִּיחַ
יִרְצוּ כָזָב
בְּפִיו יְבָרֵכוּ
וּבְקִרְבָּם יְקַלְלוּ־סֶלָה׃
ו אַךְ לֵאלֹהִים דּוֹמִּי נַפְשִׁי
כִּי־מִמֶּנּוּ תִּקְוָתִי׃
ז אַךְ־הוּא צוּרִי וִישׁוּעָתִי
מִשְׂגַּבִּי לֹא אֶמּוֹט׃
ח עַל־אֱלֹהִים יִשְׁעִי
וּכְבוֹדִי
צוּר־עֻזִּי מַחְסִי בֵּאלֹהִים׃
ט בִּטְחוּ בוֹ בְכָל־עֵת | עָם
שִׁפְכוּ־לְפָנָיו לְבַבְכֶם
אֱלֹהִים מַחֲסֶה־לָּנוּ סֶלָה׃
י אַךְ | הֶבֶל בְּנֵי־אָדָם
כָּזָב בְּנֵי אִישׁ
בְּמֹאזְנַיִם לַעֲלוֹת
הֵמָּה מֵהֶבֶל יָחַד׃

Chapter 62

1 To the Chief Musician, on yedusun,
a Psalm of David.
2 Only for God my soul waits in silence,
from Him comes my deliverance.
3 Only He is my rock and my deliverance;
my stronghold, I will not be moved greatly.
4 How long will you plan destruction
against man,
that you may all slay him
as a leaning wall, a tottering fence?
5 Only [because they fear] his lofty position
have they plotted to topple him;
delighting in lies,
with their mouth they bless [him],
but inwardly they curse [him], Selah.
6 Only for God my soul waits silently,
for my hope comes from Him.
7 He alone is my rock and my deliverance;
my stronghold, I will not be moved.
8 Upon God [rests] my deliverance
and my honor,
the rock of my strength, my refuge is in God.
9 Trust in Him at all times, people;
pour out your hearts before Him,
God is a refuge for us, Selah.
10 But the sons of man are as nothing
and deceitful are men of distinction!
[If laid] on the scales,
they and their vanity would be equal.

יא אַל־תִּבְטְחוּ בְעֹשֶׁק
וּבְגָזֵל אַל־תֶּהְבָּלוּ
חַיִל ׀ כִּי־יָנוּב
אַל־תָּשִׁיתוּ לֵב׃
יב אַחַת ׀ דִּבֶּר אֱלֹהִים
שְׁתַּיִם־זוּ שָׁמָעְתִּי
כִּי עֹז לֵאלֹהִים׃
יג וּלְךָ־אֲדֹנָי חָסֶד
כִּי־אַתָּה תְשַׁלֵּם
לְאִישׁ כְּמַעֲשֵׂהוּ׃

11 Trust not in oppression,
and in robbery do not put vain hope;
if [illegal] wealth prospers
let your heart pay it no heed.
12 Once has God spoken,
twice have I heard this;
that strength belongs to God.
13 And in You [alone] my Master, is kindness,
for You render to every man
according to his work.

פרק סג Chapter 63

Weekly Cycle	Monthly Cycle	Book Number
Tuesday	11th day of the month	Book 2

Author
דָּוִד הַמֶּלֶךְ—King David—the second king of Israel and father of the Davidic royal and messianic dynasty. David composed over seventy of the 150 psalms of Sefer Tehillim.

When & Why
King David composed this psalm while hiding in the wilderness of Judah in order to escape Saul who was plotting to kill him.

Genre
Psalm of Individual Lament - This psalm was written from the perspective of the individual worshipper, who cries out to God in his time of need. It is characterized as an address to God involving a complaint, followed by a request and ending with an expression of trust.

Chapter Summary
This and the following psalm are based on the episode of the spear and the jar which David had taken from King Saul when hiding from him. King David composed this psalm while hiding in the wilderness of Judah in order to escape. Having been forced to flee from Saul's persecution, he longs to again devote himself to Torah study and observance of the mitzvot.

This psalm consists of twelve verses, subdivided into three parts. The first verse serves as a heading.
In verses 2-6, King David yearns to be even closer to God.
In verses 7-9, he nonetheless expresses his happiness and sense of security in his current state of closeness to God.

In verses 10-12, he beseeches God to bring about a curse upon the wicked and those who utter falsehood. He further prays for a blessing for the king and for those who swear truthfully.

Introductory Words

מִזְמוֹר—Mizmor—Musical Accompaniment

Shimush Tehillim - When to Say

To separate amicably and with profit from a business partner.

For success in business—Verse 12 states: "But the king will rejoice in God, glorified will be everyone that swears by Him; for closed will be the mouth of those who speak falsehood."

Biblical Places

מִדְבַּר יְהוּדָה—The Wilderness of Judah—David compares his thirst for spiritual closeness to God and his yearning to see His splendor, to his thirst for water in the parched desert of Judea where he had hidden from his pursuers.

Talmud on Tehillim

Verse 5: "כֵּן אֲבָרֶכְךָ בְחַיָּי; בְּשִׁמְךָ, אֶשָּׂא כַפָּי"—"So will I bless You throughout my life, in Your Name will I lift my hands."

The Talmud, Berachot 16b, deduces that "כֵּן אֲבָרֶכְךָ"—"I will bless you" refers to the recitation of the Shema; "בְּשִׁמְךָ, אֶשָּׂא כַפָּי"—"I will lift my hands, invoking Your name" refers to the recitation of the Amidah (Silent Meditation). The Talmud infers from this verse that one who recites both the Shema and the Amidah will merit to have life not only in Olam Hazeh—this world, but also in Olam Habba—the World to Come.

Verse 6: "וְשִׂפְתֵי רְנָנוֹת, יְהַלֶּל פִּי"—"and with joyous language will my mouth give praise."

The Talmud, Berachot 16b, deduces that this too refers to Olam Habba.

Verse 12: "וְהַמֶּלֶךְ, יִשְׂמַח בֵּאלֹהִים: יִתְהַלֵּל, כָּל הַנִּשְׁבָּע בּוֹ: כִּי יִסָּכֵר, פִּי דוֹבְרֵי שָׁקֶר"—"But the king shall rejoice in God, glorified will be everyone that swears by Him; for closed will be the mouth of those who speak falsehood."

The Talmud, Shabbat 33b, deduces that speaking lies results in the constricting of the throat, thereby choking the slanderer.

פֶּרֶק סג

א מִזְמ֥וֹר לְדָוִ֑ד
בִּ֝הְיוֹת֗וֹ בְּמִדְבַּ֥ר יְהוּדָֽה׃
ב אֱלֹ֘הִ֤ים ׀ אֵלִ֣י אַתָּה֮ אֲֽשַׁחֲ֫רֶ֥ךָּ
צָמְאָ֬ה לְךָ֨ ׀ נַפְשִׁ֗י
כָּמַ֣הּ לְךָ֣ בְשָׂרִ֑י
בְּאֶֽרֶץ־צִיָּ֖ה וְעָיֵ֣ף בְּלִי־מָֽיִם׃
ג כֵּ֭ן בַּקֹּ֣דֶשׁ חֲזִיתִ֑יךָ
לִרְא֥וֹת עֻ֝זְּךָ֗ וּכְבוֹדֶֽךָ׃
ד כִּי־ט֣וֹב חַ֭סְדְּךָ מֵֽחַיִּ֗ים
שְׂפָתַ֥י יְשַׁבְּחֽוּנְךָ׃

Chapter 63

1 A Psalm of David,
when he was in the wilderness of Judah.
2 God, You are my Almighty, I will seek You;
my soul thirsts for You,
my flesh longs for You,
in a dry and weary land without water.
3 Thus in the Sanctuary have I perceived You,
to see Your might and Your glory.
4 For better is Your kindness than life;
my lips will praise You.

ה	כֵּן אֲבָרֶכְךָ בְחַיָּי בְּשִׁמְךָ אֶשָּׂא כַפָּי׃	5	So will I bless You throughout my life, in Your Name will I lift my hands.
ו	כְּמוֹ חֵלֶב וָדֶשֶׁן תִּשְׂבַּע נַפְשִׁי וְשִׂפְתֵי רְנָנוֹת יְהַלֶּל־פִּי׃	6	As with fat and marrow my soul will be satisfied, and with joyous language will my mouth give praise.
ז	אִם־זְכַרְתִּיךָ עַל־יְצוּעָי בְּאַשְׁמֻרוֹת אֶהְגֶּה־בָּךְ׃	7	When I remember You upon my couch, in the night watches I meditate upon You.
ח	כִּי־הָיִיתָ עֶזְרָתָה לִּי וּבְצֵל כְּנָפֶיךָ אֲרַנֵּן׃	8	For You have been a help to me, and in the shadow of Your wings I will joyfully sing.
ט	דָּבְקָה נַפְשִׁי אַחֲרֶיךָ בִּי תָּמְכָה יְמִינֶךָ׃	9	My soul cleaves after You; Your right hand supports me.
י	וְהֵמָּה לְשׁוֹאָה יְבַקְשׁוּ נַפְשִׁי יָבֹאוּ בְּתַחְתִּיּוֹת הָאָרֶץ׃	10	But those who seek destruction for my soul, they will enter into the abyss of the earth.
יא	יַגִּירֻהוּ עַל־יְדֵי־חָרֶב מְנָת שֻׁעָלִים יִהְיוּ׃	11	He will be dragged by the sword, a portion for foxes will they be.
יב	וְהַמֶּלֶךְ יִשְׂמַח בֵּאלֹהִים יִתְהַלֵּל כָּל־הַנִּשְׁבָּע בּוֹ כִּי יִסָּכֵר פִּי דוֹבְרֵי־שָׁקֶר׃	12	But the king will rejoice in God, glorified will be everyone that swears by Him; for closed will be the mouth of those who speak falsehood.

פרק סד — Chapter 64

Weekly Cycle	Monthly Cycle	Book Number
Tuesday	11th day of the month	Book 2

Author

דָּוִד הַמֶּלֶךְ—King David—the second king of Israel and father of the Davidic royal and messianic dynasty. David composed over seventy of the 150 psalms of Sefer Tehillim.

When & Why

David wrote this Psalm when he discovered that Doeg and others were plotting to kill him.

Genre

Psalm of Individual Lament - This psalm was written from the perspective of the individual worshipper, who cries out to God in his time of need. It is characterized as an address to God involving a complaint, followed by a request and ending with an expression of trust.

Chapter Summary

This and the preceding psalm are based on the episode of the spear and the jar which David had taken from King Saul while hiding from him. This psalm also alludes to our present exile. We have been driven from our land and know not what each new day brings. Nevertheless, the Psalmist concludes, "The righteous will rejoice in Adonoy, and will take refuge in Him; and all the upright in heart will glory."

This psalm consists of eleven verses, subdivided into five parts. The first verse serves as a heading.

In verses 2 & 3, King David appeals to God to protect him from the wicked.

In verses 4-7, he describes the evil deeds of the wicked and their plots against the innocent man.

In verses 8 & 9, he further depicts the downfall of the wicked.

In verse 10, the Psalmist relates how the news of the downfall will be reported throughout the world.

In verse 11, he concludes by appealing to the righteous to rejoice in God.

Introductory Words

לַמְנַצֵּחַ—Lamnatsei'ach—To the Conductor

מִזְמוֹר—Mizmor—Musical Accompaniment

Shimush Tehillim - When to Say

To safely cross a river—Verse 2 states: "Hear, God, my voice in my fervent prayer from the terror of the enemy preserve my life."

פרק סד			**Chapter 64**
לַמְנַצֵּחַ מִזְמוֹר לְדָוִד׃	א	1	To the Chief Musician, a Psalm of David.
שְׁמַע־אֱלֹהִים קוֹלִי בְשִׂיחִי מִפַּחַד אוֹיֵב תִּצֹּר חַיָּי׃	ב	2	Hear, God, my voice in my fervent prayer from the terror of the enemy preserve my life.
תַּסְתִּירֵנִי מִסּוֹד מְרֵעִים מֵרִגְשַׁת פֹּעֲלֵי אָוֶן׃	ג	3	Shelter me from the counsel of evil doers, from the gathering of workers of iniquity.
אֲשֶׁר שָׁנְנוּ כַחֶרֶב לְשׁוֹנָם דָּרְכוּ חִצָּם דָּבָר מָר׃	ד	4	Who have whet their tongue like a sword, and have aimed their arrow, a bitter word.
לִירוֹת בַּמִּסְתָּרִים תָּם פִּתְאֹם יֹרֻהוּ וְלֹא יִירָאוּ׃	ה	5	To shoot in secret at the innocent, suddenly they shoot, and are not afraid.
חַזְּקוּ־לָמוֹ ׀ דָּבָר רָע יְסַפְּרוּ לִטְמוֹן מוֹקְשִׁים אָמְרוּ מִי יִרְאֶה־לָּמוֹ׃	ו	6	They encourage each other to do evil matters, they tell of laying hidden snares, they ask, ``who would see them."

ז חָפְשׂוּ־עוֹלֹת
תַּמְנוּ חֵפֶשׂ מְחֻפָּשׂ
וְקֶרֶב אִישׁ
וְלֵב עָמֹק׃
ח וַיֹּרֵם אֱלֹהִים חֵץ
פִּתְאוֹם הָיוּ מַכּוֹתָם׃
ט וַיַּכְשִׁילוּהוּ עָלֵימוֹ
לְשׁוֹנָם
יִתְנֹדְדוּ כָּל־רֹאֵה בָם׃
י וַיִּירְאוּ כָּל־אָדָם
וַיַּגִּידוּ פֹּעַל אֱלֹהִים
וּמַעֲשֵׂהוּ הִשְׂכִּילוּ׃
יא יִשְׂמַח צַדִּיק בַּיהוָה
וְחָסָה בוֹ
וְיִתְהַלְלוּ כָּל־יִשְׁרֵי־לֵב׃

7 They devise [false] iniquities
they have completed a diligent search;
[hiding their falsehood] within themselves,
and in the depth of the heart.

8 Then God shot them with an arrow,
suddenly they were wounded.

9 And they were made to stumble
by their own tongues;
all who see them shake their heads.

10 And all men feared
and declared the work of God,
and His doing they understood.

11 The righteous will rejoice in Adonoy,
and will take refuge in Him;
and all the upright in heart will glory.

A View of the Inside of the Holy Temple

פרק סה Chapter 65

Weekly Cycle	Monthly Cycle	Book Number
Tuesday	11th day of the month	Book 2

Author

דָוִד הַמֶּלֶךְ—King David—the second king of Israel and father of the Davidic royal and messianic dynasty. David composed over seventy of the 150 psalms of Sefer Tehillim.

Genre

Psalm of Praise - This is a psalm of celebration, often the result of a victory. It declares God's goodness and urges all of creation to worship.

Chapter Summary

After God revealed the future site of the Beit HaMikdash (Temple), King David composed this psalm to express his longing for its erection and to glorify Har Tzion (Mount Zion). Taken literally, the psalm is a plea for rain in time of need, but can also be understood as alluding to the future exile of the Jewish people.

This psalm consists of fourteen verses, subdivided into three parts. The first verse serves as a heading.
In verses 2-5, the Psalmist admonishes that it is right to praise God and fulfill vows made to Him. He reminds us that God hears our prayer and forgives our sins. Closeness to Him, King David adds, leads to happiness.
In verses 6-9, King David praises God as creator and ruler of the universe.
In verses 10-14, he expresses thanksgiving for the abundant rain and a bountiful year.

Introductory Words

לַמְנַצֵּחַ—Lamnatsei'ach—To the Conductor
מִזְמוֹר—Mizmor—Musical Accompaniment

Shimush Tehillim - When to Say

For success in requesting a favor from another—Verse 6 states: "With wondrous works, through [Your] righteousness, You answer us, God of our deliverance; [You are] the trust of all [inhabitants of] the ends of the earth and of the distant seas."

Where in the Siddur

Verse 5 is recited as part of the Brit Milah (circumcision) ceremony; the first half of the verse is recited by the mohel, the second half by the congregants.

Biblical Places

הֵיכַל—Heichal—Holy Temple—a term used to refer to the inner sanctuary of the Temple in Jerusalem. The Heichal contained the Holy of Holies, the resting place of the Aron HaKodesh (Holy Ark)*. It also housed the Menorah, Altar of Incense, and Table of the Showbread.

*The Aron HaKodesh, while present in the first Beit HaMikdash (Temple), was buried, and hence its location was not known, during the period of the second Beit HaMikdash.

צִיּוֹן—Zion—a place name often used as a synonym for Jerusalem. The term Zion originally referred only to the area where a Jebbusite fortress once stood, also the location of the City of David. Zion was later used by prophets and psalmists as another name for Jerusalem.

Talmud on Tehillim

Verse 2: "לְךָ דֻמִיָּה תְהִלָּה"—"For You silence is praise."

The Talmud, Eiruvin 19a, deduces from this verse that unlike people sentenced to death by a human king, who need to be aggressively held back from cursing the king, those who are killed by Divine decree accept their punishment in silence.

פרק סה			**Chapter 65**
לַמְנַצֵּ֗חַ	א	1	To the Chief Musician,
מִזְמ֥וֹר לְדָוִ֗ד שִֽׁיר׃			a Psalm of David, a song.
לְךָ֤ דֻֽמִיָּ֪ה תְהִלָּ֓ה	ב	2	For You silence is praise,
אֱלֹהִ֣ים בְּצִיּ֑וֹן			God in Zion,
וּ֝לְךָ֗ יְשֻׁלַּם־נֶֽדֶר׃			and to You the vow is paid.
שֹׁמֵ֥עַ תְּפִלָּ֑ה	ג	3	You Who hears prayer,
עָ֝דֶ֗יךָ כָּל־בָּשָׂ֥ר יָבֹֽאוּ׃			unto You does all flesh come.
דִּבְרֵ֣י עֲ֭וֺנֹת גָּ֣בְרוּ מֶ֑נִּי	ד	4	Talk of sin has overcome me;
פְּ֝שָׁעֵ֗ינוּ			as for our transgressions,
אַתָּ֥ה תְכַפְּרֵֽם׃			You will pardon them.
אַשְׁרֵ֤י ׀ תִּֽבְחַ֣ר	ה	5	Fortunate is he whom You choose
וּתְקָרֵב֮			and bring near,
יִשְׁכֹּ֪ן חֲצֵ֫רֶ֥יךָ			that he may dwell in Your courts;
נִ֭שְׂבְּעָה			may we be satisfied
בְּט֣וּב בֵּיתֶ֑ךָ			with the goodness of Your House,
קְ֝דֹ֗שׁ הֵיכָלֶֽךָ׃			the holy place of Your Sanctuary.
נוֹרָא֤וֹת ׀	ו	6	With wondrous works,
בְּצֶ֣דֶק תַּ֭עֲנֵנוּ			through [Your] righteousness, You answer us,
אֱלֹהֵ֣י יִשְׁעֵ֑נוּ			God of our deliverance;
מִבְטָ֥ח			[You are] the trust
כָּל־קַצְוֵי־אֶ֝֗רֶץ			of all [inhabitants of] the ends of the earth
וְיָ֣ם רְחֹקִֽים׃			and of the distant seas.
מֵכִ֣ין הָרִ֣ים	ז	7	Who provides [rain] for mountains,
בְּכֹח֑וֹ			by His strength,
נֶ֝אְזָ֗ר בִּגְבוּרָֽה׃			Who is girded with might.

View of Temple Mount, Jerusalem, Israel in 1839

ח מַשְׁבִּיחַ | שְׁאוֹן יַמִּים
שְׁאוֹן גַּלֵּיהֶם
וַהֲמוֹן לְאֻמִּים׃

8 Who stills the roaring of the seas,
the roaring of their waves
and the tumult of the peoples.

ט וַיִּירְאוּ | יֹשְׁבֵי קְצָוֹת
מֵאוֹתֹתֶיךָ
מוֹצָאֵי־
בֹקֶר וָעֶרֶב
תַּרְנִין׃

9 Inhabitants of distant parts are awed
by Your signs;
with the coming and going
of morning and evening
You cause jubilation.

י פָּקַדְתָּ הָאָרֶץ | וַתְּשֹׁקְקֶהָ
רַבַּת תַּעְשְׁרֶנָּה פֶּלֶג אֱלֹהִים
מָלֵא מָיִם
תָּכִין דְּגָנָם כִּי־כֵן תְּכִינֶהָ׃

10 You remembered the earth and watered it,
greatly enriching it with the stream of God
that is full of water;
You prepare their corn, for so You prepare it.

יא תְּלָמֶיהָ רַוֵּה
נַחֵת גְּדוּדֶיהָ
בִּרְבִיבִים תְּמֹגְגֶנָּה
צִמְחָהּ תְּבָרֵךְ׃

11 Her ridges, You water abundantly,
thereby satisfying its bands of people;
with showers You make it soft,
its growth You bless.

יב עִטַּרְתָּ שְׁנַת טוֹבָתֶךָ
וּמַעְגָּלֶיךָ יִרְעֲפוּן דָּשֶׁן׃

12 You crown the year with Your goodness,
and Your paths drip with abundance.

יג יִרְעֲפוּ נְאוֹת מִדְבָּר
וְגִיל גְּבָעוֹת תַּחְגֹּרְנָה׃

13 They drip on to pastures of the wilderness,
and the hills gird themselves with joy.

יד לָבְשׁוּ כָרִים | הַצֹּאן
וַעֲמָקִים יַעַטְפוּ־בָר
יִתְרוֹעֲעוּ אַף־יָשִׁירוּ׃

14 The meadows are clothed with sheep,
and the valleys cover themselves with corn;
they shout for joy and they also sing.

פרק סו Chapter 66

Weekly Cycle	Monthly Cycle	Book Number
Tuesday	12th day of the month	Book 2

Author
Unknown

Genre
Psalm of Praise - This is a psalm of celebration, often the result of a victory. It declares God's goodness and urges all of creation to worship.
Psalm of Communal Thanksgiving - This psalm emphasizes gratitude for what God has done for the community as a whole.

Chapter Summary
In this psalm, the singer depicts the excellence of the Beit HaMikdash (Holy Temple). Here again, as in the previous chapter, the author is perhaps alluding to the exile, which he contrasts with the wonderful things that transpired beforehand. Divine deliverance, he admonishes, can come at any moment, and one must therefore not despair.

This psalm consists of twenty verses, subdivided into five parts.
In verses 1-4, the psalmist calls on all of the world's inhabitants to praise God.
In verses 5-7, he describes the wonders God performed for His people in ancient times.
In verses 8-12, he tells of the adversity that faced the people of Israel from which they were delivered.
In verses 13-15, he proclaims that he will fulfill his vows to God.
In verses 16-20, he concludes by expressing thanksgiving for the acceptance of his prayer.

Technical Terminology
סֶלָה—**Selah**—While its meaning is unclear, the most familiar opinion is that it is a musical notation, instructing the Levitical orchestra to pause its singing and playing of instruments. Alternatively, "Selah" may mean "everlasting".

Introductory Words
לַמְנַצֵּחַ—**Lamnatsei'ach**—To the Conductor
מִזְמוֹר—**Mizmor**—Musical Accompaniment
שִׁיר—**Shir**—Song

Shimush Tehillim - When to Say
To exorcise an evil spirit—Verse 12 states: "You made mortal man ride over our heads; we went through fire and water, and You brought us out to abundance."

Where in the Siddur
Verse 9 comprises one of the verses of Ve'emunah Kol Zot, the paragraph following the Shema of

Ma'ariv (evening service).

Talmud on Tehillim

Verse 18: "אָוֶן, אִם רָאִיתִי בְלִבִּי, לֹא יִשְׁמַע אֲדֹנָי"—"Even had I preceived iniquity in my heart, my Master would not have listened."

The Talmud, Kiddushin 4a, deduces that God considers one's good intentions as having been carried out, as long as, and only if, the individual has made every effort to do so.

פֶּרֶק סו			**Chapter 66**
לַמְנַצֵּחַ שִׁיר מִזְמוֹר הָרִיעוּ לֵאלֹהִים כָּל־הָאָרֶץ׃	א	1	To the Chief Musician, a song, a Psalm; shout to God all the earth.
זַמְּרוּ כְבוֹד־שְׁמוֹ שִׂימוּ כָבוֹד תְּהִלָּתוֹ׃	ב	2	Sing to the glory of His Name, make glorious His praise.
אִמְרוּ לֵאלֹהִים מַה־נּוֹרָא מַעֲשֶׂיךָ בְּרֹב עֻזְּךָ יְכַחֲשׁוּ לְךָ אֹיְבֶיךָ׃	ג	3	Say to God, "How awe_inspiring are Your works, through the greatness of Your might they have deceived You those who are Your enemies.
כָּל־הָאָרֶץ ׀ יִשְׁתַּחֲווּ לְךָ וִיזַמְּרוּ־לָךְ יְזַמְּרוּ שִׁמְךָ סֶלָה׃	ד	4	All the earth will prostrate themselves [in worship] to You, and they will sing praises to You; they will sing praises to Your Name, Selah."
לְכוּ וּרְאוּ מִפְעֲלוֹת אֱלֹהִים נוֹרָא עֲלִילָה עַל־בְּנֵי אָדָם׃	ה	5	Go and see the works of God; awe inspiring in [His] acts towards the sons of man.
הָפַךְ יָם ׀ לְיַבָּשָׁה בַּנָּהָר יַעַבְרוּ בְרָגֶל שָׁם נִשְׂמְחָה־בּוֹ׃	ו	6	He turned the sea into dry land, through the river they passed on foot; there we rejoiced in Him.
מֹשֵׁל בִּגְבוּרָתוֹ ׀ עוֹלָם עֵינָיו בַּגּוֹיִם תִּצְפֶּינָה הַסּוֹרְרִים ׀ אַל־יָרוּמוּ לָמוֹ סֶלָה׃	ז	7	He rules the world by His might, His eyes keep watch upon nations; the rebellious— let them not exalt themselves, Selah.
בָּרְכוּ עַמִּים ׀ אֱלֹהֵינוּ וְהַשְׁמִיעוּ קוֹל תְּהִלָּתוֹ׃	ח	8	Bless, peoples, our God, and let the voice of His praise be heard.
הַשָּׂם נַפְשֵׁנוּ בַּחַיִּים וְלֹא־נָתַן לַמּוֹט רַגְלֵנוּ׃	ט	9	He set our soul in life and does not allow our feet to slip.
כִּי־בְחַנְתָּנוּ אֱלֹהִים צְרַפְתָּנוּ כִּצְרָף־כָּסֶף׃	י	10	For You tried us, God; You refined us as if refining silver.

יא הֲבֵאתָנוּ בַמְּצוּדָה	11 You brought us into closed quarters,
שַׂמְתָּ מוּעָקָה בְמָתְנֵינוּ׃	You put a constraint upon our loins.
יב הִרְכַּבְתָּ אֱנוֹשׁ לְרֹאשֵׁנוּ	12 You made mortal man ride over our heads;
בָּאנוּ־בָאֵשׁ וּבַמַּיִם	we went through fire and water,
וַתּוֹצִיאֵנוּ לָרְוָיָה׃	and You brought us out to abundance.
יג אָבוֹא בֵיתְךָ	13 I will enter Your House
בְעוֹלוֹת	with burnt offerings,
אֲשַׁלֵּם לְךָ נְדָרָי׃	I will pay You my vows.
יד אֲשֶׁר־פָּצוּ שְׂפָתָי	14 That which my lips have uttered
וְדִבֶּר־פִּי בַּצַּר־לִי׃	and my mouth has spoken in my distress.
טו עֹלוֹת מֵחִים	15 Burnt offerings of fat animals
אַעֲלֶה־לָּךְ	I will offer up to You,
עִם־קְטֹרֶת אֵילִים	with the burning of rams;
אֶעֱשֶׂה בָקָר עִם־עַתּוּדִים	I will offer bullocks with goats,
סֶלָה׃	Selah.
טז לְכוּ־שִׁמְעוּ	16 Go and hearken,
וַאֲסַפְּרָה כָּל־יִרְאֵי אֱלֹהִים	and I will declare to all who fear God,
אֲשֶׁר עָשָׂה לְנַפְשִׁי׃	what He has done for my soul.
יז אֵלָיו פִּי־קָרָאתִי	17 Unto Him with my mouth I called,
וְרוֹמַם תַּחַת לְשׁוֹנִי׃	and exaltation was beneath my tongue.
יח אָוֶן אִם־רָאִיתִי בְלִבִּי	18 Even had I perceived iniquity in my heart,
לֹא יִשְׁמַע ׀ אֲדֹנָי׃	my Master would not have listened.
יט אָכֵן שָׁמַע אֱלֹהִים	19 But God has heard,
הִקְשִׁיב בְּקוֹל תְּפִלָּתִי׃	He has hearkened to the voice of my prayer.
כ בָּרוּךְ אֱלֹהִים	20 Blessed is God,
אֲשֶׁר לֹא־הֵסִיר תְּפִלָּתִי	Who has not turned away my prayer
וְחַסְדּוֹ מֵאִתִּי׃	nor His kindness from me.

Mosaic Depicting Entrance to the Holy Temple

פרק סז Chapter 67

Weekly Cycle	Monthly Cycle	Book Number
Tuesday	12th day of the month	Book 2

Author

Unknown, perhaps דָּוִד הַמֶּלֶךְ—King David—the second king of Israel and father of the Davidic royal and messianic dynasty. David composed over seventy of the 150 psalms of Sefer Tehillim.

Genre

Psalm of Communal Thanksgiving - This psalm emphasizes gratitude for what God has done for the community as a whole.

Chapter Summary

This chapter speaks of the days of the Mashiach (Messiah), when the name of God will be sanctified, and we will then be worthy of great abundance. It is a prayer for both spiritual and material deliverance.

This psalm consists of eight verses, subdivided into four parts. The first verse serves as a heading; the last as a concluding verse, in which faith is expressed that one day all nations will fear God. Verses 4 and 6 are a refrain, in which all nations acknowledge God.

In verse 2, the psalmist speaks of God's blessing to Israel.

In verse 3, he expresses his trust that God's salvation will indeed be known throughout the world.

In verse 5, he describes how God judges and governs all nations.

In verse 7, he gives thanks for an abundant harvest.

Introductory Words

לַמְנַצֵּחַ—Lamnatsei'ach—To the Conductor

מִזְמוֹר—Mizmor—Musical Accompaniment

שִׁיר—Shir—Song

Technical Terminology

נְגִינוֹת—Neginos—Tunes

סֶלָה—Selah—While its meaning is unclear, the most familiar opinion is that it is a musical notation, instructing the Levitical orchestra to pause its singing and playing of instruments. Alternatively, "Selah" may mean "everlasting".

Interesting Fact

According to tradition, King David engraved this psalm onto his shield in the shape of a seven-branch Menorah, and would study its meaning before

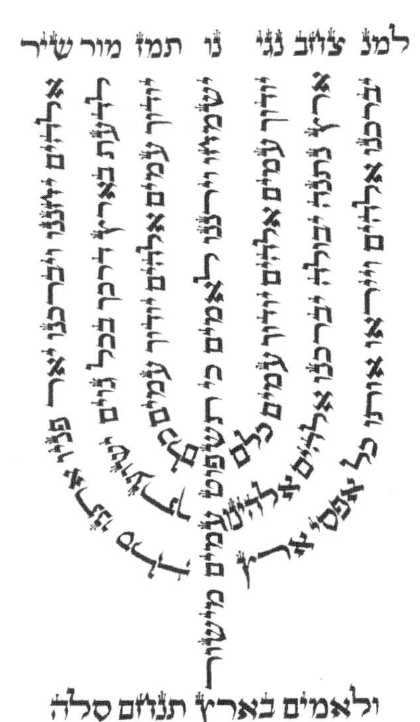

engaging in a battle.

Shimush Tehillim - When to Say

To be released from prison—Verse 2 states: " [May] God favor us and bless us, [may He] cause His countenance to shine among us."

Where in the Siddur

Recited before Ma'ariv (evening service) on Motzei Shabbat in some congregations.
Recited as one of the paragraphs of Kiddush Levanah (Sanctification of the New Moon service).
Recited by some as one of the paragraphs following Sefirat HaOmer (the counting of the Omer), a ritual connecting Pesach (Passover) and Shavu'ot.

פֶּרֶק סז

א לַמְנַצֵּחַ
בִּנְגִינֹת מִזְמוֹר שִׁיר׃
ב אֱלֹהִים יְחָנֵּנוּ וִיבָרְכֵנוּ
יָאֵר פָּנָיו
אִתָּנוּ סֶלָה׃
ג לָדַעַת בָּאָרֶץ דַּרְכֶּךָ
בְּכָל־גּוֹיִם יְשׁוּעָתֶךָ׃
ד יוֹדוּךָ עַמִּים | אֱלֹהִים
יוֹדוּךָ עַמִּים כֻּלָּם׃
ה יִשְׂמְחוּ וִירַנְּנוּ לְאֻמִּים
כִּי־תִשְׁפֹּט עַמִּים מִישׁוֹר
וּלְאֻמִּים | בָּאָרֶץ תַּנְחֵם סֶלָה׃
ו יוֹדוּךָ עַמִּים | אֱלֹהִים
יוֹדוּךָ עַמִּים כֻּלָּם׃
ז אֶרֶץ נָתְנָה יְבוּלָהּ
יְבָרְכֵנוּ אֱלֹהִים אֱלֹהֵינוּ׃
ח יְבָרְכֵנוּ אֱלֹהִים
וְיִירְאוּ אֹתוֹ
כָּל־אַפְסֵי־אָרֶץ׃

Chapter 67

1 To the Chief Musician:
a Psalm with instrumental music, a song.
2 [May] God favor us and bless us,
[may He] cause His countenance to shine
among us, Selah;
3 [So] that Your way become known on earth,
[and] Your deliverance among all nations.
4 Peoples will thank You, God,
all the peoples will thank You.
5 Nations will rejoice and sing
when You judge the peoples justly,
and lead the nations upon the earth Selah.
6 Peoples will thank You, God,
all the peoples will thank You.
7 The earth will have yielded its produce;
God, our God, will have blessed us.
8 God will bless us,
and they will fear Him—
all [men even from] the ends of the earth.

פרק סח Chapter 68

Weekly Cycle	Monthly Cycle	Book Number
Tuesday	12th day of the month	Book 2

Author
דָּוִד הַמֶּלֶךְ—King David—the second king of Israel and father of the Davidic royal and messianic dynasty. David composed over seventy of the 150 psalms of Sefer Tehillim.

Genre
Psalm of Praise - This is a psalm of celebration, often the result of a victory. It declares God's goodness and urges all of creation to worship.

Chapter Summary
King David composed this psalm as a prayer for success in all his wars. According to the view that this group of psalms is alluding to our present exile, David is referring to the wars that God will wage for Israel prior to the ultimate redemption.

This psalm consists of thirty-six verses, subdivided into three parts. The first verse serves as a heading.
In verses 2-7, King David appeals to God to arise, and for the congregation to then praise Him.
In verses 8-24, he recounts how the revelation of God's presence leads to victory.
In verses 25-36, he portrays the festive procession accompanying the Aron HaKodesh (Holy Ark) as it was brought to the Beit HaMikdash (Holy Temple). He concludes by calling upon the nation to offer praise to God and bless Him.

Introductory Words
לַמְנַצֵּחַ—Lamnatsei'ach—To the Conductor
מִזְמוֹר—Mizmor—Musical Accompaniment
שִׁיר—Shir—Song

Technical Terminology
סֶלָה—Selah—While its meaning is unclear, the most familiar opinion is that it is a musical notation, instructing the Levitical orchestra to pause its singing and playing of instruments. Alternatively, "Selah" may mean "everlasting".

Shimush Tehillim - When to Say
To exorcise an evil spirit—Verse 7 states: "God settles [lonely] individuals into a household. He brings out prisoners at appropriate times."

Where in the Siddur
Recited on Shavu'ot in some congregations.
Verses 5 and 6 comprise a part of the prayers recited upon the conclusion of Ma'ariv (evening service) of Motza'ei Shabbat in some congregations.

Verse 20 comprises one of the verses of Uva Letzion, words of praise recited prior to Aleinu on weekday mornings and Motza'ei Shabbat.
Verses 35 and 36 are found in V'hu Rachum, one of the opening paragraphs of Pesukei Dezimra (Verses of Praise which begin the Shacharit service).

Biblical Personalities

בִּנְיָמִן—Benjamin, יְהוּדָה—Yehudah—(the princes of Judah), זְבֻלוּן—(the princes of Zebulun), נַפְתָּלִי—(the princes of Naphtali)—four of the twelve sons of Jacob. They and their brothers are the ancestors of the Tribes of Israel.

Biblical Places

בָּשָׁן—Bashan—a country located in modern day Syria, not to be confused with Mount Bashan also referenced in this chapter.

כּוּשׁ—Cush—a country surrounded by the River Gihon, possibly Ethiopia of today. The Cushites were known for their beautiful appearance.

הַר־אֱלֹהִים—Har Elohim—The mountain of God, Mount Sinai, where God revealed himself.

הֵיכָל—Heichal—Holy Temple—a term used to refer to the inner sanctuary of the Temple in Jerusalem. The Heichal contained the Holy of Holies, the resting place of the Aron HaKodesh (Holy Ark)*.
It also housed the Menorah, Altar of Incense, and Table of the Showbread.
*The Aron HaKodesh, while present in the first Beit HaMikdash (Temple), was buried, and hence its location was not known, during the period of the second Beit HaMikdash.

יִשְׂרָאֵל—Yisrael—Israel - The kindgom of Israel occupied the land on the Mediterranean Sea corresponding roughly to the State of Israel of modern times. Israel developed into a united kingdom under the leadership of King David who consolidated the various tribes under his single rule.

יְרוּשָׁלָם—Yerushalayim—Jerusalem—the capital city of the kingdom of Israel, conquered by King David 3,000 years ago. David established Jerusalem as both the religious and political center of Israel.

מְעוֹן קָדְשׁוֹ—Me'on Kodsho—Holy Dwelling Place; מִקְדָּשׁ—Mikdash—Sanctuary—references to the Beit HaMikdash (Temple) in Jerusalem.

מִצְרָיִם—Mitzrayim—Egypt—the land where the Israelites sojourned and were subsequently enslaved by Pharoh until God sent Moses to redeem them. Egyptian society ran contrary to many of the ideals of the Torah. As such, the Israelite king is specifically warned not to return his nation to Egypt (a desire driven by the king's significantly increasing his cavalry).

הַר-בָּשָׁן—Mount Bashan—another name for Mount Sinai, not to be confused with Bashan proper, also referenced in this chapter.

סִינַי—Sinai—the mountain upon which God revealed himself to the Israelites and gave them the Ten Commandments.

צַלְמוֹן—Tzalmon—a mountain near Shechem, possibly a snowcapped mountain.

Talmud on Tehillim

Verse 10: "גֶּשֶׁם נְדָבוֹת, תָּנִיף אֱלֹהִים; נַחֲלָתְךָ וְנִלְאָה, אַתָּה כוֹנַנְתָּהּ"—"Bountiful rain did You pour down, God; when Your inheritance was weary, You established it firmly."

The Talmud, Shabbat 88b, allegorically explains that this verse refers to God's reviving of the Israelites after their souls were separated from their bodies upon hearing the voice of the Lord at Mount Sinai.

Verse 12: "אֲדֹנָי יִתֶּן אֹמֶר; הַמְבַשְּׂרוֹת, צָבָא רָב"—"My Master gave the word, its announcers were a great host."

The Talmud, Shabbat 88a, deduces that "each of the commandments that were uttered by God was heard in seventy languages."

Verse 13: "מַלְכֵי צְבָאוֹת, יִדֹּדוּן"—"Kings of hosts flee."

The Talmud, Shabbat 88a, allegorically explains that the souls of the Israelites at Mount Sinai retreated twelve mil (a biblical distance approximating a mile) from Mount Sinai when they heard God's voice.

Verse 14: "כַּנְפֵי יוֹנָה, נֶחְפָּה בַכֶּסֶף, וְאֶבְרוֹתֶיהָ, בִּירַקְרַק חָרוּץ"—"wings of the dove covered with silver and her pinions with the shimmer of gold."

The Talmud, Berachot 53b, states: "Just as a dove escapes danger only with its wings, so too the Israelites escape danger only by the performance of mitzvot. (See Talmud, Shabbat 49a and 103a, for further elucidation).

Verse 15: "בְּפָרֵשׂ שַׁדַּי מְלָכִים בָּהּ תַּשְׁלֵג בְּצַלְמוֹן"—"When the Almighty scatter kings therein, as snowflakes in Tzalmon."

The Talmud, Berachot 15b, explains allegorically that the fires of Geihinom (Hell) are cooled for those who recite every word of the Shema carefully.

Several other verses of this chapter are further explained in the Talmud, Pesachim 118b.

פרק סח			Chapter 68
לַמְנַצֵּחַ לְדָוִד מִזְמוֹר שִׁיר:	א	1	To the Chief Musician, a Psalm of David, a song.
יָקוּם אֱלֹהִים יָפוּצוּ אוֹיְבָיו וְיָנוּסוּ מְשַׂנְאָיו מִפָּנָיו:	ב	2	Let God arise, let His enemies be scattered, and let those who hate Him flee before Him.
כְּהִנְדֹּף עָשָׁן תִּנְדֹּף כְּהִמֵּס דּוֹנַג מִפְּנֵי־אֵשׁ יֹאבְדוּ רְשָׁעִים מִפְּנֵי אֱלֹהִים:	ג	3	As smoke is driven away, so drive [them away]; as wax melts before the fire, so let the wicked perish before the presence of God.
וְצַדִּיקִים יִשְׂמְחוּ יַעַלְצוּ לִפְנֵי אֱלֹהִים וְיָשִׂישׂוּ בְשִׂמְחָה:	ד	4	But let the righteous rejoice, let them exult before God, and let them delight with joy.
שִׁירוּ	לֵאלֹהִים זַמְּרוּ שְׁמוֹ סֹלּוּ לָרֹכֵב בָּעֲרָבוֹת בְּיָהּ שְׁמוֹ וְעִלְזוּ לְפָנָיו:	ה	5	Sing to God, compose hymns to His Name extol Him Who rides over the heavens with His Name, Yah, and exalt before Him.
אֲבִי יְתוֹמִים וְדַיַּן אַלְמָנוֹת	ו	6	A Father of orphans and a Judge of widows

אֱלֹהִים בִּמְעוֹן קָדְשׁוֹ׃	is God in His Holy Dwelling.
ז אֱלֹהִים | מוֹשִׁיב יְחִידִים |	7 God settles [lonely] individuals
בַּיְתָה	into a household.
מוֹצִיא אֲסִירִים בַּכּוֹשָׁרוֹת	He brings out prisoners at appropriate times,
אַךְ סוֹרְרִים שָׁכְנוּ צְחִיחָה׃	but the rebellious dwell in a parched land.
ח אֱלֹהִים בְּצֵאתְךָ	8 God, when You went forth
לִפְנֵי עַמֶּךָ	before Your people,
בְּצַעְדְּךָ בִישִׁימוֹן	when You marched through the wilderness,
סֶלָה׃	Selah.
ט אֶרֶץ רָעָשָׁה |	9 The earth trembled,
אַף־שָׁמַיִם נָטְפוּ	also the heavens dripped
מִפְּנֵי אֱלֹהִים	at the Presence of God;
זֶה סִינַי מִפְּנֵי אֱלֹהִים	even Sinai [trembled] at the Presence of God,
אֱלֹהֵי יִשְׂרָאֵל׃	the God of Israel.
י גֶּשֶׁם נְדָבוֹת תָּנִיף אֱלֹהִים	10 Bountiful rain did You pour down, God;
נַחֲלָתְךָ וְנִלְאָה	when Your inheritance was weary,
אַתָּה כוֹנַנְתָּהּ׃	You established it firmly.
יא חַיָּתְךָ יָשְׁבוּ־בָהּ	11 Your flock settled in it,
תָּכִין בְּטוֹבָתְךָ	You prepare in Your goodness
לֶעָנִי אֱלֹהִים׃	for the poor, God.
יב אֲדֹנָי יִתֶּן־אֹמֶר	12 My Master gave the word,
הַמְבַשְּׂרוֹת צָבָא רָב׃	its announcers were a great host.
יג מַלְכֵי צְבָאוֹת יִדֹּדוּן יִדֹּדוּן	13 "Kings of hosts flee, they flee;
וּנְוַת בַּיִת	and she that dwells within the home
תְּחַלֵּק שָׁלָל׃	apportions the booty.
יד אִם־תִּשְׁכְּבוּן בֵּין שְׁפַתָּיִם	14 Were you to lie within your boundaries,
כַּנְפֵי יוֹנָה נֶחְפָּה בַכֶּסֶף	wings of the dove covered with silver
וְאֶבְרוֹתֶיהָ בִּירַקְרַק חָרוּץ׃	and her pinions with the shimmer of gold.
טו בְּפָרֵשׂ שַׁדַּי מְלָכִים בָּהּ	15 When the Almighty scatters kings therein,
תַּשְׁלֵג בְּצַלְמוֹן׃	as snowflakes in Tzalmon.
טז הַר־אֱלֹהִים	16 A mountain of God,
הַר־בָּשָׁן	the mountain of Bashan;
הַר גַּבְנֻנִּים הַר־בָּשָׁן׃	a mountain of peaks, the mountain of Bashan.
יז לָמָּה | תְּרַצְּדוּן	17 Why do you prance—
הָרִים גַּבְנֻנִּים	You mountains of peaks?
הָהָר חָמַד אֱלֹהִים לְשִׁבְתּוֹ	God has [already] desired it for His abode
אַף־יְהוָה יִשְׁכֹּן לָנֶצַח׃	also Adonoy will dwell there forever.
יח רֶכֶב אֱלֹהִים רִבֹּתַיִם	18 The chariot of God is two myriads,
אַלְפֵי שִׁנְאָן	thousands of Shinan;

אֲדֹנָ֥י בָ֝ם	my Master is among them,
סִינַ֗י בַּקֹּֽדֶשׁ׃	at Sinai, in Holiness."
יט עָלִ֣יתָ לַמָּר֨וֹם ׀	19 You have ascended on high,
שָׁ֘בִ֤יתָ	you have captured
שֶּׁ֗בִי	what had been held captive,
לָקַ֣חְתָּ מַ֭תָּנוֹת בָּאָדָ֑ם	you have taken gifts for man,
וְאַ֥ף ס֝וֹרְרִ֗ים	that even among rebels
לִשְׁכֹּ֤ן ׀ יָ֬הּ אֱלֹהִֽים׃	God might dwell.
כ בָּ֤רוּךְ אֲדֹנָ֗י י֤וֹם ׀ י֗וֹם	20 Blessed is Adonoy day by day;
יַעֲמָס־לָ֑נוּ	He loads us,
הָאֵ֥ל יְ֝שׁוּעָתֵ֗נוּ סֶֽלָה׃	the Almighty Who is our deliverance, Selah.
כא הָאֵ֤ל ׀ לָ֗נוּ	21 The Almighty is to us
אֵ֥ל לְמוֹשָׁ֑עוֹת	an Almighty of deliverances;
וְלֵיהוִ֥ה אֲדֹנָ֑י	and through God, my Master,
לַ֝מָּ֗וֶת תּוֹצָאֽוֹת׃	are many paths to death.
כב אַךְ־אֱלֹהִ֗ים יִמְחַץ֮	22 Surely God will smash
רֹ֤אשׁ אֹ֫יְבָ֥יו	the head of His enemies,
קָדְקֹ֥ד שֵׂעָ֑ר	the hairy skull of him
מִ֝תְהַלֵּ֗ךְ בַּאֲשָׁמָֽיו׃	who goes about [untroubled] in his guilt.
כג אָמַ֣ר אֲ֭דֹנָי	23 My Master has promised,
מִבָּשָׁ֣ן אָשִׁ֑יב	"I will bring [you] back from Bashan,
אָ֝שִׁ֗יב	I will bring [you] back
מִֽמְּצֻל֥וֹת יָֽם׃	from the depths of the sea.
כד לְמַ֤עַן ׀ תִּֽמְחַ֥ץ רַגְלְךָ֗ בְּ֫דָ֥ם	24 That your foot may wade through blood;
לְשׁ֥וֹן כְּלָבֶ֑יךָ	that the tongue of your dogs
מֵאֹיְבִ֥ים מִנֵּֽהוּ׃	may have its portion from [your] enemies."
כה רָא֣וּ הֲלִיכוֹתֶ֣יךָ אֱלֹהִ֑ים	25 They have seen Your ways, God,
הֲלִ֘יכ֤וֹת אֵלִ֖י מַלְכִּ֣י בַקֹּֽדֶשׁ׃	the ways of my Almighty, my King, in Holiness.
כו קִדְּמ֣וּ שָׁ֭רִים	26 First go the singers,
אַחַ֣ר נֹגְנִ֑ים	followed by the minstrels,
בְּת֥וֹךְ עֲ֝לָמ֗וֹת תּוֹפֵפֽוֹת׃	in the midst of the maidens playing timbrels.
כז בְּֽמַקְהֵלוֹת בָּרְכ֣וּ אֱלֹהִ֑ים	27 In full assemblies bless God,
יְ֝הוָֹ֗ה	my Master—
מִמְּק֥וֹר יִשְׂרָאֵֽל׃	from the very beginning of Israel.
כח שָׁ֤ם בִּנְיָמִ֨ן ׀ צָעִ֡יר רֹדֵ֗ם	28 There Benjamin, the youngest, rules them,
שָׂרֵ֣י יְ֭הוּדָה רִגְמָתָ֑ם	the princes of Judah stoned them,
שָׂרֵ֥י זְ֝בֻל֗וּן	also the princes of Zebulun,
שָׂרֵ֥י נַפְתָּלִֽי׃	the princes of Naphtali
כט צִוָּ֣ה אֱ֭לֹהֶיךָ עֻזֶּ֑ךָ	29 Your God has commanded your strength,

עֻזָּה אֱלֹהִים	[show] Your strength, God,
זוּ פָּעַלְתָּ לָּנוּ׃	for You have wrought this for our sake.
ל מֵהֵיכָלֶךָ עַל־יְרוּשָׁלָםִ	30 Because of Your Temple at Jerusalem,
לְךָ יוֹבִילוּ מְלָכִים שָׁי׃	to You kings will bring tribute.
לא גְּעַר חַיַּת קָנֶה	31 Rebuke the wild beast of reeds,
עֲדַת אַבִּירִים |	the assembly of bulls
בְּעֶגְלֵי עַמִּים	among the calves of nations,
מִתְרַפֵּס בְּרַצֵּי־כָסֶף	each one submitting himself for pieces of silver;
בִּזַּר עַמִּים קְרָבוֹת יֶחְפָּצוּ׃	He has scattered nations that desire battles.
לב יֶאֱתָיוּ חַשְׁמַנִּים מִנִּי מִצְרָיִם	32 Nobles will come out of Egypt,
כּוּשׁ תָּרִיץ יָדָיו לֵאלֹהִים׃	Kush will hasten its hands to God.
לג מַמְלְכוֹת הָאָרֶץ	33 Kingdoms of the earth,
שִׁירוּ לֵאלֹהִים	sing to God;
זַמְּרוּ אֲדֹנָי סֶלָה׃	sing praises to my Master, Selah.
לד לָרֹכֵב בִּשְׁמֵי שְׁמֵי־	34 To the Rider upon the heaven of heavens,
קֶדֶם	[which are of] old;
הֵן יִתֵּן בְּקוֹלוֹ	behold, He utters His voice,
קוֹל עֹז׃	a mighty voice.
לה תְּנוּ עֹז לֵאלֹהִים	35 Ascribe might to God,
עַל־יִשְׂרָאֵל גַּאֲוָתוֹ	His pride [majesty] hovers over Israel,
וְעֻזּוֹ בַּשְּׁחָקִים׃	and His might is in the clouds.
לו נוֹרָא אֱלֹהִים	36 You are awesome, God,
מִמִּקְדָּשֶׁיךָ	from Your Sanctuaries
אֵל יִשְׂרָאֵל	Almighty of Israel,
הוּא נֹתֵן | עֹז וְתַעֲצֻמוֹת לָעָם	He grants might and power to the people;
בָּרוּךְ אֱלֹהִים׃	blessed is God.

Mosaic Menorah

הוא נתן
עז
ותעצמות
לעם ברוך
אלהים

He grants might and power to the people;
blessed is God.

פרק סט Chapter 69

Weekly Cycle	Monthly Cycle	Book Number
Tuesday	13th day of the month	Book 2

Author

דָּוִד הַמֶּלֶךְ—King David—the second king of Israel and father of the Davidic royal and messianic dynasty. David composed over seventy of the 150 psalms of Sefer Tehillim.

Genre

Psalm of Individual Lament - This psalm was written from the perspective of the individual worshipper, who cries out to God in his time of need. It is characterized as an address to God involving a complaint, followed by a request and ending with an expression of trust.

Chapter Summary

Continuing with the theme of the previous psalms, King David prophetically depicts the suffering that Israel will experience in the long and bitter exile which awaits it, and concludes with a plea for God's deliverance.

This psalm consists of thirty-seven verses, subdivided into three parts. The first verse serves as a heading.

In verses 2-22, King David describes his distress caused by the persecution of his enemies, and prays for deliverance from them.

In verses 23-29, he further curses his enemies.

In verses 30-37, he vows to sing a song of thanksgiving, and calls upon all who fear God to rejoice in His salvation.

Introductory Words

לַמְנַצֵּחַ—Lamnatsei'ach—To the Conductor

Musical Instrument

עַל-שׁוֹשַׁנִּים—Al Shoshanim—a musical instrument which looked like a bell with petals, likening it to a lily or a rose.

Shimush Tehillim - When to Say

For salvation from someone lustful, licentious, and sinful—Verse 15 states: "Rescue me from the mire and let me not sink; let me be rescued from my enemies and from the depths of the water."

Where in the Siddur

Verse 14 is found in the Birchot HaShachar (Morning Blessings).

Verse 14 is also recited upon removing the Torah scroll from the Aron HaKodesh (Holy Ark) in Minchah (afternoon service) of Shabbat; in Vidu (Confession service); and in Tashlich (a prayer recited in the afternoon of Rosh HaShanah, in which one petitions God to "throw his sins into the depths of the sea").

Verses 14 and 32 are included in the blessings before the Shema on the second day of Rosh HaShanah.
Verse 19 is quoted, in part, in Lechah Dodi—perhaps the most widely known song of Kabbalat Shabbat (Friday night service).
Verse 25 comprises one of the verses of Shefoch Chamatcha—a prayer beseeching the Almighty to "pour out His wrath" against His enemies, recited at the Passover Seder.

Biblical Places

עָרֵי יְהוּדָה—Arei Yehudah—The Cities of Judah—located just to the west of the Jordan River, what is referred to today as the West Bank.
צִיּוֹן—Zion—a place name often used as a synonym for Jerusalem. The term Zion originally referred only to the area where a Jebbusite fortress once stood, also the location of the City of David. Zion was later used by prophets and psalmists as another name for Jerusalem.

Talmud on Tehillim

Verse 14: "וַאֲנִי תְפִלָּתִי לְךָ יְהוָה, עֵת רָצוֹן"—"May my prayer to You, Adonoy, be at a favorable time."
The Talmud, Berachot 58a, deduces that this verse refers to a congregation that gathers to pray together.

פרק סט	Chapter 69
א לַמְנַצֵּחַ עַל־שׁוֹשַׁנִּים לְדָוִד׃	1 To the Chief Musician, upon shoshanim, [a Psalm] of David.
ב הוֹשִׁיעֵנִי אֱלֹהִים כִּי בָאוּ מַיִם עַד־נָפֶשׁ׃	2 Deliver me, God for the waters have reached until [my] soul.
ג טָבַעְתִּי ׀ בִּיוֵן מְצוּלָה וְאֵין מָעֳמָד בָּאתִי בְמַעֲמַקֵּי־מַיִם וְשִׁבֹּלֶת שְׁטָפָתְנִי׃	3 I am sunk in muddy depths without foothold; I have come into deep waters and a whirlpool has swept me away.
ד יָגַעְתִּי בְקָרְאִי נִחַר גְּרוֹנִי כָּלוּ עֵינַי מְיַחֵל לֵאלֹהָי׃	4 I am weary with my crying, my throat is parched, my eyes grow dim as I wait for my God.
ה רַבּוּ ׀ מִשַּׂעֲרוֹת רֹאשִׁי שֹׂנְאַי חִנָּם עָצְמוּ מַצְמִיתַי אֹיְבַי שֶׁקֶר אֲשֶׁר לֹא־גָזַלְתִּי אָז אָשִׁיב׃	5 More than the number of hairs on my head are those who hate me without cause; mighty are those who want to cut me off, my enemies who pursue falsehood, that which I have not robbed I am nevertheless compelled to return.
ו אֱלֹהִים אַתָּה יָדַעְתָּ לְאִוַּלְתִּי וְאַשְׁמוֹתַי מִמְּךָ לֹא־נִכְחָדוּ׃	6 God, You knew my folly, and my trespasses are not hidden from You.

ז אַל־יֵבֹשׁוּ בִי |	7 Let them not be ashamed through me
קֹוֶיךָ	those who wait for You,
אֲדֹנָי יֱהֹוִה צְבָאוֹת	my Master, God of Hosts;
אַל־יִכָּלְמוּ בִי	let them not be disgraced through me
מְבַקְשֶׁיךָ אֱלֹהֵי יִשְׂרָאֵל:	those who seek You, God of Israel.
ח כִּי־עָלֶיךָ	8 Because for Your sake
נָשָׂאתִי חֶרְפָּה	I have borne humiliation,
כִּסְּתָה כְלִמָּה פָנָי:	disgrace has covered my face.
ט מוּזָר הָיִיתִי לְאֶחָי	9 I became a stranger to my brethren,
וְנָכְרִי לִבְנֵי אִמִּי:	and an alien to my mother's children.
י כִּי־קִנְאַת בֵּיתְךָ	10 Because they envy Your House
אֲכָלָתְנִי	they have devoured me,
וְחֶרְפּוֹת חוֹרְפֶיךָ	and the humiliation of those who scorn You
נָפְלוּ עָלָי:	have fallen upon me.
יא וָאֶבְכֶּה בַצּוֹם נַפְשִׁי	11 And I wept with my fasting soul,
וַתְּהִי לַחֲרָפוֹת לִי:	and it was humiliating for me.
יב וָאֶתְּנָה לְבוּשִׁי שָׂק	12 And I made sackcloth my garment,
וָאֱהִי לָהֶם לְמָשָׁל:	and I became a byword to them.
יג יָשִׂיחוּ בִי יֹשְׁבֵי שָׁעַר	13 They talk of me, those who sit in the gate,
וּנְגִינוֹת שׁוֹתֵי שֵׁכָר:	and [about me] are the songs of drunkards.
יד וַאֲנִי תְפִלָּתִי־לְךָ | יְהֹוָה	14 May my prayer to You, Adonoy,
עֵת רָצוֹן	be at a favorable time;
אֱלֹהִים בְּרָב־חַסְדֶּךָ	God, in the abundance of Your kindness
עֲנֵנִי בֶּאֱמֶת יִשְׁעֶךָ:	answer me with the truth of Your deliverance.
טו הַצִּילֵנִי מִטִּיט	15 Rescue me from the mire
וְאַל־אֶטְבָּעָה	and let me not sink;
אִנָּצְלָה מִשֹּׂנְאַי	let me be rescued from my enemies
וּמִמַּעֲמַקֵּי־מָיִם:	and from the depths of the water.
טז אַל־תִּשְׁטְפֵנִי |	16 Let me not be carried away
שִׁבֹּלֶת מַיִם	by a whirlpool of water,
וְאַל־תִּבְלָעֵנִי מְצוּלָה	nor let the deep swallow me;
וְאַל־תֶּאְטַר־עָלַי בְּאֵר פִּיהָ:	and let not the pit close its mouth on me.
יז עֲנֵנִי יְהֹוָה	17 Answer me, Adonoy,
כִּי־טוֹב חַסְדֶּךָ	for Your kindness is good;
כְּרֹב רַחֲמֶיךָ	according to the abundance of Your mercy
פְּנֵה אֵלָי:	turn to me.
יח וְאַל־תַּסְתֵּר פָּנֶיךָ	18 And hide not Your face
מֵעַבְדֶּךָ	from Your servant,
כִּי־צַר־לִי מַהֵר עֲנֵנִי:	for I am in distress, speedily answer me.

יט	קָרְבָה אֶל־נַפְשִׁי גְאָלָהּ	19	Draw near to my soul and redeem it;
	לְמַעַן אֹיְבַי פְּדֵנִי׃		because of my enemies, ransom me.
כ	אַתָּה יָדַעְתָּ חֶרְפָּתִי	20	You know of my humilation
	וּבָשְׁתִּי וּכְלִמָּתִי		and my shame and my disgrace;
	נֶגְדְּךָ כָּל־צוֹרְרָי׃		before You are all my adversaries.
כא	חֶרְפָּה ׀ שָׁבְרָה לִבִּי	21	Humiliation has broken my heart
	וָאָנוּשָׁה		and I am very sick,
	וָאֲקַוֶּה לָנוּד		and I hoped for encouragement
	וָאַיִן		but there was none,
	וְלַמְנַחֲמִים וְלֹא מָצָאתִי׃		and for consolers, but I found none.
כב	וַיִּתְּנוּ בְּבָרוּתִי רֹאשׁ	22	And they put poison into my food,
	וְלִצְמָאִי		and for my thirst
	יַשְׁקוּנִי חֹמֶץ׃		they gave me vinegar to drink.
כג	יְהִי־שֻׁלְחָנָם לִפְנֵיהֶם לְפָח	23	Let their table before them become a snare,
	וְלִשְׁלוֹמִים לְמוֹקֵשׁ׃		and when they are at peace, let it become a trap.
כד	תֶּחְשַׁכְנָה עֵינֵיהֶם מֵרְאוֹת	24	Let their eyes be too darkened to see,
	וּמָתְנֵיהֶם תָּמִיד הַמְעַד׃		and let their loins continually totter.
כה	שְׁפָךְ־עֲלֵיהֶם זַעְמֶךָ	25	Pour out Your wrath upon them,
	וַחֲרוֹן אַפְּךָ		and let the fierceness of Your anger
	יַשִּׂיגֵם׃		overtake them.
כו	תְּהִי־טִירָתָם נְשַׁמָּה	26	Let their palace be desolate,
	בְּאָהֳלֵיהֶם אַל־יְהִי יֹשֵׁב׃		in their tents let there be no dweller.
כז	כִּי־אַתָּה אֲשֶׁר־הִכִּיתָ	27	For him whom You have smitten
	רָדָפוּ		they pursued,
	וְאֶל־מַכְאוֹב חֲלָלֶיךָ		and of the pain of those whom You wounded
	יְסַפֵּרוּ׃		they relate.
כח	תְּנָה־עָוֺן עַל־עֲוֺנָם	28	Add sin to their sin,
	וְאַל־יָבֹאוּ בְּצִדְקָתֶךָ׃		and let them not [enjoy] Your righteousness.
כט	יִמָּחוּ מִסֵּפֶר חַיִּים	29	Let them be blotted out of the Book of Life,
	וְעִם צַדִּיקִים		and with the righteous
	אַל־יִכָּתֵבוּ׃		let them not be inscribed.
ל	וַאֲנִי עָנִי וְכוֹאֵב	30	But I am afflicted and in pain;
	יְשׁוּעָתְךָ אֱלֹהִים תְּשַׂגְּבֵנִי׃		let Your deliverance, God, strengthen me.
לא	אֲהַלְלָה שֵׁם־אֱלֹהִים בְּשִׁיר	31	I will praise the Name of God with a song,
	וַאֲגַדְּלֶנּוּ בְתוֹדָה׃		and I will magnify Him with thanksgiving.
לב	וְתִיטַב לַיהוָה	32	And it will please Adonoy
	מִשּׁוֹר פָּר		more than a bullock
	מַקְרִן מַפְרִיס׃		that has horns and hoofs.
לג	רָאוּ עֲנָוִים יִשְׂמָחוּ	33	The humble will see it and be glad,

דֹּרְשֵׁי אֱלֹהִים וִיחִי לְבַבְכֶם:	those who seek God, let your hearts revive.
לד כִּי־שֹׁמֵעַ אֶל־אֶבְיוֹנִים יְהוָה	34 For God hearkens to the needy,
וְאֶת־אֲסִירָיו לֹא בָזָה:	and His prisoners He does not despise.
לה יְהַלְלוּהוּ שָׁמַיִם וָאָרֶץ	35 Heaven and earth will praise Him,
יַמִּים וְכָל־רֹמֵשׂ בָּם:	the seas and everything that moves in them.
לו כִּי אֱלֹהִים | יוֹשִׁיעַ צִיּוֹן	36 For God will deliver Zion,
וְיִבְנֶה עָרֵי יְהוּדָה	and build the cities of Judah,
וְיָשְׁבוּ שָׁם וִירֵשׁוּהָ:	and they will settle there and possess it.
לז וְזֶרַע עֲבָדָיו יִנְחָלוּהָ	37 And the seed of His servants will inherit it,
וְאֹהֲבֵי שְׁמוֹ יִשְׁכְּנוּ־בָהּ:	and those who love His Name will dwell in it.

פֶּרֶק ע Chapter 70

Weekly Cycle	Monthly Cycle	Book Number
Tuesday	13th day of the month	Book 2

Author

דָּוִד הַמֶּלֶךְ—King David—the second king of Israel and father of the Davidic royal and messianic dynasty. David composed over seventy of the 150 psalms of Sefer Tehillim.

When & Why

David wrote this psalm during a period of great suffering in his life. This period was likely when Saul was chasing him or when Absalom was trying to usurp his throne.

Genre

Psalm of Individual Lament - This psalm was written from the perspective of the individual worshipper, who cries out to God in his time of need. It is characterized as an address to God involving a complaint, followed by a request and ending with an expression of trust.

Chapter Summary

King David composed this psalm when fleeing from his enemies. In this chapter he asks God to rescue him.

This psalm and the following one are considered one unit comprised of two parts. Chapter 70 consists of six verses; chapter 71 contains twenty-four. The first verse serves as a heading. In chapter 70, verses 2-6 and chapter 71, verses 1-13, the Psalmist prays for salvation, and describes how his rescue will bring both disappointment to his enemies and joy to the righteous. In chapter 71, verses 14-24, he thanks God for his salvation and vows to tell of God's wonders to the coming generation. He further vows to praise God with singing and the playing of musical instruments.

Introductory Words

לַמְנַצֵּחַ—Lamnatsei'ach—To the Conductor

Technical Terminology

לְהַזְכִּיר—Lehazkir—For Remembrance

Shimush Tehillim - When to Say

To confront and overcome an enemy—Verses 2 and 6 state: "God, [come] to my rescue; Adonoy, to my help hasten." "God, hasten to me, my help and my rescuer are You, Adonoy, do not delay."

King David's Harp

פרק ע		Chapter 70
א לַמְנַצֵּחַ	1	To the Chief Musician,
לְדָוִד לְהַזְכִּיר׃		[a Psalm] of David, to serve as a memorial.
ב אֱלֹהִים לְהַצִּילֵנִי	2	God, [come] to my rescue;
יְהוָה לְעֶזְרָתִי חוּשָׁה׃		Adonoy, to my help hasten.
ג יֵבֹשׁוּ וְיַחְפְּרוּ	3	Let them be ashamed and humiliated
מְבַקְשֵׁי נַפְשִׁי		those who seek my soul;
יִסֹּגוּ אָחוֹר וְיִכָּלְמוּ		let them fall back and be disgraced
חֲפֵצֵי רָעָתִי׃		those who desire my hurt.
ד יָשׁוּבוּ עַל־עֵקֶב	4	Let them be turned back
בָּשְׁתָּם		because of their shame
הָאֹמְרִים הֶאָח ׀ הֶאָח׃		those who say, "Aha, aha."
ה יָשִׂישׂוּ וְיִשְׂמְחוּ ׀ בְּךָ	5	Let them exult and rejoice in You,
כָּל־מְבַקְשֶׁיךָ		all those who seek You,
וְיֹאמְרוּ תָמִיד		and let them say continually,
יִגְדַּל אֱלֹהִים		"Be magnified, God,"
אֹהֲבֵי יְשׁוּעָתֶךָ׃		those who love Your deliverance.
ו וַאֲנִי ׀ עָנִי וְאֶבְיוֹן	6	As for me, being poor and needy,
אֱלֹהִים חוּשָׁה־לִּי		God, hasten to me,
עֶזְרִי וּמְפַלְטִי אַתָּה		my help and my rescuer are You,
יְהוָה אַל־תְּאַחַר׃		Adonoy, do not delay.

פרק עא Chapter 71

Weekly Cycle	Monthly Cycle	Book Number
Tuesday	13th day of the month	Book 2

Author

Unknown; perhaps דָּוִד הַמֶּלֶךְ—King David—the second king of Israel and father of the Davidic royal and messianic dynasty. David composed over seventy of the 150 psalms of Sefer Tehillim.

When & Why

David might have written this psalm when he was elderly and fleeing from Absalom, his son. In it, he praises God for giving him the strength to escape in his weak and frail condition.

Genre

Psalm of Individual Lament - This psalm was written from the perspective of the individual worshipper, who cries out to God in his time of need. It is characterized as an address to God involving a complaint, followed by a request and ending with an expression of trust.

Chapter Summary

The psalmist speaks here about the tragedy of Absalom, an enemy and pursuer of his own father, King David. Nonetheless, declares the author, God protects the oppressed and remains a refuge for young and old alike.

This psalm and the previous one are considered one unit divided into two sections. The previous chapter consists of six verses, and this chapter consists of twenty-four verses.

In chapter 70, verses 2-6 and chapter 71, verses 1-13, the psalmist prays for salvation and describes how his rescue will bring disappointment to his enemies and joy to the righteous.

In chapter 71, verses 14-24, he thanks God for his salvation, and vows to tell of God's wonders to the coming generation. He further vows to praise God with singing and the playing of musical instruments.

Musical Instruments

נֶבֶל—Nevel—A Large Handheld Lyre - played by plucking with fingers.

כִּנּוֹר—Kinor—A Small Handheld Harp - played with a plecturm (pick).

Shimush Tehillim - When to Say

To be saved from being imprisoned—Verse 2 states: " In Your righteousness save me and rescue me, incline Your ear to me and deliver me."

Where in the Siddur

Verse 9 comprises one of the verses of Selichot (Penitential Service), recited the week of Rosh HaShanah through Yom Kippur. Selichot are not recited on Rosh HaShanah proper.

Verse 19 is one of the three verses of Tzidkatcha, recited after the Amidah (Silent Meditation) of Minchah on Shabbat afternoon.

פרק עא

א בְּךָ־יְהוָה חָסִיתִי
אַל־אֵבוֹשָׁה לְעוֹלָם:
ב בְּצִדְקָתְךָ
תַּצִּילֵנִי וּתְפַלְּטֵנִי
הַטֵּה־אֵלַי אָזְנְךָ וְהוֹשִׁיעֵנִי:
ג הֱיֵה לִי | לְצוּר מָעוֹן
לָבוֹא תָּמִיד
צִוִּיתָ לְהוֹשִׁיעֵנִי
כִּי־סַלְעִי וּמְצוּדָתִי אָתָּה:
ד אֱלֹהַי
פַּלְּטֵנִי מִיַּד רָשָׁע
מִכַּף מְעַוֵּל וְחוֹמֵץ:
ה כִּי־אַתָּה תִקְוָתִי
אֲדֹנָי יְהוִה מִבְטַחִי מִנְּעוּרָי:
ו עָלֶיךָ | נִסְמַכְתִּי מִבֶּטֶן
מִמְּעֵי אִמִּי אַתָּה גוֹזִי
בְּךָ תְהִלָּתִי תָמִיד:
ז כְּמוֹפֵת הָיִיתִי לְרַבִּים
וְאַתָּה מַחֲסִי־עֹז:
ח יִמָּלֵא פִי תְּהִלָּתֶךָ
כָּל־הַיּוֹם תִּפְאַרְתֶּךָ:
ט אַל־תַּשְׁלִיכֵנִי לְעֵת זִקְנָה
כִּכְלוֹת כֹּחִי אַל־תַּעַזְבֵנִי:
י כִּי־אָמְרוּ אוֹיְבַי לִי
וְשֹׁמְרֵי נַפְשִׁי
נוֹעֲצוּ יַחְדָּו:
יא לֵאמֹר אֱלֹהִים עֲזָבוֹ
רִדְפוּ וְתִפְשׂוּהוּ
כִּי־אֵין מַצִּיל:
יב אֱלֹהִים אַל־תִּרְחַק מִמֶּנִּי
אֱלֹהַי לְעֶזְרָתִי חוּשָׁה:
יג יֵבֹשׁוּ יִכְלוּ
שֹׂטְנֵי נַפְשִׁי
יַעֲטוּ חֶרְפָּה
וּכְלִמָּה מְבַקְשֵׁי רָעָתִי:
יד וַאֲנִי תָּמִיד אֲיַחֵל
וְהוֹסַפְתִּי עַל־כָּל־תְּהִלָּתֶךָ:

Chapter 71

1 In You, Adonoy, I have taken refuge,
let me not be ashamed, ever.
2 In Your righteousness
save me and rescue me,
incline Your ear to me and deliver me.
3 Be for me a sheltering rock
to enter at all times,
You ordered my deliverance;
for my rock and my fortress are You.
4 My God,
rescue me from the hand of the wicked,
from the hand of the scheming and the violent.
5 For You are my hope,
my Master, God, my trust since my youth.
6 On You I have relied from birth,
from my mother's womb You drew me;
of You is my praise continually.
7 I became an example for the multitude,
and You were my mighty refuge.
8 Let my mouth be filled with Your praise,
all the day long with Your glory.
9 Do not cast me off in time of old age,
when my strength fails do not forsake me.
10 For my enemies [who] speak about me,
and those who watch for my soul,
take counsel together.
11 Saying, "God has forsaken him,
pursue and take him,
for there is no one to save him."
12 God, be not far from me,
my God, hasten to help me.
13 Let them be ashamed and consumed,
the adversaries of my soul;
let them be covered with humiliation
and disgrace—those who seek my hurt.
14 But as for me, I will continually hope,
and I will add to all Your praises.

טו פִּי ׀ יְסַפֵּר צִדְקָתֶךָ
כָּל־הַיּוֹם תְּשׁוּעָתֶךָ
כִּי לֹא יָדַעְתִּי סְפֹרוֹת׃

15 My mouth will tell of Your righteousness,
all the day of Your deliverance,
for I know not [how] to count them.

טז אָבוֹא בִּגְבֻרוֹת
אֲדֹנָי יְהוִה
אַזְכִּיר צִדְקָתְךָ
לְבַדֶּךָ׃

16 I will assert the mighty acts
of my Master, God;
I will mention Your righteousness
[Yours] alone.

יז אֱלֹהִים לִמַּדְתַּנִי מִנְּעוּרָי
וְעַד־הֵנָּה אַגִּיד נִפְלְאוֹתֶיךָ׃

17 God, You have taught me from my youth,
and to this day I declare Your wonders.

יח וְגַם עַד־זִקְנָה ׀ וְשֵׂיבָה
אֱלֹהִים אַל־תַּעַזְבֵנִי
עַד־אַגִּיד זְרוֹעֲךָ לְדוֹר
לְכָל־יָבוֹא גְּבוּרָתֶךָ׃

18 And even until old age and hoary hairs,
God, do not forsake me
until I declare Your strength to the generation,
to all who are yet to come, Your might.

יט וְצִדְקָתְךָ אֱלֹהִים
עַד־מָרוֹם
אֲשֶׁר־עָשִׂיתָ גְדֹלוֹת
אֱלֹהִים מִי כָמוֹךָ׃

19 And Your righteousness God
reaches to the high heavens
for You do great things;
God, who is like You?

כ אֲשֶׁר הִרְאִיתַנִי ׀
צָרוֹת רַבּוֹת וְרָעוֹת
תָּשׁוּב תְּחַיֵּינִי
וּמִתְּהֹמוֹת הָאָרֶץ
תָּשׁוּב תַּעֲלֵנִי׃

20 You Who have caused me to see
many grievous troubles,
You will revive me once again,
and from the depths of the earth
You will raise me up again.

כא תֶּרֶב ׀ גְּדֻלָּתִי
וְתִסֹּב תְּנַחֲמֵנִי׃

21 You will increase my greatness,
and You will turn and comfort me.

כב גַּם־אֲנִי ׀ אוֹדְךָ
בִכְלִי־נֶבֶל
אֲמִתְּךָ אֱלֹהָי
אֲזַמְּרָה לְךָ בְכִנּוֹר
קְדוֹשׁ יִשְׂרָאֵל׃

22 I will also give thanks to You
with the lyre instrument,
for Your faithfulness, my God;
I will sing praises to You with the harp,
Holy One of Israel.

כג תְּרַנֵּנָּה שְׂפָתַי כִּי אֲזַמְּרָה־לָּךְ
וְנַפְשִׁי אֲשֶׁר פָּדִיתָ׃

23 My lips will rejoice when I sing to You,
and [also] my soul which You have redeemed.

כד גַּם־לְשׁוֹנִי
כָּל־הַיּוֹם תֶּהְגֶּה צִדְקָתֶךָ
כִּי־בֹשׁוּ כִי־חָפְרוּ
מְבַקְשֵׁי רָעָתִי׃

24 My tongue also,
all the day will tell of Your righteousness;
for they are ashamed for they are humiliated
those who seek my harm."

גם אני
אודך
בכלי נבל
אמתך אלהי
אזמרה לך
בכנור
קדוש
ישראל

I will also give thanks to You
with the lyre instrument,
for Your faithfulness, my God;
I will sing praises to You with the harp,
Holy One of Israel.

פרק עב Chapter 72

Weekly Cycle	Monthly Cycle	Book Number
Tuesday	14th day of the month	Book 2

Author

דָּוִד הַמֶּלֶךְ—King David—the second king of Israel and father of the Davidic royal and messianic dynasty. David composed over seventy of the 150 psalms of Sefer Tehillim.

When & Why

David wrote this psalm when he passed the throne on to Solomon. In it, he blesses Solomon that he should be a fair and merciful judge of the people.

Genre

Psalm of Royalty - This psalm describes how God reigns supreme. It focuses on the human king of Israel, or upon God as King of Israel.

Chapter Summary

King David composed this psalm in honor of his son Shlomo (Solomon), whom he crowned near the end of this life. With the influence of Ruach HaKodesh (Divine Inspiration), David foresaw that Solomon would ask God to grant him a knowing and heedful heart in judgment, and he prayed that God would in turn grant him the Torah wisdom to rule justly.

This psalm consists of twenty verses, subdivided into five parts. The last verse serves as a formal ending for the second section of the Book of Tehillim. It thus concludes with the words "Completed are the prayers of David, son of Jesse."

In verses 1-7, King David opens with a prayer to God that He will direct the new king to judge righteously.

In verses 8-11, he describes the king's greatness.

In verses 12-15, he describes how the king helps the poor.

In verses 16-17, he asks of God to bestow His blessings upon the land and the king.

In verses 18 and 19, he concludes by blessing God.

Shimush Tehillim - When to Say

To find favor amongst others

To prevent poverty—Verse 2 states: "May he judge Your people with righteousness, and Your poor with justice."

Where in the Siddur

Recited by some while visiting the cemetery.

Verses 18 and 19 comprise the third and fourth verses of Baruch Hashem Le'olam—one of the closing paragraphs of Pesukei Dezimra (Verses of Praise which begin the Shacharit morning service).

Verses 18 and 19 are also found in the longer version of Baruch Hashem Le'olam, recited upon the conclusion of Shema of Ma'ariv (evening service).

Biblical Personalities

מַלְכֵי שְׁבָא —The Kings of Sheba—perhaps a reference to the story of Malkat Sheva (Queen of Sheba). (Rashi)

מַלְכֵי תַרְשִׁישׁ—The Kings of Tarshish—they had a fleet at sea, along with the fleet of Hiram. Once every three years the fleet of Tarshish would come to the Port of Yafo (Jaffa) bearing gold, silver, ivory, monkeys and parrots.

Biblical Places

לְבָנוֹן—Lebanon—located just to the north of Israel, famous for its cedar trees. Lebanon was one of Israel's foremost trading partners.

סְבָא—Seba—believed to be located in North Africa.

שְׁבָא—Sheba—perhaps located in Ethiopia.

Talmud on Tehillim

Verse 5: "יִירָאוּךָ עִם שָׁמֶשׁ; וְלִפְנֵי יָרֵחַ, דּוֹר דּוֹרִים"—"So that they will fear You as long as the sun is upon them and as long as the moon is before them, throughout all generations."

The Talmud, Berachot 29b, deduces from this verse that it is meritorious to recite Shacharit (morning service) at sunrise. (See Talmud Shabbat 11b for further elucidation).

Verse 17: "יְהִי שְׁמוֹ, לְעוֹלָם לִפְנֵי שֶׁמֶשׁ, יִנּוֹן (ינין) שְׁמוֹ"—"May his name endure forever, as long as the sun, may His name be perpetuated."

The Talmud, Pesachim 54a, states that the phrase "May His name be eternal" refers to the Mashiach (Messiah). (See Talmud Shabbat 118b for further elucidation).

פֶּרֶק עַב

א לִשְׁלֹמֹה |
אֱלֹהִים מִשְׁפָּטֶיךָ לְמֶלֶךְ תֵּן
וְצִדְקָתְךָ לְבֶן־מֶלֶךְ׃

ב יָדִין עַמְּךָ
בְצֶדֶק
וַעֲנִיֶּיךָ בְמִשְׁפָּט׃

ג יִשְׂאוּ הָרִים שָׁלוֹם
לָעָם
וּגְבָעוֹת בִּצְדָקָה׃

ד יִשְׁפֹּט | עֲנִיֵּי־עָם
יוֹשִׁיעַ לִבְנֵי אֶבְיוֹן
וִידַכֵּא עוֹשֵׁק׃

Chapter 72

1 [A Psalm] of Solomon.
God, endow the king with Your own justice,
and Your righteousness to the king's son.

2 May he judge Your people
with righteousness,
and Your poor with justice.

3 May the mountains bear peace
to the people,
and the hills, through charity.

4 May he judge the poor of the people,
and deliver the children of the needy,
and crush the oppressor.

ה	יִירָאוּךָ	5	So that they will fear You
	עִם־שָׁמֶשׁ		as long as the sun is upon them
	וְלִפְנֵי יָרֵחַ		and as long as the moon is before them,
	דּוֹר דּוֹרִים׃		throughout all generations.
ו	יֵרֵד כְּמָטָר עַל־גֵּז	6	May he descend as rain upon mown grass,
	כִּרְבִיבִים זַרְזִיף אָרֶץ׃		as showers of rain that water the earth.
ז	יִפְרַח־בְּיָמָיו צַדִּיק	7	In his days let the righteous flourish,
	וְרֹב שָׁלוֹם		and abundance of peace,
	עַד־בְּלִי יָרֵחַ׃		until the moon will be no more.
ח	וְיֵרְדְּ מִיָּם עַד־יָם	8	And may he have dominion from sea to sea,
	וּמִנָּהָר עַד־אַפְסֵי־אָרֶץ׃		and from the river until the ends of the earth.
ט	לְפָנָיו יִכְרְעוּ צִיִּים	9	May nobles kneel before him,
	וְאֹיְבָיו עָפָר יְלַחֵכוּ׃		and his enemies lick the dust.
י	מַלְכֵי תַרְשִׁישׁ וְאִיִּים	10	The kings of Tarshish and of the isles
	מִנְחָה יָשִׁיבוּ		will return tribute;
	מַלְכֵי שְׁבָא וּסְבָא		the kings of Sheba and Seba
	אֶשְׁכָּר יַקְרִיבוּ׃		will offer gifts.
יא	וְיִשְׁתַּחֲווּ־לוֹ כָל־מְלָכִים	11	They will prostrate themselves before him—all kings,
	כָּל־גּוֹיִם יַעַבְדוּהוּ׃		all nations will serve him.
יב	כִּי־יַצִּיל אֶבְיוֹן מְשַׁוֵּעַ	12	For he will rescue the needy when he cries,
	וְעָנִי וְאֵין־עֹזֵר לוֹ׃		and the poor who has none to help him.
יג	יָחֹס עַל־דַּל וְאֶבְיוֹן	13	He will have pity on the poor and needy,
	וְנַפְשׁוֹת אֶבְיוֹנִים יוֹשִׁיעַ׃		and souls of the needy he will deliver.
יד	מִתּוֹךְ וּמֵחָמָס	14	From oppression and violence
	יִגְאַל נַפְשָׁם		he will redeem their soul,
	וְיֵיקַר דָּמָם		and precious will their blood be
	בְּעֵינָיו׃		in his eyes.
טו	וִיחִי	15	May he [Solomon] live;
	וְיִתֶּן־לוֹ מִזְּהַב שְׁבָא		and may He give him of the gold of Sheba,
	וְיִתְפַּלֵּל בַּעֲדוֹ תָמִיד		and pray for him continually
	כָּל־הַיּוֹם יְבָרֲכֶנְהוּ׃		and all the day bless him.
טז	יְהִי פִסַּת־בַּר ׀ בָּאָרֶץ	16	May an abundance of grain be in the land,
	בְּרֹאשׁ הָרִים		upon the top of the mountains,
	יִרְעַשׁ כַּלְּבָנוֹן פִּרְיוֹ		may its fruit rustle like Lebanon;
	וְיָצִיצוּ מֵעִיר		and may they [Israel] blossom out of the city
	כְּעֵשֶׂב הָאָרֶץ׃		like grass of the earth.
יז	יְהִי שְׁמוֹ לְעוֹלָם	17	May his name endure forever,
	לִפְנֵי־שֶׁמֶשׁ		as long as the sun,
	יִנּוֹן שְׁמוֹ		may his name be perpetuated;

וְיִתְבָּרְכוּ בוֹ		and may men bless themselves by him
כָּל־גּוֹיִם יְאַשְּׁרוּהוּ׃		and may all nations praise him.
יח בָּרוּךְ ׀ יְהוָה אֱלֹהִים	18	Blessed is Adonoy, God,
אֱלֹהֵי יִשְׂרָאֵל		God of Israel
עֹשֵׂה נִפְלָאוֹת לְבַדּוֹ׃		Who alone performs wonders.
יט וּבָרוּךְ ׀ שֵׁם כְּבוֹדוֹ	19	And blessed is the Name of His glory
לְעוֹלָם		forever,
וְיִמָּלֵא כְבוֹדוֹ אֶת־כֹּל־הָאָרֶץ		and may His glory fill the whole earth;
אָמֵן ׀ וְאָמֵן׃		Amen and Amen.
כ כָּלּוּ	20	Completed
תְפִלּוֹת דָּוִד בֶּן־יִשָׁי׃		are the prayers of David, son of Jesse.

The Visit of the Queen of Sheba to King Solomon

BOOK 3

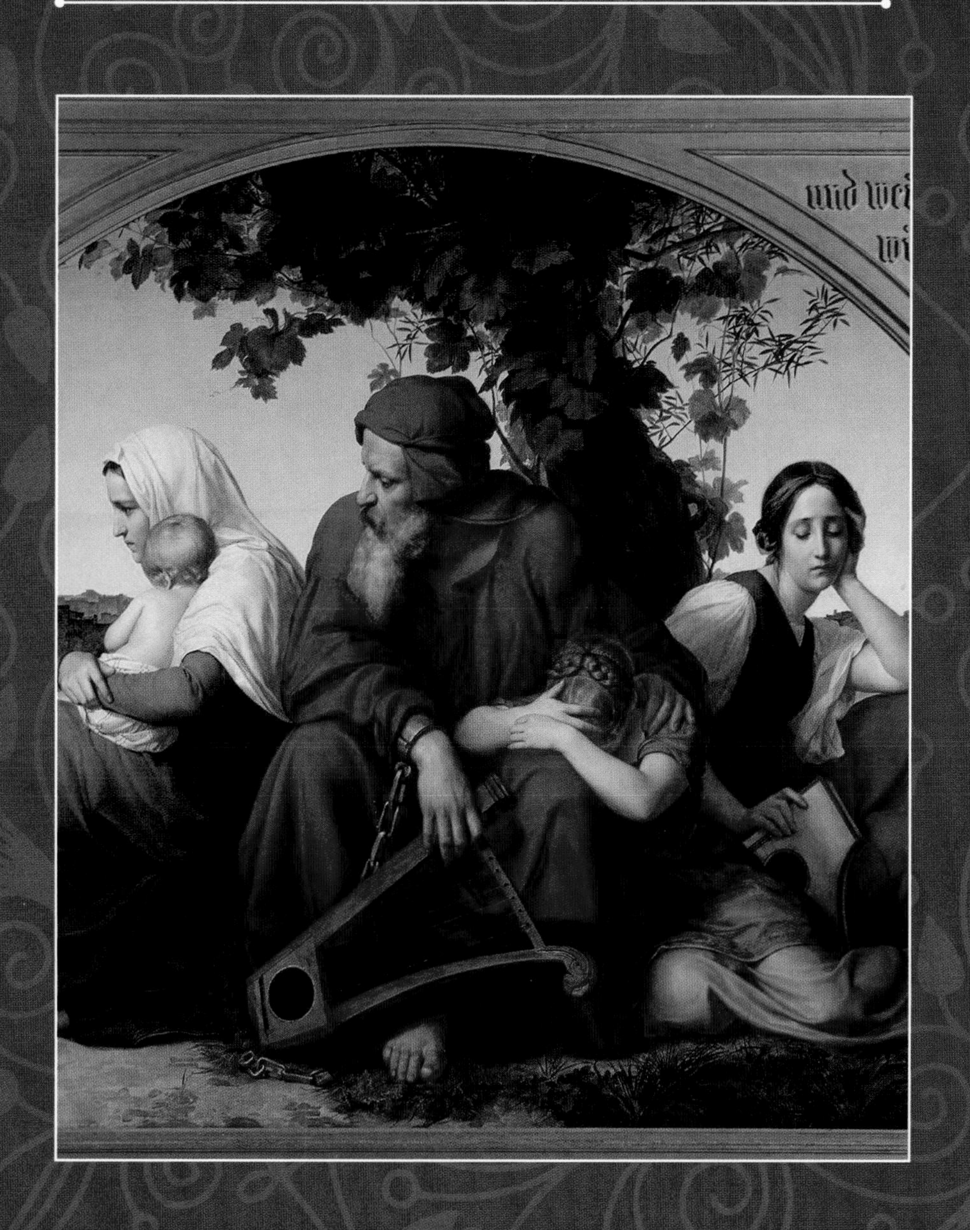

פרק עג ~ Chapter 73

Weekly Cycle	Monthly Cycle	Book Number
Wednesday	14th day of the month	Book 3

Author

אָסָף—Asaf—a composer of several psalms and patriarch of a family of singers in the Beit HaMikdash (Temple).

Genre

Psalm of Wisdom - This psalm contains teachings and wise advice and is meant to instruct people on how to live a Godly life.

Chapter Summary

In this chapter, Asaf addresses one of life's most difficult questions: Why do the righteous suffer and the wicked live well? He allegorically explains that though it seems as if the wicked are prospering, they in fact grow only as grass, and are thus easily destroyed.

This psalm consists of twenty-eight verses, subdivided into two parts. The first verse serves as a heading.

In verses 2-16, the psalmist describes the confusion of the God-fearing man, troubled by the prosperity of the wicked and suffering of the righteous.

In verses 17-28, he explains that the success of the wicked is but an illusion; all who stray from God will perish, while the righteous will indeed benefit from their closeness to God

Introductory Word

מִזְמוֹר—Mizmor—Musical Accompaniment

Shimush Tehillim - When to Say

To prevent a person from converting from Judaism (recite 7 times daily)— Verses 2 and 28 state: "But as for me, my feet had almost turned away." "But as for me, God's nearness is my good."

פרק עג

א מִזְמוֹר לְאָסָף
אַךְ טוֹב לְיִשְׂרָאֵל אֱלֹהִים
לְבָרֵי לֵבָב׃
ב וַאֲנִי
כִּמְעַט נָטָיוּ רַגְלָי
כְּאַיִן
שֻׁפְּכוּ אֲשֻׁרָי׃
ג כִּי־קִנֵּאתִי בַּהוֹלְלִים
שְׁלוֹם רְשָׁעִים אֶרְאֶה׃
ד כִּי אֵין חַרְצֻבּוֹת לְמוֹתָם
וּבָרִיא אוּלָם׃
ה בַּעֲמַל אֱנוֹשׁ אֵינֵמוֹ
וְעִם־אָדָם לֹא יְנֻגָּעוּ׃
ו לָכֵן עֲנָקַתְמוֹ גַאֲוָה
יַעֲטָף־שִׁית חָמָס לָמוֹ׃
ז יָצָא מֵחֵלֶב עֵינֵמוֹ
עָבְרוּ מַשְׂכִּיּוֹת לֵבָב׃
ח יָמִיקוּ ׀
וִידַבְּרוּ בְרָע עֹשֶׁק
מִמָּרוֹם יְדַבֵּרוּ׃
ט שַׁתּוּ בַשָּׁמַיִם פִּיהֶם
וּלְשׁוֹנָם תִּהֲלַךְ בָּאָרֶץ׃
י לָכֵן ׀ יָשׁוּב עַמּוֹ הֲלֹם
וּמֵי מָלֵא
יִמָּצוּ לָמוֹ׃
יא וְאָמְרוּ אֵיכָה יָדַע־אֵל
וְיֵשׁ דֵּעָה בְעֶלְיוֹן׃
יב הִנֵּה־אֵלֶּה רְשָׁעִים
וְשַׁלְוֵי עוֹלָם
הִשְׂגּוּ־חָיִל׃
יג אַךְ־רִיק זִכִּיתִי לְבָבִי
וָאֶרְחַץ בְּנִקָּיוֹן כַּפָּי׃
יד וָאֱהִי נָגוּעַ כָּל־הַיּוֹם
וְתוֹכַחְתִּי לַבְּקָרִים׃
טו אִם־אָמַרְתִּי אֲסַפְּרָה כְמוֹ
הִנֵּה דוֹר בָּנֶיךָ
בָגָדְתִּי׃

Chapter 73

1 A Psalm of Asaph.
Surely God is good to Israel,
to the pure of heart.
2 But as for me,
my feet had almost turned away,
in an instant,
my steps would have been swept aside.
3 For I envied the arrogant
when I saw the peace of the wicked.
4 For there is no suffering when they die
and their health is sound.
5 In the toil of man they do not suffer,
and they are not tormented as other mortals.
6 Therefore they wear pride as a necklace,
their body is enwrapped in violence.
7 Bulging from fatness, are their eyes,
they surpassed the imaginings of their heart.
8 They scoff
and speak wickedly about oppression,
out of loftiness they speak.
9 They have set their mouth against Heaven,
and their tongue walks through the earth.
10 Therefore His people will turn here,
and waters of abundance
will be drained out by them.
11 And they say, "How does God know?
Is there knowledge in the Most High?"
12 Behold, such are the wicked,
and always at ease,
they have attained much wealth.
13 Surely in vain have I kept my heart pure,
and washed my hands in cleanliness [innocence].
14 For I was plagued all the day,
and my rebuke came every morning.
15 If I had said, "I will tell how it is,
behold, the generation of Your children
I would have caused them to be faithless.

טז וָאֲחַשְּׁבָה לָדַעַת זֹאת	16 As I pondered to understand this,
עָמָל הוּא בְעֵינָי׃	it seemed as iniquity in my eyes.
יז עַד־אָבוֹא אֶל־מִקְדְּשֵׁי־אֵל	17 Until I entered into the Sanctuaries of God,
אָבִינָה לְאַחֲרִיתָם׃	then I understood what would be their end.
יח אַךְ בַּחֲלָקוֹת	18 Only in slippery places
תָּשִׁית לָמוֹ	do You set them down,
הִפַּלְתָּם לְמַשּׁוּאוֹת׃	You hurl them down to desolation.
יט אֵיךְ הָיוּ לְשַׁמָּה	19 How they have become desolate
כְרָגַע	in an instant,
סָפוּ	they come to an end,
תַּמּוּ מִן־בַּלָּהוֹת׃	they are finished through terrors.
כ כַּחֲלוֹם מֵהָקִיץ	20 As a dream without awakening,
אֲדֹנָי	[so] my Master,
בָּעִיר ׀ צַלְמָם תִּבְזֶה׃	in the city will You despise their appearance.
כא כִּי יִתְחַמֵּץ לְבָבִי	21 For my heart was in ferment
וְכִלְיוֹתַי אֶשְׁתּוֹנָן׃	and my mind was keen.
כב וַאֲנִי־בַעַר וְלֹא אֵדָע	22 And I am ignorant and know nothing,
בְּהֵמוֹת הָיִיתִי עִמָּךְ׃	as a beast was I with You.
כג וַאֲנִי תָמִיד עִמָּךְ	23 But I am continually with You,
אָחַזְתָּ בְּיַד־יְמִינִי׃	You held my right hand.
כד בַּעֲצָתְךָ תַנְחֵנִי	24 With Your counsel You will guide me,
וְאַחַר כָּבוֹד תִּקָּחֵנִי׃	and afterward, with glory You will receive me.
כה מִי־לִי בַשָּׁמָיִם	25 Whom have I in heaven [but You,]
וְעִמְּךָ לֹא־חָפַצְתִּי בָאָרֶץ׃	and besides You I desire nothing on earth.
כו כָּלָה שְׁאֵרִי וּלְבָבִי	26 My flesh and my heart yearn,
צוּר־לְבָבִי וְחֶלְקִי	the rock of my heart and my portion
אֱלֹהִים לְעוֹלָם׃	is God, forever.
כז כִּי־הִנֵּה רְחֵקֶיךָ יֹאבֵדוּ	27 For behold, those far from You will perish,
הִצְמַתָּה כָּל־זוֹנֶה מִמֶּךָּ׃	You cut down all who go astray from You.
כח וַאֲנִי ׀	28 But as for me,
קִרֲבַת אֱלֹהִים לִי־טוֹב	God's nearness is my good
שַׁתִּי ׀ בַּאדֹנָי יֱהֹוִה מַחְסִי	I have put my refuge in my Master, God,
לְסַפֵּר כָּל־מַלְאֲכוֹתֶיךָ׃	that I may tell all of Your Divine mission.

פרק עד Chapter 74

Weekly Cycle	Monthly Cycle	Book Number
Wednesday	14th day of the month	Book 3

Author

אָסָף—Asaf—a composer of several psalms and patriarch of a family of singers in the Beit HaMikdash (Temple).

Genre

Psalm of Communal Lament - This psalm contains teachings and wise advice and is meant to instruct people on how to live a Godly life.

Chapter Summary

Asaf composed this prophetic psalm as a prayer on behalf of those who are today in exile. He foresaw the calamity of the Beit HaMikdash (Holy Temple) being destroyed and burned, and Israel's subsequent exile among the nations. In the bitterness of his heart he cries out, "Why, God, have You cast [us] off forever?"

This psalm consists of twenty-three verses, subdivided into three parts.
In verses 1-11, the psalmist laments the victory of the wicked who have desecrated the Sanctuary and the name of God. He further describes the deeds of the wicked, and then directs a second lament towards God.
In verses 12-17, he praises God and tells of His mighty deeds in days of old.
In verses 18-23, he prays for mercy, asking God not to allow the wicked nations to destroy the people of Israel.

Technical Terminology

מַשְׂכִּיל—Maskil—a discerning person; alternatively, a giver of instruction, perhaps denoting a translator of the chapter (Rashi).

Shimush Tehillim - When to Say

Against enemies and evil spirits—Verse 22 states: "Arise, God, defend Your own cause; remember Your scorn from the vile person all the day."

Where in the Siddur

Recited in some congregations on the fast of Asarah B'Tevet (Tenth of Tevet), upon the conclusion of Shacharit (morning service).
Recited in some congregations on the second day of Passover, upon the conclusion of Shacharit.
Verse 2 is also found in Selichot (Penitential Service), immediately preceding Shema Koleinu (a responsive prayer beseeching God to hear our voice). Selichot are recited the week of Rosh HaShanah through Yom Kippur. Selichot are not recited on Rosh HaShanah proper.

Biblical Creatures

לִוְיָתָן—Leviathan—a large sea monster or creature.

תַּנִּינִים—Taninim—perhaps a reference to sea monsters which God created on the fifth day of creation, as recorded in Sefer Bereishit (Genesis); alternatively, a reference to crocodiles and/or alligators.

פֶּרֶק עד

א מַשְׂכִּיל לְאָסָף
לָמָה אֱלֹהִים זָנַחְתָּ לָנֶצַח
יֶעְשַׁן אַפְּךָ
בְּצֹאן מַרְעִיתֶךָ׃
ב זְכֹר עֲדָתְךָ ׀
קָנִיתָ קֶּדֶם
גָּאַלְתָּ שֵׁבֶט
נַחֲלָתֶךָ
הַר־צִיּוֹן זֶה ׀ שָׁכַנְתָּ בּוֹ׃
ג הָרִימָה פְעָמֶיךָ
לְמַשֻּׁאוֹת נֶצַח
כָּל־הֵרַע אוֹיֵב
בַּקֹּדֶשׁ׃
ד שָׁאֲגוּ צֹרְרֶיךָ
בְּקֶרֶב מוֹעֲדֶךָ
שָׂמוּ אוֹתֹתָם אֹתוֹת׃
ה יִוָּדַע
כְּמֵבִיא לְמָעְלָה
בִּסֲבָךְ־עֵץ קַרְדֻּמּוֹת׃
ו וְעַתָּה
פִּתּוּחֶיהָ יָּחַד
בְּכַשִּׁיל וְכֵילַפֹּת
יַהֲלֹמוּן׃
ז שִׁלְחוּ בָאֵשׁ מִקְדָּשֶׁךָ
לָאָרֶץ חִלְּלוּ
מִשְׁכַּן־שְׁמֶךָ׃
ח אָמְרוּ בְלִבָּם
נִינָם יָחַד
שָׂרְפוּ
כָל־מוֹעֲדֵי־אֵל
בָּאָרֶץ׃
ט אוֹתֹתֵינוּ לֹא רָאִינוּ

Chapter 74

1 A Maskil of Asaph.
Why, God, have You cast [us] off forever;
will Your anger [continue to] smolder
against the sheep of Your pasture?
2 Remember Your congregation
which You have acquired of old,
You have redeemed the tribe
of Your inheritance,
this mountain of Zion where You have dwelled.
3 Lift Your terror
to inflict perpetual desolations,
for all the evil the enemy has done
in the Sanctuary.
4 Your adversaries roared
amidst Your meeting place
they have set up their own signs as signs.
5 They considered [their blows]
as an attack against the One on high,
their axes were swallowed in a thicket of trees.
6 And now
its [the Temple's] entrance all together,
with hatchets and hammers
they strike them down.
7 They have set Your Sanctuary on fire,
to the very ground they have profaned
the Dwelling-Place of Your Name.
8 They said in their heart,
their rulers all together,
they have burned
all the meeting places of the Almighty
in the land.
9 Our signs we have not seen,

אֵין־עוֹד נָבִיא
וְלֹא־אִתָּנוּ
יֹדֵעַ עַד־מָה׃

there is no longer any prophet,
and there is none among us
who knows how long.

י עַד־מָתַי אֱלֹהִים יְחָרֶף צָר
יְנָאֵץ אוֹיֵב שִׁמְךָ לָנֶצַח׃

10 How long, God, will the adversary revile,
will the enemy blaspheme Your Name forever?

יא לָמָּה תָשִׁיב יָדְךָ
וִימִינֶךָ
מִקֶּרֶב חוקך חֵיקְךָ כַלֵּה׃

11 Why do You withdraw Your hand,
even Your right hand?
Draw it from Your bosom, consume them.

יב וֵאלֹהִים מַלְכִּי מִקֶּדֶם
פֹּעֵל יְשׁוּעוֹת
בְּקֶרֶב הָאָרֶץ׃

12 And [yet,] God is my King of old,
performing acts of deliverance
in the midst of the earth.

יג אַתָּה פוֹרַרְתָּ בְעָזְּךָ יָם
שִׁבַּרְתָּ רָאשֵׁי תַנִּינִים
עַל־הַמָּיִם׃

13 You crumbled the sea with Your strength;
You shattered the heads of the sea monsters
upon the water.

יד אַתָּה רִצַּצְתָּ רָאשֵׁי לִוְיָתָן
תִּתְּנֶנּוּ מַאֲכָל לְעָם לְצִיִּים׃

14 You crushed the heads of Leviathan,
You gave him as food to the nation of legions.

טו אַתָּה בָקַעְתָּ מַעְיָן וָנָחַל
אַתָּה הוֹבַשְׁתָּ נַהֲרוֹת אֵיתָן׃

15 You split open the fountain and brook,
You dried up mighty rivers.

טז לְךָ יוֹם אַף־לְךָ לָיְלָה
אַתָּה הֲכִינוֹתָ מָאוֹר וָשָׁמֶשׁ׃

16 Yours is the day, also Yours is the night;
You established the luminary and the sun.

יז אַתָּה הִצַּבְתָּ
כָּל־גְּבוּלוֹת אָרֶץ
קַיִץ וָחֹרֶף אַתָּה יְצַרְתָּם׃

17 You set
all the borders of the earth,
summer and winter, You formed them.

יח זְכָר־זֹאת אוֹיֵב חֵרֵף | יְהוָה
וְעַם נָבָל נִאֲצוּ שְׁמֶךָ׃

18 Remember this, the enemy reviled Adonoy,
and the vile nation blasphemed Your Name.

יט אַל־תִּתֵּן לְחַיַּת
נֶפֶשׁ תּוֹרֶךָ
חַיַּת עֲנִיֶּיךָ אַל־תִּשְׁכַּח לָנֶצַח׃

19 Do not deliver to the wild beast
the soul of Your turtledove;
the life of Your poor forget not forever.

כ הַבֵּט לַבְּרִית
כִּי מָלְאוּ מַחֲשַׁכֵּי־אֶרֶץ
נְאוֹת חָמָס׃

20 Look upon the covenant,
for the dark places of the land are full of
the habitations of violence.

כא אַל־יָשֹׁב דַּךְ נִכְלָם
עָנִי וְאֶבְיוֹן יְהַלְלוּ שְׁמֶךָ׃

21 Let not the oppressed turn back in disgrace,
let the poor and needy praise Your Name.

כב קוּמָה אֱלֹהִים רִיבָה רִיבֶךָ
זְכֹר חֶרְפָּתְךָ
מִנִּי־נָבָל כָּל־הַיּוֹם׃

22 Arise, God, defend Your own cause;
remember Your scorn
from the vile person all the day.

כג אַל־תִּשְׁכַּח קוֹל צֹרְרֶיךָ
שְׁאוֹן קָמֶיךָ
עֹלֶה תָמִיד׃

23 Forget not the voice of Your adversaries,
the tumult of those who rise up against You
which ascends continually.

פרק עה Chapter 75

Weekly Cycle	Monthly Cycle	Book Number
Wednesday	14th day of the month	Book 3

Author
אָסָף—Asaf—a composer of several psalms and patriarch of a family of singers in the Beit HaMikdash (Temple).

Genre
Psalm of Thanksgiving - This psalm emphasizes gratitude for what God has done.

Chapter Summary
Asaf offers solace to the exiles by speaking of the redemption that will surely come. Ultimately, God will exact retribution against the nations and bring about the ingathering of His beloved people.

This psalm consists of eleven verses, subdivided into four parts. The first two verses serve as a heading, in which Asaf praises God.
In verses 3-4, the psalmist tells of God's promise to judge the world righteously and to set the world firmly on its foundations.
In verses 5-8, he warns the wicked not to act arrogantly and not to put their trust in their success, as true prosperity comes only from God.
In verses 8-9, he describes how God gives the wicked poison to drink in order to punish them.
In verses 10 and 11, he concludes by expressing his desire, and subsequently vows, to sing praises to God.

Introductory Words
לַמְנַצֵּחַ—Lamnatsei'ach—To the Conductor
מִזְמוֹר—Mizmor—Musical Accompaniment
שִׁיר—Shir—Song

Technical Terminology
אַל תַּשְׁחֵת—Al Tashcheit—Do not destroy. This phrase is perhaps the author's, or printer's, notation indicating that the associated manuscript was from another source, and should not be thrown away or destroyed.
סֶלָה—Selah—While its meaning is unclear, the most familiar opinion is that it is a musical notation, instructing the Levitical orchestra to pause its singing and playing of instruments. Alternatively, "Selah" may mean "everlasting".

Shimush Tehillim - When to Say
For forgiveness of sins—Verse 11 states: "And all the horns [pride] of the wicked I will cut off, uplifted will be the pride of the righteous."

Where in the Siddur

Recited in some traditions on the third through sixth days of Passover.

Biblical Personalities

יַעֲקֹב—Yaakov—Jacob—also called Yisrael—Israel—the third patriarch, considered the father of the twelve tribes of Israel. He was married to Leah and Rachel, and was the twin brother of Eisav.

פֶּרֶק עה

א לַמְנַצֵּחַ אַל־תַּשְׁחֵת
מִזְמוֹר לְאָסָף שִׁיר:
ב הוֹדִינוּ לְּךָ | אֱלֹהִים הוֹדִינוּ
וְקָרוֹב שְׁמֶךָ
סִפְּרוּ נִפְלְאוֹתֶיךָ:
ג כִּי אֶקַּח מוֹעֵד
אֲנִי מֵישָׁרִים אֶשְׁפֹּט:
ד נְמֹגִים
אֶרֶץ וְכָל־יֹשְׁבֶיהָ
אָנֹכִי תִכַּנְתִּי עַמּוּדֶיהָ סֶּלָה:
ה אָמַרְתִּי לַהוֹלְלִים
אַל־תָּהֹלּוּ
וְלָרְשָׁעִים
אַל־תָּרִימוּ קָרֶן:
ו אַל־תָּרִימוּ לַמָּרוֹם קַרְנְכֶם
תְּדַבְּרוּ בְצַוָּאר עָתָק:
ז כִּי לֹא מִמּוֹצָא וּמִמַּעֲרָב
וְלֹא מִמִּדְבַּר הָרִים:
ח כִּי־אֱלֹהִים שֹׁפֵט
זֶה יַשְׁפִּיל וְזֶה יָרִים:
ט כִּי כוֹס בְּיַד־יְהוָה
וְיַיִן חָמַר | מָלֵא מֶסֶךְ
וַיַּגֵּר מִזֶּה
אַךְ־שְׁמָרֶיהָ יִמְצוּ יִשְׁתּוּ
כֹּל רִשְׁעֵי־אָרֶץ:
י וַאֲנִי אַגִּיד לְעֹלָם
אֲזַמְּרָה לֵאלֹהֵי יַעֲקֹב:
יא וְכָל־קַרְנֵי רְשָׁעִים
אֲגַדֵּעַ
תְּרוֹמַמְנָה קַרְנוֹת צַדִּיק:

Chapter 75

1 To the Chief Musician, Al Tashchais,
a Psalm of Asaph, a song.
2 We gave thanks to You, God, we gave thanks,
for Your Name is near;
they told of Your wonders.
3 When I celebrate the appointed Festival
I will judge [its theme] with fairness.
4 In danger of total dissolvement
was the earth and all its inhabitants,
but I firmly established its pillars, Selah.
5 I say to the arrogant,
"Deal not arrogantly";
and to the wicked, [I say]
"do not raise the horn [of arrogance]."
6 Raise not up heavenward, your horn,
nor speak insolently with a haughty neck.
7 For neither from the east nor from the west,
nor from the wilderness [comes success.]
8 For God is the Judge,
one He humbles, and one He raises.
9 For a cup is in the hand of Adonoy,
with strong wine, a full mixture,
and He pours out of this [cup];
[but] only its dregs will they drain and drink—
all the wicked of the earth.
10 But as for me, I will declare it forever,
I will sing praises to the God of Jacob.
11 And all the horns [pride] of the wicked
I will cut off,
uplifted will be the pride of the righteous.

פרק עו Chapter 76

Weekly Cycle	Monthly Cycle	Book Number
Wednesday	14th day of the month	Book 3

Author

אָסָף—Asaf—a composer of several psalms and patriarch of a family of singers in the Beit HaMikdash (Temple).

Genre

Psalm of Praise – This is a psalm of celebration, often the result of a victory. It declares God's goodness and urges all of creation to worship.
Psalm of Zion – This psalm glorifies God's city and His holy mount in which He has placed His abode.

Chapter Summary

Here too, Asaf speaks of the future redemption and God's vengeance against Israel's enemies. This psalm also alludes to the Mishkan (Tabernacle), here referred to as Sukkat David (the Sukkah of David). As such, it is recited in some communities on the holiday of Sukkot.

This psalm consists of thirteen verses, subdivided into three parts. The first verse serves as a heading.
In verses 2 and 3, the psalmist proudly declares that the name of God has become known in Israel, and that his dwelling place is set in Zion.
In verses 4-10, he further describes how God has imposed His fear upon His enemies and has delivered all humble inhabitants of the earth from the hands of their oppressors.
In verses 11-13, he speaks of the people who subjugate themselves to God, fear Him, and express their devotion by making vows to Him.

Introductory Words

לַמְנַצֵּחַ—Lamnatsei'ach—To the Conductor
מִזְמוֹר—Mizmor—Musical Accompaniment
שִׁיר—Shir—Song

Technical Terminology

נְגִינֹת—Neginos—Tunes
סֶלָה—Selah—While its meaning is unclear, the most familiar opinion is that it is a musical notation, instructing the Levitical orchestra to pause its singing and playing of instruments. Alternatively, "Selah" may mean "everlasting".

Shimush Tehillim - When to Say

For protection against fire and water—Verse 9 states: "From heaven You caused sentence to be heard, the earth feared and was still."

Where in the Siddur

Recited on the first day of Sukkot in some congregations (see "Chapter Summary" for further explanation).

Biblical Places

שָׁלֵם—Shalem—another name for Jerusalem, dating back to the time of Abraham. The name Yerushalayim itself does not appear in the Chumash.

יְהוּדָה—Yehudah—Judah - one of the twelve tribes of Israel. The Davidic dynasty descended from this tribe.

יִשְׂרָאֵל—Yisrael—Israel - The kindgom of Israel occupied the land on the Mediterranean Sea corresponding roughly to the State of Israel of modern times. Israel developed into a united kingdom under the leadership of King David who consolidated the various tribes under his single rule.

צִיּוֹן—Zion—a place name often used as a synonym for Jerusalem. The term Zion originally referred only to the area where a Jebbusite fortress once stood, also the location of the City of David. Zion was later used by prophets and psalmists as another name for Jerusalem.

Talmud on Tehillim

Verse 9: "מִשָּׁמַיִם, הִשְׁמַעְתָּ דִּין; אֶרֶץ יָרְאָה וְשָׁקָטָה"—"From heaven You caused sentence to be heard, the earth feared and was still."

The Talmud, Shabbat 88a, explains that before the Jewish nation accepted the Torah and declared: "We will do and we will listen", the earth became afraid. Had they not accepted the Torah, the world would have been returned to a state of tohu vavohu— astonishing emptiness. Once the nation indeed accepted it, the earth calmed down and became peaceful.

פרק עו	Chapter 76
א לַמְנַצֵּחַ בִּנְגִינֹת מִזְמוֹר לְאָסָף שִׁיר:	1 To the Chief Musician, with string music, a Psalm of Asaph, a song.
ב נוֹדָע בִּיהוּדָה אֱלֹהִים בְּיִשְׂרָאֵל גָּדוֹל שְׁמוֹ:	2 In Judah God is known, in Israel His Name is great.
ג וַיְהִי בְשָׁלֵם סֻכּוֹ וּמְעוֹנָתוֹ בְצִיּוֹן:	3 When His Tabernacle was in Shalem, and His dwelling place in Zion.
ד שָׁמָּה שִׁבַּר רִשְׁפֵי־קָשֶׁת מָגֵן וְחֶרֶב וּמִלְחָמָה סֶלָה:	4 There He broke the flying arrows of the bow, the shield, sword, and the battle, Selah.
ה נָאוֹר אַתָּה אַדִּיר מֵהַרְרֵי־טָרֶף:	5 Awesome are You and mightier than the mountains with their lairs.
ו אֶשְׁתּוֹלְלוּ | אַבִּירֵי לֵב	6 Deprived [of intelligence] were the stout_hearted

	נָמוּ שְׁנָתָם		they slept their sleep;
	וְלֹא־מָצְאוּ כָל־אַנְשֵׁי־חַיִל		and all the men of might found not
	יְדֵיהֶם׃		their hands [capabilities].
ז	מִגַּעֲרָתְךָ אֱלֹהֵי יַעֲקֹב	7	At Your rebuke, God of Jacob,
	נִרְדָּם		they are cast into a deep sleep,
	וְרֶכֶב וָסוּס׃		[also their] chariot and horse.
ח	אַתָּה ׀ נוֹרָא אַתָּה	8	You, awesome are You,
	וּמִי־יַעֲמֹד לְפָנֶיךָ		and who can stand before You
	מֵאָז אַפֶּךָ׃		once You are angry.
ט	מִשָּׁמַיִם	9	From heaven
	הִשְׁמַעְתָּ דִּין		You caused sentence to be heard,
	אֶרֶץ יָרְאָה וְשָׁקָטָה׃		the earth feared and was still.
י	בְּקוּם־לַמִּשְׁפָּט אֱלֹהִים	10	When God arises to pass judgment,
	לְהוֹשִׁיעַ כָּל־עַנְוֵי־אֶרֶץ		to deliver all the humble of the earth,
	סֶלָה׃		Selah.
יא	כִּי־חֲמַת אָדָם	11	For the wrath of man
	תּוֹדֶךָּ		will turn to praise You,
	שְׁאֵרִית חֵמֹת תַּחְגֹּר׃		the residue of wrath will You restrain.
יב	נִדְרוּ וְשַׁלְּמוּ	12	Vow and fulfill them
	לַיהוָה אֱלֹהֵיכֶם		to Adonoy, your God,
	כָּל־סְבִיבָיו		all you who surround Him,
	יוֹבִילוּ שַׁי לַמּוֹרָא׃		bring tribute to Him that is to be feared.
יג	יִבְצֹר רוּחַ נְגִידִים	13	He cuts down the spirit of princes,
	נוֹרָא לְמַלְכֵי־אָרֶץ׃		He is awesome to the kings of the earth.

Aquatic detail from the Lod Mosaic

פרק עז Chapter 77

Weekly Cycle	Monthly Cycle	Book Number
Wednesday	15th day of the month	Book 3

Author

אָסָף—Asaf—a composer of several psalms and patriarch of a family of singers in the Beit HaMikdash (Temple), perhaps written for יְדוּתוּן—Yedutun—a noted singer and composer of several psalms, or perhaps co-authored with Yedutun.

Genre

Psalm of Individual Lament – This psalm was written from the perspective of the individual worshipper, who cries out to God in his time of need. It is characterized as an address to God involving a complaint, followed by a request and ending with an expression of trust.

Chapter Summary

Despite the decrees and edicts that would afflict Israel in exile, Asaf does not come as one challenging and demanding of God, but rather speaks in the language of song and praise. He knows that Israel's sins are washed clean through harsh judgments.

This psalm consists of twenty-one verses, subdivided into two sections. The first verse serves as a heading.

In verses 2-10, the psalmist laments his personal distress, and then extends his lament to the distress of the entire nation. He describes how he cries out to God and prays to Him. He further complains that God seems to have forgotten his people.

In verses 11-21, he tells of God's wondrous deeds in days of old and asks that they be performed once again. He tells of how God redeemed Israel, and describes how the entire world trembled when God's glory was revealed during the period leading up to, and including, the Exodus from Egypt.

Introductory Words

לַמְנַצֵּחַ—Lamnatsei'ach—To the Conductor

מִזְמוֹר—Mizmor—Musical Accompaniment

סֶלָה—Selah—While its meaning is unclear, the most familiar opinion is that it is a musical notation, instructing the Levitical orchestra to pause its singing and playing of instruments. Alternatively, "Selah" may mean "everlasting".

Technical Terminology

יְדוּתוּן—Yedutun—a singer of unknown origin; alternatively, a musical instrument

Shimush Tehillim - When to Say

To avoid distress—Verse 3 states: " In the day of my trouble I sought my Master."

Where in the Siddur

Recited in some congregations on the Shabbat prior to the month of Nisan, in conjunction with

Parashat HaChodesh—a special Torah reading for that day.
Recited in some congregations on Chol HaMo'eid Sukkot (Intermediate Days of Sukkot).
The first three words of verse 4—"Ezkerah Elo-him ve'ehemayah"—"I shall remember God and stir"— open one of the stanzas of Ne'ilah (Closing Service) of Yom Kippur.
Verses 15 & 16 are found in the Selichot (Penitential Service) of Ta'anit Esther (Fast of Esther).

Biblical Personalities

אַהֲרֹן—Aaron—older brother of Moses and the first Kohein (Priest). The descendents of Aaron, as future kohanim, were designated to perform the ritual service in the Beit HaMikdash (Temple).
יוֹסֵף—Yosef—Joseph—the son of Jacob and Rachel. As second in command to Pharaoh, he sustained his brothers while they were in Egypt and was therefore rewarded in kind. Instead of receiving only one share in the land of Israel, as did his brothers, each of his sons, Ephraim and Menasheh, received a full share. It is also believed that the first Mashiach (Messiah) will be from the tribe of Joseph, to be followed by Mashiach from the tribe of Judah.
מֹשֶׁה—Moshe—Moses—sent by God to lead the Israelites out of Egypt. He received the Torah on behalf of the Israelites and acted as a mediator between them and God. He was closer to God than all of the other prophets who preceded and followed him.

פרק עז			**Chapter 77**
לַמְנַצֵּחַ עַל־יְדוּתוּן לְאָסָף מִזְמוֹר׃	א	1	To the Chief Musician, on Yedusun, by Asaph a Psalm,
קוֹלִי אֶל־אֱלֹהִים וְאֶצְעָקָה קוֹלִי אֶל־אֱלֹהִים וְהַאֲזִין אֵלָי׃	ב	2	[I will lift] my voice to God and cry, [I will lift] my voice to God, and He will give ear to me.
בְּיוֹם צָרָתִי אֲדֹנָי דָּרָשְׁתִּי יָדִי ׀ לַיְלָה נִגְּרָה וְלֹא תָפוּג מֵאֲנָה הִנָּחֵם נַפְשִׁי׃	ג	3	In the day of my trouble I sought my Master, my wound exudes into the night without ceasing, my soul refuses to be comforted.
אֶזְכְּרָה אֱלֹהִים וְאֶהֱמָיָה אָשִׂיחָה ׀ וְתִתְעַטֵּף רוּחִי סֶלָה׃	ד	4	I remember [how] God [favored me] and I moan, when I talk about it, my spirit faints, Selah.
אָחַזְתָּ שְׁמֻרוֹת עֵינָי נִפְעַמְתִּי וְלֹא אֲדַבֵּר׃	ה	5	You held fast the lids of my eyes; I throbbed with pain and could not speak.
חִשַּׁבְתִּי יָמִים מִקֶּדֶם שְׁנוֹת עוֹלָמִים׃	ו	6	I have pondered the days of old, the years of ancient times.
אֶזְכְּרָה נְגִינָתִי בַּלָּיְלָה עִם־לְבָבִי אָשִׂיחָה	ז	7	I recall my song into the night, with my heart I meditate

וַיְחַפֵּשׂ רוּחִי׃	and my spirit searches diligently.
ח הַלְעוֹלָמִים יִזְנַח | אֲדֹנָי	8 "Will my Master cast [me] off forever
וְלֹא־יֹסִיף לִרְצוֹת עוֹד׃	and will He no longer be favorable?
ט הֶאָפֵס לָנֶצַח חַסְדּוֹ	9 Has His kindness ceased forever?
גָּמַר אֹמֶר	Has His promise come to an end
לְדֹר וָדֹר׃	for generation upon generation?
י הֲשָׁכַח חַנּוֹת אֵל	10 Has the Almighty forgotten to be gracious?
אִם־קָפַץ בְּאַף רַחֲמָיו סֶלָה׃	Has His anger shut off His mercies, Selah?"
יא וָאֹמַר חַלּוֹתִי הִיא	11 And I said, ``It is to terrify me,
שְׁנוֹת	this changing
יְמִין עֶלְיוֹן׃	of the right hand of the Most High.
יב אֶזְכּוֹר מַעַלְלֵי־יָהּ	12 I will remember the deeds of God
כִּי־אֶזְכְּרָה מִקֶּדֶם פִּלְאֶךָ׃	when I remember Your wonders of old.
יג וְהָגִיתִי בְכָל־פָּעֳלֶךָ	13 And I will meditate upon all Your work,
וּבַעֲלִילוֹתֶיךָ אָשִׂיחָה׃	and of Your deeds I will speak."
יד אֱלֹהִים בַּקֹּדֶשׁ דַּרְכֶּךָ	14 God, in holiness is Your way,
מִי־אֵל גָּדוֹל כֵּאלֹהִים׃	what power is as great as God?
טו אַתָּה הָאֵל עֹשֵׂה פֶלֶא	15 You are the Almighty Who does wonders;
הוֹדַעְתָּ בָעַמִּים	You have let the people know
עֻזֶּךָ׃	of Your strength.
טז גָּאַלְתָּ	16 You have redeemed
בִּזְרוֹעַ	with [an outstretched] arm
עַמֶּךָ	Your people,
בְּנֵי־יַעֲקֹב וְיוֹסֵף סֶלָה׃	the sons of Jacob and Joseph, Selah.
יז רָאוּךָ מַּיִם | אֱלֹהִים	17 The waters beheld You, God,
רָאוּךָ מַּיִם יָחִילוּ	the waters beheld You, they were terrified;
אַף יִרְגְּזוּ תְהֹמוֹת׃	even the depths trembled.
יח זֹרְמוּ מַיִם | עָבוֹת	18 The clouds poured forth waters,
קוֹל נָתְנוּ שְׁחָקִים	the skies sent out a sound, [thunder]
אַף־חֲצָצֶיךָ יִתְהַלָּכוּ׃	also Your arrows [hailstones] went abroad.
יט קוֹל רַעַמְךָ |	19 The sound of Your thunder
בַּגַּלְגַּל	rolled like a wheel,
הֵאִירוּ בְרָקִים תֵּבֵל	the bolts of lightning lit up the world,
רָגְזָה וַתִּרְעַשׁ הָאָרֶץ׃	the earth trembled and shook.
כ בַּיָּם דַּרְכֶּךָ	20 In the sea was Your way,
וּשְׁבִילְךָ בְּמַיִם רַבִּים	and Your path in the great waters,
וְעִקְּבוֹתֶיךָ לֹא נֹדָעוּ׃	and Your footsteps were not known.
כא נָחִיתָ כַצֹּאן עַמֶּךָ	21 You led Your people like a flock,
בְּיַד־מֹשֶׁה וְאַהֲרֹן׃	by the hand of Moses and Aaron.

פרק עח Chapter 78

Weekly Cycle	Monthly Cycle	Book Number
Wednesday	15th day of the month	Book 3

Author

אָסָף—Asaf—a composer of several psalms and patriarch of a family of singers in the Beit HaMikdash (Temple).

Genre

Psalm of Wisdom – This psalm contains teachings and wise advice and is meant to instruct people on how to live a Godly life.

Chapter Summary

Asaf depicts all of the awesome and wondrous things that God has done on behalf of the Jewish people, from the time of the Exodus from Egypt to the reign of King David. He stresses David's greatness and the excellence of the Beit HaMikdash (Holy Temple) built by his son, King Solomon.

This psalm consists of seventy-two verses, subdivided into four parts.
In verses 1-8, the psalmist emphasizes the obligation to relate the wondrous deeds which God performed during the Exodus from Egypt. He does so not only to praise the Lord, but also in order to instill fear of God in his and future generations, so that they would not sin as did their forefathers.
In verses 9-39, he tells of the parting of the Red Sea and of the miracles performed in the desert, as well as the rebellion of that generation and their ensuing punishment. God was nonetheless compassionate, the author reminds us, and turned away his anger on numerous occasions.
In verses 40-55, he tells of the ten plaques in Egypt and the subsequent conquest of the Land of Israel. Again, he describes the rebellion of the generation.
In verses 56-72, Asaf further tells of the acts of salvation enjoyed by Israel before the selection of David as king. He continues to focus on sins committed, this time during the period of the Judges, the recent destruction of Shiloh, and continuing through the period of the anointing of David.

Technical Terminology

מַשְׂכִּיל —Maskil—a discerning person; alternatively, a giver of instruction, perhaps denoting a translator of the chapter (Rashi).

Shimush Tehillim - When to Say

To find favor in the eyes of royal authority—Verse 55 states: "And He drove out the nations before them, and allotted them as the portions of inheritance."

Where in the Siddur

Recited in some communities on Chol HaMo'eid Pesach (Intermediate Days of Passover).
Verses 36 and 37 are found in Yesod HaTeshuvah (Foundation of Repentance) recited in some

congregations on the eve of Rosh Hashanah. Some recite Yesod HaTeshuvah immediately following Hatarat Nedarim (Annulment of Vows).

Verse 38 comprises the first verse of Vehu Rachum (so named for the first two words of this verse) in Pesukei Dezimra (introductory Verses of Praise to the Shacharit morning service). It is similarly

Madaba Mosaic Map of the Old City of Jerusalem, located in Madaba, Jordan

the opening verse of the long Tachanun (Supplication service) recited on Mondays and Thursdays (this prayer too is referred to as Vehu Rachum).

Verse 38 is also found in Uva Letzion—a prayer preceding Aleinu of Shacharit, and is one of the two introductory verses to Ma'ariv (evening service). Finally, it is the penultimate verse of Yehi Chevod—the introductory prayer to Ashrei of Pesukei Dezimra.

Verse 49 is expounded upon at length in the Passover Haggadah.

Verse 54 is found in Pirkei Avot (Ethics of the Fathers), 6:10.

Verse 61 comprises one of the verses of the long Tachanun (Supplication service) recited on Mondays and Thursdays.

Biblical Personalities

חָם—Cham—one of the three sons of Noah, and as the Bible refers to him, the father of Mitzrayim (Egypt). Cham defiled Noah when the latter became intoxicated.

אֹהֶל יוֹסֵף—Ohel Yosef—Tent of Joseph—a reference to the two tribes that descended from Joseph, Menasheh and Ephraim.

בְּנֵי-אֶפְרַיִם—The Sons of Ephraim—the most prominent of the tribes located in the North of the land of Israel, they hosted the Mishkan (Tabernacle) in the city of Shiloh for 369 years. They were exiled during the Assyrians' conquest of the northern Ten Tribes of Israel, and subsequently dispersed among the nations.

יַעֲקֹב—Yaakov—Jacob—also called Israel, the third patriarch, considered the father of the twelve tribes of Israel. He was the brother of Eisav, and was married to Leah and Rachel.

יְהוּדָה—Yehudah—Judah - one of the twelve tribes of Israel. The Davidic dynasty descended from this tribe.

Biblical Places

הר צִיּוֹן—Har Tzion—Mount Zion—another name for Yerushalayim (Jerusalem).

מִשְׁכָּן—Mishkan—the Tabernacle—the portable dwelling place for the Shechinah (Divine Presence) from the time of the Exodus from Egypt through the conquering of the land of Canaan. Built to specifications revealed by God to Moses at Mount Sinai, it accompanied the Israelites on their wanderings in the wilderness.

מִצְרָיִם—Mitzrayim—Egypt—the land where Israel was enslaved until God sent Moses to redeem them. Egyptian society ran contrary to many of the ideals of the Torah. The Israelite king is thus specifically warned not to amass calvalry, lest he be tempted to return his nation to Egypt.

שְׂדֵה-צֹעַן—Sedei Tzoan—The Field of Zoan—identitifed as the city where Moses performed miracles before Pharaoh to persuade him to release Israel from his service. The Field of Zoan is thus perhaps synonymous with the Land of Goshen.

שִׁלוֹ —Shiloh—the sight of the Aron HaKodesh (Holy Ark) prior to its capture. Shiloh was located in the inheritence of the tribe of Joseph.

יַם-סוּף—Yam Suf—The Red Sea—also referred to as the Sea of Reeds, the body of water which miraculously parted for the Israelites as they fled the Egyptians, and then engulfed the pursuing Egyptian soldiers, drowning them.

יִשְׂרָאֵל—Yisrael—Israel The kindgom of Israel occupied the land on the Mediterranean Sea corresponding roughly to the State of Israel of modern times. Israel developed into a united kingdom under the leadership of King David who consolidated the various tribes under his single rule.

Talmud on Tehillim

Verse 54: "הַר-זֶה, קָנְתָה יְמִינוֹ"—"To this mountain which His right hand acquired." The Talmud, Pesachim 87b, explains that this mountain refers to Har HaBayit (the Temple Mount) in Jerusalem.

Bread Stamp with Menorah (Courtesy of Shlomo Moussaieff)

פֶּרֶק עח

Chapter 78

א מַשְׂכִּיל לְאָסָף
הַאֲזִינָה עַמִּי תּוֹרָתִי
הַטּוּ אָזְנְכֶם לְאִמְרֵי־פִי:

1 An instruction of Asaph.
Give ear, my people, to my Torah;
incline your ear to the words of my mouth.

ב אֶפְתְּחָה בְמָשָׁל פִּי
אַבִּיעָה חִידוֹת מִנִּי־קֶדֶם:

2 I will open my mouth with a parable,
I will utter riddles concerning days of old.

ג אֲשֶׁר שָׁמַעְנוּ וַנֵּדָעֵם
וַאֲבוֹתֵינוּ סִפְּרוּ־לָנוּ:

3 That which we have heard and known,
and our fathers have told us.

ד לֹא נְכַחֵד | מִבְּנֵיהֶם
לְדוֹר אַחֲרוֹן מְסַפְּרִים
תְּהִלּוֹת יְהוָה
וֶעֱזוּזוֹ וְנִפְלְאוֹתָיו אֲשֶׁר עָשָׂה:

4 We will not withhold from their children,
even to the last generation we will relate
the praises of Adonoy—
His might and His wonders that He has done.

ה וַיָּקֶם עֵדוּת | בְּיַעֲקֹב
וְתוֹרָה שָׂם בְּיִשְׂרָאֵל
אֲשֶׁר צִוָּה אֶת־אֲבוֹתֵינוּ
לְהוֹדִיעָם לִבְנֵיהֶם:

5 He has established a testimony in Jacob,
and a Torah He has appointed in Israel
which He commanded our fathers
to make them known to their sons.

ו לְמַעַן יֵדְעוּ | דּוֹר אַחֲרוֹן
בָּנִים יִוָּלֵדוּ
יָקֻמוּ וִיסַפְּרוּ לִבְנֵיהֶם:

6 That the last generation might know them,
that the sons who will be born
will rise and tell them to their own children.

ז וְיָשִׂימוּ בֵאלֹהִים כִּסְלָם
וְלֹא יִשְׁכְּחוּ מַעַלְלֵי־אֵל
וּמִצְוֹתָיו יִנְצֹרוּ:

7 And they will put their hope in God,
and not forget the deeds of the Almighty,
and His commandments, they will keep.

ח וְלֹא יִהְיוּ | כַּאֲבוֹתָם
דּוֹר סוֹרֵר וּמֹרֶה
דּוֹר לֹא־הֵכִין לִבּוֹ
וְלֹא־נֶאֶמְנָה אֶת־אֵל
רוּחוֹ:

8 And they will not be like their fathers,
a generation, stubborn and rebellious,
a generation that did not set its heart aright,
and who were not faithful with the Almighty
in their spirit.

ט בְּנֵי־אֶפְרַיִם
נוֹשְׁקֵי רוֹמֵי־קָשֶׁת
הָפְכוּ בְּיוֹם קְרָב:

9 The children of Ephraim,
armed archers,
retreated in the day of battle.

י לֹא שָׁמְרוּ
בְּרִית אֱלֹהִים
וּבְתוֹרָתוֹ מֵאֲנוּ לָלֶכֶת:

10 They [Israel] did not preserve
the covenant of God,
and refused to walk after His Torah.

יא וַיִּשְׁכְּחוּ עֲלִילוֹתָיו
וְנִפְלְאוֹתָיו אֲשֶׁר הֶרְאָם:

11 And they forgot His deeds
and His wonders which He had shown them.

יב נֶגֶד אֲבוֹתָם
עָשָׂה פֶלֶא
בְּאֶרֶץ מִצְרַיִם שְׂדֵה־צֹעַן:

12 In the presence of their fathers
He did wonders,
in the land of Egypt, in the field of Zoan.

יג בָּקַע יָם וַיַּעֲבִירֵם

13 He split the sea and brought them across

וַיַּצֶּב־מַיִם כְּמוֹ־נֵד׃
and He made the waters stand like a wall.

יד וַיַּנְחֵם בֶּעָנָן יוֹמָם
וְכָל־הַלַּיְלָה בְּאוֹר אֵשׁ׃
14 And He led them with a cloud by day,
and all night with a light of fire.

טו יְבַקַּע צֻרִים בַּמִּדְבָּר
וַיַּשְׁקְ
כִּתְהֹמוֹת רַבָּה׃
15 He cleaved rocks in the wilderness,
and gave them to drink [in abundance]
out of the great depths.

טז וַיּוֹצִא נוֹזְלִים
מִסָּלַע
וַיּוֹרֶד כַּנְּהָרוֹת מָיִם׃
16 And He brought forth streams
from the rock,
and caused waters to run down like rivers.

יז וַיּוֹסִיפוּ עוֹד לַחֲטֹא־לוֹ
לַמְרוֹת עֶלְיוֹן בַּצִּיָּה׃
17 And yet they continued to sin against Him,
to vex the Most High, in the desert.

יח וַיְנַסּוּ־אֵל בִּלְבָבָם
לִשְׁאָל־אֹכֶל לְנַפְשָׁם׃
18 And they tested the Almighty in their hearts,
by asking for food for their soul

יט וַיְדַבְּרוּ בֵּאלֹהִים
אָמְרוּ הֲיוּכַל אֵל לַעֲרֹךְ
שֻׁלְחָן בַּמִּדְבָּר׃
19 And they spoke against God,
they said, "Can the Almighty prepare
a table in the wilderness?

כ הֵן הִכָּה־צוּר ׀ וַיָּזוּבוּ מַיִם
וּנְחָלִים יִשְׁטֹפוּ
הֲגַם־לֶחֶם יוּכַל תֵּת
אִם־יָכִין שְׁאֵר לְעַמּוֹ׃
20 Behold, He struck a rock and waters flowed,
and streams burst forth;
Can He give bread also,
will He prepare meat for His people?"

כא לָכֵן ׀ שָׁמַע יְהוָה
וַיִּתְעַבָּר
וְאֵשׁ נִשְּׂקָה בְיַעֲקֹב
וְגַם־אַף עָלָה בְיִשְׂרָאֵל׃
21 Therefore, Adonoy heard
and He was enraged,
and a fire was kindled against Jacob,
and anger also went up against Israel.

כב כִּי לֹא הֶאֱמִינוּ בֵּאלֹהִים
וְלֹא בָטְחוּ בִּישׁוּעָתוֹ׃
22 For they did not have faith in God,
and did not trust in His deliverance.

כג וַיְצַו שְׁחָקִים מִמָּעַל
וְדַלְתֵי שָׁמַיִם פָּתָח׃
23 And He commanded clouds from above,
and the doors of heaven He opened.

כד וַיַּמְטֵר עֲלֵיהֶם מָן לֶאֱכֹל
וּדְגַן־שָׁמַיִם נָתַן לָמוֹ׃
24 And He rained upon them manna to eat,
and the grain of heaven He gave them.

כה לֶחֶם אַבִּירִים אָכַל אִישׁ
צֵידָה שָׁלַח לָהֶם לָשֹׂבַע׃
25 Bread of the angels man did eat,
provisions He set them for [their] satisfaction.

כו יַסַּע קָדִים בַּשָּׁמָיִם
וַיְנַהֵג בְּעֻזּוֹ תֵימָן׃
26 He made the east wind blow in heaven,
and He brought with His might, a south wind.

כז וַיַּמְטֵר עֲלֵיהֶם
כֶּעָפָר שְׁאֵר
וּכְחוֹל יַמִּים עוֹף כָּנָף׃
27 And He rained upon them
meat [plentiful] as dust
and winged fowl as the sand of the seas.

כח וַיַּפֵּל בְּקֶרֶב מַחֲנֵהוּ
סָבִיב לְמִשְׁכְּנֹתָיו׃
28 And He let it fall in the midst of His camp,
round about His dwellings.

כט	וַיֹּאכְלוּ וַיִּשְׂבְּעוּ מְאֹד	29	And they ate and were abundantly satiated,
	וְתַאֲוָתָם יָבִא לָהֶם׃		and their craving He satisfied.
ל	לֹא־זָרוּ	30	They had not yet abandoned
	מִתַּאֲוָתָם		their lust
	עוֹד אָכְלָם בְּפִיהֶם׃		their food was still in their mouth.
לא	וְאַף אֱלֹהִים ׀ עָלָה בָהֶם	31	And the anger of God rose up against them,
	וַיַּהֲרֹג בְּמִשְׁמַנֵּיהֶם		and slew their obese ones,
	וּבַחוּרֵי יִשְׂרָאֵל הִכְרִיעַ׃		and the chosen of Israel He bent low.
לב	בְּכָל־זֹאת חָטְאוּ־עוֹד	32	Despite all this they still sinned,
	וְלֹא־הֶאֱמִינוּ בְּנִפְלְאוֹתָיו׃		and had no faith in His wonders.
לג	וַיְכַל־בַּהֶבֶל יְמֵיהֶם	33	And He ended their days in vanity,
	וּשְׁנוֹתָם בַּבֶּהָלָה׃		and their years in terror.
לד	אִם־הֲרָגָם	34	When He slew them
	וּדְרָשׁוּהוּ		then they would seek Him,
	וְשָׁבוּ וְשִׁחֲרוּ־אֵל׃		and they would turn back and seek the Almighty.
לה	וַיִּזְכְּרוּ	35	And they remembered
	כִּי־אֱלֹהִים צוּרָם		that God was their rock,
	וְאֵל עֶלְיוֹן גֹּאֲלָם׃		and the Most High Almighty, their redeemer.
לו	וַיְפַתּוּהוּ בְּפִיהֶם	36	And they beguiled Him with their mouths,
	וּבִלְשׁוֹנָם יְכַזְּבוּ־לוֹ׃		and with their tongues they deceived Him.
לז	וְלִבָּם לֹא־נָכוֹן עִמּוֹ	37	And their heart was not steadfast with Him,
	וְלֹא נֶאֶמְנוּ בִּבְרִיתוֹ׃		and they were not faithful in His covenant.
לח	וְהוּא רַחוּם ׀	38	And He, the Merciful One
	יְכַפֵּר עָוֺן וְלֹא־יַשְׁחִית		atones iniquity, and does not destroy;
	וְהִרְבָּה לְהָשִׁיב אַפּוֹ		He frequently withdraws His anger,
	וְלֹא־יָעִיר כָּל־חֲמָתוֹ׃		and does not arouse all His rage.
לט	וַיִּזְכֹּר	39	And He remembered
	כִּי־בָשָׂר הֵמָּה		that they were but flesh,
	רוּחַ הוֹלֵךְ וְלֹא יָשׁוּב׃		a passing wind that does not return.
מ	כַּמָּה יַמְרוּהוּ	40	How often did they rebel against Him
	בַמִּדְבָּר		in the wilderness,
	יַעֲצִיבוּהוּ בִּישִׁימוֹן׃		and grieve Him in the desert.
מא	וַיָּשׁוּבוּ וַיְנַסּוּ אֵל	41	Again and again they tested the Almighty,
	וּקְדוֹשׁ יִשְׂרָאֵל		and of the Holy One of Israel
	הִתְווּ׃		they asked for a sign.
מב	לֹא־זָכְרוּ אֶת־יָדוֹ	42	They did not remember His hand,
	יוֹם אֲשֶׁר־פָּדָם		nor the day He redeemed them
	מִנִּי־צָר׃		from the oppressor.
מג	אֲשֶׁר־שָׂם בְּמִצְרַיִם אֹתוֹתָיו	43	[Nor] how He set His signs in Egypt,

וּמוֹפְתָיו בִּשְׂדֵה־צֹעַן׃	and His wonders in the field of Zoan.
מד וַיַּהֲפֹךְ לְדָם יְאֹרֵיהֶם	44 And He turned their rivers into blood,
וְנֹזְלֵיהֶם	and also their streams
בַּל־יִשְׁתָּיוּן׃	so that they could not drink.
מה יְשַׁלַּח בָּהֶם עָרֹב	45 He set among them swarms of beasts
וַיֹּאכְלֵם	which devoured them;
וּצְפַרְדֵּעַ וַתַּשְׁחִיתֵם	and frog[s] and it destroyed them.
מו וַיִּתֵּן לֶחָסִיל יְבוּלָם	46 And He gave the locust their produce,
וִיגִיעָם לָאַרְבֶּה׃	and [the fruit of] their labor to the grasshopper.
מז יַהֲרֹג בַּבָּרָד גַּפְנָם	47 He destroyed their vines with hail,
וְשִׁקְמוֹתָם בַּחֲנָמַל׃	and their sycamore trees with chanamal.
מח וַיַּסְגֵּר לַבָּרָד בְּעִירָם	48 And He delivered their cattle to the hail,
וּמִקְנֵיהֶם לָרְשָׁפִים׃	and their flocks to fiery bolts [lightning].
מט יְשַׁלַּח־בָּם ׀ חֲרוֹן אַפּוֹ	49 He dispatched upon them His fierce anger,
עֶבְרָה וָזַעַם וְצָרָה	wrath, and indignation, and distress,
מִשְׁלַחַת מַלְאֲכֵי רָעִים׃	a delegation of messengers of evil.
נ יְפַלֵּס נָתִיב לְאַפּוֹ	50 He levelled a path for His anger,
לֹא חָשַׂךְ מִמָּוֶת נַפְשָׁם	He spared not their soul from death,
וְחַיָּתָם לַדֶּבֶר הִסְגִּיר׃	and their bodies He gave over to pestilence.
נא וַיַּךְ כָּל־בְּכוֹר בְּמִצְרָיִם	51 And He smote every first born in Egypt,
רֵאשִׁית אוֹנִים	the first fruit of their strength,
בְּאָהֳלֵי־חָם׃	in the tents of Cham.
נב וַיַּסַּע כַּצֹּאן עַמּוֹ	52 He caused His people to journey like sheep,
וַיְנַהֲגֵם כַּעֵדֶר	and guided them like a flock
בַּמִּדְבָּר׃	in the wilderness.
נג וַיַּנְחֵם לָבֶטַח וְלֹא פָחָדוּ	53 And He led them safely so they feared not;
וְאֶת־אוֹיְבֵיהֶם כִּסָּה הַיָּם׃	for their enemies, the sea had covered.
נד וַיְבִיאֵם	54 And He brought them
אֶל־גְּבוּל קָדְשׁוֹ	to the boundary of His Sanctuary,
הַר־זֶה	to this mountain
קָנְתָה יְמִינוֹ׃	which His right hand acquired.
נה וַיְגָרֶשׁ מִפְּנֵיהֶם ׀ גּוֹיִם	55 And He drove out the nations before them,
וַיַּפִּילֵם בְּחֶבֶל נַחֲלָה	and allotted them as the portions of inheritance,
וַיַּשְׁכֵּן בְּאָהֳלֵיהֶם	And He caused them to dwell in their tents
שִׁבְטֵי יִשְׂרָאֵל׃	the tribes of Israel.
נו וַיְנַסּוּ וַיַּמְרוּ	56 And they tested and rebelled
אֶת־אֱלֹהִים עֶלְיוֹן	against God, the Most High,
וְעֵדוֹתָיו לֹא שָׁמָרוּ׃	and His testimonies they did not preserve.
נז וַיִּסֹּגוּ	57 And they turned back

וַֽיִּבְגְּדוּ כַּאֲבוֹתָם	and dealt treacherously like their fathers;
נֶהְפְּכוּ כְּקֶשֶׁת רְמִיָּה׃	they changed like a warped bow.
נח וַיַּכְעִיסוּהוּ	58 And they angered Him
בְּבָמוֹתָם	with their high altars,
וּבִפְסִילֵיהֶם יַקְנִיאוּהוּ׃	and with their idols they roused His jealousy.
נט שָׁמַע אֱלֹהִים וַיִּתְעַבָּר	59 God heard and was most angry,
וַיִּמְאַס מְאֹד בְּיִשְׂרָאֵל׃	and He greatly abhorred Israel.
ס וַיִּטֹּשׁ מִשְׁכַּן שִׁלוֹ	60 And He abandoned the Tabernacle of Shiloh,
אֹהֶל שִׁכֵּן בָּאָדָם׃	the tent wherein He dwelled among man.
סא וַיִּתֵּן לַשְּׁבִי עֻזּוֹ	61 And He delivered His might into captivity,
וְתִפְאַרְתּוֹ בְיַד־צָר׃	and His glory into the hand of the adversary.
סב וַיַּסְגֵּר לַחֶרֶב עַמּוֹ	62 And He gave over His people to the sword,
וּבְנַחֲלָתוֹ הִתְעַבָּר׃	and with His inheritance He was most angry.
סג בַּחוּרָיו אָכְלָה־אֵשׁ	63 His young men were consumed by fire,
וּבְתוּלֹתָיו לֹא הוּלָּלוּ׃	and His virgins had no marriage song.
סד כֹּהֲנָיו בַּחֶרֶב נָפָלוּ	64 His priests fell by the sword,
וְאַלְמְנֹתָיו לֹא תִבְכֶּינָה׃	and their widows did not weep.
סה וַיִּקַץ כְּיָשֵׁן ׀ אֲדֹנָי	65 And my Master awoke as one out of sleep,
כְּגִבּוֹר	like a mighty warrior
מִתְרוֹנֵן מִיָּיִן׃	rousing himself with singing, from wine.
סו וַיַּךְ־צָרָיו אָחוֹר	66 And He smote His adversaries into retreat,
חֶרְפַּת עוֹלָם נָתַן לָמוֹ׃	eternal humiliation He bestowed upon them.
סז וַיִּמְאַס בְּאֹהֶל יוֹסֵף	67 And He abhorred the tent of Joseph,
וּבְשֵׁבֶט אֶפְרַיִם לֹא בָחָר׃	and the tribe of Ephraim He did not choose.
סח וַיִּבְחַר אֶת־שֵׁבֶט יְהוּדָה	68 And He chose the tribe of Judah;
אֶת־הַר צִיּוֹן אֲשֶׁר אָהֵב׃	Mount Zion which He loves.
סט וַיִּבֶן כְּמוֹ־רָמִים	69 And like the heights of heaven, He built
מִקְדָּשׁוֹ	His Sanctuary.
כְּאֶרֶץ יְסָדָהּ לְעוֹלָם׃	like the earth which He has founded forever.
ע וַיִּבְחַר בְּדָוִד עַבְדּוֹ	70 And He chose David, His servant,
וַיִּקָּחֵהוּ מִמִּכְלְאֹת צֹאן׃	and took him from the sheepfolds.
עא מֵאַחַר עָלוֹת	71 From behind the suckling ewes
הֱבִיאוֹ	He brought him,
לִרְעוֹת בְּיַעֲקֹב עַמּוֹ	to be shepherd over Jacob, His people,
וּבְיִשְׂרָאֵל נַחֲלָתוֹ׃	and Israel His inheritance.
עב וַיִּרְעֵם	72 And he shepherded them
כְּתֹם לְבָבוֹ	according to the integrity of his heart,
וּבִתְבוּנוֹת כַּפָּיו	and by the skillfulness of his hands
יַנְחֵם׃	he led them.

פרק עט Chapter 79

Weekly Cycle	Monthly Cycle	Book Number
Wednesday	16th day of the month	Book 3

Author
אָסָף—Asaf—a composer of several psalms and patriarch of a family of singers in the Beit HaMikdash (Temple).

Genre
Psalm of Communal Lament – This psalm focuses on expressing deep sorrow for the travails of a nation and as a group asking for God's blessing or intervention.

Chapter Summary
Israel's greatest anguish comes from the defilement of God's name through the destruction of His Beit HaMikdash (Temple) by Israel's enemies. Thus, Asaf here asks that He avenge the destruction as well as the extermination of His people.

This psalm consists of thirteen verses, subdivided into two parts.
In verses 1-4, the psalmist cries out against the terrible destruction that has visited his people.
In verses 5-13, he prays for pardon for their sins, mercy, and salvation. He further beseeches God to take revenge against Israel's enemies. He ends with a vow and promise to relate the praises of God forever.

Introductory Words
מִזְמוֹר—Mizmor—Musical Accompaniment

Shimush Tehillim - When to Say
For one's enemies to perish—Verse 12 states: "And render to our neighbors sevenfold into their bosom, their humiliation with which they thought to humiliate You, my Master."

Where in the Siddur
Recited in some congregations on Shivah Asar BeTamuz (the fast of the Seventeenth of Tammuz).
Verses 6 & 7 are recited in the Passover Haggadah as the first two verses of Shefoch Chamatcha, asking God to pour out his wrath against the nations who do not recognize Him.
Verse 8 is found in the final paragraph of Tachanun (Supplication Prayer) of Shacharit (morning service) and Minchah (evening service).
Verse 9 is the final verse of Tachanun.
Verse 10 comprises one of the verses of Av HaRachamim, a prayer beseeching God to remember all martyrs who perished through Kiddush Hashem (sanctification of God's name), recited just prior to the Musaf service of Shabbat.
Verse 13 is found in Baruch Hashem Le'olam—the blessing immediately preceding the Amidah (Silent Meditation) of Ma'ariv.

The last clause of verse 13 is found in Modim—one of the final blessings of the Amidah.

Biblical Personalities

יַעֲקֹב—Yaakov—Jacob—also called Yisrael—Israel, the third patriarch, considered the father of the twelve tribes of Israel. He was the twin brother of Eisav, and married to Leah and Rachel.

Biblical Places

הֵיכָל—Heichal—Holy Temple—a term used to refer to the inner sanctuary of the Temple in Jerusalem. The Heichal contained the Holy of Holies, the resting place of the Aron HaKodesh (Holy Ark)*. It also housed the Menorah, Altar of Incense, and Table of the Showbread.

*The Aron HaKodesh, while present in the first Beit HaMikdash (Temple), was buried, and hence its location was not known, during the period of the second Beit HaMikdash.

יְרוּשָׁלָם—Yerushalayim—Jerusalem—the capital city of Israel, conquered by King David 3,000 years ago. David established Jerusalem as both the religious and political center of Israel.

פרק עט

א מִזְמוֹר לְאָסָף
אֱלֹהִים
בָּאוּ גוֹיִם | בְּנַחֲלָתֶךָ
טִמְּאוּ
אֶת־הֵיכַל קָדְשֶׁךָ
שָׂמוּ אֶת־יְרוּשָׁלַםִ לְעִיִּים:
ב נָתְנוּ אֶת־נִבְלַת עֲבָדֶיךָ
מַאֲכָל לְעוֹף הַשָּׁמָיִם
בְּשַׂר חֲסִידֶיךָ
לְחַיְתוֹ־אָרֶץ:
ג שָׁפְכוּ דָמָם | כַּמַּיִם
סְבִיבוֹת יְרוּשָׁלָםִ
וְאֵין קוֹבֵר:
ד הָיִינוּ חֶרְפָּה לִשְׁכֵנֵינוּ
לַעַג וָקֶלֶס
לִסְבִיבוֹתֵינוּ:
ה עַד־מָה יְהוָה תֶּאֱנַף
לָנֶצַח
תִּבְעַר כְּמוֹ־אֵשׁ קִנְאָתֶךָ:
ו שְׁפֹךְ חֲמָתְךָ אֶל־הַגּוֹיִם
אֲשֶׁר לֹא־יְדָעוּךָ
וְעַל מַמְלָכוֹת
אֲשֶׁר בְּשִׁמְךָ לֹא קָרָאוּ:

Chapter 79

1 A Psalm of Asaph.
God,
nations have entered into Your inheritance;
they have defiled
the Sanctuary of Your holiness,
they have made Jerusalem into heaps of ruins.
2 They have given the corpse of Your servants
as food to the birds of the heaven;
the flesh of Your devoted ones
to the beasts of the earth.
3 They have shed their blood like water,
round about Jerusalem,
with no one to bury them.
4 We were a humiliation to our neighbors,
an object of scorn and derision
to those around us.
5 How long, Adonoy, will You be angry?
Forever?
Will Your jealousy burn like fire?
6 Pour out Your wrath upon the nations
that know You not,
and upon the kingdoms
that do not call upon Your Name.

ז כִּי אָכַל אֶת־יַעֲקֹב	7 For they have devoured Jacob,
וְאֶת־נָוֵהוּ הֵשַׁמּוּ׃	and His habitation they have laid waste.
ח אַל־תִּזְכָּר־לָנוּ	8 Remember not against us
עֲוֺנֹת רִאשֹׁנִים	the sins of our ancestors;
מַהֵר יְקַדְּמוּנוּ רַחֲמֶיךָ	let Your compassion come swiftly toward us,
כִּי דַלּוֹנוּ מְאֹד׃	for we have been brought very low.
ט עָזְרֵנוּ ׀ אֱלֹהֵי יִשְׁעֵנוּ	9 Help us, God of our deliverance,
עַל־דְּבַר כְּבוֹד־שְׁמֶךָ	for the sake of the glory of Your Name;
וְהַצִּילֵנוּ וְכַפֵּר עַל־חַטֹּאתֵינוּ	save us and atone our sins,
לְמַעַן שְׁמֶךָ׃	for the sake of Your Name.
י לָמָּה ׀ יֹאמְרוּ הַגּוֹיִם	10 Why should the nations say:
אַיֵּה אֱלֹהֵיהֶם	"Where is their God?"
יִוָּדַע בַּגּוֹיִם	Let it be known among the nations
לְעֵינֵינוּ	before our eyes,
נִקְמַת דַּם־עֲבָדֶיךָ הַשָּׁפוּךְ׃	the avenging of the spilt blood of Your servants.
יא תָּבוֹא לְפָנֶיךָ	11 Let come before You
אֶנְקַת אָסִיר	the groaning of the prisoner;
כְּגֹדֶל זְרוֹעֲךָ	according to the greatness of Your power
הוֹתֵר בְּנֵי תְמוּתָה׃	set free those condemned to die.
יב וְהָשֵׁב לִשְׁכֵנֵינוּ שִׁבְעָתַיִם	12 And render to our neighbors sevenfold
אֶל־חֵיקָם	into their bosom,
חֶרְפָּתָם	their humiliation
אֲשֶׁר	with which they thought
חֵרְפוּךָ	to humiliate You,
אֲדֹנָי׃	my Master.
יג וַאֲנַחְנוּ עַמְּךָ ׀	13 And we, Your people,
וְצֹאן מַרְעִיתֶךָ	the sheep of Your pasture,
נוֹדֶה לְּךָ לְעוֹלָם	will give thanks to You forever,
לְדֹר וָדֹר	from generation to generation
נְסַפֵּר תְּהִלָּתֶךָ׃	we will recount Your praise.

פרק פ Chapter 80

Weekly Cycle	Monthly Cycle	Book Number
Wednesday	16th day of the month	Book 3

Author

אָסָף—Asaf—a composer of several psalms and patriarch of a family of singers in the Beit HaMikdash (Temple).

Genre

Psalm of Communal Lament – This psalm focuses on expressing deep sorrow for the travails of a nation and as a group asking for God's blessing or intervention.

Chapter Summary

Asaf composed this psalm as a prayer for the redemption of the exiles. He reminds the Jewish people of their earlier glory and closeness to God, assuring them that they will one day be restored.

This psalm consists of twenty verses, subdivided into three parts. The first verse serves as a heading. Verses 4, 8, and 20 are a refrain; each refrain builds upon the previous one by the addition of a description and appellation of God; verse 4 refers to "Elokim"—"God", verse 8 to "Elokim Tzeva'ot"—"God of Hosts", and verse 20 to "Hashem Elokim Tzeva'ot"— "Adonoy, God of Hosts".

In verses 2 & 3, Asaf calls upon God to shine forth and bring deliverance.

In verses 5-7, he laments: "How long?". Just how long will God reject the prayers of His people and not answer them?

In verses 9-19, the psalmist expresses his prayer through a simile in which Israel is compared to a vine, and God is compared to the one who plants and nurtures it. Asaf concludes his prayer by spelling out that the subject of the parable is man.

Introductory Words

לַמְנַצֵּחַ—Lamnatsei'ach—To the Conductor

מִזְמוֹר—Mizmor—Musical Accompaniment

Musical Instrument

אֶל שֹׁשַׁנִּים—El Shoshanim—a musical instrument that looked like a bell with petals, likening it to a lily or a rose.

Shimush Tehillim - When to Say

To avoid idol worship—Verse 19 states: "Thereby we will not turn back from You, revive us and we will invoke Your Name."

Bells - Shoshanim

Where in the Siddur

Recited on the third day of Passover in some traditions.
Recited on the second day of Sukkot in some traditions.

Biblical Personalities

אֶפְרַיִם—Ephraim, בִּנְיָמִן—Binyamin—Benjamin and מְנַשֶּׁה—Menasheh—three of the tribes of Israel. Menasheh and Ephraim were the children of Yosef (Joseph), and grandsons of Rachel; Binyamin was the younger brother of Yosef, and son of Rachel.

יוֹסֵף—Yosef—Joseph—the son of Jacob and Rachel. As second in command to Pharaoh, he sustained his brothers while they were in Egypt and was therefore rewarded in kind. Instead of receiving only one share in the land of Israel, as did his brothers, each of his sons, Ephraim and Menasheh, received a full share. It is also believed that the first Mashiach (Messiah) will be from the tribe of Joseph, to be followed by Mashiach from the tribe of Judah.

Biblical Places

מִצְרַיִם—Mitzrayim—Egypt—the land where Israel was enslaved until God sent Moses to redeem them. Egyptian society ran contrary to many of the ideals of the Torah. The Israelite king is thus specifically warned not to amass calvalry, lest he be tempted to return his nation to Egypt.

פֶּרֶק פ			**Chapter 80**
לַמְנַצֵּחַ	א	1	To the Chief Musician,
אֶל־שֹׁשַׁנִּים			to the shoshanim
עֵדוּת לְאָסָף מִזְמוֹר:			a testimony, a Psalm of Asaph.
רֹעֵה יִשְׂרָאֵל ׀ הַאֲזִינָה	ב	2	Shepherd of Israel, give ear
נֹהֵג כַּצֹּאן יוֹסֵף			You Who leads Joseph like a flock,
יֹשֵׁב הַכְּרוּבִים			You Who are enthroned upon the Cherubim
הוֹפִיעָה:			shine forth [with Your might.]
לִפְנֵי אֶפְרַיִם ׀ וּבִנְיָמִן	ג	3	Before Ephraim and Benjamin
וּמְנַשֶּׁה			and Manasseh
עוֹרְרָה אֶת־גְּבוּרָתֶךָ			stir up Your might
וּלְכָה לִישֻׁעָתָה לָּנוּ:			for it is [fitting] for You to deliver us.
אֱלֹהִים הֲשִׁיבֵנוּ	ד	4	God, lead us back
וְהָאֵר פָּנֶיךָ			and cause Your face to shine
וְנִוָּשֵׁעָה:			and [thus] will we be delivered.
יְהוָה אֱלֹהִים צְבָאוֹת	ה	5	Adonoy, God of Hosts,
עַד־מָתַי עָשַׁנְתָּ			how long will You be angry
בִּתְפִלַּת עַמֶּךָ:			[ignoring] the prayer of Your people?
הֶאֱכַלְתָּם לֶחֶם דִּמְעָה	ו	6	You have fed them the bread of tears,

וַתַּשְׁקֵמוֹ בִּדְמָעוֹת
שָׁלִישׁ׃

and You have made them drink tears
in large measures.

ז תְּשִׂימֵנוּ מָדוֹן
לִשְׁכֵנֵינוּ
וְאֹיְבֵינוּ יִלְעֲגוּ־לָמוֹ׃

7 You made us a target of strife
for our neighbors,
and our enemies mock [You] as they please.

ח אֱלֹהִים צְבָאוֹת הֲשִׁיבֵנוּ
וְהָאֵר פָּנֶיךָ
וְנִוָּשֵׁעָה׃

8 God of Hosts, lead us back,
and cause Your Presence to shine
and [thus] shall we be delivered.

ט גֶּפֶן מִמִּצְרַיִם תַּסִּיעַ
תְּגָרֵשׁ גּוֹיִם וַתִּטָּעֶהָ׃

9 A vine out of Egypt You brought,
You drove out the nations and planted it.

י פִּנִּיתָ לְפָנֶיהָ
וַתַּשְׁרֵשׁ שָׁרָשֶׁיהָ וַתְּמַלֵּא־אָרֶץ׃

10 You cleared a place before it,
and it took root and filled the land.

יא כָּסּוּ הָרִים
צִלָּהּ
וַעֲנָפֶיהָ אַרְזֵי־אֵל׃

11 The mountains were covered
with its shadow,
and its branches became mighty cedars.

יב תְּשַׁלַּח קְצִירֶהָ עַד־יָם
וְאֶל־נָהָר יוֹנְקוֹתֶיהָ׃

12 It stretched its branches until the sea,
and to the river its shoots.

יג לָמָּה פָּרַצְתָּ גְדֵרֶיהָ
וְאָרוּהָ כָּל־עֹבְרֵי דָרֶךְ׃

13 Why have You then broken down its fences,
so that all wayfarers pluck its fruit?

יד יְכַרְסְמֶנָּה חֲזִיר מִיָּעַר
וְזִיז שָׂדַי יִרְעֶנָּה׃

14 The boar of the forest ravages it,
and the wild fowl of the field feed upon it.

טו אֱלֹהִים צְבָאוֹת שׁוּב־נָא
הַבֵּט מִשָּׁמַיִם וּרְאֵה
וּפְקֹד גֶּפֶן זֹאת׃

15 God of Hosts, do return, we beseech You;
look down from heaven, and behold,
and be mindful of this vine.

טז וְכַנָּה
אֲשֶׁר־נָטְעָה יְמִינֶךָ
וְעַל־בֵּן
אִמַּצְתָּה לָּךְ׃

16 And of the foundation
which Your right hand has planted,
and upon the son
whom You strengthened for Yourself.

יז שְׂרֻפָה בָאֵשׁ כְּסוּחָה
מִגַּעֲרַת פָּנֶיךָ יֹאבֵדוּ׃

17 It is burned with fire, it is cut down,
at the rebuke of Your Presence they perish.

יח תְּהִי־יָדְךָ
עַל־אִישׁ יְמִינֶךָ
עַל־בֶּן־אָדָם
אִמַּצְתָּ לָּךְ׃

18 May Your hand rest
upon the man of Your right hand,
upon the son of man
whom You strengthened for Yourself.

יט וְלֹא־נָסוֹג מִמֶּךָּ
תְּחַיֵּנוּ וּבְשִׁמְךָ נִקְרָא׃

19 Thereby we will not turn back from You,
revive us and we will invoke Your Name.

כ יְהוָה אֱלֹהִים צְבָאוֹת הֲשִׁיבֵנוּ
הָאֵר פָּנֶיךָ
וְנִוָּשֵׁעָה׃

20 Adonoy, God of Hosts, lead us back
cause Your presence to shine
and [thus] will we be delivered.

פרק פא Chapter 81

Weekly Cycle	Monthly Cycle	Book Number
Wednesday	16th day of the month	Book 3

Author

אָסָף—Asaf—a composer of several psalms and patriarch of a family of singers in the Beit HaMikdash (Temple).

When & Why

This psalm was written by Assaf. It was read as the the Song of the Day in the Mussaf prayer on Rosh HaShanah in the Temple.

Genre

Psalm of Wisdom – This psalm contains teachings and wise advice and is meant to instruct people on how to live a Godly life.

Chapter Summary

Asaf speaks here about Rosh HaShanah and the traditional blowing of the Shofar on that day. He also celebrates the end of the Israelites' enslavement in Egypt, which, according to tradition, took place on Rosh HaShanah.

This psalm consists of seventeen verses, subdivided into two parts. The first verse serves as a heading.

In verses 2-6, the psalmist calls to the people of Israel, encouraging them to sing aloud and make joyful noise for God; to play musical instruments and to blow the Shofar, in accordance with God's command to Israel.

In verses 7-17, God, as it were, rebukes Israel, reminding them of the deliverance from Egypt, and warns them not to worship idols. He further reminds them that they have not listened to His words and that He has therefore removed His providence from them. He concludes with a wish that Israel will once again hearken to God's voice and will subsequently merit salvation and blessing.

Introductory Words

לַמְנַצֵּחַ—Lamnatsei'ach—To the Conductor

Musical Instrument

גִּתִּית—Gittis—A Stringed Instrument; perhaps from the city of Gath

תֹּף—Tof—A Drum or Tambourine

כִּנּוֹר—Kinor—A Small Handheld Harp - played with a plecturm (pick)

נֶבֶל—Nevel—A Large Handheld Lyre - played by plucking with fingers

שׁוֹפָר—Shofar—A Ram's Horn

Technical Terminology

סֶלָה—Selah—While its meaning is unclear, the most familiar opinion is that it is a musical notation, instructing the Levitical orchestra to pause its singing and playing of instruments. Alternatively, "Selah" may mean "everlasting".

Shimush Tehillim - When to Say

For protecting oneself from worshipping idols—Verse 10 states: "Let no strange god be within you, nor bow before a foreign god."

Where in the Siddur

Recited as the Shir Shel Yom (Psalm of the Day) of Thursday.
Recited on Rosh HaShanah in some traditions.
Recited on the sixth day of Sukkot in some traditions.
Verse 2 is found in Mishnah, Tamid 7:4.
Verse 3 is found in the blessings before the Shema on the second day of Rosh HaShanah.
Verses 4 & 5 comprise the introductory verses of the daytime Kiddush on Rosh HaShanah.
Verses 4 & 5 are also found in the Shofarot section of Musaf of Rosh HaShanah, as well as immediately prior to the Amidah (Silent Meditation) of Ma'ariv (evening service) of Rosh HaShanah.
Verse 11 is found in Hoshi'a et Amecha—one of the paragraphs of Pesukei Dezimra (Verses of Praise introducing the Shacharit morning service).

Biblical Personalities

יַעֲקֹב—Yaakov—Jacob—also called Yisrael—Israel, the third patriarch, recognized as the father of the twelve tribes of Israel. He was the twin brother of Eisav, and married to Leah and Rachel.
יהוֹסֵף—Joseph—Yehosef - the son of Jacob and the father of Ephraim and Menasheh. Joseph feared God's Name and refused to give in to the wiles of Potiphar's wife. Because of this, he merited that the letter ה from God's name be added to his name, making it Yehoseph.

Biblical People

יִשְׂרָאֵל—Yisrael—The Nation of Israel

Biblical Places

מֵי מְרִיבָה—Mei Merivah—Waters of Meribah—the site at which the Israelites quarreled with Moses about the lack of water, and Moses in turn rebuked them for testing God.
מִצְרָיִם—Mitzrayim—Egypt—the land where Israel was enslaved until God sent Moses to redeem them. Egyptian society ran contrary to many of the ideals of the Torah. The Israelite king is thus specifically warned not to amass calvalry, lest he be tempted to return his nation to Egypt.

Biblical Holiday

(ראש) חֹדֶשׁ—(Rosh) Chodesh—the first day of the lunar month, when the moon begins its new cycle. In Temple times, it was a holy, festive day, similar in significance to Shabbat and Festivals.

Talmud on Tehillim

Verse 2: "הַרְנִינוּ לֵאלֹהִים עוּזֵּנוּ, הָרִיעוּ לֵאלוֹקֵי יַעֲקֹב"—"Sing joyously to God, our strength, shout for joy to the God of Jacob."
The Talmud, Rosh Hashana 30b, teaches that the Levi'im (Levites) sang this psalm during the service of the Korban Musaf (additional sacrificial offering of Shabbat and Festivals) of Rosh HaShanah.

Verse 7: "הֲסִירוֹתִי מִסֵּבֶל שִׁכְמוֹ כַּפָּיו מִדּוּד תַּעֲבֹרְנָה"—"From the burden I removed his shoulder, his hands were removed from the cauldron."

The Talmud, Sukkot 55a, teaches that this psalm was sung in the Beit HaMikdash (Temple) on the sixth day of Chol HaMo'eid Sukkot (Intermediate days of Sukkot).

Verse 10: "לֹא יִהְיֶה בְךָ אֵל זָר"—"Let no strange god be within you."

The Talmud, Shabbat 105b, offers a less literal, yet more profound, interpretation of this phrase: You shall not have within yourself a strange god. This verse, then, is not warning us against worshipping external idols. Rather, it is referring to the yeitzer hara (evil inclination), admonishing us to search for it within ourselves and to root it out.

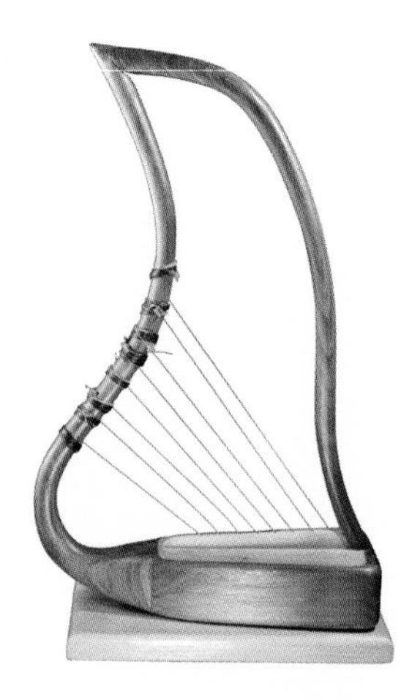

Kinor - Harp

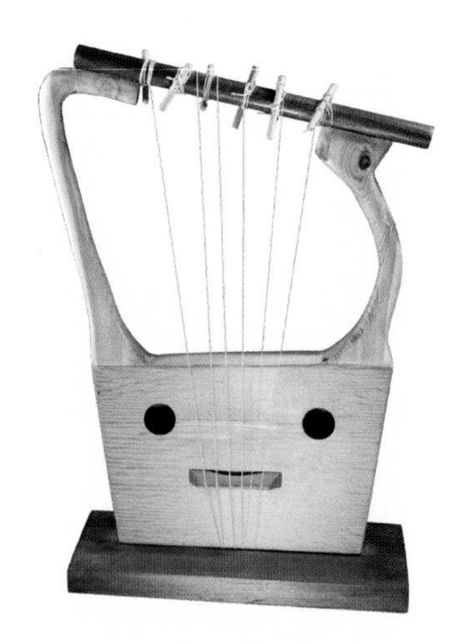

Nevel - Lyre

פֶּרֶק פא

א לַמְנַצֵּחַ ׀
עַל־הַגִּתִּית לְאָסָף׃
ב הַרְנִינוּ לֵאלֹהִים עוּזֵּנוּ
הָרִיעוּ לֵאלֹהֵי יַעֲקֹב׃
ג שְׂאוּ־זִמְרָה וּתְנוּ־תֹף
כִּנּוֹר נָעִים עִם־נָבֶל׃
ד תִּקְעוּ בַחֹדֶשׁ שׁוֹפָר
בַּכֵּסֶה לְיוֹם חַגֵּנוּ׃
ה כִּי חֹק לְיִשְׂרָאֵל הוּא
מִשְׁפָּט לֵאלֹהֵי יַעֲקֹב׃
ו עֵדוּת ׀ בִּיהוֹסֵף שָׂמוֹ
בְּצֵאתוֹ עַל־אֶרֶץ מִצְרָיִם
שְׂפַת לֹא־יָדַעְתִּי אֶשְׁמָע׃

Chapter 81

1 To the Chief Musician—
upon the Gittis, a Psalm of Asaf:
2 Sing joyously to God, our strength,
shout for joy to the God of Jacob.
3 Take up the hymn, sound the drum,
the pleasant harp and the lute.
4 Blow the shofar on Rosh Chodesh,
at the appointed time for our feast day.
5 For it is a statute for Israel,
a [day of] judgment of the God of Jacob.
6 As a testimony for Yehosef, He ordained it
when he went out over the land of Egypt,
[where] an unfamiliar language I heard.

ז הֲסִירוֹתִי מִסֵּבֶל שִׁכְמוֹ
כַּפָּיו מִדּוּד תַּעֲבֹרְנָה׃

7 From the burden I removed his shoulder,
his hands were removed from the cauldron.

ח בַּצָּרָה קָרָאתָ וָאֲחַלְּצֶךָּ
אֶעֶנְךָ
בְּסֵתֶר
רַעַם
אֶבְחָנְךָ עַל־מֵי מְרִיבָה סֶלָה׃

8 In distress you called out, and I released you,
I answered you
[though you called] in secret
[I answered you] thunderously;
I tested you at the waters of Merivah, Selah.

ט שְׁמַע עַמִּי וְאָעִידָה בָּךְ
יִשְׂרָאֵל אִם־תִּשְׁמַע־לִי׃

9 Hear, My people, I will testify about you,
Israel, if you would just listen to Me.

י לֹא־יִהְיֶה בְךָ אֵל זָר
וְלֹא תִשְׁתַּחֲוֶה לְאֵל נֵכָר׃

10 Let no strange god be within you,
nor bow before a foreign god.

Shofar - Ram's Horn

Tof - Drum

יא אָנֹכִי | יְהֹוָה אֱלֹהֶיךָ
הַמַּעַלְךָ מֵאֶרֶץ מִצְרָיִם
הַרְחֶב־פִּיךָ וַאֲמַלְאֵהוּ׃

11 I am Adonoy, your God,
Who brought you up from the land of Egypt,
open your mouth wide, and I will fill it.

יב וְלֹא־שָׁמַע עַמִּי לְקוֹלִי
וְיִשְׂרָאֵל לֹא־אָבָה לִי׃

12 But My people did not heed My voice,
and Israel did not want Me.

יג וָאֲשַׁלְּחֵהוּ בִּשְׁרִירוּת לִבָּם
יֵלְכוּ בְּמוֹעֲצוֹתֵיהֶם׃

13 So I sent them to follow their heart's desires,
let them follow their own devices.

יד לוּ עַמִּי שֹׁמֵעַ לִי
יִשְׂרָאֵל בִּדְרָכַי יְהַלֵּכוּ׃

14 If only My people would heed Me,
if Israel would walk in My ways.

טו כִּמְעַט אוֹיְבֵיהֶם אַכְנִיעַ
וְעַל צָרֵיהֶם אָשִׁיב יָדִי׃

15 I would immediately subdue their enemies,
and turn My hand against their tormentors.

טז מְשַׂנְאֵי יְהֹוָה
יְכַחֲשׁוּ־לוֹ
וִיהִי עִתָּם לְעוֹלָם׃

16 Those who cause hate of Adonoy
deceive [pretend obedience to] Him,
but their time (of punishment) will be forever.

יז וַיַּאֲכִילֵהוּ
מֵחֵלֶב חִטָּה
וּמִצּוּר
דְּבַשׁ אַשְׂבִּיעֶךָ׃

17 But He would feed him (Israel)
from the cream of the wheat,
and from the rock,
I would sate you with honey.

פרק פב Chapter 82

Weekly Cycle	Monthly Cycle	Book Number
Wednesday	16th day of the month	Book 3

Author
אָסָף—Asaf—a composer of several psalms and patriarch of a family of singers in the Beit HaMikdash (Temple).

When & Why
Assaf wrote this psalm about judges who were cheating the poor and letting people get away with theft.

Genre
Psalm of Communal Lament - This psalm focuses on expressing deep sorrow for the travails of a nation and as a group asking for God's blessing or intervention.

Chapter Summary
Asaf describes how God stands in the Divine Assembly, watching over the judges to see if they in fact administer true justice. Accordingly, this psalm warns against perversion of the law.

This psalm consists of eight verses.
In verse 1, the psalmist speaks of God as standing in judgment.
In verses 2-7, he rebukes judges who judge corruptly and do not fulfill their duty.
In verse 8, he concludes by asking God to rise and judge the earth, for He will rule over all of the nations.

Introductory Words
מִזְמוֹר—Mizmor—Musical Accompaniment

Technical Terminology
סֶלָה—Selah—While its meaning is unclear, the most familiar opinion is that it is a musical notation, instructing the Levitical orchestra to pause its singing and playing of instruments. Alternatively, "Selah" may mean "everlasting".

Shimush Tehillim - When to Say
For success on a mission—Verse 4 states: "Rescue the lowly and the needy, save them from the hand of the wicked."

Where in the Siddur
Recited as the Shir Shel Yom (Psalm of the Day) of Tuesday.
Recited in some congregations on Hoshana Rabbah (the seventh day of Sukkot).

Talmud on Tehillim
Verse 1: "אֱלֹקִים נִצָּב בַּעֲדַת קֵל"—"God stands in the congregation of the Almighty."

The Talmud, Berachot 6a, deduces from this verse that the Shechinah (Divine Presence) is always present in the synagogue. The Talmud further explains that if three judges are sitting together and learn Torah, the Shechinah is with them.

Tzelzelim - Cymbals

פֶּרֶק פב

א מִזְמוֹר לְאָסָף
אֱלֹהִים נִצָּב
בַּעֲדַת־אֵל
בְּקֶרֶב אֱלֹהִים יִשְׁפֹּט:
ב עַד־מָתַי תִּשְׁפְּטוּ־עָוֶל
וּפְנֵי רְשָׁעִים תִּשְׂאוּ־סֶלָה:
ג שִׁפְטוּ־דַל וְיָתוֹם
עָנִי וָרָשׁ הַצְדִּיקוּ:
ד פַּלְּטוּ־דַל וְאֶבְיוֹן
מִיַּד רְשָׁעִים הַצִּילוּ:
ה לֹא יָדְעוּ | וְלֹא יָבִינוּ
בַּחֲשֵׁכָה יִתְהַלָּכוּ
יִמּוֹטוּ כָּל־מוֹסְדֵי אָרֶץ:
ו אֲנִי־אָמַרְתִּי אֱלֹהִים אַתֶּם
וּבְנֵי עֶלְיוֹן כֻּלְּכֶם:
ז אָכֵן כְּאָדָם תְּמוּתוּן
וּכְאַחַד הַשָּׂרִים תִּפֹּלוּ:
ח קוּמָה אֱלֹהִים שָׁפְטָה הָאָרֶץ
כִּי־אַתָּה תִנְחַל בְּכָל־הַגּוֹיִם:

Chapter 82

1 A Psalm of Asaf
God stands
in the congregation of the Almighty,
in the midst of the judges He gives judgment.
2 How long will you judge lawlessly
and show partiality to the wicked, Selah?
3 Render justice to the lowly and the orphan,
deal righteously with the poor and destitute.
4 Rescue the lowly and the needy,
save them from the hand of the wicked.
5 They neither know nor understand,
they walk along in darkness,
all the foundations of the earth are shaken.
6 I had said "You are godlike beings,
all of you sons of the Most High."
7 Nevertheless, you shall die like men,
and fall like one of the princes.
8 Arise, God, judge the earth,
for You will inherit all the nations.

פרק פג Chapter 83

Weekly Cycle	Monthly Cycle	Book Number
Wednesday	17th day of the month	Book 3

Author

אָסָף—Asaf—a composer of several psalms and patriarch of a family of singers in the Beit HaMikdash (Temple).

When & Why

Assaf wrote this psalm about the massive war that was waged by Jehoshaphat against the armies of Ammon, Moab, and many other nations.

Genre

Psalm of Communal Lament - This psalm focuses on expressing deep sorrow for the travails of a nation and as a group asking for God's blessing or intervention.

Chapter Summary

In this psalm, Asaf addresses all of the locations of the future exile of the Jewish people. He asserts that the hatred of the nations for Israel is rooted in their hatred of God himself.

This psalm consists of nineteen verses, subdivided into four parts. The first verse serves as a heading.

In verse 2, the psalmist appeals to God to not be silent.

In verses 3-9, he details the plot of the enemies to destroy all the people of Israel, and then lists specific enemy nations.

In verses 10-16, he prays for the downfall of these enemies in the days of the Judges, by wind, fire and earthquakes.

In verses 17-19, he concludes his prayer with the hope that the enemies will be ashamed, and will thus come to know that there is but one God who rules over the entire earth.

Introductory Words

מִזְמוֹר—Mizmor—Musical Accompaniment

שִׁיר—Shir—Song

Shimush Tehillim - When to Say

For success in war—Verse 2 states: "God, do not hold Your silence; be not silent and be not still Almighty."

Where in the Siddur

Recited as one of the paragraphs of the Selichot (Penitential Service) of Tzom Gedaliah (Fast of Gedaliah), Asarah BeTeiveit (Fast of the Tenth of Teiveit), Ta'anit Esther (Fast of Esther), and Shivah Asar BeTammuz (Fast of the Seventeenth of Tammuz).

Biblical People

עֲמָלֵק—Amalek—a grandson of Esau, brother of Jacob. Immediately following the Exodus, the Amelekites attacked the weakest of the Jewish people, those trailing behind. God showed no mercy on them and declared that they and their descendants be wiped out.

All those listed below were enemies of Israel.

עַמּוֹן—Ammon—descendents of Lot, nephew of Avraham, located to the east of the Jordan River.

אַשּׁוּר—Ashur—Assyria—the nation which exiled the Ten Northern Tribes of Israel.

אֱדוֹם—Edom—descendants of Esau, brother of Jacob. Their sibling rivalry persisted for centuries, most strongly expressed when the Edomites looted Jerusalem as it was being overrun by the Babylonians.

גְּבָל—Geval—Gebal—a Phoenician city located on the coastline of the Mediterranean Sea.

הַגְרִים—Hagrim—Hagrites—an offshoot of the Ishmaelites, they inhabited the regions of Jetur, Naphish and Nodab to the east of Gilead. Their name is derived from Hagar, mother of Yishama'eil and wife of Avraham.

מִדְיָן—Midian—descendants of Midian, son of Avraham and Keturah.

מוֹאָב—Moab—located on the eastern shore of the Dead Sea.

פְּלֶשֶׁת (פְּלִשְׁתִּים)—Philistia (Phillistines)—a nation located on the southwestern coast of Israel.

בְּנֵי-לוֹט—The Sons of Lot—perhaps an additional reference to Ammon and Moab mentioned above, or a reference to other descendents of Lot, nephew of Avraham.

צוֹר—Tzor—Tyre—located on the southwestern coast of Lebanon, just to the north of Israel, particularly known for the production of a rare Tyrian royal purple used for the nobility. It was also the source of techeilet, a dye referred to in the Torah, used to color the tzizit fringes of the Tallit and other four cornered garments.

יִשְׁמְעֵאלִים—Yishme'eilim—Ishmaelites—descendants of Ishmael, son of Avraham and Hagar, a nomadic people who had an adversarial relationship with the Israelites which continued through the time of the Beit HaMikdash (Temple) in Jerusalem.

Biblical Personalities

יָבִין—Jabin—king of Chatzor, an enemy of Israel.

עֹרֵב—Oreb and זְאֵב—Ze'eb—two princes who led the Mideanites. They raided Israel with the use of swift camels, but were defeated by Gideon, Judge of Israel. Many Midianites perished in this battle.

סִיסְרָא—Sisera—a commander of the Canaanite army of King Jabin of Chatzor, mentioned in the Book of Judges. After being defeated by Barak, Sisera was killed by Yaeil (Jael), who hammered a tent peg into his temple.

זֶבַח—Zevach—Zebah and צַלְמֻנָּע—Zalmunna—two kings who led a vast host of Midianites who invaded Israel, and over whom Gideon gained a great and decisive victory.

Biblical Places

עֵין-דֹּאר—Ein Dor—located between the Hill of Moreh and Mount Tabor in Eimek Yizre'eil—the Jezreel Valley.

נַחַל קִישׁוֹן—Nachal Kishon—The Brook of Kishon—located in and running through northern Israel, where the Prophetess Devorah triumphed in the war between the Israelites and Chatzor.

פרק פג

א שִׁיר מִזְמוֹר לְאָסָף׃
ב אֱלֹהִים אַל־דֳּמִי־לָךְ
אַל־תֶּחֱרַשׁ וְאַל־תִּשְׁקֹט אֵל׃
ג כִּי־הִנֵּה אוֹיְבֶיךָ יֶהֱמָיוּן
וּמְשַׂנְאֶיךָ
נָשְׂאוּ רֹאשׁ׃
ד עַל־עַמְּךָ יַעֲרִימוּ סוֹד
וְיִתְיָעֲצוּ
עַל־צְפוּנֶיךָ׃
ה אָמְרוּ
לְכוּ וְנַכְחִידֵם מִגּוֹי
וְלֹא־יִזָּכֵר שֵׁם־יִשְׂרָאֵל עוֹד׃
ו כִּי נוֹעֲצוּ
לֵב יַחְדָּו
עָלֶיךָ בְּרִית יִכְרֹתוּ׃
ז אָהֳלֵי אֱדוֹם וְיִשְׁמְעֵאלִים
מוֹאָב וְהַגְרִים׃
ח גְּבָל וְעַמּוֹן וַעֲמָלֵק
פְּלֶשֶׁת עִם־יֹשְׁבֵי צוֹר׃
ט גַּם־אַשּׁוּר נִלְוָה עִמָּם
הָיוּ זְרוֹעַ
לִבְנֵי־לוֹט סֶלָה׃
י עֲשֵׂה־לָהֶם כְּמִדְיָן
כְּסִיסְרָא כְיָבִין
בְּנַחַל קִישׁוֹן׃
יא נִשְׁמְדוּ בְעֵין־דֹּאר
הָיוּ דֹּמֶן לָאֲדָמָה׃
יב שִׁיתֵמוֹ נְדִיבֵמוֹ
כְּעֹרֵב וְכִזְאֵב
וּכְזֶבַח וּכְצַלְמֻנָּע כָּל־נְסִיכֵמוֹ׃
יג אֲשֶׁר אָמְרוּ נִירְשָׁה לָּנוּ
אֵת נְאוֹת אֱלֹהִים׃
יד אֱלֹהַי שִׁיתֵמוֹ כַגַּלְגַּל
כְּקַשׁ לִפְנֵי־רוּחַ׃
טו כְּאֵשׁ תִּבְעַר־יָעַר
וּכְלֶהָבָה תְּלַהֵט הָרִים׃
טז כֵּן תִּרְדְּפֵם בְּסַעֲרֶךָ

Chapter 83

1 A song, a Psalm of Asaph.
2 God, do not hold Your silence;
be not silent and be not still Almighty.
3 For behold, Your enemies are in an uproar
and those who hate You
have lifted up their head.
4 Against Your people they plot deceitfully,
and they conspire against
those sheltered by You.
5 They say
"Come, let us cut them off from nationhood,
let Israel's name be remembered no more"
6 For they conspire together
with a unanimous heart,
against You they make a covenant.
7 The tents of Edom and the Ishmaelites;
Moab and the Hagrites.
8 Gebal, and Ammon, and Amalek;
Philistia with the inhabitants of Tyre.
9 Even Assyria is joined with them,
they become a supporting arm
to the children of Lot, Selah.
10 Do unto them as with Midian;
as to Sisera, as to Jabin,
at the river bed of Kishon.
11 They were destroyed at Ein Dor;
they became dung for the soil.
12 Make their nobles,
like Oreb and Zeeb,
and like Zebach and Zalmuna, all their princes.
13 Who said, "Let us inherit for ourselves
the pleasant habitations of God."
14 My God, make them like whirling chaff,
like straw before the wind.
15 Like fire that burns the forest,
and like a flame that ignites the mountains.
16 So pursue them with Your tempest,

	וּבְסוּפָתְךָ תְבַהֲלֵם:	and terrify them with Your storm.
יז / 17	מַלֵּא פְנֵיהֶם קָלוֹן	Fill their faces with shame,
	וִיבַקְשׁוּ שִׁמְךָ יְהוָה:	then they will seek Your Name, Adonoy.
יח / 18	יֵבֹשׁוּ וְיִבָּהֲלוּ עֲדֵי־עַד	Let them be ashamed and terrified, forever;
	וְיַחְפְּרוּ וְיֹאבֵדוּ:	and let them be humiliated and perish.
יט / 19	וְיֵדְעוּ כִּי־אַתָּה	Then they will know that You,
	שִׁמְךָ יְהוָה לְבַדֶּךָ	Whose Name is Adonoy, are alone,
	עֶלְיוֹן עַל־כָּל־הָאָרֶץ:	the Most High over all the earth.

פרק פד — Chapter 84

Weekly Cycle	Monthly Cycle	Book Number
Wednesday	17th day of the month	Book 3

Author

בְּנֵי-קֹרַח—Sons of Korach—Korach rebelled against his cousins Moshe and Aharon (Moses and Aaron) and challenged their authority. Korach and his cohorts perished in the aftermath of the rebellion, yet his sons, who repented, survived.

When & Why

The sons of Korach wrote this psalm prophetically about the exile from Israel and the people of Israel's longing to reconnect to God in their homeland.

Genre

Psalm of Praise – This is a psalm of celebration, often the result of a victory. It declares God's goodness and urges all of creation to worship.

Psalm of Zion - This psalm glorifies God's city and His holy mount in which He has placed His abode.

Chapter Summary

The composers of this psalm express their own personal yearning, as well as that of all exiles, for the redemption of Zion and rebuilding of the Beit HaMikdash (Holy Temple). The sons of Korach further pray for the knowledge to fathom the glory of the Creator to the utmost limit of human intelligence.

This psalm consists of thirteen verses, subdivided into four parts. The first verse serves as a heading.

In verses 2-4, the psalmists express their yearning for the Beit HaMikdash (Temple).

In verses 5-8, they describe the good fortune of those who dwell in the house of God and those who come on pilgrimages before Him.

In verses 9-10, they request that their prayer be heard and that God extend His protection to the king of Israel.

In verses 11-13, they conclude by declaring that it is good to be in the house of God and to trust in Him.

Introductory Words

לַמְנַצֵּחַ—Lamnatsei'ach—To the Conductor

מִזְמוֹר—Mizmor—Musical Accompaniment

Musical Instrument

גִּתִּית—Gittis—A Stringed Instrument; perhaps from the city of Gath

Technical Terminology

סֶלָה—Selah—While its meaning is unclear, the most familiar opinion is that it is a musical notation, instructing the Levitical orchestra to pause its singing and playing of instruments. Alternatively, "Selah" may mean "everlasting".

Shimush Tehillim - When to Say

For a debilitating disease—Verses 8 & 9 state: "They go from strength to strength, [every one] appears before God in Zion. Adonoy, God of Hosts, hear my prayer, give ear, God of Jacob."

Where in the Siddur

Verse 5 is the first verse of Ashrei, one of the central prayers of Shacharit (morning service) and Minchah (afternoon service).

Verse 13 comprises one of the verses of Vehu Rachum, one of the paragraphs of Pesukei Dezimra (introductory Verses of Praise to Shacharit).

Verse 13 is also found in Uva Letzion, one of the closing prayers of both Shacharit and Ma'ariv (evening service) of Motza'ei Shabbat, as well as in the Motza'ei Shabbat Havdalah service.

Biblical Personalities

יַעֲקֹב—Ya'akov—Jacob—also called Yisrael—Israel, the third patriarch, considered the father of the twelve tribes of Israel. He was the brother of Eisav, and married to Leah and Rachel.

Biblical Places

בֵּית אֱלֹהַי—Beit Elokai—House of My God—a reference to the Beit HaMikdash (Temple) in Jerusalem.

עֵמֶק הַבָּכָא—Eimek Habacha—the Valley of Baca, also called the Valley of Tears (the word "bacha" being a play on the root meaning "cry"). It is thus viewed not only as a place name, but as a state of mind, encouraging one who is going through difficult times to make God a wellspring of hope and encouragment.

צִיּוֹן—Zion—a place name often used as a synonym for Jerusalem. The term Zion originally referred only to the area where a Jebbusite fortress once stood, also the location of the City of David. Zion was later used by prophets and psalmists as another name for Jerusalem.

Talmud on Tehillim

Verse 5: "אַשְׁרֵי יוֹשְׁבֵי בֵיתֶךָ"—"Fortunate are those who dwell in Your house."

The Talmud, Berachot 32b, infers from this verse that one should wait a few moments upon arriving in the synagogue before commencing prayers. The Talmud further elaborates that the early pious and righteous Jews would meditate and ready themselves for "one hour" before and after they prayed, in order to both prepare for prayer and to contemplate what they had gained during prayer.

Verse 8: "יֵלְכוּ מֵחַיִל אֶל חָיִל"—"They go from strength to strength."

The Talmud, Berachot 64a, teaches that "one who leaves a house of prayer and [immediately] enters a house of study, will merit to receive the Shechinah (Divine Presence)."

פֶּרֶק פד

א לַמְנַצֵּחַ
עַל־הַגִּתִּית
לִבְנֵי־קֹרַח מִזְמוֹר:
ב מַה־יְּדִידוֹת מִשְׁכְּנוֹתֶיךָ
יְהוָה צְבָאוֹת:
ג נִכְסְפָה וְגַם־כָּלְתָה | נַפְשִׁי
לְחַצְרוֹת יְהוָה
לִבִּי וּבְשָׂרִי יְרַנְּנוּ
אֶל אֵל־חָי:
ד גַּם־צִפּוֹר | מָצְאָה בַיִת
וּדְרוֹר | קֵן לָהּ
אֲשֶׁר־שָׁתָה אֶפְרֹחֶיהָ
אֶת־מִזְבְּחוֹתֶיךָ
יְהוָה צְבָאוֹת מַלְכִּי וֵאלֹהָי:
ה אַשְׁרֵי
יוֹשְׁבֵי בֵיתֶךָ
עוֹד יְהַלְלוּךָ סֶּלָה:
ו אַשְׁרֵי אָדָם
עוֹז־לוֹ בָךְ
מְסִלּוֹת בִּלְבָבָם:
ז עֹבְרֵי |
בְּעֵמֶק הַבָּכָא
מַעְיָן יְשִׁיתוּהוּ
גַּם־בְּרָכוֹת
יַעְטֶה מוֹרֶה:

Chapter 84

1 To the Chief Musician,
upon the winepress,
a Psalm of the sons of Korach.
2 How beloved are Your dwelling places,
Adonoy of Hosts.
3 My soul yearns and even pines
for the courtyards of Adonoy;
my heart and my flesh will sing for joy
to the living Almighty.
4 Even the bird has found a house,
and the swallow a nest for herself,
where she places her young
on the ruins of Your Altars,
Adonoy of Hosts, my King and my God.
5 Fortunate are those
who dwell in Your house;
may they continue to praise You, Selah.
6 Fortunate is the man
whose strength is in You;
ways [of uprightness are] in his heart.
7 Those who pass through
the Valley of Weeping,
make it into a spring [with their tears];
even with their blessings
they enwrap their Teacher.

	Hebrew	English
ח / 8	יֵלְכוּ מֵחַיִל אֶל־חָיִל	They go from strength to strength,
	יֵרָאֶה אֶל־אֱלֹהִים בְּצִיּוֹן׃	[every one] appears before God in Zion.
ט / 9	יְהוָה אֱלֹהִים צְבָאוֹת	Adonoy, God of Hosts,
	שִׁמְעָה תְפִלָּתִי	hear my prayer,
	הַאֲזִינָה אֱלֹהֵי יַעֲקֹב סֶלָה׃	give ear, God of Jacob, Selah.
י / 10	מָגִנֵּנוּ רְאֵה אֱלֹהִים	Behold our shield [the temple] O' God
	וְהַבֵּט פְּנֵי מְשִׁיחֶךָ׃	and look upon the face of Your annointed.
יא / 11	כִּי טוֹב־יוֹם בַּחֲצֵרֶיךָ	For better a day in Your courtyards
	מֵאָלֶף	than a thousand [days elsewhere],
	בָּחַרְתִּי הִסְתּוֹפֵף	I would rather stand at the threshold
	בְּבֵית אֱלֹהַי	of the House of my God,
	מִדּוּר בְּאָהֳלֵי־רֶשַׁע׃	than to dwell in the tents of wickedness.
יב / 12	כִּי שֶׁמֶשׁ | וּמָגֵן	For [my] sun and [my] shield
	יְהוָה אֱלֹהִים	is Adonoy, God;
	חֵן וְכָבוֹד יִתֵּן יְהוָה	Adonoy bestows favor and glory,
	לֹא יִמְנַע־טוֹב	He will not withhold goodness
	לַהֹלְכִים בְּתָמִים׃	from those who walk wholeheartedly.
יג / 13	יְהוָה צְבָאוֹת	Adonoy of Hosts,
	אַשְׁרֵי אָדָם בֹּטֵחַ בָּךְ׃	fortunate is the man who trusts in You.

Maccabean Menorah Coin

פרק פה Chapter 85

Weekly Cycle	Monthly Cycle	Book Number
Wednesday	17th day of the month	Book 3

Author

בְּנֵי-קֹרַח—Sons of Korach—Korach rebelled against his cousins Moshe and Aharon (Moses and Aaron) and challenged their authority. Korach and his cohorts perished in the aftermath of the rebellion, yet his sons, who repented, survived.

When & Why

The sons of Korach wrote this psalm prophetically about the exile from Israel. In it, they pray to God to return the people of Israel to their homeland.

Genre

Psalm of Communal Lament –This psalm focuses on expressing deep sorrow for the travails of a nation and as a group asking for God's blessing or intervention.

Chapter Summary

The sons of Korach composed this psalm regarding the present exile. It is a plea for the Jewish people's redemption and return to their land. "Will You forever be angry with us?", they boldly declare.

This psalm consists of fourteen verses, subdivided into two parts. The first verse serves as a heading.

In verses 2-8, the sons of Korach offer a prayer of thanks for the salvation that occurred in the past, and proceed with a request regarding the future.

In verses 9-14, God, as it were, responds to the prayer with words of hope.

Introductory Words

לַמְנַצֵּחַ—Lamnatsei'ach—To the Conductor

מִזְמוֹר—Mizmor—Musical Accompaniment

Technical Terminology

סֶלָה—Selah—While its meaning is unclear, the most familiar opinion is that it is a musical notation, instructing the Levitical orchestra to pause its singing and playing of instruments. Alternatively, "Selah" may mean "everlasting".

Shimush Tehillim - When to Say

To find favor in the eyes of a friend—Verses 4 & 5 state: "You have withdrawn all Your wrath, You have turned back from the fierceness of Your anger. Return to us, God of our deliverance, and annul Your anger toward us."

Where in the Siddur

Verse 8 comprises one of the verses of Hoshia et Amecha, a paragraph of Pesukei Dezimra

(introductory Verses of Praise to the Shacharit morning service).
Verse 14 is found in the funeral service.

Biblical Personalities

יַעֲקֹב—Ya'akov—Jacob—also called Yisrael—Israel, the third patriarch, considered the father of the twelve tribes of Israel. He was the brother of Eisav, and married to Leah and Rachel.

פרק פה	**Chapter 85**
א לַמְנַצֵּחַ ׀	1 1. To the Chief Musician,
לִבְנֵי־קֹרַח מִזְמוֹר׃	a Psalm of the sons of Korach.
ב רָצִיתָ יְהֹוָה	2 Adonoy, You have shown favor
אַרְצֶךָ	to Your land,
שַׁבְתָּ שְׁבִית יַעֲקֹב׃	You have returned the captivity of Jacob.
ג נָשָׂאתָ עֲוֹן	3 You have forgiven the iniquity
עַמֶּךָ	of Your people,
כִּסִּיתָ כָל־חַטָּאתָם	You have concealed [pardoned] all their sins,
סֶלָה׃	Selah.
ד אָסַפְתָּ כָל־עֶבְרָתֶךָ	4 You have withdrawn all Your wrath,
הֱשִׁיבוֹתָ	You have turned back
מֵחֲרוֹן אַפֶּךָ׃	from the fierceness of Your anger.
ה שׁוּבֵנוּ אֱלֹהֵי יִשְׁעֵנוּ	5 Return to us, God of our deliverance,
וְהָפֵר כַּעַסְךָ עִמָּנוּ׃	and annul Your anger toward us.
ו הַלְעוֹלָם תֶּאֱנַף־בָּנוּ	6 Will You forever be angry with us?
תִּמְשֹׁךְ אַפְּךָ	Will You draw out Your anger
לְדֹר וָדֹר׃	to all generations?
ז הֲלֹא־אַתָּה תָּשׁוּב תְּחַיֵּנוּ	7 Will You not indeed revive us again
וְעַמְּךָ יִשְׂמְחוּ־בָךְ׃	that Your people may rejoice in You?
ח הַרְאֵנוּ יְהֹוָה חַסְדֶּךָ	8 Show us Your kindness, Adonoy,
וְיֶשְׁעֲךָ תִּתֶּן־לָנוּ׃	and grant us Your salvation.
ט אֶשְׁמְעָה	9 Let me hear
מַה־יְדַבֵּר הָאֵל ׀ יְהֹוָה	what the Almighty, Adonoy will speak,
כִּי ׀ יְדַבֵּר שָׁלוֹם אֶל־עַמּוֹ	for He will speak of peace to His people
וְאֶל־חֲסִידָיו	and to His devoted ones,
וְאַל־יָשׁוּבוּ לְכִסְלָה׃	so that they do not turn back to folly.
י אַךְ ׀ קָרוֹב לִירֵאָיו	10 Near to those who fear Him
יִשְׁעוֹ	is His deliverance,
לִשְׁכֹּן כָּבוֹד בְּאַרְצֵנוּ׃	that glory may dwell in our land.

יא חֶסֶד־וֶאֱמֶת נִפְגָּשׁוּ
צֶדֶק וְשָׁלוֹם נָשָׁקוּ׃

11 Kindness and truth are met together,
righteousness and peace have kissed.

יב אֱמֶת מֵאֶרֶץ תִּצְמָח
וְצֶדֶק מִשָּׁמַיִם נִשְׁקָף׃

12 Truth will sprout from the earth,
and righteousness will look down from heaven.

יג גַּם־יְהוָה יִתֵּן הַטּוֹב
וְאַרְצֵנוּ תִּתֵּן יְבוּלָהּ׃

13 Also, Adonoy will give that which is good,
and our land will yield its produce.

יד צֶדֶק לְפָנָיו יְהַלֵּךְ
וְיָשֵׂם לְדֶרֶךְ פְּעָמָיו׃

14 Righteousness will precede Him
and He will set His footsteps upon the way.

פרק פו Chapter 86

Weekly Cycle	Monthly Cycle	Book Number
Wednesday	17th day of the month	Book 3

Author

דָּוִד הַמֶּלֶךְ—King David—the second king of Israel and father of the Davidic royal and messianic dynasty. David composed over seventy of the 150 psalms of Sefer Tehillim.

When & Why

David wrote this psalm when he was in exile escaping Saul. In it, he prays that God save him from the people who are trying to kill him.

Genre

Psalm of Individual Lament – This psalm was written from the perspective of the individual worshipper, who cries out to God in his time of need. It is characterized as an address to God involving a complaint, followed by a request and ending with an expression of trust.

Chapter Summary

This psalm was composed by King David while fleeing from Saul. He prays, as we all must, for Divine deliverance from the power of those who sought his life. He then acknowledges all of the loving kindness already bestowed upon him by God.

This psalm consists of seventeen verses, subdivided into four parts. The first verse serves as a heading.

In verses 1-7, King David requests of God to hear his prayer and save him.

In verses 8-10, he praises God.

In verses 11-13, he once again prays, focusing on his present troubles. He beseeches God to assist him in following in His path. He then proceeds by making a vow to God.

In verses 14-17, the Psalmist reaches out yet again to God. He asks God to have mercy on him and bring him salvation.

Introductory Words

תְּפִלָּה—Tefilah—Prayer

Shimush Tehillim - When to Say

To be saved from an evil spirit— Verse 2 states: "Preserve my soul for I am devoted, deliver Your servant, my God, who trusts in You."

Where in the Siddur

Verse 5 comprises one of the verses of Uva Letzion—a closing prayer of Shacharit (morning service).

Verse 8 is recited, often sung, prior to the opening of the Aron (Holy Ark) on Shabbat and Festivals.

Verse 8 is also found in Atah Horeita, the prayer introducing the Hakafot (dancing with the Torah scrolls) on Simchat Torah.

Verses 9 & 10 are part of Baruch Hashem Le'olam of Ma'ariv (evening service).

Biblical Places

שְׁאוֹל—Sheol—Lower or Underworld; abode of the dead.

Talmud on Tehillim

Verse 2: "שָׁמְרָה נַפְשִׁי, כִּי חָסִיד אָנִי"—"Preserve my soul for I am devoted."

The Talmud, Berachot 4a, deduces that King David said to God: "All the kings of the east and west (denoting the entire civilized world) sleep until three hours into the day, but I arise at midnight to give thanks to You." Tradition tells us that before midnight, David dedicated himself to his own spiritual growth through Torah study. But after midnight, he would compose lofty songs of praise and thanksgiving.

Verse 17:"עֲשֵׂה עִמִּי אוֹת לְטוֹבָה וְיִרְאוּ שֹׂנְאַי וְיֵבֹשׁוּ, כִּי אַתָּה יְהֹוָה עֲזַרְתַּנִי וְנִחַמְתָּנִי" "Give me a sign of Your kindness, that my enemies may see it and be ashamed, for You, Adonoy, have helped me and comforted me."

The Talmud, Shabbat 30a, teaches that King David here is asking God to display a clear sign of favor for him, indicating forgiveness for his sin regarding Bath Sheba. Such a public sign would lead all who had assailed and denounced David to feel ashamed of their actions. God informed David that he was indeed forgiven, but that this forgiveness would not be made public during his lifetime. Rather, his exoneration would become known to all only in the time of the reign of his son Solomon. Indeed, when Solomon finished building the Temple, he was unable to place the Aron HaKodesh (Holy Ark) into the Holy of Holies, for the Temple gates blocked the way! Nothing helped, until the king beseeched God for the sake of his father and implored: "Remember the righteousness of Your servant David." Only then did the gates relent, allowing the Ark to be placed in its proper location. At that time, we are told, "the faces of David's enemies darkened like the undersides of a kettle, and all of Israel knew that God had forgiven David for the sin of Bath Sheba ."

BOOK
WEEKLY
MONTHLY
CHAPTER
BOOK 3
WEDNESDAY
17
86

פרק פו

א תְּפִלָּה לְדָוִד
הַטֵּה־יְהוָה אָזְנְךָ עֲנֵנִי
כִּי־עָנִי וְאֶבְיוֹן אָנִי:
ב שָׁמְרָה נַפְשִׁי כִּי־חָסִיד אָנִי
הוֹשַׁע עַבְדְּךָ אַתָּה אֱלֹהַי
הַבּוֹטֵחַ אֵלֶיךָ:
ג חָנֵּנִי אֲדֹנָי
כִּי אֵלֶיךָ אֶקְרָא כָּל־הַיּוֹם:
ד שַׂמֵּחַ נֶפֶשׁ עַבְדֶּךָ
כִּי אֵלֶיךָ אֲדֹנָי
נַפְשִׁי אֶשָּׂא:
ה כִּי־אַתָּה אֲדֹנָי
טוֹב וְסַלָּח
וְרַב־חֶסֶד
לְכָל־קֹרְאֶיךָ:
ו הַאֲזִינָה יְהוָה תְּפִלָּתִי
וְהַקְשִׁיבָה בְּקוֹל תַּחֲנוּנוֹתָי:
ז בְּיוֹם צָרָתִי אֶקְרָאֶךָּ
כִּי תַעֲנֵנִי:
ח אֵין־כָּמוֹךָ
בָאֱלֹהִים | אֲדֹנָי
וְאֵין כְּמַעֲשֶׂיךָ:
ט כָּל־גּוֹיִם | אֲשֶׁר עָשִׂיתָ
יָבוֹאוּ | וְיִשְׁתַּחֲווּ
לְפָנֶיךָ אֲדֹנָי
וִיכַבְּדוּ לִשְׁמֶךָ:
י כִּי־גָדוֹל אַתָּה
וְעֹשֵׂה נִפְלָאוֹת
אַתָּה אֱלֹהִים לְבַדֶּךָ:
יא הוֹרֵנִי יְהוָה | דַּרְכֶּךָ
אֲהַלֵּךְ בַּאֲמִתֶּךָ
יַחֵד לְבָבִי לְיִרְאָה שְׁמֶךָ:
יב אוֹדְךָ | אֲדֹנָי אֱלֹהַי
בְּכָל־לְבָבִי
וַאֲכַבְּדָה שִׁמְךָ לְעוֹלָם:
יג כִּי־חַסְדְּךָ
גָּדוֹל עָלָי
וְהִצַּלְתָּ נַפְשִׁי

Chapter 86

1 A Prayer of David.
Incline Your ear Adonoy, and answer me,
for poor and needy am I.
2 Preserve my soul for I am devoted,
deliver Your servant, my God,
who trusts in You.
3 Be gracious to me my Master,
for to You I cry out all the day.
4 Make glad the soul of Your servant,
for, to You, my Master,
I lift up my soul.
5 For You, my Master,
are good and forgiving,
and abounding in kindness
to all who call upon You.
6 Give ear, Adonoy, to my prayer,
and listen to the voice of my supplications.
7 In the day of my distress I call out to You,
for You will answer me.
8 There is none like You
among gods, my Master,
and there is nothing like Your works.
9 All nations which You have made
will come and bow down
before You, my Master,
and they will give honor to Your Name.
10 For You are great
and do wondrous things,
You alone God.
11 Teach me, Adonoy, Your way
that I may walk in Your truth;
let me be of one heart to fear Your Name.
12 I will thank You, my Master, my God,
with all my heart,
and I will glorify Your Name, forever.
13 For Your kindness
has been great toward me,
and You have rescued my soul

מִשְּׁאוֹל תַּחְתִּיָּה׃			from the lowest depths of the grave.
אֱלֹהִים ׀ זֵדִים קָמוּ־עָלַי	יד	14	God, the insolent have risen up against me,
וַעֲדַת עָרִיצִים			and a company of violent men
בִּקְשׁוּ נַפְשִׁי			have sought my soul,
וְלֹא שָׂמוּךָ			and they have not set [the fear of] You
לְנֶגְדָּם׃			before them.
וְאַתָּה אֲדֹנָי	טו	15	But You, my Master,
אֵל־רַחוּם וְחַנּוּן			are the Almighty Who is Merciful and Gracious,
אֶרֶךְ אַפַּיִם וְרַב־חֶסֶד וֶאֱמֶת׃			Slow to Anger and Full of Kindness and Truth.
פְּנֵה אֵלַי וְחָנֵּנִי	טז	16	Turn to me and be gracious to me,
תְּנָה־עֻזְּךָ לְעַבְדֶּךָ			give Your strength to Your servant,
וְהוֹשִׁיעָה לְבֶן־אֲמָתֶךָ׃			and deliver the son of Your handmaid.
עֲשֵׂה־עִמִּי אוֹת לְטוֹבָה	יז	17	Give me a sign of Your kindness,
וְיִרְאוּ שֹׂנְאַי וְיֵבֹשׁוּ			that my enemies may see it and be ashamed,
כִּי־אַתָּה יְהוָה עֲזַרְתַּנִי			for You, Adonoy, have helped me
וְנִחַמְתָּנִי׃			and comforted me.

Mosaic Floor from a Bathhouse in Herod's Temple

פרק פז Chapter 87

Weekly Cycle	Monthly Cycle	Book Number
Wednesday	17th day of the month	Book 3

Author

בְּנֵי-קֹרַח—Sons of Korach—Korach rebelled against his cousins Moshe and Aharon (Moses and Aaron) and challenged their authority. Korach and his cohorts perished in the aftermath of the rebellion, yet his sons, who repented, survived.

Genre

Psalm of Praise – This is a psalm of celebration, often the result of a victory. It declares God's goodness and urges all of creation to worship.

Psalm of Zion – This psalm glorifies God's city and His holy mount in which He has placed His abode.

Chapter Summary

In this psalm, the singers praise the excellent qualities of Jerusalem. They proclaim that the holy city is the source of Divine Inspiration and refinement of the intellect.

This psalm consists of seven verses, subdivided into two parts. The beginning of the first verse serves as a heading.

In verses 1 & 2, the sons of Korach sing praises of Zion.

In verses 4-7, they proclaim that Zion is the birthplace of all who come to it to serve God, Jews and non-Jews alike, including those who come from far off lands. All peoples of the world, they assert, have the right to be considered natives of Zion. Verse 7 further describes the scene of celebration and joy when the pilgrims gather in Zion.

Introductory Words

מִזְמוֹר—Mizmor—Musical Accompaniment

שִׁיר—Shir—Song

Technical Terminology

סֶלָה—Selah—While its meaning is unclear, the most familiar opinion is that it is a musical notation, instructing the Levitical orchestra to pause its singing and playing of instruments. Alternatively, "Selah" may mean "everlasting".

Shimush Tehillim - When to Say

To protect a city or community (say this and the following chapter)—Verse 3 states: "Glorious things are spoken of you, [for you are] the city of God."

Biblical Places

בָּבֶל—Babylon—led by King Nebuchadnezzar, who destroyed the Beit HaMikdash (Temple) and exiled the Jews to his land.

כּוּשׁ—Cush—a country surrounded by the River Gihon, possibly Ethiopia of today.

עִיר הָאֱלֹהִים—Ir HaElokim—the City of God—a reference to Jerusalem.

פְּלֶשֶׁת (פְּלִשְׁתִּים)—Philistia (Phillistines)—an enemy nation which dwelled on the southwestern coast of Israel.

רַהַב—Rahab—another name for Egypt

צֹר—Tyre—located on the southwestern coast of Lebanon, just to the north of Israel, particularly known for the production of a rare Tyrian royal purple used for the nobility. It was also the source of techeilet, a dye referred to in the Torah, used to color the tzizit fringes of the Tallit and other four cornered garments.

צִיּוֹן—Zion—often used as a synonym for Jerusalem. The term Zion originally referred only to the area where a Jebbusite fortress once stood, which was also the location of the City of David. Zion was later used by prophets and psalmists as another name for Jerusalem.

Talmud on Tehillim

Verse 2: "אֹהֵב יְהוָה שַׁעֲרֵי צִיּוֹן, מִכֹּל מִשְׁכְּנוֹת יַעֲקֹב"—"Adonoy loves the gates of Zion more than all the dwellings of Jacob."

The Talmud, Berachot 8a, deduces from here that as of the time of the destruction of the Beit

HaMikdash (Temple), God loves the study of his laws even more than the act of going to a house of worship. We are told that from the day that the Beit HaMikdash was destroyed, the Holy One has in this world only the "four cubits" of halachah (Jewish law). When the Beit HaMikdash existed, it was there that the Shechinah (Divine Presence) dwelled in this world. In its absence, the Beit Midrash (house of study) takes its place. Accordingly, one who prays after engaging in words of Torah is considered as if he has prayed in the Beit HaMikdash itself.

Mosaic with Menorah, Shofar and Palm Branch

פרק פז	**Chapter 87**
א לִבְנֵי־קֹרַח מִזְמוֹר שִׁיר יְסוּדָתוֹ בְּהַרְרֵי־קֹדֶשׁ׃	1 A Psalm of the sons of Korach, a song, its foundation is in the holy mountains.
ב אֹהֵב יְהוָה שַׁעֲרֵי צִיּוֹן מִכֹּל מִשְׁכְּנוֹת יַעֲקֹב׃	2 Adonoy loves the gates of Zion more than all the dwellings of Jacob.
ג נִכְבָּדוֹת מְדֻבָּר בָּךְ עִיר הָאֱלֹהִים סֶלָה׃	3 Glorious things are spoken of you, [for you are] the city of God, Selah.
ד אַזְכִּיר ׀ רַהַב וּבָבֶל לְיֹדְעָי הִנֵּה פְלֶשֶׁת וְצוֹר עִם־כּוּשׁ זֶה יֻלַּד־שָׁם׃	4 "I will make mention of Rahav and Babylon to my friends; behold Philistia, and Tyre, with Cush, `this one was born there.'"
ה וּלְצִיּוֹן ׀ יֵאָמַר אִישׁ וְאִישׁ יֻלַּד־בָּהּ וְהוּא יְכוֹנְנֶהָ עֶלְיוֹן׃	5 But of Zion it will be said "This man and that man was born there, and He will establish her above [all others].
ו יְהוָה יִסְפֹּר בִּכְתוֹב עַמִּים זֶה יֻלַּד־שָׁם סֶלָה׃	6 When Adonoy records the peoples [for everlasting disgrace, He will count the Jews among them, saying,]: this one was born there Selah.
ז וְשָׁרִים כְּחֹלְלִים כָּל־מַעְיָנַי בָּךְ׃	7 And singers and dancers alike [will chant], all my innermost thoughts are of You.

פרק פח Chapter 88

Weekly Cycle	Monthly Cycle	Book Number
Wednesday	18th day of the month	Book 3

Authors

בְּנֵי-קֹרַח—Sons of Korach—Korach rebelled against his cousins Moshe and Aharon (Moses and Aaron) and challenged their authority. Korach and his cohorts perished in the aftermath of the rebellion, yet his sons, who repented, survived; co-authored with הֵימָן הָאֶזְרָחִי—Heiman the Ezrahite—a composer and singer in the Beit HaMikdash (Temple), perhaps the brother of Eitan the Ezrahite. He is also referred to in the Talmud as Chozeh HaMelech (the Seer of the King).

When & Why

This psalm was written about the suffering that Israel will undergo while in exile.

Genre

Psalm of Individual Lament - This psalm was written from the perspective of the individual worshipper, who cries out to God in his time of need. It is characterized as an address to God involving a complaint, followed by a request and ending with an expression of trust.

Chapter Summary

In this psalm, the authors aim to humble the spirit of the listener. As it is conducive to subduing man's pride, it, as several others, is titled a "maskil"—"(for a) discerning individual", indicating that a man acts wisely by enlightening his soul and striving towards proper conduct.

This psalm consists of nineteen verses, subdivided into three parts. The first verse serves as a heading.

In verses 2-9, the psalmists request that their prayer be accepted. They display their inner conflict, lamenting that it seems as if they are dead.

In verses 10-13, they continue to pray, declaring that God's salvation is for the living and not for the dead.

In verses 14-19, the psalmists again cry out, this time directly to God, and describe their distress in even starker terms.

Introductory Words

שִׁיר—Shir—Song

מִזְמוֹר—Mizmor—Musical Accompaniment

לַמְנַצֵּחַ—Lamnatsei'ach—To the Conductor

Technical Terminology

לְעַנּוֹת—La'anot—to responsively chant

מָחֲלַת—Machalat—a musical instrument; alternatively, a prayer for forgiveness

מַשְׂכִּיל—Maskil—a discerning person; alternatively, a giver of instruction, perhaps denoting a translator of the chapter (Rashi).

סֶלָה—Selah—While its meaning is unclear, the most familiar opinion is that it is a musical notation, instructing the Levitical orchestra to pause its singing and playing of instruments. Alternatively, "Selah" may mean "everlasting".

Shimush Tehillim - When to Say

To protect a city or community (say this and the previous chapter)—Verses 3 and 18 state: " Let my prayer come before You, incline Your ear to my song". "They encompassed me like water all the day, they engulf me at once."

Biblical Places

שְׁאוֹל—Sheol—Lower or Underworld; abode of the dead.

Talmud on Tehillim

Verse 6: "בְּמֵתִים חָפְשִׁי"—"I am [considered] among the dead who are free."
The Talmud, Shabbat 30a, states: "One should engage in Torah and good deeds before he dies, for as soon as he dies he can no longer study Torah or perform meritorious deeds."

פֶּרֶק פּזז			Chapter 88
שִׁיר מִזְמוֹר לִבְנֵי קֹרַח לַמְנַצֵּחַ עַל־מָחֲלַת לְעַנּוֹת מַשְׂכִּיל לְהֵימָן הָאֶזְרָחִי׃	א	1	A song, a Psalm of the sons of Korach, to the Chief Musician, upon machalas leanos, an instruction of Heiman the Ezrahite.
יְהוָה אֱלֹהֵי יְשׁוּעָתִי יוֹם־צָעַקְתִּי בַלַּיְלָה נֶגְדֶּךָ׃	ב	2	Adonoy, God of my deliverance; by day I cried [before You], at night I stood before You [in prayer].
תָּבוֹא לְפָנֶיךָ תְּפִלָּתִי הַטֵּה־אָזְנְךָ לְרִנָּתִי׃	ג	3	Let my prayer come before You, incline Your ear to my song.
כִּי־שָׂבְעָה בְרָעוֹת נַפְשִׁי וְחַיַּי לִשְׁאוֹל הִגִּיעוּ׃	ד	4	For my soul is satiated with troubles, and my life approaches the grave.
נֶחְשַׁבְתִּי עִם־יוֹרְדֵי בוֹר הָיִיתִי כְּגֶבֶר אֵין־אֱיָל׃	ה	5	I am counted with those who go down to the pit, I have become like a man without strength.
בַּמֵּתִים חָפְשִׁי כְּמוֹ חֲלָלִים ׀ שֹׁכְבֵי קֶבֶר אֲשֶׁר לֹא זְכַרְתָּם עוֹד וְהֵמָּה מִיָּדְךָ נִגְזָרוּ׃	ו	6	I am [considered] among the dead who are free as the slain that lie in the grave, whom You no longer remember, and who are cut off by Your hand.
שַׁתַּנִי בְּבוֹר תַּחְתִּיּוֹת בְּמַחֲשַׁכִּים בִּמְצֹלוֹת׃	ז	7	You have put me into the lowest pit, into dark places, into depths.

עָלַי סָמְכָה חֲמָתֶךָ וְכָל־מִשְׁבָּרֶיךָ עִנִּיתָ סֶּלָה׃	ח	8	Your wrath lies hard upon me, and with all Your waves [of anger] You have afflicted me, Selah.
הִרְחַקְתָּ מְיֻדָּעַי מִמֶּנִּי שַׁתַּנִי תוֹעֵבוֹת לָמוֹ כָּלֻא וְלֹא אֵצֵא׃	ט	9	You have estranged my friends from me, You have made me an abomination to them; I am imprisoned and cannot go out.
עֵינִי דָאֲבָה מִנִּי עֹנִי קְרָאתִיךָ יְהוָה בְּכָל־יוֹם שִׁטַּחְתִּי אֵלֶיךָ כַפָּי׃	י	10	My eyes grieved because of such affliction; I have called upon You, Adonoy, every day, I have stretched out my hands to You.
הֲלַמֵּתִים תַּעֲשֶׂה־פֶּלֶא אִם־רְפָאִים יָקוּמוּ ׀ יוֹדוּךָ סֶּלָה׃	יא	11	Will You work wonders for the dead? Will the lifeless rise and thank You, Selah?
הַיְסֻפַּר בַּקֶּבֶר חַסְדֶּךָ אֱמוּנָתְךָ בָּאֲבַדּוֹן׃	יב	12	Will Your kindness be declared in the grave? Your faithfulness in [our] destruction?
הֲיִוָּדַע בַּחֹשֶׁךְ פִּלְאֶךָ וְצִדְקָתְךָ בְּאֶרֶץ נְשִׁיָּה׃	יג	13	Will Your wonders be known in the dark and Your righteousness in the land of oblivion?
וַאֲנִי ׀ אֵלֶיךָ יְהוָה שִׁוַּעְתִּי וּבַבֹּקֶר תְּפִלָּתִי תְקַדְּמֶךָּ׃	יד	14	But as for me, to You, Adonoy, I cry, and in the morning my prayer will be early to greet You.
לָמָה יְהוָה תִּזְנַח נַפְשִׁי תַּסְתִּיר פָּנֶיךָ מִמֶּנִּי׃	טו	15	Why, Adonoy, do You cast off my soul? [Why] do You hide Your face from me?
עָנִי אֲנִי וְגֹוֵעַ מִנֹּעַר נָשָׂאתִי אֵמֶיךָ אָפוּנָה׃	טז	16	I am afflicted and at the point of sudden death; I have borne Your sudden terrors which have become part of me.
עָלַי עָבְרוּ חֲרוֹנֶיךָ בִּעוּתֶיךָ צִמְּתוּתֻנִי׃	יז	17	I am overwhelmed by Your fierce wrath, Your frightening attacks have cut me off.
סַבּוּנִי כַמַּיִם כָּל־הַיּוֹם הִקִּיפוּ עָלַי יָחַד׃	יח	18	They encompassed me like water all the day, they engulf me at once.
הִרְחַקְתָּ מִמֶּנִּי אֹהֵב וָרֵעַ מְיֻדָּעַי מַחְשָׁךְ׃	יט	19	You have estranged from me, friend and companion, from my acquaintances, I am [abandoned] in darkness.

פרק פט Chapter 89

Weekly Cycle	Monthly Cycle	Book Number
Wednesday	18th day of the month	Book 3

Author

אֵיתָן הָאֶזְרָחִי—Eitan the Ezrahite—a composer and singer in the Beit HaMikdash (Temple), perhaps the brother of Heiman the Ezrahite. Alternatively, the Talmud identifies him with Avraham (Abraham) our forefather.

When & Why

This psalm was written as a lament over the prolonged exile and the termination of Davidic rule over Israel.

Genre

Psalm of Communal Lament - This psalm focuses on expressing deep sorrow for the travails of a nation and as a group asking for God's blessing or intervention.

Psalm of Royalty - This psalm describes how God reigns supreme. It focuses on the human king of Israel, or upon God as King of Israel.

Chapter Summary

God's kindness to the Jewish people, and to the royal line of David in particular, is eternal. Israel's confidence that all of His assurances will surely be fulfilled has historically given the nation the strength to endure.

This psalm consists of fifty-three verses, subdivided into six parts. The first verse serves as a heading.

In verses 2-5, the psalmist takes it upon himself to sing forever of God's acts of lovingkindness. He also acknowledges God's eternal covenant with David.

In verses 6-19, he recounts the praises of God as the One who rules the swelling of the sea, has crushed Rahab (Egypt), has created the world and rules over it justly. He further describes the happiness of the people who crown God as King.

In verses 20-38, he expresses and expounds upon the promise to David that he has been chosen for an everlasting monarchy.

In verses 39-46, he laments that God's promise to David has in fact not been fulfilled. He describes at length the downfall of the Davidic kingdom, in contrast to its promised greatness.

In verses 47-52, the psalmist cries out to God. He asks what has become of the previous promises to David, and boldly declares that enemies are vilifying the servants of God, God Himself, and His anointed.

In verse 53, Eitan concludes with blessing the name of God for all eternity.

Technical Terminology

מַשְׂכִּיל—Maskil—a discerning person; alternatively, a giver of instruction, perhaps denoting a translator of the chapter (Rashi).

סֶלָה—Selah—While its meaning is unclear, the most familiar opinion is that it is a musical notation, instructing the Levitical orchestra to pause its singing and playing of instruments. Alternatively, "Selah" may mean "everlasting".

Shimush Tehillim - When to Say

To prevent loss of organs or limbs due to disease.

To avoid imprisonment—Verse 19 states: "For Adonoy is our shield, and the Holy One of Israel is our King."

Where in the Siddur

Most of the verses are found in the introduction to Selichot (Penitential Service).

Verse 53 is the first verse of Baruch Hashem Le'olam—one of the closing paragraphs of Pesukei Dezimra (introductory Verses of Praise to the Shacharit morning service). It also opens Baruch Hashem Le'olam of the weekday Ma'ariv (evening service).

Verses 16-18 are recited following the blowing of the Shofar on Rosh HaShanah.

Biblical Places

חֶרְמוֹן—Chermon—Hermon—a tall mountain in the most northern part of israel.

רָהַב—Rahab—another name for Egypt.

שְׁאוֹל—Sheol—Lower or Underworld; abode of the dead.

תָּבוֹר—Tabor—a low mountain where the battle took place between the Israelite army led by Barak and his wife Deborah the Judge, against the army of Jabin, King of Chazor, and his commander Sisera. Descending from the mountain, the Israelites attacked and vanquished Sisera and the Canaanites.

Talmud on Tehillim

Verse 1: "מַשְׂכִּיל לְאֵיתָן הָאֶזְרָחִי"—"An instruction of Ethan the Ezrahite."

The Talmud, Bava Batra 15a, teaches that Eitan HaEzrachi actually refers to our forefather, Avraham Avinu (Abraham), so called as the meaning of the word eitan is "strength".

Verse 33: "וּפָקַדְתִּי בְשֵׁבֶט פִּשְׁעָם"—"Then I will punish them with the rod for their sins."

The Talmud, Yoma 86a, explains that there are three levels of atonement. If one transgresses a positive commandment and then repents, he is forgiven immediately; if one transgresses a negative commandment and then repents, his punishment is suspended and the day of Yom Kippur atones for the sin; finally, if one commits sins of such gravity as to be punishable by death or excommunication, and then repents, both his repentance and Yom Kippur suspend God's punishment, and only suffering purges the sin.

Carved Menorah from Hammat, Tiberius

פֶּרֶק פּט

א לַמְנַצֵּחַ עַל־שׁוֹשַׁנִּים לְדָוִד׃
ב חַסְדֵי יְהוָה
עוֹלָם אָשִׁירָה
לְדֹר וָדֹר | אוֹדִיעַ
אֱמוּנָתְךָ בְּפִי׃
ג כִּי־אָמַרְתִּי
עוֹלָם חֶסֶד
יִבָּנֶה
שָׁמַיִם |
תָּכִן אֱמוּנָתְךָ בָהֶם׃
ד כָּרַתִּי בְרִית לִבְחִירִי
נִשְׁבַּעְתִּי לְדָוִד עַבְדִּי׃
ה עַד־עוֹלָם אָכִין זַרְעֶךָ
וּבָנִיתִי לְדֹר־וָדוֹר
כִּסְאֲךָ סֶלָה׃
ו וְיוֹדוּ שָׁמַיִם פִּלְאֲךָ
יְהוָה
אַף־אֱמוּנָתְךָ
בִּקְהַל קְדֹשִׁים׃
ז כִּי מִי בַשַּׁחַק
יַעֲרֹךְ לַיהוָה
יִדְמֶה לַיהוָה
בִּבְנֵי אֵלִים׃
ח אֵל נַעֲרָץ
בְּסוֹד־קְדֹשִׁים רַבָּה
וְנוֹרָא
עַל־כָּל־סְבִיבָיו׃
ט יְהוָה | אֱלֹהֵי צְבָאוֹת
מִי־כָמוֹךָ חֲסִין | יָהּ
וֶאֱמוּנָתְךָ סְבִיבוֹתֶיךָ׃
י אַתָּה מוֹשֵׁל בְּגֵאוּת הַיָּם
בְּשׂוֹא גַלָּיו אַתָּה תְשַׁבְּחֵם׃
יא אַתָּה דִכִּאתָ כֶחָלָל רָהַב
בִּזְרוֹעַ עֻזְּךָ
פִּזַּרְתָּ אוֹיְבֶיךָ׃
יב לְךָ שָׁמַיִם
אַף־לְךָ אָרֶץ

Chapter 89

1 An instruction of Ethan the Ezrahite.
2 Of the kindness of Adonoy,
forever I will sing,
throughout all generations will I make known
Your faithfulness with my mouth.
3 For I have said,
"A world which manifests Your lovingkindness
You did build";
in the heavens
You established Your faithfulness in them.
4 I have made a covenant with My chosen,
I have sworn to David, My servant.
5 `Forever will I establish your seed,
and build up throughout all generations,
your throne, Selah."
6 And the heavens will praise Your wonders,
Adonoy,
and Your faithfulness [will be praised]
in the assembly of holy ones.
7 For who in the skies
can be compared to Adonoy,
who can be likened to Adonoy
among the sons of the mighty?
8 The Almighty, revered
in the great council of the holy ones,
and awe inspiring
over all that are round about Him.
9 Adonoy, God of Hosts,
who is like You a mighty One, God;
and Your faithfulness is round about You.
10 You rule over the majesty of the sea;
when it raises its waves, You still them.
11 You crushed Rahav like a corpse;
with the arm of Your strength
You scattered Your enemies.
12 Yours are the heavens,
also Yours is the earth,

	תֵּבֵל וּמְלֹאָהּ		the inhabited world and its fullness,
	אַתָּה יְסַדְתָּם׃		You have founded them.
יג	צָפוֹן וְיָמִין	13	The north and the south,
	אַתָּה בְרָאתָם		You have created them,
	תָּבוֹר וְחֶרְמוֹן בְּשִׁמְךָ יְרַנֵּנוּ׃		[Mt.] Tabor and Hermon rejoice in Your Name.
יד	לְךָ זְרוֹעַ עִם־גְּבוּרָה	14	Yours is an arm with might;
	תָּעֹז יָדְךָ תָּרוּם יְמִינֶךָ׃		strong is Your hand, exalted is Your right hand.
טו	צֶדֶק וּמִשְׁפָּט	15	Righteousness and justice
	מְכוֹן כִּסְאֶךָ		are the foundations of Your throne,
	חֶסֶד וֶאֱמֶת יְקַדְּמוּ פָנֶיךָ׃		kindness and truth precede Your Presence.
טז	אַשְׁרֵי הָעָם	16	Fortunate is the people
	יוֹדְעֵי תְרוּעָה		that understand the call of teruah
	יְהוָה		Adonoy,
	בְּאוֹר־פָּנֶיךָ יְהַלֵּכוּן׃		in the light of Your Presence they walk.
יז	בְּשִׁמְךָ יְגִילוּן כָּל־הַיּוֹם	17	In Your Name they exult all the day,
	וּבְצִדְקָתְךָ		and through Your righteousness
	יָרוּמוּ׃		they are uplifted.
יח	כִּי־תִפְאֶרֶת עֻזָּמוֹ אָתָּה	18	For the glory of their might is You,
	וּבִרְצֹנְךָ תָּרוּם קַרְנֵנוּ׃		and through Your favor, our horn is exalted.
יט	כִּי לַיהוָה מָגִנֵּנוּ	19	For Adonoy is our shield,
	וְלִקְדוֹשׁ יִשְׂרָאֵל מַלְכֵּנוּ׃		and the Holy One of Israel is our King.
כ	אָז דִּבַּרְתָּ־	20	Then You spoke
	בְחָזוֹן לַחֲסִידֶיךָ וַתֹּאמֶר		in a vision to Your devoted ones and said,
	שִׁוִּיתִי עֵזֶר		"I have set forth [My] help
	עַל־גִּבּוֹר		upon one [David] who is mighty,
	הֲרִימוֹתִי בָחוּר מֵעָם׃		I have exalted one chosen from the people.
כא	מָצָאתִי דָּוִד עַבְדִּי	21	I have found David, My servant,
	בְּשֶׁמֶן קָדְשִׁי מְשַׁחְתִּיו׃		with My holy oil I have annointed him.
כב	אֲשֶׁר יָדִי תִּכּוֹן עִמּוֹ	22	With whom My hand will be established,
	אַף זְרוֹעִי תְאַמְּצֶנּוּ׃		also My arm will strengthen him.
כג	לֹא־יַשִּׁא אוֹיֵב בּוֹ	23	The enemy will not extort from him
	וּבֶן־עַוְלָה לֹא יְעַנֶּנּוּ׃		and the son of wickedness will not afflict him.
כד	וְכַתּוֹתִי מִפָּנָיו צָרָיו	24	And I will crush his adversaries before him,
	וּמְשַׂנְאָיו אֶגּוֹף׃		and his enemies, I will smite.
כה	וֶאֱמוּנָתִי וְחַסְדִּי	25	And My faithfulness and My kindness
	עִמּוֹ		will be with him,
	וּבִשְׁמִי תָּרוּם קַרְנוֹ׃		and through My Name his horn will be exalted.
כו	וְשַׂמְתִּי בַיָּם יָדוֹ	26	And I will set his hand upon the sea,
	וּבַנְּהָרוֹת יְמִינוֹ׃		and upon the rivers his right hand.

כז הוּא יִקְרָאֵנִי
אָבִי אָתָּה
אֵלִי וְצוּר יְשׁוּעָתִי׃
כח אַף־אָנִי בְּכוֹר אֶתְּנֵהוּ
עֶלְיוֹן לְמַלְכֵי־אָרֶץ׃
כט לְעוֹלָם אֶשְׁמָר־לוֹ חַסְדִּי
וּבְרִיתִי נֶאֱמֶנֶת לוֹ׃
ל וְשַׂמְתִּי לָעַד זַרְעוֹ
וְכִסְאוֹ כִּימֵי שָׁמָיִם׃
לא אִם־יַעַזְבוּ בָנָיו תּוֹרָתִי
וּבְמִשְׁפָּטַי לֹא יֵלֵכוּן׃
לב אִם־חֻקֹּתַי יְחַלֵּלוּ
וּמִצְוֹתַי לֹא יִשְׁמֹרוּ׃
לג וּפָקַדְתִּי בְשֵׁבֶט
פִּשְׁעָם
וּבִנְגָעִים עֲוֺנָם׃
לד וְחַסְדִּי לֹא־אָפִיר מֵעִמּוֹ
וְלֹא־אֲשַׁקֵּר בֶּאֱמוּנָתִי׃
לה לֹא־אֲחַלֵּל בְּרִיתִי
וּמוֹצָא שְׂפָתַי
לֹא אֲשַׁנֶּה׃
לו אַחַת נִשְׁבַּעְתִּי בְקָדְשִׁי
אִם־לְדָוִד אֲכַזֵּב׃
לז זַרְעוֹ לְעוֹלָם יִהְיֶה
וְכִסְאוֹ
כַשֶּׁמֶשׁ נֶגְדִּי׃
לח כְּיָרֵחַ יִכּוֹן עוֹלָם
וְעֵד בַּשַּׁחַק נֶאֱמָן סֶלָה׃
לט וְאַתָּה זָנַחְתָּ וַתִּמְאָס
הִתְעַבַּרְתָּ עִם־מְשִׁיחֶךָ׃
מ נֵאַרְתָּה
בְּרִית עַבְדֶּךָ
חִלַּלְתָּ לָאָרֶץ נִזְרוֹ׃
מא פָּרַצְתָּ כָל גְּדֵרֹתָיו
שַׂמְתָּ מִבְצָרָיו מְחִתָּה׃
מב שַׁסֻּהוּ כָּל־עֹבְרֵי דָרֶךְ
הָיָה חֶרְפָּה לִשְׁכֵנָיו׃
מג הֲרִימוֹתָ יְמִין
צָרָיו

27 He will call unto Me [saying],
`You are my Father,
my Almighty and the Rock of my deliverance.'
28 I will also make him great,
the highest of the kings of the earth.
29 Forever will I preserve for him My kindness,
and My covenant will be steadfast with him.
30 And I will make His seed endure forever,
and his throne as the days of heaven.
31 If his sons ever forsake My Torah,
and in My mandates they will not walk;
32 If My statutes they will profane,
and My commandments they will not preserve;
33 Then I will punish them with the rod
for their sins,
and with plagues because of their iniquity.
34 But My kindness I will not cancel from him,
and I will not be false in My faithfulness.
35 I will not profane My covenant,
and that which is uttered from My lips
I will not alter.
36 One thing I have sworn by My holiness,
unto David I will not be false.
37 His seed forever will endure,
and his throne [will stand]
as the sun before Me.
38 As the moon, it will be established forever,
and as a faithful witness in the sky, Selah.
39 But You have abandoned and reviled,
You are filled with anger against Your annointed.
40 You have rejected
the covenant of Your servant,
You have profaned his crown to the ground.
41 You have broken down all his fences,
You have brought his strongholds to ruin.
42 They trampled him, all the wayfarers;
he was a humiliation to his neighbors.
43 You exalted the right hand
of his adversaries,

הִשְׂמַחְתָּ כָּל־אוֹיְבָיו׃	You made all his enemies rejoice.
מד אַף־תָּשִׁיב	44 You also turned back
צוּר חַרְבּוֹ	the sharp edge of his sword,
וְלֹא הֲקֵימֹתוֹ בַּמִּלְחָמָה׃	and did not keep him upright in battle.
מה הִשְׁבַּתָּ מִטְּהָרוֹ	45 You have made his brightness cease,
וְכִסְאוֹ	and his throne
לָאָרֶץ מִגַּרְתָּה׃	You have cast down to the ground.
מו הִקְצַרְתָּ יְמֵי עֲלוּמָיו	46 You have shortened the days of his youth,
הֶעֱטִיתָ עָלָיו בּוּשָׁה סֶלָה׃	You have enwrapped him with shame, Selah.
מז עַד־מָה יְהוָה	47 How long, Adonoy,
תִּסָּתֵר לָנֶצַח	will You hide Yourself forever?
תִּבְעַר כְּמוֹ־אֵשׁ חֲמָתֶךָ׃	[How long] will Your wrath burn like fire?
מח זְכָר־אֲנִי מֶה־חָלֶד	48 I remember how short is my life-span
עַל־מַה־שָּׁוְא	for what vanity
בָּרָאתָ כָל־בְּנֵי־אָדָם׃	have You created all the children of man.
מט מִי גֶבֶר יִחְיֶה	49 What man is he that lives,
וְלֹא יִרְאֶה־מָּוֶת	and will not see death,
יְמַלֵּט נַפְשׁוֹ	that will rescue his soul
מִיַּד־שְׁאוֹל סֶלָה׃	from the grasp of the grave, Selah?
נ אַיֵּה ׀ חֲסָדֶיךָ הָרִאשֹׁנִים ׀	50 Where are Your former acts of kindness,
אֲדֹנָי	my Master,
נִשְׁבַּעְתָּ לְדָוִד	which You swore to David
בֶּאֱמוּנָתֶךָ׃	in Your faithfulness?
נא זְכֹר אֲדֹנָי	51 Remember, my Master,
חֶרְפַּת עֲבָדֶיךָ	the humiliation of Your servants,
שְׂאֵתִי בְחֵיקִי	I bear in my bosom
כָּל־רַבִּים עַמִּים׃	[the burdens of] all the many peoples.
נב אֲשֶׁר חֵרְפוּ אוֹיְבֶיךָ ׀ יְהוָה	52 That Your enemies have reviled, Adonoy,
אֲשֶׁר חֵרְפוּ	that they have reviled
עִקְּבוֹת מְשִׁיחֶךָ׃	the footsteps of Your annointed.
נג בָּרוּךְ יְהוָה לְעוֹלָם	53 Blessed is Adonoy, forever,
אָמֵן ׀ וְאָמֵן׃	Amen and Amen.

BOOK 4

פרק צ Chapter 90

Weekly Cycle	Monthly Cycle	Book Number
Thursday	19th day of the month	Book 4

Author

מֹשֶׁה—Moshe—Moses—the leader of the Israelites and receiver of the Torah at Sinai, a shepherd chosen by God for his humility and loyalty to his sheep. The penultimate verse of the Torah describes him as the greatest prophet of all time.

When & Why

Moses is castigating the people. He speaks of the weaknessness of man and the shortness of his days. The years that one is alive, can either be misused tools resulting in futility, or with spiritual purposfullness, man can fulfill the reason he was created.

Genre

Psalm of Communal Lament –This psalm focuses on expressing deep sorrow for the travails of a nation and as a group asking for God's blessing or intervention.

Chapter Summary

This psalm opens the fourth book of the Book of Psalms. The first of eleven psalms which tradition attributes to Moses, it is a lament over the frailty of man and the short span of his days.

This psalm consists of seventeen verses, subdivided into two parts. The first clause of verse 1 serves as a heading.

In verses 1-10, the psalmist, through the use of simile, focuses on God's eternity, and contrasts it to the shortness and suffering of the life of man.

In verses 11-17, he turns to prayer, asking for a life of contentment and joy. He petitions God with a request for the attainment of wisdom, and ends with a prayer on behalf of the servants of God, that they will be privileged to merit His lovingkindness, loyalty and pleasantness.

Introductory Word

תְּפִלָּה—Tefilah—Prayer

Shimush Tehillim - When to Say

To repel an evil spirit—Verse 17 states: "May the pleasantness of my Master our God be upon us, and the work of our hands established for us, and the work of our hands—establish it."

Where in the Siddur

Recited as one of the paragraphs of Pesukei Dezimra (introductory Verses of Praise to the Shacharit morning service) of Shabbat, Yom Tov (Festivals), and Hoshana Rabbah (the seventh day of Sukkot). Recited on Shabbat Nachamu (the Shabbat following Tisha Be'Av) in some traditions.

Verse 17 is the first verse of Viy'hi No'am, recited following the Amidah of Ma'ariv (nighttime service) of Motza'ei Shabbat.

Verse 17 is also recited by some as part of the bedtime Shema service.

Talmud of Tehillim

Verse 10: "יְמֵי שְׁנוֹתֵינוּ בָהֶם שִׁבְעִים שָׁנָה וְאִם בִּגְבוּרֹת שְׁמוֹנִים שָׁנָה"—"The days of our years in them [total] seventy years, and with strength, eighty years."

The Talmud, Pesachim 94b, uses this verse to relate how Nebuchadnezzar, the greatest king of ancient Babylonia, was the master of self-deception. Evil and wicked, he perceived himself to be so great and lofty that he could ascend the heights of the "Most High." In actuality, he too was subject to the rules of man and his finality, and quite small in comparison to the vast world and heavens which God had created. Man is temporal, inasmuch as he is here on earth for a mere seventy or eighty years and eventually destined to die. Accordingly, no man should think of himself as so great, as only God is everlasting.

פֶּרֶק צ

א תְּפִלָּה לְמֹשֶׁה אִישׁ־הָאֱלֹהִים
אֲדֹנָי
מָעוֹן אַתָּה הָיִיתָ לָּנוּ
בְּדֹר וָדֹר:

ב בְּטֶרֶם | הָרִים יֻלָּדוּ
וַתְּחוֹלֵל אֶרֶץ
וְתֵבֵל
וּמֵעוֹלָם עַד־עוֹלָם
אַתָּה אֵל:

ג תָּשֵׁב אֱנוֹשׁ
עַד־דַּכָּא
וַתֹּאמֶר
שׁוּבוּ בְנֵי־אָדָם:

ד כִּי אֶלֶף שָׁנִים בְּעֵינֶיךָ
כְּיוֹם אֶתְמוֹל כִּי יַעֲבֹר
וְאַשְׁמוּרָה בַלָּיְלָה:

ה זְרַמְתָּם שֵׁנָה יִהְיוּ
בַּבֹּקֶר
כֶּחָצִיר יַחֲלֹף:

ו בַּבֹּקֶר יָצִיץ
וְחָלָף
לָעֶרֶב יְמוֹלֵל וְיָבֵשׁ:

ז כִּי־כָלִינוּ בְאַפֶּךָ
וּבַחֲמָתְךָ נִבְהָלְנוּ:

Chapter 90

1 A prayer of Moses, the man of God:
My Master
a dwelling[-place] have You been for us
in every generation.

2 Before the mountains were born,
and You brought forth the earth
and the inhabited world;
from world to world
You are Almighty.

3 You push man down
until the crushing point
and You say,
"Return, children of man!"

4 For a thousand years are in Your eyes
like the yesterday that has just passed,
and like a night watch.

5 The stream of their life is [but] slumber,
in the morning
they are as grass, freshly grown.

6 [If] in the morning it blossoms,
and grows afresh
by evening it is cut off and shriveled.

7 So are we consumed by Your anger
and by Your rage are we terrified.

שַׁתָּה עֲוֺנֹתֵינוּ לְנֶגְדֶּךָ	ח	8	You have set our iniquities before You,
עֲלֻמֵנוּ			the sins of our youth
לִמְאוֹר פָּנֶיךָ׃			before the light of Your countenance.
כִּי כָל־יָמֵינוּ	ט	9	For all our days
פָּנוּ בְעֶבְרָתֶךָ			vanish in Your wrath;
כִּלִּינוּ שָׁנֵינוּ			we terminate our years
כְמוֹ־הֶגֶה׃			like an unspoken word.
יְמֵי־שְׁנוֹתֵינוּ בָהֶם	י	10	The days of our years in them
שִׁבְעִים שָׁנָה			[total] seventy years,
וְאִם בִּגְבוּרֹת ׀ שְׁמוֹנִים שָׁנָה			and with strength, eighty years,
וְרָהְבָּם עָמָל וָאָוֶן			and their pride is frustration and falsehood;
כִּי־גָז חִישׁ וַנָּעֻפָה׃			for, cut off quickly, we fly away.
מִי־יוֹדֵעַ	יא	11	Who can [get to] know
עֹז אַפֶּךָ			the force of Your anger?
וּכְיִרְאָתְךָ עֶבְרָתֶךָ׃			And like the fear of You so is Your wrath.
לִמְנוֹת יָמֵינוּ כֵּן הוֹדַע	יב	12	To count our days, teach us
וְנָבִא לְבַב חָכְמָה׃			and we will acquire a heart of wisdom.
שׁוּבָה יְהוָה עַד־מָתָי	יג	13	Turn Adonoy—how long?
וְהִנָּחֵם עַל־עֲבָדֶיךָ׃			And change Your mind about Your servants.
שַׂבְּעֵנוּ בַבֹּקֶר	יד	14	Satisfy us in the morning
חַסְדֶּךָ			with Your kindliness,
וּנְרַנְּנָה וְנִשְׂמְחָה			and we will sing and rejoice
בְּכָל־יָמֵינוּ׃			throughout our days.
שַׂמְּחֵנוּ	טו	15	Make us rejoice
כִּימוֹת עִנִּיתָנוּ			like the days You afflicted us,
שְׁנוֹת רָאִינוּ רָעָה׃			the years [when] we saw evil.
יֵרָאֶה אֶל־עֲבָדֶיךָ	טז	16	Let be revealed to Your servants,
פָעֳלֶךָ			Your deeds
וַהֲדָרְךָ עַל־בְּנֵיהֶם׃			and Your splendor be upon their children.
וִיהִי ׀ נֹעַם אֲדֹנָי אֱלֹהֵינוּ	יז	17	May the pleasantness of my Master our God
עָלֵינוּ			be upon us,
וּמַעֲשֵׂה יָדֵינוּ כּוֹנְנָה עָלֵינוּ			and the work of our hands established for us,
וּמַעֲשֵׂה יָדֵינוּ כּוֹנְנֵהוּ׃			and the work of our hands—establish it.

פרק צא Chapter 91

Weekly Cycle	Monthly Cycle	Book Number
Thursday	19th day of the month	Book 4

Author
מֹשֶׁה—Moshe—Moses—the leader of the Israelites and receiver of the Torah at Sinai, a shepherd chosen by God for his humility and loyalty to his sheep. The penultimate verse of the Torah describes him as the greatest prophet of all time.

When & Why
Moses wrote this psalm prophetically about the difficulty that Israel will face in exile. In it, he tells Israel to remain faithful that the ultimate redemption will eventually arrive.

Genre
Psalm of Individual Confidence – In this psalm, the worshipper expresses absolute certainty that his prayers will be heard.

Chapter Summary
Moses describes here the excellence of the Tzaddik (righteous individual) who trusts in God. He further depicts four levels of cleaving to God and of Divine Supervision. He also speaks out against plagues, and concludes with offering a song of thanksgiving.

This psalm consists of sixteen verses, subdivided into two sections.
In verses 1-8, the author proclaims that God will protect the one who trusts in Him. Accordingly, such an individual has no need to fear the darkness. He asserts, too, that God will destroy the wicked.
In verses 9-16, he declares that God will send his angels to guard the Tzaddik on his path. One who believes in the Lord's protection, Moses assures the reader, will be awarded with long days and seeing true salvation.

Shimush Tehillim - When to Say
To ward off evil spirits—Verse 3 states: "For He will save you from the snare trap, from destructive pestilence."
To alleviate fear—Verse 5 states: "You will not fear the terror of night, nor the arrow that flies by day."

Where in the Siddur
Recited as part of Pesukei Dezimra (introductory Verses of Praise to the Shacharit morning service) of Shabbat, Yom Tov (Festivals), and Hoshana Rabbah (the seventh day of Sukkot).
Recited following the Amidah (Silent Meditation) of Ma'ariv (nighttime service) of Motza'ei Shabbat.
Recited by some as part of the bedtime Shema service.
Recited as part of the burial ceremony at the graveside (some recite it seven times).

Talmud on Tehillim

Verse 6: "מְדֶּבֶר, בָּאֹפֶל יַהֲלֹךְ; מִקֶּטֶב, יָשׁוּד צָהֳרָיִם"—"The pestilence that prowls in darkenss, nor the deadly plague that ravages at noon."

This verse speaks of the various demons which lurk at nighttime and at noontime.

The Talmud, Pesachim 111b, informs us that it is important to know the difference between the various types of demons, in order to utilize the proper wording for an amulet used to ward off the evil spirits. (Such amulets, while not common in Ashkenazic circles, are still found in some Sefardic communities).

Verse 10: "לֹא תְאֻנֶּה אֵלֶיךָ רָעָה; וְנֶגַע, לֹא יִקְרַב בְּאָהֳלֶךָ"—"No evil shall befall you, and no plague shall come near your tent."

The Talmud, Berachot 55b, deduces that "No harm will befall you" refers to the rewards given to a righteous individual. A deserving person, suggests the Talmud, is shown good dreams, while a non-deserving person is shown bad dreams.

פרק צא			Chapter 91
יֹשֵׁב	א	1	He who dwells
בְּסֵתֶר עֶלְיוֹן			in the shelter of the Supreme One,
בְּצֵל שַׁדַּי יִתְלוֹנָן׃			under the protection of Shadai he will abide.
אֹמַר לַיהוָה	ב	2	I say of Adonoy,
מַחְסִי וּמְצוּדָתִי			[He is] my refuge and my stronghold,
אֱלֹהַי אֶבְטַח־בּוֹ׃			my God in Whom I trust.
כִּי הוּא יַצִּילְךָ מִפַּח יָקוּשׁ	ג	3	For He will save you from the snare-trap,
מִדֶּבֶר הַוּוֹת׃			from destructive pestilence.
בְּאֶבְרָתוֹ ׀ יָסֶךְ לָךְ	ד	4	With His wings He will cover you
וְתַחַת־כְּנָפָיו תֶּחְסֶה			and beneath His wings, you will find refuge;
צִנָּה וְסֹחֵרָה אֲמִתּוֹ׃			His truth is a shield, a full shield.
לֹא־תִירָא מִפַּחַד לָיְלָה	ה	5	You will not fear the terror of night,
מֵחֵץ יָעוּף יוֹמָם׃			nor the arrow that flies by day.
מִדֶּבֶר בָּאֹפֶל יַהֲלֹךְ	ו	6	The pestilence that prowls in darkness,
מִקֶּטֶב יָשׁוּד צָהֳרָיִם׃			nor the deadly plague that ravages at noon.
יִפֹּל מִצִּדְּךָ ׀ אֶלֶף	ז	7	A thousand will fall at your [left] side,
וּרְבָבָה מִימִינֶךָ			and ten thousand at your [right] side
אֵלֶיךָ לֹא יִגָּשׁ׃			but it shall not come near you.
רַק בְּעֵינֶיךָ תַבִּיט	ח	8	Only with your eyes will you behold
וְשִׁלֻּמַת רְשָׁעִים תִּרְאֶה׃			and see the punishment of the wicked.
כִּי־אַתָּה	ט	9	For you [have proclaimed]:
יְהוָה מַחְסִי			"Adonoy is my refuge,"
עֶלְיוֹן			the Supreme One

שַׂמְתָּ מְעוֹנֶךָ׃	you have made your dwelling.
י לֹא־תְאֻנֶּה אֵלֶיךָ רָעָה	10 No evil shall befall you,
וְנֶגַע לֹא־יִקְרַב בְּאָהֳלֶךָ׃	and no plague shall come near your tent.
יא כִּי מַלְאָכָיו	11 For His angels
יְצַוֶּה־לָּךְ	He will command on your behalf—
לִשְׁמָרְךָ בְּכָל־דְּרָכֶיךָ׃	to guard you in all your ways.
יב עַל־כַּפַּיִם יִשָּׂאוּנְךָ	12 They will carry you upon their hands,
פֶּן־תִּגֹּף בָּאֶבֶן רַגְלֶךָ׃	lest you hurt your foot on a rock.
יג עַל־שַׁחַל וָפֶתֶן תִּדְרֹךְ	13 You will tread upon lion and snake,
תִּרְמֹס כְּפִיר וְתַנִּין׃	you will trample young lion and serpent.
יד כִּי בִי חָשַׁק	14 Because he clings to Me with desire,
וַאֲפַלְּטֵהוּ	I will save him;
אֲשַׂגְּבֵהוּ כִּי־יָדַע שְׁמִי׃	I will strengthen him, for he knows My Name.
טו יִקְרָאֵנִי ׀ וְאֶעֱנֵהוּ	15 When he calls upon Me, I will answer him;
עִמּוֹ־אָנֹכִי בְצָרָה	I am with him in distress,
אֲחַלְּצֵהוּ וַאֲכַבְּדֵהוּ׃	I will free him and honor him.
טז אֹרֶךְ יָמִים אַשְׂבִּיעֵהוּ	16 I will satiate him with longevity,
וְאַרְאֵהוּ בִּישׁוּעָתִי׃	and will let him see My deliverance.

פרק צב ~ Chapter 92

Weekly Cycle	Monthly Cycle	Book Number
Thursday	19th day of the month	Book 4

Author

מֹשֶׁה—Moshe—Moses—the leader of the Israelites and receiver of the Torah at Sinai, a shepherd chosen by God for his humility and loyalty to his sheep. The penultimate verse of the Torah describes him as the greatest prophet of all time.

Genre

Psalm of Praise – This is a psalm of celebration, often the result of a victory. It declares God's goodness and urges all of creation to worship.

Chapter Summary

This psalm was sung by the Levi'im (Levites) in the Beit HaMikdash (Temple) on Shabbat. It is viewed as an allusion to Olam Haba (the World to Come), an entirely spiritual existence, and thus referred to as "Yom Shekulo Shabbat"—a "day which is entirely Shabbat". While it is generally acknowledged that this chapter was authored by Moses, some suggest that it was composed by Adam upon being granted forgiveness for eating from the Tree of Knowledge.

This psalm consists of sixteen verses, subdivided into three parts. The first verse serves as a heading.

In verses 2-6, the psalmist asserts that it is good to give thanks to God. The Lord's deeds are great and profound, he declares, and as such they arouse in his heart feelings of joy and thanks. He prosaically speaks of recounting God's acts of kindness—of singing about them with the accompaniment of musical instruments—morning and evening.

In verses 7-15, the wicked and their fleeting success are contrasted with the righteous and their lasting success. The wicked will be destroyed, suggests the author, yet the righteous will flourish.

In verse 16, Moses proudly proclaims that God is his rock, righteous and upright.

Introductory Words

מִזְמוֹר—Mizmor—Musical Accompaniment
שִׁיר—Shir—Song

Musical Instruments

עָשׂוֹר—Asor—A Ten-Stringed Lyre
נֶבֶל—Nevel—A Large Handheld Lyre - played by plucking with fingers
כִּנּוֹר—Kinor—A Small Handheld Harp - played with a plecturm (pick)

Technical Terminology

הִגָּיוֹן—Higayon—Meditation or Singing

Golden Jug

Shimush Tehillim - When to Say

To rise to greatness—Verse 13 states: "The righteous will blossom like a date palm, like a cedar in Lebanon, he will grow tall."

Where in the Siddur

Recited as one of the paragraphs of Kabbalat Shabbat (Friday night service), ushering in the Shabbat.

Recited as one of the paragraphs of Pesukei Dezimra (Verses of Praise introducing the Shacharit morning service) of Shabbat and Yom Tov (Festivals).

Recited as the Shir Shel Yom (Psalm of the Day) for Shabbat.

Verse 1 is found in the Mishnah, Tamid 7:4.

Verses 1 and 2 are found in the blessings preceding the Shema of Shacharit (morning service) of Shabbat.

Biblical Places

לְבָנוֹן—Lebanon—located just to the north of Israel, famous for its cedar trees. Lebanon was one of Israel's foremost trading partners.

Contemporary Songs

Verses 2 & 3; 13-16

Talmud on Tehillim

Verse 1: "מִזְמוֹר שִׁיר לְיוֹם הַשַּׁבָּת"—"A song for the Shabbos day."

The Talmud, Rosh Hashana 31a, states that this psalm was sung in the Beit HaMikdash (Temple) on Shabbat by the Levi'im (Levites).

Verse 13: "צַדִּיק כַּתָּמָר יִפְרָח, כְּאֶרֶז בַּלְּבָנוֹן יִשְׂגֶּה"—"The righteous will blossom like a date palm like a cedar in Lebanon, he will grow tall."

The Talmud, Bava Batra 90b, suggests that the Tzaddik (righteous man) is likened to both the cedar and the date palm precisely because each possesses only one of two praiseworthy qualities.

A date palm produces fruit but does not regenerate itself; a cedar, on the other hand, regenerates itself but does not bear fruit. The psalmist therefore compares the righteous to both, thereby implying that the Tzaddik both "produces fruit" and "regenerates".

Verse 16: "לְהַגִּיד, כִּי-יָשָׁר יְהוָה"—"To declare that Adonoy is upright."

The Talmud, Kiddushin 82a, deduces that man's primary motivation in life should be "attesting to the uprightness and greatness of God". While one must have an occupation and earn his keep, some individuals mistakenly believe that success and happiness are determined by precisely how much wealth they amass. The psalmist reminds us that such success, however, is fleeting. True happiness and success, we are admonished, result only from the learning of Torah and the observing of mitzvot, as only they are everlasting.

פֶּרֶק צב

א מִזְמוֹר שִׁיר לְיוֹם הַשַּׁבָּת׃
ב טוֹב לְהֹדוֹת לַיהוָה
וּלְזַמֵּר לְשִׁמְךָ עֶלְיוֹן׃
ג לְהַגִּיד בַּבֹּקֶר חַסְדֶּךָ
וֶאֱמוּנָתְךָ בַּלֵּילוֹת׃
ד עֲלֵי־עָשׂוֹר וַעֲלֵי־נָבֶל
עֲלֵי הִגָּיוֹן בְּכִנּוֹר׃
ה כִּי שִׂמַּחְתַּנִי יְהוָה
בְּפָעֳלֶךָ
בְּמַעֲשֵׂי יָדֶיךָ אֲרַנֵּן׃
ו מַה־גָּדְלוּ מַעֲשֶׂיךָ יְהוָה
מְאֹד עָמְקוּ מַחְשְׁבֹתֶיךָ׃
ז אִישׁ־בַּעַר לֹא יֵדָע
וּכְסִיל לֹא־יָבִין אֶת־זֹאת׃
ח בִּפְרֹחַ רְשָׁעִים | כְּמוֹ עֵשֶׂב
וַיָּצִיצוּ כָּל־פֹּעֲלֵי אָוֶן
לְהִשָּׁמְדָם עֲדֵי־עַד׃
ט וְאַתָּה מָרוֹם לְעֹלָם יְהוָה׃

Chapter 92

1 A Psalm, a song for the Shabbos day.
2 It is good to thank Adonoy,
and sing praise to Your Name, Most High.
3 To relate Your kindliness in the morning,
and Your faithfulness in the nights.
4 Upon a ten-stringed instrument and lute,
in meditation upon the harp.
5 For You have given me joy, Adonoy,
with Your deeds,
at the work of Your hands I sing joyously.
6 How great are Your works, Adonoy;
how infinitely profound are Your thoughts.
7 An empty-headed man cannot know,
nor does a fool understand this:
8 When the wicked bloom like grass,
and all the evildoers blossom—
it is so that they may be destroyed forever.
9 But You will remain on high forever Adonoy.

כִּי הִנֵּה אֹיְבֶיךָ ׀ יְהוָה	For behold, Your enemies, Adonoy;
י כִּי־הִנֵּה אֹיְבֶיךָ יֹאבֵדוּ	10 For behold, Your enemies shall perish;
יִתְפָּרְדוּ כָּל־פֹּעֲלֵי אָוֶן׃	dispersed shall be all evildoers.
יא וַתָּרֶם כִּרְאֵים קַרְנִי	11 You uplifted my horn like that of a unicorn;
בַּלֹּתִי בְּשֶׁמֶן רַעֲנָן׃	I am saturated with fresh oil.
יב וַתַּבֵּט עֵינִי	12 My eye has seen [the defeat of]
בְּשׁוּרָי	those who spy on me;
בַּקָּמִים עָלַי מְרֵעִים	of the wicked who rise against me,
תִּשְׁמַעְנָה אָזְנָי׃	my ears have heard [that they are doomed].
יג צַדִּיק כַּתָּמָר יִפְרָח	13 The righteous will blossom like a date palm,
כְּאֶרֶז בַּלְּבָנוֹן יִשְׂגֶּה׃	like a cedar in Lebanon, he will grow tall.
יד שְׁתוּלִים בְּבֵית יְהוָה	14 Planted in the House of Adonoy,
בְּחַצְרוֹת אֱלֹהֵינוּ יַפְרִיחוּ׃	in the courtyards of our God they will blossom.
טו עוֹד יְנוּבוּן בְּשֵׂיבָה	15 They will still be fruitful in old age;
דְּשֵׁנִים וְרַעֲנַנִּים יִהְיוּ׃	they will be full of sap and freshness.
טז לְהַגִּיד כִּי־יָשָׁר יְהוָה	16 To declare that Adonoy is upright;
צוּרִי	He is my Stronghold;
וְלֹא־עַוְלָתָה בּוֹ׃	in Whom there is no injustice.

פרק צג Chapter 93

Weekly Cycle	Monthly Cycle	Book Number
Thursday	19th day of the month	Book 4

Author

מֹשֶׁה—Moshe—Moses—the leader of the Israelites and receiver of the Torah at Sinai, a shepherd chosen by God for his humility and loyalty to his sheep. The penultimate verse of the Torah describes him as the greatest prophet of all time.

When & Why

Moses wrote this psalm prophetically about the days of Messiah, when God's glory will be revealed in full to the entire world and all of humanity will recognize that God rules the universe.

Genre

Psalm of Enthronement – This psalm extols God's royal role in the universe,

Psalm of Praise – This is a psalm of celebration, often the result of a victory. It declares God's goodness and urges all of creation to worship.

Chapter Summary

Moses here glorifies God's kingship, mighty strength, and total dominion. The series of psalms attributed to Moses (90-100) allude, among other things, to the Days of the Mashiach (Messiah), when all mankind will recognize that "the Lord is King" over all the land.

This psalm consists of five verses, subdivided into three sections.
In verses 1 & 2, the psalmist assures the reader that God's kingdom endures forever.
In verse 3 & 4, he asserts that God is mightier than His enemies.
In verse 5, he further proclaims that God will dwell in His house "for the length of days".

Shimush Tehillim - When to Say

To defeat an opponent in court—Verse 5 states: "Your testimonies are extremely faithful, holiness is becoming to Your House, Adonoy—for the length of days."

Where in the Siddur

Recited as the Shir Shel Yom (Psalm of the Day) for Friday.
Recited as part of Kabbalat Shabbat (Friday night service).
Recited as one of the paragraphs of Pesukei Dezimra (Verses of Praise introducing the Shacharit morning service) of Shabbat, Yom Tov (Festivals), and Hoshana Rabbah (seventh day of Sukkot).
Verse 1 is found in the Musaf Amidah (Silent Meditation) of Rosh Hashanah.

Biblical Places

בֵּיתְךָ—Your House—a reference to the Beit HaMikdash (Temple) in Jerusalem.

Talmud on Tehillim

Verse 1: "ה' מָלָךְ, גֵּאוּת לָבֵשׁ"—"Adonoy had begun His reign He has clothed Himself in majesty."
The Talmud, Rosh Hashana 31b, teaches that this psalm was sung by the Levi'im (Levites) in the Beit HaMikdash (Temple) on Friday.

פרק צג	Chapter 93
א יְהוָה מָלָךְ	1 Adonoy had begun His reign
גֵּאוּת לָבֵשׁ	He has clothed Himself with majesty;
לָבֵשׁ יְהוָה	Adonoy has clothed Himself,
עֹז הִתְאַזָּר	He has girded Himself with strength.
אַף־תִּכּוֹן תֵּבֵל	He has firmly established the world
בַּל־תִּמּוֹט׃	so that it cannot be moved.
ב נָכוֹן כִּסְאֲךָ מֵאָז	2 Your throne stands firm from of old,
מֵעוֹלָם אָתָּה׃	You are from eternity.
ג נָשְׂאוּ נְהָרוֹת ׀ יְהוָה	3 The rivers have raised—Adonoy—
נָשְׂאוּ נְהָרוֹת קוֹלָם	the rivers have raised their voice,
יִשְׂאוּ נְהָרוֹת דָּכְיָם׃	the rivers raise their raging waves.
ד מִקֹּלוֹת ׀ מַיִם רַבִּים	4 More than the sound of many waters,

אַדִּירִים מִשְׁבְּרֵי־יָם		mightier than the breakers of the sea
אַדִּיר בַּמָּרוֹם יְהוָה׃		Mighty on high, are You, Adonoy.
עֵדֹתֶיךָ ׀ נֶאֶמְנוּ מְאֹד	ה / 5	Your testimonies are extremely faithful,
לְבֵיתְךָ נַאֲוָה־קֹדֶשׁ		holiness is becoming to Your House,
יְהוָה לְאֹרֶךְ יָמִים׃		Adonoy—for the length of days.

פרק צד ~ Chapter 94

Weekly Cycle	Monthly Cycle	Book Number
Thursday	19th day of the month	Book 4

Author

מֹשֶׁה—Moshe—Moses—the leader of the Israelites and receiver of the Torah at Sinai, a shepherd chosen by God for his humility and loyalty to his sheep. The penultimate verse of the Torah describes him as the greatest prophet of all time.

When & Why

Moses wrote this psalm as a prayer for the coming of the Messiah and the ultimate redemption.

Genre

Psalm of Communal Lament – This psalm focuses on expressing deep sorrow for the travails of a nation and as a group asking for God's blessing or intervention.

Chapter Summary

Moses appeals to God to obliterate the wicked who rise up against Israel. He further requests that His nation be fortified while in exile. God, the author assures the reader, will not abandon His people.

This psalm consists of twenty-three verses, subdivided into three parts.
In verses 1-7, the psalmist laments the deeds of the wicked, and calls upon God to take vengeance upon them. He describes how they arrogantly boast of their success and speak out against God. He further bemoans their oppression and affliction of Israel.
In verses 8-15, Moses reminds the reader that God observes our actions and judges us accordingly.
In verses 16-23, the psalmist describes how God helps those who trust in Him.

Shimush Tehillim - When to Say

To rise to greatness (see Chapter 92)
To ward off and defeat an enemy—Verse 16 states: "Who will rise up for me against the wicked, who will stand up for me against the evildoers?"

Where in the Siddur

Recited—along with the first three verses of Psalm 95—as the Shir Shel Yom (Psalm of the Day) for Wednesday.

Recited on the fifth day of Sukkot in some communities.

Verse 1 is quoted in the Mishnah, Tamid 7:4.

Verse 1 and 2 are found in Vehu Rachum, one of the paragraphs of Pesukei Dezimra (Verses of Praise introducing the Shacharit morning service).

Verse 14 is found in Yehi Chevod, one of the paragraphs of Pesukei Dezimra.

Biblical Personalities

יַעֲקֹב—Jacob—also called Yisrael—Israel, the third patriarch, considered the father of the twelve tribes of Israel. He was the twin brother of Eisav, and married to Leah and Rachel.

Contemporary Song

Verse 14

Talmud on Tehillim

Verse 12: "אַשְׁרֵי הַגֶּבֶר אֲשֶׁר־תְּיַסְּרֶנּוּ יָּהּ"—"Fortunate is the man whom You chastise, God, and whom You instruct from Your Torah." The Talmud, Berachot 5a, deduces that if one is afflicted with suffering, he should turn to the study of Torah.

פרק צד			Chapter 94
אֵל־נְקָמוֹת יְהוָה אֵל נְקָמוֹת הוֹפִיַע׃	א	1	Almighty of vengeance, Adonoy, Almighty of vengeance, reveal Yourself.
הִנָּשֵׂא שֹׁפֵט הָאָרֶץ הָשֵׁב גְּמוּל עַל־גֵּאִים׃	ב	2	Arise, Judge of the earth, repay the arrogant their just reward.
עַד־מָתַי רְשָׁעִים | יְהוָה עַד־מָתַי רְשָׁעִים יַעֲלֹזוּ׃	ג	3	How long shall the wicked— Adonoy— how long shall the wicked exult?
יַבִּיעוּ יְדַבְּרוּ עָתָק יִתְאַמְּרוּ כָּל־פֹּעֲלֵי אָוֶן׃	ד	4	They express, they speak with arrogance; all the evildoers are boastful.
עַמְּךָ יְהוָה יְדַכְּאוּ וְנַחֲלָתְךָ יְעַנּוּ׃	ה	5	Adonoy, they crush Your people and Your heritage they oppress.
אַלְמָנָה וְגֵר יַהֲרֹגוּ וִיתוֹמִים יְרַצֵּחוּ׃	ו	6	The widow and stranger they kill, and orphans they murder.
וַיֹּאמְרוּ לֹא יִרְאֶה־יָּהּ וְלֹא־יָבִין אֱלֹהֵי יַעֲקֹב׃	ז	7	And they say, "God does not see, the God of Jacob is not concerned."
בִּינוּ בֹּעֲרִים בָּעָם וּכְסִילִים מָתַי תַּשְׂכִּילוּ׃	ח	8	Consider, [you] stupid [ones] among the people, and you fools, when will you become wise?

ט הֲנֹטַע אֹזֶן
הֲלֹא יִשְׁמָע
אִם־יֹצֵר עַיִן הֲלֹא יַבִּיט׃

9 He Who implanted the ear,
does He not hear?
He Who formed the eye, does He not see?

י הֲיֹסֵר גּוֹיִם
הֲלֹא יוֹכִיחַ
הַמְלַמֵּד אָדָם דָּעַת׃

10 He Who chastises nations,
does He not reprove—
He that teaches man knowledge?

יא יְהֹוָה יֹדֵעַ מַחְשְׁבוֹת אָדָם
כִּי־הֵמָּה הָבֶל׃

11 Adonoy knows the thoughts of men,
that they are vanity.

יב אַשְׁרֵי | הַגֶּבֶר
אֲשֶׁר־תְּיַסְּרֶנּוּ יָּהּ
וּמִתּוֹרָתְךָ תְלַמְּדֶנּוּ׃

12 Fortunate is the man
whom You chastise, God,
and whom You instruct from Your Torah.

יג לְהַשְׁקִיט לוֹ מִימֵי רָע
עַד יִכָּרֶה לָרָשָׁע שָׁחַת׃

13 To grant him tranquility from days of evil,
until the pit is dug for the wicked.

יד כִּי | לֹא־יִטֹּשׁ יְהֹוָה עַמּוֹ
וְנַחֲלָתוֹ לֹא יַעֲזֹב׃

14 For Adonoy will not abandon His people
and His inheritance, He will not forsake.

טו כִּי־עַד־צֶדֶק יָשׁוּב מִשְׁפָּט
וְאַחֲרָיו כָּל־יִשְׁרֵי־לֵב׃

15 For justice shall return unto righteousness,
and all the upright in heart will follow it.

טז מִי־יָקוּם לִי עִם־מְרֵעִים
מִי־יִתְיַצֵּב לִי
עִם־פֹּעֲלֵי אָוֶן׃

16 Who will rise up for me against the wicked,
who will stand up for me
against the evildoers?

יז לוּלֵי יְהֹוָה עֶזְרָתָה לִּי
כִּמְעַט |
שָׁכְנָה דוּמָה נַפְשִׁי׃

17 Had Adonoy not been my help,
in an instant
my soul would have dwelt in the silent grave.

יח אִם־אָמַרְתִּי מָטָה רַגְלִי
חַסְדְּךָ יְהֹוָה יִסְעָדֵנִי׃

18 If [whenever] I said, ``My foot has slipped,"
Your kindliness, Adonoy upheld me.

יט בְּרֹב שַׂרְעַפַּי
בְּקִרְבִּי
תַּנְחוּמֶיךָ יְשַׁעַשְׁעוּ נַפְשִׁי׃

19 When (worrisome) thoughts multiply
within me,
Your consolations soothe my soul.

כ הַיְחָבְרְךָ כִּסֵּא הַוּוֹת
יֹצֵר עָמָל עֲלֵי־חֹק׃

20 Can an evil tribunal have accord with You—
[a tribunal] that makes iniquity into law?

כא יָגוֹדּוּ עַל־נֶפֶשׁ צַדִּיק
וְדָם נָקִי יַרְשִׁיעוּ׃

21 They gang up against the life of the righteous,
and blood of the innocent they condemn.

כב וַיְהִי יְהֹוָה לִי לְמִשְׂגָּב
וֵאלֹהַי לְצוּר מַחְסִי׃

22 Adonoy has been my stronghold,
my God the Rock of my refuge.

כג וַיָּשֶׁב עֲלֵיהֶם | אֶת־אוֹנָם
וּבְרָעָתָם יַצְמִיתֵם
יַצְמִיתֵם יְהֹוָה אֱלֹהֵינוּ׃

23 He turns their violence against them,
and destroys them with their own wickedness;
Adonoy, my God, destroys them.

Adonoy has been my stronghold,
my God the Rock of my refuge.

פרק צה Chapter 95

Weekly Cycle	Monthly Cycle	Book Number
Thursday	19th day of the month	Book 4

Author

משה—Moshe—Moses—the leader of the Israelites and receiver of the Torah at Sinai, a shepherd chosen by God for his humility and loyalty to his sheep. The penultimate verse of the Torah describes him as the greatest prophet of all time.

When & Why

Moses wrote this psalm prophetically about the coming of the Messiah, when God will gather the people of Israel from among the nations and bring them to their homeland.

Genre

Psalm of Praise – This is a psalm of celebration, often the result of a victory. It declares God's goodness and urges all of creation to worship.

Chapter Summary

This psalm speaks of the Days of Mashiach (Messiah) and of the ingathering of exiles preceding his arrival. Some view this psalm (and the following psalms through chapter 100) as addressing two methods by which God conducts the world—the natural and the miraculous. Others see it as praise of the righteous who, by accepting their suffering, hasten the redemption.

This psalm consists of eleven verses, subdivided into two parts.
In verses 1- 7, Moses calls out to all to sing God's praises and shout out to Him with joy, for He is the creator of the entire world. Let us therefore bow to Him, implores the author.
In verses 8- 11, the psalmist rebukes the congregation, reminding them that they must now fulfill their promise to obey God. They must take care not to act as the generation that wandered in the wilderness, who, as a result of their rebellious behavior, were not privileged to enter Israel and God's "place of rest"—the Beit HaMikdash (Temple).

Shimush Tehillim - When to Say

To avoid being led astray—Verse 8 states: "Do not harden your heart as at Merivah, as on the day of Massah in the desert."

Where in the Siddur

Recited as the opening paragraph of Kabbalat Shabbat (Friday night service).
Recited on Shabbat Hagadol (the Shabbat before Passover) in some congregations.
The first three verses comprise part of the Shir Shel Yom (Psalm of the Day) for Wednesday.
This is the only Shir Shel Yom composed of a compilation of verses from multiple psalms (with the intent of creating an inspiring message), rather than the normative singular psalm.

Biblical Places

מַסָּה—Massah—located in the wilderness, where the Israelites complained to Moses about the lack of water. He in turn rebuked them for testing God; hence the name Massah, meaning "testing".

מְרִיבָה—Meribah—also located in the wilderness, where the Israelites similarly quarreled with Moses about the lack of water, and he in turn rebuked them; hence the name Merivah, meaning "quarreling". The verses describing these events (Exodus, 17:1-7) seem to imply that "Massah and Merivah" are indeed one location.

פֶּרֶק צה

א לְכוּ נְרַנְּנָה לַיהוָה
נָרִיעָה
לְצוּר יִשְׁעֵנוּ:
ב נְקַדְּמָה פָנָיו
בְּתוֹדָה
בִּזְמִרוֹת נָרִיעַ לוֹ:
ג כִּי אֵל גָּדוֹל יְהוָה
וּמֶלֶךְ גָּדוֹל עַל־כָּל־אֱלֹהִים:
ד אֲשֶׁר בְּיָדוֹ מֶחְקְרֵי־אָרֶץ
וְתוֹעֲפוֹת הָרִים לוֹ:
ה אֲשֶׁר־לוֹ הַיָּם וְהוּא עָשָׂהוּ
וְיַבֶּשֶׁת יָדָיו יָצָרוּ:
ו בֹּאוּ נִשְׁתַּחֲוֶה וְנִכְרָעָה
נִבְרְכָה
לִפְנֵי־יְהוָה עֹשֵׂנוּ:
ז כִּי הוּא אֱלֹהֵינוּ
וַאֲנַחְנוּ עַם מַרְעִיתוֹ
וְצֹאן יָדוֹ
הַיּוֹם אִם־בְּקֹלוֹ תִשְׁמָעוּ:
ח אַל־תַּקְשׁוּ לְבַבְכֶם כִּמְרִיבָה
כְּיוֹם מַסָּה בַּמִּדְבָּר:
ט אֲשֶׁר נִסּוּנִי אֲבוֹתֵיכֶם
בְּחָנוּנִי גַּם־רָאוּ פָעֳלִי:
י אַרְבָּעִים שָׁנָה | אָקוּט בְּדוֹר
וָאֹמַר
עַם תֹּעֵי לֵבָב הֵם
וְהֵם לֹא־יָדְעוּ דְרָכָי:
יא אֲשֶׁר־נִשְׁבַּעְתִּי בְאַפִּי
אִם־יְבֹאוּן אֶל־מְנוּחָתִי:

Chapter 95

1 Come, let us sing to Adonoy;
let us sound the shofar
to the Rock of our deliverance.
2 Let us greet His Presence
with thanksgiving,
with hymns let us raise our voices unto Him.
3 For a great Almighty is Adonoy
and a great King over all gods.
4 For in His hands are the depths of the earth,
and the heights of the mountains are His;
5 For the sea is His, and He made it,
and the dry land, His hands formed.
6 Come, let us prostrate ourselves and bow;
let us kneel
before Adonoy, our Maker.
7 For He is our God
and we are the people of His pasture,
and the flock of His hand,
[even] today if you will heed His voice.
8 Do not harden your heart as at Merivah,
as on the day of Massah in the desert.
9 When your fathers tested Me,
they tried Me, though they had seen My work.
10 Forty years I quarreled with that generation;
and I said,
"They are a people of erring hearts,
and they did not know my ways."
11 Therefore I swore in My anger,
"They shall not enter My resting place."

פרק צו Chapter 96

Weekly Cycle	Monthly Cycle	Book Number
Thursday	19th day of the month	Book 4

Author
מֹשֶׁה—Moshe—Moses—the leader of the Israelites and receiver of the Torah at Sinai, a shepherd chosen by God for his humility and loyalty to his sheep. The penultimate verse of the Torah describes him as the greatest prophet of all time.

When & Why
Moses wrote this psalm about how the people of Israel will sing in joy when they are redeemed from exile.

Genre
Psalm of Enthronement - This psalm extols God's royal role in the universe.
Psalm of Praise – This is a psalm of celebration, often the result of a victory. It declares God's goodness and urges all of creation to worship.

Chapter Summary
The psalmist sings a song for the future, when God will deliver Israel from evil persecutors. In this and the following psalm, the singer further declares that the Lord will perform miracles transcending nature in order to conform to the deliverance of His servants.

This psalm consists of thirteen verses, subdivided into four parts.
In verses 1-3, Moses calls out to all to sing to God.
In verses 4-6, he asserts that God is great and should be feared.
In verses 7-10, he further calls upon all the nations of the world to fear God.
In verses 11-13, he assures the reader that even the mighty forces of creation will rejoice and raise their voices in song in God's honor on the day that He judges all peoples of the earth.

Introductory Word
שִׁיר—Shir—Song

Shimush Tehillim - When to Say
To help one's family rejoice—Verse 1 states: "Sing to Adonoy a new song Sing to Adonoy all the [inhabitants of] earth."

Where in the Siddur
Recited as the second paragraph of Kabbalat Shabbat (Friday night service).
Recited on the first day of Sukkot in some congregations.
Verse 4 is found in Selichot (Penitential Service) of Ma'ariv (evening service) of Yom Kippur.

Biblical Places
חֲצְרוֹתָיו—His Courtyards—a reference to the Beit HaMikdash (Temple) in Jerusalem.

Contemporary Song
Verse 11

פרק צו

א שִׁירוּ לַיהוָה שִׁיר חָדָשׁ
שִׁירוּ לַיהוָה כָּל־הָאָרֶץ׃
ב שִׁירוּ לַיהוָה בָּרְכוּ שְׁמוֹ
בַּשְּׂרוּ מִיּוֹם־לְיוֹם יְשׁוּעָתוֹ׃
ג סַפְּרוּ בַגּוֹיִם כְּבוֹדוֹ
בְּכָל־הָעַמִּים נִפְלְאוֹתָיו׃
ד כִּי גָדוֹל יְהוָה וּמְהֻלָּל מְאֹד
נוֹרָא הוּא עַל־כָּל־אֱלֹהִים׃
ה כִּי | כָּל־אֱלֹהֵי הָעַמִּים אֱלִילִים
וַיהוָה שָׁמַיִם עָשָׂה׃
ו הוֹד־וְהָדָר לְפָנָיו
עֹז וְתִפְאֶרֶת בְּמִקְדָּשׁוֹ׃
ז הָבוּ לַיהוָה מִשְׁפְּחוֹת עַמִּים
הָבוּ לַיהוָה כָּבוֹד וָעֹז׃
ח הָבוּ לַיהוָה כְּבוֹד שְׁמוֹ
שְׂאוּ־מִנְחָה וּבֹאוּ לְחַצְרוֹתָיו׃
ט הִשְׁתַּחֲווּ לַיהוָה
בְּהַדְרַת־קֹדֶשׁ
חִילוּ מִפָּנָיו כָּל־הָאָרֶץ׃
י אִמְרוּ בַגּוֹיִם |
יְהוָה מָלָךְ
אַף־תִּכּוֹן תֵּבֵל
בַּל־תִּמּוֹט
יָדִין עַמִּים בְּמֵישָׁרִים׃
יא יִשְׂמְחוּ הַשָּׁמַיִם
וְתָגֵל הָאָרֶץ
יִרְעַם הַיָּם וּמְלֹאוֹ׃
יב יַעֲלֹז שָׂדַי וְכָל־אֲשֶׁר־בּוֹ
אָז יְרַנְּנוּ כָּל־עֲצֵי־יָעַר׃
יג לִפְנֵי יְהוָה | כִּי בָא
כִּי בָא לִשְׁפֹּט הָאָרֶץ
יִשְׁפֹּט־תֵּבֵל בְּצֶדֶק
וְעַמִּים בֶּאֱמוּנָתוֹ׃

Chapter 96

1 Sing to Adonoy a new song
Sing to Adonoy all the [inhabitants of] earth.
2 Sing to Adonoy, bless His Name,
proclaim His deliverance from day to day.
3 Recount His glory among the nations,
His wonders among all the peoples.
4 For Adonoy is great and most extolled;
He is awesome above all gods.
5 For all the gods of the nations are idols,
whereas Adonoy made the heavens.
6 Beauty and splendor are before Him,
strength and glory are in His Sanctuary.
7 Ascribe to Adonoy—families of peoples—
—ascribe to Adonoy honor and might!
8 Ascribe to Adonoy the honor due His Name,
bring an offering and come to His courtyards.
9 Prostrate yourselves before Adonoy
in the splendor of holiness;
tremble before Him all (peoples of) the earth!
10 Declare among the nations,
"Adonoy reigns!"
for He established the world
so that it cannot be moved,
He will judge the peoples with uprightness.
11 The heavens will rejoice,
the earth will exult,
the sea and its fullness will roar.
12 The field and all that is in it will jubilate,
then all the trees of the forest will sing for joy.
13 Before Adonoy when He comes—
when He comes to judge the earth;
He will judge mankind with justice,
and peoples with His truth.

פרק צז Chapter 97

Weekly Cycle	Monthly Cycle	Book Number
Thursday	20th day of the month	Book 4

Author

מֹשֶׁה—Moshe—Moses—the leader of the Israelites and receiver of the Torah at Sinai, a shepherd chosen by God for his humility and loyalty to his sheep. The penultimate verse of the Torah describes him as the greatest prophet of all time.

When & Why

Moses wrote this psalm to encourage the people of Israel while in the Babylonian exile to maintain their devotion to God. Their faithfulness will cause the redemption and return to the Land of Israel.

Genre

Psalm of Enthronement - This psalm extols God's royal role in the universe.

Psalm of Praise – This is a psalm of celebration, often the result of a victory. It declares God's goodness and urges all of creation to worship.

Chapter Summary

Moses, once again through beautiful imagery, depicts how the earth and the heavens will rejoice when God will reign supreme. The singer then admonishes even those adhering to the Torah, that they should despise evil and wickedness.

This psalm consists of twelve verses, subdivided into three parts.

In verses 1-6, the psalmist speaks of the revelation of the glory of God's kingdom.

In verses 7-9, he addresses the humiliation suffered by idol-worshipers and the joy of those who worship God.

In verses 10-12, he implores the righteous to hate evil, and assures them of God's promised salvation in return. Moses concludes this psalm by admonishing the congregation to rejoice in God and give thanks to His name.

Shimush Tehillim - When to Say

To help one's family rejoice—Verse 8 states: "Zion will hear and rejoice, and the daughters [cities] of Judah will exult because of Your judgments, Adonoy."

Where in the Siddur

Recited as the third paragraph of Kabbalat Shabbat (Friday night service).

Recited on the third through sixth days of Sukkot in some congregations.

Verse 1 is found in the repetition of the Musaf Amidah (Silent Meditation) of Rosh HaShanah.

Verse 11 is the opening verse of the Kol Nidrei Yom Kippur service.

Biblical Places

בְּנוֹת יְהוּדָה—**Daughters of Judah**—Judean villages surrounding Jerusalem.

צִיּוֹן—**Zion**—often used as a synonym for Jerusalem, the term Zion originally referred only to the area where a Jebbusite fortress once stood, also the location of the City of David. Zion was later used by prophets and psalmists as another name for Jerusalem.

Contemporary Song
Verse 11

פֶּרֶק צ״ז

א יְהֹוָה מָלָךְ
תָּגֵל הָאָרֶץ
יִשְׂמְחוּ אִיִּים רַבִּים׃
ב עָנָן וַעֲרָפֶל סְבִיבָיו
צֶדֶק וּמִשְׁפָּט
מְכוֹן כִּסְאוֹ׃
ג אֵשׁ לְפָנָיו תֵּלֵךְ
וּתְלַהֵט סָבִיב צָרָיו׃
ד הֵאִירוּ בְרָקָיו
תֵּבֵל
רָאֲתָה וַתָּחֵל הָאָרֶץ׃
ה הָרִים כַּדּוֹנַג נָמַסּוּ
מִלִּפְנֵי יְהֹוָה
מִלִּפְנֵי אֲדוֹן כָּל־הָאָרֶץ׃
ו הִגִּידוּ הַשָּׁמַיִם צִדְקוֹ
וְרָאוּ כָל־הָעַמִּים כְּבוֹדוֹ׃
ז יֵבֹשׁוּ |
כָּל־עֹבְדֵי פֶסֶל
הַמִּתְהַלְלִים בָּאֱלִילִים
הִשְׁתַּחֲווּ־לוֹ כָּל־אֱלֹהִים׃
ח שָׁמְעָה וַתִּשְׂמַח | צִיּוֹן
וַתָּגֵלְנָה בְּנוֹת יְהוּדָה
לְמַעַן מִשְׁפָּטֶיךָ יְהֹוָה׃
ט כִּי־אַתָּה יְהֹוָה עֶלְיוֹן
עַל־כָּל־הָאָרֶץ
מְאֹד נַעֲלֵיתָ עַל־כָּל־אֱלֹהִים׃
י אֹהֲבֵי יְהֹוָה שִׂנְאוּ רָע
שֹׁמֵר נַפְשׁוֹת חֲסִידָיו
מִיַּד רְשָׁעִים יַצִּילֵם׃
יא אוֹר זָרֻעַ לַצַּדִּיק
וּלְיִשְׁרֵי־לֵב שִׂמְחָה׃
יב שִׂמְחוּ צַדִּיקִים בַּיהֹוָה
וְהוֹדוּ לְזֵכֶר קָדְשׁוֹ׃

Chapter 97

1 When Adonoy is [universally accepted as] King
the earth will exult;
the multitudes of islands will rejoice.
2 Clouds and dense darkness surround Him;
righteousness and justice
are the foundations of His throne.
3 Fire will go before Him
to surround and burn His antagonists.
4 His lightning illuminates
the inhabited world,
the earth sees and trembles.
5 The mountains melt like wax
before Adonoy,
before the Master of all the earth.
6 The heavens will declare His righteousness
and all the peoples will behold His glory.
7 Humiliated will be
all who serve graven images,
who are proud of idols;
before Him all gods will bow.
8 Zion will hear and rejoice,
and the daughters [cities] of Judah will exult
because of Your judgments, Adonoy.
9 For You, Adonoy, are most high
over all the earth;
You are greatly exalted above all gods.
10 Lovers of Adonoy, hate evil!
He preserves the souls of His pious ones;
from the hand of the wicked, He saves them.
11 Light is sown for the righteous,
and for the upright in heart—joy.
12 Rejoice, righteous ones, in Adonoy,
and give thanks to His holy Name.

פרק צח Chapter 98

Weekly Cycle	Monthly Cycle	Book Number
Thursday	20th day of the month	Book 4

Author

מֹשֶׁה—Moshe—Moses—the leader of the Israelites and receiver of the Torah at Sinai, a shepherd chosen by God for his humility and loyalty to his sheep. The penultimate verse of the Torah describes him as the greatest prophet of all time.

When & Why

Moses wrote this psalm prophetically about the great joy that Israel will experience after the coming of the Messiah.

Genre

Psalm of Enthronement - This psalm extols God's royal role in the universe.

Psalm of Praise – This is a psalm of celebration, often the result of a victory. It declares God's goodness and urges all of creation to worship.

Chapter Summary

Continuing the theme of the previous psalm, Moses, through beautiful imagery, alludes to the messianic era. Of interesting note is that both their opening and closing verses are quite similar. The singer composed this as a song for that future time, when we will have witnessed God's performing many miraculous deeds for our sake.

This psalm consists of nine verses, subdivided into three parts.

In verses 1-3, the psalmist begins with a command to the congregation to sing a new song to God for His marvels and victories He has bestowed upon Israel. He further beautifully describes the manifestation of God's salvation.

In verses 4-6, he calls upon all the inhabitants of the earth to make joyful music in honor of God and to crown Him as King.

In verses 7-9, He addresses the forces of nature: the sea, land, rivers and mountains to sing praises in honor of God's arrival as judge of the earth.

Introductory Words

שִׁיר—Shir—Song

מִזְמוֹר—Mizmor—Musical Accompaniment

Musical Instruments

חֲצֹצְרוֹת—Chatzotzrot—A pair of non-musical, signaling devices used by the Kohanim to signal the assembly of the nation, the breaking of camp and in conjunction with various ritual functions.

כִּנּוֹר—Kinor—A Small Handheld Harp - played with a plecturm (pick)

שׁוֹפָר—Shofar—A Ram's Horn

Shimush Tehillim - When to Say

To make peace between two parties—Verse 8 states: "Rivers will clap hands, together, mountains will sing."

Where in the Siddur

Recited as the fourth paragraph of Kabbalat Shabbat (Friday night service).
Verse 6 is found in the Mussaf Amidah (Silent Meditation) of Rosh HaShanah.

Biblical Personalities

בֵּית יִשְׂרָאֵל—Beit Yisroel—House of Israel.

פֶּרֶק צ״ח

א מִזְמ֡וֹר
שִׁ֤ירוּ לַיהֹוָ֨ה ׀ שִׁ֣יר חָ֭דָשׁ
כִּֽי־נִפְלָא֣וֹת עָשָׂ֑ה
הוֹשִׁיעָה־לּ֥וֹ יְ֝מִינ֗וֹ
וּזְר֥וֹעַ קָדְשֽׁוֹ׃
ב הוֹדִ֣יעַ יְ֭הֹוָה יְשׁוּעָת֑וֹ
לְעֵינֵ֥י הַ֝גּוֹיִ֗ם
גִּלָּ֥ה צִדְקָתֽוֹ׃
ג זָ֘כַ֤ר חַסְדּ֨וֹ ׀
וֶ֥אֱֽמוּנָתוֹ֮
לְבֵ֪ית יִשְׂרָ֫אֵ֥ל
רָא֥וּ כָל־אַפְסֵי־אָ֑רֶץ
אֵ֝֗ת יְשׁוּעַ֥ת אֱלֹהֵֽינוּ׃
ד הָרִ֣יעוּ לַ֭יהֹוָה
כָּל־הָאָ֑רֶץ
פִּצְח֖וּ
וְרַנְּנ֣וּ וְזַמֵּֽרוּ׃
ה זַמְּר֣וּ לַיהֹוָ֣ה בְּכִנּ֑וֹר
בְּ֝כִנּ֗וֹר וְק֣וֹל זִמְרָֽה׃
ו בַּחֲצֹ֣צְרוֹת וְק֣וֹל שׁוֹפָ֑ר
הָ֝רִ֗יעוּ לִפְנֵ֤י ׀ הַמֶּ֬לֶךְ יְהֹוָֽה׃
ז יִרְעַ֣ם הַ֭יָּם וּמְלֹא֑וֹ
תֵּ֝בֵ֗ל וְיֹ֣שְׁבֵי בָֽהּ׃
ח נְהָר֥וֹת יִמְחֲאוּ־כָ֑ף
יַ֝֗חַד הָרִ֥ים יְרַנֵּֽנוּ׃
ט לִֽפְנֵי־יְהֹוָ֗ה כִּ֢י בָ֡א
לִשְׁפֹּ֫ט הָאָ֥רֶץ
יִשְׁפֹּֽט־תֵּבֵ֥ל בְּצֶ֑דֶק
וְ֝עַמִּ֗ים בְּמֵישָׁרִֽים׃

Chapter 98

1 A Psalm.
Sing to Adonoy, a new song
for He has performed wonders;
His right hand effected deliverance for Him
[as did] His holy arm.
2 Adonoy has made known His deliverance,
before the eyes of the nations
He has revealed His justice.
3 He remembered His kindliness
and faithfulness
to the House of Israel;
all the ends of the earth have seen
the deliverance of our God.
4 Raise your voice unto Adonoy
all [inhabitants of] the earth!
burst forth into exultation,
sing, and play music!
5 Play to Adonoy with a harp,
with harp and the sound of music.
6 With trumpets and the sound of the shofar
raise your voices before the King, Adonoy.
7 The sea and its fullness, will roar with joy!
[also] the world and those who dwell therein.
8 Rivers will clap hands,
together, mountains will sing.
9 Before Adonoy
when He comes to judge the earth;
He will judge mankind with righteousness
and peoples with uprightness.

פרק צט Chapter 99

Weekly Cycle	Monthly Cycle	Book Number
Thursday	20th day of the month	Book 4

Author

מֹשֶׁה—Moshe—Moses—the leader of the Israelites and receiver of the Torah at Sinai, a shepherd chosen by God for his humility and loyalty to his sheep. The penultimate verse of the Torah describes him as the greatest prophet of all time.

When & Why

Moses wrote this psalm propheticaly about the war between Gog and Magog in the end of days. This war will be fought by these two world super powers in Jerusalem. Then God's kingship will be fully manifest at this time.

Genre

Psalm of Enthronement - This psalm extols God's royal role in the universe.

Psalm of Praise – This is a psalm of celebration, often the result of a victory. It declares God's goodness and urges all of creation to worship.

Chapter Summary

As in the previous two psalms, here too Moses speaks of the future revelation of God's kingship, as well as His returning to Zion. When that time arrives, asserts the psalmist, the nations will be seized with fear.

This psalm consists of nine verses, subdivided into three parts, each of which ends with the refrain "Kadosh"—"[God is] holy".

In verses 1-3, the psalmist depicts God as ruling from Zion over all peoples of the earth, and how the earth itself trembles in fear of Him.

In verses 4 & 5, he describes the holiness of God as manifesting itself in His sovereignty over Israel. He further reminds the reader that God dealt in a just and righteous manner with Jacob.

In verses 6-9, he again describes the holiness of God, this time as manifesting itself through His nearness to His chosen who in turn fear Him.

Shimush Tehillim - When to Say

For assistance in becoming pious—Verse 6 states: "Moses and Aaron among His priests, and Samuel among those who invoke His Name, called to Adonoy, and He answered them."

Where in the Siddur

Recited as one of the paragraphs of Kabbalat Shabbat (Friday night service).

Verse 5 is one of the verses recited following the removal of the Torah from the Aron Kodesh (Holy Ark).

Verse 5 also comprises one of the verses of Hodu—a central prayer of Pesukei DeZimra (Verses of Praise introducing the Shacharit morning service).

Biblical Personalities

אַהֲרֹן—Aaron—Moses' older brother and the first Kohein Gadol (High Priest). The descendents of Aaron were designated to perform the ritual service in the Beit HaMikdash (Temple).

יַעֲקֹב—Jacob—also called Yisrael—Israel, the third patriarch, considered the father of the twelve tribes of Israel. He was the twin brother of Esau, and was married to Leah and Rachel.

מֹשֶׁה—Moses—sent by God to redeem the Israelites from Egypt. He received the Torah on behalf of the Israelites and acted as a mediator between them and God.

שְׁמוּאֵל—Samuel—a prophet and the last of the Judges who led Israel in the period prior to the institution of a monarchy. He conceded to the Israelites' demand for a king, and subsequently anointed Saul as the first king of Israel. When King Saul rebelled against God's command to obliterate the entirety of Amaleik, Samuel anointed David to start a new monarchic line.

Biblical Places

הַר קָדְשׁוֹ—(His) Holy Mount—a reference to the Beit HaMikdash (Temple) in Jerusalem.

צִיּוֹן—Zion—often used as a synonym for Jerusalem, the term Zion originally referred only to the area where a Jebbusite fortress once stood, also the location of the City of David. Zion was later used by prophets and psalmists as another name for Jerusalem.

Biblical Creatures

כְּרוּבִים—Cherubim—were golden angelic winged infants positioned upon the Ark of the Covenant, which contained the two Tablets with the Ten Commandments on them.

פרק צט	Chapter 99
א יְהוָה	1 When Adonoy is [universally accepted as]
מָלָךְ	King,
יִרְגְּזוּ עַמִּים	peoples will tremble;
יֹשֵׁב	[Before Him Who is] enthroned
כְּרוּבִים	on Cherubim,
תָּנוּט הָאָרֶץ׃	the earth will quake.
ב יְהוָה בְּצִיּוֹן גָּדוֹל	2 Adonoy, is great in Zion,
וְרָם הוּא עַל־כָּל־הָעַמִּים׃	and is high above all the peoples.
ג יוֹדוּ שִׁמְךָ	3 They will pay homage to Your Name,
גָּדוֹל וְנוֹרָא קָדוֹשׁ הוּא׃	[saying], great and awesome, It is holy.
ד וְעֹז מֶלֶךְ	4 The might of the King
מִשְׁפָּט אָהֵב	is [evidenced in] His love of justice,
אַתָּה כּוֹנַנְתָּ מֵישָׁרִים	You have established uprightness,
מִשְׁפָּט וּצְדָקָה בְּיַעֲקֹב	justice and charity amid Jacob
אַתָּה עָשִׂיתָ׃	You have instituted.

ה רוֹמְמוּ יְהֹוָה אֱלֹהֵינוּ
וְהִשְׁתַּחֲווּ לַהֲדֹם רַגְלָיו
קָדוֹשׁ הוּא׃

5 Exalt Adonoy, our God,
and prostrate yourselves at His footstool,
holy is He.

ו מֹשֶׁה וְאַהֲרֹן | בְּכֹהֲנָיו
וּשְׁמוּאֵל
בְּקֹרְאֵי שְׁמוֹ
קֹרְאִים אֶל־יְהֹוָה וְהוּא יַעֲנֵם׃

6 Moses and Aaron among His priests,
and Samuel
among those who invoke His Name,
called to Adonoy, and He answered them.

ז בְּעַמּוּד עָנָן יְדַבֵּר אֲלֵיהֶם
שָׁמְרוּ עֵדֹתָיו
וְחֹק נָתַן־לָמוֹ׃

7 In a pillar of cloud He spoke to them;
they preserved His testimonies
and the statute which He gave them.

ח יְהֹוָה אֱלֹהֵינוּ אַתָּה עֲנִיתָם
אֵל נֹשֵׂא הָיִיתָ לָהֶם
וְנֹקֵם עַל־עֲלִילוֹתָם׃

8 Adonoy, our God, You answered them;
You were a forgiving God to them,
[yet] You took vengeance for their misdeeds.

ט רוֹמְמוּ יְהֹוָה אֱלֹהֵינוּ
וְהִשְׁתַּחֲווּ לְהַר קָדְשׁוֹ
כִּי־קָדוֹשׁ יְהֹוָה אֱלֹהֵינוּ׃

9 Exalt Adonoy, our God,
and prostrate yourselves at His holy mountain;
for Adonoy, our God, is holy.

פרק ק — Chapter 100

Weekly Cycle	Monthly Cycle	Book Number
Thursday	20th day of the month	Book 4

Author

מֹשֶׁה—Moshe—Moses—the leader of the Israelites and receiver of the Torah at Sinai, a shepherd chosen by God for his humility and loyalty to his sheep. The penultimate verse of the Torah describes him as the greatest prophet of all time.

When & Why

This psalm was written to be said by someone who brings a thanksgiving offering in the Temple.

Genre

Psalm of Thanksgiving – This is a psalm of celebration, often the result of a victory. It declares God's goodness and urges all of creation to worship.

Prayer of Communal Thanksgiving - This psalm emphasizes gratitude for what God has done for the community.

Chapter Summary

This psalm was chanted in conjunction with the Korban Todah (Thanksgiving offering) in the Beit

HaMikdash (Temple). It also serves as a general call to all Israel to offer thanks to God for all the good He has bestowed upon His people.

This psalm consists of five verses, subdivided into three parts. The first half of verse 1 serves as a heading.
In verses 1 & 2, the psalmist bids "the land" to shout out to God and serve Him with joy.
In verse 3, he admonishes us to know that God is the Lord and that we are His nation.
In verses 4 & 5, he further encourages us to thank God, praise Him, and bless His name.

Introductory Word

מִזְמוֹר—Mizmor—Musical Accompaniment

Shimush Tehillim - When to Say

To rise to greatness—Verse 1 states: "A Psalm of thanksgiving: Shout for joy to Adonoy, everyone on earth."

Where in the Siddur

Recited as part of Pesukei Dezimra (Verses of Praise introducing the Shacharit morning service) of weekdays. It is omitted on Erev (the eve of) Yom Kippur, Erev Pesach (Passover), and Chol Hamo'eid (Intermediate Days of) Pesach, as the Korban Todah (Thanksgiving offering) was not offered in the Beit HaMikdash (Temple) on those days. (See "Chapter Summary" for more information).

Contemporary Song

Verse 2

פֶּרֶק ק

א מִזְמ֥וֹר לְתוֹדָ֑ה
הָרִ֥יעוּ לַ֝יהֹוָ֗ה כָּל־הָאָֽרֶץ׃
ב עִבְד֣וּ אֶת־יְהֹוָ֣ה בְּשִׂמְחָ֑ה
בֹּ֥אוּ לְ֝פָנָ֗יו בִּרְנָנָֽה׃
ג דְּע֗וּ כִּֽי־יְהֹוָ֗ה ה֥וּא אֱלֹ֫הִ֥ים
הֽוּא־עָ֭שָׂנוּ וְלֹ֣א אֲנַ֑חְנוּ
עַ֝מּ֗וֹ וְצֹ֣אן מַרְעִיתֽוֹ׃
ד בֹּ֤אוּ שְׁעָרָ֨יו ׀ בְּתוֹדָ֗ה
חֲצֵרֹתָ֥יו בִּתְהִלָּ֑ה
הֽוֹדוּ־ל֝֗וֹ בָּרְכ֥וּ שְׁמֽוֹ׃
ה כִּי־ט֣וֹב יְ֭הֹוָה
לְעוֹלָ֣ם חַסְדּ֑וֹ
וְעַד־דֹּ֥ר וָ֝דֹ֗ר
אֱמוּנָתֽוֹ׃

Chapter 100

1 A Psalm of thanksgiving:
Shout for joy to Adonoy, everyone on earth.
2 Serve Adonoy with joy
come before Him with exultation.
3 Know that Adonoy is God
He has made us and we are His,
His people and the sheep of His pasturing.
4 Enter His gates with thanksgiving,
His courtyards with praise.
Give thanks to Him, bless His Name.
5 For Adonoy is good,
His loving kindness is eternal
and to every generation
His faithfulness [extends.]

פרק קא Chapter 101

Weekly Cycle	Monthly Cycle	Book Number
Thursday	20th day of the month	Book 4

Author

דָּוִד הַמֶּלֶךְ—King David—the second king of Israel and father of the Davidic royal and messianic dynasty. David composed over seventy of the 150 psalms of Sefer Tehillim.

When & Why

David wrote this psalm to explain how he ruled his kingdom and led the people of Israel.

Genre

Psalm of Royalty - This psalm describes how God reigns supreme. It focuses on the human king of Israel, or upon God as King of Israel.

Chapter Summary

This psalm depicts David's conduct both in his home and in ruling his kingdom. It emphasizes the kindness and just judgment which he practiced towards Israel. Some suggest that David composed this psalm when he beseeched God to allow him build the Beit HaMikdash (Temple).

This psalm consists of eight verses, subdivided into two parts.

The first verse serves as an introduction, in which King David proclaims that he will sing of lovingkindness and justice.

In verses 2-4, the Psalmist contemplates how he conducts himself with integrity and distances himself from evil deeds.

In verses 5-8, he speaks of the members of his household, asserting that he makes sure that they too walk with integrity. He declares that he sends away the wicked and draws the righteous near to him.

Introductory Word

מִזְמוֹר—Mizmor—Musical Accompaniment

Shimush Tehillim - When to Say

To ward off an evil spirit—Verse 3 states: "I will not set before my eyes works of wickedness the doing of crooked things I hate; [thus] it will not cleave to me."

Ennion Glass Pitcher

פֶּרֶק קא

Chapter 101

א לְדָוִד מִזְמוֹר
חֶסֶד־וּמִשְׁפָּט אָשִׁירָה
לְךָ יְהוָה אֲזַמֵּרָה׃

1 A Psalm of David.
I will sing of kindness and judgment;
to You, Adonoy, I will sing praises.

ב אַשְׂכִּילָה ׀ בְּדֶרֶךְ תָּמִים
מָתַי תָּבוֹא אֵלָי
אֶתְהַלֵּךְ בְּתָם־לְבָבִי
בְּקֶרֶב בֵּיתִי׃

2 I will concern myself in the way of integrity,
when will [the opportunity] come to me—
I will walk in the integrity of my heart
within my house.

ג לֹא־אָשִׁית ׀ לְנֶגֶד עֵינַי
דְּבַר־בְּלִיָּעַל
עֲשֹׂה־סֵטִים שָׂנֵאתִי
לֹא יִדְבַּק בִּי׃

3 I will not set before my eyes
works of wickedness
the doing of crooked things I hate;
[thus] it will not cleave to me.

ד לֵבָב עִקֵּשׁ יָסוּר מִמֶּנִּי
רָע לֹא אֵדָע׃

4 A perverse heart will be estranged from me,
I will know no evil.

ה מְלָשְׁנִי בַסֵּתֶר ׀ רֵעֵהוּ
אוֹתוֹ אַצְמִית
גְּבַהּ־עֵינַיִם
וּרְחַב לֵבָב
אֹתוֹ לֹא אוּכָל׃

5 He who slanders his neighbor in secret,
him will I cut down;
he who is haughty of eye
and proud of heart,
him will I not tolerate [as a friend].

ו עֵינַי ׀ בְּנֶאֶמְנֵי־אֶרֶץ
לָשֶׁבֶת עִמָּדִי
הֹלֵךְ בְּדֶרֶךְ תָּמִים
הוּא יְשָׁרְתֵנִי׃

6 My eyes are upon the faithful of the land,
that they may dwell with me;
he who walks in the way of integrity,
he will minister to me.

ז לֹא־יֵשֵׁב ׀ בְּקֶרֶב בֵּיתִי
עֹשֵׂה רְמִיָּה
דֹּבֵר שְׁקָרִים
לֹא־יִכּוֹן לְנֶגֶד עֵינָי׃

7 He will not dwell within my house,
one who works deceit;
he who tells lies
will have no place before my eyes.

ח לַבְּקָרִים
אַצְמִית כָּל־רִשְׁעֵי־אָרֶץ
לְהַכְרִית מֵעִיר־יְהוָה
כָּל־פֹּעֲלֵי אָוֶן׃

8 Each morning
I will cut down all the wicked of the land,
to cut off from the city of Adonoy
all those who do evil.

Royal Golden Menorah Ring (Courtesy of the Shlomo Moussaieff Collection)

פרק קב Chapter 102

Weekly Cycle	Monthly Cycle	Book Number
Thursday	20th day of the month	Book 4

Author

Unknown; perhaps דָּוִד הַמֶּלֶךְ—King David—the second king of Israel and father of the Davidic royal and messianic dynasty. David composed over seventy of the 150 psalms of Sefer Tehillim.

When & Why

David might have written this psalm about his own suffering and about the future suffering of the people of Israel who will be in exile.

Genre

Psalm of Individual Lament - This psalm was written from the perspective of the individual worshipper, who cries out to God in his time of need. It is characterized as an address to God involving a complaint, followed by a request and ending with an expression of trust.

Chapter Summary

The psalmist, according to tradition, would chant this psalm whenever he would turn inside himself and vanish from before his pursuers. He would then pour forth this prayer before the Lord, pleading for deliverance from his troubles. Some explain that he is also speaking on behalf of future exiles who, like he, would be victimized and agonized by their enemies.

This psalm consists of twenty-nine verses, subdivided into four parts. The first verse serves as a heading, in which the psalmist depicts his lament as that of a suffering man who pours out his speech to God.

In verses 2-3, the author requests that his prayer be accepted.

In verses 4-12, he describes his distress and grief.

In verses 13-23, he prays for the rebuilding of Zion.

In verses 24-29, he concludes by speaking of the shortness of man's life in contrast to God's eternity.

Introductory Word

תְּפִלָּה—Tefilah—Prayer

Shimush Tehillim - When to Say

For a woman who is barren—Verses 18, 21 and 29 state: " He has turned to the prayer of the lonely one and has not despised their prayer". "To hear the anguished cry of the prisoner, to liberate those who are doomed to die". "Your servant's children will be securely settled, and their seed will be established before You."

Where in the Siddur

Verse 3 is found in the prayer recited by the congegation during the Birkat Kohanim (Priestly Blessing).

Verse 14 is found in the introductory paragraphs of Selichot (Penitential Service).
Verse 14 also appears in one of the Kinot (Elegies) of Tishah BeAv (the Fast of the Ninth of Av).
Verse 28 is found in the introduction to the Viduy (Confession Service) of Yom Kippur.

Biblical Places

יְרוּשָׁלַיִם—Jerusalem—the capital city of Israel, conquered by King David 3,000 years ago. David established Jerusalem as both the religious and political center of Israel.

צִיּוֹן—Zion—often used as a synonym for Jerusalem, the term Zion originally referred only to the area where a Jebbusite fortress once stood, also the location of the City of David. Zion was later used by prophets and psalmists as another name for Jerusalem.

Contemporary Song

Verse 14

Talmud on Tehillim

Verse 24: "עִנָּה בַדֶּרֶךְ כֹּחִי; קִצַּר יָמָי"—"He weakened my strength in the way, He shortened my days." The Talmud, Gittin 70a, teaches that three things weaken a person's strength: anxiety, traveling and sin.

פֶּרֶק קב

א תְּפִלָּה לְעָנִי
כִי־יַעֲטֹף
וְלִפְנֵי יְהֹוָה
יִשְׁפֹּךְ שִׂיחוֹ:
ב יְהֹוָה שִׁמְעָה תְפִלָּתִי
וְשַׁוְעָתִי אֵלֶיךָ תָבוֹא:
ג אַל־תַּסְתֵּר פָּנֶיךָ ׀ מִמֶּנִּי
בְּיוֹם צַר לִי
הַטֵּה־אֵלַי אָזְנֶךָ
בְּיוֹם אֶקְרָא מַהֵר עֲנֵנִי:
ד כִּי כָלוּ בְעָשָׁן יָמָי
וְעַצְמוֹתַי כְּמוֹקֵד נִחָרוּ:
ה הוּכָּה כָעֵשֶׂב וַיִּבַשׁ לִבִּי
כִּי־שָׁכַחְתִּי מֵאֲכֹל לַחְמִי:
ו מִקּוֹל אַנְחָתִי
דָּבְקָה עַצְמִי לִבְשָׂרִי:
ז דָּמִיתִי לִקְאַת מִדְבָּר
הָיִיתִי כְּכוֹס חֳרָבוֹת:
ח שָׁקַדְתִּי וָאֶהְיֶה
כְּצִפּוֹר בּוֹדֵד עַל־גָּג:

Chapter 102

1 A prayer of the poor
when he is enwrapped [with affliction],
and before Adonoy
he pours out his thoughts [prayers].
2 Adonoy, hear my prayer,
and let my cry come to You.
3 Hide not Your face from me,
in the day of my distress,
incline Your ear to me;
in the day when I call answer me speedily.
4 For my days are consumed as smoke,
and my bones are dried up as a hearth.
5 Smitten like grass and withered is my heart,
for I have forgotten to eat my bread.
6 From the sound of my sighing
my bone clung to my flesh.
7 I am like a pelican of the wilderness,
I have become like an owl of the wasteland.
8 I meditated and realized that I am
like a bird that is alone on the roof.

ט	כָּל־הַיּוֹם חֵרְפוּנִי אוֹיְבָי מְהוֹלָלַי בִּי נִשְׁבָּעוּ׃	9	All day my enemies taunt me; those who mock me, swear by me.
י	כִּי־אֵפֶר כַּלֶּחֶם אָכָלְתִּי וְשִׁקֻּוַי בִּבְכִי מָסָכְתִּי׃	10	For I have eaten ashes like bread, and mixed my drink with tears.
יא	מִפְּנֵי־זַעַמְךָ וְקִצְפֶּךָ כִּי נְשָׂאתַנִי וַתַּשְׁלִיכֵנִי׃	11	Because of Your indignation and Your wrath, for You have lifted me up and then You cast me down.
יב	יָמַי כְּצֵל נָטוּי וַאֲנִי כָּעֵשֶׂב אִיבָשׁ׃	12	My days are like a lengthened shadow, and I, like grass, wither away.
יג	וְאַתָּה יְהוָה לְעוֹלָם תֵּשֵׁב וְזִכְרְךָ לְדֹר וָדֹר׃	13	But You, Adonoy, will be enthroned forever, and Your memorial is for all generations.
יד	אַתָּה תָקוּם תְּרַחֵם צִיּוֹן כִּי־עֵת לְחֶנְנָהּ כִּי־בָא מוֹעֵד׃	14	You will arise and have compassion on Zion, for it is time to be gracious to her, for the appointed time has come.
טו	כִּי־רָצוּ עֲבָדֶיךָ אֶת־אֲבָנֶיהָ וְאֶת־עֲפָרָהּ יְחֹנֵנוּ׃	15	For Your servants take pleasure in her stones and bestow their favor on her dust.
טז	וְיִירְאוּ גוֹיִם אֶת־שֵׁם יְהוָה וְכָל־מַלְכֵי הָאָרֶץ אֶת־כְּבוֹדֶךָ׃	16	And nations will fear the Name of Adonoy and all the kings of the earth, Your glory.
יז	כִּי־בָנָה יְהוָה צִיּוֹן נִרְאָה בִּכְבוֹדוֹ׃	17	When Adonoy has built up Zion, He will have appeared in His glory.
יח	פָּנָה אֶל־תְּפִלַּת הָעַרְעָר וְלֹא־בָזָה אֶת־תְּפִלָּתָם׃	18	He has turned to the prayer of the lonely one and has not despised their prayer.
יט	תִּכָּתֶב זֹאת לְדוֹר אַחֲרוֹן וְעַם נִבְרָא יְהַלֶּל־יָהּ׃	19	This will be written for the generation to come, and a newly created people will praise God.
כ	כִּי־הִשְׁקִיף מִמְּרוֹם קָדְשׁוֹ יְהוָה מִשָּׁמַיִם ׀ אֶל־אֶרֶץ הִבִּיט׃	20	For He observed from the height of His Sanctuary, Adonoy from heaven, looked down to the earth.
כא	לִשְׁמֹעַ אֶנְקַת אָסִיר לְפַתֵּחַ בְּנֵי תְמוּתָה׃	21	To hear the anguished cry of the prisoner, to liberate those who are doomed to die.
כב	לְסַפֵּר בְּצִיּוֹן שֵׁם יְהוָה וּתְהִלָּתוֹ בִּירוּשָׁלִָם׃	22	To recount in Zion the Name of Adonoy, and His praise in Jerusalem.
כג	בְּהִקָּבֵץ עַמִּים יַחְדָּו	23	When peoples gather together,

Ir David - The City of David

וּמַמְלָכוֹת לַעֲבֹד אֶת־יהוה׃
כד עִנָּה בַדֶּרֶךְ כֹּחִי
קִצַּר יָמָי׃
כה אֹמַר אֵלִי
אַל־תַּעֲלֵנִי בַּחֲצִי יָמָי
בְּדוֹר דּוֹרִים
שְׁנוֹתֶיךָ׃
כו לְפָנִים
הָאָרֶץ יָסַדְתָּ
וּמַעֲשֵׂה יָדֶיךָ שָׁמָיִם׃
כז הֵמָּה ׀ יֹאבֵדוּ וְאַתָּה תַעֲמֹד
וְכֻלָּם כַּבֶּגֶד יִבְלוּ
כַּלְּבוּשׁ תַּחֲלִיפֵם
וְיַחֲלֹפוּ׃
כח וְאַתָּה־הוּא
וּשְׁנוֹתֶיךָ לֹא יִתָּמּוּ׃
כט בְּנֵי־עֲבָדֶיךָ
יִשְׁכּוֹנוּ
וְזַרְעָם לְפָנֶיךָ יִכּוֹן

and kingdoms, to serve Adonoy.
24 He weakened my strength in the way,
He shortened my days.
25 I say [to God], ``My Almighty,
do not remove me in the midst of my days,
throughout all generations
do Your years endure.
26 In the beginning
You laid the foundations of the earth,
and the work of Your hands are the heavens.
27 They will perish but You will endure;
all of them will wear out like a garment;
as a garment You will change them
and they shall vanish.
28 But You are the same,
and Your years will not end.
29 Your servant's children
will be securely settled,
and their seed will be established before You.

פרק קג Chapter 103

Weekly Cycle	Monthly Cycle	Book Number
Thursday	20th day of the month	Book 4

Author

דָוִד הַמֶּלֶךְ—King David—the second king of Israel and father of the Davidic royal and messianic dynasty. David composed over seventy of the 150 psalms of Sefer Tehillim.

When & Why

David wrote this psalm to thank God for all of the good that God had granted him in his life.

Genre

Psalm of Praise – This is a psalm of celebration, often the result of a victory. It declares God's goodness and urges all of creation to worship.

Chapter Summary

King David composed this psalm in praise of God for all the kindnesses that He performed, and continues to perform, for him and for all of Israel. He challenges the reader, indeed all Jews, to know the good ways of the Holy One and to serve Him out of love.

This psalm consists of twenty-two verses, subdivided into five parts.
In verses 1-5, King David instructs his soul to bless God, and tells of the good that God has done for him.
In verses 6-9, he further tells of God's mercy.
In verses 10-14, he praises God as compassionate to those who fear Him.
In verses 15-19, the Psalmist contrasts the shortness of man's life with that of the Almighty who is everlasting.
In verses 20-22, King David concludes by calling upon all living creatures to bless God.

Introductory Word

בָּרְכִי—Barchi—Blessing

Shimush Tehillim - When to Say

For a woman who is barren—Verse 4 states: "Who redeems your life from destruction, Who crowns you with kindliness and compassion."

Where in the Siddur

Verse 1 serves as the final verse of Nishmat Kol Chai, the closing paragraph of Pesukei Dezimra (Verses of Praise introducing the Shacharit morning service) of Shabbat and Yom Tov (Festivals).
Verse 10 is found in the opening paragraph of the long Tachanun (Supplication Service) recited on Mondays and Thursdays.
Verse 13 is paraphrased in the long Tachanun recited on Mondays and Thursdays.
Verse 14 is the penultimate verse of the regular Tachanun.

Verse 17 is included in the blessings before the Shema of Shacharit (morning service) of the second day of Rosh HaShanah.

Verse 19 comprises one of the verses of Yehi Chevod, one of the paragraphs of Pesukei Dezimra.

Biblical Personalities

מֹשֶׁה—Moses—sent by God to redeem the Israelites from Egypt. He received the Torah on behalf of the Israelites, and acted as a mediator between them and God.

Talmud on Tehillim

Verse 1: "לְדָוִד: בָּרְכִי נַפְשִׁי, אֶת יְהוָה; וְכָל קְרָבַי, אֶת שֵׁם קָדְשׁוֹ"—"[A Psalm] of David. my soul, bless Adonoy; and all that is within me [bless] His holy Name."

The Talmud, Berachot 10a, teaches that King David dwelled in "five worlds", corresponding to the five aspects of the human soul: nefesh (soul), ruach (spirit), neshamah (breath), chaya (living essence), and yechidah (unity). The nefesh, explains the Talmud, is instilled while one is but a fetus in the womb. King David therefore offered praise for his time in his mother's womb, when he was infused with a soul.

Verse 20: "גִּבֹּרֵי כֹחַ, עֹשֵׂי דְבָרוֹ; לִשְׁמֹעַ בְּקוֹל דְּבָרוֹ"—"mighty in strength who fulfill His word, to hearken to the voice of His word."

The Talmud, Kiddushin 40a, infers from this verse that "one who has an opportunity to have an illicit relationship and overcomes his desire, a miracle will happen for him".

פֶּרֶק קג	**Chapter 103**
א לְדָוִד ׀	1 [A Psalm] of David.
בָּרְכִי נַפְשִׁי אֶת־יְהוָה	my soul, bless Adonoy;
וְכָל־קְרָבַי	and all that is within me [bless]
אֶת־שֵׁם קָדְשׁוֹ׃	His holy Name.
ב בָּרְכִי נַפְשִׁי אֶת־יְהוָה	2 My soul, bless Adonoy;
וְאַל־תִּשְׁכְּחִי כָּל־גְּמוּלָיו׃	and forget not all His beneficial deeds.
ג הַסֹּלֵחַ לְכָל־עֲוֺנֵכִי	3 Who forgives all your iniquity,
הָרֹפֵא לְכָל־תַּחֲלֻאָיְכִי׃	Who heals all your diseases.
ד הַגּוֹאֵל מִשַּׁחַת חַיָּיְכִי	4 Who redeems your life from destruction,
הַמְעַטְּרֵכִי	Who crowns you
חֶסֶד וְרַחֲמִים׃	with kindliness and compassion.
ה הַמַּשְׂבִּיעַ בַּטּוֹב עֶדְיֵךְ	5 Who satisfies your mouth with goodness,
תִּתְחַדֵּשׁ כַּנֶּשֶׁר נְעוּרָיְכִי׃	that your youth renews itself like the eagle.
ו עֹשֵׂה צְדָקוֹת יְהוָה	6 Adonoy does deeds of righteousness,
וּמִשְׁפָּטִים לְכָל־עֲשׁוּקִים׃	and deeds of justice to all the oppressed.
ז יוֹדִיעַ דְּרָכָיו לְמֹשֶׁה	7 He made known His ways to Moses,
לִבְנֵי יִשְׂרָאֵל עֲלִילוֹתָיו׃	to the children of Israel, His deeds.
ח רַחוּם וְחַנּוּן יְהוָה	8 Compassionate and gracious is Adonoy,

אֶרֶךְ אַפַּיִם וְרַב־חָסֶד׃	slow in anger and abundant in kindliness.
ט לֹא־לָנֶצַח יָרִיב	9 Not always will He contend [with us],
וְלֹא לְעוֹלָם יִטּוֹר׃	and not forever will He keep ill will.
י לֹא כַחֲטָאֵינוּ עָשָׂה לָנוּ	10 Not according to our sins has He treated us,
וְלֹא כַעֲוֹנֹתֵינוּ	and not according to our iniquities
גָּמַל עָלֵינוּ׃	has He dealt with us.
יא כִּי כִגְבֹהַּ שָׁמַיִם עַל־הָאָרֶץ	11 For as high as heaven is above the earth,
גָּבַר חַסְדּוֹ	has His kindliness been strengthened
עַל־יְרֵאָיו׃	toward those who fear Him.
יב כִּרְחֹק מִזְרָח מִמַּעֲרָב	12 As far as the east is from the west,
הִרְחִיק מִמֶּנּוּ	so far has He removed from us
אֶת־פְּשָׁעֵינוּ׃	our transgressions.
יג כְּרַחֵם אָב	13 As a father has compassion
עַל־בָּנִים	upon [his] children,
רִחַם יְהוָה	so has Adonoy compassion
עַל־יְרֵאָיו׃	upon those who fear Him.
יד כִּי־הוּא יָדַע יִצְרֵנוּ	14 For He knows our nature,
זָכוּר כִּי־עָפָר אֲנָחְנוּ׃	He is mindful that we are but dust.
טו אֱנוֹשׁ כֶּחָצִיר יָמָיו	15 As for man, his days are as grass;
כְּצִיץ הַשָּׂדֶה כֵּן יָצִיץ׃	as a flower of the field, so he flourishes.
טז כִּי רוּחַ עָבְרָה־בּוֹ	16 If a deathly wind passes over him,
וְאֵינֶנּוּ	he is gone,
וְלֹא־יַכִּירֶנּוּ עוֹד מְקוֹמוֹ׃	and his place knows him no more.
יז וְחֶסֶד יְהוָה ׀	17 But the kindliness of Adonoy is
מֵעוֹלָם	from everlasting to everlasting
וְעַד־עוֹלָם עַל־יְרֵאָיו	upon those who fear Him,
וְצִדְקָתוֹ לִבְנֵי בָנִים׃	and His righteousness unto children's children.
יח לְשֹׁמְרֵי בְרִיתוֹ	18 To those who preserve His covenant,
וּלְזֹכְרֵי פִקֻּדָיו	and to those who remember His precepts
לַעֲשׂוֹתָם׃	to do them.
יט יְהוָה	19 Adonoy
בַּשָּׁמַיִם הֵכִין כִּסְאוֹ	has established His throne in heaven,
וּמַלְכוּתוֹ בַּכֹּל מָשָׁלָה׃	[but] His dominion rules over all.
כ בָּרְכוּ יְהוָה מַלְאָכָיו	20 Bless Adonoy, His angels,
גִּבֹּרֵי כֹחַ עֹשֵׂי דְבָרוֹ	mighty in strength who fulfill His word,
לִשְׁמֹעַ בְּקוֹל דְּבָרוֹ׃	to hearken to the voice of His word.
כא בָּרְכוּ יְהוָה כָּל־צְבָאָיו	21 Bless Adonoy, all His hosts,
מְשָׁרְתָיו עֹשֵׂי רְצוֹנוֹ׃	His servants who do His will.
כב בָּרְכוּ יְהוָה ׀ כָּל־מַעֲשָׂיו	22 Bless Adonoy, all His works,

בְּכָל־מְקֹמוֹת מֶמְשַׁלְתּוֹ	in all places of His dominion;
בָּרְכִי נַפְשִׁי אֶת־יְהוָה:	my soul, bless Adonoy.

פרק קד Chapter 104

Weekly Cycle	Monthly Cycle	Book Number
Thursday	21st day of the month	Book 4

Author
Unknown

Genre
Psalm of Praise - This is a psalm of celebration, often the result of a victory. It declares God's goodness and urges all of creation to worship.

Chapter Summary
In this psalm, the author sings the praises of God for all that He included in nature, and for His continued conduct of the world as set during the Six Days of Creation. He concludes with a prayer for the downfall of the wicked, at which time all will proclaim "Halleluyah!"

This psalm consists of thirty-five verses, subdivided into five parts.
In verses 1-6, the psalmist pays homage to light, the heavens, water, clouds, wind and earth, and is thus filled with admiration and awe. He praises God for His wisdom and glory, revealed to us daily through nature.
In verses 7-18, he continues his praise, referring to the land, sea and rivers, fruits, trees, and animals.
In verses 19-26, he further speaks of the wonders of the sun and moon, day and night, and all living creatures of the sea.
In verses 27-30, he references the cycles of decay and renewal in the natural order.
In verses 31-35, the singer concludes by extolling God's joy in His world, which he correlates with his own rejoicing in the Lord.

Introductory Word
בָּרְכִי—Barchi—Blessing

Shimush Tehillim - When to Say
To be free of a harmful force—Verse 35 states: "Sin will be excised from the earth, and the wicked will be no more."

Where in the Siddur
Recited on Rosh Chodesh (New Moon), following the Shir Shel Yom (Psalm of the Day).

Recited following the Shabbat afternoon Minchah service between Sukkot and Shabbat Hagadol (the Shabbat preceding Passover) in some congregations.
Verses 1 & 2 are recited upon donning the Tallit prior to Shacharit (morning service).
Verse 24 is found in the blessings before the Shema of Shacharit.
Verse 24 is also referenced in Pirkei Avot (Ethics of Our Fathers), 6:10.
Verse 31 is the first verse of Yehi Chevod, one of the paragraphs of Pesukei Dezimra (Verses of Praise introducing the Shacharit morning service).
Verse 31 is also found in Baruch Hashem Le'olam, one of the paragraphs of the weekday Ma'ariv (evening service). It is also one of the verses of Atah Horeita (the introduction to the Hakafot dancing ceremony) recited on Simchat Torah.

Biblical Places

לְבָנוֹן—Lebanon—located just to the north of Israel, famous for its cedar trees. Lebanon was one of Israel's foremost trading partners.

Biblical Creatures

לִוְיָתָן—Leviathan—a large sea monster or creature.

Contemporary Song

Verses 33–35

Talmud on Tehillim

Verse 35: "יִתַּמּוּ חַטָּאִים מִן הָאָרֶץ"—"Sin will be excised from the earth."
The Talmud, Berachot 9b, teaches that King David recited one hundred three chapters of Tehillim (Psalms), but did not proclaim "Halleluyah" in any of them, until he prophetically perceived the downfall of the wicked and was then moved to sing Halleluyah!

פרק קד			**Chapter 104**
בָּרְכִ֥י נַפְשִׁ֗י אֶת־יְה֫וָ֥ה יְהוָ֣ה אֱ֭לֹהַי גָּדַ֣לְתָּ מְּאֹ֑ד ה֖וֹד וְהָדָ֣ר לָבָֽשְׁתָּ׃	א	1	My soul bless Adonoy; Adonoy, my God, You are greatly exalted; with beauty and splendor are You clothed.
עֹֽטֶה־א֭וֹר כַּשַּׂלְמָ֑ה נוֹטֶ֥ה שָׁ֝מַ֗יִם כַּיְרִיעָֽה׃	ב	2	Enwrapped in light, garment-like, He spreads out the heavens like a curtain.
הַֽמְקָ֘רֶ֤ה בַמַּ֗יִם עֲֽלִיּ֫וֹתָ֥יו הַשָּׂם־עָבִ֥ים רְכוּב֑וֹ הַ֝מְהַלֵּ֗ךְ עַל־כַּנְפֵי־רֽוּחַ׃	ג	3	He Who covers with water, His upper chambers; He Who makes clouds His chariot, He Who walks upon wings of wind.
עֹשֶׂ֣ה מַלְאָכָ֣יו רוּח֑וֹת מְ֝שָׁרְתָ֗יו אֵ֣שׁ לֹהֵֽט׃	ד	4	He Who makes winds His messengers, flaming fires His servants.
יָֽסַד־אֶ֭רֶץ עַל־מְכוֹנֶ֑יהָ	ה	5	He Who established the earth upon its foundations,

בַּל־תִּמּוֹט עוֹלָם וָעֶד׃	[so] that it shall never be moved.
ו תְּהוֹם	6 The deep
כַּלְּבוּשׁ כִּסִּיתוֹ	He covered as with a garment;
עַל־הָרִים יַעַמְדוּ־מָיִם׃	waters remain on mountains.
ז מִן־גַּעֲרָתְךָ יְנוּסוּן	7 At Your shout they retreated,
מִן־קוֹל רַעַמְךָ יֵחָפֵזוּן׃	at Your thunderous voice they hastened away.
ח יַעֲלוּ הָרִים יֵרְדוּ בְקָעוֹת	8 They go up mountains, down into valleys,
אֶל־מְקוֹם זֶה ׀ יָסַדְתָּ לָהֶם׃	to the specific place You founded for them.
ט גְּבוּל־שַׂמְתָּ	9 You set a boundary
בַּל־יַעֲבֹרוּן	[which] they may not cross,
בַּל־יְשׁוּבוּן לְכַסּוֹת הָאָרֶץ׃	lest they return to cover the earth.
י הַמְשַׁלֵּחַ מַעְיָנִים בַּנְּחָלִים	10 He Who sends springs into streams
בֵּין הָרִים יְהַלֵּכוּן׃	to flow between the mountains;
יא יַשְׁקוּ כָּל־חַיְתוֹ שָׂדָי	11 to water all the beasts of the fields;
יִשְׁבְּרוּ פְרָאִים צְמָאָם׃	the wild ones quench their thirst.
יב עֲלֵיהֶם עוֹף־הַשָּׁמַיִם יִשְׁכּוֹן	12 Over them dwell the birds of the sky,
מִבֵּין עֳפָאִים יִתְּנוּ־קוֹל׃	from among the branches, they give voice.
יג מַשְׁקֶה הָרִים	13 [You] Who waters the mountains
מֵעֲלִיּוֹתָיו	from His upper chambers,
מִפְּרִי מַעֲשֶׂיךָ	from the fruit of Your works
תִּשְׂבַּע הָאָרֶץ׃	the earth is sated.
יד מַצְמִיחַ חָצִיר ׀ לַבְּהֵמָה	14 [You] Who causes grass to sprout for cattle,
וְעֵשֶׂב לַעֲבֹדַת הָאָדָם	and vegetation for the labor of man,
לְהוֹצִיא לֶחֶם מִן־הָאָרֶץ׃	to bring forth bread from the earth;
טו וְיַיִן ׀ יְשַׂמַּח לְבַב־אֱנוֹשׁ	15 and wine to cheer the heart of man,
לְהַצְהִיל פָּנִים מִשָּׁמֶן	to make [his] face shine from oil,
וְלֶחֶם לְבַב־אֱנוֹשׁ יִסְעָד׃	and bread to sustain the heart of man.
טז יִשְׂבְּעוּ עֲצֵי יְהוָה	16 Adonoy's trees are sated,
אַרְזֵי לְבָנוֹן אֲשֶׁר נָטָע׃	the cedars of Lebanon that He planted;
יז אֲשֶׁר־שָׁם צִפֳּרִים יְקַנֵּנוּ	17 where birds make their nests,
חֲסִידָה בְּרוֹשִׁים בֵּיתָהּ׃	the stork—the firs are her home.
יח הָרִים הַגְּבֹהִים לַיְּעֵלִים	18 The high mountains [are] for the wild goats,
סְלָעִים מַחְסֶה לַשְׁפַנִּים׃	the rocks a refuge for the rabbits.
יט עָשָׂה יָרֵחַ לְמוֹעֲדִים	19 He made the moon to fix seasons
שֶׁמֶשׁ יָדַע מְבוֹאוֹ׃	the sun knows its place to set.
כ תָּשֶׁת־חֹשֶׁךְ וִיהִי לָיְלָה	20 You make darkness and night comes
בּוֹ־תִרְמֹשׂ כָּל־חַיְתוֹ־יָעַר׃	in which all the beasts of the forest move about.
כא הַכְּפִירִים שֹׁאֲגִים לַטָּרֶף	21 The young lions roar for prey,
וּלְבַקֵּשׁ מֵאֵל אָכְלָם׃	and seek their food from the Almighty.

כב תִּזְרַח הַשֶּׁמֶשׁ יֵאָסֵפוּן
וְאֶל־מְעוֹנֹתָם יִרְבָּצוּן׃

22 [When] the sun rises, they gather
and come into their dens to lie.

כג יֵצֵא אָדָם לְפָעֳלוֹ
וְלַעֲבֹדָתוֹ עֲדֵי־עָרֶב׃

23 Man goes out to his work,
to his labor until evening.

כד מָה־רַבּוּ מַעֲשֶׂיךָ ׀ יְהוָה
כֻּלָּם בְּחָכְמָה עָשִׂיתָ
מָלְאָה הָאָרֶץ קִנְיָנֶךָ׃

24 How many are Your works, Adonoy!
You made them all with wisdom;
the earth is full of Your possessions!

כה זֶה ׀ הַיָּם גָּדוֹל וּרְחַב יָדָיִם
שָׁם־רֶמֶשׂ וְאֵין מִסְפָּר
חַיּוֹת קְטַנּוֹת עִם־גְּדֹלוֹת׃

25 This sea, great and wide—
therein are innumerable creeping things,
animals small and great.

כו שָׁם אֳנִיּוֹת יְהַלֵּכוּן
לִוְיָתָן זֶה־
יָצַרְתָּ לְשַׂחֶק־בּוֹ׃

26 There ships travel;
this Leviathan
You formed to frolic with.

כז כֻּלָּם אֵלֶיךָ יְשַׂבֵּרוּן
לָתֵת אָכְלָם בְּעִתּוֹ׃

27 They all look to You expectantly,
to provide their food in its time.

כח תִּתֵּן לָהֶם
יִלְקֹטוּן
תִּפְתַּח יָדְךָ
יִשְׂבְּעוּן טוֹב׃

28 [When] You give it to them,
they gather it in;
[when] You open Your hand
they are sated with goodness.

כט תַּסְתִּיר פָּנֶיךָ
יִבָּהֵלוּן
תֹּסֵף רוּחָם יִגְוָעוּן
וְאֶל־עֲפָרָם יְשׁוּבוּן׃

29 When You hide Your face,
they are panic_stricken;
when You gather in their breath, they perish,
and to their dust they return.

ל תְּשַׁלַּח רוּחֲךָ
יִבָּרֵאוּן
וּתְחַדֵּשׁ פְּנֵי אֲדָמָה׃

30 When You send Your spirit,
they will be created [anew];
and You will renew the face of the earth.

לא יְהִי כְבוֹד יְהוָה לְעוֹלָם
יִשְׂמַח יְהוָה בְּמַעֲשָׂיו׃

31 The glory of Adonoy will endure forever,
Adonoy will rejoice in His works—

לב הַמַּבִּיט לָאָרֶץ וַתִּרְעָד
יִגַּע בֶּהָרִים וְיֶעֱשָׁנוּ׃

32 He Who gazes upon the earth and it trembles;
He Who touches the mountains and they erupt.

לג אָשִׁירָה לַיהוָה בְּחַיָּי
אֲזַמְּרָה לֵאלֹהַי
בְּעוֹדִי׃

33 I will sing to Adonoy with my life;
I will offer hymns to my God
as long as I am alive.

לד יֶעֱרַב עָלָיו שִׂיחִי
אָנֹכִי אֶשְׂמַח בַּיהוָה׃

34 May my words be pleasant to Him;
I will rejoice in Adonoy.

לה יִתַּמּוּ חַטָּאִים ׀ מִן־הָאָרֶץ
וּרְשָׁעִים ׀ עוֹד אֵינָם
בָּרְכִי נַפְשִׁי אֶת־יְהוָה
הַלְלוּ־יָהּ׃

35 Sin will be excised from the earth,
and the wicked will be no more;
My soul bless Adonoy,
Praise God.

פרק קה Chapter 105

Weekly Cycle	Monthly Cycle	Book Number
Thursday	21st day of the month	Book 4

Author
Unknown

When & Why
David might have written this psalm about the bringing up of the Ark from the house of Oved to the City of David in Jerusalem.

Genre
Psalm of Wisdom - This psalm contains teachings and wise advice and is meant to instruct people on how to live a Godly life.

Chapter Summary
The psalmist, perhaps King David, composed this psalm when he joyously brought up the Aron HaKodesh (Holy Ark) to the City of David. He describes all that transpired with Israel from the time they descended to Egypt until they entered the Holy Land, and enjoins all adherents of the Torah to make God's glory known to the world.

This psalm consists of forty-five verses, subdivided into four parts.
In verses 1-6, the psalmist calls upon the congregation to thank God and tell of His wonders.
In verses 7-25, he describes the attributes of God in the fulfillment of His convenant with the patriarchs, and further speaks of the substance of the covenant. He pays homage to the patriarchs, Joseph as the viceroy of Egypt, and the Israelites as a whole in their enslavement.
In verses 26-43, he details the plagues in Egypt, the subsequent exodus, and the wandering in the wilderness.
In verses 44 & 45, the singer concludes with praises of God as the driving force behind the conquest of the Promised Land.

Shimush Tehillim - When to Say
To relieve a fever (some say this in the 4th hour of the day)—Verse 20 states: "The king sent messengers and released him, the ruler of the peoples, and set him free."

Where in the Siddur
Recited on the first day of Passover in some congregations.
Verses 8-10 comprise part of the recitation of the baby naming ceremony at a Brit Milah (circumcision).
Verses 8 and 42 are each found in the repetition of the Musaf Amidah (Silent Meditation) of Rosh HaShanah.
Verse 24 is also referenced in Pirkei Avot (Ethics of Our Fathers), 6:10.

Biblical Personalities

אַהֲרֹן—Aaron—older brother of Moses and the first Kohein (Priest). The descendents of Aaron, as future kohanim, were designated to perform the ritual service in the Beit HaMikdash (Temple).

אַבְרָהָם—Abraham—Together with his wife Sarah, the first to actively spread the idea of monotheism throughout the world, and the first to enter into a covenant with God. The first of the forefathers, today he is considered the founder of the world's three monotheistic religions: Judaism, Christianity and Islam.

יַעֲקֹב—Jacob—also called Yisrael—Israel, the third patriarch, considered the father of the twelve tribes of Israel. He was the twin brother of Esau, and married to Leah and Rachel.

מֹשֶׁה—Moshe—Moses—sent by God to lead the Israelites out of Egypt. He received the Torah on behalf of the Israelites and acted as a mediator between them and God. He was closer to God than all of the other prophets who preceded and followed him.

יִשְׂרָאֵל—Yisrael—Israel—also called Jacob, the third patriarch— considered the father of the twelve tribes of Israel. He was the twin brother of Esau, and married to Leah and Rachel.

יִשְׂחָק—Yitzchak—Isaac was the second son of Abraham, and the father of Jacob and Esau. Isaac was one of the three patriarchs of the Israelites.

יוֹסֵף—Yosef—Joseph—the son of Jacob and Rachel. As second in command to Pharaoh, he sustained his brothers while they were in Egypt and was therefore rewarded in kind. Instead of receiving only one share in the land of Israel, as did his brothers, each of his sons, Ephraim and Menasheh, received a full share. It is also believed that the first Mashiach (Messiah) will be from the tribe of Joseph, to be followed by Mashiach from the tribe of Judah.

Biblical Places

כְּנָעַן—Canaan—the biblical name of the Land of Israel.

מִצְרַיִם—Egypt—where Israel was enslaved until God sent Moses to redeem them. Egyptian society ran contrary to many of the ideals of the Torah. As such, the Israelite king is specifically warned not to amass cavalry, lest he be tempted to return his nation to Egypt.

אֶרֶץ-חָם—Land of Ham—a synonym for Egypt, as the Egyptians were descedants of Ham.

Aquatic detail from the Lod Mosaic

פרק קה

א הוֹדוּ לַיהוָה קִרְאוּ בִּשְׁמוֹ
הוֹדִיעוּ בָעַמִּים עֲלִילוֹתָיו׃
ב שִׁירוּ־לוֹ זַמְּרוּ־לוֹ
שִׂיחוּ בְּכָל־נִפְלְאוֹתָיו׃
ג הִתְהַלְלוּ בְּשֵׁם קָדְשׁוֹ
יִשְׂמַח לֵב ׀
מְבַקְשֵׁי יְהוָה׃
ד דִּרְשׁוּ יְהוָה וְעֻזּוֹ
בַּקְּשׁוּ פָנָיו תָּמִיד׃
ה זִכְרוּ נִפְלְאוֹתָיו
אֲשֶׁר־עָשָׂה
מֹפְתָיו וּמִשְׁפְּטֵי־פִיו׃
ו זֶרַע אַבְרָהָם עַבְדּוֹ
בְּנֵי יַעֲקֹב בְּחִירָיו׃
ז הוּא יְהוָה אֱלֹהֵינוּ
בְּכָל־הָאָרֶץ מִשְׁפָּטָיו׃
ח זָכַר לְעוֹלָם בְּרִיתוֹ
דָּבָר צִוָּה
לְאֶלֶף דּוֹר׃
ט אֲשֶׁר כָּרַת אֶת־אַבְרָהָם
וּשְׁבוּעָתוֹ לְיִשְׂחָק׃
י וַיַּעֲמִידֶהָ לְיַעֲקֹב לְחֹק
לְיִשְׂרָאֵל בְּרִית עוֹלָם׃
יא לֵאמֹר
לְךָ אֶתֵּן אֶת־אֶרֶץ־כְּנָעַן
חֶבֶל נַחֲלַתְכֶם׃
יב בִּהְיוֹתָם מְתֵי מִסְפָּר
כִּמְעַט וְגָרִים בָּהּ׃
יג וַיִּתְהַלְּכוּ מִגּוֹי אֶל־גּוֹי
מִמַּמְלָכָה אֶל־עַם אַחֵר׃
יד לֹא־הִנִּיחַ אָדָם לְעָשְׁקָם
וַיּוֹכַח עֲלֵיהֶם מְלָכִים׃
טו אַל־תִּגְּעוּ בִמְשִׁיחָי
וְלִנְבִיאַי אַל־תָּרֵעוּ׃
טז וַיִּקְרָא רָעָב עַל־הָאָרֶץ
כָּל־מַטֵּה־לֶחֶם שָׁבָר׃
יז שָׁלַח לִפְנֵיהֶם אִישׁ
לְעֶבֶד נִמְכַּר יוֹסֵף׃

Chapter 105

1 Give thanks to Adonoy, proclaim His Name,
make His deeds known among the nations.
2 Sing to Him, compose songs to Him,
speak of all His wonders.
3 Take pride in [uttering] His Holy Name,
let the heart rejoice
of those who seek Adonoy.
4 Search for Adonoy and His might,
seek His Presence continually.
5 Remember His wonders
that He has performed,
His miracles, and the laws from His mouth.
6 [You] the seed of Abraham His servant,
children of Jacob, His chosen ones.
7 He is Adonoy, our God,
the entire earth is governed by His laws.
8 He remembered His covenant forever,
the word which He commanded
to a thousand generations.
9 Which He made as a treaty with Abraham
and which was His oath to Isaac.
10 And He established it for Jacob as a statute,
for Israel as an everlasting covenant.
11 Saying
"To you I will give the Land of Canaan,
the portion of your inheritance."
12 When they were only few in number,
very few and strangers in it.
13 And they wandered from nation to nation,
from one kingdom to another people.
14 He permitted no one to oppress them,
and admonished kings for their sake.
15 "Do not touch My anointed ones,
and to My prophets do no harm."
16 And He called for a famine upon the land,
every staff [supply] of bread He broke.
17 He sent before them a man,
as a slave was Joseph sold.

יח עִנּוּ בַכֶּבֶל רַגְלוֹ	18	They afflicted his foot with fetters,
בַּרְזֶל בָּאָה נַפְשׁוֹ׃		an iron chain was laid on his soul.
יט עַד־עֵת בֹּא־דְבָרוֹ	19	Until the time that His word came to pass,
אִמְרַת יְהוָה צְרָפָתְהוּ׃		the word of Adonoy tested [purified] him.
כ שָׁלַח מֶלֶךְ וַיַּתִּירֵהוּ	20	The king sent messengers and released him,
מֹשֵׁל עַמִּים וַיְפַתְּחֵהוּ׃		the ruler of the peoples, and set him free.
כא שָׂמוֹ אָדוֹן לְבֵיתוֹ	21	He appointed him master of his house,
וּמֹשֵׁל בְּכָל־קִנְיָנוֹ׃		and ruler over all his possessions.
כב לֶאְסֹר שָׂרָיו בְּנַפְשׁוֹ	22	To endear his soul to his princes,
וּזְקֵנָיו יְחַכֵּם׃		and make his elders wise.
כג וַיָּבֹא יִשְׂרָאֵל מִצְרָיִם	23	And Israel came to Egypt,
וְיַעֲקֹב גָּר בְּאֶרֶץ־חָם׃		and Jacob sojourned in the land of Ham.
כד וַיֶּפֶר אֶת־עַמּוֹ מְאֹד	24	And He made His people extremely fruitful,
וַיַּעֲצִמֵהוּ מִצָּרָיו׃		and made them mightier than their adversaries.
כה הָפַךְ לִבָּם לִשְׂנֹא עַמּוֹ	25	He turned their heart to hate His people,
לְהִתְנַכֵּל בַּעֲבָדָיו׃		to conspire against His servants.
כו שָׁלַח מֹשֶׁה עַבְדּוֹ	26	He sent Moses, His servant,
אַהֲרֹן אֲשֶׁר בָּחַר־בּוֹ׃		Aaron, whom He had chosen.
כז שָׂמוּ־בָם	27	They placed among them
דִּבְרֵי אֹתוֹתָיו		words of His signs,
וּמֹפְתִים בְּאֶרֶץ חָם׃		and wonders in the land of Ham.
כח שָׁלַח חֹשֶׁךְ וַיַּחְשִׁךְ	28	He sent darkness and made it dark,
וְלֹא־מָרוּ אֶת־דְּבָרוֹ׃		and they rebelled not against His word.
כט הָפַךְ אֶת־מֵימֵיהֶם לְדָם	29	He turned their waters into blood,
וַיָּמֶת אֶת־דְּגָתָם׃		and killed their fish.
ל שָׁרַץ אַרְצָם צְפַרְדְּעִים	30	Their land swarmed with frogs,
בְּחַדְרֵי מַלְכֵיהֶם׃		in the very chambers of their kings.
לא אָמַר וַיָּבֹא עָרֹב	31	He spoke and hordes of wild beasts came;
כִּנִּים בְּכָל־גְּבוּלָם׃		vermin within all their borders.
לב נָתַן גִּשְׁמֵיהֶם בָּרָד	32	He gave their rain in the form of hail,
אֵשׁ לֶהָבוֹת בְּאַרְצָם׃		flaming fire in their land.
לג וַיַּךְ גַּפְנָם וּתְאֵנָתָם	33	And it smote their vine and their fig tree,
וַיְשַׁבֵּר עֵץ גְּבוּלָם׃		and broke the tree[s] within their border.
לד אָמַר וַיָּבֹא אַרְבֶּה	34	He spoke and the locust came,
וְיֶלֶק וְאֵין מִסְפָּר׃		and the beetle without number.
לה וַיֹּאכַל כָּל־עֵשֶׂב בְּאַרְצָם	35	And it ate up every herb in their land,
וַיֹּאכַל פְּרִי אַדְמָתָם׃		and it ate up the fruit of their soil.
לו וַיַּךְ כָּל־בְּכוֹר	36	And He smote all the first born
בְּאַרְצָם		in their land,

רֵאשִׁית לְכָל־אוֹנָם׃
לז וַיּוֹצִיאֵם
בְּכֶסֶף וְזָהָב
וְאֵין בִּשְׁבָטָיו כּוֹשֵׁל׃
לח שָׂמַח מִצְרַיִם בְּצֵאתָם
כִּי־נָפַל פַּחְדָּם עֲלֵיהֶם׃
לט פָּרַשׂ עָנָן
לְמָסָךְ
וְאֵשׁ לְהָאִיר לָיְלָה׃
מ שָׁאַל וַיָּבֵא שְׂלָו
וְלֶחֶם שָׁמַיִם
מא יַשְׂבִּיעֵם׃
מב פָּתַח צוּר וַיָּזוּבוּ מָיִם
הָלְכוּ בַּצִּיּוֹת נָהָר׃
מג כִּי־זָכַר אֶת־דְּבַר קָדְשׁוֹ
אֶת־אַבְרָהָם עַבְדּוֹ׃
מד וַיּוֹצִא עַמּוֹ
בְשָׂשׂוֹן
בְּרִנָּה אֶת־בְּחִירָיו׃
מה וַיִּתֵּן לָהֶם אַרְצוֹת גּוֹיִם
וַעֲמַל לְאֻמִּים יִירָשׁוּ׃
מו בַּעֲבוּר | יִשְׁמְרוּ חֻקָּיו
וְתוֹרֹתָיו יִנְצֹרוּ הַלְלוּ־יָהּ׃

the prime of all their strength,
37 And He brought them out
with silver and gold,
and none among His tribes stumbled.
38 Egypt rejoiced when they departed,
for their fear had fallen upon them.
39 He spread out a cloud
for a [protective] shelter,
and a fire to give light in the night.
40 They [Israel] asked and He brought quail,
and [with] bread from heaven
He satisfied them.
41 He opened a rock and waters flowed out,
they ran through dry places like a river.
42 For He remembered His holy word,
to Abraham, His servant.
43 And He brought forth His people
with gladness
His chosen ones with singing.
44 And He gave them the lands of nations,
and the labor of the peoples they inherited.
45 So that they might preserve His statutes
and treasure His laws, praise God.

Synagogue Floor Mosaic from Roman Period

פרק קו Chapter 106

Weekly Cycle	Monthly Cycle	Book Number
Thursday	22nd day of the month	Book 4

Author

Unknown; perhaps דָּוִד הַמֶּלֶךְ—King David—the second king of Israel and father of the Davidic royal and messianic dynasty. David composed over seventy of the 150 psalms of Sefer Tehillim.

When & Why

David might have written this psalm with regards to the bringing up of the Ark from the house of Oved to the City of David in Jerusalem.

Genre

Psalm of Wisdom - This psalm contains teachings and wise advice and is meant to instruct people on how to live a Godly life.

Chapter Summary

The singer continues to depict the many beneficent acts performed by God for Israel. He warns the Jewish people not to be ungrateful as their forefathers, and reminds them that God's abundant kindness is nevertheless unconditional.

This psalm consists of forty-eight verses, subdivided into three parts.
In verses 1-5, the psalmist praises God for His lovingkindness extended to those who maintain justice. He adds a supplication to be privileged to witness Israel's salvation.
In verses 6-46, he engages in a lengthy confession on behalf of God's people. He introduces his words by stating that the people of Israel and their fathers have sinned. He then lists many of the sins committed by the generations that left Egypt and wandered in the wilderness, as well as sins committed by subsequent generations in Israel.
In verses 47 and 48, he concludes with a prayer for deliverance, and offers a blessing to God corresponding to the words of praise with which he opened the psalm.

Introductory Words

הַלְלוּ-יָ-ה—Halleluyah—Praise God
הודו—Hodu—Give thanks

Shimush Tehillim - When to Say

For a fever (some recite this in the 3rd hour of the day)—Verse 44 states: "And He regarded their affliction, when He heard their cry."

Where in the Siddur

Recited on the second day of Passover in some traditions.
Verse 2 is the final verse of Anim Zemirot—a responsive poem of praise, usually sung towards the conlusion of the Shabbat and Yom Tov (Festivals) morning service.

Verse 2 is also recited by some upon the conclusion of Shir HaMa'alot (Song of Ascent; Psalm 126) preceding Birkat HaMazon (Grace After Meals) of Shabbat and Yom Tov.
Verse 11 is found in the blessing following the Shema of Shacharit (morning service).
Verse 45 is found in the Musaf Amidah (Silent Meditation) of Rosh HaShanah.
Verse 47 is found in the long Tachanun (Supplication Service) recited on Mondays and Thursdays.
Verse 47 is also found in Baruch Hashem Le'olam of the weekday Ma'ariv (evening service).

Biblical Personalities

אַהֲרֹן—Aaron—the older brother of Moses, and the first Kohein Gadol (High Priest). The descendents of Aaron were designated to perform the ritual service in the Beit HaMikdash (Temple).

דָּתָן וַאֲבִירָם— Dathan and Abiram—two brothers, who, along with Korach the Levite and others, rebelled against Moses and Aaron. God punished Dathan and Abiram, thereby proving that Moses was the chosen leader of Israel, by opening the ground underneath them and burying them and their possessions.

מֹשֶׁה—Moses—sent by God to redeem the Israelites from Egypt. He received the Torah on Sinai, and acted as a mediator between the people and God.

פִּינְחָס—Phinehas—a Kohein Gadol (High Priest), the grandson of Aaron and son of Eleazar. He distinguished himself as a youth by his zeal against the heresy and idolatry of Ba'al Pe'or. The Moabites and Midianites had successfully tempted the people to worship Ba'al Pe'or, whereby Phinehas personally speared an Israelite prince and a Midianite woman while engaged in illicit sexual activity. This brave act of Phinehas ended a plague sent by God to punish the Israelites for their sexual promiscuity with the Midianites. Phinehas is commended for having stopped Israel's fall to these idolatrous practices and for stemming God's wrath.

Biblical Places

מִצְרַיִם—Egypt—the land where Israel was enslaved until God sent Moses to redeem them. Egyptian society ran contrary to many of the ideals of the Torah, and the Israelite king is thus specifically warned not to amass cavalry, lest he be tempted to return his nation to Egypt.

חֹרֵב—Horeb—synonymous with Mount Sinai, the mountain upon which the Ten Commandments were given to Moses by God. While waiting for Moses to descend, the nation of Israel committed the sin of the Golden Calf.

אֶרֶץ חָם—Land of Ham—another name for Egypt, as the Egyptians were descendants of Ham.

יַם-סוּף—The Red Sea or the Sea of Reeds—the waters which parted for the Israelites as they escaped the pursuing Egyptians. The waters then engulfed and drowned all of the Egyptians soldiers.

מֵי מְרִיבָה—Waters of Meribah—where the Israelites quarreled with Moses about the lack of water, and Moses in turn rebuked them for testing God.

Foreign Worship

בַּעַל פְּעוֹר—Ba'al Pe'or—a pagan deity of either agriculture or fertility, in which its followers engaged in acts of promiscuity and immorality. It was perhaps limited in its following to the area of Pe'or, perhaps more widespread. Some identify Ba'al Pe'or with Chemosh, referred to elsewhere as the god of Moab.

שֵׁדִים—Sheidim—demons worshipped by idolators.

תַבְנִית שׁוֹר—Tavnit Shor—literally meaning a "form of an ox", a reference to the golden calf worshipped by the Israelites following the revelation at Sinai.

Talmud on Tehillim

Verse 30: "וַיַּעֲמֹד פִּינְחָס, וַיְפַלֵּל"—"And Pinchos stood up and wrought judgment."
The Talmud, Berachot 6b and 26d, deduces that the word "vay'fallel" ("he intervened"), can also be understood as "he prayed", and that Pinchas thus stood when he prayed. The title "Amidah" (Silent Meditation), the central, private prayer of each of the daily services, literally means "standing", as one stands during its recitation. The Amidah is also referred to as Shemoneh Esrei; literally meaning "eighteen", the weekday Amidah originally contained eighteen blessings.

פֶּרֶק קו	Chapter 106
א הַלְלוּיָהּ |	1 Praise God.
הוֹדוּ לַיהוָה כִּי־טוֹב	Give thanks to Adonoy, for He is good,
כִּי לְעוֹלָם חַסְדּוֹ:	for His kindness is everlasting.
ב מִי יְמַלֵּל גְּבוּרוֹת יְהוָה	2 Who can recount the mighty acts of Adonoy,
יַשְׁמִיעַ כָּל־תְּהִלָּתוֹ:	or make heard all His praise?
ג אַשְׁרֵי שֹׁמְרֵי מִשְׁפָּט	3 Fortunate are those who preserve justice,
עֹשֵׂה צְדָקָה בְכָל־עֵת:	that do righteousness at all times.
ד זָכְרֵנִי יְהוָה	4 Remember me, Adonoy,
בִּרְצוֹן עַמֶּךָ	when You favor Your people,
פָּקְדֵנִי בִּישׁוּעָתֶךָ:	be mindful of me with Your deliverance.
ה לִרְאוֹת | בְּטוֹבַת בְּחִירֶיךָ	5 To behold the good [fortune] of Your chosen,
לִשְׂמֹחַ בְּשִׂמְחַת גּוֹיֶךָ	to rejoice in the rejoicing of Your nation,
לְהִתְהַלֵּל עִם־נַחֲלָתֶךָ:	to glory with Your inheritance.
ו חָטָאנוּ עִם־אֲבוֹתֵינוּ	6 We have sinned with our fathers,
הֶעֱוִינוּ הִרְשָׁעְנוּ:	we have committed iniquity, and wickedness.
ז אֲבוֹתֵינוּ בְמִצְרַיִם |	7 Our fathers in Egypt
לֹא־הִשְׂכִּילוּ נִפְלְאוֹתֶיךָ	did not understand Your wonders,
לֹא זָכְרוּ	they did not remember
אֶת־רֹב חֲסָדֶיךָ	the multitude of Your kindnesses;
וַיַּמְרוּ עַל־יָם	but they rebelled at the sea,
בְּיַם־סוּף:	at the Sea of Reeds.
ח וַיּוֹשִׁיעֵם לְמַעַן שְׁמוֹ	8 And He delivered them for His Name's sake,
לְהוֹדִיעַ אֶת־גְּבוּרָתוֹ:	to make known His mighty power.
ט וַיִּגְעַר בְּיַם־סוּף	9 And He rebuked the Sea of Reeds

וַיֶּחֱרָב
וַיּוֹלִיכֵם בַּתְּהֹמוֹת
כַּמִּדְבָּר׃

and it dried up,
and He led them through the depths
as through a wilderness.

י וַיּוֹשִׁיעֵם
מִיַּד שׂוֹנֵא
וַיִּגְאָלֵם
מִיַּד אוֹיֵב׃

10 And He delivered them
from the hand of the enemy,
and He redeemed them
from the hand of the foe.

יא וַיְכַסּוּ־מַיִם צָרֵיהֶם
אֶחָד מֵהֶם לֹא נוֹתָר׃

11 And the waters covered their adversaries;
not one of them remained.

יב וַיַּאֲמִינוּ בִדְבָרָיו
יָשִׁירוּ תְּהִלָּתוֹ׃

12 Then they believed in His words,
they sang His praise.

יג מִהֲרוּ שָׁכְחוּ מַעֲשָׂיו
לֹא־חִכּוּ לַעֲצָתוֹ׃

13 They soon forgot His works,
they waited not for His counsel.

יד וַיִּתְאַוּוּ תַאֲוָה
בַּמִּדְבָּר
וַיְנַסּוּ־אֵל
בִּישִׁימוֹן׃

14 And they lusted exceedingly
in the wilderness,
and they put the Almighty to the test
in the desolations.

טו וַיִּתֵּן לָהֶם שֶׁאֱלָתָם
וַיְשַׁלַּח רָזוֹן בְּנַפְשָׁם׃

15 And He gave them their request,
but sent emaciation into their souls.

טז וַיְקַנְאוּ לְמֹשֶׁה
בַּמַּחֲנֶה
לְאַהֲרֹן קְדוֹשׁ יְהוָה׃

16 And they were jealous of Moses
in the camp,
of Aaron, the holy one of Adonoy.

יז תִּפְתַּח־אֶרֶץ וַתִּבְלַע דָּתָן
וַתְּכַס עַל־עֲדַת אֲבִירָם׃

17 The earth opened and swallowed up Dathan,
and covered the company of Abiram.

יח וַתִּבְעַר־אֵשׁ בַּעֲדָתָם
לֶהָבָה תְּלַהֵט רְשָׁעִים׃

18 And a fire burned in their company,
a flame ignited the wicked.

יט יַעֲשׂוּ־עֵגֶל בְּחֹרֵב
וַיִּשְׁתַּחֲווּ
לְמַסֵּכָה׃

19 They made a calf in Horeb,
and they prostrated themselves
before a molten image.

כ וַיָּמִירוּ אֶת־כְּבוֹדָם
בְּתַבְנִית שׁוֹר אֹכֵל עֵשֶׂב׃

20 And they exchanged their Glory [God]
for the likeness of an ox that eats grass.

כא שָׁכְחוּ אֵל מוֹשִׁיעָם
עֹשֶׂה גְדֹלוֹת בְּמִצְרָיִם׃

21 They forgot the Almighty, their Deliverer,
Who had done great things in Egypt.

כב נִפְלָאוֹת בְּאֶרֶץ חָם
נוֹרָאוֹת עַל־יַם־סוּף׃

22 Wonders in the land of Ham,
awe inspiring deeds at the Sea of Reeds.

כג וַיֹּאמֶר לְהַשְׁמִידָם
לוּלֵי מֹשֶׁה בְחִירוֹ
עָמַד בַּפֶּרֶץ לְפָנָיו
לְהָשִׁיב חֲמָתוֹ מֵהַשְׁחִית׃

23 And He said that He would destroy them,
had not Moses, His chosen one,
stood in the breach before Him,
to turn back His wrath from destruction.

כד וַיִּמְאֲסוּ בְּאֶרֶץ חֶמְדָּה
לֹא־הֶאֱמִינוּ לִדְבָרוֹ׃

24 And they despised the desirable land,
they believed not His word.

כה וַיֵּרָגְנוּ בְאָהֳלֵיהֶם
לֹא שָׁמְעוּ בְּקוֹל יְהוָה׃

25 And they murmured in their tents,
they hearkened not to the voice of Adonoy.

כו וַיִּשָּׂא יָדוֹ לָהֶם
לְהַפִּיל אוֹתָם בַּמִּדְבָּר׃

26 And He raised up His hand against them,
to cause them to fall in the wilderness.

כז וּלְהַפִּיל זַרְעָם בַּגּוֹיִם
וּלְזָרוֹתָם בָּאֲרָצוֹת׃

27 And to fell their seed among the nations,
and to scatter them in the lands.

כח וַיִּצָּמְדוּ לְבַעַל פְּעוֹר
וַיֹּאכְלוּ זִבְחֵי מֵתִים׃

28 And they joined themselves to Baal Peor,
and they ate the sacrifices of the dead.

כט וַיַּכְעִיסוּ בְּמַעַלְלֵיהֶם
וַתִּפְרָץ־בָּם מַגֵּפָה׃

29 And they provoked Him with their doings,
and a plague broke out in their midst.

ל וַיַּעֲמֹד פִּינְחָס
וַיְפַלֵּל
וַתֵּעָצַר הַמַּגֵּפָה׃

30 And Pinchos stood up
and wrought judgment,
and the plague was held back.

לא וַתֵּחָשֶׁב לוֹ
לִצְדָקָה
לְדֹר וָדֹר עַד־עוֹלָם׃

31 And it was accounted to him
as righteousness,
throughout all generations, forever.

לב וַיַּקְצִיפוּ
עַל־מֵי מְרִיבָה
וַיֵּרַע לְמֹשֶׁה בַּעֲבוּרָם׃

32 And they provoked Him
at the waters of Merivah,
and Moses suffered harm because of them.

לג כִּי־הִמְרוּ אֶת־רוּחוֹ
וַיְבַטֵּא בִּשְׂפָתָיו׃

33 For they defied His spirit,
and He swore with His lips.

לד לֹא־הִשְׁמִידוּ אֶת־הָעַמִּים
אֲשֶׁר אָמַר יְהוָה לָהֶם׃

34 They did not destroy the peoples
as Adonoy had commanded them.

לה וַיִּתְעָרְבוּ בַגּוֹיִם
וַיִּלְמְדוּ מַעֲשֵׂיהֶם׃

35 But they mingled with the nations,
and they learned their deeds.

לו וַיַּעַבְדוּ אֶת־עֲצַבֵּיהֶם
וַיִּהְיוּ לָהֶם לְמוֹקֵשׁ׃

36 And they worshipped their idols,
which became a snare for them.

לז וַיִּזְבְּחוּ אֶת־בְּנֵיהֶם
וְאֶת־בְּנוֹתֵיהֶם לַשֵּׁדִים׃

37 And they sacrificed their sons
and their daughters to the demons.

לח וַיִּשְׁפְּכוּ דָם נָקִי
דַּם־בְּנֵיהֶם וּבְנוֹתֵיהֶם
אֲשֶׁר זִבְּחוּ לַעֲצַבֵּי כְנָעַן
וַתֶּחֱנַף הָאָרֶץ בַּדָּמִים׃

38 And they shed innocent blood,
the blood of their sons and of their daughters,
whom they sacrificed to the idols of Canaan;
and the land was polluted with blood.

לט וַיִּטְמְאוּ בְמַעֲשֵׂיהֶם
וַיִּזְנוּ בְּמַעַלְלֵיהֶם׃

39 And they were defiled by their deeds,
and went astray through their actions.

מ וַיִּחַר־אַף יְהוָה
בְּעַמּוֹ

40 And Adonoy's fury blazed
against His people,

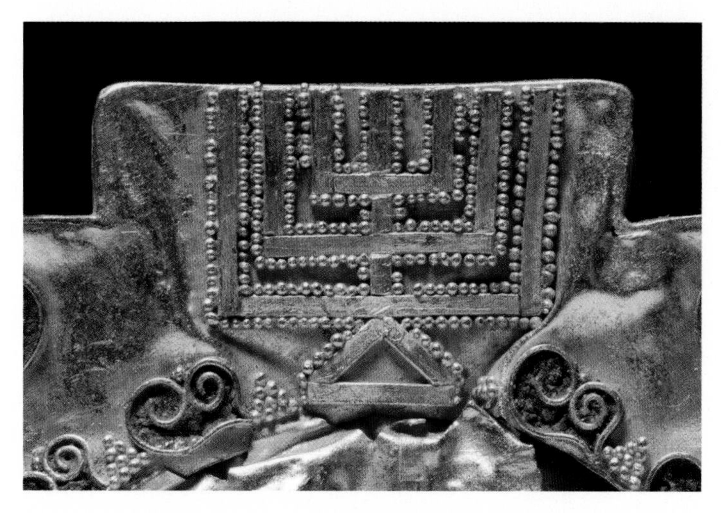

Golden Menorah (Courtesy of Shlomo Moussaieff Collection)

וַיְתָעֵב אֶת־נַחֲלָתוֹ׃	and He abhorred His inheritance.
מא וַיִּתְּנֵם	41 And He placed them
בְּיַד־גּוֹיִם	into the hand of the nations,
וַיִּמְשְׁלוּ בָהֶם שֹׂנְאֵיהֶם׃	and their enemies ruled over them.
מב וַיִּלְחָצוּם אוֹיְבֵיהֶם	42 And their enemies oppressed them,
וַיִּכָּנְעוּ תַּחַת יָדָם׃	and they were humbled under their hand.
מג פְּעָמִים רַבּוֹת יַצִּילֵם	43 Many times did He rescue them,
וְהֵמָּה יַמְרוּ בַעֲצָתָם	yet they were rebellious in their counsel,
וַיָּמֹכּוּ בַּעֲוֹנָם׃	and they were brought low by their iniquity.
מד וַיַּרְא בַּצַּר לָהֶם	44 And He regarded their affliction,
בְּשָׁמְעוֹ אֶת־רִנָּתָם׃	when He heard their cry.
מה וַיִּזְכֹּר לָהֶם	45 And He remembered
בְּרִיתוֹ	His covenant with them.
וַיִּנָּחֵם	and He relented
כְּרֹב חֲסָדָיו׃	in accordance with His multitude of kindness.
מו וַיִּתֵּן אוֹתָם לְרַחֲמִים	46 And He caused them to be pitied
לִפְנֵי כָּל־שׁוֹבֵיהֶם׃	by all their captors.
מז הוֹשִׁיעֵנוּ | יְהוָה אֱלֹהֵינוּ	47 Deliver us, Adonoy, our God;
וְקַבְּצֵנוּ מִן־הַגּוֹיִם	and gather us from the nations,
לְהֹדוֹת לְשֵׁם קָדְשֶׁךָ	to give thanks to Your holy Name,
לְהִשְׁתַּבֵּחַ בִּתְהִלָּתֶךָ׃	to be extolled in Your praise.
מח בָּרוּךְ־יְהוָה אֱלֹהֵי יִשְׂרָאֵל	48 Blessed is Adonoy, God of Israel,
מִן־הָעוֹלָם | וְעַד הָעוֹלָם	from this world to the world [to come],
וְאָמַר כָּל־הָעָם אָמֵן	and let all the people say, "Amen,"
הַלְלוּ־יָהּ׃	praise God.

BOOK 5

פרק קז Chapter 107

Weekly Cycle	Monthly Cycle	Book Number
Friday	22nd day of the month	Book 5

Author

Unknown

When & Why

This psalm was written about the four types of people who need to formally thank God for his kindness to them; someone who crosses a desert, someone who is released from prison, someone who recovers from a sickness and someone who crosses the sea and arrives on dry land.

Genre

Psalm of Thanksgiving - This psalm emphasizes gratitude for what God has done.

Chapter Summary

This psalm opens the fifth book of Tehillim (Psalms), comprised primarily of praise and thanksgiving. It speaks of the miracles and splendor of the messianic age. Viewed by some as an allusion to the ingathering of past exiles, it perhaps also refers to the war of Gog and Magog preceding and ushering in Mashiach (Messiah). It is against this backdrop that the singer calls upon those worthy of God's deliverance to proclaim their thanks.

This psalm consists of forty-three verses, subdivided into four parts.

In verses 1-3, the psalmist proclaims: "Hodu LaHashem ki tov"—"Give thanks to Adonoy, for He is good", an oft repeated refrain of Tehillim. He then declares that in the future, all ingrathered exiles will indeed fulfill this charge.

In verses 4-32, the body of the psalm, he describes the four categories of individuals who must thank God for delivery: those who cross the desert, prisoners, the sick, and those who descend to the sea.

In verses 33-41, he describes God's acts of lovingkindness, expressed in His overseeing the natural order in the world.

In verses 42 & 43, the singer closes with a recognition of how the righteous rejoice while the wicked are silenced, and thus calls upon the congregation to contemplate God's acts of lovingkindness.

Introductory Words

הודו—Hodu—Give thanks

Shimush Tehillim - When to Say

For a chronic fever—Verse 20 states: "He sends His word and heals them, and delivers them from their destruction."

Where in the Siddur

Verses 10, 14 and 17-21 are found in Kapparot (Atonement Service) recited by some on Erev (the eve of) Yom Kippur.

Talmud on Tehillim

Verse 6: "וַיִּצְעֲקוּ אֶל יְהוָה, בַּצַּר לָהֶם"—"Then they cried out to Adonoy in their distress."

The Talmud, Rosh HaShanah 16b, infers that prayers indeed have the capacity to change one's fate for the positive and even to cancel an evil decree.

Verse 23: "יוֹרְדֵי הַיָּם, בָּאֳנִיּוֹת"—"Those who go down to the sea in ships."

The Talmud, Berachot 54b, deduces that one must give thanks to God for surviving a dangerous predicament, specifically the four described here: one who crossed the desert, one who completed a sea voyage, one who was imprisoned, and one who was ill. Originally one fulfilled this obligation by offering a Korban Todah (Thanksgiving sacrifice) in the Beit HaMikdash (Temple). Today one manifests this gratitude by reciting Birkat HaGomeil, a blessing thanking God for seeing one through this difficult time. Birkat HaGomeil is often recited by women after childbirth, as well as one who survived an auto accident.

פרק קז	Chapter 107
א הֹדוּ לַיהוָה כִּי־טוֹב	1 Give thanks to Adonoy, for He is good,
כִּי לְעוֹלָם חַסְדּוֹ׃	for His kindness endures forever.
ב יֹאמְרוּ גְּאוּלֵי יְהוָה	2 Let those redeemed by Adonoy say it,
אֲשֶׁר גְּאָלָם מִיַּד־צָר׃	those He redeemed from the adversary's hand.
ג וּמֵאֲרָצוֹת קִבְּצָם	3 And from the lands He gathered them,
מִמִּזְרָח וּמִמַּעֲרָב	from the east and from the west,
מִצָּפוֹן וּמִיָּם׃	from the north and from the south.
ד תָּעוּ בַמִּדְבָּר	4 They wandered in the wilderness,
בִּישִׁימוֹן דָּרֶךְ	in a path of desolation;
עִיר מוֹשָׁב לֹא מָצָאוּ׃	an inhabited city they did not find.
ה רְעֵבִים גַּם־צְמֵאִים	5 Hungry, also thirsty
נַפְשָׁם בָּהֶם תִּתְעַטָּף׃	their soul fainted within them.
ו וַיִּצְעֲקוּ אֶל־יְהוָה	6 Then they cried out to Adonoy
בַּצַּר לָהֶם	in their distress;
מִמְּצוּקוֹתֵיהֶם יַצִּילֵם׃	from their anguish He rescued them.
ז וַיַּדְרִיכֵם בְּדֶרֶךְ יְשָׁרָה	7 And He led them in a straight path,
לָלֶכֶת אֶל־עִיר מוֹשָׁב׃	that they might go to an inhabited city.
ח יוֹדוּ לַיהוָה חַסְדּוֹ	8 Let them thank Adonoy for His kindness,
וְנִפְלְאוֹתָיו לִבְנֵי אָדָם׃	and for His wonders to the children of man.
ט כִּי־הִשְׂבִּיעַ נֶפֶשׁ שֹׁקֵקָה	9 For He satisfied the longing soul,
וְנֶפֶשׁ רְעֵבָה מִלֵּא־טוֹב׃	and the hungry soul He filled with good.
י יֹשְׁבֵי חֹשֶׁךְ	10 Those who sit in darkness
וְצַלְמָוֶת	and in the shadow of death,
אֲסִירֵי עֳנִי וּבַרְזֶל׃	bound in affliction and iron.
יא כִּי־הִמְרוּ אִמְרֵי־אֵל	11 For they defied the words of the Almighty,

וַעֲצַת עֶלְיוֹן
נָאָצוּ׃

and the counsel of the Most High
they scorned.

יב וַיַּכְנַע בֶּעָמָל לִבָּם
כָּשְׁלוּ וְאֵין עֹזֵר׃

12 And He humbled their heart with hard labor,
they stumbled and there was none to help.

יג וַיִּזְעֲקוּ אֶל־יְהוָה
בַּצַּר לָהֶם
מִמְּצֻקוֹתֵיהֶם יוֹשִׁיעֵם׃

13 Then they cried out to Adonoy
in their distress;
from their anguish He delivered them.

יד יוֹצִיאֵם מֵחֹשֶׁךְ
וְצַלְמָוֶת
וּמוֹסְרוֹתֵיהֶם יְנַתֵּק׃

14 He brought them out from darkness
and from the shadow of death,
and their shackles He broke.

טו יוֹדוּ לַיהוָה חַסְדּוֹ
וְנִפְלְאוֹתָיו לִבְנֵי אָדָם׃

15 Let them thank Adonoy for His kindness,
and for His wonders to the children of man.

טז כִּי־שִׁבַּר דַּלְתוֹת נְחֹשֶׁת
וּבְרִיחֵי בַרְזֶל גִּדֵּעַ׃

16 For He has broken the gates of bronze,
and the bars of iron He has cut asunder.

יז אֱוִלִים
מִדֶּרֶךְ פִּשְׁעָם
וּמֵעֲוֺנֹתֵיהֶם
יִתְעַנּוּ׃

17 They are fools—
because of the way of their transgression
and their iniquities,
they cause their own affliction.

יח כָּל־אֹכֶל תְּתַעֵב נַפְשָׁם
וַיַּגִּיעוּ עַד־שַׁעֲרֵי מָוֶת׃

18 Their soul abhors all food,
and they drew near to the gates of death.

יט וַיִּזְעֲקוּ אֶל־יְהוָה
בַּצַּר לָהֶם
מִמְּצֻקוֹתֵיהֶם יוֹשִׁיעֵם׃

19 Then they cried out to Adonoy
in their distress;
from their anguish He delivered them.

כ יִשְׁלַח דְּבָרוֹ וְיִרְפָּאֵם
וִימַלֵּט מִשְּׁחִיתוֹתָם׃

20 He sends His word and heals them,
and delivers them from their destruction.

כא יוֹדוּ לַיהוָה חַסְדּוֹ
וְנִפְלְאוֹתָיו לִבְנֵי אָדָם׃

21 Let them thank Adonoy for His kindness,
and for His wonders to the children of man.

כב וְיִזְבְּחוּ זִבְחֵי תוֹדָה
וִיסַפְּרוּ מַעֲשָׂיו בְּרִנָּה׃

22 And let them offer sacrifices of thanksgiving,
and declare His works with singing.

כג יוֹרְדֵי הַיָּם בָּאֳנִיּוֹת
עֹשֵׂי מְלָאכָה בְּמַיִם רַבִּים׃

23 Those who go down to the sea in ships,
that do work in mighty waters.

כד הֵמָּה רָאוּ מַעֲשֵׂי יְהוָה
וְנִפְלְאוֹתָיו בִּמְצוּלָה׃

24 They saw the works of Adonoy,
and His wonders in the deep.

כה וַיֹּאמֶר וַיַּעֲמֵד רוּחַ סְעָרָה
וַתְּרוֹמֵם גַּלָּיו׃

25 He spoke and raised the stormwind,
and lifted up its waves.

כו יַעֲלוּ שָׁמַיִם
יֵרְדוּ תְהוֹמוֹת
נַפְשָׁם בְּרָעָה תִתְמוֹגָג׃

26 They rise to the heavens,
they descend to the depths,
their soul melts away because of trouble.

כז יָחוֹגּוּ וְיָנוּעוּ כַּשִּׁכּוֹר

27 They reel and stagger like a drunkard,

וְכָל־חָכְמָתָם תִּתְבַּלָּע׃	and all their skills are swallowed up [i.e. useless]
כח וַיִּצְעֲקוּ אֶל־יְהוָה	28 Then they cried out to Adonoy
בַּצַּר לָהֶם	in their distress,
וּמִמְּצוּקֹתֵיהֶם יוֹצִיאֵם׃	from their anguish He rescued them.
כט יָקֵם סְעָרָה לִדְמָמָה	29 He turned the storm into calmness,
וַיֶּחֱשׁוּ גַּלֵּיהֶם׃	and their waves were stilled.
ל וַיִּשְׂמְחוּ כִי־יִשְׁתֹּקוּ	30 They rejoiced because the waves were quieted,
וַיַּנְחֵם אֶל־מְחוֹז חֶפְצָם׃	and He led them to their desired border.
לא יוֹדוּ לַיהוָה חַסְדּוֹ	31 Let them thank Adonoy for His kindness,
וְנִפְלְאוֹתָיו לִבְנֵי אָדָם׃	and for His wonders to the children of man.
לב וִירֹמְמוּהוּ	32 Let them exalt Him
בִּקְהַל־עָם	in an assembly of people,
וּבְמוֹשַׁב זְקֵנִים יְהַלְלוּהוּ׃	and at a sitting of elders, praise Him.
לג יָשֵׂם נְהָרוֹת לְמִדְבָּר	33 He turns rivers into a wilderness,
וּמֹצָאֵי מַיִם לְצִמָּאוֹן׃	and springs of water into an arid place.
לד אֶרֶץ פְּרִי לִמְלֵחָה	34 A fruitful land into a salt waste,
מֵרָעַת יֹשְׁבֵי בָהּ׃	because of the wickedness of its inhabitants.
לה יָשֵׂם מִדְבָּר לַאֲגַם־מַיִם	35 He turns a wilderness into a pool of water,
וְאֶרֶץ צִיָּה לְמֹצָאֵי מָיִם׃	and a dry land into springs of water.
לו וַיּוֹשֶׁב שָׁם רְעֵבִים	36 And He made the hungry settle there,
וַיְכוֹנְנוּ עִיר מוֹשָׁב׃	and they established an inhabited city.
לז וַיִּזְרְעוּ שָׂדוֹת וַיִּטְּעוּ כְרָמִים	37 And they sowed fields and planted vineyards,
וַיַּעֲשׂוּ פְּרִי תְבוּאָה׃	which yielded fruit for harvest.
לח וַיְבָרְכֵם	38 And He blessed them
וַיִּרְבּוּ מְאֹד	and they multiplied greatly,
וּבְהֶמְתָּם לֹא יַמְעִיט׃	and their cattle, He did not diminish.
לט וַיִּמְעֲטוּ	39 And they were reduced in numbers
וַיָּשֹׁחוּ	and brought low,
מֵעֹצֶר רָעָה וְיָגוֹן׃	from oppression, calamity, and sorrow.
מ שֹׁפֵךְ בּוּז עַל־נְדִיבִים	40 He pours contempt upon nobles,
וַיַּתְעֵם בְּתֹהוּ	and causes them to wander in the wasteland
לֹא־דָרֶךְ׃	where there is no path.
מא וַיְשַׂגֵּב אֶבְיוֹן מֵעוֹנִי	41 And He lifted up the needy from affliction,
וַיָּשֶׂם כַּצֹּאן מִשְׁפָּחוֹת׃	and he established families like a flock.
מב יִרְאוּ יְשָׁרִים וְיִשְׂמָחוּ	42 The upright will see it and rejoice,
וְכָל־עַוְלָה קָפְצָה פִּיהָ׃	and all iniquity will shut its mouth.
מג מִי־חָכָם וְיִשְׁמָר־אֵלֶּה	43 Whoever is wise, let him note these things,
וְיִתְבּוֹנְנוּ	and they will understand
חַסְדֵי יְהוָה׃	the kindnesses of Adonoy.

פרק קט Chapter 108

Weekly Cycle	Monthly Cycle	Book Number
Friday	23rd day of the month	Book 5

Author

דָּוִד הַמֶּלֶךְ—King David—the second king of Israel and father of the Davidic royal and messianic dynasty. David composed over seventy of the 150 psalms of Sefer Tehillim.

Genre

Psalm of Praise - This is a psalm of celebration, often the result of a victory. It declares God's goodness and urges all of creation to worship.

Chapter Summary

Continuing with the theme of the previous psalm, the Singer encourages all exiles, present and future, to thank God for His everlasting compassion and salvation. David also composed this psalm to express his gratitude to God for personal deliverance.

This psalm consists of fourteen verses, subdivided into three parts. Verse 1 serves as a heading.
In verses 2-6, King David sings God's praises, accompanied with the playing of musical instruments, and offers thanks to Him.
In verses 7-10, he prays for personal salvation and for the fulfillment of God's promises to the patriarchs.
In verses 11-14, he expresses his confidence that God will indeed honor His word.

Introductory Words

מִזְמוֹר—Mizmor—Musical Accompaniment
שִׁיר—Shir—Song

Musical Instruments

נֵבֶל—Nevel—A Large Handheld Lyre - played by plucking with fingers
כִּנּוֹר—Kinor—A Small Handheld Harp - played with a plecturm (pick).

Shimush Tehillim - When to Say

For success against one's enemies—Verse 14 states: "Through God we will do valiantly and He will trample our adversaries."

Where in the Siddur: Verse 7 comprises one of the verses of the closing paragraph of the Amidah (Silent Meditation).

Biblical Personalities

אֱדוֹם—Edom—descendants of Esau, brother of Jacob. Their sibling rivalry persisted for centuries, most strongly expressed when the Edomites looted Jerusalem as it was being overrun by the Babylonians.

מְנַשֶּׁה אֶפְרַיִם וִיהוּדָה—Manasseh, Ephraim, and Judah—three of the twelve tribes of Israel.

מוֹאָב—Moab—an enemy nation located on the eastern shore of the Dead Sea.

פְּלֶשֶׁת—Philistia—an enemy nation which dwelled on the southwestern coast of Israel.

Biblical Places

גִּלְעָד—Gilead—located to the east of the Jordan River, it was divided among the tribes of Gad and Manasseh.

עֵמֶק סֻכּוֹת—Valley of Sukkot—identified with Shechem, located just to the east of the Jordan river.

Contemporary Song

Verse 3

פרק קח

א שִׁיר מִזְמוֹר לְדָוִד׃

ב נָכוֹן לִבִּי אֱלֹהִים
אָשִׁירָה וַאֲזַמְּרָה
אַף־כְּבוֹדִי׃

ג עוּרָה הַנֵּבֶל וְכִנּוֹר
אָעִירָה שָּׁחַר׃

ד אוֹדְךָ בָעַמִּים ׀ יְהֹוָה
וַאֲזַמֶּרְךָ
בַּלְאֻמִּים׃

ה כִּי־גָדוֹל מֵעַל־שָׁמַיִם
חַסְדֶּךָ
וְעַד־שְׁחָקִים אֲמִתֶּךָ׃

ו רוּמָה עַל־שָׁמַיִם אֱלֹהִים
וְעַל כָּל־הָאָרֶץ כְּבוֹדֶךָ׃

ז לְמַעַן יֵחָלְצוּן יְדִידֶיךָ
הוֹשִׁיעָה יְמִינְךָ וַעֲנֵנִי׃

ח אֱלֹהִים ׀ דִּבֶּר בְּקָדְשׁוֹ
אֶעְלֹזָה
אֲחַלְּקָה שְׁכֶם
וְעֵמֶק סֻכּוֹת אֲמַדֵּד׃

ט לִי גִלְעָד ׀ לִי מְנַשֶּׁה
וְאֶפְרַיִם מָעוֹז רֹאשִׁי
יְהוּדָה מְחֹקְקִי׃

י מוֹאָב ׀ סִיר רַחְצִי
עַל־אֱדוֹם אַשְׁלִיךְ נַעֲלִי
עֲלֵי־פְלֶשֶׁת אֶתְרוֹעָע׃

Chapter 108

1 A song, a Psalm of David.

2 My heart is steadfast, God,
I will sing and I will offer hymns,
this too is my glory.

3 Awake, lyre and harp;
and I will awaken the dawn.

4 I will thank You among peoples, Adonoy,
and I will sing praises to You
among the nations.

5 For great aboved the heavens
is Your kindness,
and until the skies is Your truth.

6 Exalted above the heavens is God,
and above all the earth is Your glory.

7 In order that Your loved ones be released,
deliver [with] Your right hand and answer me.

8 God spoke in His holiness
that I would exult,
that I would divide a portion,
and the valley of Succoth I would mete out.

9 Mine is Gilad, mine is Menashe,
and Ephraim is the stronghold of my head;
Judah is my lawgiver.

10 Moav is my wash basin,
upon Edom I will cast my lock,
at Philistia I will shout.

יא מִי יֹבִלֵנִי עִיר מִבְצָר מִי נָחַנִי עַד־אֱדוֹם׃	11 Who will bring me into the fortified city, who will lead me unto Edom?
יב הֲלֹא־אֱלֹהִים זְנַחְתָּנוּ וְלֹא־תֵצֵא אֱלֹהִים בְּצִבְאֹתֵינוּ׃	12 Has God not forsaken us, and God does not go forth with our hosts?
יג הָבָה־לָּנוּ עֶזְרָת מִצָּר וְשָׁוְא תְּשׁוּעַת אָדָם׃	13 Give us help against the adversary, futile is the help of man.
יד בֵּאלֹהִים נַעֲשֶׂה־חָיִל וְהוּא יָבוּס צָרֵינוּ׃	14 Through God we will do valiantly and He will trample our adversaries.

פֶּרֶק קט Chapter 109

Weekly Cycle	Monthly Cycle	Book Number
Friday	23rd day of the month	Book 5

Author
דָּוִד הַמֶּלֶךְ—King David—the second king of Israel and father of the Davidic royal and messianic dynasty. David composed over seventy of the 150 psalms of Sefer Tehillim.

When & Why
David wrote this psalm when he passed the throne on to Solomon. In it, he blesses Solomon that he should be a fair and merciful judge of the people.

Genre
Psalm of Individual Lament - This psalm was written from the perspective of the individual worshipper, who cries out to God in his time of need. It is characterized as an address to God involving a complaint, followed by a request and ending with an expression of trust.

Chapter Summary
King David again speaks harshly of those who rise up against him. At the same time, he speaks on behalf of all Jews who have suffered harsh burdens and and have been vilified by the nations. He implores God to aid him, because he is poor and needy, and his heart in broken.

This psalm consists of thrity-one verses, subdivided into five parts. The first half of verse 1 serves as an introduction.

In verse 1, the Psalmist beseeches God to not be silent.

In verses 2-5, he laments his being pursed by enemies without cause.

In verses 6-20, he further curses the wicked enemies.

In verses 21-29, he then prays for God's help.

In verses 30 & 31, he concludes with a vow to offer his thanks to God after He sends salvation.

Introductory Words

לַמְנַצֵּחַ—Lamnatsei'ach—To the Conductor

מִזְמוֹר—Mizmor—Musical Accompaniment

Shimush Tehillim - When to Say

To ward off an enemy—Verse 6 states: "Appoint over him a wicked man, and may an adversary stand at his right."

Where in the Siddur

Recited on Shabbat Zachor (the Shabbat preceding Purim) in some congregations.

Talmud om Tehillim

Verse 22:"וְלִבִּי, חָלַל בְּקִרְבִּי."—"and my heart is dead within me."

The Talmud, Berachot 61b, deduces from this verse that the righteous are ruled entirely by their good inclination, whereas the wicked are ruled entirely by their evil inclination. David, explains the Talmud, had such mastery over his evil inclination that it was as if it had died inside of him.

פֶּרֶק קט			**Chapter 109**
לַמְנַצֵּחַ	א	1	To the Chief Musician,
לְדָוִד מִזְמוֹר			a Psalm of David.
אֱלֹהֵי תְהִלָּתִי אַל־תֶּחֱרַשׁ׃			God of my praise, keep not silent.
כִּי פִי רָשָׁע	ב	2	For the mouth of the wicked
וּפִי־מִרְמָה			and the mouth of the deceitful
עָלַי פָּתָחוּ			have opened against me;
דִּבְּרוּ אִתִּי			they have spoken to me
לְשׁוֹן שָׁקֶר׃			the language of falsehood.
וְדִבְרֵי שִׂנְאָה	ג	3	And with words of hatred
סְבָבוּנִי			they surrounded me,
וַיִּלָּחֲמוּנִי חִנָּם׃			and fought against me without cause.
תַּחַת־אַהֲבָתִי יִשְׂטְנוּנִי	ד	4	In return for my love they accuse me,
וַאֲנִי תְפִלָּה׃			but I am [all] prayer.
וַיָּשִׂימוּ עָלַי רָעָה	ה	5	And they have imposed upon me evil

תַּחַת טוֹבָה	in return for good,
וְשִׂנְאָה תַּחַת אַהֲבָתִי׃	and hatred in return for my love.
ו הַפְקֵד עָלָיו רָשָׁע	6 Appoint over him a wicked man,
וְשָׂטָן יַעֲמֹד עַל־יְמִינוֹ׃	and may an adversary stand at his right.
ז בְּהִשָּׁפְטוֹ	7 When he is judged,
יֵצֵא רָשָׁע	may he go forth condemned,
וּתְפִלָּתוֹ תִּהְיֶה לַחֲטָאָה׃	and may his prayer be turned into sin.
ח יִהְיוּ־יָמָיו מְעַטִּים	8 May his days be few,
פְּקֻדָּתוֹ יִקַּח אַחֵר׃	may another take his [high] position.
ט יִהְיוּ־בָנָיו יְתוֹמִים	9 May his children be orphans,
וְאִשְׁתּוֹ אַלְמָנָה׃	and his wife a widow.
י וְנוֹעַ יָנוּעוּ בָנָיו וְשִׁאֵלוּ	10 May his children wander about and beg
וְדָרְשׁוּ	and may they [have to] search
מֵחָרְבוֹתֵיהֶם׃	among their ruins.
יא יְנַקֵּשׁ נוֹשֶׁה לְכָל־אֲשֶׁר־לוֹ	11 May the creditor seize all that he has,
וְיָבֹזּוּ זָרִים יְגִיעוֹ׃	and may strangers make spoils of his labor.
יב אַל־יְהִי־לוֹ מֹשֵׁךְ חָסֶד	12 May he have none who extends kindness,
וְאַל־יְהִי חוֹנֵן לִיתוֹמָיו׃	and may none be gracious to his orphans.
יג יְהִי־אַחֲרִיתוֹ לְהַכְרִית	13 May his posterity be cut off,
בְּדוֹר אַחֵר	in the generation following
יִמַּח שְׁמָם׃	let their name be blotted out.
יד יִזָּכֵר ׀ עֲוֹן אֲבֹתָיו	14 May his iniquity against his father
אֶל־יְהוָה	be remembered to Adonoy,
וְחַטַּאת אִמּוֹ	and may the sin against his mother
אַל־תִּמָּח׃	not be erased.
טו יִהְיוּ נֶגֶד־יְהוָה תָּמִיד	15 May they be before Adonoy continually,
וְיַכְרֵת מֵאֶרֶץ	and may He cut off from the earth.
זִכְרָם׃	their memory.
טז יַעַן	16 Because
אֲשֶׁר ׀ לֹא זָכַר עֲשׂוֹת חָסֶד	he remembered not to do kindness,
וַיִּרְדֹּף אִישׁ־עָנִי וְאֶבְיוֹן	but pursued the poor and needy man,
וְנִכְאֵה לֵבָב לְמוֹתֵת׃	and the broken in heart unto death.
יז וַיֶּאֱהַב קְלָלָה	17 And he loved the curse
וַתְּבוֹאֵהוּ	and now it has come upon him;
וְלֹא־חָפֵץ בִּבְרָכָה	and he desired not blessing,
וַתִּרְחַק מִמֶּנּוּ׃	and it remained far from him.
יח וַיִּלְבַּשׁ קְלָלָה	18 And he clothed himself with cursing
כְּמַדּוֹ	as with a garment,
וַתָּבֹא כַמַּיִם בְּקִרְבּוֹ	and it came like water into his innards,

וְכַשֶּׁמֶן בְּעַצְמוֹתָיו׃	and like oil into his bones.
יט תְּהִי־לוֹ כְּבֶגֶד	19 May it be to him like a garment
יַעְטֶה	in which he wraps himself,
וּלְמֵזַח	and a belt
תָּמִיד יַחְגְּרֶהָ׃	with which he continually girds himself.
כ זֹאת	20 This [is the just reward]
פְּעֻלַּת שֹׂטְנַי	for the deed of my adversaries,
מֵאֵת יְהוָה	from Adonoy—
וְהַדֹּבְרִים רָע עַל־נַפְשִׁי׃	and for those who speak evil against my soul.
כא וְאַתָּה | יְהֹוִה אֲדֹנָי	21 But You, God, my Master,
עֲשֵׂה־אִתִּי לְמַעַן שְׁמֶךָ	deal with me for Your Name's sake,
כִּי־טוֹב חַסְדְּךָ הַצִּילֵנִי׃	because of Your good kindness, rescue me.
כב כִּי־עָנִי וְאֶבְיוֹן אָנֹכִי	22 For poor and needy am I,
וְלִבִּי חָלַל בְּקִרְבִּי׃	and my heart is dead within me.
כג כְּצֵל־כִּנְטוֹתוֹ	23 Like a shadow when it is lengthened,
נֶהֱלָכְתִּי	I am gone;
נִנְעַרְתִּי כָּאַרְבֶּה׃	I am stirred up like the locust.
כד בִּרְכַּי כָּשְׁלוּ מִצּוֹם	24 My knees totter from fasting,
וּבְשָׂרִי כָּחַשׁ מִשָּׁמֶן׃	and my flesh is lean without fat.
כה וַאֲנִי | הָיִיתִי חֶרְפָּה לָהֶם	25 And I have become a disgrace to them;
יִרְאוּנִי יְנִיעוּן רֹאשָׁם׃	[when] they see me they shake their head.
כו עָזְרֵנִי יְהוָה אֱלֹהָי	26 Help me Adonoy, my God;
הוֹשִׁיעֵנִי כְחַסְדֶּךָ׃	deliver me according to Your kindness.
כז וְיֵדְעוּ כִּי־יָדְךָ זֹּאת	27 May they know that this is Your hand;
אַתָּה יְהוָה עֲשִׂיתָהּ׃	that You, Adonoy, have done it.
כח יְקַלְלוּ־הֵמָּה	28 Let them curse, but You will bless [me];
וְאַתָּה תְבָרֵךְ	they arose [against me]
קָמוּ | וַיֵּבֹשׁוּ	but they will be put to shame,
וְעַבְדְּךָ יִשְׂמָח׃	and Your servant will rejoice.
כט יִלְבְּשׁוּ שׂוֹטְנַי	29 May my adversaries be clothed
כְּלִמָּה	with humiliation,
וְיַעֲטוּ	and may they enwrap themselves
כַמְעִיל בָּשְׁתָּם׃	in their shame as in a cloak.
ל אוֹדֶה יְהוָה מְאֹד	30 I will thank Adonoy exceedingly
בְּפִי	with my mouth,
וּבְתוֹךְ רַבִּים אֲהַלְלֶנּוּ׃	and among the multitude I will praise Him.
לא כִּי־יַעֲמֹד לִימִין אֶבְיוֹן	31 For He stands at the right of the needy,
לְהוֹשִׁיעַ מִשֹּׁפְטֵי נַפְשׁוֹ׃	to deliver him from the judges of his soul.

פרק ק׳ Chapter 110

Weekly Cycle	Monthly Cycle	Book Number
Friday	23rd day of the month	Book 5

Author

דָּוִד הַמֶּלֶךְ—King David—the second king of Israel and father of the Davidic royal and messianic dynasty. David composed over seventy of the 150 psalms of Sefer Tehillim. There is a second opinion that this psalm was not written by King David, but rather addressed to King David.

When & Why

David might have written this psalm about how God helped him defeat the Philistines in battle at the very beginning of his reign.

Genre

Psalm of Royalty - This psalm describes how God reigns supreme. It focuses on the human king of Israel, or upon God as King of Israel.

Chapter Summary

King David speaks here of God's promise to come to his aid in defeating his enemies. This psalm is understood by some as a reference to God's kindness to our forefather Abraham, upon successfully defeating the "four kings". Still others see the singer as addressing the future victories of Mashiach (Messiah), the son of David.

This psalm consists of seven verses, subdivided into two parts.

In verses 1-3, King David speaks of God's assurance that He will defeat his enemies, through the imagery of symbols of royalty.

In verses 4-7, he addresses the obligations imposed upon the king: to judge his people righteously and to fight the enemies of Israel.

Introductory Words

מִזְמוֹר—Mizmor—Musical Accompaniment

Shimush Tehillim - When to Say

For peace with one's enemies—Verse 1 states: "Wait at My right until I make your enemies a stool for your feet."

Where in the Siddur

Verses 6 & 7 comprise part of Av HaRachamim, a memorial prayer recited towards the conclusion of Shacharit (morning service) of Shabbat.

Biblical Personalities

מַלְכִּי-צֶדֶק—Malchizedek—a religious leader in Jerusalem, then Shalem, in the time of Abraham. He blessed Abraham upon Abraham's returning victorious from war.

Biblical Places

צִיּוֹן—Zion—often used as a synonym for Jerusalem, Zion originally referred only to the area where a Jebbusite fortress once stood, also the location of the City of David. Zion was later used by prophets and psalmists as another name for Jerusalem.

Ring with Four Menorahs
(Courtesy of Shlomo Moussaieff Collection)

פֶּרֶק קי			**Chapter 110**
לְדָוִד מִזְמוֹר	א	1	A Psalm of David.
נְאֻם יְהוָה | לַאדֹנִי			Adonoy said to my master,
שֵׁב לִימִינִי			"Wait at My right
עַד־אָשִׁית אֹיְבֶיךָ			until I make your enemies
הֲדֹם לְרַגְלֶיךָ׃			a stool for your feet."
מַטֵּה־עֻזְּךָ	ב	2	The staff of your strength,
יִשְׁלַח יְהוָה מִצִּיּוֹן			Adonoy will send from Zion,
רְדֵה בְּקֶרֶב אֹיְבֶיךָ׃			"Rule in the midst of your enemies."
עַמְּךָ נְדָבֹת	ג	3	Your people offered themselves willingly
בְּיוֹם חֵילֶךָ			in the days of your campaign,
בְּהַדְרֵי־קֹדֶשׁ			[because of your] holy splendors
מֵרֶחֶם מִשְׁחָר			from [the time you] emerged from the womb,
לְךָ טַל יַלְדֻתֶיךָ׃			you still possess the dew of your youth.
נִשְׁבַּע יְהוָה | וְלֹא יִנָּחֵם	ד	4	Adonoy has sworn and will not rescind,
אַתָּה־כֹהֵן לְעוֹלָם			"You are a priest forever,
עַל־דִּבְרָתִי מַלְכִּי־צֶדֶק׃			according to the word of Malkizedek."
אֲדֹנָי עַל־יְמִינְךָ	ה	5	My Master at your right,
מָחַץ בְּיוֹם־אַפּוֹ מְלָכִים׃			has crushed kings in the day of His wrath.
יָדִין בַּגּוֹיִם	ו	6	He will judge the nations [the battlefield will be]
מָלֵא גְוִיּוֹת			filled with their corpses;
מָחַץ רֹאשׁ עַל־אֶרֶץ רַבָּה׃			He will crush heads on the earth many times.
מִנַּחַל בַּדֶּרֶךְ	ז	7	From the brook by the wayside
יִשְׁתֶּה			will He drink,
עַל־כֵּן יָרִים רֹאשׁ׃			therefore [Israel] will hold its head high.

פרק קי״א Chapter 111

Weekly Cycle	Monthly Cycle	Book Number
Friday	23rd day of the month	Book 5

Author
Unknown

Genre
Psalm of Praise – This is a psalm of celebration, often the result of a victory. It declares God's goodness and urges all of creation to worship.

Psalm of Individual Thanksgiving - This psalm emphasizes gratitude for what God has done for the individual.

Acrostic - A literary composition in which the writer has used the letters of the Hebrew alphabet in their order as the initial letters for a sequence of verses. i.e. א.ב.ג.ד

Chapter Summary
This psalm, written in alphabetical order, calls upon man to look closely at the works of God, to remember His wonders and the might of His powerful deeds. The psalmist seeks to implant in our hearts faith in God and hope in the final redemption.

This psalm consists of ten verses, comprised of twenty-two clauses, corresponding to the twenty-two letters of the Hebrew alphabet. The first eight verses are made up of two clauses each; the last two each contain three clauses. Each clause is viewed as an independent statement of praise. The psalmist begins by thanking God for His wondrous works of creation. He further praises the Lord for His providence over all His creatures, particularly those who fear Him. He concludes by declaring that there is a direct relationship between God's actions and the actions of the God fearing man.

Introductory Word
הַלְלוּיָ-הּ—Halleluyah—Praise God

Shimush Tehillim - When to Say
To have many friends—Verse 1 states: "I will thank Adonoy with all my heart, in the council of the upright and in the congregation."

Where in the Siddur
Verses 4 & 5 are found in the Musaf Amidah (Silent Meditation) of Rosh HaShanah.

Verse 10 is recited together with Modeh Ani upon awakening in the morning, in which one thanks God for returning the soul to the body.

פֶּרֶק קי״א

א הַ֥לְלוּ יָ֨הּ ׀
אוֹדֶ֣ה יְ֭הוָה בְּכָל־לֵבָ֑ב
בְּס֖וֹד יְשָׁרִ֣ים
וְעֵדָֽה׃
ב גְּ֭דֹלִים מַעֲשֵׂ֣י יְהוָ֑ה
דְּ֝רוּשִׁ֗ים לְכָל־חֶפְצֵיהֶֽם׃
ג הוֹד־וְהָדָ֥ר פָּעֳל֑וֹ
וְ֝צִדְקָת֗וֹ עֹמֶ֥דֶת לָעַֽד׃
ד זֵ֭כֶר עָשָׂ֣ה לְנִפְלְאֹתָ֑יו
חַנּ֖וּן וְרַח֣וּם יְהוָֽה׃
ה טֶ֭רֶף נָתַ֣ן לִירֵאָ֑יו
יִזְכֹּ֖ר לְעוֹלָ֣ם בְּרִיתֽוֹ׃
ו כֹּ֣חַ מַ֭עֲשָׂיו
הִגִּ֣יד לְעַמּ֑וֹ
לָתֵ֥ת לָ֝הֶ֗ם נַחֲלַ֥ת גּוֹיִֽם׃
ז מַעֲשֵׂ֣י יָ֭דָיו אֱמֶ֣ת וּמִשְׁפָּ֑ט
נֶ֝אֱמָנִ֗ים כָּל־פִּקּוּדָֽיו׃
ח סְמוּכִ֣ים לָעַ֣ד לְעוֹלָ֑ם
עֲ֝שׂוּיִ֗ם בֶּאֱמֶ֥ת וְיָשָֽׁר׃
ט פְּד֤וּת ׀ שָׁ֘לַ֤ח לְעַמּ֗וֹ
צִוָּֽה־לְעוֹלָ֥ם בְּרִית֑וֹ
קָד֖וֹשׁ וְנוֹרָ֣א שְׁמֽוֹ׃
י רֵאשִׁ֤ית חָכְמָ֨ה ׀
יִרְאַ֬ת יְהוָ֗ה
שֵׂ֣כֶל ט֭וֹב
לְכָל־עֹשֵׂיהֶ֑ם
תְּ֝הִלָּת֗וֹ עֹמֶ֥דֶת לָעַֽד׃

Chapter 111

1 Praise God.
I will thank Adonoy with all my heart,
in the council of the upright
and in the congregation.
2 Great are the works of Adonoy;
available to all who desire them.
3 Beauty and splendor is His work,
and His righteousness endures forever.
4 He made a memorial for His wonders,
gracious and merciful is Adonoy.
5 He gave food to those who fear Him;
He is ever mindful of His covenant.
6 The power of His works
He has declared to His people,
to give them the inheritance of the nations.
7 The works of His hands are truth and justice,
faithful are all His precepts.
8 They are established forever, for eternity;
they are achieved in truth and uprightness.
9 Redemption He sent to His people,
He commanded His covenant for eternity;
holy and awe_inspiring is His Name.
10 The beginning of wisdom
is the fear of Adonoy,
good understanding
to all who perform [His commandments],
His praise endures forever.

פרק קי״ב Chapter 112

Weekly Cycle	Monthly Cycle	Book Number
Friday	23rd day of the month	Book 5

Author
Unknown

Genre
Psalm of Wisdom - This psalm contains teachings and wise advice and is meant to instruct people on how to live a Godly life.
Acrostic - A literary composition in which the writer has used the letters of the Hebrew alphabet in their order as the initial letters for a sequence of verses. i.e. א.ב.ג.ד

Chapter Summary
The singer continues the theme of the upright man, whose reward is complete both in this world and in the World to Come. As his heart is steadfast, he has no need to fear his enemies.

This psalm consists of ten verses and, like the previous psalm, is written in alphabetical order. The psalmist tells of the fortunate man who fears God and is devoted to His commandments. Such a man is blessed with might, children and wealth, boldly declares the author, and will eventually overcome his enemies, in turn causing them to perish.

Introductory Word
הַלְלוּיָ-ה—Halleluyah—Praise God
אַשְׁרֵי—Ashrei—Praiseworthy—Happy

Shimush Tehillim - When to Say
To maximize one's personal strength—Verse 2 states: "Mighty upon the earth will be his seed, a generation of the upright who will be blessed."

Where in the Siddur
Verse 9 is found in Selichot (Penitential Service) of the Ta'anit Esther (the Fast of Esther).

פרק קי״ב	Chapter 112
א הַלְלוּ יָהּ אַשְׁרֵי־אִישׁ יָרֵא אֶת־יְהוָה בְּמִצְוֹתָיו חָפֵץ מְאֹד׃	1 Praise God. Fortunate is the man who fears Adonoy; His commandments, he greatly desires.
ב גִּבּוֹר בָּאָרֶץ יִהְיֶה זַרְעוֹ דּוֹר יְשָׁרִים יְבֹרָךְ׃	2 Mighty upon the earth will be his seed, a generation of the upright who will be blessed.

ג הוֹן־וָעֹשֶׁר בְּבֵיתוֹ וְצִדְקָתוֹ עֹמֶדֶת לָעַד׃	3 Wealth and riches are in his house, and his righteousness endures forever.
ד זָרַח בַּחֹשֶׁךְ אוֹר לַיְשָׁרִים חַנּוּן וְרַחוּם וְצַדִּיק׃	4 He causes to shine in the darkness a light for the upright [for He is] gracious, compassionate and righteous.
ה טוֹב־אִישׁ חוֹנֵן וּמַלְוֶה יְכַלְכֵּל דְּבָרָיו בְּמִשְׁפָּט׃	5 Good is the man who is gracious and lends, who conducts his affairs with justice.
ו כִּי־לְעוֹלָם לֹא־יִמּוֹט לְזֵכֶר עוֹלָם יִהְיֶה צַדִּיק׃	6 For he will never be moved, as an everlasting remembrance will the righteous remain.
ז מִשְּׁמוּעָה רָעָה לֹא יִירָא נָכוֹן לִבּוֹ בָּטֻחַ בַּיהוָה׃	7 He will not fear evil tidings, steadfast is his heart, trusting in Adonoy;
ח סָמוּךְ לִבּוֹ לֹא יִירָא עַד אֲשֶׁר־יִרְאֶה בְצָרָיו׃	8 His heart is steadfast, he will not fear, even before he sees his adversaries' [downfall]
ט פִּזַּר ׀ נָתַן לָאֶבְיוֹנִים צִדְקָתוֹ עֹמֶדֶת לָעַד קַרְנוֹ תָּרוּם בְּכָבוֹד׃	9 [Widely distributed charity] he dispersed to the needy; his righteousness endures forever, his horn will be exalted with honor.
י רָשָׁע יִרְאֶה ׀ וְכָעָס שִׁנָּיו יַחֲרֹק וְנָמָס תַּאֲוַת רְשָׁעִים תֹּאבֵד׃	10 The wicked will see it and be angered, he will gnash his teeth and melt away; the desire of the wicked will perish.

Tel Dan Stele

פרק קי״ג Chapter 113

Weekly Cycle	Monthly Cycle	Book Number
Friday	24th day of the month	Book 5

Author
Unknown

When & Why
The psalm is a preface to the story of the miracles the Israelites witnessed during the Exodus from Egypt and the splitting of the Sea of Reeds.

Genre
Psalm of Praise – This is a psalm of celebration, often the result of a victory. It declares God's goodness and urges all of creation to worship.

Chapter Summary
This is the first of the six psalms of Hallel (Service of Praise), recited on Yom Tov (Festivals) and Rosh Chodesh (New Moon), commemorating both past and future redemptions. Recognizing God's Divine Supervision over all creatures, the singer turns to Israel and declares: "Praise God! Praise, you servants of Adonoy, praise the Name of Adonoy."

Hallel is divided into three parts. The first section, chapters 113-115, consists of praises and blessings of God's name pronounced by "His servants". The second section, chapter 116, was to be sung in conjunction with the Korban Todah (Thanksgiving offering). The third section, chapters 117 and 118, is a song of praise uttered by those who enter "Adonoy's House", a reference to the Beit HaMikdash (Temple).

Psalm 113 consists of nine verses, subdivided into three stanzas of three verses each.
In verses 1-3, the psalmist calls upon all servants of God to praise Him, adding that God's name shall be praised forever.
In verses 4-6, he praises God as dwelling on high and watching over the entire world.
In verses 7-9, he further extolls God as the One who raises the poor from their degradation and enables barren women to conceive and subsequently rejoice.

Introductory Word
הַלְלוּיָ-ה—Halleluyah—Praise God
הַלְלוּ—Hallelu—Praise

Shimush Tehillim - When to Say
To destroy idolatry—Verses 5 & 6 state: "Who is like Adonoy, our God, Who dwells on high, [yet] looks down so low in the heavens and [upon] the earth?"

Where in the Siddur
Recited as the opening paragraph of Hallel, immediately following the Amidah (Silent Meditation)

of Shacharit (morning service). Hallel is also recited following the Amidah of Ma'ariv (evening service) of the first two nights of Passover in some congregations. It is also recited by all as one of the steps of the Passover Seder.
Verse 2 is found in Baruch Hashem Le'olam, one of the blessings ofMa'ariv.
Verse 2 also comprises part of the Zimmun, a responsive recitation preceding Birkat HaMazon (Grace after Meals), as well as one of the verses of Atah Horeita, the introductory paragraph to Hakafot (dancing with the Torah ceremony) on Simchat Torah.
Verse 2 is also found in the repetition of the Musaf Amidah (Silent Meditation) of Rosh HaShanah.
Verses 2-4 comprise two of the verses of Yehi Chevod, one of the paragraphs of Pesukei Dezimra (Verses of Praise introducing the Shacharit morning service).

Talmud on Tehillim

The Talmud, Pesachim 117a, after a lengthy debate as to the authorship of Hallel (Service of Praise), comprised of psalms 113-118, concludes that Moshe (Moses) is indeed its author. Also referred to as Hallel HaMitzri (the Egyptian Hallel), it was, according to tradition, sung by the Israelites upon successfully crossing the Red Sea.
Verses 7-9: "מְקִימִי מֵעָפָר דָּל... מוֹשִׁיבִי, עֲקֶרֶת הַבַּיִת"—"He raises up the poor from the dust; He returns the barren woman to the home."
The Talmud, Pesachim 118b, infers that these verses refer to God as the source of all blessings. He has the capacity to change a pauper to a prince and a barren woman to a happy mother of children.

פֶּרֶק קי״ג	**Chapter 113**
א הַֽלְלוּ יָהּ ׀	1 Praise God!
הַֽלְלוּ עַבְדֵי יְהוָה	Praise, you servants of Adonoy,
הַֽלְלוּ אֶת־שֵׁם יְהוָה׃	praise the Name of Adonoy.
ב יְהִי שֵׁם יְהוָה מְבֹרָךְ	2 The Name of Adonoy will be blessed
מֵעַתָּה וְעַד־עוֹלָם׃	from now forever.
ג מִמִּזְרַח־שֶׁמֶשׁ עַד־מְבוֹאוֹ	3 From the rising of the sun to its setting,
מְהֻלָּל שֵׁם יְהוָה׃	praised is the Name of Adonoy.
ד רָם עַל־כׇּל־גּוֹיִם ׀ יְהוָה	4 High above all nations is Adonoy
עַל הַשָּׁמַיִם כְּבוֹדוֹ׃	above the heavens is His Glory.
ה מִי כַּיהוָה אֱלֹהֵינוּ	5 Who is like Adonoy, our God,
הַמַּגְבִּיהִי לָשָׁבֶת׃	Who dwells on high,
ו הַמַּשְׁפִּילִי לִרְאוֹת	6 [yet] looks down so low
בַּשָּׁמַיִם וּבָאָרֶץ׃	in the heavens and [upon] the earth?
ז מְקִימִי מֵעָפָר דָּל	7 He raises up the poor from the dust,
מֵאַשְׁפֹּת יָרִים אֶבְיוֹן׃	from the dunghills He lifts up the needy;
ח לְהוֹשִׁיבִי עִם־נְדִיבִים	8 to seat [them] with nobles,

עִם נְדִיבֵי עַמּוֹ:		with the nobles of His people.
מוֹשִׁיבִי | עֲקֶרֶת הַבַּיִת	ט 9	He returns the barren woman to the home
אֵם־הַבָּנִים שְׂמֵחָה		[as] a joyful mother of children.
הַלְלוּ־יָהּ:		Praise God!

פרק קי״ד Chapter 114

Weekly Cycle	Monthly Cycle	Book Number
Friday	24th day of the month	Book 5

Author
Unknown

Genre
Psalm of Praise – This is a psalm of celebration, often the result of a victory. It declares God's goodness and urges all of creation to worship.

Psalm of Wisdom – This psalm contains teachings and wise advice and is meant to instruct people on how to live a Godly life.

Summary
Linked to the preceding psalm, the singer here, through stunning imagery, describes the "responses" of God's creations to the miracles He performed for Israel when they came forth from Egypt, when the sea "fled" at the sight of the Israelites' arrival, and when God turned the rock into a "pool of water".

This psalm consists of eight verses, subdivided into four stanzas.
In verses 1 & 2, the psalmist describes how Israel left its servitude to become a holy dominion for God.
In verses 3 & 4, he depicts how God's creations were terrified of His might.
In verses 5 & 6, he rhetorically asks why the works of creation were indeed filled with dread.
In verses 7 & 8, he concludes by answering that they fear from the acts of the Master of the world, the God of Jacob.

Shimush Tehillim - When to Say
For success in business—Verse 8 states: "Who turns the rock into a pool of water, the flintstone into a fountain of water."

Where in the Siddur
Recited as one of the six psalms of Hallel (Service of Praise), upon the conclusion of the Amidah

of Shacharit (morning service) of Yom Tov (Festivals) and Rosh Chodesh (New Moon). Hallel is also recited following the Amidah of Ma'ariv (evening service) of the first two nights of Passover in some congregations. It is also recited by all as one of the steps of the Passover Seder.
Recited in some congregations on the first and/or last days of Passover at the conclusion of the Musaf service.

Biblical Personalities

בֵּית אַהֲרֹן—House of Aaron—a reference to the Kohanim (Priests) who served God in the Beit HaMikdash (Temple) in Jerusalem and functioned as the religious leaders of Israel.
יַעֲקֹב—Jacob—also called Israel, the third patriarch, known as the father of the twelve tribes of Israel. He was the twin brother of Esau, and married to Leah and Rachel.

Biblical Places

מִצְרָיִם—Egypt—the land where Israel was enslaved until God sent Moses to redeem them. Egyptian society ran contrary to many of the ideals of the Torah. The Israelite king is thus specifically warned not to amass calvalry, lest he be tempted to return his nation to Egypt.
יַרְדֵּן—Jordan River—located on the eastern border of Israel. God stopped the flow of the Jordan to enable the Israelites to cross into Israel.
יַם-סוּף—[Red] Sea— also referred to as the Sea of Reeds, the body of water which miraculously parted for the Israelites as they fled the Egyptians, and then engulfed and drowned the pursuing Egyptian soldiers.

Talmud on Tehillim

The Talmud, Pesachim 117a, teaches that Moses and the Israelites recited Hallel upon successfully crossing the Red Sea. The Talmud adds that the Prophets instituted that Hallel is to be recited on Yom Tov (Festivals), Rosh Chodesh (New Moon), and occasions when one is redeemed from trouble. While the Talmud refers to the holidays of Pesach, Shavu'ot and Sukkot, and by extension to Chanukah, many congregations today also recite Hallel on Yom Ha'Atzma'ut (Israel Indepence Day) and Yom Yerushalayim (Jerusalem Reunification Day).

Chapter 114

פרק קיד

א בְּצֵאת יִשְׂרָאֵל מִמִּצְרָיִם בֵּית יַעֲקֹב מֵעַם לֹעֵז:	1 When Israel went out of Egypt, the House of Jacob from a people of an alien language.
ב הָיְתָה יְהוּדָה לְקָדְשׁוֹ יִשְׂרָאֵל מַמְשְׁלוֹתָיו:	2 Judah became His holy nation, Israel, His dominion.
ג הַיָּם רָאָה וַיָּנֹס הַיַּרְדֵּן יִסֹּב לְאָחוֹר:	3 The sea saw and fled, the Jordan turned back.
ד הֶהָרִים רָקְדוּ כְאֵילִים גְּבָעוֹת כִּבְנֵי־צֹאן:	4 The mountains skipped like rams, the hills like young sheep.

ה מַה־לְּךָ הַיָּם
כִּי תָנוּס
הַיַּרְדֵּן תִּסֹּב לְאָחוֹר:
ו הֶהָרִים תִּרְקְדוּ כְאֵילִים
גְּבָעוֹת כִּבְנֵי־צֹאן:
ז מִלִּפְנֵי אָדוֹן חוּלִי אָרֶץ
מִלִּפְנֵי אֱלוֹהַּ יַעֲקֹב:
ח הַהֹפְכִי הַצּוּר
אֲגַם־מָיִם
חַלָּמִישׁ לְמַעְיְנוֹ־מָיִם:

5 What bothers you, sea,
that you flee;
Jordan, that you turn backwards?
6 Mountains, that you skip like rams
hills, like young sheep?
7 Tremble, earth, before the Master,
from before the God of Jacob,
8 Who turns the rock
into a pool of water,
the flintstone into a fountain of water.

פרק קטו Chapter 115

Weekly Cycle	Monthly Cycle	Book Number
Friday	24th day of the month	Book 5

Author
Unknown

Genre
Psalm of Praise – This is a psalm of celebration, often the result of a victory. It declares God's goodness and urges all of creation to worship.

Chapter Summary
The singer beseeches God to relieve the Jewish people of their troubles, act mercifully towards them, and bless them. He also ridicules idolaters who seek to undermine Israel's faith in the Lord.

This psalm consists of eighteen verses. Several clauses, such as "ezram umaginam Hu"—"He is their help and their shield", serve as a refrain, perhaps indicating that these verses were originally intended to be recited responsively.

Shimush Tehillim - When to Say
To refute idolatry—Verses 4-8 state: "Their idols are silver and gold, products of human hands. They have a mouth but cannot speak, they have eyes but cannot see. They have ears but cannot hear, they have a nose, but cannot smell. Their hands cannot feel their feet cannot walk, they cannot speak with their throat. Like them shall be their makers—all who put their trust in them."

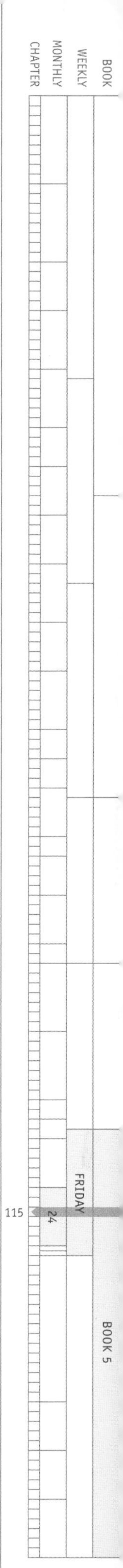

Where in the Siddur

Recited as one of the six psalms of Hallel (Service of Praise), upon the conclusion of the Amidah of Shacharit (morning service) of Yom Tov (Festivals) and Rosh Chodesh (New Moon). Verses 1-11 are omitted on Rosh Chodesh and the last six days of Pesach (Passover). Hallel is also recited following the Amidah of Ma'ariv (evening service) of the first two nights of Passover in some congregations. It is also recited by all as one of the steps of the Passover Seder.

Verse 2 is found in the long Tachanun (Supplication Service) recited on Mondays and Thursdays..

Verse 18 is the final verse of Ashrei, a central prayer of Shacharit (morning service) and Minchah (evening service).

Verse 18 is also recited by some as a conclusion to Shir HaMa'alot (Psalm 126) preceding Birkat HaMazon (Grace after Meals).

Biblical Personalities

אַהֲרֹן—Aaron—older brother of Moses, and the first Kohein Gadol (High Priest). The descendents of Aaron were designated to perform the ritual service in the Beit HaMikdash (Temple).

Contemporary Song

Verse 9

Talmud on Tehillim

Verse 1:"לֹא לָנוּ יְהוָה"—"Not for our sake, Adonoy, not for our sake."

The Talmud, Pesachim 117a, informs us that Hallel was historically recited on many occasions, most notably by Moses and the Israelites upon successfully crossing the Red Sea. We're further told that they exclaimed: "Not for our sake, O Lord, not for our sake; rather for Your name give glory." God then responded: "For my sake, for my sake I shall give glory, for how can I allow my name to be profaned." The new Jewish nation thereby acknowledged that it was God who freed them and that they were but His beneficiaries.

Others, according to the Talmudic passage, who recited Hallel:

Joshua and the Israelites upon successfully facing the kings of Canaan.

Devorah and Barak after the defeat of Sisera.

Chizkiyah and his entourage after facing Sancheriv.

Chananyah, Mishael and Azariah after being thrown into the "fiery furnace" by Nebuchadnezzar.

Mordechai and Esther upon defeating the evil Haman.

See Pesachim, 118a, for a fuller treatment of the involvement of Chananyah, Mishael and Azariah in the recitation of Hallel.

פֶּרֶק קטו		**Chapter 115**
לֹא לָנוּ יְהוָה לֹא לָנוּ כִּי־לְשִׁמְךָ תֵּן כָּבוֹד עַל־חַסְדְּךָ	א / 1	Not for our sake, Adonoy, not for our sake, but unto Your Name give honor, for the sake of Your kindliness,

עַל־אֲמִתֶּךָ׃	for the sake of Your truth.
ב לָמָּה יֹאמְרוּ הַגּוֹיִם	2 Why should the nations say,
אַיֵּה־נָא אֱלֹהֵיהֶם׃	"Where now is their God?"
ג וֵאלֹהֵינוּ בַשָּׁמָיִם	3 And [indeed,] our God is in heaven,
כֹּל אֲשֶׁר־חָפֵץ עָשָׂה׃	whatever He desires, He does.
ד עֲצַבֵּיהֶם כֶּסֶף וְזָהָב	4 Their idols are silver and gold,
מַעֲשֵׂה יְדֵי אָדָם׃	products of human hands.
ה פֶּה־לָהֶם וְלֹא יְדַבֵּרוּ	5 They have a mouth but cannot speak,
עֵינַיִם לָהֶם וְלֹא יִרְאוּ׃	they have eyes but cannot see.
ו אָזְנַיִם לָהֶם וְלֹא יִשְׁמָעוּ	6 They have ears but cannot hear,
אַף לָהֶם וְלֹא יְרִיחוּן׃	they have a nose, but cannot smell.
ז יְדֵיהֶם | וְלֹא יְמִישׁוּן	7 Their hands cannot feel
רַגְלֵיהֶם וְלֹא יְהַלֵּכוּ	their feet cannot walk,
לֹא־יֶהְגּוּ בִּגְרוֹנָם׃	they cannot speak with their throat.
ח כְּמוֹהֶם יִהְיוּ עֹשֵׂיהֶם	8 Like them shall be their makers—
כֹּל אֲשֶׁר־בֹּטֵחַ בָּהֶם׃	all who put their trust in them.
ט יִשְׂרָאֵל בְּטַח בַּיהוָה	9 Israel, trust in Adonoy;
עֶזְרָם וּמָגִנָּם הוּא׃	He is their help and their shield.
י בֵּית אַהֲרֹן בִּטְחוּ בַיהוָה	10 House of Aaron, trust in Adonoy;
עֶזְרָם וּמָגִנָּם הוּא׃	He is their help and their shield.
יא יִרְאֵי יְהוָה בִּטְחוּ בַיהוָה	11 [You] who fear Adonoy, trust in Adonoy;
עֶזְרָם וּמָגִנָּם הוּא׃	He is their help and their shield.
יב יְהוָה זְכָרָנוּ יְבָרֵךְ	12 Adonoy, mindful of us, will bless—
יְבָרֵךְ אֶת־בֵּית יִשְׂרָאֵל	He will bless the House of Israel;
יְבָרֵךְ אֶת־בֵּית אַהֲרֹן׃	He will bless the House of Aaron.
יג יְבָרֵךְ יִרְאֵי יְהוָה	13 He will bless those who fear Adonoy,
הַקְּטַנִּים עִם־הַגְּדֹלִים׃	the small ones along with the great.
יד יֹסֵף יְהוָה עֲלֵיכֶם	14 May Adonoy increase you,
עֲלֵיכֶם וְעַל־בְּנֵיכֶם׃	you and your children.
טו בְּרוּכִים אַתֶּם לַיהוָה	15 Blessed are you unto Adonoy,
עֹשֵׂה שָׁמַיִם וָאָרֶץ׃	the Maker of heaven and earth.
טז הַשָּׁמַיִם שָׁמַיִם לַיהוָה	16 The heaven is the heaven of Adonoy,
וְהָאָרֶץ נָתַן לִבְנֵי־אָדָם׃	but the earth He gave to mankind.
יז לֹא הַמֵּתִים יְהַלְלוּ־יָהּ	17 The dead do not praise God,
וְלֹא כָּל־יֹרְדֵי	nor do those who go down
דוּמָה׃	into the silence [of the grave].
יח וַאֲנַחְנוּ | נְבָרֵךְ יָהּ	18 But we will bless God
מֵעַתָּה וְעַד־עוֹלָם	from now forever.
הַלְלוּ־יָהּ׃	Praise God!

פרק קטז Chapter 116

Weekly Cycle	Monthly Cycle	Book Number
Friday	24th day of the month	Book 5

Author

Unknown; perhaps דָּוִד הַמֶּלֶךְ—King David—the second king of Israel and father of the Davidic royal and messianic dynasty. David composed over seventy of the 150 psalms of Sefer Tehillim.

When & Why

David might have written this psalm after he was finally saved from Saul. The psalmist thanks God for saving him in his time of great distress and he reaffirms his belief that true salvation can only come from God.

Genre

Psalm of Thanksgiving - This psalm emphasizes gratitude for what God has done.

Chapter Summary

This psalm depicts the power of prayer as entreaty. The singer, tradition tells us, foresaw that the nations would eventually claim that the prayers of Israel are in vain. He therefore composed this psalm in an attempt to disprove this assertion, as he believed that his prayers would not be returned empty. Rather, he reasoned, God would hear the voice of the Israelites as they sing this psalm, and then redeem them.

This psalm consists of nineteen verses, subdivided into three parts. A section of Hallel, it gives expression to the psalmist's gratitude to the Almighty, as he vows to bring a Korban Todah (Thanksgiving offering). Like the previous psalm, this one too contains several refrains and repetitions, perhaps indicating that it was originally intended to be recited responsively.

In verses 1-4, the psalmist proudly exclaims that God hears his voice, and further calls out to God to heed his prayer now, as he is in great distress.

In verses 5-11, he recognizes God's mercy and salvation.

In verses 12-19, he vows to fulfill his promise of a peace offering and to call out in the name of God.

Shimush Tehillim - When to Say

To prevent unnatural or sudden death—Verse 8 states: "For You freed my soul from death, my eye from tears, my foot from stumbling."

Where in the Siddur

Recited as one of the six psalms of Hallel (Service of Praise), upon the conclusion of the Amidah of Shacharit (morning service) of Yom Tov (Festivals) and Rosh Chodesh (New Moon). Verses 1-11 are omitted on Rosh Chodesh and the last six days of Pesach (Passover). Hallel is also recited following the Amidah of Ma'ariv (evening service) of the first two nights of Passover in some congregations. It is also recited by all as one of the steps of the Passover Seder.

Verse 13 is part of the Havdalah service recited upon the conclusion of Shabbat.

Biblical Places

בֵּית יְהוָה—House of God—a reference to the Beit HaMikdash (Temple) in Jerusalem.
יְרוּשָׁלָם—Jerusalem—the capital city of Israel, conquered by King David 3,000 years ago. David established Jerusalem as both the religious and political center of Israel.

Talmud on Tehillim

Verse 1: "אָהַבְתִּי, כִּי יִשְׁמַע יְהוָה אֶת קוֹלִי, תַּחֲנוּנָי"—"I love when Adonoy hears my voice, my prayers."
The Talmud, Pesachim 118b, in expounding upon this verse, tells us that the Israelites asked God: When are they beloved? God in turn responded: "When I hear their voice, their supplication."
Verse 13: "כּוֹס יְשׁוּעוֹת אֶשָּׂא"—"The cup of deliverance I will raise."
The Talmud, Pesachim 119b, teaches that at the Seudat Mashiach (festive meal in honor of Messiah's arrival), King David himself will lead all present in Birkat HaMazon (Grace after Meals). As David incorporated many psalms of thanksgiving in Sefer Tehillim (Book of Psalms), built the City of David (Jerusalem), and was privileged to have his son erect the Beit HaMikdash (Temple), it is only fitting that he was bestowed with this honor, as all three of these themes are central to Birkat HaMazon.

פֶּרֶק קטז			**Chapter 116**
אָהַבְתִּי כִּי־יִשְׁמַע | יְהוָה	א	1	I love when Adonoy hears
אֶת־קוֹלִי תַּחֲנוּנָי׃			my voice, my prayers.
כִּי־הִטָּה אָזְנוֹ לִי	ב	2	Because He turned His ear to me,
וּבְיָמַי אֶקְרָא׃			throughout my days I will call [upon Him].
אֲפָפוּנִי | חֶבְלֵי־מָוֶת	ג	3	I am encompassed with pangs of death
וּמְצָרֵי שְׁאוֹל			and the narrow confines of the grave
מְצָאוּנִי			come upon me;
צָרָה וְיָגוֹן אֶמְצָא׃			trouble and sorrow I encounter.
וּבְשֵׁם־יְהוָה אֶקְרָא	ד	4	And upon the Name, Adonoy, I call
אָנָּה יְהוָה מַלְּטָה נַפְשִׁי׃			"I beseech You, Adonoy, save my soul."
חַנּוּן יְהוָה וְצַדִּיק	ה	5	Gracious is Adonoy and righteous,
וֵאלֹהֵינוּ מְרַחֵם׃			and our God is compassionate.
שֹׁמֵר פְּתָאיִם יְהוָה	ו	6	Adonoy protects the simple;
דַּלֹּתִי וְלִי יְהוֹשִׁיעַ׃			I was brought low and He delivered me.
שׁוּבִי נַפְשִׁי לִמְנוּחָיְכִי	ז	7	Return, my soul, to your restfulness,
כִּי־יְהוָה גָּמַל עָלָיְכִי׃			for Adonoy has rewarded you bountifully.
כִּי חִלַּצְתָּ נַפְשִׁי מִמָּוֶת	ח	8	For You freed my soul from death,
אֶת־עֵינִי מִן־דִּמְעָה			my eye from tears,
אֶת־רַגְלִי מִדֶּחִי׃			my foot from stumbling.
אֶתְהַלֵּךְ לִפְנֵי יְהוָה	ט	9	I will walk before Adonoy

Fresco of King David Rejoicing with the Ark in Jerusalem

בְּאַרְצוֹת הַחַיִּים׃	in the land of the living.
י הֶאֱמַנְתִּי כִּי אֲדַבֵּר	10 I had faith (even) when I said,
אֲנִי עָנִיתִי מְאֹד׃	"I suffer greatly."
יא אֲנִי אָמַרְתִּי בְחָפְזִי	11 I said in my haste,
כָּל־הָאָדָם כֹּזֵב׃	"All men are deceitful."
יב מָה־אָשִׁיב לַיהוָה	12 How can I repay Adonoy
כָּל־תַּגְמוּלוֹהִי עָלָי׃	for all the rewards He bestowed on me?
יג כּוֹס־יְשׁוּעוֹת אֶשָּׂא	13 The cup of deliverance I will raise,
וּבְשֵׁם יְהוָה אֶקְרָא׃	and upon the Name, Adonoy, I will call.
יד נְדָרַי לַיהוָה אֲשַׁלֵּם	14 My vows to Adonoy I will fulfill
נֶגְדָה־נָּא לְכָל־עַמּוֹ׃	in the presence of all His people.
טו יָקָר בְּעֵינֵי יְהוָה	15 Precious in the eyes of Adonoy
הַמָּוְתָה לַחֲסִידָיו׃	is the death of His pious ones.
טז אָנָּה יְהוָה	16 I beseech You, Adonoy,
כִּי־אֲנִי עַבְדֶּךָ	for I am Your servant—
אֲנִי־עַבְדְּךָ	I am Your servant,
בֶּן־אֲמָתֶךָ	the son of Your handmaid;
פִּתַּחְתָּ לְמוֹסֵרָי׃	You have loosened my bonds.
יז לְךָ־אֶזְבַּח זֶבַח תּוֹדָה	17 To You I will offer offerings of thanksgiving,
וּבְשֵׁם יְהוָה אֶקְרָא׃	and upon the Name, Adonoy, I will call.
יח נְדָרַי לַיהוָה אֲשַׁלֵּם	18 My vows to Adonoy I will fulfill.
נֶגְדָה־נָּא לְכָל־עַמּוֹ׃	in the presence of all His people.
יט בְּחַצְרוֹת | בֵּית יְהוָה	19 In the courtyards of the House of God,
בְּתוֹכֵכִי יְרוּשָׁלָ͏ִם	in your midst, Jerusalem.
הַלְלוּ־יָהּ׃	Praise God!

פרק קיז Chapter 117

Weekly Cycle	Monthly Cycle	Book Number
Friday	24th day of the month	Book 5

Author
Unknown

Genre
Psalm of Praise - This is a psalm of celebration, often the result of a victory. It declares God's goodness and urges all of creation to worship.

Chapter Summary
Having previously called upon Israel to praise the Lord, the singer now turns to the nations of the world to do the same. The author is perhaps alluding here to the days of Mashiach (Messiah), when, tradition tells us, Israel will praise the Lord from its perspective, and the nations from theirs.

This psalm consists of two verses, and as such is the shortest chapter of Sefer Tehillim (Book of Psalms). Along with the following chapter, it comprises the final part of Hallel. In its two verses, the psalmist calls upon the nations to praise God.

Introductory Word
הַלְלוּ—Hallelu—Praise

Shimush Tehillim - When to Say
For an innocent person wrongly blamed—Verse 2 states: "For His kindness overwhelmed us, and Adonoy's truth is forever. Praise God!"

Where in the Siddur
Recited as one of the six psalms of Hallel (Service of Praise), upon the conclusion of the Amidah of Shacharit (morning service) of Yom Tov (Festivals) and Rosh Chodesh (New Moon). Hallel is also recited following the Amidah of Ma'ariv (evening service) of the first two nights of Passover in some congregations. It is also recited by all as one of the steps of the Passover Seder.

Talmud on Tehillim
Verse 1: "הַלְלוּ אֶת־יְהוָה כָּל־גּוֹיִם"—"Praise Adonoy, all nations."

The Talmud, Pesachim 118b, infers that when Mashiach (Messiah) arrives, all the nations of the world will bring gifts of tribute to him.

פרק קיז	Chapter 117
א הַלְלוּ אֶת־יְהוָה כָּל־גּוֹיִם שַׁבְּחוּהוּ כָּל־הָאֻמִּים:	1 Praise Adonoy, all nations extol Him, all peoples.
ב כִּי גָבַר עָלֵינוּ ׀ חַסְדּוֹ וֶאֱמֶת־יְהוָה לְעוֹלָם הַלְלוּ־יָהּ:	2 For His kindness overwhelmed us,{and Adonoy's truth is forever. Praise God!

פרק קיח Chapter 118

Weekly Cycle	Monthly Cycle	Book Number
Friday	24th day of the month	Book 5

Author

Unknown; perhaps דָּוִד הַמֶּלֶךְ—King David—the second king of Israel and father of the Davidic royal and messianic dynasty. David composed over seventy of the 150 psalms of Sefer Tehillim.

Genre

Psalm of Thanksgiving - This psalm emphasizes gratitude for what God has done for the community as a whole.

Chapter Summary

According to tradition, this chapter, like the previous one, was prophetically written as thanksgiving for future acts of deliverance of the Jewish people, perhaps an allusion to the days of Mashiach (Messiah). Alternatively, it may be referring to none other than King David himself, who gave thanks to the Almighty upon his being anointed as king.

This psalm consists of twenty-nine verses, subdivided into four parts. Together with the previous psalm, it comprises the final section of Hallel.

In verses 1-4, the psalmist calls upon the Jewish people to give thanks to God for His eternal kindness.

In verses 5-14, he proudly proclaims that he has placed his trust in God, his savior.

In verses 15-18, he tells of singing which can be heard among the righteous.

In verses 19-29, he beautifully crafts communal, responsive exclamations of praise to the Almighty for His salvation.

Introductory Word

הוֹדוּ—Hodu—Give thanks

Shimush Tehillim - When to Say

For appearing before a judge (say verses 26-29)—Verse 26 states: "Blessed be he who comes in the Name of Adonoy; we bless you from Adonoy's House."

To hope for a heretic to repent—Verse 8 states: "It is better to take refuge in Adonoy than to trust in man."

Where in the Siddur

Recited as one of the six psalms of Hallel (Service of Praise), upon the conclusion of the Amidah of Shacharit (morning service) of Yom Tov (Festivals) and Rosh Chodesh (New Moon). Hallel is also recited following the Amidah of Ma'ariv (evening service) of the first two nights of Passover in some congregations. It is also one of the steps of the Passover Seder.

Verse 1 is recited by some following Shir HaMa'a lot (Psalm 126) preceding Birkat HaMazon (Grace after Meals).

Verse 1 is also recited at the Brit Milah (circumcision) ceremony.

Verse 5 is one of several verses recited responsively prior to the blowing of the Shofar on Rosh HaShanah.

Verses 5-9 are found in Tashlich—a prayer recited on Rosh HaShanah afternoon, usually by a body of water, in which we beseech God to "cast away" our sins into the depths of the sea.

Verse 25 is part of the long Tachanun (Supplication Service) recited on Mondays and Thursdays.

Biblical Personalities

אַהֲרֹן—Aaron—older brother of Moses and the first Kohein Gadol (High Priest). The descendents of Aaron, as future Kohanim, were designated to perform the ritual service in the Beit HaMikdash (Temple).

Biblical People

יִשְׂרָאֵל—Yisrael—The Nation of Israel

Contemporary Song

verse 5; verses 19 & 20

Talmud on Tehillim

Verse 21: "אוֹדְךָ, כִּי עֲנִיתָנִי"—"I thank You for You answered me."

The Talmud, Pesachim 119a, records that King David offered this verse in thanks to the Almighty for his being anointed as king by the prophet Shmuel (Samuel). Samuel was dispatched by God to anoint one of—without specification as to which—Yishai's (Jesse's) eight sons as king. David, a humble shepherd and the youngest of them, was thought to be the least qualified for the post. He thus thanked God upon being chosen for this lofty position. (See the above Talmudic passage for an elaborate treatment of the ensuing verses as a conversation between Shmuel, Yishai, David, and his brothers).

Verse 27: "אִסְרוּ־חַג בַּעֲבֹתִים עַד־קַרְנוֹת הַמִּזְבֵּחַ:"—"Bind the festival sacrifices with ropes (until they are brought) to the corners of the Altar."

The Talmud, Sukkah 45a, teaches that one who takes the Lulav (palm branch) with its accompanying species—Etrog (citron), Hadas (myrtle) and Aravah (willow)—on the holiday of Sukkot is regarded as if he has personally built an altar and offered a sacrifice upon it. The Talmud here is employing a play on words, as "avotim" ("ropes") in the above verse is the same word used in the Torah to describe the hadas (myrtle).

פרק קיח	Chapter 118
א הוֹדוּ לַיהוָה כִּי־טוֹב כִּי לְעוֹלָם חַסְדּוֹ׃	1 Thank Adonoy for He is good, for His kindness endures forever.
ב יֹאמַר־נָא יִשְׂרָאֵל כִּי לְעוֹלָם חַסְדּוֹ׃	2 Let Israel declare: "For His kindness endures forever."
ג יֹאמְרוּ־נָא בֵית־אַהֲרֹן כִּי לְעוֹלָם חַסְדּוֹ׃	3 Let the House of Aaron declare: "For His kindness endures forever."
ד יֹאמְרוּ־נָא יִרְאֵי יְהוָה כִּי לְעוֹלָם חַסְדּוֹ׃	4 Let those who fear Adonoy declare: "For His kindness endures forever."
ה מִן־הַמֵּצַר קָרָאתִי יָּהּ עָנָנִי בַמֶּרְחָב יָהּ׃	5 From the narrowness (of distress) I called [to] God, He answered me with the breadth of Divine relief.
ו יְהוָה לִי לֹא אִירָא מַה־יַּעֲשֶׂה לִי אָדָם׃	6 Adonoy is with me, I will not fear, what can man do to me?
ז יְהוָה לִי בְּעֹזְרָי וַאֲנִי אֶרְאֶה בְשֹׂנְאָי׃	7 Adonoy is with me, to help me, and I will see my enemies' (defeat).
ח טוֹב לַחֲסוֹת בַּיהוָה מִבְּטֹחַ בָּאָדָם׃	8 It is better to take refuge in Adonoy than to trust in man.
ט טוֹב לַחֲסוֹת בַּיהוָה מִבְּטֹחַ בִּנְדִיבִים׃	9 It is better to take refuge in Adonoy than to trust in nobles.
י כָּל־גּוֹיִם סְבָבוּנִי בְּשֵׁם יְהוָה כִּי אֲמִילַם׃	10 All nations surround me; in Adonoy's Name, I cut them down.
יא סַבּוּנִי גַם־סְבָבוּנִי בְּשֵׁם יְהוָה כִּי אֲמִילַם׃	11 They surrounded me, they surround me; in Adonoy's Name, I cut them down.
יב סַבּוּנִי כִדְבוֹרִים דֹּעֲכוּ כְּאֵשׁ קוֹצִים בְּשֵׁם יְהוָה כִּי אֲמִילַם׃	12 They surrounded me like bees, [but] they were extinguished like a thorn fire; in Adonoy's Name, I cut them down.
יג דַּחֹה דְחִיתַנִי לִנְפֹּל וַיהוָה עֲזָרָנִי׃	13 You pushed me again and again to fall, but Adonoy helped me.
יד עָזִּי וְזִמְרָת יָהּ וַיְהִי־לִי לִישׁוּעָה׃	14 The strength and retribution of God was (the cause of) my deliverance.

טו קוֹל ׀ רִנָּה וִישׁוּעָה	15 The sound of joyous song and deliverance
בְּאׇהֳלֵי צַדִּיקִים	is in the tents of the righteous:
יְמִין יְהוָה	"The right hand of Adonoy
עֹשָׂה חָיִל׃	performs deeds of valor.
טז יְמִין יְהוָה רוֹמֵמָה	16 The right hand of Adonoy is exalted,
יְמִין יְהוָה	the right hand of Adonoy
עֹשָׂה חָיִל׃	performs deeds of valor."
יז לֹא אָמוּת כִּי־אֶחְיֶה	17 I shall not die; for I shall live
וַאֲסַפֵּר מַעֲשֵׂי יָהּ׃	and relate the deeds of God.
יח יַסֹּר יִסְּרַנִּי יָּהּ	18 God has severely chastised me,
וְלַמָּוֶת לֹא נְתָנָנִי׃	but unto death He has not handed me.
יט פִּתְחוּ־לִי שַׁעֲרֵי־צֶדֶק	19 Open for me the gates of righteousness;
אָבֹא־בָם	I will enter them,
אוֹדֶה יָהּ׃	I will give thanks unto God.
כ זֶה־הַשַּׁעַר לַיהוָה	20 This gate is Adonoy's
צַדִּיקִים יָבֹאוּ בוֹ׃	the righteous shall enter it.
כא אוֹדְךָ כִּי עֲנִיתָנִי	21 I thank You for You answered me,
וַתְּהִי־לִי לִישׁוּעָה׃	and You have been my deliverance.
כב אֶבֶן מָאֲסוּ הַבּוֹנִים	22 The stone which the builders scorned
הָיְתָה לְרֹאשׁ פִּנָּה׃	became the cornerstone.
כג מֵאֵת יְהוָה הָיְתָה זֹּאת	23 This is Adonoy's doing,
הִיא נִפְלָאת בְּעֵינֵינוּ׃	it is a marvel in our eyes.
כד זֶה־הַיּוֹם עָשָׂה יְהוָה	24 This day was made by Adonoy,
נָגִילָה וְנִשְׂמְחָה בוֹ׃	let us exult and rejoice in Him.
כה אָנָּא יְהוָה הוֹשִׁיעָה נָּא	25 We beseech You, Adonoy, deliver us!
אָנָּא יְהוָה הַצְלִיחָה נָּא׃	We beseech You, Adonoy, make us successful!
כו בָּרוּךְ הַבָּא	26 Blessed be he who comes
בְּשֵׁם יְהוָה	in the Name of Adonoy;
בֵּרַכְנוּכֶם מִבֵּית יְהוָה׃	we bless you from Adonoy's House.
כז אֵל ׀ יְהוָה וַיָּאֶר לָנוּ	27 Almighty, Adonoy, He gave us light;
אִסְרוּ־חַג בַּעֲבֹתִים	bind the festival sacrifices with ropes
עַד־קַרְנוֹת	(until they are brought) to the corners
הַמִּזְבֵּחַ׃	of the Altar.
כח אֵלִי אַתָּה	28 You are my Almighty
וְאוֹדֶךָּ	and I will give thanks to You;
אֱלֹהַי אֲרוֹמְמֶךָּ׃	My God, I will exalt You.
כט הוֹדוּ לַיהוָה כִּי־טוֹב	29 Thank Adonoy for He is good;
כִּי לְעוֹלָם חַסְדּוֹ׃	for His kindness endures forever.

פרק קיט Chapter 119

Weekly Cycle	Monthly Cycle	Book Number
Friday	Letters א-ל - 25th day of the month Letters מ-ת - 26th day of the month	Book 5

Author

Unknown; perhaps דָּוִד הַמֶּלֶךְ—King David—the second king of Israel and father of the Davidic royal and messianic dynasty. David composed over seventy of the 150 psalms of Sefer Tehillim.

When & Why

The author of this psalm did not incorporate his name into the text of the chapter. The Rabbis of the Talmud and Midrash believed it was composed by King David.

This is the most uplifting, dear and important of all psalms. It was understood to be King David's personal prayer to God. David deeply desired to permanently cleave unto God's ways and comandments, so that he would be meritorious of God's eternal sweetness.

Genre

Psalm of Wisdom - This psalm contains teachings and wise advice and is meant to instruct people on how to live a Godly life.

Acrostic - A literary composition in which the writer has used the letters of the Hebrew alphabet in their order as the initial letters for a sequence of verses. i.e. א.ב.ג.ד

Chapter Summary

This psalm was composed as a prayer for success in spiritual matters and completeness in Torah achievement. It is arranged in alphabetical order, eight verses per letter, totaling one hundred seventy-six verses. As such, it is the longest chapter of Tehillim (Psalms). Each verse contains one of the following ten words: Torah, derech (path), chok (law), mitzvah (command), mishpat (judgment), eidut (testimony), pekud (precept), tzedek (righteousness), dibbur (speech), and amirah (recitation). All of the above refer to the Torah and its laws. The singer here intends to strengthen the hand of those who study and observe the Torah, to help them persevere and overcome all trials.

Introductory Word

אַשְׁרֵי—Ashrei—Fortunate—Praiseworthy—Happy

Shimush Tehillim - When to Say

For the healing of one's arm—Say the entire psalm, but in the following order of the letters: alef/tav, bet/shin, gimel/resh, dalet/kof, hei/tzadi, vav/pei, zayin/ayin, chet/samech, tet/nun, yud/mem, kaf/lamed.

א **For trembling**—Verse 1 states: "Fortunate are they who are "wholehearted in their way [of life], who walk in the Torah of Adonoy."
For one who wishes to fulfill a mitzvah—Verse 8 states: "Your statutes, I will preserve, do not forsake me, entirely."

ב **To heal forgetfulness**—Verse 16 states: "In Your statutes, I will be engrossed, [therefore] I will not forget Your word."
For inspiration of the heart—Verse 11 states: "In my heart, I have treasured Your word, that I might not sin against You."

ג **To heal one's right eye**—Verse 18 states: "Unveil my eyes that I may behold [understand] the unexplained things of Your Torah."

ד **To heal one's left eye**—Verse 25 states: "My soul clings to the dust sustain me in life according to Your word."

ה **For protection against sin**—Verse 37 states: "Turn away my eyes from beholding vanity, in Your ways, give me life."

ו **To assuage anger of an authority**—Verse 42 states: "That I may answer him who taunts me, for I have trusted in Your word."

ז **For healing of the spleen**—Verse 50 states: "This is my consolation in my affliction, for Your word [promise] has given me life."

ח **For healing of the upper abdomen**—Verse 58 states: "I have entreated the favor of Your countenance with my whole heart, be gracious unto me according to Your promise."

ט **For healing of the upper kidneys**—Verse 71 states: "It is good for me to have been afflicted in order that I learn Your statutes."

י **To be judged favorably** (say after the Minchah afternoon sevice)—Verse 75 states: " I know Adonoy that Your mandates are just, and I believe that you afflicted me [justly]."

כ **For inflammation of the right nostril** (say 7 times)—Verse 83 states: "For I have become [dry] like a leather skin in the smoke, [yet] Your statutes I have not forgotten."

ל **To be judged favorably** (say after the Shacharit morning service)—Verse 94 states: "I am Yours, deliver me, for Your precepts I have sought [to fulfill]."

מ **For healing of the right hand**—The verses of this letter, verses 97-104, use only the six direct depictions of the ten mentioned above (see Chapter Summary). As such, they reflect a direct connection to God. It is thus inferred that these verses refer to man's right hand, as David placed God "on his right side" (see Psalm 16:8).

נ **For traveling**—Verse 110 states: "The wicked have laid a snare for me, yet from Your precepts I have not strayed."

ס **To say before any request**—Verse 114 states: "You are my hidden fortress and shield, [only] in Your word do I hope."

ע **For healing of the left hand**—Verse 124 states: "Do with Your servant according to Your kindness, and Your statutes—teach them to me."

פ **For inflammation of the left nostril**—Verse 131 states: " I opened my mouth and eagerly swallowed them, because for Your commandments, I yearned."

צ For healing of the right leg (say 7 times)—Verse 143 states: "Distress and anguish have found me, [yet in] Your commandments I am engrossed."

ק For healing of the left leg—Verse 145 states: "I have called with my whole heart, answer me Adonoy; Your statutes I will treasure."

ר For healing of the right ear—Verse 153 states: "See my affliction and free me from it for Your Torah I have not forgotten."

ש For healing a headache—Verse 166 states: "I have hoped for Your deliverance Adonoy, and Your commandments I have done."

ת For healing of the left ear—Verse 170 states: "May my supplication come before You; according to Your word [promise], save me."

Where in the Siddur

Verses 66, 108, 122 and 160 are recited responsively prior to the blowing of the Shofar on Rosh HaShanah.
Verse 72 is found in Pirkei Avot (Ethics of Our Fathers), 6:9.
Verses 89–91 are recited as part of the blessings before the Shema on the second day of Rosh HaShanah.
Verse 99 is found in Pirkei Avot (Ethics of Our Fathers), 4:1.
Verse 142 is found in Uva Letzion, one of the closing prayers of Shacharit (morning service), as well as in Tzidkatcha, recited following the Minchah Amidah (Silent Meditation) of Shabbat afternoon.
Verses 153 and 154 serve as the textual basis for the blessing "Re'eh" of the weekday Amidah.
Verse 165 is recited upon the conclusion of Ein K'Eilokeinu, following the Musaf Amidah of Shabbat.
Verses 166, 162, and 165 are recited, in that order, by the Mohel (circumcisor) at a Brit Milah (circumcision).

Talmud on Tehillim

Verse 162: "שָׂשׂ אָנֹכִי, עַל אִמְרָתֶךָ כְּמוֹצֵא, שָׁלָל רָב"—"I am happy with Your word like one who finds great gain." The Talmud, Shabbat 130a, teaches that any commandment which the Jewish people accepted upon themselves with great joy, such as Brit Milah (circumcision), is still being performed with joy today. Brit Milah, in particular, is a constant testimony that the Jewish people have been sanctified by God's commandments, and as such calls for special joyfulness.

פרק קיט

א אַשְׁרֵי
תְמִימֵי־דָרֶךְ
הַהֹלְכִים בְּתוֹרַת יְהוָה:
ב אַשְׁרֵי
נֹצְרֵי עֵדֹתָיו
בְּכָל־לֵב יִדְרְשׁוּהוּ:
ג אַף לֹא־פָעֲלוּ עַוְלָה
בִּדְרָכָיו הָלָכוּ:
ד אַתָּה צִוִּיתָה
פִקֻּדֶיךָ לִשְׁמֹר מְאֹד:

Chapter 119

1 Fortunate are they
who are wholehearted in their way [of life],
who walk in the Torah of Adonoy.
2 Fortunate are they
that keep His testimonies,
with their whole heart, they seek Him.
3 Not only do they refrain from wrong doings
[but] they walk in His ways [and do good].
4 You have commanded Your precepts
that we should preserve them diligently.

אַחֲלַי	ה	5	This is my fervent wish—
יִכֹּנוּ דְרָכָי			may my ways be firmly established—
לִשְׁמֹר חֻקֶּיךָ׃			to preserve Your statutes.
אָז לֹא־אֵבוֹשׁ	ו	6	Then I will not be ashamed,
בְּהַבִּיטִי			when I behold [understand]
אֶל־כָּל־מִצְוֺתֶיךָ׃			all Your commandments.
אוֹדְךָ	ז	7	I will [be able to] give thanks to You
בְּיֹשֶׁר לֵבָב			with an upright heart,
בְּלָמְדִי מִשְׁפְּטֵי צִדְקֶךָ׃			when I learn Your righteous mandates.
אֶת־חֻקֶּיךָ אֶשְׁמֹר	ח	8	Your statutes, I will preserve,
אַל־תַּעַזְבֵנִי עַד־מְאֹד׃			do not forsake me, entirely.
בַּמֶּה יְזַכֶּה־נַּעַר אֶת־אָרְחוֹ	ט	9	How can a young man keep his way pure?
לִשְׁמֹר כִּדְבָרֶךָ׃			By preserving it according to Your word.
בְּכָל־לִבִּי דְרַשְׁתִּיךָ	י	10	With my whole heart, I have sought You,
אַל־תַּשְׁגֵּנִי מִמִּצְוֺתֶיךָ׃			let me not err from Your commandments.
בְּלִבִּי צָפַנְתִּי אִמְרָתֶךָ	יא	11	In my heart, I have treasured Your word,
לְמַעַן לֹא אֶחֱטָא־לָךְ׃			that I might not sin against You.
בָּרוּךְ אַתָּה יְהוָֹה	יב	12	Blessed are You Adonoy,
לַמְּדֵנִי חֻקֶּיךָ׃			teach me Your statutes.
בִּשְׂפָתַי סִפַּרְתִּי	יג	13	With my lips I have recounted (taught)
כֹּל מִשְׁפְּטֵי־פִיךָ׃			all the mandates of Your mouth.
בְּדֶרֶךְ עֵדְוֺתֶיךָ	יד	14	[Walking] in the way of Your testimonies,
שַׂשְׂתִּי			I have been gladdened
כְּעַל כָּל־הוֹן׃			as much as over all riches.
בְּפִקֻּדֶיךָ אָשִׂיחָה	טו	15	In Your precepts I will meditate,
וְאַבִּיטָה			and [thereby] look upon [understand]
אֹרְחֹתֶיךָ׃			Your ways.
בְּחֻקֹּתֶיךָ אֶשְׁתַּעֲשָׁע	טז	16	In Your statutes, I will be engrossed,
לֹא אֶשְׁכַּח דְּבָרֶךָ׃			[therefore] I will not forget Your word.
גְּמֹל עַל־עַבְדְּךָ	יז	17	Deal kindly with Your servant,
אֶחְיֶה וְאֶשְׁמְרָה דְבָרֶךָ׃			that I may live and preserve Your word.
גַּל־עֵינַי	יח	18	Unveil my eyes
וְאַבִּיטָה			that I may behold [understand]
נִפְלָאוֹת מִתּוֹרָתֶךָ׃			the unexplained things of Your Torah.
גֵּר אָנֹכִי בָאָרֶץ	יט	19	I am a stranger upon the earth,
אַל־תַּסְתֵּר מִמֶּנִּי מִצְוֺתֶיךָ׃			do not conceal from me Your commandments.
גָּרְסָה נַפְשִׁי לְתַאֲבָה	כ	20	My soul is crushed from its longing
אֶל־מִשְׁפָּטֶיךָ בְכָל־עֵת׃			to [study] Your mandates at all times.
גָּעַרְתָּ זֵדִים	כא	21	You have rebuked the insolent,

אֲרוּרִים		accursed sinners,
הַשֹּׁגִים מִמִּצְוֺתֶיךָ׃		who err [stray] from Your commandments.
גַּל מֵעָלַי	כב / 22	Remove from me
חֶרְפָּה וָבוּז		humiliation and contempt
כִּי עֵדֹתֶיךָ נָצָרְתִּי׃		for I have kept Your testimonies.
גַּם יָשְׁבוּ שָׂרִים	כג / 23	Even though princes sit
בִּי נִדְבָּרוּ		and talk against me,
עַבְדְּךָ יָשִׂיחַ בְּחֻקֶּיךָ׃		Your servant meditates in Your statutes.
גַּם־עֵדֹתֶיךָ	כד / 24	Indeed in Your testimonies
שַׁעֲשֻׁעָי		I am engrossed,
אַנְשֵׁי עֲצָתִי׃		they are my counsellors.
דָּבְקָה לֶעָפָר נַפְשִׁי	כה / 25	My soul clings to the dust
חַיֵּנִי כִּדְבָרֶךָ׃		sustain me in life according to Your word.
דְּרָכַי סִפַּרְתִּי	כו / 26	My ways [needs] have I recounted
וַתַּעֲנֵנִי		and You answered me,
לַמְּדֵנִי חֻקֶּיךָ׃		teach me Your statutes.
דֶּרֶךְ־פִּקּוּדֶיךָ	כז / 27	The way of Your precepts
הֲבִינֵנִי		let me understand,
וְאָשִׂיחָה		and I will [be able to] speak
בְּנִפְלְאוֹתֶיךָ׃		of Your wonders.
דָּלְפָה נַפְשִׁי מִתּוּגָה	כח / 28	My soul is diminished from grief,
קַיְּמֵנִי כִּדְבָרֶךָ׃		sustain me according to Your word.
דֶּרֶךְ־שֶׁקֶר הָסֵר מִמֶּנִּי	כט / 29	The way of falsehood, remove from me,
וְתוֹרָתְךָ חׇנֵּנִי׃		and with Your Torah, be gracious to me.
דֶּרֶךְ־אֱמוּנָה בָחָרְתִּי	ל / 30	The way of trust, I have chosen,
מִשְׁפָּטֶיךָ שִׁוִּיתִי׃		Your mandates, I have set before me.
דָּבַקְתִּי בְעֵדְוֺתֶיךָ	לא / 31	I have attached myself to Your testimonies,
יְהֹוָה אַל־תְּבִישֵׁנִי׃		Adonoy, do not cause me to be ashamed.
דֶּרֶךְ־מִצְוֺתֶיךָ	לב / 32	In the way of Your commandments
אָרוּץ		I will run,
כִּי תַרְחִיב לִבִּי׃		for You have expanded my heart.
הוֹרֵנִי יְהֹוָה	לג / 33	Teach me, Adonoy,
דֶּרֶךְ חֻקֶּיךָ		the way of Your statutes,
וְאֶצְּרֶנָּה עֵקֶב׃		and I will keep them [at every] step.
הֲבִינֵנִי	לד / 34	Give me understanding
וְאֶצְּרָה תוֹרָתֶךָ		and I will keep Your Torah,
וְאֶשְׁמְרֶנָּה בְכׇל־לֵב		and preserve it with my whole heart.
הַדְרִיכֵנִי	לה / 35	Guide me
בִּנְתִיב מִצְוֺתֶיךָ		in the path of Your commandments,

כִּי־בוֹ חָפָצְתִּי׃		for therein is my desire.
לו הַט־לִבִּי אֶל־עֵדְוֺתֶיךָ	36	Incline my heart to Your testimonies,
וְאַל אֶל־בָּצַע׃		and not to [selfish] gain.
לז הַעֲבֵר עֵינַי מֵרְאוֹת שָׁוְא	37	Turn away my eyes from beholding vanity,
בִּדְרָכֶךָ חַיֵּנִי׃		in Your ways, give me life.
לח הָקֵם לְעַבְדְּךָ	38	Fulfill for Your servant,
אִמְרָתֶךָ		Your word [promise]
אֲשֶׁר לְיִרְאָתֶךָ׃		that You gave [to me] who fears You.
לט הַעֲבֵר חֶרְפָּתִי אֲשֶׁר יָגֹרְתִּי	39	Turn away my humiliation which I dread,
כִּי מִשְׁפָּטֶיךָ טוֹבִים׃		because Your mandates are good.
מ הִנֵּה תָּאַבְתִּי לְפִקֻּדֶיךָ	40	Behold, I long [to fulfill] Your precepts,
בְּצִדְקָתְךָ חַיֵּנִי׃		in Your righteousness, give me life.
מא וִיבֹאֻנִי חֲסָדֶךָ יְהוָה	41	May Your kindness come to me, Adonoy.
תְּשׁוּעָתְךָ		Your deliverance,
כְּאִמְרָתֶךָ׃		according to Your word [promise].
מב וְאֶעֱנֶה חֹרְפִי דָבָר	42	That I may answer him who taunts me,
כִּי־בָטַחְתִּי בִּדְבָרֶךָ׃		for I have trusted in Your word.
מג וְאַל־תַּצֵּל מִפִּי	43	Take not from my mouth,
דְבַר־אֱמֶת עַד־מְאֹד		the word of truth to the full,
כִּי לְמִשְׁפָּטֶךָ יִחָלְתִּי׃		for in Your mandates I have hoped.
מד וְאֶשְׁמְרָה תוֹרָתְךָ	44	And [then] I will preserve Your Torah
תָמִיד לְעוֹלָם וָעֶד׃		constantly, forever and ever.
מה וְאֶתְהַלְּכָה בָרְחָבָה	45	And I will walk in widely accepted ways
כִּי פִקֻּדֶיךָ דָרָשְׁתִּי׃		for Your precepts, have I sought.
מו וַאֲדַבְּרָה בְעֵדֹתֶיךָ	46	And I will speak of Your testimonies
נֶגֶד מְלָכִים		in the presence of kings
וְלֹא אֵבוֹשׁ׃		and I will not be ashamed.
מז וְאֶשְׁתַּעֲשַׁע	47	And I will be engrossed
בְּמִצְוֺתֶיךָ		in Your commandments
אֲשֶׁר אָהָבְתִּי׃		which I have loved.
מח וְאֶשָּׂא־כַפַּי	48	And I will lift my hands
אֶל־מִצְוֺתֶיךָ		to Your commandments
אֲשֶׁר אָהָבְתִּי		which I have loved,
וְאָשִׂיחָה בְחֻקֶּיךָ׃		and I will meditate in Your statutes.
מט זְכֹר־דָּבָר לְעַבְדֶּךָ	49	Remember [Your] word to Your servant,
עַל אֲשֶׁר		through which
יִחַלְתָּנִי׃		You have given me cause to hope.
נ זֹאת נֶחָמָתִי בְעָנְיִי	50	This is my consolation in my affliction,
כִּי אִמְרָתְךָ חִיָּתְנִי׃		for Your word [promise] has given me life.

נא זֵדִים הֱלִיצֻנִי עַד־מְאֹד
מִתּוֹרָתְךָ לֹא נָטִיתִי׃

51 Insolent sinners have derided me greatly,
[but] from Your Torah I have not turned.

נב זָכַרְתִּי מִשְׁפָּטֶיךָ מֵעוֹלָם ׀
יְהוָה
וָאֶתְנֶחָם׃

52 I remembered Your mandates of old,
Adonoy,
and I found myself consoled.

נג זַלְעָפָה אֲחָזַתְנִי
מֵרְשָׁעִים
עֹזְבֵי תּוֹרָתֶךָ׃

53 Burning indignation gripped me
because of the wicked
who forsake Your Torah.

נד זְמִרוֹת הָיוּ־לִי חֻקֶּיךָ
בְּבֵית מְגוּרָי׃

54 Your statutes have been my songs
in the house of my wanderings.

נה זָכַרְתִּי בַלַּיְלָה
שִׁמְךָ יְהוָה
וָאֶשְׁמְרָה תּוֹרָתֶךָ׃

55 I remembered in the night,
Your Name, Adonoy,
and I have preserved Your Torah.

נו זֹאת הָיְתָה־לִּי
כִּי פִקֻּדֶיךָ נָצָרְתִּי׃

56 This [crown of royalty] has been mine,
because Your precepts, I have kept.

נז חֶלְקִי יְהוָה
אָמַרְתִּי לִשְׁמֹר דְּבָרֶיךָ׃

57 My portion is [in] Adonoy,
I have said, ``I will preserve Your word."

נח חִלִּיתִי
פָנֶיךָ
בְכָל־לֵב
חָנֵּנִי
כְּאִמְרָתֶךָ׃

58 I have entreated the favor
of Your countenance
with my whole heart,
be gracious unto me
according to Your promise.

נט חִשַּׁבְתִּי דְרָכָי
וָאָשִׁיבָה רַגְלַי אֶל־עֵדֹתֶיךָ׃

59 I considered my ways [my opinions]
and I turned my feet to Your testimonies.

ס חַשְׁתִּי וְלֹא הִתְמַהְמָהְתִּי
לִשְׁמֹר מִצְוֹתֶיךָ׃

60 I hurried and did not delay
to preserve Your commandments.

סא חֶבְלֵי רְשָׁעִים עִוְּדֻנִי
תּוֹרָתְךָ לֹא שָׁכָחְתִּי׃

61 Bands of wicked [men] have robbed me,
but Your Torah, I have not forgotten.

סב חֲצוֹת־לַיְלָה אָקוּם
לְהוֹדוֹת לָךְ
עַל מִשְׁפְּטֵי צִדְקֶךָ׃

62 At midnight I rise
to thank You
for Your righteous mandates.

סג חָבֵר אָנִי לְכָל־אֲשֶׁר יְרֵאוּךָ
וּלְשֹׁמְרֵי פִּקּוּדֶיךָ׃

63 I am a companion to all who fear You,
and to those who preserve Your precepts.

סד חַסְדְּךָ יְהוָה מָלְאָה הָאָרֶץ
חֻקֶּיךָ לַמְּדֵנִי׃

64 Your kindness, Adonoy, fills the earth,
teach me Your statutes.

סה טוֹב עָשִׂיתָ עִם־עַבְדְּךָ
יְהוָה כִּדְבָרֶךָ׃

65 You have done good with Your servant,
Adonoy, according to Your word.

סו טוּב טַעַם וָדַעַת
לַמְּדֵנִי

66 Good [Torah] reasoning and knowledge,
teach me,

Hebrew			English
כִּי בְמִצְוֺתֶיךָ הֶאֱמָנְתִּי׃			for in Your commandments I have believed.
טֶרֶם אֶעֱנֶה	סז	67	Before I afflicted myself [in Torah study]
אֲנִי שֹׁגֵג			I erred [in the performance of commandments],
וְעַתָּה אִמְרָתְךָ שָׁמָרְתִּי׃			but afterwards I was able to preserve Your word.
טוֹב־אַתָּה וּמֵטִיב	סח	68	You are good and You do good,
לַמְּדֵנִי חֻקֶּיךָ׃			teach me Your statutes.
טָפְלוּ עָלַי שֶׁקֶר	סט	69	They have slandered me falsely—
זֵדִים			the insolent—
אֲנִי בְּכָל־לֵב |			but with my whole heart
אֶצֹּר פִּקּוּדֶיךָ׃			I will keep Your precepts.
טָפַשׁ כַּחֵלֶב לִבָּם	ע	70	Thick like fat is their heart,
אֲנִי תּוֹרָתְךָ שִׁעֲשָׁעְתִּי׃			but I am engrossed in Your Torah.
טוֹב־לִי כִי־עֻנֵּיתִי	עא	71	It is good for me to have been afflicted
לְמַעַן אֶלְמַד חֻקֶּיךָ׃			in order that I learn Your statutes. [see v. 67]
טוֹב־לִי	עב	72	It is better for me
תוֹרַת־פִּיךָ			the teachings of Your mouth,
מֵאַלְפֵי זָהָב וָכָסֶף׃			than thousands of gold and silver.
יָדֶיךָ עָשׂוּנִי	עג	73	Your hands have made me
וַיְכוֹנְנוּנִי			and established me;
הֲבִינֵנִי			give me understanding
וְאֶלְמְדָה מִצְוֺתֶיךָ׃			and I will learn Your commandments.
יְרֵאֶיךָ	עד	74	Those who fear You
יִרְאוּנִי			will see me [in my glory]
וְיִשְׂמָחוּ			and they will rejoice
כִּי			because [they know]
לִדְבָרְךָ יִחָלְתִּי׃			in Your word I had hoped.
יָדַעְתִּי יְהוָה	עה	75	I know Adonoy
כִּי־צֶדֶק מִשְׁפָּטֶיךָ			that Your mandates are just,
וֶאֱמוּנָה עִנִּיתָנִי׃			and I believe that you afflicted me [justly].
יְהִי־נָא חַסְדְּךָ לְנַחֲמֵנִי	עו	76	Please! may Your kindness console me,
כְּאִמְרָתְךָ לְעַבְדֶּךָ׃			according to Your promise to Your servant.
יְבֹאוּנִי רַחֲמֶיךָ	עז	77	May Your compassion come to me
וְאֶחְיֶה			that I might live
כִּי־תוֹרָתְךָ שַׁעֲשֻׁעָי׃			for in Your Torah I am engrossed.
יֵבֹשׁוּ זֵדִים	עח	78	Let the insolent sinners be ashamed
כִּי־שֶׁקֶר עִוְּתוּנִי			for falsely have they distorted my sins,
אֲנִי אָשִׂיחַ			but I will [continue] to meditate
בְּפִקּוּדֶיךָ׃			in Your precepts.
יָשׁוּבוּ לִי	עט	79	Let them return to me,

רחמיך
רבים יהוה
כמשפטיך
חיני

Your mercies are great, Adonoy,
as is Your custom, give me life.

יְרֵאֶיךָ
וְיֹדְעֵי עֵדֹתֶיךָ׃

those who fear You,
and those who know Your testimonies.

פ יְהִי־לִבִּי תָמִים בְּחֻקֶּיךָ
לְמַעַן לֹא אֵבוֹשׁ׃

80 May my heart be whole in Your statutes
in order that I may not be ashamed.

פא כָּלְתָה לִתְשׁוּעָתְךָ נַפְשִׁי
לִדְבָרְךָ יִחָלְתִּי׃

81 My soul yearns for Your deliverance,
in Your word I had hoped.

פב כָּלוּ עֵינַי
לְאִמְרָתֶךָ לֵאמֹר
מָתַי תְּנַחֲמֵנִי׃

82 My eyes yearn [to see the fulfillment]
of Your promise—saying—
when will You console me?

פג כִּי־הָיִיתִי כְּנֹאד
בְּקִיטוֹר
חֻקֶּיךָ לֹא שָׁכָחְתִּי׃

83 For I have become [dry] like a leather skin
in the smoke,
[yet] Your statutes I have not forgotten.

פד כַּמָּה יְמֵי־עַבְדֶּךָ
מָתַי תַּעֲשֶׂה בְרֹדְפַי מִשְׁפָּט׃

84 How many are the days of Your servant—
when will You judge those who pursue me?

פה כָּרוּ־לִי זֵדִים שִׁיחוֹת
אֲשֶׁר
לֹא כְתוֹרָתֶךָ׃

85 Insolent sinners have dug pits for me,
because [they say]:
I am not fit according to Your Torah.

פו כָּל־מִצְוֺתֶיךָ אֱמוּנָה
שֶׁקֶר רְדָפוּנִי עָזְרֵנִי׃

86 All Your commandments are faithful,
with falsehood they pursue me, help me.

פז כִּמְעַט כִּלּוּנִי בָאָרֶץ
וַאֲנִי לֹא־עָזַבְתִּי פִקֻּדֶיךָ׃

87 They have almost destroyed me on earth—
and [yet] I did not forsake Your precepts.

פח כְּחַסְדְּךָ חַיֵּנִי
וְאֶשְׁמְרָה
עֵדוּת פִּיךָ׃

88 According to Your kindness, give me life,
and I will preserve
[the testimony] of Your mouth.

פט לְעוֹלָם יְהוָה
דְּבָרְךָ נִצָּב בַּשָּׁמָיִם׃

89 [You] are forever Adonoy,
Your word stands [eternal as] the heavens.

צ לְדֹר וָדֹר
אֱמוּנָתֶךָ
כּוֹנַנְתָּ אֶרֶץ וַתַּעֲמֹד׃

90 From generation to generation
is Your faithfulness,
You established the earth and it endures.

צא לְמִשְׁפָּטֶיךָ
עָמְדוּ הַיּוֹם
כִּי הַכֹּל עֲבָדֶיךָ׃

91 [To carry out] Your judgments,
they [the heavenly hosts] stand ready this day,
for they are all Your servants.

צב לוּלֵי תוֹרָתְךָ
שַׁעֲשֻׁעָי
אָז אָבַדְתִּי בְעָנְיִי׃

92 Were it not for Your Torah
in which I was [constantly] engrossed,
I would have perished in my affliction.

צג לְעוֹלָם לֹא־אֶשְׁכַּח פִּקּוּדֶיךָ
כִּי בָם חִיִּיתָנִי׃

93 I will never forget Your precepts
for with them You have given me life.

צד לְךָ־אֲנִי הוֹשִׁיעֵנִי
כִּי פִקּוּדֶיךָ דָרָשְׁתִּי׃

94 I am Yours, deliver me,
for Your precepts I have sought [to fulfill].

צה לִי קִוּוּ רְשָׁעִים לְאַבְּדֵנִי
עֵדֹתֶיךָ אֶתְבּוֹנָן׃

95 The wicked have hoped to destroy me,
but Your testimonies I strive to understand.

צו לְכָל תִּכְלָה רָאִיתִי קֵץ
רְחָבָה
מִצְוָתְךָ מְאֹד׃

96 To every purpose I have seen an end:
exceedingly broad, however,
is Your commandment.

צז מָה־אָהַבְתִּי תוֹרָתֶךָ
כָּל־הַיּוֹם הִיא שִׂיחָתִי׃

97 How much have I loved Your Torah!
All the day it is my meditation.

צח מֵאֹיְבַי
תְּחַכְּמֵנִי מִצְוֺתֶךָ
כִּי לְעוֹלָם הִיא־לִי׃

98 [I am superior to] my enemies
[because] Your commandments made me wise.
for they are always with me.

צט מִכָּל־מְלַמְּדַי
הִשְׂכַּלְתִּי
כִּי עֵדְוֺתֶיךָ שִׂיחָה לִּי׃

99 From all my teachers,
I have learned understanding,
for Your testimonies are my meditation.

ק מִזְּקֵנִים אֶתְבּוֹנָן
כִּי פִקּוּדֶיךָ נָצָרְתִּי׃

100 I understand more than my elders
for I have kept Your precepts [from my youth].

קא מִכָּל־אֹרַח רָע
כָּלִאתִי רַגְלָי
לְמַעַן אֶשְׁמֹר דְּבָרֶךָ׃

101 From every evil path,
I have restrained my feet,
in order to preserve Your word.

קב מִמִּשְׁפָּטֶיךָ
לֹא־סָרְתִּי
כִּי־אַתָּה הוֹרֵתָנִי׃

102 From Your mandates
I have not turned away,
for You have instructed me.

קג מַה־נִּמְלְצוּ לְחִכִּי אִמְרָתֶךָ
מִדְּבַשׁ לְפִי׃

103 How sweet to my palate are Your words!
[they are] sweeter than honey to my mouth!

קד מִפִּקּוּדֶיךָ
אֶתְבּוֹנָן
עַל־כֵּן שָׂנֵאתִי | כָּל־אֹרַח שָׁקֶר׃

104 From Your precepts
I acquire understanding,
therefore I hate every path of falsehood.

קה נֵר־לְרַגְלִי דְבָרֶךָ
וְאוֹר לִנְתִיבָתִי׃

105 A lamp for my feet is Your word
and a light for my path.

קו נִשְׁבַּעְתִּי
וָאֲקַיֵּמָה
לִשְׁמֹר מִשְׁפְּטֵי צִדְקֶךָ׃

106 I have sworn
and I have fulfilled [my oath]
to preserve Your righteous mandates.

קז נַעֲנֵיתִי עַד־מְאֹד
יְהוָה חַיֵּנִי כִדְבָרֶךָ׃

107 I am afflicted greatly,
Adonoy, give me life according to Your word.

קח נִדְבוֹת פִּי
רְצֵה־נָא יְהוָה
וּמִשְׁפָּטֶיךָ לַמְּדֵנִי׃

108 [With] the offerings of my mouth
be pleased, I beseech You, Adonoy,
and Your mandates teach me.

קט נַפְשִׁי בְכַפִּי תָמִיד
וְתוֹרָתְךָ לֹא שָׁכָחְתִּי׃

109 My soul is in my hand constantly,
yet Your Torah I have not forgotten.

קי נָתְנוּ רְשָׁעִים פַּח לִי

110 The wicked have laid a snare for me,

Hebrew	English
וּמִפִּקּוּדֶיךָ לֹא תָעִיתִי׃	yet from Your precepts I have not strayed.
קיא נָחַלְתִּי עֵדְוֺתֶיךָ לְעוֹלָם	111 Your testimonies are my heritage forever,
כִּי־שְׂשׂוֹן לִבִּי הֵמָּה׃	for they are the gladness of my heart.
קיב נָטִיתִי לִבִּי	112 I have inclined my heart
לַעֲשׂוֹת חֻקֶּיךָ	to do [fulfill] Your statutes,
לְעוֹלָם עֵקֶב׃	forever, at every step.
קיג סֵעֲפִים שָׂנֵאתִי	113 Those who think evil thoughts, I hate,
וְתוֹרָתְךָ אָהָבְתִּי׃	and Your Torah I love.
קיד סִתְרִי וּמָגִנִּי אָתָּה	114 You are my hidden fortress and shield,
לִדְבָרְךָ יִחָלְתִּי׃	[only] in Your word do I hope.
קטו סוּרוּ מִמֶּנִּי מְרֵעִים	115 Depart from me [you] evil_doers,
וְאֶצְּרָה מִצְוֺת	and I will keep the commandments
אֱלֹהָי׃	of my God.
קטז סָמְכֵנִי	116 Assist me
כְאִמְרָתְךָ	according to Your word [promise]
וְאֶחְיֶה	and I will live,
וְאַל־תְּבִישֵׁנִי מִשִּׂבְרִי׃	and do not shame me in my hope.
קיז סְעָדֵנִי וְאִוָּשֵׁעָה	117 Support me and I will be delivered,
וְאֶשְׁעָה	and I will be engrossed
בְחֻקֶּיךָ תָמִיד׃	in Your statutes always.
קיח סָלִיתָ	118 You trample
כָּל־שׁוֹגִים מֵחֻקֶּיךָ	all who [say they] erred in Your statutes
כִּי־שֶׁקֶר תַּרְמִיתָם׃	for false is their deceitful claim.
קיט סִגִים הִשְׁבַּתָּ	119 Like ashes have You nullified
כָל־רִשְׁעֵי־אָרֶץ	all the wicked of the earth,
לָכֵן אָהַבְתִּי עֵדֹתֶיךָ׃	therefore, I love Your testimonies.
קכ סָמַר מִפַּחְדְּךָ בְשָׂרִי	120 My flesh shuddered for dread of You
וּמִמִּשְׁפָּטֶיךָ יָרֵאתִי׃	and of Your judgments, I was afraid.
קכא עָשִׂיתִי מִשְׁפָּט וָצֶדֶק	121 I have done justice and righteousness,
בַּל־תַּנִּיחֵנִי לְעֹשְׁקָי׃	do not leave me to my oppressors.
קכב עֲרֹב עַבְדְּךָ לְטוֹב	122 Be surety for Your servant for good.
אַל־יַעַשְׁקֻנִי זֵדִים׃	Let me not be oppressed by insolent sinners.
קכג עֵינַי כָּלוּ לִישׁוּעָתֶךָ	123 My eyes yearn to [see] Your deliverance,
וּלְאִמְרַת צִדְקֶךָ׃	and [the fulfillment of] Your righteous word.
קכד עֲשֵׂה עִם־עַבְדְּךָ	124 Do with Your servant
כְחַסְדֶּךָ	according to Your kindness,
וְחֻקֶּיךָ לַמְּדֵנִי׃	and Your statutes—teach them to me.
קכה עַבְדְּךָ־אָנִי	125 I am your servant—
הֲבִינֵנִי	give me understanding

Hebrew	English
וְאֵדְעָה עֵדֹתֶיךָ׃	and I will know Your testimonies.
קכו עֵת לַעֲשׂוֹת לַיהוָה	126 It is a time to act for Adonoy,
הֵפֵרוּ תּוֹרָתֶךָ׃	they have made void Your Torah.
קכז עַל־כֵּן	127 Therefore
אָהַבְתִּי מִצְוֹתֶיךָ	I have loved Your commandments
מִזָּהָב וּמִפָּז׃	more than gold and even refined gold.
קכח עַל־כֵּן ׀ כָּל־פִּקּוּדֵי	128 Therefore all [Your] precepts
כֹל	regarding all things;
יִשָּׁרְתִּי	I consider [them] upright;
כָּל־אֹרַח שֶׁקֶר שָׂנֵאתִי׃	every path of falsehood I hate.
קכט פְּלָאוֹת	129 Wonderfully concealed
עֵדְוֹתֶיךָ	are [the rewards of] Your testimonies,
עַל־כֵּן נְצָרָתַם נַפְשִׁי׃	therefore my soul has treasured [all of] them.
קל פֵּתַח דְּבָרֶיךָ יָאִיר	130 Your opening words give light
מֵבִין פְּתָיִים׃	they give understanding to the simple.
קלא פִּי־פָעַרְתִּי	131 I opened my mouth
וָאֶשְׁאָפָה	and eagerly swallowed them,
כִּי לְמִצְוֹתֶיךָ יָאָבְתִּי׃	because for Your commandments, I yearned.
קלב פְּנֵה־אֵלַי וְחָנֵּנִי	132 Turn to me and be gracious to me,
כְּמִשְׁפָּט	as is Your custom
לְאֹהֲבֵי שְׁמֶךָ׃	with those who love Your Name.
קלג פְּעָמַי הָכֵן בְּאִמְרָתֶךָ	133 Train my steps by Your word,
וְאַל־תַּשְׁלֶט־בִּי כָל־אָוֶן׃	and may I not be dominated by any iniquity.
קלד פְּדֵנִי מֵעֹשֶׁק אָדָם	134 Redeem me from the oppression of man,
וְאֶשְׁמְרָה פִּקּוּדֶיךָ׃	and I will preserve Your precepts.
קלה פָּנֶיךָ	135 Your face—
הָאֵר בְּעַבְדֶּךָ	make it shine upon Your servant
וְלַמְּדֵנִי אֶת־חֻקֶּיךָ׃	and teach me Your statutes.
קלו פַּלְגֵי־מַיִם	136 Rivers of water [tears]
יָרְדוּ עֵינָי	stream from my eyes,
עַל לֹא־שָׁמְרוּ תוֹרָתֶךָ׃	because they have not preserved Your Torah.
קלז צַדִּיק אַתָּה יְהוָה	137 Righteous are You, Adonoy,
וְיָשָׁר מִשְׁפָּטֶיךָ׃	and upright are Your mandates.
קלח צִוִּיתָ	138 You have commanded
צֶדֶק עֵדֹתֶיךָ	the righteousness of Your testimonies
וֶאֱמוּנָה מְאֹד׃	and they are exceedingly faithful.
קלט צִמְּתַתְנִי קִנְאָתִי	139 I am ruined by my zealousness [that]
כִּי־שָׁכְחוּ דְבָרֶיךָ צָרָי׃	my adversaries have forgotten Your words.
קמ צְרוּפָה אִמְרָתְךָ מְאֹד	140 Your word is refined to the utmost,

וְעַבְדְּךָ אֲהֵבָהּ:	and Your servant loves it.
קמא צָעִיר אָנֹכִי וְנִבְזֶה	141 I am young and despised [by my enemies]
פִּקֻּדֶיךָ לֹא שָׁכָחְתִּי:	yet, Your precepts I have not forgotten.
קמב צִדְקָתְךָ	142 Your righteousness
צֶדֶק לְעוֹלָם	is righteousness everlasting,
וְתוֹרָתְךָ אֱמֶת:	and Your Torah is truth.
קמג צַר־וּמָצוֹק מְצָאוּנִי	143 Distress and anguish have found me,
מִצְוֹתֶיךָ שַׁעֲשֻׁעָי:	[yet in] Your commandments I am engrossed.
קמד צֶדֶק עֵדְוֹתֶיךָ לְעוֹלָם	144 Righteous are Your testimonies forever,
הֲבִינֵנִי וְאֶחְיֶה:	let me understand [them] and I will live.
קמה קָרָאתִי בְכָל־לֵב	145 I have called with my whole heart,
עֲנֵנִי יְהֹוָה	answer me Adonoy;
חֻקֶּיךָ אֶצֹּרָה:	Your statutes I will treasure.
קמו קְרָאתִיךָ הוֹשִׁיעֵנִי	146 I have called You—deliver me,
וְאֶשְׁמְרָה עֵדֹתֶיךָ:	and I will preserve Your testimonies.
קמז קִדַּמְתִּי בַנֶּשֶׁף וָאֲשַׁוֵּעָה	147 I rose before dawn, and cried;
לִדְבָרְךָ יִחָלְתִּי:	in Your word I hoped.
קמח קִדְּמוּ עֵינַי	148 My eyes were [opened] early
אַשְׁמֻרוֹת	[even] before the [last two] night watches
לָשִׂיחַ בְּאִמְרָתֶךָ:	to meditate in Your word.
קמט קוֹלִי שִׁמְעָה כְחַסְדֶּךָ	149 Hear my voice according to Your kindness,
יְהֹוָה כְּמִשְׁפָּטֶךָ חַיֵּנִי:	Adonoy, as is Your custom, give me life.
קנ קָרְבוּ	150 They draw near,
רֹדְפֵי זִמָּה	those who pursue lewdness,
מִתּוֹרָתְךָ רָחָקוּ:	[but] from Your Torah, they remain far.
קנא קָרוֹב אַתָּה יְהֹוָה	151 You are near Adonoy [to those who repent]
וְכָל־מִצְוֹתֶיךָ אֱמֶת:	and all Your commandments are true.
קנב קֶדֶם	152 From the beginning
יָדַעְתִּי מֵעֵדֹתֶיךָ	I have known [wisdom] from Your testimonies,
כִּי לְעוֹלָם יְסַדְתָּם:	because You established them forever.
קנג רְאֵה־עָנְיִי וְחַלְּצֵנִי	153 See my affliction and free me from it
כִּי־תוֹרָתְךָ לֹא שָׁכָחְתִּי:	for Your Torah I have not forgotten.
קנד רִיבָה רִיבִי וּגְאָלֵנִי	154 Defend my cause and redeem me,
לְאִמְרָתְךָ חַיֵּנִי:	for the sake of Your word, give me life.
קנה רָחוֹק מֵרְשָׁעִים	155 Far removed from the wicked
יְשׁוּעָה	is deliverance,
כִּי־חֻקֶּיךָ לֹא דָרָשׁוּ:	for Your statutes they have not sought.
קנו רַחֲמֶיךָ רַבִּים ׀ יְהֹוָה	156 Your mercies are great, Adonoy,
כְּמִשְׁפָּטֶיךָ חַיֵּנִי:	as is Your custom, give me life.

קנז רַבִּים רֹדְפַי וְצָרָי
מֵעֵדְוֺתֶיךָ לֹא נָטִיתִי׃

157 Many are my pursuers and adversaries,
yet from Your testimonies I have not turned.

קנח רָאִיתִי בֹגְדִים
וָאֶתְקוֹטָטָה
אֲשֶׁר אִמְרָתְךָ לֹא שָׁמָרוּ׃

158 I have seen men without faith [in Torah]
and I quarrelled with them,
for Your word they did not preserve.

קנט רְאֵה כִּי־פִקּוּדֶיךָ אָהָבְתִּי
יְהוָה כְּחַסְדְּךָ
חַיֵּנִי׃

159 See how I loved Your precepts;
Adonoy, according to Your kindness,
give me life.

קס רֹאשׁ־דְּבָרְךָ אֱמֶת
וּלְעוֹלָם כָּל־מִשְׁפַּט צִדְקֶךָ׃

160 The beginning of Your word is truth,
and forever are all Your righteous mandates.

קסא שָׂרִים רְדָפוּנִי חִנָּם
וּמִדְּבָרְךָ פָּחַד לִבִּי׃

161 Princes have pursued me without cause,
but only of Your words am I in awe.

קסב שָׂשׂ אָנֹכִי עַל־אִמְרָתֶךָ
כְּמוֹצֵא שָׁלָל רָב׃

162 I am happy with Your word
like one who finds great gain.

קסג שֶׁקֶר שָׂנֵאתִי וַאֲתַעֵבָה
תּוֹרָתְךָ אָהָבְתִּי׃

163 Falsehood I hate, and it is despicable:
Your Torah do I love.

קסד שֶׁבַע בַּיּוֹם הִלַּלְתִּיךָ
עַל מִשְׁפְּטֵי צִדְקֶךָ׃

164 Seven [many] times a day I praise You
because of Your righteous mandates.

קסה שָׁלוֹם רָב
לְאֹהֲבֵי תוֹרָתֶךָ
וְאֵין־לָמוֹ מִכְשׁוֹל׃

165 Great is the peace
of those who love Your Torah,
and there is no stumbling for them.

קסו שִׂבַּרְתִּי לִישׁוּעָתְךָ
יְהוָה
וּמִצְוֺתֶיךָ עָשִׂיתִי׃

166 I have hoped for Your deliverance
Adonoy,
and Your commandments I have done.

קסז שָׁמְרָה נַפְשִׁי עֵדֹתֶיךָ
וָאֹהֲבֵם מְאֹד׃

167 My soul has preserved Your testimonies
and I love them greatly.

קסח שָׁמַרְתִּי פִקּוּדֶיךָ
וְעֵדֹתֶיךָ
כִּי כָל־דְּרָכַי
נֶגְדֶּךָ׃

168 I have preserved Your precepts
and Your testimonies;
[You know this] because all my ways
are before You.

קסט תִּקְרַב רִנָּתִי
לְפָנֶיךָ יְהוָה
כִּדְבָרְךָ
הֲבִינֵנִי׃

169 May my song of prayer come near
before You Adonoy;
according to Your word,
give me understanding.

קע תָּבוֹא תְּחִנָּתִי לְפָנֶיךָ
כְּאִמְרָתְךָ הַצִּילֵנִי׃

170 May my supplication come before You;
according to Your word [promise], save me.

קעא תַּבַּעְנָה שְׂפָתַי תְּהִלָּה
כִּי תְלַמְּדֵנִי חֻקֶּיךָ׃

171 My lips will utter praise,
when You will have taught me Your statutes.

קעב תַּעַן לְשׁוֹנִי אִמְרָתֶךָ

172 My tongue will give voice to Your word,

כִּי כָל־מִצְוֺתֶיךָ צֶּדֶק׃	for all Your commandments are righteous.
קעג תְּהִי־יָדְךָ לְעָזְרֵנִי	173 May Your hand [be ready to] help me,
כִּי פִקּוּדֶיךָ בָחָרְתִּי׃	for Your precepts I have chosen.
קעד תָּאַבְתִּי לִישׁוּעָתְךָ	174 I have yearned for Your deliverance,
יְהֹוָה	Adonoy,
וְתוֹרָתְךָ שַׁעֲשֻׁעָי׃	and in Your Torah I am engrossed.
קעה תְּחִי־נַפְשִׁי	175 May my soul live
וּתְהַלְלֶךָּ	that it might praise You,
וּמִשְׁפָּטֶךָ יַעֲזְרֻנִי׃	and may Your judgments help me.
קעו תָּעִיתִי כְּשֶׂה אֹבֵד	176 I have strayed like a lost sheep,
בַּקֵּשׁ עַבְדֶּךָ	seek Your servant [bring him back to You]
כִּי מִצְוֺתֶיךָ לֹא שָׁכָחְתִּי׃	for Your commandments I have not forgotten.

פרק קכ Chapter 120

Weekly Cycle	Monthly Cycle	Book Number
Saturday	27th day of the month	Book 5

Author

Unknown; perhaps דָּוִד הַמֶּלֶךְ—King David—the second king of Israel and father of the Davidic royal and messianic dynasty. David composed over seventy of the 150 psalms of Sefer Tehillim.

Genre

Psalm of Individual Lament - This psalm was written from the perspective of the individual worshipper, who cries out to God in his time of need. It is characterized as an address to God involving a complaint, followed by a request and ending with an expression of trust.

Psalm of Pilgrimage - These psalms were used at the beginning of pilgrimages as well as once the Pilgrim had reached his or her destination.

Song of Ascents - A title given to fifteen of the Psalms, 120-134, that each starts with the ascription Shir HaMa'alot, meaning "Song of Ascents". These psalms praise, exult, and "elevate" God.

Chapter Summary

The following fifteen psalms (120-134) are considered one series, each opening with the words "Shir HaMa'a lot" (Song of Ascents). Their number corresponds to the fifteen steps between the men's and women's galleries of the Beit HaMikdash (Temple), as it was there that they were recited by the Levi'im (Levites).

The Levi'im would recite each psalm while ascending from the first step to the next. Rav Sa'adiyah Ga'on wrote that the name "Song of Ascents" was titled so, because each psalm was sung louder than the previous one. It was the Levi'im's voices that were ascending louder and louder.

This psalm consists of seven verses, subdivided into two parts.
Verse 1 serves as an introduction, in which the psalmist proclaims that God answers his calls.
In verses 2-4, he appeals for deliverance from a deceitful tongue.
In verses 5-7, he rants against those who prefer war over peaceful relations.

Introductory Word

שִׁיר—Shir—Song

Shimush Tehillim - When to Say

For protection from a snake or scorpion (say seven times)—Verse 1 states: "In my great distress I called to Adonoy and He answered me."

Where in the Siddur

Recited together with the entire Shir HaMa'alot series, following the Shabbat afternoon Minchah service, on the weeks between Sukkot and Pesach (Passover).

Biblical Places

מֶשֶׁךְ וְקֵדָר—Meshech and Keidar—foreign nations which had no contact with Israel. They are mentioned here as an example of people with a poor reputation for their lack of trustworthiness. It is understood that one had to lie in order to coexist with such people.

פֶּרֶק קכ		**Chapter 120**
א שִׁיר הַמַּעֲלוֹת אֶל־יְהוָה בַּצָּרָתָה לִּי קָרָאתִי וַיַּעֲנֵנִי׃	1	A Song of Ascents. In my great distress I called to Adonoy and He answered me.
ב יְהוָה הַצִּילָה נַפְשִׁי מִשְּׂפַת־שֶׁקֶר מִלָּשׁוֹן רְמִיָּה׃	2	Adonoy, deliver my soul from lying lips, from a deceitful tongue.
ג מַה־יִּתֵּן לְךָ וּמַה־יֹּסִיף לָךְ לָשׁוֹן רְמִיָּה׃	3	What will He give you and what more will He add to a deceitful tongue?
ד חִצֵּי גִבּוֹר שְׁנוּנִים עִם גַּחֲלֵי רְתָמִים׃	4	Sharp arrows of a warrior with burning coals of a broom.
ה אוֹיָה־לִי כִּי־גַרְתִּי מֶשֶׁךְ שָׁכַנְתִּי עִם־אָהֳלֵי קֵדָר׃	5	Woe is me that I dwell in Meschech, that I reside among Kedar's tents.
ו רַבַּת שָׁכְנָה־לָּהּ נַפְשִׁי עִם שׂוֹנֵא שָׁלוֹם׃	6	Too long has my soul dwelt with those who hate peace.
ז אֲנִי־שָׁלוֹם וְכִי אֲדַבֵּר הֵמָּה לַמִּלְחָמָה׃	7	I am for peace; but when I speak they are for war.

פרק קכא Chapter 121

Weekly Cycle	Monthly Cycle	Book Number
Saturday	27th day of the month	Book 5

Author

Unknown; perhaps דָּוִד הַמֶּלֶךְ—King David—the second king of Israel and father of the Davidic royal and messianic dynasty. David composed over seventy of the 150 psalms of Sefer Tehillim.

Genre

Psalm of Individual Confidence - In this psalm, the worshipper expresses absolute certainty that his prayers will be heard.

Psalm of Pilgrimage - These psalms were used at the beginning of pilgrimages as well as once the Pilgrim had reached his or her destination.

Song of Ascents - A title given to fifteen of the Psalms, 120-134, that each starts with the ascription Shir HaMa'alot, meaning "Song of Ascents". These psalms praise, exult, and "elevate" God.

Chapter Summary

This psalm, the second in the series of Shir HaMa'alot (Song of Ascents), in contrast to the previous one, is one of consolation. The singer raises his eyes to the mountains, asking who will heed his appeal for help. He concludes that his help comes from none other than the Lord.

This psalm consists of eight verses, viewed metaphorically as a dialogue between one embarking on a journey and the other wishing him well.

In verses 1 & 2, the traveler lifts his eyes to the mountains, asking who will come to his rescue. He concludes that his help comes from God.

In verse 3, the well-wisher exclaims that God, as the traveler's guardian, will not slumber.

In verse 4, the traveler acknowledges the above assertion.

In verses 5-8, the well-wisher reaffirms that God will protect the traveler from all evil, from his departure until his return.

Pool of Siloam

Introductory Word

שִׁיר—Shir—Song

Shimush Tehillim - When to Say

To go out alone at night (say seven times)—Verse 6 states: "By day the sun will not smite you, nor the moon at night."

Additionally, some communities have the custom to recite this psalm for a public time of distress.

Where in the Siddur

Recited together with the entire Shir HaMa'alot series, following the Shabbat afternoon Minchah service, on the weeks between Sukkot and Pesach (Passover).

Recited as part of Kiddush Levanah (Sanctification of the New Moon service).

Recited as part of Tashlich, a prayer recited on Rosh HaShanah afternoon, usually by a body of water, in which we beseech God to "cast away" our sins into the depths of the sea.

Verses 4 and 8 are found in the bedtime Shema service.

Verse 7 is part of the blessing given by the Kohein (Priest) at a Pidyon HaBein (Redemption of the First Born) ceremony.

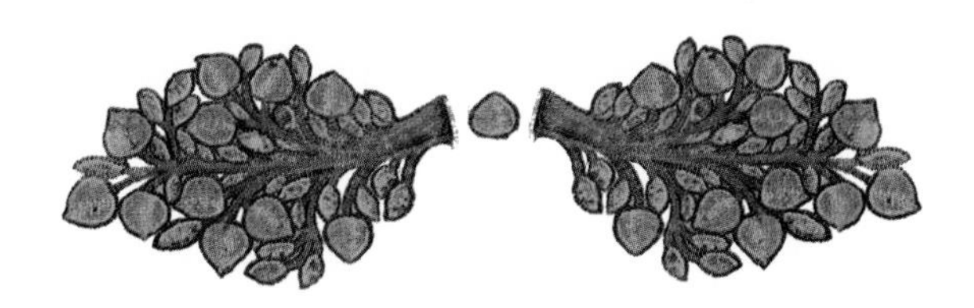

פֶּרֶק קכא		Chapter 121
א שִׁיר לַמַּעֲלוֹת אֶשָּׂא עֵינַי אֶל־הֶהָרִים מֵאַיִן יָבֹא עֶזְרִי:	1	A Song of Ascents. I will lift my eyes to the mountains: from where will my help come?
ב עֶזְרִי מֵעִם יְהוָה עֹשֵׂה שָׁמַיִם וָאָרֶץ:	2	My help comes from Adonoy, Maker of heaven and earth.
ג אַל־יִתֵּן לַמּוֹט רַגְלֶךָ אַל־יָנוּם שֹׁמְרֶךָ:	3	He will not let your foot slip, He will not slumber—your Guardian.
ד הִנֵּה לֹא־יָנוּם וְלֹא יִישָׁן שׁוֹמֵר יִשְׂרָאֵל:	4	Behold, He does not slumber nor does He sleep—the Guardian of Israel!
ה יְהוָה שֹׁמְרֶךָ יְהוָה צִלְּךָ עַל־יַד יְמִינֶךָ:	5	Adonoy is your Guardian, Adonoy is your shelter at your right hand.
ו יוֹמָם הַשֶּׁמֶשׁ לֹא־יַכֶּכָּה וְיָרֵחַ בַּלָּיְלָה:	6	By day the sun will not smite you, nor the moon at night.
ז יְהוָה יִשְׁמָרְךָ מִכָּל־רָע יִשְׁמֹר אֶת־נַפְשֶׁךָ:	7	Adonoy will guard you from all evil; He will preserve your soul.
ח יְהוָה יִשְׁמָר־צֵאתְךָ וּבוֹאֶךָ מֵעַתָּה וְעַד־עוֹלָם:	8	Adonoy will guard your going and coming, from now and forever.

פרק קכב Chapter 122

Weekly Cycle	Monthly Cycle	Book Number
Saturday	27th day of the month	Book 5

Author

דָוִד הַמֶּלֶךְ—King David—the second king of Israel and father of the Davidic royal and messianic dynasty. David composed over seventy of the 150 psalms of Sefer Tehillim.

When & Why

This psalm was written about the Jewish people's yearning to return to Israel from exile.

Genre

Psalm of Pilgrimage - These psalms were used at the beginning of pilgrimages as well as once the Pilgrim had reached his or her destination.

Psalm of Praise – This is a psalm of celebration, often the result of a victory. It declares God's goodness and urges all of creation to worship.

Psalm of Zion - This psalm glorifies God's city and His holy mount in which He has placed His abode.

Song of Ascents - A title given to fifteen of the Psalms, 120-134, that each starts with the ascription Shir HaMa'alot, meaning "Song of Ascents". These psalms praise, exult, and "elevate" God.

Chapter Summary

This psalm, the third in the series of Shir HaMa'alot (Song of Ascents), speaks of the excellence of Jerusalem and of Israel's yearning to travel there for the Shalosh Regalim (three Pilgrimage Festivals). King David prophetically takes pride in how the Jewish people will recall the days of yore when they would ascend to Jerusalem as one.

This psalm consists of nine verses, subdivided into three parts.

In verses 1-3, the Psalmist expresses the joy of the pilgrims who ascend to the built Jerusalem.

In Verses 4 & 5, King David reflects upon Jerusalem as the place where Israel worships God and the place of judgment for the House of David.

In Verses 6-9, King David prays for the continued peace of Jerusalem.

Introductory Word

שִׁיר—Shir—Song

Shimush Tehillim - When to Say

To face an important person (say three times)—Verse 7 states: "Peace be within your walls, serenity within your palaces."

Where in the Siddur

Recited together with the entire Shir HaMa'alot series, following the Shabbat afternoon Minchah service, on the weeks between Sukkot and Pesach (Passover).

Recited on Shabbat Nachamu (the Shabbat following Tishah BeAv) in some traditions.
Verses 7-9 are recited upon the conclusion of Ein K'Eilokeinu, following the Musaf Amidah (Silent Meditation) of Shabbat.

Biblical Places

בֵּית דָּוִד—House of David—a reference to the Davidic dynasty.
בֵּית יְהוָֹה—House of God—a reference to the Beit HaMikdash (Temple) in Jerusalem.
יְרוּשָׁלָם—Yerushalayim—Jerusalem—the capital city of Israel, conquered by King David 3,000 years ago. David established Jerusalem as both the religious and political center of Israel.

Contemporary Songs

verses 2 & 3; 7-9

Talmud on Tehillim

Verse 1: "שָׂמַחְתִּי, בְּאֹמְרִים לִי בֵּית יְהוָֹה נֵלֵךְ"—"I rejoiced when they said to me, 'To the House of Adonoy let us go.'"
David composed this psalm for the people to sing as they ascended to Jerusalem for the Shalosh Regalim (three Pilgrimage Festivals). (See "Chapter Summary"). As the city was not completed in David's day, he perhaps wrote it prophetically, alluding to the built city in the time of his son Solomon.
The Talmud Yerushalmi (Jerusalem Talmud), Shekalim 2, teaches that evil men of King David's generation would purposefully stand near his windows and inquire loudly as to when he would build the Beit HaMikdash (Temple), knowing fully well that God had informed David that his son Solomon, and not he, would be the Temple builder. Instead of becoming angry at their taunting as they had hoped, David instead was happy when they said to him: "We are going to the House of the Lord!"

פֶּרֶק קכב			Chapter 122
שִׁיר הַמַּעֲלוֹת לְדָוִד שָׂמַחְתִּי בְּאֹמְרִים לִי בֵּית יְהוָֹה נֵלֵךְ:	א	1	A Song of Ascents of David. I rejoiced when they said to me, "To the House of Adonoy let us go."
עֹמְדוֹת הָיוּ רַגְלֵינוּ בִּשְׁעָרַיִךְ יְרוּשָׁלָם:	ב	2	Our feet stood within your gates, Jerusalem.
יְרוּשָׁלַם הַבְּנוּיָה כְּעִיר שֶׁחֻבְּרָה־לָּהּ יַחְדָּו:	ג	3	Jerusalem which is built as a city that fosters togetherness.
שֶׁשָּׁם עָלוּ שְׁבָטִים שִׁבְטֵי־יָהּ עֵדוּת לְיִשְׂרָאֵל	ד	4	There the tribes went up, the tribes of God, as a testimony of Israel;

לְהֹדוֹת לְשֵׁם יְהוָה׃		to give thanks to the Name of Adonoy.
כִּי שָׁמָּה |	ה / 5	For there,
יָשְׁבוּ כִסְאוֹת לְמִשְׁפָּט		were set thrones for judgment,
כִּסְאוֹת לְבֵית דָּוִיד׃		thrones of the House of David.
שַׁאֲלוּ שְׁלוֹם יְרוּשָׁלָםִ	ו / 6	Inquire after the peace of Jerusalem;
יִשְׁלָיוּ אֹהֲבָיִךְ׃		may those who love you enjoy serenity.
יְהִי־שָׁלוֹם בְּחֵילֵךְ	ז / 7	Peace be within your walls,
שַׁלְוָה בְּאַרְמְנוֹתָיִךְ׃		serenity within your palaces.
לְמַעַן אַחַי וְרֵעָי	ח / 8	For the sake of my brethren and companions,
אֲדַבְּרָה־נָּא שָׁלוֹם בָּךְ׃		I will say, "Peace be with you."
לְמַעַן בֵּית־יְהוָה	ט / 9	For the sake of the House of Adonoy
אֱלֹהֵינוּ		our God,
אֲבַקְשָׁה טוֹב לָךְ׃		I will seek your good.

פרק קכג Chapter 123

Weekly Cycle	Monthly Cycle	Book Number
Saturday	27th day of the month	Book 5

Author
Unknown; perhaps דָּוִד הַמֶּלֶךְ—King David—the second king of Israel and father of the Davidic royal and messianic dynasty. David composed over seventy of the 150 psalms of Sefer Tehillim.

When & Why
This psalm was written about the trials and tribulations of Israel's long exile.

Genre
Psalm of Individual Lament - This psalm was written from the perspective of the individual worshipper, who cries out to God in his time of need. It is characterized as an address to God involving a complaint, followed by a request and ending with an expression of trust.

Psalm of Pilgrimage - These psalms were used at the beginning of pilgrimages as well as once the Pilgrim had reached his or her destination.

Song of Ascents - A title given to fifteen of the Psalms, 120-134, that each starts with the ascription Shir HaMa'alot, meaning "Song of Ascents". These psalms praise, exult, and "elevate" God.

Chapter Summary
This psalm, the fourth in the series of Shir HaMa'alot (Song of Ascents), was composed with an

eye toward any and all future exiles of the Jewish people. The psalmist expresses his faith that at such times, every Jew will declare: "To You I will lift my eyes, [to You] Who dwells in heaven."

This psalm consists of four verses, subdivided into two parts.
In verses 1 & 2, the psalmist lifts up his eyes to the Lord, asking for His mercy.
In verses 3 & 4, he describes his feelings as he reaches out to God in relation to those who mock him and treat him with contempt.

Introductory Word

שִׁיר—Shir—Song

Shimush Tehillim - When to Say

For a servant who has fled —Verse 2 states: "Behold, as the eyes of servants [look] toward the hand of their master, as the eyes of a maiden [look] toward the hand of her mistress; so our eyes [look] toward Adonoy our God until he is gracious to us."

Where in the Siddur

Recited together with the entire Shir HaMa'alot series, following the Shabbat afternoon Minchah service, on the weeks between Sukkot and Pesach (Passover).
Verse 3 is found in the final paragraph of Tachanun (Supplication Service) of the weekday Shacharit (morning service).

פרק קכג

א שִׁיר הַֽמַּעֲלוֹת
אֵלֶיךָ נָשָׂאתִי אֶת־עֵינַי
הַיֹּשְׁבִי בַּשָּׁמָיִם:
ב הִנֵּה כְעֵינֵי עֲבָדִים
אֶל־יַד אֲדוֹנֵיהֶם
כְּעֵינֵי שִׁפְחָה
אֶל־יַד גְּבִרְתָּהּ
כֵּן עֵינֵינוּ אֶל־יְהוָה אֱלֹהֵינוּ
עַד שֶׁיְּחָנֵּנוּ:
ג חָנֵּנוּ יְהוָה חָנֵּנוּ
כִּי־רַב שָׂבַעְנוּ בוּז:
ד רַבַּת שָׂבְעָה־לָּהּ נַפְשֵׁנוּ
הַלַּעַג הַשַּׁאֲנַנִּים
הַבּוּז
לִגְאֵי יוֹנִים:

Chapter 123

1 A Song of Ascents.
To You I will lift my eyes,
[to You] Who dwells in heaven.
2 Behold, as the eyes of servants [look]
toward the hand of their master,
as the eyes of a maiden [look]
toward the hand of her mistress;
so our eyes [look] toward Adonoy our God
until he is gracious to us.
3 Be gracious to us, Adonoy, be gracious to us
for we are fully satiated with humiliation.
4 Our soul is fully satiated
with the scorning of those who are at ease,
with the humiliation
of the arrogant oppressors.

פרק קכד Chapter 124

Weekly Cycle	Monthly Cycle	Book Number
Saturday	27th day of the month	Book 5

Author

דָוִד הַמֶּלֶךְ—King David—the second king of Israel and father of the Davidic royal and messianic dynasty. David composed over seventy of the 150 psalms of Sefer Tehillim.

When & Why

This psalm informs us as to how God will ensure the survival and continuity of the Jewish people when they are in exile.

Genre

Psalm of Pilgrimage - These psalms were used at the beginning of pilgrimages as well as once the Pilgrim had reached his or her destination.

Song of Ascents - A title given to fifteen of the Psalms, 120-134, that each starts with the ascription Shir HaMa'alot, meaning "Song of Ascents". These psalms praise, exult, and "elevate" God.

Chapter Summary

King David composed this song, the fifth in the series of Shir HaMa'alot (Song of Ascents), for future exiles to recite upon their redemption. It gives expression to their trust in the Lord, as they recognize that if not for His help, they would have perished under the immense burden of their toil and despair.

This psalm consists of eight verses, subdivided into two parts.

In verses 1-5, the Psalmist describes the danger of annihilation faced by the Israelites, and how they were miraculously saved by God.

In verses 6-8, he offers a blessing to God for their rescue.

Introductory Word

שִׁיר—Shir—Song

Shimush Tehillim - When to Say

Before crossing a river or traveling by boat—Verse 4 states: "The waters would have then swept us away, affliction would have passed over our soul."

Where in the Siddur

Recited together with the entire Shir HaMa'alot series, following the Shabbat afternoon Minchah service, on the weeks between Sukkot and Pesach (Passover).

The Birds Mosaic, Caesarea

פֶּרֶק קכד

א שִׁיר הַמַּעֲלוֹת לְדָוִד
לוּלֵי יְהוָה שֶׁהָיָה לָנוּ
יֹאמַר־נָא יִשְׂרָאֵל׃
ב לוּלֵי יְהוָה
שֶׁהָיָה לָנוּ
בְּקוּם עָלֵינוּ אָדָם׃
ג אֲזַי חַיִּים בְּלָעוּנוּ
בַּחֲרוֹת אַפָּם בָּנוּ׃
ד אֲזַי הַמַּיִם שְׁטָפוּנוּ
נַחְלָה עָבַר עַל־נַפְשֵׁנוּ׃
ה אֲזַי עָבַר עַל־נַפְשֵׁנוּ
הַמַּיִם הַזֵּידוֹנִים׃
ו בָּרוּךְ יְהוָה
שֶׁלֹּא נְתָנָנוּ
טֶרֶף לְשִׁנֵּיהֶם׃
ז נַפְשֵׁנוּ כְּצִפּוֹר נִמְלְטָה
מִפַּח יוֹקְשִׁים
הַפַּח נִשְׁבָּר וַאֲנַחְנוּ נִמְלָטְנוּ׃
ח עֶזְרֵנוּ בְּשֵׁם יְהוָה
עֹשֵׂה שָׁמַיִם וָאָרֶץ׃

Chapter 124

1 A Song of Ascents of David.
"Had it not been for Adonoy Who was for us,"
let Israel now say.
2 "Had it not been for Adonoy
Who was for us,
when men rose up against us.
3 They would have then swallowed us alive,
when their wrath blazed against us.
4 The waters would have then swept us away,
affliction would have passed over our soul.
5 Then over our soul would have gone
the impetuous waters.
6 Blessed is Adonoy,
Who did not give us
as prey to their teeth.
7 Our soul escaped as a bird
out of the fowler's snare;
the snare is broken and we escaped.
8 Our help is in the Name of Adonoy,
Maker of heaven and earth."

פרק קכה Chapter 125

Weekly Cycle	Monthly Cycle	Book Number
Saturday	27th day of the month	Book 5

Author

Unknown; perhaps דָּוִד הַמֶּלֶךְ—King David—the second king of Israel and father of the Davidic royal and messianic dynasty. David composed over seventy of the 150 psalms of Sefer Tehillim.

Genre

Psalm of Communal Confidence - In this psalm, the community expresses absolute certainty that their prayers will be heard.

Psalm of Pilgrimage - These psalms were used at the beginning of pilgrimages as well as once the Pilgrim had reached his or her destination.

Song of Ascents - A title given to fifteen of the Psalms, 120-134, that each starts with the ascription Shir HaMa'alot, meaning "Song of Ascents". These psalms praise, exult, and "elevate" God.

Chapter Summary

In this chapter, the sixth in the series of Shir HaMa'alot (Song of Ascents), the psalmist emphasizes that the aforementioned final redemption will, indeed, endure. Unlike all earlier redemptions, this one will be eternal, he assures us, and the Jewish people will never again be exiled.

This psalm consists of five verses, subdivided into three parts.

In verses 1 & 2, the singer declares that those who trust in God will be protected from evil.

In verse 3, he adds that evildoers will not succeed in enslaving the righteous.

In verses 4 & 5, he concludes by proclaiming that the good will be well rewarded, the wicked will perish, and peace will at last be upon Israel.

Introductory Word

שִׁיר—Shir—Song

Shimush Tehillim - When to Say

If confronted by enemies while traveling (say this 7 times while holding salt)—Verse 3 states: "For it will not rest [for long] the reign of wickedness upon the lot of the righteous."

Where in the Siddur

Recited together with the entire Shir HaMa'alot series, following the Shabbat afternoon Minchah service, on the weeks between Sukkot and Pesach (Passover).

Biblical People

יִשְׂרָאֵל—Yisrael—The Nation of Israel.

Biblical Places

יְרוּשָׁלַיִם—Yerushalayim—Jerusalem—the capital city of the kingdom of Israel, conquered by King David 3,000 years ago. David established Jerusalem as both the religious and political center of

Israel.

צִיּוֹן—Zion—a place name often used as a synonym for Jerusalem. The term Zion originally referred only to the area where a Jebbusite fortress once stood, also the location of the City of David. Zion was later used by prophets and psalmists as another name for Jerusalem.

Talmud on Tehillim

Verse 1: "שִׁיר הַמַּעֲלוֹת. הַבֹּטְחִים בַּיהוָה כְּהַר צִיּוֹן"—"A Song of Ascents. Those who trust in Adonoy are as Mount Zion." The Talmud, Berachot 58b, explains that just as Mount Zion will never be destroyed, so too will those who trust in God remain equally firm and strong.

Verse 5: "וְהַמַּטִּים עֲקַלְקַלּוֹתָם יוֹלִיכֵם יְהוָה, אֶת פֹּעֲלֵי הָאָוֶן, שָׁלוֹם עַל יִשְׂרָאֵל"—"And as for those who turn aside to their crooked ways, Adonoy will lead them away together with the workers of iniquity."

The Talmud, Berachot 19a, deduces that those who speak ill of Talmidei Chachamim (Torah scholars) after their death will fall into Geihinom (Hell), even if their words are true.

פֶּרֶק קכה

א שִׁיר הַמַּעֲלוֹת
הַבֹּטְחִים בַּיהוָה
כְּהַר־צִיּוֹן לֹא־יִמּוֹט
לְעוֹלָם יֵשֵׁב:

ב יְרוּשָׁלַם הָרִים סָבִיב לָהּ
וַיהוָה סָבִיב לְעַמּוֹ
מֵעַתָּה וְעַד־עוֹלָם:

ג כִּי לֹא יָנוּחַ
שֵׁבֶט הָרֶשַׁע
עַל גּוֹרַל הַצַּדִּיקִים
לְמַעַן לֹא־יִשְׁלְחוּ הַצַּדִּיקִים ׀
בְּעַוְלָתָה יְדֵיהֶם:

ד הֵיטִיבָה יְהוָה לַטּוֹבִים
וְלִישָׁרִים בְּלִבּוֹתָם:

ה וְהַמַּטִּים ׀
עֲקַלְקַלּוֹתָם
יוֹלִיכֵם יְהוָה
אֶת פֹּעֲלֵי הָאָוֶן
שָׁלוֹם עַל־יִשְׂרָאֵל:

Chapter 125

1 A Song of Ascents.
Those who trust in Adonoy
are as Mount Zion which cannot be moved,
but abides forever.

2 Jerusalem is surrounded by mountains,
and Adonoy is around His people,
from now forever.

3 For it will not rest [for long]
the reign of wickedness
upon the lot of the righteous;
in order that the righteous will not put forth
their hands unto iniquity.

4 Do good, Adonoy, to those who are good,
and to those who are upright in their hearts.

5 And as for those who turn aside
to their crooked ways,
Adonoy will lead them away
together with the workers of iniquity;
peace be upon Israel.

פרק קכו Chapter 126

Weekly Cycle	Monthly Cycle	Book Number
Saturday	27th day of the month	Book 5

Author
Unknown; perhaps דָּוִד הַמֶּלֶךְ—King David—the second king of Israel and father of the Davidic royal and messianic dynasty. David composed over seventy of the 150 psalms of Sefer Tehillim.

When & Why
This psalm describes the great joy that the people of Israel will experience when they are returned to their homeland.

Genre
Psalm of Pilgrimage - These psalms were used at the beginning of pilgrimages as well as once the Pilgrim had reached his or her destination.
Song of Ascents - A title given to fifteen of the Psalms, 120-134, that each starts with the ascription Shir HaMa'alot, meaning "Song of Ascents". These psalms praise, exult, and "elevate" God.

Chapter Summary
Like the previous psalm, this one too, the seventh in the series of Shir HaMa'alot (Song of Ascents), speaks of the future eternal redemption, when the Lord will return the captivity of Zion. Then, the singer proclaims, we will be like dreamers.

This psalm consists of six verses, subdivided into two parts.
In verses 1-3, the psalmist expresses his thanks for all that God has done for us in the past.
In verses 4-6, with an eye towards the future, he prays for the ultimate redemption.

Introductory Word
שִׁיר—Shir—Song

Shimush Tehillim - When to Say
For a woman whose children pass away—Verse 6 states: "[Though] he walks along weeping, carrying the bag of seed, he will return with joyous song carrying his sheaves."

Where in the Siddur
Sung in a fast, joyous, often upbeat tune preceding Birkat HaMazon (Grace after Meals) on Shabbat, Festivals, Rosh Chodesh (First of the Month), Chol HaMo'eid (Intermediate Days of Pesach and Sukkot), and other joyous occasions. While fourteen consecutive psalms actually begin with the words "Shir HaMa'alot" (Song of Ascents), this is the one commonly referred to as "Shir HaMa'alot", due to its inclusion on the above occasions.
Recited together with the entire Shir HaMa'alot series, following the Shabbat afternoon Minchah service, on the weeks between Sukkot and Pesach (Passover).

Biblical Places

צִיּוֹן—Zion—a place name often used as a synonym for Jerusalem. The term Zion originally referred only to the area where a Jebbusite fortress once stood, also the location of the City of David. Zion was later used by prophets and psalmists as another name for Jerusalem.

Talmud on Tehillim

Verse 2: "אָז יִמָּלֵא שְׂחוֹק פִּינוּ, וּלְשׁוֹנֵנוּ רִנָּה"—"Then will our mouths be filled with laughter, and our tongue with joyous song."

The Talmud, Berachot 31a, teaches that in the future, when Mashiach (Messiah) arrives, our mouths will indeed "be filled with laughter and our tongues with glad song". But as long as we are in exile, we are instructed, it is forbidden to only rejoice. Rather, we must always be mindful of the destruction of the Beit HaMikdash (Temple) and yet-to-be fulfilled promise of its rebuilding.

פרק קכו	Chapter 126
א שִׁיר הַמַּעֲלוֹת בְּשׁוּב יְהוָה אֶת־שִׁיבַת צִיּוֹן הָיִינוּ כְּחֹלְמִים׃	1 A Song of Ascents. When Adonoy brings about the return to Zion we will have been like dreamers.
ב אָז יִמָּלֵא שְׂחוֹק פִּינוּ וּלְשׁוֹנֵנוּ רִנָּה אָז יֹאמְרוּ בַגּוֹיִם הִגְדִּיל יְהוָה לַעֲשׂוֹת עִם־אֵלֶּה׃	2 Then will our mouths be filled with laughter, and our tongue with joyous song. Then they will say among the nations: `Adonoy has done great things for them.'
ג הִגְדִּיל יְהוָה לַעֲשׂוֹת עִמָּנוּ הָיִינוּ שְׂמֵחִים׃	3 Adonoy had done great things for us; we will [then] rejoice.
ד שׁוּבָה יְהוָה אֶת־שְׁבִיתֵנוּ כַּאֲפִיקִים בַּנֶּגֶב׃	4 Adonoy! bring back our exiles like springs in the desert.
ה הַזֹּרְעִים בְּדִמְעָה בְּרִנָּה יִקְצֹרוּ׃	5 Those who sow in tears will reap with joyous song.
ו הָלוֹךְ יֵלֵךְ | וּבָכֹה נֹשֵׂא מֶשֶׁךְ־הַזָּרַע בֹּא־יָבֹא בְרִנָּה נֹשֵׂא אֲלֻמֹּתָיו׃	6 [Though] he walks along weeping, carrying the bag of seed, he will return with joyous song carrying his sheaves.

פרק קכז Chapter 127

Weekly Cycle	Monthly Cycle	Book Number
Saturday	27th day of the month	Book 5

Author
Probably written by דָּוִד הַמֶּלֶךְ—King David—the second king of Israel and father of the Davidic royal and messianic dynasty. It is likely that David dedicated this to his son Shlomo - Solomon.

When & Why
It is plausible that David wrote this psalm after hearing from the prophet Nathan that his son Solomon will build the Temple.

Genre
Psalm of Pilgrimage - These psalms were used at the beginning of pilgrimages as well as once the Pilgrim had reached his or her destination.
Psalm of Wisdom - This psalm contains teachings and wise advice and is meant to instruct people on how to live a Godly life.
Song of Ascents - A title given to fifteen of the Psalms, 120-134, that each starts with the ascription Shir HaMa'alot, meaning "Song of Ascents". These psalms praise, exult, and "elevate" God.

Chapter Summary
As the opening verse indicates, it appears that King David composed this psalm, the eighth in the series of Shir HaMa'alot (Song of Ascents), regarding his son Solomon. The Psalmist specifically speaks of the Beit HaMikdash (Holy Temple) that Solomon would build and the royal dynasty of the House of David that would be passed down through him for all future generations. These accomplishments, the Psalmist reminds us, are dependent upon God's help, and not due solely to human endeavor.

This psalm consists of five verses, subdivided into two parts.
In verses 1 & 2, the psalmist emphasizes that the help of God is needed if man is to succeed in his efforts.
In verses 3-5, he further describes the benefit and happiness enjoyed by the one to whom God has granted children.

Introductory Word
שִׁיר—Shir—Song

Shimush Tehillim - When to Say
For protection of a child in utero—Verses 3 and 4 state: "Behold, a heritage of Adonoy, are children a reward [from Him] is the fruit of the womb. As arrows in the hand of a mighty man, so are the children of one's youth."

Where in the Siddur

Recited together with the entire Shir HaMa'alot series, following the Shabbat afternoon Minchah service, on the weeks between Sukkot and Pesach (Passover).

Talmud on Tehillim

Verse 2: "שָׁוְא לָכֶם מַשְׁכִּימֵי קוּם, מְאַחֲרֵי שֶׁבֶת" —"It is in vain for you that you rise early, sit up late." The Talmud, Ketubot 62a, deduces that this refers to the wives of Talmidei Chachamim (Torah scholars), who lose sleep each night as they patiently await the return of their husbands from the study hall. They too will merit life in the World to Come, as they are considered partners in their husbands' pursuit of Torah study.

פרק קכז

א שִׁיר הַֽמַּעֲלוֹת לִשְׁלֹמֹה
אִם־יְהֹוָה ׀ לֹא־יִבְנֶה בַיִת
שָׁוְא ׀ עָמְלוּ בוֹנָיו בּוֹ
אִם־יְהֹוָה לֹֽא־יִשְׁמָר־עִיר
שָׁוְא ׀ שָׁקַד שׁוֹמֵֽר׃
ב שָׁוְא לָכֶם ׀
מַשְׁכִּימֵי קוּם מְאַֽחֲרֵי־שֶׁבֶת
אֹכְלֵי לֶחֶם הָעֲצָבִים
כֵּן יִתֵּן
לִֽידִידוֹ
שֵׁנָֽא׃
ג הִנֵּה נַחֲלַת יְהֹוָה בָּנִים
שָׂכָר פְּרִי הַבָּֽטֶן׃
ד כְּחִצִּים בְּיַד־גִּבּוֹר
כֵּן בְּנֵי הַנְּעוּרִֽים׃
ה אַשְׁרֵי הַגֶּבֶר
אֲשֶׁר מִלֵּא אֶת־אַשְׁפָּתוֹ מֵהֶם
לֹא־יֵבֹשׁוּ
כִּֽי־יְדַבְּרוּ אֶת־אוֹיְבִים
בַּשָּֽׁעַר׃

Chapter 127

1 A Song of Ascents of Solomon.
If Adonoy will not build a house,
then in vain have its builders toiled upon it;
if Adonoy will not preserve the city,
in vain does the watchman keep vigil.

2 It is in vain for you
that you rise early, sit up late,
who eat the bread of toil;
but He will surely give [sustenance]
to His loved ones
to those who banish sleep from themselves.

3 Behold, a heritage of Adonoy, are children
a reward [from Him] is the fruit of the womb.

4 As arrows in the hand of a mighty man,
so are the children of one's youth.

5 Fortunate is the man
who has filled his quiver with them;
they will not be ashamed
when they speak with their enemies
in the gate.

פרק קכח Chapter 128

Weekly Cycle	Monthly Cycle	Book Number
Saturday	27th day of the month	Book 5

Author

Unknown; perhaps דָּוִד הַמֶּלֶךְ—King David—the second king of Israel and father of the Davidic royal and messianic dynasty. David composed over seventy of the 150 psalms of Sefer Tehillim.

Genre

Psalm of Pilgrimage - These psalms were used at the beginning of pilgrimages as well as once the Pilgrim had reached his or her destination.

Song of Ascents - A title given to fifteen of the Psalms, 120-134, that each starts with the ascription Shir HaMa'alot, meaning "Song of Ascents". These psalms praise, exult, and "elevate" God.

Chapter Summary

In this psalm, the ninth in the series of Shir HaMa'alot (Song of Ascents), the singer praises the excellence of the God-fearing man, sustained by the labor of his hands. Happy is he, the author proclaims, who not only does not transgress, but who fears the Lord, walks in His ways and keeps His commandments.

This psalm consists of six verses, subdivided into two parts.

In verses 1-3, the psalmist extols the happiness of the God-fearing man.

In verses 4-6, he delineates the blessings which this individual is granted by God.

Introductory Word

שִׁיר—Shir—Song

Shimush Tehillim - When to Say

For protection during pregnancy—Verse 3 states: "Your wife is a fruitful vine in the innermost parts of your home, your children are like olive plants around your table."

Where in the Siddur

Recited together with the entire Shir HaMa'alot series, following the Shabbat afternoon Minchah service, on the weeks between Sukkot and Pesach (Passover).

Recited prior to Aleinu of the Motza'ei Shabbat Ma'ariv (nighttime service).

Recited by some as one of the prayers of the bedtime Shema.

Verse 2 is found in Pirkei Avot (Ethics of the Fathers), 4:1 and 6:4.

Biblical Places

יְרוּשָׁלַםִ—Yerushalayim—Jerusalem—the capital city of the kingdom of Israel, conquered by King David 3,000 years ago. David established Jerusalem as both the religious and political center of Israel.

צִיּוֹן—Zion—a place name often used as a synonym for Jerusalem. The term Zion originally referred only to the area where a Jebbusite fortress once stood, also the location of the City of David. Zion was later used by prophets and psalmists as another name for Jerusalem.

Contemporary Song

Verses 5 & 6

Talmud on Tehillim

Verse 3: "אֶשְׁתְּךָ כְּגֶפֶן פֹּרִיָּה בְּיַרְכְּתֵי בֵיתֶךָ"—"Your wife is a fruitful vine in the innermost parts of your home."

The Talmud, Berachot 57a, infers from this verse that if one sees a vine laden with grapes in a dream, it is an omen that his wife will not miscarry.

פרק קכח	Chapter 128
א שִׁיר הַֽמַּֽעֲלוֹת אַשְׁרֵי כָּל־יְרֵא יְהֹוָה הַהֹלֵךְ בִּדְרָכָיו׃	1 A Song of Ascents. Fortunate is everyone who fears Adonoy, who walks in His ways.
ב יְגִיעַ כַּפֶּיךָ כִּי תֹאכֵל אַשְׁרֶיךָ וְטוֹב לָךְ׃	2 The toil of your hands, when you eat thereof— fortunate are you, good will be yours.
ג אֶשְׁתְּךָ ׀ כְּגֶפֶן פֹּרִיָּה בְּיַרְכְּתֵי בֵיתֶךָ בָּנֶיךָ כִּשְׁתִלֵי זֵיתִים סָבִיב לְשֻׁלְחָנֶךָ׃	3 Your wife is a fruitful vine in the innermost parts of your home, your children are like olive plants around your table.
ד הִנֵּה כִי־כֵן יְבֹרַךְ גָּבֶר יְרֵא יְהֹוָה׃	4 Behold, so is blessed the man who fears Adonoy.
ה יְבָרֶכְךָ יְהֹוָה מִצִּיּוֹן וּרְאֵה בְּטוּב יְרוּשָׁלָםִ כֹּל יְמֵי חַיֶּיךָ׃	5 May Adonoy bless you out of Zion, and may you look upon the good of Jerusalem all the days of your life.
ו וּרְאֵה־בָנִים לְבָנֶיךָ שָׁלוֹם עַל־יִשְׂרָאֵל׃	6 May you see [the] children of your children, peace upon Israel.

פרק קכט Chapter 129

Weekly Cycle	Monthly Cycle	Book Number
Saturday	27th day of the month	Book 5

Author

Unknown; perhaps דָּוִד הַמֶּלֶךְ—King David—the second king of Israel and father of the Davidic royal and messianic dynasty. David composed over seventy of the 150 psalms of Sefer Tehillim.

Genre

Psalm of Communal Confidence - In this psalm, the community expresses absolute certainty that their prayers will be heard.

Psalm of Pilgrimage - These psalms were used at the beginning of pilgrimages as well as once the Pilgrim had reached his or her destination.

Song of Ascents - A title given to fifteen of the Psalms, 120-134, that each starts with the ascription Shir HaMa'alot, meaning "Song of Ascents". These psalms praise, exult, and "elevate" God.

Chapter Summary

This psalm, the tenth in the series of Shir HaMa'alot (Song of Ascents), was composed for the exiles, to be recited in the aftermath of the ultimate redemption.

This psalm consists of eight verses, subdivided into two parts.

In verses 1-4, the psalmist describes Israel's suffering and subsequent salvation.

In verses 5-8, he levels a curse against those who hate Zion.

Introductory Word

שִׁיר—Shir—Song

Shimush Tehillim - When to Say

For diligence in perfoming mitzvot (recite daily)—Verse 2 states: "Much have they afflicted me from my youth; but also they have not prevailed against me."

The Silver Scroll, Oldest Existing Written Piece of Birkat Kohanim, discovered by Dr. Gabriel Barkay in 1979

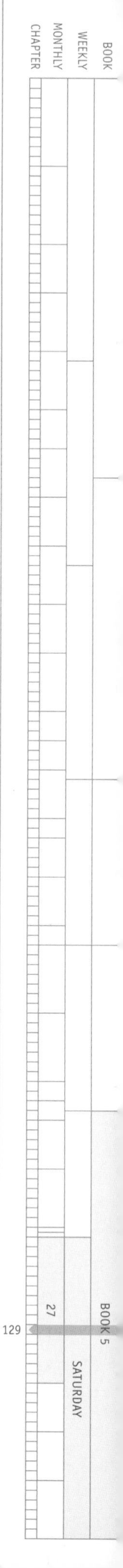

Where in the Siddur

Recited together with the entire Shir HaMa'alot series, following the Shabbat afternoon Minchah service, on the weeks between Sukkot and Pesach (Passover).

Biblical Places

צִיּוֹן—Zion—a place name often used as a synonym for Jerusalem. The term Zion originally referred only to the area where a Jebbusite fortress once stood, also the location of the City of David. Zion was later used by prophets and psalmists as another name for Jerusalem.

פֶּרֶק קכט

א שִׁיר הַמַּעֲלוֹת
רַבַּת צְרָרוּנִי מִנְּעוּרָי
יֹאמַר־נָא יִשְׂרָאֵל:
ב רַבַּת צְרָרוּנִי מִנְּעוּרָי
גַּם לֹא־יָכְלוּ לִי:
ג עַל־גַּבִּי חָרְשׁוּ חֹרְשִׁים
הֶאֱרִיכוּ לְמַעֲנִיתָם:
ד יְהוָה צַדִּיק
קִצֵּץ עֲבוֹת רְשָׁעִים:
ה יֵבֹשׁוּ וְיִסֹּגוּ אָחוֹר
כֹּל שֹׂנְאֵי צִיּוֹן:
ו יִהְיוּ כַּחֲצִיר גַּגּוֹת
שֶׁקַּדְמַת שָׁלַף יָבֵשׁ:
ז שֶׁלֹּא מִלֵּא כַפּוֹ קוֹצֵר
וְחִצְנוֹ מְעַמֵּר:
ח וְלֹא אָמְרוּ | הָעֹבְרִים
בִּרְכַּת־יְהוָה אֲלֵיכֶם
בֵּרַכְנוּ אֶתְכֶם בְּשֵׁם יְהוָה:

Chapter 129

1 A Song of Ascents.
"Much have they afflicted me from my youth,"
let Israel now say.
2 "Much have they afflicted me from my youth;
but also they have not prevailed against me.
3 The plowers plowed on my back;
they made long their furrows.
4 Adonoy is righteous,
He has cut the cords of the wicked.
5 Let them be ashamed and turned backward,
all haters of Zion.
6 Let them be as grass upon the roofs,
before it springs up it withers.
7 With which the reaper does not fill his hand,
nor the sheath binder his bosom."
8 And the passers by did not say:
"The blessing of Adonoy be upon you;
"we bless you in the Name of Adonoy."

פרק קל Chapter 130

Weekly Cycle	Monthly Cycle	Book Number
Saturday	27th day of the month	Book 5

Author
Unknown; perhaps דָּוִד הַמֶּלֶךְ—King David—the second king of Israel and father of the Davidic royal and messianic dynasty. David composed over seventy of the 150 psalms of Sefer Tehillim.

When & Why
David might have written this psalm as a prayer to God to forgive the sins that the people of Israel will commit when they are in exile.

Genre
Psalm of Individual Lament - This psalm was written from the perspective of the individual worshipper, who cries out to God in his time of need. It is characterized as an address to God involving a complaint, followed by a request and ending with an expression of trust.
Psalm of Pilgrimage - These psalms were used at the beginning of pilgrimages as well as once the Pilgrim had reached his or her destination.
Song of Ascents - A title given to fifteen of the Psalms, 120-134, that each starts with the ascription Shir HaMa'alot, meaning "Song of Ascents". These psalms praise, exult, and "elevate" God.

Chapter Summary
In this psalm, the eleventh in the series of Shir HaMa'alot (Song of Ascents), the singer calls upon future exiles to call out to God in times of distress. God, in turn, he assures the reader, will have mercy upon them. The psalmist concludes by pleading for forgiveness for the iniquities of future exiles, as well as for their subsequent deliverance, even if undeserved.

This psalm consists of eight verses, subdivided into two parts.
In verses 1-4, the psalmist cries out to God "out of the depths", and asks that his requests be heard.
In verses 5-8, he places his hope in God and proclaims that God will indeed redeem Israel.

Introductory Word
שִׁיר—Shir—Song

Shimush Tehillim - When to Say
In times of distress—Verse 5 states: "I hope for Adonoy, my soul hopes; and for His word, I wait."

Where in the Siddur
Recited responsively as an addition to the daily liturgy of the High Holidays season, from Rosh HaShanah through Yom Kippur, immediately following Pesukei Dezimra (introductory Verses of Praise to the Shacharit morning service). It is customary for the Ark to be opened for its recitation. Recited together with the entire Shir HaMa'alot series, following the Shabbat afternoon Minchah

service, on the weeks between Sukkot and Pesach (Passover).

Recited as part of Tashlich—a prayer recited on Rosh HaShanah afternoon, usually by a body of water, in which we beseech God to "cast away" our sins into the depths of the sea.

Recited traditionally, together with select other psalms, as a prayer for the ill, as well as for Israel in times of distress.

Recited in some congregations every weekday upon the conclusion of Shacharit.

Verses 3 & 4 are found in the opening paragraph of the long Tachanun (Supplication Service) recited on Mondays and Thursdays.

Biblical People

יִשְׂרָאֵל—Yisrael—The Nation of Israel.

Talmud on Tehillim

Verse 1: "מִמַּעֲמַקִּים קְרָאתִיךָ יְהוָה"—"Out of the depths I have called to You, Adonoy."

The Talmud, Berachot 10b, infers that "one should not stand in a high place and pray, but rather in a low place, as it states 'From the depths I called you, O God." It is for this reason that in some synagogues the platform where the Chazzan (leader) stands is lower than the floor of the main sanctuary.

פֶּרֶק קל			**Chapter 130**
שִׁיר הַמַּעֲלוֹת	א	1	A Song of Ascents.
מִמַּעֲמַקִּים			Out of the depths
קְרָאתִיךָ יְהוָה:			I have called to You, Adonoy.
אֲדֹנָי שִׁמְעָה בְקוֹלִי	ב	2	My Master, hear my voice;
תִּהְיֶינָה אָזְנֶיךָ קַשֻּׁבוֹת			let Your ears be attentive
לְקוֹל תַּחֲנוּנָי:			to the voice of my supplications.
אִם־עֲוֺנוֹת תִּשְׁמָר־יָהּ	ג	3	If You God should take account of iniquities,
אֲדֹנָי מִי יַעֲמֹד:			my Master, who could survive?
כִּי־עִמְּךָ הַסְּלִיחָה	ד	4	For with You is forgiveness,
לְמַעַן תִּוָּרֵא:			in order that You be feared.
קִוִּיתִי יְהוָה קִוְּתָה נַפְשִׁי	ה	5	I hope for Adonoy, my soul hopes;
וְלִדְבָרוֹ הוֹחָלְתִּי:			and for His word, I wait
נַפְשִׁי לַאדֹנָי	ו	6	My soul [waits] for my Master
מִשֹּׁמְרִים			more than the watchman [waits]
לַבֹּקֶר			for the morning,
שֹׁמְרִים			[more than] the watchman [waits]
לַבֹּקֶר:			for the morning.
יַחֵל יִשְׂרָאֵל אֶל־יְהוָה	ז	7	Wait, Israel, upon Adonoy
כִּי־עִם־יְהוָה הַחֶסֶד			for with Adonoy there is loving_kindness
וְהַרְבֵּה עִמּוֹ פְדוּת:			and with Him there is much redemption.
וְהוּא יִפְדֶּה אֶת־יִשְׂרָאֵל	ח	8	And He will redeem Israel
מִכֹּל עֲוֺנֹתָיו:			from all its iniquities.

פרק קלא Chapter 131

Weekly Cycle	Monthly Cycle	Book Number
Saturday	27th day of the month	Book 5

Author

דָּוִד הַמֶּלֶךְ—King David—the second king of Israel and father of the Davidic royal and messianic dynasty. David composed over seventy of the 150 psalms of Sefer Tehillim.

When & Why

David might have written this psalm as a prayer to God to forgive the sins that the people of Israel will commit when they are in exile.

Genre

Psalm of Pilgrimage - These psalms were used at the beginning of pilgrimages as well as once the Pilgrim had reached his or her destination.

Song of Ascents - A title given to fifteen of the Psalms, 120-134, that each starts with the ascription Shir HaMa'alot, meaning "Song of Ascents". These psalms praise, exult, and "elevate" God.

Chapter Summary

In this psalm, the twelfth in the series of Shir HaMa'alot (Song of Ascents), King David once again points to himself, depicting the humility of his soul and his subjugation before God. He concludes by admonishing the Jewish people to conduct themselves in the same manner. Only then, he declares, can they in turn trust in God for deliverance, for everything comes from Him.

This psalm consists of a mere three verses.

In verses 1 & 2, the Psalmist rejects the path of human arrogance and describes his own devotion to God.

In verse 3, he prays that Israel, like he, place their hope in God.

Introductory Word

שִׁיר—Shir—Song

Biblical People

יִשְׂרָאֵל—Yisrael—The Nation of Israel.

Shimush Tehillim - When to Say

For one with too much pride (say 3 times daily)—Verse 1 states: "Adonoy, my heart was not haughty nor my eyes lofty; and I did not concern myself with things too great and too wonderful for me."

Where in the Siddur

Recited together with the entire Shir HaMa'alot series, following the Shabbat afternoon Minchah service, on the weeks between Sukkot and Pesach (Passover).

פֶּרֶק קלא

א שִׁ֗יר הַֽמַּֽעֲל֗וֹת לְדָ֫וִ֥ד
יְהֹוָ֤ה | לֹא־גָבַ֣הּ לִ֭בִּי
וְלֹא־רָמ֣וּ עֵינַ֑י
וְלֹא־הִלַּ֓כְתִּי
בִּגְדֹל֖וֹת
וּבְנִפְלָא֣וֹת מִמֶּֽנִּי׃
ב אִם־לֹ֤א שִׁוִּ֨יתִי |
וְדוֹמַ֗מְתִּי נַ֫פְשִׁ֥י
כְּ֭גָמֻל עֲלֵ֣י אִמּ֑וֹ
כַּגָּמֻ֖ל עָלַ֣י נַפְשִֽׁי׃
ג יַחֵ֣ל יִ֭שְׂרָאֵל אֶל־יְהֹוָ֑ה
מֵ֝עַתָּ֗ה וְעַד־עוֹלָֽם׃

Chapter 131

1 A Song of Ascents of David.
Adonoy, my heart was not haughty
nor my eyes lofty;
and I did not concern myself
with things too great
and too wonderful for me.
2 Have I not calmed
and quieted my soul,
like a child that is weaned from his mother,
like a weaned child my soul is with me.
3 Wait Israel upon Adonoy,
from now and forever.

פֶּרֶק קלב Chapter 132

Weekly Cycle	Monthly Cycle	Book Number
Saturday	27th day of the month	Book 5

Author

דָּוִד הַמֶּלֶךְ—King David—the second king of Israel and father of the Davidic royal and messianic dynasty. David composed over seventy of the 150 psalms of Sefer Tehillim.

When & Why

David wrote this psalm when he built an altar and brought sacrifices to God in the field of Goren, which was where the Temple would ultimately be built.

Genre

Psalm of Pilgrimage - These psalms were used at the beginning of pilgrimages as well as once the Pilgrim had reached his or her destination.

Psalm of Royalty - This psalm describes how God reigns supreme. It focuses on the human king of Israel, or upon God as King of Israel.

Song of Ascents - A title given to fifteen of the Psalms, 120-134, that each starts with the ascription Shir HaMa'alot, meaning "Song of Ascents". These psalms praise, exult, and "elevate" God.

Chapter Summary

King David composed this the thirteenth in the series of Shir HaMa'alot (Song of Ascents), when he built the altar on the threshing floor of Aravna the Yebusite, destined to become the site of the Beit HaMikdash (Holy Temple), as instructed by the prophet Gad. Until that time, its location was not yet known by David.

This psalm consists of eighteen verses, subdivided into three parts.
In verses 1-6, King David beseeches the Almighty to remember his efforts to locate the place to be designated for God's dwelling.
In verses 7-10, the Psalmist records the song to be sung by those going up to the Beit HaMikdash (Holy Temple) with the Aron HaKodesh (Holy Ark).
In verses 11-18, God keeps His oath and informs David of the selection of Jerusalem as the place of the Divine Presence.

Introductory Word

שִׁיר—Shir—Song

Shimush Tehillim - When to Say

For one finding it hard to honor a vow (say daily)—Verses 2 and 12 state: "How he swore to Adonoy and vowed to the Mighty One of Jacob." "If your children will preserve My covenant and My testimony that I will teach them then their children will sit on your throne."

Where in the Siddur

Recited together with the entire Shir HaMa'alot series, following the Shabbat afternoon Minchah service, on the weeks between Sukkot and Pesach (Passover).
Verses 8-10 comprise part of the paragraph recited as the Torah scroll is returned to the Aron HaKodesh (Holy Ark) .
Verses 8-10 also comprise part of Atah Horeita, the paragraph introducing Hakafot (dancing with the Torah scrolls) on Simchat Torah.
Verse 13 is found in Yehi Chevod, the paragraph introducing Ashrei of Pesukei Dezimra (introductory Verses of Praise to the Shacharit morning service).

Biblical Personalities

יַעֲקֹב—Jacob, also called Yisrael—Israel, the third patriarch, and known as the father of the twelve tribes of Israel. He was married to Rachel and Leah, and was the brother of Eisav.

Biblical Places

אֶפְרָתָה—Ephrat—also referred to as Bethlehem, located in or near the modern day city of the same name.
הֲדֹם רַגְלָיו מִשְׁכְּנוֹתָיו—His Tabernacles; His Footstool—references to the Beit HaMikdash (Holy Temple).
צִיּוֹן—Zion—a place name often used as a synonym for Jerusalem. The term Zion originally referred only to the area where a Jebbusite fortress once stood, also the location of the City of David. Zion was later used by prophets and psalmists as another name for Jerusalem.

פרק קלב

א שִׁיר הַמַּעֲלוֹת
ב זְכוֹר־יְהוָה לְדָוִד
אֵת כָּל־עֻנּוֹתוֹ:
ג אֲשֶׁר נִשְׁבַּע לַיהוָה
נָדַר לַאֲבִיר יַעֲקֹב:
ד אִם־אָבֹא
בְּאֹהֶל בֵּיתִי
אִם־אֶעֱלֶה
עַל־עֶרֶשׂ יְצוּעָי:
ה אִם־אֶתֵּן שְׁנַת לְעֵינָי
לְעַפְעַפַּי תְּנוּמָה:
ו עַד־אֶמְצָא מָקוֹם לַיהוָה
מִשְׁכָּנוֹת לַאֲבִיר יַעֲקֹב:
ז הִנֵּה־שְׁמַעֲנוּהָ בְאֶפְרָתָה
מְצָאנוּהָ בִּשְׂדֵי־יָעַר:
ח נָבוֹאָה לְמִשְׁכְּנוֹתָיו
נִשְׁתַּחֲוֶה לַהֲדֹם רַגְלָיו:
ט קוּמָה יְהוָה לִמְנוּחָתֶךָ
אַתָּה וַאֲרוֹן עֻזֶּךָ:
י כֹּהֲנֶיךָ
יִלְבְּשׁוּ־צֶדֶק
וַחֲסִידֶיךָ יְרַנֵּנוּ:
יא בַּעֲבוּר דָּוִד עַבְדֶּךָ
אַל־תָּשֵׁב פְּנֵי מְשִׁיחֶךָ:
יב נִשְׁבַּע־יְהוָה | לְדָוִד
אֱמֶת לֹא־יָשׁוּב מִמֶּנָּה
מִפְּרִי בִטְנְךָ
אָשִׁית לְכִסֵּא־לָךְ:
יג אִם־יִשְׁמְרוּ בָנֶיךָ | בְּרִיתִי
וְעֵדֹתִי זוֹ אֲלַמְּדֵם
גַּם־בְּנֵיהֶם
עֲדֵי־עַד יֵשְׁבוּ לְכִסֵּא־לָךְ:
יד כִּי־בָחַר יְהוָה בְּצִיּוֹן
אִוָּהּ לְמוֹשָׁב לוֹ:
טו זֹאת־מְנוּחָתִי עֲדֵי־עַד
פֹּה־אֵשֵׁב כִּי אִוִּתִיהָ:
טז צֵידָהּ בָּרֵךְ אֲבָרֵךְ

Chapter 132

1 A Song of Ascents.
Remember, Adonoy, unto David
all his afflictions.
2 How he swore to Adonoy
and vowed to the Mighty One of Jacob.
3 Surely I will not enter
into the tent of my house;
nor will I go up
into the bed that is spread for me.
4 Surely I will not give sleep to my eyes,
nor slumber to my eyelids.
5 Until I find a place for Adonoy,
dwelling places for the Mighty One of Jacob.
6 Behold, we heard of it as being in Ephrath;
we found it in the fields of the forest.
7 Let us come to His Tabernacles,
let us prostrate ourselves at His footstool.
8 Arise Adonoy to Your resting place,
You and the Ark of Your strength.
9 Let Your priests
clothe themselves in righteousness,
and let Your devoted ones sing in joy.
10 For the sake of David Your servant,
do not reject Your annointed.
11 Adonoy swore to David,
a truth from which He will not turn back,
"Of the fruit of your womb
I will set upon your throne.
12 If your children will preserve My covenant
and My testimony that I will teach them;
then their children too
will forever sit on your throne."
13 For Adonoy has chosen Zion;
He desired it for His Dwelling Place.
14 "This is My resting place forever,
here I will dwell for I have desired it.
15 Her provision I will abundantly bless;

אֶ֝בְיוֹנֶ֗יהָ אַשְׂבִּ֥יעַ לָֽחֶם׃		her needy I will satiate with bread.
וְ֭כֹהֲנֶיהָ	יז / 16	And her priests
אַלְבִּ֣ישׁ יֶ֑שַׁע		I will clothe with deliverance
וַ֝חֲסִידֶ֗יהָ רַנֵּ֥ן יְרַנֵּֽנוּ׃		and her devoted ones will sing for joy.
שָׁ֤ם אַצְמִ֣יחַ	יח / 17	There will I cause to spring up
קֶ֣רֶן לְדָוִ֑ד		the horn of David
עָרַ֥כְתִּי נֵ֝֗ר לִמְשִׁיחִֽי׃		[there] have I ordered a lamp for my annointed.
א֭וֹיְבָיו אַלְבִּ֣ישׁ בֹּ֑שֶׁת	יט / 18	His enemies I will clothe with shame,
וְ֝עָלָ֗יו יָצִ֥יץ נִזְרֽוֹ׃		but upon him his crown will shine."

פרק קל״ג Chapter 133

Weekly Cycle	Monthly Cycle	Book Number
Saturday	27th day of the month	Book 5

Author

דָוִד הַמֶּלֶךְ—King David—the second king of Israel and father of the Davidic royal and messianic dynasty. David composed over seventy of the 150 psalms of Sefer Tehillim.

Genre

Psalm of Pilgrimage - These psalms were used at the beginning of pilgrimages as well as once the Pilgrim had reached his or her destination.

Psalm of Wisdom - This psalm contains teachings and wise advice and is meant to instruct people on how to live a Godly life.

Song of Ascents - A title given to fifteen of the Psalms, 120-134, that each starts with the ascription Shir HaMa'alot, meaning "Song of Ascents". These psalms praise, exult, and "elevate" God.

Chapter Summary

In this psalm, the fourteenth in the series of Shir HaMa'a lot (Song of Ascents), King David, filled with hope, now speaks of the love and unity among the Kohanim (Priests) serving God in the Mikdash (Sanctuary). Some suggest that he composed this song after the kingdom of Saul united with the kingdom of David upon the death of Mefiboshet, grandson of Saul.

This psalm, like psalm 131, consists of only three verses, subdivided into two parts.
In verse 1, the Psalmist speaks of the beauty and pleasantness of brothers dwelling in harmony.
In verses 2 & 3, he expands upon this idea through beautiful imagery.

Introductory Word

שִׁיר—Shir—Song

Shimush Tehillim - When to Say

For developing friendship; to like or be liked by others—Verse 1 states: "Behold, how good and how pleasant it is when brethren also dwell together in unity."

Where in the Siddur

Recited together with the entire Shir HaMa'alot series, following the Shabbat afternoon Minchah service, on the weeks between Sukkot and Pesach (Passover).

Verse 2 is found in Tashlich—a prayer recited on Rosh HaShanah afternoon, usually by a body of water, in which we beseech God to "cast away" our sins into the depths of the sea.

Biblical Personalities

אַהֲרֹן—Aaron—older brother of Moses and the first Kohein (Priest). The descendents of Aaron, as future Kohanim, were designated to perform the ritual service in the Beit HaMikdash (Temple).

Biblical Places

חֶרְמוֹן—Hermon—a tall mountain in the most northern part of israel.

הַרְרֵי צִיּוֹן—Mountains of Zion—a reference to Jerusalem.

Contemporary Song

Verse 1

פרק קלג	Chapter 133
א שִׁיר הַמַּעֲלוֹת לְדָוִד	1 A Song of Ascents of David.
הִנֵּה מַה־טּוֹב וּמַה־נָּעִים	Behold, how good and how pleasant it is
שֶׁבֶת אַחִים גַּם־יָחַד:	when brethren also dwell together in unity.
ב כַּשֶּׁמֶן הַטּוֹב | עַל־הָרֹאשׁ	2 Like the precious oil upon the head
יֹרֵד עַל־הַזָּקָן	coming down upon the beard,
זְקַן־אַהֲרֹן	the beard of Aaron
שֶׁיֹּרֵד	that comes down
עַל־פִּי מִדּוֹתָיו:	upon the edge of his garments.
ג כְּטַל־חֶרְמוֹן	3 Like the dew of Hermon
שֶׁיֹּרֵד עַל־הַרְרֵי צִיּוֹן	that comes down upon the mountains of Zion;
כִּי שָׁם | צִוָּה יְהוָה אֶת־הַבְּרָכָה	for there Adonoy commanded the blessing,
חַיִּים עַד־הָעוֹלָם:	life for evermore.

פרק קלד Chapter 134

Weekly Cycle	Monthly Cycle	Book Number
Saturday	27th day of the month	Book 5

Author

Unknown; perhaps דָוִד הַמֶּלֶךְ—King David—the second king of Israel and father of the Davidic royal and messianic dynasty. David composed over seventy of the 150 psalms of Sefer Tehillim.

Genre

Psalm of Pilgrimage - These psalms were used at the beginning of pilgrimages as well as once the Pilgrim had reached his or her destination.

Song of Ascents - A title given to fifteen of the Psalms, 120-134, that each starts with the ascription Shir HaMa'alot, meaning "Song of Ascents". These psalms praise, exult, and "elevate" God.

Chapter Summary

In this fifteenth and final psalm of the series of Shir HaMa'alot (Song of Ascents), the singer once again turns to the Kohanim (Priests) and declares: "Behold, bless the Lord, all you servants of the Lord." As the previous psalm concluded with praises of Jerusalem and the land of Israel when the Jewish people will dwell there, the psalmist concludes the series by proclaiming that its excellence stems from the righteous, who praise and worship God "by the night".

This psalm, like the previous one, consists of a mere three verses, subdivided into two sections. In verses 1 & 2, the singer calls upon all "servants of Adonoy" to lift their hands and bless God. In verse 3, he boldly declares that God will in turn bless those who bless Him.

Introductory Word

שִׁיר—Shir—Song

Shimush Tehillim - When to Say

Before studying Torah—Verse 1 states: "Behold, bless Adonoy all [you] servants of Adonoy, who stand in the House of Adonoy in the night."

Where in the Siddur

Recited together with the entire Shir HaMa'alot series, following the Shabbat afternoon Minchah service, on the weeks between Sukkot and Pesach (Passover).

Biblical Places

בֵּית-יְהוָה—House of God—a reference to the Beit HaMikdash (Temple) in Jerusalem.

צִיּוֹן—Zion—a place name often used as a synonym for Jerusalem. The term Zion originally referred only to the area where a Jebbusite fortress once stood, also the location of the City of David. Zion was later used by prophets and psalmists as another name for Jerusalem.

פרק קלד

א שִׁיר הַמַּעֲלוֹת

ב הִנֵּה | בָּרְכוּ אֶת־יְהוָה

כָּל־עַבְדֵי יְהוָה

הָעֹמְדִים בְּבֵית־יְהוָה

בַּלֵּילוֹת׃

ג שְׂאוּ־יְדֵכֶם קֹדֶשׁ

וּבָרְכוּ אֶת־יְהוָה׃

ד יְבָרֶכְךָ יְהוָה מִצִּיּוֹן

עֹשֵׂה שָׁמַיִם וָאָרֶץ׃

Chapter 134

1 A Song of Ascents.
Behold, bless Adonoy
all [you] servants of Adonoy,
who stand in the House of Adonoy
in the night.

2 Lift your hands to the Sanctuary
and bless Adonoy.

3 Adonoy will bless you out of Zion,
[He Who is] Maker of heaven and earth.

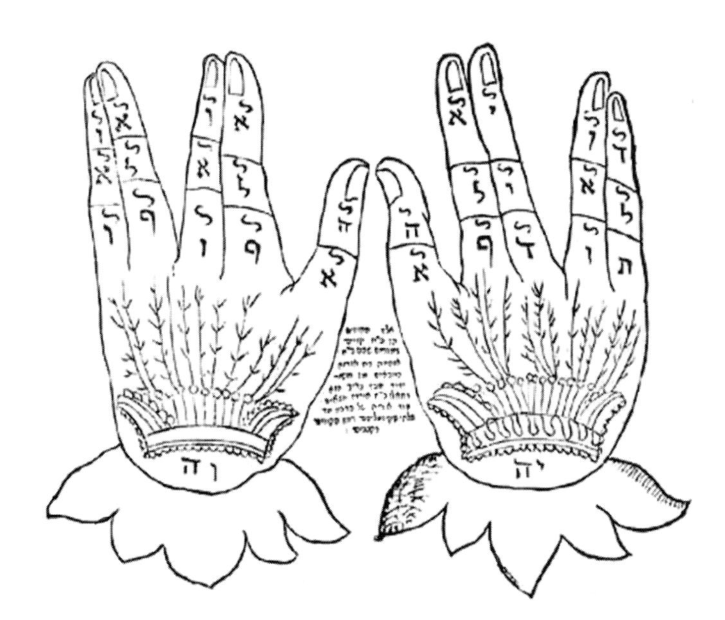

Duchan Hands

פרק קלה Chapter 135

Weekly Cycle	Monthly Cycle	Book Number
Saturday	28th day of the month	Book 5

Author
Unknown

When & Why
This psalm was read aloud to the Priests and Levites in the Temple as an accompaniment to their prayers.

Genre
Psalm of Praise – This is a psalm of celebration, often the result of a victory. It declares God's goodness and urges all of creation to worship.

Chapter Summary
The singer now bids the House of Israel to praise God for all he has wrought on our behalf throughout history. Miracles of the ten plagues, the Exodus from Egypt, the Israelites' sojourn in the wilderness and subsequesnt entry into the Holy Land are all recounted, as evidence that God supervises and guides the unfolding of history. By contrast, worship of false Gods, the author asserts, is worthless.

This psalm consists of twenty-one verses, subdivided into three sections.
In verses 1-3, the psalmist calls upon the congregation to praise God.
In verses 4-18, he describes the greatness and power of God, expressed through the wonders of creation, the plagues in Egypt and the conquest of Canaan. He further contrasts God's being eternal with idols, the mere handiwork of man.
In verses 19-21, the psalmist comes full circle and once again calls upon the congregation to bless God.

Introductory Word
הַלְלוּיָ-ה—Halleluyah—Praise God

Shimush Tehillim - When to Say
To inspire one towards repentance (say daily after morning prayers)—Verse 3 states: "Praise God, for Adonoy is good, sing to His Name which is pleasant."

Where in the Siddur
Recited as part of Pesukei Dezimra (introductory Verses of Praise to the Shacharit morning service) on Shabbat, Yom Tov (Festivals), and Hoshana Rabbah (the seventh day of Sukkot).
Recited on the fifth day of Pesach (Passover) in some traditions.
Verses 4 and 13 are found in Yehi Chevod, the introductory paragraph to Ashrei of Pesukei Dezimra.
Verse 21 is the second verse of Baruch Hashem Le'olam of Pesukei Dezimra, as well as Baruch

Hashem Le'olam recited upon the conclusion of Shema of Ma'ariv (evening service).

Biblical Personalities

אַהֲרֹן—Aaron—older brother of Moses and the first Kohein (Priest). The descendents of Aaron, as future Kohanim, were designated to perform the ritual service in the Beit HaMikdash (Temple).

עוֹג—Og—an Amorite King of the country Bashan, he was a mighty giant whose defeat is considered one of many great victories for Moses and the Israelites in the wilderness.

פַּרְעֹה—Pharoah—a title of the rulers of ancient Egyptian dynasties. It perhaps has its origin in another Egyptian term of the same root, meaning "great house", referring to the royal palace.

סִיחוֹן—Sihon—an Amorite king, whose country Heshbon was just east of the Jordan River. After he refused to allow the Israelites to pass through his land, they fought the Amorites in battle and emerged victorious. His walled towns were captured and the complete Amorite country was taken by the Israelites, who killed the king and all his people.

יַעֲקֹב—Yaakov—Jacob, also called Yisrael—Israel—the third patriarch, known as the father of the twelve tribes of Israel. He was married to Rachel and Leah, and was the twin brother of Eisav.

Biblical People

יִשְׂרָאֵל—Yisrael—The Nation of Israel.

Biblical Places

כְּנָעַן—Canaan—the biblical name of the Land of Israel.

בֵּית-יְהוָה—House of God—a reference to the Beit HaMikdash (Temple) in Jerusalem.

מִצְרָיִם—Mitzrayim—Egypt—the land where the Israelites sojourned and were subsequently enslaved by Pharoh until God sent Moses to redeem them. Egyptian society ran contrary to many of the ideals of the Torah. As such, the Israelite king is specifically warned not to amass cavalry, lest he be tempted to return his nation to Egypt.

יְרוּשָׁלִָם—Yerushalayim—Jerusalem—the capital city of the kingdom of Israel, conquered by King David 3,000 years ago. David established Jerusalem as both the religious and political center of Israel.

צִיּוֹן—Zion—a place name often used as a synonym for Jerusalem. The term Zion originally referred only to the area where a Jebbusite fortress once stood, also the location of the City of David. Zion was later used by prophets and psalmists as another name for Jerusalem.

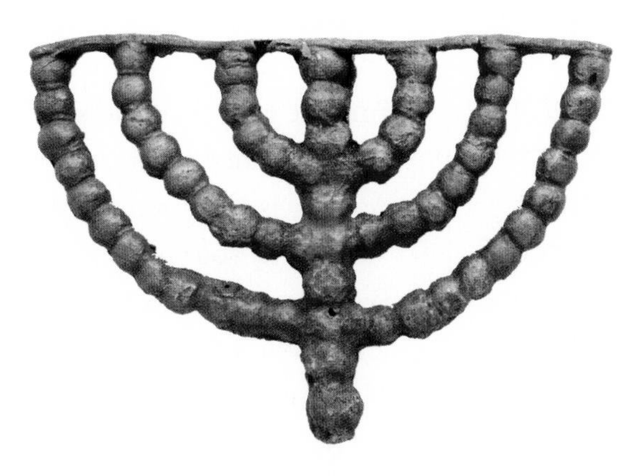

Seven-branched Menorah

פֶּרֶק קלה

א הַֽלְלוּ יָהּ ׀

ב הַֽלְלוּ אֶת־שֵׁם יְהוָה
הַֽלְלוּ עַבְדֵי יְהוָה׃

ג שֶׁעֹמְדִים בְּבֵית יְהוָה
בְּחַצְרוֹת בֵּית אֱלֹהֵינוּ׃

ד הַֽלְלוּ־יָהּ כִּי־טוֹב יְהוָה
זַמְּרוּ לִשְׁמוֹ כִּי נָעִים׃

ה כִּי־יַעֲקֹב בָּחַר לוֹ יָהּ
יִשְׂרָאֵל לִסְגֻלָּתוֹ׃

ו כִּי אֲנִי יָדַעְתִּי
כִּי־גָדוֹל יְהוָה
וַאֲדֹנֵינוּ מִכָּל־אֱלֹהִים׃

ז כֹּל אֲשֶׁר־חָפֵץ יְהוָה
עָשָׂה בַּשָּׁמַיִם וּבָאָרֶץ
בַּיַּמִּים וְכָל־תְּהוֹמוֹת׃

ח מַעֲלֶה נְשִׂאִים
מִקְצֵה הָאָרֶץ
בְּרָקִים לַמָּטָר עָשָׂה
מוֹצֵא־רוּחַ מֵאוֹצְרוֹתָיו׃

ט שֶׁהִכָּה בְּכוֹרֵי מִצְרָיִם
מֵאָדָם עַד־בְּהֵמָה׃

י שָׁלַח ׀ אֹתוֹת וּמֹפְתִים
בְּתוֹכֵכִי מִצְרָיִם
בְּפַרְעֹה וּבְכָל־עֲבָדָיו׃

יא שֶׁהִכָּה גּוֹיִם רַבִּים
וְהָרַג מְלָכִים עֲצוּמִים׃

יב לְסִיחוֹן ׀ מֶלֶךְ הָאֱמֹרִי
וּלְעוֹג מֶלֶךְ הַבָּשָׁן
וּלְכֹל מַמְלְכוֹת כְּנָעַן׃

יג וְנָתַן אַרְצָם נַחֲלָה
נַחֲלָה לְיִשְׂרָאֵל עַמּוֹ׃

יד יְהוָה שִׁמְךָ לְעוֹלָם
יְהוָה זִכְרְךָ לְדֹר־וָדֹר׃

טו כִּי־יָדִין יְהוָה עַמּוֹ
וְעַל־עֲבָדָיו יִתְנֶחָם׃

טז עֲצַבֵּי הַגּוֹיִם
כֶּסֶף וְזָהָב
מַעֲשֵׂה יְדֵי אָדָם׃

Chapter 135

1 Praise God,

2 Praise the Name of Adonoy,
Praise [Him], servants of Adonoy.

3 [You] who stand in the House of Adonoy,
in the courtyards of the House of our God.

4 Praise God, for Adonoy is good,
sing to His Name which is pleasant.

5 For God chose Jacob to be His,
Israel for His treasure.

6 For I know
that Adonoy is great,
our Master [is greater] than all gods.

7 All that was desired by Adonoy,
He has done in heaven and on earth,
in the seas and all the depths.

8 He causes clouds to rise
from the ends of the earth;
lightning for the rain He makes;
He brings forth winds from His vaults.

9 He struck down the firstborn of Egypt
both man and beast.

10 He sent signs and wonders
into the midst of Egypt,
upon Pharaoh and upon all his servants.

11 For He smote many nations,
and slew mighty kings:

12 Sichon, King of the Amorites,
and Og, King of the Bashan,
and all the kingdoms of Canaan.

13 And He gave their lands as an inheritance,
an inheritance to Israel, His people.

14 Adonoy is Your Name forever,
Adonoy is Your mention for generations.

15 For Adonoy judges His people,
and upon His servants will He relent.

16 The idols of the nations,
are of silver and gold,
products of human hands:

יז פֶּה־לָהֶם וְלֹא יְדַבֵּרוּ	17 They have a mouth but do not speak;
עֵינַיִם לָהֶם וְלֹא יִרְאוּ׃	they have eyes but do not see.
יח אָזְנַיִם לָהֶם וְלֹא יַאֲזִינוּ	18 They have ears but do not listen;
אַף אֵין־יֶשׁ־רוּחַ בְּפִיהֶם׃	nor is there any breath in their mouth.
יט כְּמוֹהֶם יִהְיוּ עֹשֵׂיהֶם	19 Like them let their makers be—
כֹּל אֲשֶׁר־בֹּטֵחַ בָּהֶם׃	all who trust in them.
כ בֵּית יִשְׂרָאֵל בָּרְכוּ אֶת־יְהוָה	20 House of Israel, bless Adonoy!
בֵּית אַהֲרֹן בָּרְכוּ אֶת־יְהוָה׃	House of Aaron, bless Adonoy!
כא בֵּית הַלֵּוִי בָּרְכוּ אֶת־יְהוָה	21 House of Levi, bless Adonoy!
יִרְאֵי יְהוָה בָּרְכוּ אֶת־יְהוָה׃	[You] who fear Adonoy, bless Adonoy!
כב בָּרוּךְ יְהוָה | מִצִּיּוֹן	22 Blessed is Adonoy from Zion,
שֹׁכֵן יְרוּשָׁלָם	He Who dwells in Jerusalem.
הַלְלוּ־יָהּ׃	Praise God.

פרק קלו ~ Chapter 136

Weekly Cycle	Monthly Cycle	Book Number
Saturday	28th day of the month	Book 5

Author
Unknown

Genre
Psalm of Praise – This is a psalm of celebration, often the result of a victory. It declares God's goodness and urges all of creation to worship.

Psalm of Communal Thanksgiving - This psalm emphasizes gratitude for what God has done for the community as a whole.

Chapter Summary
This psalm is known as the Hallel Hagadol, the great praise, because it describes how God, enthroned in the high heavens is concerned with every living creature.

Written in poetic, responsive form, this psalm maintains the theme, even the details, of the previous one. Each line ends with the words "for His kindness is eternal." Its twenty-six verses correspond to the twenty-six generations from Creation until the receiving of the Torah at Sinai. The refrain indicates that as those generations did not have the Torah through which to merit God's beneficence, God nonetheless sustained them due to His pure loving kindness.

This psalm consists of twenty-six verses, subdivided into three sections.
In verses 1-3, the psalmist calls upon the congregation to praise God.
In verses 4-25, he describes the wonders of God through the creation of the world, the Exodus from Egypt, and the conquest of Israel. The singer further celebrates God's remembering and saving His creatures, provding them with sustenance.
In verse 26, the psalmist comes full circle, once again calling upon the congregation to bless God.

Introductory Word

הוֹדוּ—Hodu—Give thanks

Shimush Tehillim - When to Say

To help one admit sins and confess—Each verse states: "for His kindliness endures forever."

Interesting Fact

The word "hodu" means both "give thanks" and "admit", as thanking can only come from appreciation and subsequent admission.

Where in the Siddur

Recited as part of Pesukei Dezimra (introductory Verses of Praise to the Shacharit morning service) on Shabbat, Yom Tov (Festivals), and Hoshana Rabbah (the seventh day of Sukkot).
Recited in the section of Hallel at the Pesach (Passover) Seder.
Recited on the eighth day of Pesach in some traditions.
Verse 1 is found in the final paragraph of Birkat HaMazon (Grace after Meals). Verse 25 is found in its opening paragraph.
Verse 4 is recited as one of the verses of Atah Horeita, a responsive reading introducing the Hakafot dancing ceremony on Simchat Torah.
Verse 6 is included in one of the blessings of Birchot HaShachar (Morning Blessings).
Verse 7 is found in La'Keil Baruch, one of the blessings preceding Shema of Shacharit (morning service).

Biblical Personalities

עוֹג—Og—an Amorite King of the country Bashan, he was a mighty giant whose defeat is considered one of many great victories for Moses and the Israelites in the wilderness.
פַּרְעֹה—Pharoah—a title of the rulers of ancient Egyptian dynasties. It perhaps has its origin in another Egyptian term of the same root, meaning "great house", referring to the royal palace.
סִיחוֹן—Sihon—an Amorite king, whose country Heshbon was just east of the Jordan River. After he refused to allow the Israelites to pass through his land, they fought the Amorites in battle and emerged victorious. His walled towns were captured and the complete Amorite country was taken by the Israelites, who killed the king and all his people.

Biblical People

בֵּית יִשְׂרָאֵל—Beit Yisroel— The House of Israel.

Biblical Places

מִצְרָיִם—Mitzrayim—Egypt—the land where the Israelites sojourned and were subsequently enslaved by Pharoh until God sent Moses to redeem them. Egyptian society ran contrary to many of the ideals of the Torah. As such, the Israelite king is specifically warned not to amass cavalry, lest he be tempted to return his nation to Egypt.

מִדְבָּר—Wilderness—a reference to the desert the Israelites traversed for forty years on their way to Israel.

יַם-סוּף—Yam Suf—The Red Sea—also referred to as the Sea of Reeds, the body of water which miraculously parted for the Israelites as they fled the Egyptians, and then engulfed the pursuing Egyptian soldiers, drowning them.

פֶּרֶק קלו

א הוֹדוּ לַיהוָה כִּי־טוֹב
כִּי לְעוֹלָם חַסְדּוֹ׃
ב הוֹדוּ לֵאלֹהֵי הָאֱלֹהִים
כִּי לְעוֹלָם חַסְדּוֹ׃
ג הוֹדוּ לַאֲדֹנֵי הָאֲדֹנִים
כִּי לְעוֹלָם חַסְדּוֹ׃
ד לְעֹשֵׂה נִפְלָאוֹת גְּדֹלוֹת לְבַדּוֹ
כִּי לְעוֹלָם חַסְדּוֹ׃
ה לְעֹשֵׂה הַשָּׁמַיִם
בִּתְבוּנָה
כִּי לְעוֹלָם חַסְדּוֹ׃
ו לְרֹקַע הָאָרֶץ עַל־הַמָּיִם
כִּי לְעוֹלָם חַסְדּוֹ׃
ז לְעֹשֵׂה אוֹרִים גְּדֹלִים
כִּי לְעוֹלָם חַסְדּוֹ׃
ח אֶת־הַשֶּׁמֶשׁ לְמֶמְשֶׁלֶת בַּיּוֹם
כִּי לְעוֹלָם חַסְדּוֹ׃
ט אֶת־הַיָּרֵחַ וְכוֹכָבִים
לְמֶמְשְׁלוֹת בַּלָּיְלָה
כִּי לְעוֹלָם חַסְדּוֹ׃
י לְמַכֵּה מִצְרַיִם
בִּבְכוֹרֵיהֶם
כִּי לְעוֹלָם חַסְדּוֹ׃
יא וַיּוֹצֵא יִשְׂרָאֵל מִתּוֹכָם
כִּי לְעוֹלָם חַסְדּוֹ׃
יב בְּיָד חֲזָקָה וּבִזְרוֹעַ נְטוּיָה
כִּי לְעוֹלָם חַסְדּוֹ׃
יג לְגֹזֵר יַם־סוּף לִגְזָרִים
כִּי לְעוֹלָם חַסְדּוֹ׃

Chapter 136

1 Thank Adonoy for He is good,
for His kindliness endures forever.
2 Thank the God of gods,
for His kindliness endures forever.
3 Thank the Master of masters,
for His kindliness endures forever.
4 He Who does great wonders, alone,
for His kindliness endures forever.
5 He Who makes the heavens,
with understanding,
for His kindliness endures forever.
6 He Who spreads the earth over the waters,
for His kindliness endures forever.
7 He Who makes the great luminaries,
for His kindliness endures forever.
8 The sun to rule by day,
for His kindliness endures forever.
9 The moon and stars
to rule by night,
for His kindliness endures forever.
10 He Who struck Egypt
through their firstborn,
for His kindliness endures forever.
11 He brought Israel out of their midst,
for His kindliness endures forever.
12 With a strong hand and outstretched arm,
for His kindliness endures forever.
13 He Who parted the Sea of Reeds into parts,
for His kindliness endures forever.

יד וְהֶעֱבִיר יִשְׂרָאֵל בְּתוֹכוֹ
כִּי לְעוֹלָם חַסְדּוֹ׃

14 And He made Israel pass through it
for His kindliness endures forever.

טו וְנִעֵר פַּרְעֹה וְחֵילוֹ
בְיַם־סוּף
כִּי לְעוֹלָם חַסְדּוֹ׃

15 And He threw Pharaoh and his army
into the Sea of Reeds,
for His kindliness endures forever.

טז לְמוֹלִיךְ עַמּוֹ
בַּמִּדְבָּר
כִּי לְעוֹלָם חַסְדּוֹ׃

16 He Who led His people
through the wilderness
for His kindliness endures forever.

יז לְמַכֵּה מְלָכִים גְּדֹלִים
כִּי לְעוֹלָם חַסְדּוֹ׃

17 He Who struck great kings,
for His kindliness endures forever.

יח וַיַּהֲרֹג מְלָכִים אַדִּירִים
כִּי לְעוֹלָם חַסְדּוֹ׃

18 And He slew mighty kings,
for His kindliness endures forever.

יט לְסִיחוֹן מֶלֶךְ הָאֱמֹרִי
כִּי לְעוֹלָם חַסְדּוֹ׃

19 Sichon, king of the Amorites,
for His kindliness endures forever.

כ וּלְעוֹג מֶלֶךְ הַבָּשָׁן
כִּי לְעוֹלָם חַסְדּוֹ׃

20 And Og, king of the Bashan,
for His kindliness endures forever.

כא וְנָתַן אַרְצָם לְנַחֲלָה
כִּי לְעוֹלָם חַסְדּוֹ׃

21 And gave their land as an inheritance,
for His kindliness endures forever.

כב נַחֲלָה לְיִשְׂרָאֵל עַבְדּוֹ
כִּי לְעוֹלָם חַסְדּוֹ׃

22 An inheritance to Israel, His servant,
for His kindliness endures forever.

כג שֶׁבְּשִׁפְלֵנוּ זָכַר לָנוּ
כִּי לְעוֹלָם חַסְדּוֹ׃

23 In our lowliness, He remembered us,
for His kindliness endures forever.

כד וַיִּפְרְקֵנוּ מִצָּרֵינוּ
כִּי לְעוֹלָם חַסְדּוֹ׃

24 And He freed us from our oppressors,
for His kindliness endures forever.

כה נֹתֵן לֶחֶם לְכָל־בָּשָׂר
כִּי לְעוֹלָם חַסְדּוֹ׃

25 He gives food to all flesh,
for His kindliness endures forever.

כו הוֹדוּ לְאֵל הַשָּׁמָיִם
כִּי לְעוֹלָם חַסְדּוֹ׃

26 Thank the Almighty of heaven
for His kindliness endures forever.

Aquatic detail from the Lod Mosaic

פרק קלז Chapter 137

Weekly Cycle	Monthly Cycle	Book Number
Saturday	28th day of the month	Book 5

Author

Unknown; perhaps דָּוִד הַמֶּלֶךְ—King David—the second king of Israel and father of the Davidic royal and messianic dynasty. David composed over seventy of the 150 psalms of Sefer Tehillim.

When & Why

David might have written this psalm prophetically as a lament over the destruction of the first and second Temples.

Genre

Psalm of Communal Lament - This psalm focuses on expressing deep sorrow for the travails of a nation and as a group asking for God's blessing or intervention.

Chapter Summary

The psalmist composed this psalm in the aftermath of the destruction of the first Beit HaMikdash (Temple). He laments the destruction, beseeching the Almighty to recompence with justice.

This psalm consists of nine verses, subdivided into three parts.
In verses 1-3, the psalmist describes the calamities of the past, when the exiles sat and wept beside the rivers of Babylon.
In verses 4-6, he speaks of the present, remanding the exiles to fulfill their oath to remember Jerusalem.
In verses 7-9, he directs his thoughts to the future, and further pronounces a curse upon the enemies who destroyed Jerusalem.

Shimush Tehillim - When to Say

To remove hatred from the world—Verse 5 states: "If I ever forget you, Jerusalem, may my right hand forget [its movement]."

Musical Instruments

כִּנּוֹר—Kinor—A Small Handheld Harp - played with a plecturm (pick)

Where in the Siddur

Recited by some as an introduction to Birkat HaMazon (Grace after Meals) on all of the days on which Psalm 126 (Shir HaMa'alot) is not recited.
Verse 7 is found in the repetition of the Musaf Amidah (Silent Meditation) of Rosh HaShanah.
Verses 5 & 6 are customarily recited by the groom, and in some circles sung by all present, immediately prior to the breaking of the glass at the conclusion of the Jewish wedding ceremony.

Biblical Personalities

אֱדוֹם—Edom—descendants of Eisav (Esau), the brother of Yaakov (Jacob). The sibling rivalry between them persisted for centuries, most strongly expressed when the Edomites looted Jerusalem as it was being overrun by the Babylonians.

בָּבֶל—Babylon—led by King Nebuchadnezzar, the Babylonians destroyed the Beit HaMikdash (Temple) and exiled the Jews to his land.

יְרוּשָׁלַםִ—Yerushalayim—Jerusalem—the capital city of the kingdom of Israel, conquered by King David 3,000 years ago. David established Jerusalem as both the religious and political center of Israel.

צִיּוֹן—Zion—a place name often used as a synonym for Jerusalem. The term Zion originally referred only to the area where a Jebbusite fortress once stood, also the location of the City of David. Zion was later used by prophets and psalmists as another name for Jerusalem.

Talmud on Tehillim

Verses 5 & 6: "אִם אֶשְׁכָּחֵךְ יְרוּשָׁלָםִ תִּשְׁכַּח יְמִינִי... אִם לֹא אַעֲלֶה אֶת יְרוּשָׁלַםִ עַל רֹאשׁ שִׂמְחָתִי"—"If I ever forget you, Jerusalem, may my right hand forget [its movement]...if I set not Jerusalem above my highest joy." The Talmud, Bava Batra 60b, explains the words "at the head of my joy" as a reference to placing crushed ashes on the head of the bridegroom as a sign of mourning for Jerusalem and the Beit HaMikdash (Temple).

פֶּרֶק קלז	Chapter 137
א עַל נַהֲרוֹת | בָּבֶל	1 By the rivers of Babylon,
שָׁם יָשַׁבְנוּ גַּם־בָּכִינוּ	there we sat and we also wept,
בְּזָכְרֵנוּ אֶת־צִיּוֹן׃	when we remembered Zion.
ב עַל־עֲרָבִים בְּתוֹכָהּ	2 Upon the willows in its midst,
תָּלִינוּ כִּנֹּרוֹתֵינוּ׃	we hung our harps.
ג כִּי שָׁם שְׁאֵלוּנוּ שׁוֹבֵינוּ	3 For there our captors demanded of us
דִּבְרֵי־שִׁיר	words of song,
וְתוֹלָלֵינוּ שִׂמְחָה	and our tormentors asked of us [with] mirth;
שִׁירוּ לָנוּ מִשִּׁיר צִיּוֹן׃	"Sing to us from the song[s] of Zion."
ד אֵיךְ נָשִׁיר אֶת־שִׁיר־יְהוָה	4 How shall we sing the song of Adonoy
עַל אַדְמַת נֵכָר׃	on alien soil?
ה אִם־אֶשְׁכָּחֵךְ יְרוּשָׁלִָם	5 If I ever forget you, Jerusalem,
תִּשְׁכַּח יְמִינִי׃	may my right hand forget [its movement].
ו תִּדְבַּק־לְשׁוֹנִי | לְחִכִּי	6 May my tongue cleave to my palate,
אִם־לֹא אֶזְכְּרֵכִי	if I remember you not;
אִם־לֹא אַעֲלֶה אֶת־יְרוּשָׁלִַם	if I set not Jerusalem
עַל רֹאשׁ שִׂמְחָתִי׃	above my highest joy.

ז זְכֹר יְהוָה ׀ לִבְנֵי אֱדוֹם אֵת יוֹם יְרוּשָׁלִָם הָאֹמְרִים עָרוּ ׀ עָרוּ עַד הַיְסוֹד בָּהּ:	7 Remember, Adonoy, to the sons of Edom the day of Jerusalem, [it was they] who said, "Raze it, raze it to its very foundation."
ח בַּת־בָּבֶל הַשְּׁדוּדָה אַשְׁרֵי שֶׁיְשַׁלֶּם־לָךְ אֶת־גְּמוּלֵךְ שֶׁגָּמַלְתְּ לָנוּ:	8 Daughter of Babylon, it is you who is the annihilated one; fortunate is he who will repay you for all you have done to us.
ט אַשְׁרֵי ׀ שֶׁיֹּאחֵז וְנִפֵּץ אֶת־עֹלָלַיִךְ אֶל־הַסָּלַע:	9 Fortunate is he who will take and dash your little ones against the rock.

פרק קלח — Chapter 138

Weekly Cycle
Saturday

Monthly Cycle
28th day of the month

Book Number
Book 5

Author

דָּוִד הַמֶּלֶךְ—King David—the second king of Israel and father of the Davidic royal and messianic dynasty. David composed over seventy of the 150 psalms of Sefer Tehillim.

When & Why

David wrote this psalm to thank God for saving him from his enemies and establishing his kingdom.

Genre

Psalm of Communal Thanksgiving - This psalm emphasizes gratitude for what God has done for the community.

Chapter Summary

King David composed this psalm to give thanks to God for all the good He has bestowed upon him. He thereby addresses God's Divine Supervision and care for mankind.

This psalm consists of eight verses, subdivided into three parts.
In verses 1-3, King David praises and thanks God for answering his prayers.
In verses 4-6, he asserts that all kings of the earth will similarly praise Him.
In verses 7 & 8, the Psalmist concludes with a prayer for salvation.

Shimush Tehillim - When to Say

To encourage love—Verse 7 states: "If I walk in the midst of distress You keep me alive, against the wrath of my enemies You stretch forth Your hand, and Your right hand delivers me."

Biblical Places

הֵיכָל—Heichal—Holy Temple—a term used to refer to the inner sanctuary of the Temple in Jerusalem. The Heichal contained the Holy of Holies, the resting place of the Aron HaKodesh (Holy Ark)*. It also housed the Menorah, Altar of Incense, and Table of the Showbread.

*The Aron HaKodesh, while present in the first Beit HaMikdash (Temple), was buried, and hence its location was not known, during the period of the second Beit HaMikdash.

פרק קל״ח			**Chapter 138**
לְדָוִד ׀	א	1	[A Psalm] of David.
אוֹדְךָ בְכָל־לִבִּי			I will thank You with all my heart,
נֶגֶד אֱלֹהִים			in the presence of the mighty
אֲזַמְּרֶךָּ׃			will I sing praises to You.
אֶשְׁתַּחֲוֶה	ב	2	I will prostrate myself
אֶל־הֵיכַל קָדְשְׁךָ			toward Your Holy Sanctuary,
וְאוֹדֶה אֶת־שְׁמֶךָ			and give thanks to Your Name,
עַל־חַסְדְּךָ וְעַל־אֲמִתֶּךָ			for Your kindness and for Your truth;
כִּי־הִגְדַּלְתָּ			for You have magnified
עַל־כָּל־שִׁמְךָ אִמְרָתֶךָ׃			Your word far beyond Your Name.
בְּיוֹם קָרָאתִי וַתַּעֲנֵנִי	ג	3	In the day I called, You answered me;
תַּרְהִבֵנִי בְנַפְשִׁי עֹז׃			You uplifted me—You strengthened my soul.
יוֹדוּךָ יְהוָה	ד	4	They thanked You Adonoy—
כָּל־מַלְכֵי־אָרֶץ			all the kings of the earth,
כִּי שָׁמְעוּ אִמְרֵי־פִיךָ׃			when they heard the words of Your mouth.
וְיָשִׁירוּ בְּדַרְכֵי יְהוָה	ה	5	And they will sing of the ways of Adonoy,
כִּי גָדוֹל כְּבוֹד יְהוָה׃			for great is the glory of Adonoy.
כִּי־רָם יְהוָה	ו	6	For though Adonoy is exalted,
וְשָׁפָל יִרְאֶה			He still regards the lowly;
וְגָבֹהַּ מִמֶּרְחָק יְיֵדָע׃			but the haughty, from afar He admonishes.
אִם־אֵלֵךְ ׀ בְּקֶרֶב צָרָה	ז	7	If I walk in the midst of distress
תְּחַיֵּנִי			You keep me alive,
עַל אַף אֹיְבַי			against the wrath of my enemies
תִּשְׁלַח יָדֶךָ			You stretch forth Your hand,
וְתוֹשִׁיעֵנִי יְמִינֶךָ׃			and Your right hand delivers me.
יְהוָה יִגְמֹר	ח	8	Adonoy will accomplish

בְּעֲדִי	that which concerns me;
יְהוָה חַסְדְּךָ לְעוֹלָם	Adonoy, Your kindness endures forever,
מַעֲשֵׂי יָדֶיךָ אַל־תֶּרֶף׃	the work of Your hands forsake not.

פרק קלט Chapter 139

Weekly Cycle	Monthly Cycle	Book Number
Saturday	28th day of the month	Book 5

Author
דָוִד הַמֶּלֶךְ—King David—the second king of Israel and father of the Davidic royal and messianic dynasty. David composed over seventy of the 150 psalms of Sefer Tehillim.

Genre
Psalm of Individual Lament - This psalm was written from the perspective of the individual worshipper, who cries out to God in his time of need. It is characterized as an address to God involving a complaint, followed by a request and ending with an expression of trust.

Chapter Summary
As in the previous psalm, David speaks of individual Divine Supervision in this lowly world. He thereby reminds the reader that one cannot flee from God nor hide from His presence.

This psalm consists of twenty-four verses, subdivided into three parts.
In verses 1-18, King David praises God as man's creator, possessing knowledge of all of man's affairs.
In verses 19-23, he requests of God to continue to protect him from the wicked.
In verse 24, he thanks God for seeing him through in times of hardship, and affirms that He will indeed continue to protect him.

Introductory Words
לַמְנַצֵּחַ —Lamnatsei'ach—To the Conductor
מִזְמוֹר—Mizmor—Musical Accompaniment

Shimush Tehillim - When to Say
For love between husband and wife—Verse 5 states: "The back and front [of me] You have fashioned and You laid upon me Your hand." This verse is understood to be an allusion to Adam, originally created as a hybrid of both male and female traits. Man and woman were later split, but remained destined for each other.

Talmud on Tehillim
Verse 11: "וָאֹמַר, אַךְ חֹשֶׁךְ יְשׁוּפֵנִי; וְלַיְלָה, אוֹר בַּעֲדֵנִי"—"And if I were to say, 'Surely the darkness will envelop

me, the night would be as light about me."
The Talmud, Pesachim 2b, elucidates that King David at first thought that, as a result of his sins, it will be dark for him in the World to Come. But now that he sees that he had been forgiven, as God has clearly seen him through, he realizes that even in this world he will have "light".

פרק קלט	Chapter 139
א לַמְנַצֵּחַ לְדָוִד מִזְמוֹר יְהוָה חֲקַרְתַּנִי וַתֵּדָע׃	1 To the Chief Musician, a Psalm of David. Adonoy, You have searched me and [You] know [me].
ב אַתָּה יָדַעְתָּ שִׁבְתִּי וְקוּמִי בַּנְתָּה לְרֵעִי מֵרָחוֹק׃	2 You know my sitting down and my rising, You understand [how to draw me near to You] from afar.
ג אָרְחִי וְרִבְעִי זֵרִיתָ וְכָל־דְּרָכַי הִסְכַּנְתָּה׃	3 My going about and my lying down You have encompassed, and all my ways You recognize.
ד כִּי אֵין מִלָּה בִּלְשׁוֹנִי הֵן יְהוָה יָדַעְתָּ כֻלָּהּ׃	4 For there is [yet] no word on my tongue, behold, Adonoy, You know it all.
ה אָחוֹר וָקֶדֶם צַרְתָּנִי וַתָּשֶׁת עָלַי כַּפֶּכָה׃	5 The back and front [of me] You have fashioned and You laid upon me Your hand.
ו פְּלִיאָה דַעַת מִמֶּנִּי נִשְׂגְּבָה לֹא־אוּכַל לָהּ׃	6 Such knowledge is concealed from me, it is too high, I cannot [understand] it.
ז אָנָה אֵלֵךְ מֵרוּחֶךָ וְאָנָה מִפָּנֶיךָ אֶבְרָח׃	7 Where could I go from Your spirit, or where could I flee from Your Presence?
ח אִם־אֶסַּק שָׁמַיִם שָׁם אָתָּה וְאַצִּיעָה שְּׁאוֹל הִנֶּךָּ׃	8 If I would ascend to heaven, You are there; and if I were to make my bed in the grave, You are there.
ט אֶשָּׂא כַנְפֵי־שָׁחַר אֶשְׁכְּנָה בְּאַחֲרִית יָם׃	9 If I were to take the wings of the dawn, and dwell in the uttermost part of the sea.
י גַּם־שָׁם יָדְךָ תַנְחֵנִי וְתֹאחֲזֵנִי יְמִינֶךָ׃	10 Even there Your hand would lead me, and Your right hand would hold me.
יא וָאֹמַר אַךְ־חֹשֶׁךְ יְשׁוּפֵנִי וְלַיְלָה אוֹר בַּעֲדֵנִי׃	11 And if I were to say, "Surely the darkness will envelop me, the night would be as light about me."
יב גַּם־חֹשֶׁךְ לֹא־יַחְשִׁיךְ מִמֶּךָ	12 Even the darkness conceals nothing from You,

וְלַיְלָה כַּיּוֹם יָאִיר	but the night shines as the day;
כַּחֲשֵׁיכָה כָּאוֹרָה׃	the darkness is as the light.
יג כִּי־אַתָּה קָנִיתָ כִלְיֹתָי	13 For You have fashioned my mind,
תְּסֻכֵּנִי בְּבֶטֶן אִמִּי׃	You covered me in my mother's stomach.
יד אוֹדְךָ	14 I will thank You,
עַל כִּי נוֹרָאוֹת	for in an awesome [and wondrous] way
נִפְלֵיתִי	was I formed
נִפְלָאִים מַעֲשֶׂיךָ	wonderful are Your works,
וְנַפְשִׁי יֹדַעַת מְאֹד׃	and my soul is well aware of this.
טו לֹא־נִכְחַד עָצְמִי מִמֶּךָּ	15 My essence was not hidden from You,
אֲשֶׁר־עֻשֵּׂיתִי בַסֵּתֶר	when I was made in secret,
רֻקַּמְתִּי בְּתַחְתִּיּוֹת אָרֶץ׃	wrought in the lowest parts.
טז גָּלְמִי ׀ רָאוּ עֵינֶיךָ	16 My unformed substance Your eyes did see,
וְעַל־סִפְרְךָ כֻּלָּם יִכָּתֵבוּ	and in Your book they are all written,
יָמִים יֻצָּרוּ	even the days are fashioned;
וְלוֹ אֶחָד בָּהֶם׃	and He chose for Himself one among them.
יז וְלִי מַה־יָּקְרוּ	17 How precious to me
רֵעֶיךָ אֵל	are the thoughts of You, Almighty;
מֶה עָצְמוּ רָאשֵׁיהֶם׃	how overwhelming [even] their beginnings.
יח אֶסְפְּרֵם	18 If I were to count them,
מֵחוֹל יִרְבּוּן	they are more in number than the sand;
הֱקִיצֹתִי	were I to reach their end,
וְעוֹדִי עִמָּךְ׃	I would still be bound up with You.
יט אִם־תִּקְטֹל אֱלוֹהַּ ׀ רָשָׁע	19 If You God, would slay the wicked,
וְאַנְשֵׁי דָמִים סוּרוּ מֶנִּי׃	and men of blood depart from me.
כ אֲשֶׁר יֹאמְרֻךָ	20 They utter Your Name
לִמְזִמָּה	with wicked thought,
נָשֻׂא לַשָּׁוְא	they have borne it for falsehood,
עָרֶיךָ׃	those who are Your enemies.
כא הֲלוֹא־מְשַׂנְאֶיךָ יְהוָה ׀	21 Behold those who hate You Adonoy
אֶשְׂנָא	I hate
וּבִתְקוֹמְמֶיךָ אֶתְקוֹטָט׃	with those who rise up against You I contend.
כב תַּכְלִית שִׂנְאָה שְׂנֵאתִים	22 With the utmost hatred, I hate them
לְאוֹיְבִים הָיוּ לִי׃	they have come to be my enemies.
כג חָקְרֵנִי אֵל וְדַע לְבָבִי	23 Search me, Almighty, and know my heart,
בְּחָנֵנִי וְדַע שַׂרְעַפָּי׃	try me and know my thoughts.
כד וּרְאֵה	24 And see
אִם־דֶּרֶךְ־עֹצֶב בִּי	if there be any degenerate way in me,
וּנְחֵנִי בְּדֶרֶךְ עוֹלָם׃	and lead me in the way of eternity.

פרק קמ Chapter 140

Weekly Cycle	Monthly Cycle	Book Number
Saturday	29th day of the month	Book 5

Author

דָּוִד הַמֶּלֶךְ—King David—the second king of Israel and father of the Davidic royal and messianic dynasty. David composed over seventy of the 150 psalms of Sefer Tehillim.

When & Why

David wrote this psalm when Doeg the Edomite and the people of Zif pretended to ally with him, but then betrayed him to Saul.

Genre

Psalm of Individual Lament - This psalm was written from the perspective of the individual worshipper, who cries out to God in his time of need. It is characterized as an address to God involving a complaint, followed by a request and ending with an expression of trust.

Chapter Summary

King David entreats God to rescue him from his evil pursuers and to exact vengeance upon them for His sake. This psalm is viewed by some as an allusion to the afflictions of the Jewish people in exile.

This psalm consists of fourteen verses, subdivided into two parts. The first verse serves as a heading.

In verses 2-9, King David prays for deliverance from the evil designs of the wicked.

In verses 10-14, He contrasts the fate of the wicked with the fate of the righteous. The wicked will face destruction, he boldly declares, and the righteous will be rewarded with salvation.

Introductory Words

לַמְנַצֵּחַ—Lamnatsei'ach—To the Conductor

מִזְמוֹר—Mizmor—Musical Accompaniment

Technical Terminology

סֶלָה—Selah—While its meaning is unclear, the most familiar opinion is that it is a musical notation, instructing the Levitical orchestra to pause its singing and playing of instruments. Alternatively, "Selah" may mean "everlasting".

Shimush Tehillim - When to Say

To remove hatred between husband and wife—Verse 9 states: "Grant not, Adonoy, the desires of the wicked; let not his aspiration succeed so that they exalt themselves."

פֶּרֶק קמ

Chapter 140

א לַמְנַצֵּחַ
מִזְמוֹר לְדָוִד׃

1 To the Chief Musician,
a Psalm of David.

ב חַלְּצֵנִי יְהוָה מֵאָדָם רָע
מֵאִישׁ חֲמָסִים תִּנְצְרֵנִי׃

2 Free me, Adonoy, from the evil man,
from the violent man preserve me.

ג אֲשֶׁר חָשְׁבוּ רָעוֹת בְּלֵב
כָּל־יוֹם יָגוּרוּ מִלְחָמוֹת׃

3 Who devised evil things in [their] heart,
every day they gather together for wars.

ד שָׁנְנוּ לְשׁוֹנָם
כְּמוֹ־נָחָשׁ
חֲמַת עַכְשׁוּב תַּחַת שְׂפָתֵימוֹ
סֶלָה׃

4 They have sharpened their tongue
like a serpent,
viper's venom is under their lips,
Selah.

ה שָׁמְרֵנִי יְהוָה ׀
מִידֵי רָשָׁע
מֵאִישׁ חֲמָסִים תִּנְצְרֵנִי
אֲשֶׁר חָשְׁבוּ לִדְחוֹת פְּעָמָי׃

5 Guard me, Adonoy,
from the hands of the wicked,
from the violent man preserve me,
who have conspired to divert my steps.

ו טָמְנוּ־גֵאִים ׀ פַּח לִי
וַחֲבָלִים
פָּרְשׂוּ רֶשֶׁת לְיַד־מַעְגָּל
מֹקְשִׁים שָׁתוּ־לִי סֶלָה׃

6 The proud have hidden a snare for me,
and with cords
they have spread a net by the wayside,
traps they have set for me, Selah.

ז אָמַרְתִּי לַיהוָה אֵלִי אָתָּה
הַאֲזִינָה יהוה
קוֹל תַּחֲנוּנָי׃

7 I have said to Adonoy, "You are my God,"
give ear, Adonoy,
to the voice of my supplications.

ח יֱהוִה אֲדֹנָי
עֹז יְשׁוּעָתִי
סַכֹּתָה לְרֹאשִׁי
בְּיוֹם נָשֶׁק׃

8 God, my Master,
the strength of my deliverance,
You have protected my head
in the day of battle.

ט אַל־תִּתֵּן יְהוָה
מַאֲוַיֵּי רָשָׁע
זְמָמוֹ אַל־תָּפֵק
יָרוּמוּ סֶלָה׃

9 Grant not, Adonoy,
the desires of the wicked;
let not his aspiration succeed
so that they exalt themselves, Selah.

י רֹאשׁ מְסִבָּי
עֲמַל שְׂפָתֵימוֹ יְכַסֵּמוֹ׃

10 [As for] the head of those who surround me,
let the mischief of their own lips cover them.

יא יִמּוֹטוּ עֲלֵיהֶם גֶּחָלִים
בָּאֵשׁ יַפִּלֵם
בְּמַהֲמֹרוֹת בַּל־יָקוּמוּ׃

11 Let burning coals settle on them,
let them be cast into the fire,
into conflicts from which they cannot rise.

יב אִישׁ לָשׁוֹן
בַּל־יִכּוֹן בָּאָרֶץ
אִישׁ־חָמָס רָע

12 A slanderer
will not be established in the earth;
an evil man of violence

יְצוּדֶנּוּ לְמַדְחֵפֹת׃	will be trapped by his own evil in the pits.
יג יָדַעְתִּי כִּי־יַעֲשֶׂה יְהוָה	13 I know that Adonoy will perform
דִּין עָנִי	judgment for the poor,
מִשְׁפַּט אֶבְיֹנִים׃	the justice of the needy.
יד אַךְ צַדִּיקִים	14 Surely the righteous
יוֹדוּ לִשְׁמֶךָ	will give thanks to Your Name;
יֵשְׁבוּ יְשָׁרִים אֶת־פָּנֶיךָ׃	the upright will dwell in Your Presence.

פרק קמא Chapter 141

Weekly Cycle	Monthly Cycle	Book Number
Saturday	29th day of the month	Book 5

Author

דָּוִד הַמֶּלֶךְ—King David—the second king of Israel and father of the Davidic royal and messianic dynasty. David composed over seventy of the 150 psalms of Sefer Tehillim.

When & Why

David wrote this psalm when he went to Philistia to escape Saul. In it, he prays that he should not be tempted to adopt the beliefs and practices of the Philistines.

Genre

Psalm of Individual Lament - This psalm was written from the perspective of the individual worshipper, who cries out to God in his time of need. It is characterized as an address to God involving a complaint, followed by a request and ending with an expression of trust.

Chapter Summary

King David asks of God to safeguard him from sinning with his tongue. Let him not be like the man of evil speech, of whom he spoke in the previous psalm, the Psalmist prays; nor let him sin in thought and by deed.

This psalm consists of ten verses, subdivided into three parts.
In verses 1 & 2, King David requests of God that his prayer be accepted.
In verses 3-7, he asks God to protect him from the temptations to join the wicked and act accordingly.
In verses 8-10, he further petitions the Almighty to save him from falling into the traps set by the wicked.

Introductory Words

לַמְנַצֵּחַ —Lamnatsei'ach—To the Conductor
מִזְמוֹר—Mizmor—Musical Accompaniment

Shimush Tehillim - When to Say

To heal one's heart—verse 4 states: "Let my heart not turn to anything evil, to occupy itself in deeds of wickedness."

	פרק קמא		Chapter 141
א	מִזְמוֹר לְדָוִד	1	A Psalm of David.
	יְהוָה קְרָאתִיךָ		Adonoy, I have called out to You,
	חוּשָׁה לִּי		hurry to my help;
	הַאֲזִינָה קוֹלִי בְּקָרְאִי־לָךְ׃		give ear to my voice when I call out to You.
ב	תִּכּוֹן תְּפִלָּתִי	2	Let my prayer
	קְטֹרֶת לְפָנֶיךָ		be as the incense offering before You,
	מַשְׂאַת כַּפַּי		[and let] the lifting up of my hands
	מִנְחַת־עָרֶב׃		[be] as the evening offering.
ג	שִׁיתָה יְהוָה שָׁמְרָה לְפִי	3	Adonoy, set a guard to my mouth,
	נִצְּרָה עַל־דַּל שְׂפָתָי׃		keep watch over the doors of my lips.
ד	אַל־תַּט־לִבִּי לְדָבָר ׀ רָע	4	Let my heart not turn to anything evil,
	לְהִתְעוֹלֵל עֲלִלוֹת ׀ בְּרֶשַׁע		to occupy itself in deeds of wickedness
	אֶת־אִישִׁים פֹּעֲלֵי־אָוֶן		with men who work iniquity;
	וּבַל־אֶלְחַם		and let me not partake of food
	בְּמַנְעַמֵּיהֶם׃		in their feasts of pleasure.
ה	יֶהֶלְמֵנִי־צַדִּיק ׀ חֶסֶד	5	Let the righteous smite me in kindness,
	וְיוֹכִיחֵנִי		and let him correct me;
	שֶׁמֶן רֹאשׁ		as oil that annoints the head,
	אַל־יָנִי רֹאשִׁי		let not my head refuse it,
	כִּי־עוֹד וּתְפִלָּתִי		but my only prayer is
	בְּרָעוֹתֵיהֶם׃		[against involvement in] their evil doings.
ו	נִשְׁמְטוּ בִידֵי־סֶלַע	6	[When they are] cast onto the rocks
	שֹׁפְטֵיהֶם		[by] their judges
	וְשָׁמְעוּ אֲמָרַי		they will hear my words
	כִּי נָעֵמוּ׃		[and understand] how pleasing they are.
ז	כְּמוֹ פֹלֵחַ וּבֹקֵעַ בָּאָרֶץ	7	As one who loosens and breaks up the earth,
	נִפְזְרוּ עֲצָמֵינוּ		are our bones scattered
	לְפִי שְׁאוֹל׃		at the mouth of the grave.
ח	כִּי אֵלֶיךָ ׀ יְהוִה אֲדֹנָי	8	For to You, God, my Master,
	עֵינָי		are my eyes [lifted];
	בְּכָה חָסִיתִי		in You have I taken refuge,
	אַל־תְּעַר נַפְשִׁי׃		pour not out my soul.
ט	שָׁמְרֵנִי מִידֵי פַח	9	Preserve me from the snare

יָקְשׁוּ לִי		which they have laid for me,
וּמֹקְשׁוֹת פֹּעֲלֵי אָוֶן:		and from the traps of the workers of iniquity.
יִפְּלוּ בְמַכְמֹרָיו רְשָׁעִים	10	Let the wicked fall into their own nets
יַחַד		together,
אָנֹכִי עַד־אֶעֱבוֹר:		until I pass over.

פרק קמב Chapter 142

Weekly Cycle	Monthly Cycle	Book Number
Saturday	29th day of the month	Book 5

Author

דָּוִד הַמֶּלֶךְ—King David—the second king of Israel and father of the Davidic royal and messianic dynasty. David composed over seventy of the 150 psalms of Sefer Tehillim.

When & Why

David wrote this psalm when Saul and his men were chasing after him. In order to avoid being captured, David hid himself, crouching in a cave. Saul entered into this same cave. While Saul stood there David thought to cut the corner of Saul's royal robe so that if he would ever be captured, David would avoid execution by showing Saul the missing piece of the robe. The swatch of cloth would be proof that David had the opportunity to kill Saul but spared him. So too, "measure for measure", Saul should spare David's life.

Genre

Psalm of Individual Lament - This psalm was written from the perspective of the individual worshipper, who cries out to God in his time of need. It is characterized as an address to God involving a complaint, followed by a request and ending with an expression of trust.

Chapter Summary

King David composed this psalm when hiding from Saul in a cave, at which time he offered a prayer to God to bring him out of the cave safely. This incident imparted to David the notion, which he often returns to throughout the book of Psalms, that one need never despair of Divine Compassion.

This psalm consists of eight verses, subdivided into three sections. Verse 1 serves as a heading.
In verses 2 & 3, King David cries out to God.
In verses 4 & 5, he describes his troubles.
In verses 6-8, he pleads for deliverance.

Introductory Words

תְּפִלָּה—Tefilah—Prayer

Technical Terminology

מַשְׂכִּיל—Maskil—a discerning person; alternatively, a giver of instruction, perhaps denoting a translator of the chapter (Rashi).

Shimush Tehillim - When to Say

To heal one's legs—Verse 4 states: "When around me, enwraps itself my spirit and You know my path; in the path in which I walk they have hidden a trap for me."
In times of distress—Verse 3 states:" I pour out before Him my prayerful meditation, my distress, before Him, I declare."

Biblical Places

מְעָרָה—Cave—a reference to the cave in which David hid from King Saul. Saul wanted to murder David, as he was paranoid that David would try to overthrow him.

פרק קמב			Chapter 142
מַשְׂכִּיל לְדָוִד	א	1	An instruction of David,
בִּהְיוֹתוֹ בַמְּעָרָה תְפִלָּה׃			when he was in the cave, a Prayer.
קוֹלִי אֶל־יְהוָה אֶזְעָק	ב	2	With my voice I cry out to Adonoy;
קוֹלִי אֶל־יְהוָה אֶתְחַנָּן׃			with my voice I supplicate to Adonoy.
אֶשְׁפֹּךְ לְפָנָיו	ג	3	I pour out before Him
שִׂיחִי			my prayerful meditation,
צָרָתִי לְפָנָיו אַגִּיד׃			my distress, before Him, I declare.
בְּהִתְעַטֵּף עָלַי |	ד	4	When around me, enwraps itself
רוּחִי			my spirit
וְאַתָּה יָדַעְתָּ נְתִיבָתִי			and You know my path;
בְּאֹרַח־זוּ אֲהַלֵּךְ			in the path in which I walk
טָמְנוּ פַח לִי׃			they have hidden a trap for me.
הַבֵּיט יָמִין | וּרְאֵה	ה	5	Look to the right and see,
וְאֵין־לִי מַכִּיר			that no one recognizes me;
אָבַד מָנוֹס מִמֶּנִּי			refuge is lost for me,
אֵין דּוֹרֵשׁ לְנַפְשִׁי׃			no one cares for my soul.
זָעַקְתִּי אֵלֶיךָ יְהוָה	ו	6	I have cried out to You, Adonoy;
אָמַרְתִּי אַתָּה מַחְסִי			I have said, "You are my refuge,
חֶלְקִי בְּאֶרֶץ הַחַיִּים׃			my portion in the land of the living."
הַקְשִׁיבָה | אֶל־רִנָּתִי	ז	7	Listen to my cry
כִּי־דַלּוֹתִי מְאֹד			for I have been brought very low,
הַצִּילֵנִי מֵרֹדְפַי			rescue me from my pursuers
כִּי אָמְצוּ מִמֶּנִּי׃			for they are mightier than me.
הוֹצִיאָה מִמַּסְגֵּר | נַפְשִׁי	ח	8	Bring my soul out of prison,
לְהוֹדוֹת אֶת־שְׁמֶךָ			that I may give thanks to Your Name;
בִּי יַכְתִּרוּ צַדִּיקִים			because of me the righteous will crown [You],
כִּי תִגְמֹל עָלָי׃			when You will have dealt kindly with me.

let me know the way in which I should walk,
for to You have I lifted my soul.

פרק קמג Chapter 143

Weekly Cycle	Monthly Cycle	Book Number
Saturday	29th day of the month	Book 5

Author
דָּוִד הַמֶּלֶךְ—King David—the second king of Israel and father of the Davidic royal and messianic dynasty. David composed over seventy of the 150 psalms of Sefer Tehillim.

When & Why
David wrote this psalm as a prayer that he be saved from his enemies.

Genre
Psalm of Individual Lament - This psalm was written from the perspective of the individual worshipper, who cries out to God in his time of need. It is characterized as an address to God involving a complaint, followed by a request and ending with an expression of trust.

Chapter Summary
Speaking on behalf of himself and the Jewish people, King David now asks that God answer our prayers simply in response to our desire to be upright, even if we do not have sufficient merit. If not for our human frailty and laxity, we would serve God perfectly.

This psalm consists of twelve verses, subdivided into two parts.
In verses 1-6, King David cries out to God in distress, and asks Him to respond.
In verses 7-12, he prays for personal salvation and the demise of his enemies. He further entreaties the Almighty on behalf of the entire Jewish people.

Introductory Words
מִזְמוֹר—Mizmor—Musical Accompaniment

Technical Terminology
סֶלָה—Selah—While its meaning is unclear, the most familiar opinion is that it is a musical notation, instructing the Levitical orchestra to pause its singing and playing of instruments. Alternatively, "Selah" may mean "everlasting".

Shimush Tehillim - When to Say
For healing of the upper arm—Verse 6 states: "I spread out my hands to You, my soul, as an arid land yearns for You."

Where in the Siddur
Verse 2 is found in the repetition of the Musaf Amidah (Silent Meditation) of Rosh HaShanah.

פֶּרֶק קמ״ג			**Chapter 143**
מִזְמוֹר לְדָוִד	א	1	A Psalm of David.
יְהוָה ׀ שְׁמַע תְּפִלָּתִי			Adonoy, hear my prayer,
הַאֲזִינָה אֶל־תַּחֲנוּנַי			give ear to my supplications;
בֶּאֱמֻנָתְךָ			[show me] Your faithfulness
עֲנֵנִי בְּצִדְקָתֶךָ׃			answer me with Your righteousness.
וְאַל־תָּבוֹא בְמִשְׁפָּט	ב	2	And enter not into judgment
אֶת־עַבְדֶּךָ			with Your servant,
כִּי לֹא־יִצְדַּק לְפָנֶיךָ כָל־חָי׃			for no living soul will be justified before You.
כִּי רָדַף אוֹיֵב ׀ נַפְשִׁי	ג	3	For the enemy has pursued my soul,
דִּכָּא לָאָרֶץ חַיָּתִי			he has crushed my life to the ground;
הוֹשִׁיבַנִי בְמַחֲשַׁכִּים			he has made me dwell in dark places
כְּמֵתֵי עוֹלָם׃			as those who are dead forever.
וַתִּתְעַטֵּף עָלַי רוּחִי	ד	4	A faintness is upon my soul,
בְּתוֹכִי יִשְׁתּוֹמֵם לִבִּי׃			within me my heart is appalled.
זָכַרְתִּי יָמִים ׀ מִקֶּדֶם	ה	5	I remembered the days of old,
הָגִיתִי בְכָל־פָּעֳלֶךָ			I meditated on all Your doings,
בְּמַעֲשֵׂה יָדֶיךָ אֲשׂוֹחֵחַ׃			of the work of Your hands I speak.
פֵּרַשְׂתִּי יָדַי אֵלֶיךָ	ו	6	I spread out my hands to You,
נַפְשִׁי ׀ כְּאֶרֶץ־עֲיֵפָה			my soul, as an arid land
לְךָ סֶלָה׃			yearns for You, Selah.
מַהֵר עֲנֵנִי ׀ יְהוָה	ז	7	Speedily answer me, Adonoy,
כָּלְתָה רוּחִי			my spirit is stymied;
אַל־תַּסְתֵּר פָּנֶיךָ מִמֶּנִּי			hide not Your face from me,
וְנִמְשַׁלְתִּי			for then I would be
עִם־יֹרְדֵי בוֹר׃			as those who go down into the pit.
הַשְׁמִיעֵנִי בַבֹּקֶר ׀ חַסְדֶּךָ	ח	8	Let me hear Your kindness in the morning,
כִּי־בְךָ בָטָחְתִּי			for in You have I trusted;
הוֹדִיעֵנִי דֶּרֶךְ־זוּ אֵלֵךְ			let me know the way in which I should walk,
כִּי־אֵלֶיךָ נָשָׂאתִי נַפְשִׁי׃			for to You have I lifted my soul.
הַצִּילֵנִי מֵאֹיְבַי ׀ יְהוָה	ט	9	Rescue me from my enemies, Adonoy,
אֵלֶיךָ			to You [do I tell my troubles that]
כִסִּתִי׃			I have hidden [from others].
לַמְּדֵנִי ׀ לַעֲשׂוֹת רְצוֹנֶךָ	י	10	Teach me to do Your will,
כִּי־אַתָּה אֱלוֹהָי			for You are my God;
רוּחֲךָ טוֹבָה			let Your good spirit
תַּנְחֵנִי בְּאֶרֶץ מִישׁוֹר׃			lead me in a land of uprightness.
לְמַעַן־שִׁמְךָ יְהוָה	יא	11	For the sake of Your Name, Adonoy,
תְּחַיֵּנִי			revive me;

בְּצִדְקָתְךָ |		in Your righteousness
תּוֹצִיא מִצָּרָה נַפְשִׁי:		bring my soul out of distress.
וּבְחַסְדְּךָ תַּצְמִית אֹיְבָי	יב / 12	And in Your kindness cut off my enemies,
וְהַאֲבַדְתָּ כָּל־צֹרְרֵי נַפְשִׁי		and destroy all the oppressors of my soul,
כִּי אֲנִי עַבְדֶּךָ:		for I am Your servant.

פרק קמד Chapter 144

Weekly Cycle	Monthly Cycle	Book Number
Saturday	29th day of the month	Book 5

Author
דָּוִד הַמֶּלֶךְ—King David—the second king of Israel and father of the Davidic royal and messianic dynasty. David composed over seventy of the 150 psalms of Sefer Tehillim.

When & Why
David wrote this psalm after defeating all of his enemies in battle and when the people of Israel were finally living in peace.

Genre
Psalm of Royalty - This psalm describes how God reigns supreme. It focuses on the human king of Israel, or upon God as King of Israel.

Musical Instruments
נֵבֶל עָשׂוֹר—Nevel Asor—A Ten Stringed Handheld Lyre

Chapter Summary
King David now expresses his gratitude to God for having given him the strength to wage war against his enemies. He specifically mentions his battle against Goliath, and thanks Him for helping him emerge victorious.

This psalm consists of fifteen verses, subdivided into two parts.
In verses 1-11, King David prays to the Almighty to rescue him from his enemies, and further blesses God for granting him victory and proctecting him.
In verses 12-15, he describes the future blessings of peace and plenty to be enjoyed after the defeat of one's pursuers.

Introductory Word
בָּרוּךְ—Baruch—Blessed

Shimush Tehillim - When to Say

For a broken hand—Verse 11 states: "Deliver me and rescue me from the hand of strangers."

For protection against damaging forces and demons—Verse 11 continues: "Whose mouth speaks deceit, whose right hand is a right hand of falsehood."

Where in the Siddur

Recited in some congregations just prior to Ma'ariv (nighttime service) of Motza'ei Shabbat (Saturday night).

Verses 3 & 4 are found in the introductory verses of the Yizkor memorial service.

Verse 15 comprises one of the verses of Ashrei.

Verse 15 is also found in Hoshia et Amecha of Pesukei Dezimra (introductory Verses of Praise to the Shacharit morning service).

Talmud on Tehillim

Verse 12: "אֲשֶׁר בָּנֵינוּ, כִּנְטִעִים... בְּנוֹתֵינוּ כְזָוִיֹּת"—"So that our sons are [pure] as plants...our daughters are as cornerpillars."

The Talmud Pesachim 87a, explains that: "So that our sons are [pure] as plants" refers to young Jewish men who have not sinned; "Our daughters are as cornerpillars", continues the Talmud, refers to the purity and conduct of Jewish women. Women, asserts the Talmud, are the cornerstone of the Jewish family and home.

King Hezekiah's Seal

פרק קמד			**Chapter 144**
לְדָוִד ׀ בָּרוּךְ יְהוָה ׀ צוּרִי הַמְלַמֵּד יָדַי לַקְרָב אֶצְבְּעוֹתַי לַמִּלְחָמָה:	א	1	A Psalm of David. Blessed is Adonoy, my Rock, Who trains my hands for battle, my fingers for war.
חַסְדִּי וּמְצוּדָתִי מִשְׂגַּבִּי וּמְפַלְטִי לִי מָגִנִּי וּבוֹ חָסִיתִי הָרוֹדֵד עַמִּי תַחְתָּי:	ב	2	My Kindness and my Fortress, my Stronghold and my Rescuer, my Shield and in Whom I take refuge, Who subdues my people under me.
יְהוָה מָה־אָדָם וַתֵּדָעֵהוּ בֶּן־אֱנוֹשׁ וַתְּחַשְּׁבֵהוּ:	ג	3	Adonoy, what is man that You acknowledge him, or the son of man that You are mindful of him?

ד אָדָם לַהֶבֶל דָּמָה
יָמָיו כְּצֵל עוֹבֵר:

4 Man is compared to a breath,
his days are as a shadow that passes over.

ה יְהוָה הַט־שָׁמֶיךָ וְתֵרֵד
גַּע בֶּהָרִים
וְיֶעֱשָׁנוּ:

5 Adonoy, bend Your heavens and descend;
touch the mountains
and they will vanish like smoke.

ו בְּרוֹק בָּרָק וּתְפִיצֵם
שְׁלַח חִצֶּיךָ וּתְהֻמֵּם:

6 Cast forth lightning and scatter them,
send out Your arrows and confound them.

ז שְׁלַח יָדֶיךָ מִמָּרוֹם
פְּצֵנִי וְהַצִּילֵנִי מִמַּיִם רַבִּים
מִיַּד בְּנֵי נֵכָר:

7 Stretch forth Your hands from on high;
deliver and rescue me from powerful waters,
from the hand of strangers.

ח אֲשֶׁר פִּיהֶם דִּבֶּר־שָׁוְא
וִימִינָם יְמִין שָׁקֶר:

8 Whose mouth speaks deceit,
and their right hand is a right hand of falsehood.

ט אֱלֹהִים
שִׁיר חָדָשׁ אָשִׁירָה לָּךְ
בְּנֵבֶל עָשׂוֹר
אֲזַמְּרָה־לָּךְ:

9 God,
a new song I will sing to You,
upon a lyre of ten strings
will I sing praises to You.

י הַנּוֹתֵן תְּשׁוּעָה לַמְּלָכִים
הַפּוֹצֶה אֶת־דָּוִד עַבְדּוֹ
מֵחֶרֶב רָעָה:

10 He Who gives deliverance to kings,
He Who delivers David, His servant,
from the evil sword.

יא פְּצֵנִי וְהַצִּילֵנִי
מִיַּד בְּנֵי־נֵכָר
אֲשֶׁר פִּיהֶם דִּבֶּר־שָׁוְא
וִימִינָם יְמִין שָׁקֶר:

11 Deliver me and rescue me
from the hand of strangers,
Whose mouth speaks deceit,
whose right hand is a right hand of falsehood.

יב אֲשֶׁר בָּנֵינוּ | כִּנְטִעִים
מְגֻדָּלִים בִּנְעוּרֵיהֶם
בְּנוֹתֵינוּ כְזָוִיֹּת
מְחֻטָּבוֹת תַּבְנִית הֵיכָל:

12 So that our sons are [pure] as plants,
grown up in their youth;
our daughters are as cornerpillars,
lauded as the edifice of a palace.

יג מְזָוֵינוּ מְלֵאִים
מְפִיקִים מִזַּן אֶל־זַן
צֹאונֵנוּ מַאֲלִיפוֹת
מְרֻבָּבוֹת בְּחוּצוֹתֵינוּ

13 Our garners are full,
providing nourishment from harvest to harvest,
our sheep increase by the thousands
and ten thousands in our fields.

יד אַלּוּפֵינוּ מְסֻבָּלִים
אֵין־פֶּרֶץ וְאֵין יוֹצֵאת
וְאֵין צְוָחָה בִּרְחֹבֹתֵינוּ:

14 Our leaders are tolerated,
with no breach and no bad tidings,
and no outcry in our streets.

טו אַשְׁרֵי הָעָם
שֶׁכָּכָה לּוֹ
אַשְׁרֵי הָעָם
שֶׁיְהוָה אֱלֹהָיו:

15 Fortunate is the people
whose lot is thus;
Fortunate is the people
for whom Adonoy is their God.

פרק קמה Chapter 145

Weekly Cycle	Monthly Cycle	Book Number
Saturday	30th day of the month	Book 5

Author

דָּוִד הַמֶּלֶךְ—King David—the second king of Israel and father of the Davidic royal and messianic dynasty. David composed over seventy of the 150 psalms of Sefer Tehillim.

Genre

Psalm of Praise – This is a psalm of celebration, often the result of a victory. It declares God's goodness and urges all of creation to worship.

Acrostic - A literary composition in which the writer has used the letters of the Hebrew alphabet in their order as the initial letters for a sequence of verses. i.e. א.ב.ג.ד

Chapter Summary

In this psalm, which comprises most of the famous prayer Ashrei, King David proclaims and highlights God's kindnesses and compassion, as well as His constant overseeing of, and involvement in, nature. Written in acrostic form (with the exception of a verse beginning with the letter nun), it contains only pure, unadulterated praise to the Almighty, thus serving as a fitting opening to the final unit of Songs of Praise of David's magnum opus.

This psalm consists of twenty-one verses, subdivided into four parts. It is the first of the final collection of Songs of Praise.

In verses 1-7, King David proclaims God's greatness, boldly declaring that his praise joins with the praises of God that have been and will be spoken in every generation.

In verses 8-14, he describes the glory of the kingdom of God.

In verses 15-20, the Psalmist proclaims that God is close to all who cry out to Him, providing for all of their needs.

In verse 21, he comes full circle and declares that he, and indeed all flesh, will continue to praise and bless the Almighty.

Introductory word

תְּהִלָּה—Tehilah—Praise

Shimush Tehillim - When to Say

To overcome fear—Verse 19 states: "The will of those who fear Him He fulfills; He hears their cry and delivers them."

Where in the Siddur

Recited as the bulk of Ashrei, a prayer recited three times daily—in Pesukei Dezimra (Verses of Praise introducing the Shacharit morning service); as one of the concluding prayers of Shacharit (morning service); and as the opening prayer of Minchah (afternoon service). In its appearance in

Pesukei Dezimra, it is recited together as a unit of Psalms 145-150, viewed as a daily recitation of Hallel (Praise Service).
Verse 13 is found in the repetition of the Musaf Amidah (Silent Meditation) of Rosh HaShanah.
Verse 16 is found in the final paragraph of Birkat HaMazon (Grace after Meals).
Verse 16 is recited after securing the head Tefillin (phylacteries) in place.
Verse 21 is recited by some following Psalm 126 (Shir HaMa'alot) preceding Birkat HaMazon.

Talmud on Tehillim

Verse 1: "תְּהִלָּה, לְדָוִד"—"A praise by David!"
The Talmud, Berachot 4b, states that one who says this verse three times daily is guaranteed to merit a place in the World to Come.
Verse 15: "עֵינֵי כֹל, אֵלֶיךָ יְשַׂבֵּרוּ, וְאַתָּה נוֹתֵן לָהֶם אֶת אָכְלָם בְּעִתּוֹ"—"The eyes of all look to You expectantly, and You give them their food in its proper time."
The Talmud, Ketubot 67b, noting that the verse states "in its (his) time" and not "in their time", deduces that God provides for every individual based upon his specific needs.
Verse 17: "צַדִּיק יְהוָה בְּכָל דְּרָכָיו, וְחָסִיד בְּכָל מַעֲשָׂיו"—"Adonoy is just in all His ways and benevolent in all His deeds."
The Talmud, Rosh HaShanah 17b, infers that the term "Tzaddik" ("righteous") ascribes to God the attribute of passing true judgment; the term "Chasid" ("faithful"), the attribute of God's mercy. The Talmud further explains that God as Chasid prevails over God as Tzaddik, for man cannot measure up to the demands of strict justice. Indeed, the Almighty judges and interacts with his creatures with kindness and compassion.

פֶּרֶק קמה

א תְּהִלָּה לְדָוִד
אֲרוֹמִמְךָ אֱלוֹהַי הַמֶּלֶךְ
וַאֲבָרְכָה שִׁמְךָ לְעוֹלָם וָעֶד:
ב בְּכָל־יוֹם אֲבָרְכֶךָּ
וַאֲהַלְלָה שִׁמְךָ לְעוֹלָם וָעֶד:
ג גָּדוֹל יְהוָה וּמְהֻלָּל מְאֹד
וְלִגְדֻלָּתוֹ אֵין חֵקֶר:
ד דּוֹר לְדוֹר
יְשַׁבַּח מַעֲשֶׂיךָ
וּגְבוּרֹתֶיךָ יַגִּידוּ:
ה הֲדַר כְּבוֹד הוֹדֶךָ
וְדִבְרֵי נִפְלְאוֹתֶיךָ אָשִׂיחָה:

Chapter 145

1 A praise by David!
I will exalt You, my God, the King,
and bless Your Name forever and ever.
2 Every day I will bless You
and extol Your Name forever and ever.
3 Adonoy is great and highly extolled,
and His greatness is unfathomable.
4 One generation to another
will praise Your works
and Your mighty acts they will declare.
5 The splendor of Your glorious majesty,
and the words of Your wonders I will speak.

ו וֶעֱזוּז נוֹרְאֹתֶיךָ יֹאמֵרוּ
וּגְדוּלָּתְךָ אֲסַפְּרֶנָּה׃

6 Of Your awesome might, they will speak
and Your greatness I will recount.

ז זֵכֶר רַב־טוּבְךָ
יַבִּיעוּ
וְצִדְקָתְךָ יְרַנֵּנוּ׃

7 Mention of Your bountifulness
they will express,
and in Your righteousness joyfully exult.

ח חַנּוּן וְרַחוּם יְהוָה
אֶרֶךְ אַפַּיִם וּגְדָל־חָסֶד׃

8 Adonoy is gracious and merciful,
slow to anger and great in kindliness.

ט טוֹב־יְהוָה לַכֹּל
וְרַחֲמָיו עַל־כָּל־מַעֲשָׂיו׃

9 Adonoy is good to all,
His mercy encompasses all His works.

י יוֹדוּךָ יְהוָה כָּל־מַעֲשֶׂיךָ
וַחֲסִידֶיךָ יְבָרְכוּכָה׃

10 All Your works will thank You, Adonoy,
and Your pious ones will bless You.

יא כְּבוֹד מַלְכוּתְךָ
יֹאמֵרוּ
וּגְבוּרָתְךָ יְדַבֵּרוּ׃

11 Of the honor of Your kingship,
they will speak
and Your might they will declare.

יב לְהוֹדִיעַ ׀ לִבְנֵי הָאָדָם
גְּבוּרֹתָיו
וּכְבוֹד הֲדַר מַלְכוּתוֹ׃

12 To reveal to men
His mighty acts,
and the glorious splendor of His kingship.

יג מַלְכוּתְךָ מַלְכוּת כָּל־עֹלָמִים
וּמֶמְשַׁלְתְּךָ בְּכָל־דּוֹר וָדֹר׃

13 Your kingship is the kingship for all times,
and Your dominion is in every generation.

יד סוֹמֵךְ יְהוָה לְכָל־הַנֹּפְלִים
וְזוֹקֵף לְכָל־הַכְּפוּפִים׃

14 Adonoy supports all the fallen,
and straightens all the bent.

טו עֵינֵי־כֹל אֵלֶיךָ יְשַׂבֵּרוּ
וְאַתָּה נוֹתֵן־לָהֶם
אֶת־אָכְלָם בְּעִתּוֹ׃

15 The eyes of all look expectantly to You,
and You give them
their food at its proper time.

טז פּוֹתֵחַ אֶת־יָדֶךָ
וּמַשְׂבִּיעַ לְכָל־חַי רָצוֹן׃

16 You open Your hand
and satisfy the desire of every living being.

יז צַדִּיק יְהוָה בְּכָל־דְּרָכָיו
וְחָסִיד בְּכָל־מַעֲשָׂיו׃

17 Adonoy is just in all His ways
and benevolent in all His deeds.

יח קָרוֹב יְהוָה לְכָל־קֹרְאָיו
לְכֹל אֲשֶׁר יִקְרָאֻהוּ בֶאֱמֶת׃

18 Adonoy is near to all who call upon Him,
to all who call upon Him in truth.

יט רְצוֹן־יְרֵאָיו יַעֲשֶׂה
וְאֶת־שַׁוְעָתָם יִשְׁמַע וְיוֹשִׁיעֵם׃

19 The will of those who fear Him He fulfills;
He hears their cry and delivers them.

כ שׁוֹמֵר יְהוָה
אֶת־כָּל־אֹהֲבָיו
וְאֵת כָּל־הָרְשָׁעִים יַשְׁמִיד׃

20 Adonoy watches over
all those who love Him,
and will destroy all the wicked.

כא תְּהִלַּת יְהוָה יְדַבֶּר־פִּי
וִיבָרֵךְ כָּל־בָּשָׂר
שֵׁם קָדְשׁוֹ לְעוֹלָם וָעֶד׃

21 Praise of Adonoy, my mouth will declare
and all flesh will bless
His holy Name forever and ever.

Adonoy is near to all who call upon Him,
to all who call upon Him in truth.

פרק קמו Chapter 146

Weekly Cycle	Monthly Cycle	Book Number
Saturday	30th day of the month	Book 5

Author
Unknown

Genre
Psalm of Praise – This is a psalm of celebration, often the result of a victory. It declares God's goodness and urges all of creation to worship.

Chapter Summary
The psalmist exhorts man to perform good deeds while still in possession of his soul. He further urges the reader not to place his full trust in human beings, who cannot provide ultimate deliverance, but rather in the Lord.

This psalm consists of ten verses, subdivided into two parts. It is the second in the final collection of Songs of Praise.
In verses 1-5, the singer speaks of God's greatness in contrast to the weakness of man. He calls on the congregation to praise God, and proclaims the happiness of the person who puts his trust in Him.
In verses 6-10, he elaborates upon God's praises as the One who delivers the weak and oppressed. He concludes by declaring that God's kingdom in Zion is everlasting.

Introductory Word
הַלְלוּיָ-ה—Halleluyah—Praise God

Shimush Tehillim - When to Say
For recovering from a stabbing—Verse 8 states: "Adonoy gives sight to the blind; Adonoy straightens the bent."

Where in the Siddur
Recited together as a unit of Psalms 145-150, beginning with Ashrei of Pesukei Dezimra (Verses of Praise introducing the Shacharit morning service), viewed as a daily recitation of Hallel (Praise Service).
Verse 8 serves as the basis for three of the blessings—Pokei'ach Ivrim (He gives sight to the blind), Matir Asurim (He unbinds the bound), and Zokeif Kefufim (He straightens the bent)—of Birchot HaShachar (Morning Blessings).
Verse 10 is the final verse of Kedushah (Sanctification Prayer) recited in the repetition of the Amidah (Silent Meditation), as well as the final verse of the third blessing of the High Holidays Amidah.
Verse 10 is part of the prayers recited in Sefardic communities upon returning the Sefer Torah to the Aron HaKodesh (Holy Ark).

Biblical Personalities
יַעֲקֹב—Yaakov—Jacob, also called Yisrael—Israel—the third patriarch, known as the father of the

twelve tribes of Israel. He was married to Rachel and Leah, and was the twin brother of Eisav.

Biblical People

יִשְׂרָאֵל—Yisrael—The Nation of Israel.

Biblical Places

צִיּוֹן—Zion—a place name often used as a synonym for Jerusalem. The term Zion originally referred only to the area where a Jebbusite fortress once stood, also the location of the City of David. Zion was later used by prophets and psalmists as another name for Jerusalem.

פֶּרֶק קמו	Chapter 146
א הַֽלְלוּ־יָ֨הּ הַלְלִ֥י נַ֝פְשִׁ֗י אֶת־יְהֹוָֽה׃	1 Praise God! My soul, praise Adonoy.
ב אֲהַלְלָ֣ה יְהֹוָ֣ה בְּחַיָּ֑י אֲזַמְּרָ֖ה לֵאלֹהַ֣י בְּעוֹדִֽי׃	2 I will praise Adonoy with my life; I will sing to my God as long as I live.
ג אַל־תִּבְטְח֥וּ בִנְדִיבִ֑ים בְּבֶן־אָדָ֓ם ׀ שֶׁ֤אֵ֖ין ל֣וֹ תְשׁוּעָֽה׃	3 Do not place your trust [even] in noble men, in man who has no [power of] deliverance.
ד תֵּצֵ֣א ר֭וּחוֹ יָשֻׁ֣ב לְאַדְמָת֑וֹ בַּיּ֥וֹם הַ֝ה֗וּא אָבְד֥וּ עֶשְׁתֹּנֹתָֽיו׃	4 [When] his spirit departs, he returns to his earth; on that day his plans come to naught.
ה אַשְׁרֵ֗י שֶׁ֤אֵ֣ל יַעֲקֹ֣ב בְּעֶזְר֑וֹ שִׂ֝בְר֗וֹ עַל־יְהֹוָ֥ה אֱלֹהָֽיו׃	5 Fortunate [is he] when the Almighty of Jacob is his help whose expectation is on Adonoy, his God.
ו עֹשֶׂ֤ה ׀ שָׁ֘מַ֤יִם וָאָ֗רֶץ אֶת־הַיָּ֥ם וְאֶת־כָּל־אֲשֶׁר־בָּ֑ם הַשֹּׁמֵ֖ר אֱמֶ֣ת לְעוֹלָֽם׃	6 He makes heaven and earth, the sea and all that is in them; He keeps His promises faithfully forever.
ז עֹשֶׂ֤ה מִשְׁפָּ֨ט ׀ לָעֲשׁוּקִ֗ים נֹתֵ֣ן לֶ֭חֶם לָרְעֵבִ֑ים יְ֝הֹוָ֗ה מַתִּ֥יר אֲסוּרִֽים׃	7 He performs justice for the oppressed; He gives bread to the hungry; Adonoy releases the imprisoned.
ח יְהֹוָ֤ה ׀ פֹּ֘קֵ֤חַ עִוְרִ֗ים יְ֭הֹוָה זֹקֵ֣ף כְּפוּפִ֑ים יְ֝הֹוָ֗ה אֹהֵ֥ב צַדִּיקִֽים׃	8 Adonoy gives sight to the blind; Adonoy straightens the bent. Adonoy loves the righteous.
ט יְהֹוָ֤ה ׀ שֹׁ֘מֵ֤ר אֶת־גֵּרִ֗ים יָת֣וֹם וְאַלְמָנָ֣ה יְעוֹדֵ֑ד וְדֶ֖רֶךְ רְשָׁעִ֣ים יְעַוֵּֽת׃	9 Adonoy protects strangers; the orphan and widow He enables to stand firm; and the way of the wicked He thwarts.
י יִמְלֹ֤ךְ יְהֹוָ֨ה ׀ לְעוֹלָ֗ם אֱלֹהַ֣יִךְ צִ֭יּוֹן לְדֹ֣ר וָדֹ֑ר הַֽלְלוּ־יָֽהּ׃	10 Adonoy will reign forever; your God, Zion, throughout all generations. Praise God.

פרק קמז Chapter 147

Weekly Cycle	Monthly Cycle	Book Number
Saturday	30th day of the month	Book 5

Author
Unknown

When & Why
This psalm was written as a praise to God for redeeming Israel from among the nations and returning them to their homeland.

Genre
Psalm of Praise – This is a psalm of celebration, often the result of a victory. It declares God's goodness and urges all of creation to worship.

Chapter Summary
The singer extols the wondrous works of God in heaven and on earth, as well as His kindness to His creatures. He further exalts the holy city of Jerusalem and speaks of the future ingathering of the exiles.

This psalm consists of twenty verses, subdivided into three parts. It is the third in the final collection of Songs of Praise.
In verses 1-6, the psalmist praises God for His power and righteousness.
In verses 7-11, he praises God for His providence over His creations and His lovingkindness towards all who fear Him.
In verses 12-20, he continues his praise of the Lord as the One who blesses Jerusalem, sends rain in its time, and who gave the precious Torah to Israel.

Introductory Word
הַלְלוּ-יָ-ה—Halleluyah—Praise God

Musical Instruments
כִּנּוֹר—Kinor—A Small Handheld Harp - played with a plecturm (pick)

Shimush Tehillim - When to Say
For a snakebite—Verse 3 states: "[He is] the Healer of the broken hearted and [also] binds up their wounds."

Where in the Siddur
Recited together as a unit of Psalms 145-150, beginning with Ashrei of Pesukei Dezimra (Verses of Praise introducing the Shacharit morning service), viewed as a daily recitation of Hallel (Praise service).

Biblical Personalities
יַעֲקֹב—Yaakov—Jacob, also called Yisrael—Israel—the third patriarch, known as the father of the

twelve tribes of Israel. He was married to Rachel and Leah, and was the twin brother of Eisav.

Biblical People

יִשְׂרָאֵל—Yisrael—The Nation of Israel.

Biblical Places

יְרוּשָׁלַם—Yerushalayim—Jerusalem—the capital city of the kingdom of Israel, conquered by King David 3,000 years ago. David established Jerusalem as both the religious and political center of Israel.

צִיּוֹן—Zion—a place name often used as a synonym for Jerusalem. The term Zion originally referred only to the area where a Jebbusite fortress once stood, also the location of the City of David. Zion was later used by prophets and psalmists as another name for Jerusalem.

Contemporary Song

Verse 12

Talmud on Tehillim

Verse 2: "בּוֹנֵה יְרוּשָׁלַם יְהוָה; נִדְחֵי יִשְׂרָאֵל יְכַנֵּס"—"The builder of Jerusaelm is Adonoy; the banished ones of Israel He will gather."

The Talmud, Berachot 49a, notes that the third blessing of Birkat HaMazon (Grace after Meals) concludes with the words "בּוֹנֵה יְרוּשָׁלַם"—"He builds Jerusalem", as the above verse states that God is the "builder" of Jerusalem. The Talmud further explains that God will rebuild Jerusalem when he gathers in the dispersed of Israel, thereby taking them from galut to geulah, from exile to redemption.

Verse 14:"הַשָּׂם גְּבוּלֵךְ שָׁלוֹם; חֵלֶב חִטִּים, יַשְׂבִּיעֵךְ"—"He established peace at your border; with prime wheat He satisfies you."

The Talmud, Berachot 56a, infers that one who sees wheat in his dream, peace awaits him.

The Talmud, Bava Metzia 49a, further deduces that one should always be careful to have adequate grain in his home, as quarrels in one's home typically relate to grain (finance).

פֶּרֶק קמז

א הַֽלְלוּ יָ֨הּ ׀
כִּי־ט֭וֹב זַמְּרָ֣ה אֱלֹהֵ֑ינוּ
כִּֽי־נָ֝עִ֗ים נָאוָ֥ה תְהִלָּֽה׃
ב בּוֹנֵ֣ה יְרוּשָׁלַ֣ם יְהוָ֑ה
נִדְחֵ֖י יִשְׂרָאֵ֣ל יְכַנֵּֽס׃
ג הָ֭רֹפֵא לִשְׁב֣וּרֵי לֵ֑ב
וּ֝מְחַבֵּ֗שׁ לְעַצְּבוֹתָֽם׃
ד מוֹנֶ֣ה ֭מִסְפָּר לַכּוֹכָבִ֑ים
לְ֝כֻלָּ֗ם שֵׁמ֥וֹת יִקְרָֽא׃
ה גָּד֣וֹל אֲדוֹנֵ֣ינוּ וְרַב־כֹּ֑חַ
לִ֝תְבוּנָת֗וֹ אֵ֣ין מִסְפָּֽר׃

Chapter 147

1 Praise God!
for it is good to sing to our God;
for [His] praise is pleasant, befitting.

2 The builder of Jerusalem is Adonoy;
the banished ones of Israel He will gather.

3 [He is] the Healer of the broken-hearted
and [also] binds up their wounds.

4 He fixes the number of stars;
He calls all of them by names.

5 Great is our Master and abundant in power;
His understanding is beyond reckoning.

ו מְעוֹדֵד עֲנָוִים יְהוָה	6 Adonoy causes the humble to stand firm;
מַשְׁפִּיל רְשָׁעִים עֲדֵי־אָרֶץ׃	He casts down the wicked to the ground.
ז עֱנוּ לַיהוָה בְּתוֹדָה	7 Cry out to Adonoy in thanksgiving;
זַמְּרוּ לֵאלֹהֵינוּ בְכִנּוֹר׃	sing to our God with the harp.
ח הַמְכַסֶּה שָׁמַיִם ׀	8 [The One] Who covers the heavens
בְּעָבִים	with clouds,
הַמֵּכִין לָאָרֶץ מָטָר	Who prepares rain for the earth;
הַמַּצְמִיחַ הָרִים חָצִיר׃	Who causes grass to grow upon the hills.
ט נוֹתֵן לִבְהֵמָה לַחְמָהּ	9 Who gives the animal its fodder;
לִבְנֵי עֹרֵב אֲשֶׁר יִקְרָאוּ׃	[also] to the young ravens which call.
י לֹא בִגְבוּרַת הַסּוּס יֶחְפָּץ	10 Not the power of the horse does He desire,
לֹא־בְשׁוֹקֵי הָאִישׁ יִרְצֶה׃	nor the thighs of man does He want.
יא רוֹצֶה יְהוָה אֶת־יְרֵאָיו	11 Adonoy wants those who fear Him,
אֶת־הַמְיַחֲלִים לְחַסְדּוֹ׃	those who hope for His kindliness.
יב שַׁבְּחִי יְרוּשָׁלַםִ אֶת־יְהוָה	12 Jerusalem, praise Adonoy;
הַלְלִי אֱלֹהַיִךְ צִיּוֹן׃	Zion, extol your God.
יג כִּי־חִזַּק בְּרִיחֵי שְׁעָרָיִךְ	13 For He has fortified the bars of your gates;
בֵּרַךְ בָּנַיִךְ בְּקִרְבֵּךְ׃	He has blessed your children in your midst.
יד הַשָּׂם־גְּבוּלֵךְ שָׁלוֹם	14 He established peace at your border;
חֵלֶב חִטִּים יַשְׂבִּיעֵךְ׃	with prime wheat He satisfies you.
טו הַשֹּׁלֵחַ אִמְרָתוֹ אָרֶץ	15 He dispatches His command earthward;
עַד־מְהֵרָה יָרוּץ דְּבָרוֹ׃	His word races swiftly.
טז הַנֹּתֵן שֶׁלֶג כַּצָּמֶר	16 He provides snow like fleece,
כְּפוֹר כָּאֵפֶר יְפַזֵּר׃	He scatters frost like ashes.
יז מַשְׁלִיךְ קַרְחוֹ כְפִתִּים	17 He hurls His ice like crumbs;
לִפְנֵי קָרָתוֹ מִי יַעֲמֹד׃	who can withstand His cold?
יח יִשְׁלַח דְּבָרוֹ וְיַמְסֵם	18 He dispatches His word and melts them;
יַשֵּׁב רוּחוֹ יִזְּלוּ־מָיִם׃	He blows His wind, they flow as water.
יט מַגִּיד דְּבָרָיו לְיַעֲקֹב	19 He declares His word to Jacob,
חֻקָּיו וּמִשְׁפָּטָיו לְיִשְׂרָאֵל׃	His statutes and His laws to Israel
כ לֹא עָשָׂה כֵן ׀ לְכָל־גּוֹי	20 He did not do so to any [other] nation;
וּמִשְׁפָּטִים בַּל־יְדָעוּם	and of His laws they were not informed.
הַלְלוּ־יָהּ׃	Praise God.

פרק קמח Chapter 148

Weekly Cycle	Monthly Cycle	Book Number
Saturday	30th day of the month	Book 5

Author
Unknown

Genre
Psalm of Praise – This is a psalm of celebration, often the result of a victory. It declares God's goodness and urges all of creation to worship.

Chapter Summary
The psalmist now calls out to all creatures, on high and below, each in accordance with its level and degree of completeness, to offer acclaim and praise to God.

This psalm consists of fourteen verses, subdivided into two parts. It is the fourth in the final collection of Songs of Praise.
In verses 1-6, the singer addresses the heavenly beings, admonishing them to praise God.
In verses 7-14, he specifies twenty-three earthly beings that must also praise the Almighty, thereby encompassing the entire universe.

Introductory Word
הַלְלוּיָ-הּ—Halleluyah—Praise God

Shimush Tehillim - When to Say
For protection from a damaging fire—Verse 8 states: "Fire and hail, snow and vapor, stormwind, [all] fulfilling His word."

Where in the Siddur
Recited together as a unit of Psalms 1465-150, beginning with Ashrei of Pesukei Dezimra (Verses of Praise introducing the Shacharit morning service), viewed as a daily recitation of Hallel (Praise service).
Verses 1-6 are recited as the introduction to Kiddush Levanah (Sanctification of the New Moon service).
Verses 13-14 are recited by the congregation as the Torah scroll is returned to the Aron HaKodesh (Holy Ark).

Biblical People
יִשְׂרָאֵל—Yisrael—The Nation of Israel.

Biblical Cretures
תַּנִּינִים—Taninim—perhaps a reference to sea monsters which God created on the fifth day of creation, as recorded in Sefer Bereishit (Genesis); alternatively, a reference to crocodiles and/or alligators.

Talmud on Tehillim

Verse 3: ''הַלְלוּהוּ, שֶׁמֶשׁ וְיָרֵחַ; הַלְלוּהוּ, כָּל כּוֹכְבֵי אוֹר''—"Praise Him, sun and moon; Praise Him, all the stars of light."

The Talmud, Pesachim 2a, infers that these words are addressing only the stars which continue to provide light. Stars which no longer give light needn't praise Him, as they have already fulfilled their charge.

פֶּרֶק קמח			**Chapter 148**
הַלְלוּ יָהּ	א	1	Praise God.
הַלְלוּ אֶת־יְהוָה מִן־הַשָּׁמַיִם			Praise Adonoy from the sky;
הַלְלוּהוּ בַּמְּרוֹמִים׃			Praise Him in the heights!
הַלְלוּהוּ כָל־מַלְאָכָיו	ב	2	Praise Him, all His angels,
הַלְלוּהוּ כָּל־צְבָאָיו׃			praise Him, all His hosts!
הַלְלוּהוּ שֶׁמֶשׁ וְיָרֵחַ	ג	3	Praise Him, sun and moon;
הַלְלוּהוּ כָּל־כּוֹכְבֵי אוֹר׃			Praise Him, all the stars of light.
הַלְלוּהוּ שְׁמֵי הַשָּׁמָיִם	ד	4	Praise Him, skies of skies,
וְהַמַּיִם אֲשֶׁר | מֵעַל הַשָּׁמָיִם׃			and the waters that are above the skies.
יְהַלְלוּ אֶת־שֵׁם יְהוָה	ה	5	They will praise the Name of Adonoy,
כִּי הוּא צִוָּה וְנִבְרָאוּ׃			for He commanded and they were created.
וַיַּעֲמִידֵם לָעַד	ו	6	He established them for all time,
לְעוֹלָם			for as long as the world exists;
חָק־נָתַן וְלֹא יַעֲבוֹר׃			He decreed it and it is unalterable.
הַלְלוּ אֶת־יְהוָה מִן־הָאָרֶץ	ז	7	Praise Adonoy from the earth
תַּנִּינִים וְכָל־תְּהֹמוֹת׃			sea-monsters and all [that dwell in] the depths.
אֵשׁ וּבָרָד שֶׁלֶג וְקִיטוֹר	ח	8	Fire and hail, snow and vapor,
רוּחַ סְעָרָה עֹשָׂה דְבָרוֹ׃			stormwind, [all] fulfilling His word.
הֶהָרִים וְכָל־גְּבָעוֹת	ט	9	The mountains and all the hills,
עֵץ פְּרִי וְכָל־אֲרָזִים׃			fruit trees and all cedars.
הַחַיָּה וְכָל־בְּהֵמָה	י	10	Wild beasts and all animals,
רֶמֶשׂ וְצִפּוֹר כָּנָף׃			creeping things and winged fowl.
מַלְכֵי־אֶרֶץ וְכָל־לְאֻמִּים	יא	11	Earthly kings and all peoples,
שָׂרִים וְכָל־שֹׁפְטֵי אָרֶץ			ministers and all earthly judges.
בַּחוּרִים וְגַם־בְּתוּלוֹת	יב	12	Young men and also maidens,
זְקֵנִים עִם־נְעָרִים׃			elders together with lads.
יְהַלְלוּ | אֶת־שֵׁם יְהוָה	יג	13	They will praise the Name of Adonoy,
כִּי־נִשְׂגָּב שְׁמוֹ לְבַדּוֹ			for His Name alone is exalted;
הוֹדוֹ עַל־אֶרֶץ וְשָׁמָיִם׃			His majesty is over the earth and the skies.
וַיָּרֶם קֶרֶן | לְעַמּוֹ	יד	14	He will raise the might of His people,

תְּהִלָּה לְכָל־חֲסִידָיו	[which is] praise for all His pious ones,
לִבְנֵי יִשְׂרָאֵל	for the children of Israel,
עַם־קְרֹבוֹ	the people near to Him.
הַלְלוּ־יָהּ׃	Praise God.

פרק קמט Chapter 149

Weekly Cycle	Monthly Cycle	Book Number
Saturday	30th day of the month	Book 5

Author
Unknown; perhaps דָּוִד הַמֶּלֶךְ—King David—the second king of Israel and father of the Davidic royal and messianic dynasty. David composed over seventy of the 150 psalms of Sefer Tehillim.

When & Why
David might have written this psalm which describes the time of the Messiah, when the people of Israel will compose new prayers to sing to God to praise Him for all of the miracles that He performs.

Genre
Psalm of Praise – This is a psalm of celebration, often the result of a victory. It declares God's goodness and urges all of creation to worship.

Chapter Summary
The singer now speaks of the future redemption. At that time, he boldly proclaims, there will be many saintly individuals, and the praise of God will indeed be widespread.

This psalm consists of nine verses, subdivided into two parts. It is the fifth in the final collection of Songs of Praise.

In verses 1-4, the psalmist calls upon the congregation to praise God for delivering His people.

In verses 5-9, he speaks of the joy brought about by the victory of the pious over the foreign nations.

Introductory Word
הַלְלוּיָ-ה—Halleluyah—Praise God

שִׁיר—Shir—Song

Musical Instruments
מָחוֹל—Machol—A reedless wind instrument or possibly a dance.

תֹּף—Tof—Drum - A large, thin drum, made with wood and animal hide, in conjunction with dance, and often played by women. The frame-drum was held with the left hand and played by striking the head of the drum with the alternating thumb and forefingers of the right hand in various rhythmic patterns.

כִּנּוֹר—Kinor—Harp - A generic term for an ancient class of 'gut' string instruments used to accompany the voice or another instrument. Along with the lyre and melodic cymbals, the harp was one of the three primary instruments of song used by the Levites in their musical ensembles.

Shimush Tehillim - When to Say

To prevent a fire from spreading—Verse 8 states: "To bind their kings with chains, and their nobles with iron fetters."

Where in the Siddur

Recited together as a unit of Psalms 145-150, beginning with Ashrei of Pesukei Dezimra (Verses of Praise introducing the Shacharit morning service), viewed as a daily recitation of Hallel (Praise service).

Biblical Places

צִיּוֹן—Zion—a place name often used as a synonym for Jerusalem. The term Zion originally referred only to the area where a Jebbusite fortress once stood, also the location of the City of David. Zion was later used by prophets and psalmists as another name for Jerusalem.

Talmud on Tehillim

Verse 6: "וְחֶרֶב פִּיפִיּוֹת בְּיָדָם"— "and a double-edged sword in their hand."

The Talmud, Berachot 5a, infers that "whoever recites the Shema at his bedside before going to sleep is considered as if he is wielding a double-edged sword in his hand." The recital of the bedtime Shema, then, has the power to protect both one's body from demons and soul from the Yeitzer Hara (evil inclination). It is therefore compared to a double-edged sword.

פרק קמט	Chapter 149
א הַלְלוּ יָהּ |	1 Praise God.
שִׁירוּ לַיהוָה שִׁיר חָדָשׁ	Sing a new song to Adonoy,
תְּהִלָּתוֹ בִּקְהַל חֲסִידִים׃	His praise in the assembly of the pious.
ב יִשְׂמַח יִשְׂרָאֵל בְּעֹשָׂיו	2 Israel will rejoice in its Maker;
בְּנֵי־צִיּוֹן יָגִילוּ בְמַלְכָּם׃	the children of Zion will exult in their King.
ג יְהַלְלוּ שְׁמוֹ בְמָחוֹל	3 They will praise His Name with dance;
בְּתֹף וְכִנּוֹר	with drum and harp
יְזַמְּרוּ־לוֹ׃	they will make music to Him.
ד כִּי־רוֹצֶה יְהוָה בְּעַמּוֹ	4 Because Adonoy desires His people;
יְפָאֵר עֲנָוִים בִּישׁוּעָה׃	He will adorn the humble with deliverance.
ה יַעְלְזוּ חֲסִידִים בְּכָבוֹד	5 The pious will rejoice in honor;
יְרַנְּנוּ עַל־מִשְׁכְּבוֹתָם׃	they will sing joyously upon their beds.

ו רוֹמְמוֹת אֵל בִּגְרוֹנָם וְחֶרֶב פִּיפִיּוֹת בְּיָדָם:	6 High praises of the Almighty in their throats, and a double-edged sword in their hand.
ז לַעֲשׂוֹת נְקָמָה בַּגּוֹיִם תּוֹכֵחֹת בַּל־אֻמִּים:	7 To perform vengeance upon the nations, chastisement upon the peoples.
ח לֶאְסֹר מַלְכֵיהֶם בְּזִקִּים וְנִכְבְּדֵיהֶם בְּכַבְלֵי בַרְזֶל:	8 To bind their kings with chains, and their nobles with iron fetters.
ט לַעֲשׂוֹת בָּהֶם ׀ מִשְׁפָּט כָּתוּב הָדָר הוּא לְכָל־חֲסִידָיו הַלְלוּ־יָהּ:	9 To execute upon them [the] written judgment; it is the splendor of all His pious ones. Praise God.

פרק קנ Chapter 150

Weekly Cycle	Monthly Cycle	Book Number
Saturday	30th day of the month	Book 5

Author
Unknown

Genre
Psalm of Praise – This is a psalm of celebration, often the result of a victory. It declares God's goodness and urges all of creation to worship.

Chapter Summary
This, the final psalm, is one of thanksgiving and praise to God. The psalmist thus begins and concludes with "Halleluyah—Praise the Lord!"

This psalm consists of six verses, subdivided into two parts. It is the sixth and final psalm in the closing unit of Songs of Praise.

In verses 1-5, the psalmist poetically describes ten methods with which to praise the Lord.

In verse 6, he concludes this magnificent work with a call to all living creatures to indeed praise Him.

Introductory Word
הַלְלוּיָ-ה—Halleluyah—Praise God

שִׁיר—Shir—Song

Musical Instruments
שׁוֹפָר—Shofar—A non-musical signaling device made from the hollow horn of a kosher animal,

traditionally a ram. It was light, portable, easy to make, and was readily available to the common people. It's distinctive and piercing sound , varying sequences of long and short tone, could be heard over long distances.

נֵבֶל—Nevel—Lyre—An ancient string instrument of ten or more strings used to accompany the vocal presentations of the Levites. Standing almost three feet tall, the nevel had strings that were played in much the same manner as a modern harp - by plucking with the fingers.

כִּנּוֹר—Kinor—Harp - A generic term for an ancient class of 'gut' string instruments used to accompany the voice or another instrument. Along with the lyre and melodic cymbals, the harp was one of the three primary instruments of song used used by the Levites in their musical ensembles.

תֹּף—Tof—Drum - A large, thin drum, made with wood and animal hide, in conjunction with dance, and often played by women. The frame-drum was held with the left hand and played by striking the head of the drum with the alternating thumb and forefingers of the right hand in various rhythmic patterns.

מָחוֹל—Machol—A reedless wind instrument or possibly a dance.

מִנִּים— Minim—Referred to as a category or group of stringed instruments used by the Levi'im in the Orchestra of the Beit HaMikdash.

עֻגָב—Ugav—A generic name for a family of hollow, tubular musical wind instruments. Closed on one end and made of bone, bamboo, wood, or metal its sound is created by gently blowing across the tube. Mentioned only five times within the Bible in limited contexts, the ugav is one of the instruments of the scriptures we know very little about. Due to the inconsistent renderings as a string instrument, harp, pipe, organ, and even a song in various translations, an exact description and classification of this instrument is problematic.

צִלְצְלֵי-שָׁמַע—Tsel-Tselai Shama—Cymbals of melodious sounds.

צִלְצְלֵי תְרוּעָה—Tselai Teruah—A pair of small cymbals (1½" to 2½"), individually mounted on flexible prongs that would be shaken rapidly (the teruah) causing the cymbal plates to concussively strike each other. Unlike finger cymbals, this cymbal clapper requires very little skill to execute.

Shimush Tehillim - When to Say

To give praise to the Almighty—Verse 6 states: "Let every soul praise God. Praise God."

Where in the Siddur

Recited together as a unit of Psalms 145-150, beginning with Ashrei of Pesukei Dezimra (Verses of Praise introducing the Shacharit morning service), viewed as a daily recitation of Hallel (Praise service).

Recited in its entirety in the Musaf Amidah (Silent Meditation) of Rosh HaShanah.

Talmud on Tehillim

Verse 3: "הַלְלוּהוּ, בְּתֵקַע שׁוֹפָר"—"Praise Him with the blowing of the shofar."

This final psalm contains ten mentions of "Hallelu"—"Praise" (or its variant "Halleluhu"—"Praise Him"). The Talmud, Rosh HaShanah 32a, presents a disagreement as to the significance of the number ten here. Perhaps it corresponds to the Aseret HaDibrot (the Ten Commandments), or, alternatively, to the "ten utterances with which the world was created". (See Pirkei Avot, Ethics of

Our Fathers, 5:1 for further explanation).

Verse 6: ''כֹּל הַנְּשָׁמָה, תְּהַלֵּל יָהּ: הַלְלוּ יָ-הּ''—"Let every soul praise God. Praise God."

The Talmud, Berachot 43b, deduces from this verse that one is required to bless God for the bad which befalls him, just as he blesses for the good. The Talmud further deduces that there is a fitting blessing to be recited for every benefit to man, however minute, even, for example, an aromatic fragrance.

The Talmud, Eiruvin 18b, adds: "Rabbi Yirmiyah ben Elazar said: From the day that the Beit HaMikdash (Temple) was destroyed, only the first two letters of the name of God, "yud" and "hei", are used." For this reason, Sefer Tehillim—the Book of Psalms comes to a close by praising God with the name "Yah", spelled with only these two letters.

פרק קנ	Chapter 150
א הַלְלוּ יָהּ |	1 Praise God.
הַלְלוּ־אֵל בְּקָדְשׁוֹ	Praise the Almighty in His Sanctuary
הַלְלוּהוּ	Praise God
בִּרְקִיעַ עֻזּוֹ:	in the firmament of His might
ב הַלְלוּהוּ בִגְבוּרֹתָיו	2 Praise Him for His mighty deeds;
הַלְלוּהוּ	praise Him
כְּרֹב גֻּדְלוֹ:	according to the abundance of His greatness.
ג הַלְלוּהוּ בְּתֵקַע שׁוֹפָר	3 Praise Him with the blowing of the shofar;
הַלְלוּהוּ בְּנֵבֶל וְכִנּוֹר:	Praise Him with lyre and harp.
ד הַלְלוּהוּ בְתֹף וּמָחוֹל	4 Praise Him with drum and dance.
הַלְלוּהוּ	Praise Him
בְּמִנִּים וְעוּגָב:	with stringed instruments and flute.
ה הַלְלוּהוּ בְצִלְצְלֵי־שָׁמַע	5 Praise Him with resounding cymbals.
הַלְלוּהוּ בְּצִלְצְלֵי תְרוּעָה:	Praise Him with clanging cymbals.
ו כֹּל הַנְּשָׁמָה תְּהַלֵּל יָהּ	6 Let every soul praise God.
הַלְלוּ־יָהּ:	Praise God.

PRAYERS TO BE RECİTED AFTER SAYİNG TEHİLLİM - PSALMS

תפילה לאחר אמירת תהלים - Prayer After Reciting Tehillim

מִי יִתֵּן מִצִּיּוֹן יְשׁוּעַת יִשְׂרָאֵל	O that the salvation of Israel would come out of Zion
בְּשׁוּב יהוה שְׁבוּת עַמּוֹ	When the Lord returns the captivity of His people,
יָגֵל יַעֲקֹב יִשְׂמַח יִשְׂרָאֵל.	Jacob shall rejoice, Israel shall be glad.
וּתְשׁוּעַת צַדִּיקִים מֵיהוה	But the salvation of the righteous is from the Lord,
מָעוּזָּם בְּעֵת צָרָה.	their stronghold in time of distress.
וַיַּעְזְרֵם יהוה וַיְפַלְּטֵם;	The Lord helped them and rescued them;
יְפַלְּטֵם מֵרְשָׁעִים וְיוֹשִׁיעֵם,	He rescued them from the wicked and saved them
כִּי חָסוּ בוֹ.	because they took refuge in Him.
יְהִי רָצוֹן מִלְּפָנֶיךָ,	May it be your will,
יהוה אֱלֹהֵינוּ וֵאלֹהֵי אֲבוֹתֵינוּ,	Hashem our God and the God of our forefathers,
בִּזְכוּת:	in the merit of:

Upon completing an entire Book of Tehillim say:

Book V	Book IV	Book III	Book II	Book I
ספר חמישי	ספר רביעי	ספר שלישי	ספר שני	ספר ראשון
Psalms 107-150	Psalms 90-106	Psalms 73-89	Psalms 42-72	Psalms 1-41

שֶׁבַּתְּהִלִּים שֶׁקָּרָאנוּ לְפָנֶיךָ,	Of Tehillim that we read before you,
שֶׁהוּא כְּנֶגֶד:	that corresponds to the book of:

Deuteronomy	Numbers	Leviticus	Exodus	Genesis
ספר דברים	ספר במדבר	ספר ויקרא	ספר שמות	ספר בראשית
Psalms 107-150	Psalms 90-106	Psalms 73-89	Psalms 42-72	Psalms 1-41

בִּזְכוּת מִזְמוֹרָיו	In the merit of its psalms,
וּבִזְכוּת פְּסוּקָיו וּבִזְכוּת תֵּבוֹתָיו	and verses, and words,

Upon reciting less than an entire book say:

מִזְמוֹרֵי תְהִלִּים שֶׁקָּרָאנוּ לְפָנֶיךָ,	The psalms of Tehillim that we read before you,
וּבִזְכוּת פְּסוּקֵיהֶם וּבִזְכוּת תֵּבוֹתֵיהֶם,	and in the merit of its verses and words,

On weekdays, all continue here (For the Sabbath and Festivals, skip below):

וּבִזְכוּת שְׁמוֹתֶיךָ הַקְּדוֹשִׁים וְהַטְּהוֹרִים	And in the merit of the holy pure names
הַיּוֹצְאִים מֵהֶם,	that emanate from them,
שֶׁתְּכַפֵּר לָנוּ עַל כָּל חַטֹּאתֵינוּ	That You grant atonement for all of our transgressions,
וְתִמְחַל לָנוּ עַל כָּל עֲוֹנוֹתֵינוּ	pardon us for all our inequities,
וְתִסְלַח לָנוּ עַל כָּל פְּשָׁעֵינוּ	and forgive us for all our sins,
שֶׁחָטָאנוּ וְשֶׁעָוִינוּ	that we have transgressed,
וְשֶׁפָּשַׁעְנוּ לְפָנֶיךָ	been iniquitous, and sinned before You.
וְתַחֲזִירֵנוּ בִּתְשׁוּבָה שְׁלֵמָה לְפָנֶיךָ	Return us to You in complete repentance,
וְתַדְרִיכֵנוּ לַעֲבוֹדָתֶךָ	guide us in Your service,
וְתִפְתַּח לִבֵּנוּ בְּתַלְמוּד תּוֹרָתֶךָ	and open our hearts to the study of Your Torah.
וְתִשְׁלַח רְפוּאָה שְׁלֵמָה לְחוֹלֵי עַמֶּךָ	Send a full recovery to the sick of Your nation.

One reciting for a particular sick person adds:

For a Female	For a Male
Insert Patient's Name (Cholah)	Insert Patient's Name (Choleh)
____ bat (daughter of) ____	____ ben (son of) ____
Insert Mother's Hebrew Name	Insert Mother's Hebrew Name

וְתִקְרָא לִשְׁבוּיִם דְּרוֹר	Proclaim liberty for the captives,
וְלַאֲסוּרִים פְּקַח קוֹחַ	and freedom for prisoners
וּלְכָל הוֹלְכֵי דְרָכִים	And for all the wayfarers
וְעוֹבְרֵי יַמִּים וּנְהָרוֹת	and travelers of seas and rivers
מֵעַמְּךָ יִשְׂרָאֵל	of Your nation Israel,
תַּצִּילֵם מִכָּל צַעַר וָנֶזֶק	Save them from all pain and damage,
וְתַגִּיעֵם לִמְחוֹז חֶפְצָם	and bring them to their desired destination
לְחַיִּים וּלְשָׁלוֹם	for life and for peace.
וְתִפְקוֹד לְכָל	May You remember to all
חֲשׂוּכֵי בָנִים	who are childless,
בְּזֶרַע שֶׁל קְיָמָא	[to grant] them children that are healthy
לַעֲבוֹדָתֶךָ וּלְיִרְאָתֶךָ	to serve and fear You.
וְעֻבָּרוֹת שֶׁל עַמְּךָ בֵּית יִשְׂרָאֵל	And the pregnant women of Your nation Israel,
תַּצִּילֵן	you shall protect,
שֶׁלֹּא תַפֵּלְנָה וְלָדוֹתֵיהֶן	that they do not miscarry,
וְהַיּוֹשְׁבוֹת עַל הַמַּשְׁבֵּר בְּרַחֲמֶיךָ הָרַבִּים	And for those on the birth stool,
תַּצִּילֵן מִכָּל רָע	protect them from all evil,
וְאֶל הַמֵּינִיקוֹת תַּשְׁפִּיעַ	And may You cause the nursing mothers
שֶׁלֹּא יֶחְסַר חָלָב מִדַּדֵּיהֶן	not to lack milk in their breasts.

וְאַל יִמְשׁוֹל אַסְכְּרָה	And not hold any sway over
וְשֵׁדִין וְכָל פְּגָעִים וּמַרְעִין בִּישִׁין	diphtheria, demons, evil sprits and occurrences
בְּכָל יַלְדֵי עַמְּךָ	any children of Your nation,
בֵּית יִשְׂרָאֵל	the house of Israel.
וּתְגַדְּלֵם לְתוֹרָתֶךָ לִלְמוֹד תּוֹרָה	Raise them to study Torah for its own sake,
לִשְׁמָהּ וְתַצִּילֵם מֵעַיִן הָרָע	and protect them from the evil eye,
וּמִדֶּבֶר וּמִמַּגֵּפָה	pestilence, plague,
וּמִשָּׂטָן וּמִיֵּצֶר הָרָה	Satan, and the evil inclination.
וּתְבַטֵּל מֵעָלֵינוּ	Cancel from upon us
וּמִכָּל עַמְּךָ בֵּית יִשְׂרָאֵל	and Your whole nation of Israel,
בְּכָל מָקוֹם שֶׁהֵם	wherever they are,
כָּל גְּזֵרוֹת קָשׁוֹת וְרָעוֹת	all harsh and evil decrees.
וְתַטֶּה לֵב הַמַּלְכוּת	May You sway the hearts of the government
עָלֵינוּ לְטוֹבָה	regarding us for good,
וְתִגְזוֹר עָלֵינוּ גְּזֵרוֹת טוֹבוֹת	so that they decree upon us favorable laws.
וְתִשְׁלַח בְּרָכָה וְהַצְלָחָה	May You send blessing and success
בְּכָל מַעֲשֵׂה יָדֵינוּ	upon all our handiwork.
וְהָכֵן פַּרְנָסָתֵנוּ	Prepare our livelihood
מִיָּדְךָ הָרְחָבָה וְהַמְּלֵאָה	from Your open and generous hand,
וְלֹא יִצְטָרְכוּ עַמְּךָ יִשְׂרָאֵל	so that Your nation Israel
זֶה לָזֶה וְלֹא לְעַם אַחֵר	do not need to rely on each other or another nation.
וְתֵן לְכָל אִישׁ וְאִישׁ דֵּי פַּרְנָסָתוֹ	Give to every person ample livelihood,
וּלְכָל גְּוִיָּה וּגְוִיָּה דֵּי מַחְסוֹרָהּ	and everybody what it lacks,
וּתְמַהֵר וְתָחִישׁ לְגָאֳלֵנוּ	And may You speedily hurry to redeem us,

Recite only in the presence of a Minyan:

וְתִבְנֶה בֵּית מִקְדָּשֵׁנוּ וְתִפְאַרְתֵּנוּ	and build our Temple of holiness and splendor.
וּבִזְכוּת שְׁלֹשׁ עֶשְׂרֵה מִדּוֹתֶיךָ	And in the merit of the Thirteen Attributes
שֶׁל רַחֲמִים הַכְּתוּבוֹת בְּתוֹרָתֶךָ כְּמוֹ	of Your Mercy that are recorded in Your Torah,
שֶׁנֶּאֱמַר:	as it is said:
יהוה יהוה	Hashem, Hashem,
אֵל רַחוּם וְחַנּוּן	God, Compassionate, and Gracious,
אֶרֶךְ אַפַּיִם	Slow to anger,
וְרַב חֶסֶד וֶאֱמֶת	and Abundant in Kindness and Truth,
נֹצֵר חֶסֶד לָאֲלָפִים	Preserver of Kindness for thousands [of generations],
נֹשֵׂא עָוֹן וָפֶשַׁע	Forgiver of Inequity, Willful sin,
וְחַטָּאָה וְנַקֵּה	and Inadvertent sin, and Who Absolves
שֶׁאֵינָן חוֹזְרוֹת	Those that are never turned away

<table>
<tr><td>empty-handed from You.</td><td>רֵיקָם מִלְּפָנֶיךָ.</td></tr>
<tr><td>Assist us,</td><td>עָזְרֵנוּ</td></tr>
<tr><td>God of our salvations,</td><td>אֱלֹהֵי יִשְׁעֵנוּ</td></tr>
<tr><td>for the sake of the glory of Your Name,</td><td>עַל דְּבַר כְּבוֹד שְׁמֶךָ</td></tr>
<tr><td>and rescue us and atone for our sins,</td><td>וְהַצִּילֵנוּ וְכַפֵּר עַל חַטֹּאתֵינוּ</td></tr>
<tr><td>for the sake of the glory of Your Name.</td><td>לְמַעַן שְׁמֶךָ.</td></tr>
<tr><td>Blessed is Hashem, forever,</td><td>בָּרוּךְ יהוה לְעוֹלָם</td></tr>
<tr><td>Amen and Amen.</td><td>אָמֵן וְאָמֵן.</td></tr>
</table>

On Sabbath and Festivals all continue here:

<table>
<tr><td>And in the merit of the holy,</td><td>וּבִזְכוּת שְׁמוֹתֶיךָ הַקְּדוֹשִׁים וְהַטְּהוֹרִים</td></tr>
<tr><td>pure names that emanate from them,</td><td>הַיּוֹצְאִים מֵהֶם שֶׁתְּהֵא נֶחְשֶׁבֶת לָנוּ</td></tr>
<tr><td>That the recital of these psalms</td><td>אֲמִירַת מִזְמוֹרֵי תְהִלִּים</td></tr>
<tr><td>should be as if David, King of Israel,</td><td>אֵלּוּ כְּאִלּוּ אֲמָרָם דָּוִד מֶלֶךְ יִשְׂרָאֵל</td></tr>
<tr><td>of blessed memory,</td><td>עָלָיו הַשָּׁלוֹם</td></tr>
<tr><td>had said them himself,</td><td>בְּעַצְמוֹ</td></tr>
<tr><td>may his merit shield us.</td><td>זְכוּתוֹ יָגֵן עָלֵינוּ</td></tr>
<tr><td>May it stand in our favor</td><td>וְיַעֲמוֹד לָנוּ</td></tr>
<tr><td>to unite the Bride of Youth with her Beloved,</td><td>לְחַבֵּר אֵשֶׁת נְעוּרִים עִם דּוֹדָהּ</td></tr>
<tr><td>in love, comradeship, and companionship.</td><td>בְּאַהֲבָה וְאַחֲוָה וְרֵעוּת.</td></tr>
<tr><td>And from this,</td><td>וּמִשָּׁם</td></tr>
<tr><td>may abundant blessing be drawn</td><td>יִמָּשֵׁךְ לָנוּ שֶׁפַע</td></tr>
<tr><td>unto our spirit, breath, and soul,</td><td>לְנֶפֶשׁ רוּחַ וּנְשָׁמָה.</td></tr>
<tr><td>And just as we recite songs</td><td>וּכְשֵׁם שֶׁאָנוּ אוֹמְרִים</td></tr>
<tr><td>before You in this world,</td><td>לְפָנֶיךָ שִׁירָה בָּעוֹלָם הַזֶּה</td></tr>
<tr><td>May we merit to recite before You,</td><td>כַּךְ נִזְכֶּה לוֹמַר לְפָנֶיךָ</td></tr>
<tr><td>Hashem our God, and God of our forefathers</td><td>יהוה אֱלֹהֵינוּ וֵאלֹהֵי אֲבוֹתֵינוּ</td></tr>
<tr><td>songs and praise in the next world.</td><td>שִׁיר וּשְׁבָחָה לָעוֹלָם הַבָּא.</td></tr>
<tr><td>And though the recitation of psalms</td><td>וְעַל יְדֵי אֲמִירַת תְּהִלִּים</td></tr>
<tr><td>may the Rose of Sharon awaken</td><td>תִּתְעוֹרֵר חֲבַצֶּלֶת הַשָּׁרוֹן</td></tr>
<tr><td>to sing with a pleasant voice,</td><td>וְלַשִׁיר בְּקוֹל נָעִים</td></tr>
<tr><td>in ecstasy and joy.</td><td>בְּגִילַת וְרַנֵּן,</td></tr>
<tr><td>May you give her Lebanon's glory,</td><td>כְּבוֹד הַלְּבָנוֹן נִתַּן לָהּ,</td></tr>
<tr><td>majesty, and splendor</td><td>הוֹד וְהָדָר</td></tr>
<tr><td>in the House of our God,</td><td>בְּבֵית אֱלֹהֵינוּ</td></tr>
<tr><td>speedily in our days.</td><td>בִּמְהֵרָה בְיָמֵינוּ</td></tr>
<tr><td>Amen. Selah.</td><td>אָמֵן סֶלָה.</td></tr>
</table>

OBSCURE PHRASES

Obscure Phrases Explained

1st Appearance	Occurrences	Hebrew	Transliteration
3:3	74	רַבִּים אֹמְרִים לְנַפְשִׁי אֵין יְשׁוּעָתָה לּוֹ בֵאלֹהִים סֶלָה׃	Selah
5:1	1	לַמְנַצֵּחַ אֶל־הַנְּחִילוֹת מִזְמוֹר לְדָוִד׃	El-Hanechilot
7:1	1	שִׁגָּיוֹן לְדָוִד אֲשֶׁר־שָׁר לַיהוָה עַל־דִּבְרֵי־כוּשׁ בֶּן־יְמִינִי׃	Shiggayon
8:1	3	לַמְנַצֵּחַ עַל־הַגִּתִּית מִזְמוֹר לְדָוִד׃	Al-Hagitit
9:1	1	לַמְנַצֵּחַ עַלְמוּת לַבֵּן מִזְמוֹר לְדָוִד׃	Al-mut Labain
9:17	1	נוֹדַע ׀ יְהוָה מִשְׁפָּט עָשָׂה בְּפֹעַל כַּפָּיו נוֹקֵשׁ רָשָׁע הִגָּיוֹן סֶלָה׃	Higgayon Selah

Translation	Translation
Forever	This word is some form of musical instruction. The word "Selah" is found only in the book of Psalms with one exception; the third chapter of the Book Habakkuk. It is used as a pause between chapters or within a composition. It can also mean "evermore" or, "so it is" or, "it is certainly true". There are those who say that "Selah" means that whatever King David said endures for eternity.
On a musical instrument in the temple	A wind instrument that produced a sound akin to the buzzing of bees.
A song of lament	It is either a musical instrument or a particular tune used to accompany this psalm. Another interpretation cites it as a penitential or lamenting song. The Gemara understands the word as a derivative of שגיאה, error.
On the Gittis	Possibly a harp that came from the Philistine city of Gath. Alternatively, this is a reference to the nation of Edom which God will ultimately trod upon like a gath, Hebrew for "winepress".
Upon the death of Labain	"The phrase "al-mut" is problematical. Opinions differ as to whether "al-mut" is one word - a musical instrument or set of chords - or two words as translated here, "upon the death of Labain". There are multiple opinions as to who Labain was. A few possibilities were; King David's son Absalom, Nebal, Goliath, or a man named Labain who was David's enemy.
Reflective interlude	"Higgayon", like the word selah that immediately follows it, is some type of musical sign for a singer or an instrumentalist. One opinion says that the Levitical orchestra paused playing while everyone in attendance reflected on the word that had just been sung.

1st Appearance	Occurrences	Hebrew	Transliteration
16:1	6	מִכְתָּם לְדָוִד שָׁמְרֵנִי אֵל כִּי־חָסִיתִי בָךְ׃	Michtam
22:1	1	לַמְנַצֵּחַ עַל־אַיֶּלֶת הַשַּׁחַר מִזְמוֹר לְדָוִד׃	Al-Ayelet Hashachar
32:1	13	לְדָוִד מַשְׂכִּיל אַשְׁרֵי נְשׂוּי־פֶּשַׁע כְּסוּי חֲטָאָה׃	Maskil
38:1	2	מִזְמוֹר לְדָוִד לְהַזְכִּיר׃	Lehazkir
45:1	2	לַמְנַצֵּחַ עַל־שֹׁשַׁנִּים לִבְנֵי־קֹרַח מַשְׂכִּיל שִׁיר יְדִידֹת׃	Al-Shoshannim
46:1	1	לַמְנַצֵּחַ לִבְנֵי־קֹרַח עַל־עֲלָמוֹת שִׁיר׃	Al-Alamot
53:1	2	לַמְנַצֵּחַ עַל־מָחֲלַת מַשְׂכִּיל לְדָוִד׃	Al-Machalat

Translation	Translation
An engraving	The name of a type of psalm. Similar to the Hebrew word מכתב (michtav) a written "letter", "מכתם" (michtam) is believed to be an inscription that was engraved into a stone or tablet. The Levi'im would conduct the services utilizing them.
On the doe (female deer) of the dawn	Rashi is of the opinion that it is either the name of a musical instrument or the congregation of Israel that is a beloved doe that comes into view at dawn. Another opinion is that the term means "the morning star", the sight of which inspired David to compose this psalm.
A discerning person or giver of instruction	A musical composition that required either one or more of the following; thought, understanding, insight, cleverness or some special skill regarding giving instructions to others.
For remembrance	An instruction for the congregation to reflect on their troubles and to pray to Hashem for salvation.
On the roses or lilies	Some say it's a musical instrument that looked like a bell with petals likening it to a lily or a rose. Others interpret it to mean honoring the torah scholars that are likened to roses that are considered to be beautiful.
An unidentified instrument or sung in a falsetto voice	Some says it's either a musical instrument or a musical direction indicating that the associated work should be sung in falsetto, mimicking the sound of a maiden's voice.
On the Machalat	The name of a musical instrument or the name of the melody to which this song was to be sung. Alternatively it could mean either מחילה - mechilah, forgiveness or מחלה - machalah, regarding the illness.

1st Appearance	Occurrences	Hebrew	Transliteration
54:1	6	לַמְנַצֵּחַ בִּנְגִינֹת מַשְׂכִּיל לְדָוִד׃	B'Neginot
56:1	1	לַמְנַצֵּחַ | עַל־יוֹנַת אֵלֶם רְחֹקִים לְדָוִד מִכְתָּם בֶּאֱחֹז אֹתוֹ פְלִשְׁתִּים בְּגַת׃	Al-Yonath Elem Rechokim
57:1	4	לַמְנַצֵּחַ אַל־תַּשְׁחֵת לְדָוִד מִכְתָּם בְּבָרְחוֹ מִפְּנֵי־שָׁאוּל בַּמְּעָרָה׃	Al-Tashchet
60:1	1	לַמְנַצֵּחַ עַל־שׁוּשַׁן עֵדוּת מִכְתָּם לְדָוִד לְלַמֵּד׃	Lelamed
62:1	3	לַמְנַצֵּחַ עַל־יְדוּתוּן מִזְמוֹר לְדָוִד׃	Al-Yedutun
88:1	1	שִׁיר מִזְמוֹר לִבְנֵי קֹרַח לַמְנַצֵּחַ עַל־מָחֲלַת לְעַנּוֹת מַשְׂכִּיל לְהֵימָן הָאֶזְרָחִי׃	Le'Anot

Translation	Translation
With tunes	The psalms at times were sung solo, as a choir, with and without musical accompaniment. At times an individual instrument was played and at its greatest moment the Levi'im played as a full orchestra and sang as a large choir.
Over a silent dove in the distance	King David referring to himself for he was distant from the land of Israel when he composed this psalm.
Do not destroy	Most likely indicates that the manuscript was from an original text and it should not be thrown awat or destroyed.
To teach	May indicate that this manuscript was used in some manner to teach. The psalmist bids the Levite musician to teach the people the theme of this psalm - namely, that God brought military victory to King David and that all events are determined by Divine Providence.
"For Yedutun or on the Yedutun"	Yedutun was one of the leaders of the Levitical orchestra. Alternatively this is the name of a musical instrument that was crafted by Yedutun or his close family members hence the Yedutun. i.e. the Stradivarius of it's time.
To responsively chant	May have indicated that the work that follows was to be sung responsively.

TEHILLIM AND TEMPLE SERVICE

THROUGHOUT THE TEMPLE SERVICE, THE LEVITES WOULD PLAY INSTRUMENTS AND RECITE DIFFERENT PSALMS IN ACCOMPANIMENT. SOME TEHILLIM WERE SAID WHILE OFFERING SACRIFICES, SOME UPON ENTERING AND LEAVING DIFFERENT SECTIONS OF THE BEIT HAMIKDASH (TEMPLE), AND SOME, IN CONJUNCTION WITH PARTICULAR DAYS OF THE WEEK.

The Sound of Music in the Temple

What did the music in the Temple sound like? We are familiar with the pronunciation of the Hebrew words in the Book of Tehillim and with the help of the te'amim- the graphic signs or accents that come underneath and on top of the text, we know how they are to be sung. The one question that remained unanswered was how did the music of the Levitical orchestra sound?
"The Davidic Cipher," written by Mr. Dennis McCorkle, introduces and confirms a plausible theory as to how the music in the temple sounded. Just as our own system of music notation utilizes a unique set of symbols to represent the notes to be played, McCorkle claims that the Hebrew system of musical notation also uses a set of symbols (i.e., the cantillation symbols or te'amim).
By associating or mapping the letters of the Hebrew alphabet with the traditional system of music notation, he was able to link the music to the te'amim. Applying his theory, Tehillim primarily viewed as a literary text is now able to be understood as songs that were sung while the music was played.

Halleluyah

Halleluyah is a transliteration of the Hebrew word הַלְלוּ-יָה, occuring only in the Book of Psalms 24 times. The phrase consists of two Hebrew words Hallelu, meaning Praise and Yah, the name of God, short for YHVH, the unspeakable holy name of God.
The word Halleluyah was sometimes used as an invocation for an individual to Praise God for something specific. One would be asked to think of something that they were grateful for and to acknowledge God as the source of that blessing. Halleluyah!

Poetry and Parallelism

Traditional English poetry commonly uses two distinctive methods: meter and rhyme. Meter has to do with the number of 'beats' in a line and rhyming usually involves ending two clauses with words that sound similar. Hebrew poetry in the Book of Psalms is different. It does use meter, although that is not easily reflected in translation. It does not, however, use rhyme.
The Biblical poetry of Psalms uses parallelism as its primary poetic device. Parallelism involves using relatively short sentences, usually made up of two brief clauses that parallel one another in some way. Parallelism is a kind of rhyme, in which an idea is developed by the use of repetition, synonyms, or opposites. Sometimes the parallel elements are synonymous terms and the idea expressed in both clauses is the same, repeated twice, in different but nearly the same words, as in Psalm 104:33, "I will sing to Adonoy with my life; / I will offer hymns to my God."
Sometimes the parallel elements complement each other, as in; Psalm 1:1, "who has not walked in the counsel of the wicked, / and in the way of the sinful he has not stood, / and in the seat of the scornful he has not sat." Sometimes they explain each other, as in; Psalm 18:15, "And He sent out His arrows and scattered them; / and He shot forth lightning and confounded them." At times the second part is the opposite of the first, expressing opposite ideas, as in; Psalm 20:9, "They have bowed down and fallen, / but we have risen and stand firm."
Many lines are composed of two parallel clauses, as in; Psalm 2:3, "Let us remove their bands / and cast away from us their cords." There are also lines composed of three parallel clauses, as in; Psalm 18:9, "Smoke arose from His nostrils, / devouring fire from His mouth; / coals flamed

forth from Him." Sometimes there are four parallel clauses, two parallel lines joining together to form a stanza as in; Psalm 18:5 & 6, "I was often surrounded by bands of death, / and floods of despicable people alarmed me. / Bands of the wicked surrounded me, / I was confronted by the snares of death."

Psalmultaneously

When reading the Five Books of Moses, for the most part, the storyline appears in chronological order with some exceptions. Psalms on the other hand is another story, actually three stories. Taking place at the same time as Sefer Tehillim are two other books that run concurrently; Sefer Shmuel or The Book of Samuel and Divrei Hayamim or The Book of Chronicles.
Recorded in the Book of Samuel are events in King David's life that are alluded to in the heading of 12 Psalms in Sefer Tehillim. The wording of these headings is sometimes very similar to the language of Samuel.
The Book of Chronicles expands on information that is sparsely provided in the Book of Samuel and the Book of Psalms. Therein, we learn what families the Levitical singers and musicians came from, their role and function in the temple, whether it be composer, conductor, part of the choir or orchestra. Therefore, it could be said that Tehillim, Shmuel and Divrei Hayamim occurred Psalmultaneously.

Doxology

Sefer Tehillim – The Book of Psalms is divided into five books or sections, similar to that of the Five Books of Moses. At the conclusion of each of the five books of Tehillim, there is a short hymn of praise to God, known as a doxology.

Lcation	Hebrew	English
Ch. 41, V. 14	בָּר֘וּךְ יְהֹוָ֤ה | אֱלֹהֵ֣י יִשְׂרָאֵ֗ל מֵֽהָעוֹלָם וְעַ֬ד הָעוֹלָ֗ם אָ֘מֵ֥ן | וְאָמֵֽן׃	Blessed is Adonoy, the God of Israel, from all times past, throughout all times to come, Amen and Amen.
Ch. 72, V. 20	כָּלּ֥וּ תְפִלּ֑וֹת דָּ֝וִ֗ד בֶּן־יִשָֽׁי׃	Completed are the prayers of David, son of Jesse.
Ch. 89 V. 53	בָּר֖וּךְ יְהֹוָ֥ה לְעוֹלָ֗ם אָ֘מֵ֥ן | וְאָמֵֽן׃	Blessed is Adonoy, forever, Amen and Amen
Ch. 106 V. 48	בָּֽרוּךְ־יְהֹוָ֨ה אֱלֹהֵ֪י יִשְׂרָאֵ֡ל מִן־הָעוֹלָ֨ם וְעַ֬ד הָעוֹלָ֗ם וְאָמַ֣ר כָּל־הָעָ֣ם אָ֭מֵן הַֽלְלוּ־יָֽהּ׃	Blessed is Adonoy, God of Israel, from this world to the world (to come), and let the people say "Amen," praise God.
Ch. 150 V. 6	כֹּ֣ל הַ֭נְּשָׁמָה תְּהַלֵּ֥ל יָ֗הּ הַֽלְלוּ־יָֽהּ׃	Let every soul praise God. Praise God.

Shir Shel Yom (Song of the Day)

Corresponding to the Days of Creation

Day of the Week	Chapter and Corresponding Phrase to the Day of the Week
Sunday 1st day of creation	Chapter 24 לְדָוִד מִזְמוֹר לַיהוָה הָאָרֶץ וּמְלוֹאָהּ תֵּבֵל וְיֹשְׁבֵי בָהּ: "Of David, the earth is Adonay's and the fullness thereof, the inhabited world and those who dwell in it."
Connection to the Day of Creation	On the 1st day of creation God created the universe and ruled over it. He also predestined man to acquire the universe and have dominion over it upon his creation.
Monday 2nd day of creation	Chapter 48 גָּדוֹל יְהוָה וּמְהֻלָּל מְאֹד בְּעִיר אֱלֹהֵינוּ הַר־קָדְשׁוֹ: "Adonoy is great and highly extolled, in the city of our God, the mountain of His Sanctuary."
Connection to the Day of Creation	On the 2nd day of creation God created the firmament, separating the waters below from the waters above, thereby displaying His greatness.
Tuesday 3rd day of creation	Chapter 82 מִזְמוֹר לְאָסָף אֱלֹהִים נִצָּב בַּעֲדַת־אֵל בְּקֶרֶב אֱלֹהִים יִשְׁפֹּט: "A Psalm of Asaf. God stands in the congregation of the almighty, in the midst of judges He gives judgment."
Connection to the Day of Creation	On the 3rd day of creation God gathered together all the waters below the firmament, exposing dry land and subsequently creating vegetation, thereby preparing the world for His assembly.
Wednesday 4th day of creation	Chapter 94 אֵל־נְקָמוֹת יְהוָה אֵל נְקָמוֹת הוֹפִיעַ: "Almighty of vengeance, Adonoy, Almighty of vengeance, reveal Yourself."
Connection to the Day of Creation	On the 4th day of creation God created the sun, moon and stars, yet at the same time He determined to hold accountable and exact punishment from, all who worship them.

Day of the Week	Chapter and Corresponding Phrase to the Day of the Week
Thursday 5th day of creation	Chapter 81 **הַרְנִינוּ לֵאלֹהִים עוּזֵּנוּ הָרִיעוּ לֵאלֹהֵי יַעֲקֹב:** "Sing joyously to the God, our strength, shout for the joy to the God of Jacob."
Connection to the Day of Creation	On the 5th day of creation God created the birds and fish, which in turn sing the praises of God.
Friday 6th day of creation	Chapter 93 **יְהוָה מָלָךְ גֵּאוּת לָבֵשׁ לָבֵשׁ יְהוָה עֹז הִתְאַזָּר** "Adonoy has begun his reign He has clothed Himself with majesty; Adonoy has clothed Himself, He has girded Himself with strength."
Connection to the Day of Creation	On the 6th day of creation God completed His work and reigned over it in its entirety.
Shabbat 7th day of creation	Chapter 92 **מִזְמוֹר שִׁיר לְיוֹם הַשַּׁבָּת:** "A Psalm, a song for the Sabbath day."
Connection to the Day of Creation	On the 7th day God created the Shabbat, which He subsequently blessed and sanctified. As it is a day of rest for mankind, it is deserving of its own special "melodious song".

Tehillim for Shabbat

Some have the custom to say an extra chapter of Tehillim on Shabbat which corresponds to the weekly Parashah (Torah portion).

Parasha	Chapter	Parasha	Chapter	Parasha	Chapter	Parasha	Chapter
Bereishit	139	Beshalach	66	Emor	42	Ki Tavo	75
Noach	29	Yitro	19	Behar	112	Nitzavim	97
Lech Lecha	110	Mishpatim	72	Shelach	105	Vayeilech	17
Vayeira	11	Terumah	26	Korach	112	Ha'azinu	32
Chayei Sarah	45	Tetzaveh	65	Chukat	67	Vezot - Haberachah	51
Toldot	36	Ki Tisa	75	Balak	68	Bechukotai	81
Vayeitzei	3	Vayakhel	61	Pinchas	64	Bamidbar	65
Vayishlach	140	Pekudei	45	Matot	5	Naso	71
Vayeishev	112	Vayikra	50	Mas'ei	95	Beha'alotcha	12
Mikeitz	40	Tzav	107	Devarim	79		
Vayigash	48	Shemini	128	Va'etchanan	50		
Vayechi	41	Tazria	106	Eikev	111		
Shemot	99	Metzora	120	Re'ei	49		
Va'eira	46	Acharei Mot	26	Shoftim	137		
Bo	77	Kedoshim	15	Ki Teitzei	90		

Tehillim for Other Special Days

Some have the custom to recite a chapter of Tehillim which corresponds to the particular theme of that day. There are three major sources which list the appropriate Psalms: Avodat Yisrael by Rav Yisrael of Koznitz, Beit Yaakov by Rav Yosef Karo, and Ma'ase Rav by the Vilna Gaon.

Special Days	Avodat Yisrael	Beit Yaakov	Ma'ase Rav
Rosh Chodesh	104	104	104
Shabbat HaGadol	95	95	
Pesach (Passover)-1st Day	105	105	114
Pesach - 2nd Day	66	106	74
Pesach - 3rd Day	78	75	80
Pesach - 4th Day	78	75	75
Pesach - 5th Day	78	75	135
Pesach - 6th Day	78	75	66
Pesach - 7th Day	18	18	18
Pesach - 8th Day	114	136 or 114	136
Isru Chag (the day after) Pesach	118	118	

Special Days	Avodat Yisrael	Beit Yaakov	Ma'ase Rav
Fast of BeHa"B (days following Pesach)	33	33	19
Shavu'ot - 1st Day	68	29	68
Shavu'ot - 2nd Day	29	68	
17th of Tammuz	79	79	
9th of Av	137	137	
Shabbat Nachamu	90	122	
Slichot days before Rosh HaShanah	89	89	
Erev (Eve of) Rosh HaShanah	98	95	81
Rosh HaShanah - 1st Day	81	47	81
Rosh HaShanah - 2nd Day	47	81	
10 Days of Repentance	10	130	
Shabbat Shuvah	32	32	
Erev (Eve of) Yom Kippur	107	100	
Kol Nidrei Night	99	97	32
Yom Kippur	65	32	76
Succot - 1st Day	76	96	42
Succot - 2nd Day	66	80	29
Succot - 3rd Day	97	77	50
Succot - 4th Day	97	77	04
Succot - 5th Day	97	77	81
Succot - 6th Day	97	77	82
Hoshana Rabbah	88	88 or 61	12
Shemini Atzeret	65	65	8
Simchat Torah	147	147	
Shabbat Bereishit	139	8	30
Chanukah	30	30	
10th of Teiveit	74	74	
Parashat Shekalim	49	49	
Parashat Zachor	109	109	
Fast of Esther	22	22	22
Purim	7	7	
Shushan Purim	60	60	
Parashat Parah	51	51	
Parashat HaChodesh	77	77	
House of Mourning		49	
Wedding	19	19	
Brit Milah	12	12	

BIBLIOGRAPHY

Bibliography

Alter, Robert, *The Book of Psalms: A Translation with Commentary.* W.N. Norton & Company, Inc. 2007, New York.

Baumol, Rabbi Avi, *The Poetry of Prayer: Tehillim in Tefillah. Gefen Publishing House.* 2009, Jerusalem.

Braun, Joachim, *Music In Ancient Israel/Palestine* Wm. B. Eerdmans Publishing Co. 2002, Grand Rapids, MI.

Brown, Francis, DD., D. Litt, *The New Brown-Driver-Briggs-Gesenius Hebrew- English Lexicon. Hendrickson Publishers.* 1979, Peabody, MA.

Chasidah, Yisahai, *Ishei Hatanach/Encyclopedia of Biblical Personalities: Anthologized from the Talmud, Midrash and Rabbinic Writings.* Shaar Press, 1994, Jerusalem.

Dahood, Mitchell, *The Anchor Bible Psalms I, II, III.* Doubleday, 1965, New York.

Davis, Rabbi Avrohom, *The Metsudah Tehillim.* Mitsudah Ktav, 1995, Hoboken, NJ.

Davis, Rabbi Menachem, *Tehillim Simchat Yehoshua: The ArtScroll Interlinear Tehillim - Psalms* Mesorah Publications, Ltd. 2002, Brooklyn, NY.

Deutsch, Rabbi Shaul Shimon, *Parasha Series: Sefer Bereishis.* The Living Torah Museum, 2012, Israel.

Feuer, Rabbi Avrohom Chaim, *Artscroll Tanach Series: Tehillim/Psalms.* Mesorah Publications, Ltd. 2002, Brooklyn, NY.

Fisch, Harold, *The Koren Jerusalem Bible.* Koren Publishers. 2008, Jerusalem.

Fishbane, Michael, *The Jewish Study Bible: featuring the Jewish Publication Society Tanakh Translation.* Jewish Publication Society - Oxford University Press, Inc. 2004, New York.

Frumin, Moshe, *Musical Instruments Of the Ancient World and According to the Holy Scriptures.* Moshe / Idan Frumin. 2005, Israel.

Hakham, Amos, *The Bible/Psalms with the Jerusalem Commentary.* Mosad Harav Kook. 2003, Jerusalem.

Heber, Rabbi Shmuel, *Yashmia Kol Tehiloto al Tehillim.* Graphidia, 2011, Israel.

Hendin, David, *Guide to Biblical Coins.* Amphora 2010. Nyack, NY.

Herczeg, Rabbi Yisrael Isser Zvi, *Tehillim with Rashi's Commentary.* Feldheim Publishers, 2009, Jerusalem.

Hirsch, Rabbi Samson Raphael, *The Hirsch Psalms.* Feldheim Publishers. 1997, Jerusalem.

Idelsohn, Abraham Z, *Jewish Music: It's Historical Development.* Dover Publications, Inc. 1992, New York.

Keel, Othmar, *The Symbolism of the Biblical World: Ancient Near Eastern Iconography and The Book of Psalms.* The Seabury Press. 1978, New York.

Mannn, Jacob & Sonne, Isaiah, *The Bible as Read and Preached in the Old Synagogue.* The Mann-Sonne Publication Committee. 1966, Cincinnati, OH.

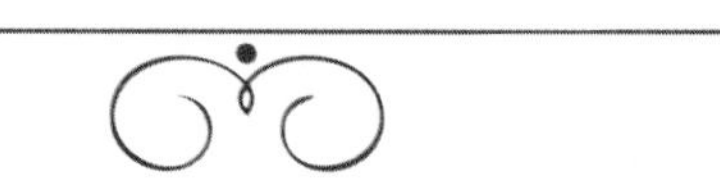

McCorkle, Dennis, *The Davidic Cipher: Unlocking the Hidden Music of Psalms*. Outskirts Press, Inc. 2010, Denver, Co.

Mykoff, M. H., Rubin, Gavriel, Schapiro, Moshe, *The Living Nach: Sacred Writings*. Moznaim Publishing Corporation. 1998, Brooklyn, NY.

Nulman, Macy, *The Encyclopedia of Jewish Prayer: The Ashkenazic and Sephardic Rites*. Jason Aronson Inc. 1993, Northvale, NJ.

Rabinowitz, Rabbi Chaim Dov, *Da'ath Sofrim: Book of Tehillim (Psalms)*. Moznaim Publishing Corporation. 2010, Jerusalem.

Sarna, Nahum M, *On the Book of Psalms: Exploring the Prayers of Ancient Israel*. Schocken Books, 1993, New York.

Scherman, Rabbi Nosson, *The Stone Edition Tanach*. Mesorah Publications, Ltd. 1996, Brooklyn, NY.

Scherman, Rabbi Nosson, *The Artscroll Siddur*. Mesorah Publications, Ltd. 1991, Brooklyn, NY.

Schneersohn, Rabbi Yosef Yitzchak, *Tehillim Ohel Yosef Yitzchak*. Kehot Publishing Society, 2010, Brooklyn, NY.

Sendrey, Alfred, *Music In Ancient Israel*. Philosophical Library, Inc. 1969, New York.

Strickman, Norman H, *Rabbi Abraham Ibn Ezra's Commentary on the Book of Psalms*. Academic Studies Press. 2009, Boston, MA.

Vermes, Geza, *The Complete Dead Sea Scrolls In English*. Allen Lane, The Penguin Press. 1997, New York.

Waxman, Ephraim, *Dor L'Dor Timeline*. Feldheim Publishers. 2006, Brooklyn, NY.

Westenholz, Joan Goodnick, *Sounds of Ancient Music*. Bible Lands Museum Jerusalem, 2007, Jerusalem.

Yerushalmi, Rabbi Shmuel, *The Torah Anthology: Yalkut Me'am Lo'ez*. Moznaim Publishing Corporation, 1989, Brooklyn, NY.

Encyclopedia Judaica: Book of Psalms - CD ROM Edition Judaica Multimedia (Israel) Ltd. 1997, Israel.

JPS *Hebrew English Tanakh*. The Jewish Publication Society. 1999, Philadelphia, PA.

כולי, יעקב רבי. *ילקוט מעם לועז ספר תהלים*. וגשל, תשמ״ב, ירושלים.

אשלג, יחזקאל וסף הלוי. *ספר הזהר עם פירוש ״הסולם״ על תהלים*. מכן עטרת שלמה. תשס״א, בני ברק, ישראל.

ספר תהלים אור ליהודה. עטרת פז. 5767, ירושלים.

סדור רינת ישראל ספרדי ועדות המזרח*. מורשת. תשל״ו, ישראל.

ספר תהלים יסד מלכות. אשכול. תשנ״ה, ירושלים, ישראל.

גמליאל הכהן רבינוביץ. *ספר תהלים עם טיב התחילות שימוש תהלים*. גמליאל הכהן רבינוביץ. תשס״ב, ירושלים.

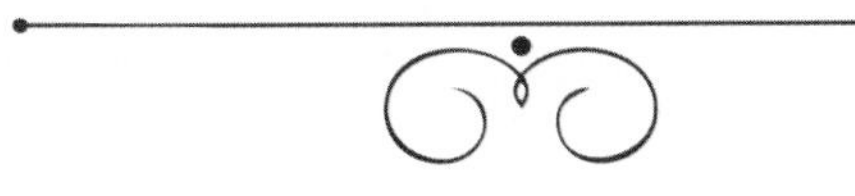

About the Author

Reuben Ebrahimoff is a trailblazer. A native New Yorker and the son of immigrants, he was the first Mashadi Jew from Persia to attend a yeshiva day school in the U.S.

A student of Brooklyn's esteemed Rabbi Shimon Kessin, Reuben embarked on his inspirational journey to seek knowledge of the Biblical Prophets. Realizing the beauty of each week's Haftorah portion, Reuben sought to share his insight and is affectionately known as "Haftorahman". Gifted with extraordinary oratory and people skills, Reuben has enthralled 100+ congregational audiences across the globe with his cherished and entertaining interpretations of the Haftorah. His weekly seven Haftorah facts reach an audience of over 2000+ and are available online as a handout or on video at OU.Org https://www.youtube.com/user/Haftorahman

"From Your Lips to God's Ears", is a comprehensive and notable publication that chronicles the history, the authors, the locations and even the musical instruments featured throughout the beloved book of Psalms. Reuben's 10-step guide to understanding this revered collection of prayers used through the ages in times of joy and sorrow will be a necessary classic featured in every home, Jewish and non-Jewish alike.

Reuben is the proud father of a daughter and President of Brilliant I.D.E.A.S., a jewelry manufacturing company in New York. For over a decade, he has spent every summer season teaching a Shabbat series on "The World of the Prophets" at The Hampton Synagogue in Westhampton Beach.

Reuben Ebrahimoff
Email. reuben@fromyourlipstogodsears.com

Photo Credits

p. 23 Cover of Handwritten Tehillim - *Moshe Weinberg*
p. 29 Tehillim Scroll - *Israeli Antiquities Authority*
p. 27 Mosaic - *Israel Antiquities Authority*
p. 42a Harp - *David Henden*
p. 42a Coin - *David Henden*
p. 42b Drum - *Moshe Frumin*
p. 42b Clay Drummer - *Israel Museum, Jerusalem*
p. 42c Coin - *David Henden*
p. 42c Lyre - *Moshe Frumin*
p. 42d Hand Drum - *Moshe Frumin*
p. 42d Female Playing Drum - *Israel Antiquities Authority*
p. 43e Shofar - *Dennis McCorkle, The Davidic Cipher*
p. 43e Mosaic with Shofar - *Israel Antiquities Authority*
p. 43f Cymbals - *Dennis McCorkle, The Davidic Cipher*
p. 43f Oil Lamp - *Ardon Bar Hama (Courtesy of Shlomo Moussaieff Collection)*
p. 43g Chatzotrot - *Image taken from Israel Stamp*
p. 43g Coin - *David Henden*
p. 43h Hand Cymbals - *Israel Stamp*
p. 43h Oil Lamp - *Ardon Bar Hama (Courtesy of Shlomo Moussaieff Collection)*
p. 44 Shofar - *Rabbi Avraham Mishar Aryeh, The Music in the Temple*
p. 44 Chatzotzrot - *Rabbi Avraham Mishar Aryeh, The Music in the Temple*
p. 45 Harp - *Rabbi Avraham Mishar Aryeh, The Music in the Temple*
p. 45 Alamos - *Rabbi Avraham Mishar Aryeh, The Music in the Temple*
p. 46 Nevel - *Rabbi Avraham Mishar Aryeh, The Music in the Temple*
p. 46 Nevel Asor - *Rabbi Avraham Mishar Aryeh, The Music in the Temple*
p. 47 Sheminit - *Rabbi Avraham Mishar Aryeh, The Music in the Temple*
p. 48 Ugav - *Rabbi Avraham Mishar Aryeh, The Music in the Temple*
p. 49 Nechilot - *Rabbi Avraham Mishar Aryeh, The Music in the Temple*
p. 50 Melodic Cymbals - *Rabbi Avraham Mishar Aryeh, The Music in the Temple*
p. 50 Pitched Cymbals - *Rabbi Avraham Mishar Aryeh, The Music in the Temple*
p. 51 Framed Hand Drum - *Rabbi Avraham Mishar Aryeh, The Music in the Temple*
p. 51 Cymbal Clappers - *Rabbi Avraham Mishar Aryeh, The Music in the Temple*
p. 69 David Accompanies Transportation of Ark of the Covenant - *(1816), scene from Hall of Ark, by Luigi Ademollo (1764-1849), fresco, Italy, Florence, Palazzo Pitti*
p. 71 Amulet Plaque - *Limestone, 4th-5th centuries, C.E. Institute of Archeology, Hebrew University, Jerusalem*
p. 73 Royal Capital - *Amalyah Oren, Israel Antiquities Authority (awaiting photo and caption*
p. 81 Sheminit - *Rabbi Avraham Mishar Aryeh, The Music in the Temple*
p. 90 Glass Jar with Menorah, Ardon Bar Hama (Courtesy of Shlomo Moussaieff Collection)
p. 92 *Mosaic from Colonia Aelia Augusta Italica depicting a Lion, 176-275 AD, Archeological Museum, Seville*
p. 95 Tiberius Synagogue Menorahs and Ark - *Zev Radovan*
p. 98 Mosaic - *Beth Alpha Synagogue Nave Mosaics*

p. 318 Maccabean Menorah Coin - *Ardon Bar Hama (Courtesy of Shlomo Moussaieff Collection)*
p. 324 Mosaic Floor - *Israel Antiquities Authority*
p. 326 Mosaic - *Herodium 1st century B.C.E., Israel Museum*
p. 329 Lion - *Yitzhak Magen, Israel Antiquities Authority*
p. 331 Carved Menorah - *Israel Museum*
p. 335 Leaves Mosaic - Yitzhak Magen, *Israel Antiquities Authority*
p. 337 Arch of Titus - *Rome, Italy*
p. 340 Mosaic Motif - *Yitzhak Magen, Israel Antiquities Authority*
p. 344 Golden Jug - *Ardon Bar Hama (Courtesy of Shlomo Moussaieff Collection)*
p. 364 Ennion Glass Pitcher - *Ardon Bar Hama (Courtesy of Shlomo Moussaieff Collection)*
p. 365 Menorah Ring - *Ardon Bar Hama (Courtesy of Shlomo Moussaieff Collection)*
p. 369 City of David - *Ir David*
p. 378 Lod Mosaic - *Israel Antiquities Authority*
p. 381 Synagogue Floor Mosaic - *Israel Antiquities Authority*
p. 387 Golden Menorah - *Ardon Bar Hama (Courtesy of Shlomo Moussaieff Collection)*
p. 389 Israel in Egypt - *Edward Poynter*
p. 396 Guilloche Pattern - *Yitzhak Magen, Israel Antiquities Authority*
p. 401 Ring with Four Menorahs - *Ardon Bar Hama (Courtesy of Shlomo Moussaieff Collection)*
p. 403 Mosaic Motif - *Yitzhak Magen, Israel Antiquities Authority*
p. 405 Tel Dan Stele - *Oren Rozen*
p. 415 Fresco of King David - *Renata Sedmakova*
p. 438 Pool of Siloam - *Pablo Betzer*
p. 439 Leaves Mosaic - Yitzhak Magen, *Israel Antiquities Authority*
p. 445 Mosaic Bird - *The Birds Mosaic, Caesarea*
p. 447 Guilloche Pattern - *Yitzhak Magen, Israel Antiquities Authority*
p. 449 Grapes Mosaic - *Yitzhak Magen, Israel Antiquities Authority*
p. 451 Grapes Mosaic - *Yitzhak Magen, Israel Antiquities Authority*
p. 453 Mosaic - *Yitzhak Magen, The Good Samaritan Inn Museum*
p. 454 Silver Scroll - *Bruce Zuckerman, West Semitic Research Project*
p. 455 Tree Mosaic - Yitzhak Magen, *Israel Antiquities Authority*
p. 465 Duchan Hands - *Shefa Tal, Hanau, 1612. Hebraic Section*
p. 467 Seven-branched Menorah - *Israel Antiquities Authority*
p. 472 Lod Mosaic - *Israel Antiquities Authority*
p. 490 King Hezekiah's Seal - *Eilat Mazar (Courtesy of Shlomo Moussaieff Collection)*
p. 500 Mosaic - *Yitzhak Magen, Israel Antiquities Authority*
p. 507 Stamps - *Israeli Postal Service*